THE

NAVY LIST

2006

Corrected to 1st April 2006

LONDON: TSO

Crown copyright 2006
Published for Ministry of Defence under licence from the Controller of Her Majesty's Stationery Office
Applications for reproduction should be made in writing to The Copyright Unit, Her Majesty's Stationery Office,
St Clements House, 2-16 Colegate, Norwich NR3 1BQ

ISBN 978 0 11 773057 1
ISBN 0 11 773057 2

The Navy List is compiled and published by order of the Defence Council for the convenience of the Naval Service, but as errors may occasionally occur the Council must expressly reserve the right to determine the status of any Officer according to the actual circumstances of the case, independently of any entry in the Navy List

By Command of the Defence Council,

SIR KEVIN TEBBIT

Published by TSO (The Stationery Office) and available from:

Online
www.tso.co.uk/bookshop

Mail, Telephone, Fax & E-mail
TSO
PO Box 29, Norwich, NR3 1GN
Telephone orders/General enquiries: 0870 600 5522
Fax orders: 0870 600 5533
E-mail: customer.services@tso.co.uk
Textphone 0870 240 3701

TSO Shops
123 Kingsway, London, WC2B 6PQ
020 7242 6393 Fax 020 7242 6394
68-69 Bull Street, Birmingham B4 6AD
0121 236 9696 Fax 0121 236 9699
9-21 Princess Street, Manchester M60 8AS
0161 834 7201 Fax 0161 833 0634
16 Arthur Street, Belfast BT1 4GD
028 9023 8451 Fax 028 9023 5401
18-19 High Street, Cardiff CF10 1PT
029 2039 5548 Fax 029 2038 4347
71 Lothian Road, Edinburgh EH3 9AZ
0870 606 5566 Fax 0870 606 5588

TSO Accredited Agents
(see Yellow Pages)

and through good booksellers

Printed in the United Kingdom by The Stationery Office
ID188361 C15 6/06 19585 340024

PREFACE

This edition of the Navy List has been produced largely from the information held in the Naval Manpower Management Information System and is corrected to include those promotions, appointments etc. promulgated on or before 1 April 2006 as becoming effective on or before 30 June 2006. Only Flag rank entries in Section one will be corrected after this date.

Serving officers who notice errors or omissions in Sections 2 and 3 of the List should complete the form on the final page of the Navy List and forward it to their Career Manager. Other errors or omissions should be brought to the attention of the Editor of the Navy List. All other readers who should notice errors or omissions are invited to write to:

Mr Andrew Hiscutt
The Editor of the Navy List
DNCM
Room 208
Jago Road
HM Naval Base
PORTSMOUTH
Hants, PO1 3LU

quoting the page(s) in question. Every effort will be made to include corrections and omissions received by the Editor before 28 March 2007. Regrettably, letters cannot be acknowledged.

Officers who succeed to peerages, baronetcies or courtesy titles should notify their Career Manager so that their computer records can be updated and the changes reflected in the Navy List. The degrees shown after Active Service Officers' names are not necessarily a complete list of those held, but are generally confined to degrees of an honorary nature conferred specially upon an Officer, and those that are so related to the professional duties of an Officer as to give some indication of his professional qualifications.

The Editor controls the master Allowance List for the free distribution of the Navy List. DSDC(L) at Llangennech is responsible for the issue of this publication strictly according to the Allowance List. Units are asked to ensure that the Editor and DSDC(L) are informed of any reduction in requirement. Requests for additional copies and amendment to the master Allowance List should be addressed to DSDC(L) at Llangennech (using RN Form 53001(Demand for Naval Books)). Firmly attached to this demand should be a letter addressed to the Editor with a clear supporting case.

The Ministry of Defence is investing in the replacement to the Naval Manpower Management Information systems. The new system is a Tri-service initiative and is called "the Joint Pay and Administration system" (JPA). JPA will radically enhance all areas of service administration. However, JPA will not record information in the same, format and/or content as its predecessor, consequently the 2007 edition of the Navy List will evolve to reflect these changes.

The 2007 Retired Officers and Emergency list will equally be affected by the inception of JPA and this will be addressed separately as to any changes in content and/or format.

CONTENTS

Section 8

Section 9

Abbreviations-

Index

HER MAJESTY THE QUEEN

LORD HIGH ADMIRAL OF THE UNITED KINGDOM 1964

MEMBERS OF THE ROYAL FAMILY

HIS ROYAL HIGHNESS THE PRINCE PHILIP, DUKE OF EDINBURGH, KG, KT, OM, GBE, AC, QSO

Admiral of the Fleet .... 15 Jan 53
Captain General Royal Marines .... 1 Jun 53
Admiral of the Fleet Royal Australian Navy .... 1 Apr 54
Admiral of the Fleet Royal New Zealand Navy .... 15 Jan 53
Admiral of the Royal Canadian Sea Cadets .... 15 Jan 53

HIS ROYAL HIGHNESS THE PRINCE OF WALES, KG, KT, OM, GCB, AK, QSO, ADC

Vice Admiral .... 14 Nov 02

HIS ROYAL HIGHNESS THE DUKE OF YORK, KCVO, ADC

Admiral of the Sea Cadet Corps .... 11 May 92
Honorary Captain Royal Navy .... 27 Jun 05

HER ROYAL HIGHNESS THE PRINCESS ROYAL, KG, GCVO, QSO

Rear Admiral Chief Commandant for Women in the Royal Navy .... 1 Nov 93

HIS ROYAL HIGHNESS PRINCE MICHAEL OF KENT, GCVO

Honorary Rear Admiral Royal Naval Reserve .... 1 Jun 04

HER ROYAL HIGHNESS PRINCESS ALEXANDRA THE HON LADY OGILVY, KG GCVO

Patron, Queen Alexandra's Royal Naval Nursing Service .... 12 Nov 55

VICE ADMIRAL OF THE UNITED KINGDOM

Admiral Sir James Burnell-Nugent KCB CBE

PERSONAL AIDES-DE-CAMP TO THE QUEEN

Vice Admiral His Royal Highness The Prince of Wales, KG, KT, OM, GCB, AK, QSO, ADC
Honorary Captain His Royal Highness The Duke of York, KCVO, ADC

FIRST AND PRINCIPAL NAVAL AIDE-DE-CAMP TO THE QUEEN

Admiral Sir Jonathon Band KCB ADC .... 02 Aug 02

FLAG AIDE-DE-CAMP TO THE QUEEN

Vice Admiral A.J. Johns CBE ADC.. 25 Oct 05

NAVAL AND MARINE AIDES-DE-CAMP TO THE QUEEN

Commodore G.J. Thwaites	Appointed 24 Mar 05	Seniority	1 Apr 03
Commodore P.K. Walpole	Appointed 13 Sep 05	Seniority	7 Jul 03
Commodore C.J. Stait, OBE	Appointed 15 Mar 05	Seniority	22 Jun 04
Commodore D.G. Steel	Appointed 1 Mar 06	Seniority	21 Nov 05
Captain W.M. Covington, CBE (Commodore)	Appointed 11 May 04	Seniority	31 Dec 96
Captain M.J. Potter (Commodore)	Appointed 27 Sep 02	Seniority	30 Jun 97

EXTRA NAVAL AND MARINE EQUERRIES TO THE QUEEN

Vice Admiral Sir James Weatherall, KCVO, KBE
Vice Admiral T Blackburn, CB LVO
Lieutenant General Sir John Richards, KCB, KCVO
Rear Admiral Sir Paul Greening, GCVO
Rear Admiral Sir John Garnier, KCVO, CBE
Rear Admiral Sir Robert Woodard, KCVO
Commodore A.J.C.Morrow, CVO Royal Navy

NAVAL AND MARINE RESERVE AIDES-DE-CAMP TO THE QUEEN

Commodore N.J E Reynolds, RD, ADC RNR	Appointed 01 Feb 04	Seniority	30 Sep 99
Colonel B.L. Hough, RD, ADC RMR	Appointed 20 Jun 03	Seniority	01 Jun 97
Captain S.P. Thorne, RD, RNR	Appointed 01 Mar 05	Seniority	30 Sep 03

HONORARY CHAPLAINS TO THE QUEEN

The Venerable J Green QHC
The Reverend Monsignor B.R.Madders, MBE, QHC, VG
The Reverend D Barlow, QHC, MA
The Reverend S M Rae, MBE, QHC, BD

HONORARY PHYSICIANS TO THE QUEEN

Surgeon Commodore N.E.Baldock, QHP, MB, ChB, FRCP, FFOM, MRCS, DipAvMed
Surgeon Commodore P.F.R. Tolley, OBE, QHP, MB, BCh
Surgeon Commodore T.R. Douglas-Riley, QHP, MB, BS, MRCS, LRCP, MRCGP, DA, jsdc
Surgeon Captain O.M. Howard, QHP, MB, BS, FRCP,

HONORARY SURGEONS TO THE QUEEN

Surgeon Vice Admiral I.L.Jenkins, CB, CVO, QHS, MB, BCH, FRCS
Surgeon Rear Admiral M.A.Farquharson-Roberts, CBE, QHS, MB, BS, MA, LRCP, FRCS, rcds

HONORARY DENTAL SURGEON TO THE QUEEN

Surgeon Commodore (D) G.L. Morrison, QHDS, BDS, FDS, MBA, DRDRCS

NAVAL RESERVE HONORARY PHYSICIAN TO THE QUEEN

Surgeon Captain J.A. McM Turner, RD, QHP, FRCP

HONORARY NURSE TO THE QUEEN

Captain L. Gibbon, ARRC, QHN, QARNNS

HONORARY OFFICERS IN HER MAJESTY'S FLEET

ADMIRAL

His Majesty King Karl XVI Gustav of Sweden, KG ....25 Jun 75
His Majesty Sultan Haji Hassanal Bolkiah Mu'izzaddin Waddaulah Sultan and Yang Di-pertuan of
Brunei Darussalam, GCB, GCMG .... 4 Aug 01

HONORARY OFFICERS IN HER MAJESTY'S ROYAL MARINES

COLONEL

His Majesty King Harald V of Norway, KG, GCVO..18 Mar 81

THE DEFENCE COUNCIL

Chairman
THE RIGHT HONOURABLE DES BROWNE MP
(Secretary of State for Defence)

THE RIGHT HONOURABLE ADAM INGRAM JP MP
(Minister of State for the Armed Forces)

LORD DRAYSON
(Parliamentary Under Secretary of State and Minister for Defence Procurement)

MR TOM WATSON MP
(Under-Secretary of State for Defence and Minister for Veterans)

SIR JOCK STIRRUP, KCB, AFC, ADC, FRAeS, FCMI
(Chief of Defence Staff)

MR BILL JEFFERY, CB
(Permanent Under-Secretary of State)

ADMIRAL SIR JONATHON BAND, KCB, ADC
(First Sea Lord and Chief of the Naval Staff)

GENERAL SIR MIKE JACKSON, GCB, CBE, DSO, ADC, Gen
(Chief of the General Staff)

*AIR CHIEF MARSHAL SIR GLENN TORPY, KCB, CBE, DSO
(Chief of the Air Staff)

GENERAL SIR TIMOTHY GRANVILLE-CHAPMAN, KCB, CBE, ADC, Gen
(Vice Chief of the Defence Staff)

SIR PETER SPENCER, KCB
(Chief of Defence Procurement)

PROFESSOR ROY ANDERSON
(Chief Scientific Adviser)

MR IAN ANDREWS, CBE, TD
(Second Permanent Under-Secretary of State)

GENERAL SIR KEVIN O'DONOGHUE, KCB, CBE
(Chief of Defence Logistics)

THE ADMIRALTY BOARD

Chairman
THE RIGHT HONOURABLE DES BROWNE MP
(Secretary of State for Defence)
(Chairman of the Defence Council and Chairman of the
Admiralty Board of the Defence Council)

THE RIGHT HONORABLE ADAM INGRAM JP MP
(Minister of State for the Armed Forces)

LORD DRAYSON
(Parliamentary Under Secretary of State and Minister for Defence Procurement)

MR TOM WATSON MP
(Under-Secretary of State for Defence and Minister for Veterans)

ADMIRAL SIR JONATHON BAND, KCB, ADC
(First Sea Lord and Chief of the Naval Staff)

ADMIRAL SIR JAMES BURNELL-NUGENT, KCB, CBE
(Commander in Chief Fleet/Commander Allied Naval Forces North)

VICE ADMIRAL ADRIAN J JOHNS, CBE, ADC
(Second Sea Lord and Commander in Chief Naval Home Command)

REAR ADMIRAL A D H MATHEWS
(Director Land and Maritime, Controller of the Navy)

REAR ADMIRAL R PAUL BOISSIER
(Director General Logistics Fleet, Navy Board Member for Logistics)

REAR ADMIRAL ALAN M MASSEY, CBE
(Assistant Chief of Naval Staff)

MR IAN ANDREWS, CBE, TD
(Second Permanent Under-Secretary of State and Secretary of the Admiralty Board)

OFFICERS ON THE ACTIVE LIST
OF THE ROYAL NAVY, THE ROYAL MARINES,
THE QUEEN ALEXANDRA'S
ROYAL NAVAL NURSING SERVICE;
AND RETIRED AND EMERGENCY OFFICERS
SERVING AND LIST OF RFA OFFICERS' NAMES

Name	Rank	Branch Spec	Seniority	Where Serving

A

Name	Rank	Branch	Spec	Seniority	Where Serving
Abbey, Michael Keith, MSc, CEng, MIMarEST	CDR(FTC)	E	MESM	31.12.00	DLO BRISTOL
Abbey, Michael Peter, MBE, pcea	LT CDR(FTC(A)	X	P	01.10.88	FLEET AV VL
Abbot, Sir Peter (Charles), GBE, KCB, MA, rcds, pce	ADM			03.10.95	
Abbot, Richard Leslie, BSc, PGDip	LT(IC)	X	HM2	01.09.03	ENDURANCE
Abbott, David,	CAPT RM(CC)	-	SO(LE)	01.04.03	846 SQN
Abbott, David Anthony, BTech	LT CDR(FTC)	E	WE	01.10.04	CAPT MCTA
Abbott, Duncan Alexander James, BA	SLT(IC)	X		01.11.04	DARTMOUTH BRNC
Abbott, Grant Paul, MA	CAPT RM(CC)	-		01.09.02	PSYOPS TEAM
Abbotts, Michael Charles, BEng, MRAeS	LT(CC)	E	AE	01.04.02	824 SQN
Abel, James Andrew, MEng	LT(IC)	E	WESM	01.11.05	VIGILANT(STBD)
Abel, Lucy, BSc	LT(IC)	X		01.09.02	NP IRAQ
Abel, Nigel Philip,	LT(FTC)	X	P	16.08.96	BULWARK
Abernethy, James Richard Gordon, MA, PGDIPAN, pce, psc(j)	CDR(FTC)	X	PWO(N)	30.06.04	FLEET COSCAP
Abernethy, Lee John Francis, pce	CDR(FTC)	X	PWO(C)	30.06.05	HQ SACT
Abey, John Ashton,	LT(IC)	MS		01.07.04	DRAKE COB
Ablett, Eleanor Louise, BA	LT CDR(FTC)	S		01.10.02	FLEET COSP&S
Ablett, Simon David, BEng, CEng, MIEE	LT CDR(FTC)	E	WE	01.01.06	DLO BRISTOL
Abraham, Paul, pce(sm)	CDR(FTC)	X	SM	31.12.96	FLEET COMOPS NWD
Ackland, Heber Kemble, MA(OXON), psc(j)	CDR(FTC)	S		30.06.06	MOD (LONDON)
Acland, David Daniel, pce, pcea	CDR(FTC)	X	P	30.06.06	JCA IPT USA
Adair, Allan Alexander Shafto, rcds, pce, psc(a)	CDRE(FTC)	X	PWO	04.11.03	RN GIBRALTAR
Adam, Ian Kennedy, pce	LT CDR(FTC)	X	PWO(A)	01.01.97	GRAFTON
Adam, Murray William, BSc	SLT(IC)	X		01.11.03	ATHERSTONE
Adams, Alistair John, BSc, pce	CAPT(FTC)	X	PWO(C)	30.06.06	FLEET COSCAP
Adams, Andrew Mark, BEng, MA, CEng, MIMarEST, psc(j)	CDR(FTC)	E	MESM	30.06.02	MOD (LONDON)
Adams, Edwin Smyth, BEng	LT(CC)	X	P	16.09.99	846 SQN
Adams, Geoffrey Hugh, BEng, MSc, CEng, MIMarEST	LT CDR(FTC)	E	ME	01.04.01	DARTMOUTH BRNC
Adams, George, MIMarEST	LT(FTC)	E	ME	01.05.97	SULTAN
Adams, Peter, BSc, PGCE	CDR(FTC)	E	TM	30.06.03	NEPTUNE DLO
Adams, Richard Joseph, BEng, CEng, MIMarEST	LT CDR(FTC)	E	MESM	01.03.03	VANGUARD(STBD)
Adams, Samantha Anna,	LT(SC(MD)	Q	(RGN)	01.06.03	RH HASLAR
Adams, Sarah Jayne, MBE	SLT(IC)	S		01.01.05	DARTMOUTH BRNC
Adams, William John,	LT(CC)	X		01.05.02	NEPTUNE DLO
Adamson, Hazel Josie, BEng	SLT(IC)	E	ME U/T	01.03.04	NORTHUMBERLAND
Adamson, Stephen Edward,	LT(IC)	X		01.05.02	JFC HQ AGRIPPA
Adcock, Graham Edward,	CAPT RM(FTC)	-		01.01.01	RMR BRISTOL
Ahlgren, Edward Graham, SM(n), SM	LT CDR(FTC)	X	SM	01.10.00	FOST SM SEA
Ahuja, Vijay,	SURG SLT(SCC)	-		22.01.05	DARTMOUTH BRNC
Aiken, Stephen Ronald, OBE, BSc, MA, pce, pce(sm), psc(j)	CDR(FTC)	X	SM	30.06.03	SOVEREIGN
Ainscow, Anthony James,	LT(IC)	E	ME	01.05.02	SULTAN
Ainsley, Andrew Malcolm James, n	LT(FTC)	X		01.08.00	SEVERN
Ainsley, Roger Stewart, MA, jsdc, pce, hcsc	RADM	-	AWO(A)	27.04.04	FOST SEA

Name	Rank	Branch	Spec	Seniority	Where Serving
(FLAG OFFICER SEA TRAINING APR 04)					
Ainsworth, Alan J, ...LT(IC)	E	WE		01.07.04	DLO BRISTOL
Air, Christopher, ...2LT(IC)	-			01.08.01	FPGRM
Airey, Simon Edward, MA, jsdc.........................CDR(FTC) (Act Capt)	S		31.12.94	DA KIEV	
Aitchison, Kenneth James, MB, CHB, MRCGP, DObstRCOG........... SURG CDR(SCC)	-		GMPP	04.02.96	MWS COLLINGWOOD
Aitken, Andrew John, BA, SM(n), SM.................................LT CDR(FTC)	X	SM		01.09.02	SUPERB
Aitken, Kenneth Matthew, MAPM ....CDR(FTC)	S	(S)		30.06.03	AFPAA(CENTURION)
Aitken, Lee-Anne, BSc, ...LT(IC)	X			01.01.05	BLYTH
Aitken, Neil Donald, BEng ....SLT(IC)	X	O U/T		01.05.04	DARTMOUTH BRNC
Aitken, Steven Robert, MSc...LT(CC)	X	P		01.01.01	JSCSC
Ajala, Ahmed Rufai Abiodun, BEng, MSc gw....................LT CDR(FTC)	E	WE		01.10.04	MOD (LONDON)
Akers, Samuel John, ...LT(IC)	X	P		01.01.06	RNAS YEOVILTON
Alabaster, Martin Brian, MA, MSc, rcds, psc.....................CDRE(FCC)	E	WE		30.04.02	FLEET COSP&S
Alberts, Paul William, ...LT(FTC)	E	WE		01.04.01	SCU SHORE
Albon, Mark, BSc, Cert Ed, PGDip...................................CDR(FTC)	X	HM		30.06.06	JHQ/CIS LISBON
Albon, Ross, OBE, BSc, MBA, rcds(fm).............CAPT(FTC) (Barrister)	S	BAR		30.06.02	DLO/DG LOG (SC)
Alcindor, David John, BSc, SM(n)......................................LT(CC)	X	SM		01.04.97	SUPERB
Alcock, Christopher, OBE, pce, pcea, psc..........................CDR(FTC)	X	O		30.06.98	FLEET COSCAP
Alder, Mark Christian, BEng, MSc, CEng, PGDip....................LT(IC)	E	MESM		01.05.04	TALENT
Alderson, Richard James, BA..MAJ(FTC)	-			01.10.04	45 CDO RM
Alderton, Paul Alexander, BSc, BTech..............................LT(CC)	X	WE		01.01.03	JSCSC
Aldous, Benjamin Walker, LLB ....LT(FTC)	X			01.11.99	MWS COLLINGWOOD
Aldous, Robert James, ...LT(IC)	X			01.10.04	MWS COLLINGWOOD
Aldwinckle, Terence William, ...LT CDR(FCC)	Q	IC		01.10.01	RH HASLAR
Alexander, Amy Louisa, BA...LT(FTC)	E	WE		01.09.99	DLO BRISTOL
Alexander, Oliver Douglas Dudley, ...LT(FTC)	X	MCD		01.11.97	SDG PLYMOUTH
Alexander, Phillip Michael Duncan, MEng, PGDip ....LT(FTC)	E	MESM		01.01.01	NP DNREAY
Alexander, Robert Stuart, MA, pce, pcea, psc....................CDR(FTC)	X	P		30.06.99	MOD (LONDON)
Alexander, William Augustus Dudley, BSc.............................LT(IC)	X			01.01.06	MONMOUTH
Alison, Lynn Alexander, ...LT CDR(FTC)	E	WE		01.10.94	FLEET COSP&S
Allan, Chris Ruthven, BSc, n......................................LT CDR(FTC)	X			01.12.05	MWS COLLINGWOOD
Allan, Fraser Stuart, ...CAPT RM(CC)	-			01.09.03	CTCRM
Allan, Owen James, ...LT(IC)	E	WE		01.01.05	DARTMOUTH BRNC
Allan, Victoria Elizabeth, BA ....SLT(IC)	X			01.09.03	BLYTH
Allcock, Edward Charles, BM ....SURG LT(SCC)	-			07.08.02	MDHU PORTSMOUTH
Allen, Alexander Paul, BEng ....SLT(IC)	E	ME U/T		01.01.04	SULTAN
Allen, Anthony David, PGDIPAN, pce..............................LT CDR(FTC)	X	PWO(N)		01.02.98	EXCHANGE AUSTLIA
Allen, David Peter, ...LT(FTC)	E	WE		15.06.90	CAPT MCTA
Allen, Douglas James Keith, BEng ....LT CDR(CC)	X	P		01.10.03	JHCHQ
Allen, Leslie Bernard, FInstLM..LT CDR(CC)	X	MW		01.10.04	RALEIGH
Allen, Patrick Lyons, pce, pcea.....................................LT CDR(FTC)	X	O		01.06.99	MIDDLETON
Allen, Paul Miles, MBA, MSc ....LT CDR(FTC)	X	O		01.10.04	LOAN JTEG BSC DN
Allen, Richard, pce(sm), SM(n), SM..................................CDR(FTC)	X	SM		30.06.06	MWS COLLINGWOOD
Allen, Richard Mark, pce, pce(sm) ....CDR(FTC)	X	SM		30.06.99	MWS COLLINGWOOD
Allen, Russell William, ...LT(IC)	X	EW		01.07.04	RNU RAF DIGBY
Allen, Stephen Michael, pce, pcea.................................CDR(FTC)	X	O		30.06.04	JSCSC
Allfree, Joseph, BSc, n...LT CDR(FTC)	X	PWO(A)		01.01.03	MWS COLLINGWOOD
Allibon, Mark Christopher, pce, psc(j), MA ....CDR(FTC)	X	PWO(A)		30.06.00	MWS COLLINGWOOD
Allinson, Michael David, BSc ....SLT(IC)	X			01.03.04	SOUTHAMPTON
Allison, Aubrey Stuart Crawford, MSc, MB, ...SURG CAPT(FCC)	-	(CO/M)		30.06.03	FLEET COSP&S
BS, MRCS, LRCP, MFOM, MRCGP, psc					
Allison, Glenn, ...LT(FTC)	X	P		16.11.94	848 SQN HERON
Allison, Graham, EDINBURGH, BSc....................................SLT(IC)	X			01.02.05	DARTMOUTH BRNC
Allkins, Helen Louise, BSc..CDR(FC(MD)	Q	ACC/EM		30.06.03	RCDM
Allsop, Alistair Roos Lonsdale, MB, BSc, BCH, ... SURG LTCDR(FCC)				05.08.03	
MRCGP, Dip OM, Dip FFP, DipIMC RCSED					
Allwood, Christopher, BSc, PGCE, adp ....CAPT(FTC)	E	IS		30.06.04	SULTAN AIB
Almond, David Edwin Magor, BA, psc ....LT CDR(FTC)	S			01.07.89	MOD (LONDON)
Almond, Nicholas Andrew Barrie, BEng................................LT(IC)	E	AE		01.09.04	DLO YEO
Alsop, Sweyn Hamish, ...LT(CC)	X	P		01.12.98	750 SQN HERON
Alston, Richard, BA..CAPT RM(CC)	-	C		01.09.02	CDO LOG REGT RM
Ambrose, Rachael Elizabeth Frakes, MB, BS....................SURG LT(MC(MD)	-			07.08.02	MDHU DERRIFORD

Name	Rank	Branch	Spec	Seniority	Where Serving
Ameye, Christopher Robin, pce, psc(j)o	CDR(FTC)	X	MCD	31.12.97	SUPT OF DIVING
Amorosi, Riccardo Guy Filippo Luigi, BA, MEng	LT(IC)	E	WE	01.09.05	NORTHUMBERLAND
Amos, John Louis,	SLT(IC)	X		01.09.05	RALEIGH
Amos, Julian Harvey James,	MAJ(FTC)	-		01.09.98	COM MCC NWD
Amphlett, Nigel Gavin, BSc, MA, pce, pcea, psc(j)	CDR(FTC)	X	O	30.06.03	FLEET COSCAP
Ancona, Simon James, MA, pce, pcea, psc, hcsc	CAPT(FTC)	X	O	30.06.03	CUMBERLAND
Anderson, Andrew,	LT(CC)	X	ATC	01.05.03	OCEAN
Anderson, Bruce William Drysdale,	CAPT RM(IC)	-		01.09.05	42 CDO RM
Anderson, Christopher John, BSc, IEng, MIIE	LT(IC)	E	WE	13.04.01	JES IPT
Anderson, Fraser Boyd, BSc, gdas	LT CDR(FTC)	X	O	01.10.93	LOAN JTEG BSC DN
Anderson, Garry Stephen, SM(n), SM	LT(FTC)	X	SM	01.10.98	SOVEREIGN
Anderson, Hugh Alastair, LLB	CDR(FTC) (Barrister)	S	BAR	30.06.02	FLEET COSP&S
Anderson, Jon Harvey,	2LT(IC)	-		01.08.01	42 CDO RM
Anderson, Kevin, BSc	LT(IC)	E	TM	01.06.03	RNICG
Anderson, Lindsy Claire,	LT(FTC)	E	WE	01.09.03	CV(F) IPT
Anderson, Lynne Ann, BA	LT(IC)	S		01.12.02	FLEET FOTR
Anderson, Mark, BSc, pce, pce(sm)	CDRE(FTC)	X		30.03.04	MOD (LONDON)
Anderson, Michael Ian Christopher, BSc, MSc(Econ)	SLT(IC)	X	O U/T	01.05.04	RNAS CULDROSE
Anderson, Neil,	LT(IC)	E	WE	09.04.04	CHATHAM
Anderson, Robert Gordon, MSc, psc	CDR(FTC) (Act Capt)	E	WE	31.12.95	SHAPE BELGIUM
Anderson, Stephen Ronald,	LT(CC)	X	O	01.08.00	MWS COLLINGWOOD
Anderson-Cooke, Darren Christopher James, BSc	LT(IC)	E	TM	01.05.02	RNICG
Anderson-Hanney, Philip,	LT(IC)	X		01.10.04	SDG PORTSMOUTH
Andersson, James Laverock, MB, CHB	SURG SLT(SCC) (Act Surg Lt)	-		02.08.05	DARTMOUTH BRNC
Andrew, Peter, BEng	LT(CC)	E	MESM	01.11.99	TALENT
Andrews, Christopher, BSc	LT(CC)	E	IS	01.05.00	ALBION
Andrews, Dominic Michel,	LT(IC)	E	WE	01.05.03	CHATHAM
Andrews, Iain Stuart, DipEd	LT(CC)	X	MW	01.09.01	ATHERSTONE
Andrews, Justin Pierre,	LT(IC)	E	WE	01.05.02	EXETER
Andrews, Paul Nicholas, DipEcon, pce	LT CDR(FTC)	X	PWO(A)	01.06.94	FLEET HQ WI
Andrews, Rick, BEng	SLT(IC)	E	MESMUT	01.09.04	IRON DUKE
Angliss, Roger John,	LT(IC)	X		08.04.05	824 SQN
Angus, Donald Joshua Charles,	SURG SLT(SCC)	-		28.09.04	DARTMOUTH BRNC
Aniyi, Christopher Bamidele Jost, BEng, MA, MSc, CEng, MIMarEST, psc(j)	LT CDR(FTC)	E	ME	01.10.00	FOST SEA
Ankah, Gregory Kofi Esiaw, BEng, MSc	LT CDR(FTC)	E	ME	01.12.04	NORTHUMBERLAND
Annett, Ian Gordon, BEng, MSc, CEng, FRGS, MIEE, psc(j), gw	CDR(FTC)	E	WE	30.06.02	ILLUSTRIOUS
Ansell, Christopher Neil, BA, SM(n), SM	LT(IC)	X	SM	01.01.99	VENGEANCE(STBD)
Anstey, Robert James, pce(sm), pce, SM(n), SM	CDR(FTC)	X	SM	30.06.05	VIGILANT(PORT)
Antrobus, Stuart Ronald, BEM	LT(IC) (Act Lt Cdr)	X	AV	05.08.01	MOD (BATH)
Aplin, Adrian Trevor, MBE, MA, MCIT, MILT, psc(j), ESLog	CDR(FTC)	S		30.06.02	RNAS YEOVILTON
Appelquist, Paul, BSc, MAPM, CEng, MIEE	LT CDR(FTC)	E	WESM	01.10.99	NAVSEC
Apps, Julian Crawford,	CAPT RM(IC)	-		01.09.04	NP IRAQ
Arbuthnott, Edward Alexander Hugh, MEng	LT(IC)	X	P U/T	01.02.06	RNAS YEOVILTON
Archdale, Peter Mervyn,	LT CDR(FTC)	X	PWO(U)	16.03.85	NEPTUNE
Archer, Graham William, BEng	CDR(FTC)	E	AE	30.06.02	IA BRISTOL
Archer, Timothy William Kendray,	CAPT RM(CC)	-		01.09.03	CTCRM
Archibald, Brian Robert, BSc, pce, psc(j)	CAPT(FTC)	X	PWO(A)	30.06.04	DLO BRISTOL
Archibald, Kirsty Elaine,	SLT(IC)	E	WE U/T	01.09.04	CAMPBELTOWN
Arend, Faye Marie, BA	LT(IC)	S		01.01.99	DARTMOUTH BRNC
Argent, Daniel John Thomas Cecil, BSc	LT(IC)	E	IS	01.12.04	DARTMOUTH BRNC
Argent-Hall, Dominic, BSc, CEng, MIEE, psc	CDR(FTC)	E	WE	30.06.00	MOD (LONDON)
Argles, Edward,	2LT(IC)	-		01.08.04	45 CDO RM
Arkle, Nicholas James, BA	LT(CC)	X	P	01.09.98	LOAN OTHER SVCE
Armand-Smith, Penelope Harriet, MSc(Econ)	LT(IC)	X		01.01.05	SUTHERLAND
Armour, Graeme Alexander, MA, psc(j)	LT COL(FTC)	-		30.06.06	FLEET COSP&S
Armstrong, Colin David,	LT(CC)	X		01.09.00	MWS COLLINGWOOD
Armstrong, David Morgan, BA	LT(IC)	X		01.01.04	MWS COLLINGWOOD
Armstrong, Euan McAlpine, MB, ChB, MRCS	SURG LT(FCC)	-		05.02.02	NELSON (PAY)
Armstrong, Nicholas Peter Bruce, MSc, pcea, gdas	LT CDR(FTC)	X	O	01.10.96	829 SQN HQ
Armstrong, Roger Ian, psc(m),	LT COL(FTC)	-		31.12.92	COS 2SL/CNH
Armstrong, Rory James, BSc	LT(IC)	X		01.01.03	MWS COLLINGWOOD

Name	Rank	Branch	Spec	Seniority	Where Serving
Armstrong, Russell Freddie,	CAPT RM(IC)	-		01.09.05	29 CDO REGT RA
Armstrong, Scott Thomas,	LT CDR(FTC)	X	P	01.10.04	EXCHANGE RAF UK
Armstrong, Stuart McAlpine, BSc, SM(n), SM	LT(FTC)	X	SM	01.09.00	VANGUARD(STBD)
Arnall-Culliford, Edward Charles, BA	SLT(IC)	X		01.11.04	DARTMOUTH BRNC
Arnold, Andrew Stewart,	LT CDR(FTC)	S	(W)	01.10.02	FLEET COSP&S
Arnold, Bruce William Henry, MSc, CEng, MIMechE	CDR(FTC)	E	MESM	31.12.92	DLO BRISTOL
Arthur, Calum Hugh Charles, MB, ChB	SURG LT(SCC)	-		01.08.01	MDHU DERRIFORD
Arthur, Iain Davidson, OBE, pce(sm)	CAPT(FTC)	X	SM	30.06.06	ACDS(POL) USA
Asbridge, Jonathan Ian, MA, MHCIMA, MILT, psc(j)	LT CDR(FTC)	S	SM	16.11.97	PJHQ
Ash, Timothy Claudius Vincent, psc(j), MA	LT CDR(FTC)	X	MW	01.10.99	FLEET HQ PORTS 2
Ashby, Keith John, BEng, MIEE	LT(CC)	E	WE	01.09.97	SAT IPT
Ashcroft, Adam Charles, MA, Hf, pce, pcea, psc(j)	CDR(FTC)	X	P	31.12.00	CENTCOM USA
Ashcroft, Kieran Thomas, BEng	LT(IC)	E	TM	01.04.04	RNICG
Ashley, Paul David,	LT(CC)	X		01.05.00	ILLUSTRIOUS
Ashlin, James Matthew, BSc	LT(CC)	X	P	16.09.98	RAF CRANWELL EFS
Ashman, Rodney Guy, ACMA	LT CDR(FTC)	S	CMA	28.02.00	JSCSC
Ashmore, Sir Edward (Beckwith), GCB, DSC, IRs, jssc, psc	ADM OF FLEET	-		09.02.77	
Ashton, James, BEng, PGDip	LT(FTC)	E	MESM	01.09.02	VIGILANT(PORT)
Ashton, Richard Eric, MA, MD, MB, BCh, FRCP	SURG CAPT(FCC)	-	(CK)	01.04.03	RH HASLAR
Ashton Jones, Geraint, MSc, PGCE	LT CDR(FTC)	E	IS	01.10.96	FLEET HQ WI
Ashworth, Helen Joanne, BEng	LT CDR(FTC)	E	ME	01.10.04	ILLUSTRIOUS
Askew, Daniel Thomas,	MID(NE)(IC)	X	O U/T	01.01.06	DARTMOUTH BRNC
Askham, Mathew Thomas, BA	SLT(IC)	X	P U/T	01.06.03	RNAS YEOVILTON
Aspden, Andrew Mark, MA, pce, pcea, psc(j)	CDR(FTC)	X	O	30.06.03	BULWARK
Asquith, Simon Phillip, SM(n), SM	LT CDR(FTC)	X	SM	01.06.03	NAVSEC
Astle, Dawn Sandra,	LT(FTC)	X	AAWO	01.12.98	NOTTINGHAM
Aston, Mark William, BDS, MSc, MGDS RCS	SGCDR(D)(FCC)	-		30.06.97	EXCH ARMY SC(G)
Athayde Banazol, Claire Victoria Norsworthy, ACIS	LT CDR(FTC)	S		04.04.99	RNP TEAM
Atherton, Bruce William,	MAJ(FTC)	-	P	01.10.04	EXCHANGE USA
Atherton, Martin John, MA, psc(j)	CAPT(FTC)	S		30.06.03	NEPTUNE DLO
Atkins, Ian, BEng, MA, MSc, CEng, MIMarEST, psc(j), Eur Ing	LT CDR(FTC)	E	ME	01.07.00	MOD (BATH)
Atkins, Paul Ronald,	LT(IC)	E	MESM	01.05.03	FWO DEVONPORT
Atkinson, Anthony,	LT(IC)	E	TM	01.06.03	CTCRM
Atkinson, Charlotte Penelope, BSc	LT CDR(FTC)	X	HM2	01.10.04	MWS COLLINGWOOD
Atkinson, Garth Carson, BSc	LT CDR(FTC)	X	PWO(U)	01.02.04	ST ALBANS
Atkinson, Lee Vickerman,	LT(CC)	X		01.05.02	MWS COLLINGWOOD
Atkinson, Mark, pce,	LT CDR(FTC)	X	MCD	01.02.96	JSCSC
Atkinson, Neil Craig, BPh	CAPT RM(FTC)	-		01.05.00	UNOMIG
Atkinson, Richard Jonathan, pce	LT CDR(FTC)	X	AAWO	01.07.04	ARK ROYAL
Atkinson, Simon Reay, BSc, MPhil, CEng, FIEE, Eur Ing	CDR(FTC)	E	WE	30.06.00	NBC PORTSMOUTH
Attwater, Richard Phillip,	LT(IC)	X		01.01.05	EXETER
Attwood, Keith Alistair, BEng	LT(IC)	X	P	01.09.04	RNAS YEOVILTON
Atwal, Kamaldip Singh, BSc	LT(IC)	E	TM	01.01.02	DEF SCH OF LANG
Auld, Douglas Martin, BEng	LT(FTC)	E	MESM	01.01.98	NEPTUNE BNSL
Austen, Richard Mark,	LT(FTC) (Act Lt Cdr)	S	(W)	08.04.94	MAS BRUSSELS
Austen, Tiffany Victoria,	LT(IC)	S		01.04.05	801 NAS (GR7)
Austin, Peter Nigel, BSc, BA(OU), IEng, MIIE	LT(FTC)	E	WESM	09.01.01	NEPTUNE SWS
Austin, Simon Alexander,	SLT(IC)	X		01.09.03	MWS COLLINGWOOD
Austin, Stephen Timothy, MSc, CEng, MIMarEST	LT(FTC)	E	ME	01.05.00	DRAKE SFM
Avery, Malcolm Byrne, BSc, pce, pce(sm), psc	CDRE(FTC)	X	SM	24.06.02	NAVSEC
Avison, Matthew James, pcea	LT CDR(FTC)	X	O	01.10.99	JSCSC
Axcell, Matthew Frederick, BSc	CAPT RM(CC)	-		01.09.03	RNAS YEOVILTON
Axon, David Brian, pce, psc(j), MA	CDR(FTC)	X	AAWO	30.06.03	MOD (LONDON)
Axon, Gail Margaret, BA	LT CDR(FTC) (Barrister)	S	BAR	01.10.00	MOD (LONDON)
Ayers, Dominic Edwin Bodkin, BA, MB, BS, MRCS	SURG LTCDR(FCC)	-		03.08.00	NELSON (PAY)
Ayers, Oliver Richard Beedom, BA	SLT(IC)	X		01.11.03	RAMSEY
Ayers, Richard Peter Beedom, BSc, CEng, MIEE, psc	CDR(FTC)	E	WE	31.12.92	NC3 AGENCY
Aylott, Peter Richard Frank Dobson, MA, PGDIPAN, pce, n	LT CDR(FTC)	X	PWO(N)	29.01.00	MWS COLLINGWOOD
Ayres, Christopher Paul, BSc, pce, psc, psc(j)	CDR(FTC)	X	PWO(U)	30.06.96	MOD (LONDON)
Ayrton, Robert Edward,	LT(IC)	X		01.12.02	FWO DEVPT SEA

Name	Rank	Branch	Spec	Seniority	Where Serving

B

Name	Rank	Branch	Spec	Seniority	Where Serving
Backus, Robert Ian Kirkwood, BEng	LT CDR(FTC)	X	PWO(U)	01.10.03	ARGYLL
Baddeley, Robert,	LT(IC)	E	TM	01.11.03	RALEIGH
Baden, James Martin, MB, BS, BDS, BMS, MRCS, FDS RCPSGlas	SURG LTCDR(MCC)	-		17.03.99	NELSON (PAY)
Badenoch, William,	2LT(IC)	-		01.08.02	CTCRM LYMPSTONE
Badrock, Bruce, n.	LT CDR(FTC)	X	H CH	05.07.98	ECHO
Baggaley, Jason Antony Lloyd, BSc, CEng, MIEE	LT CDR(FTC)	E	WE	01.10.01	LANCASTER
Bagnall, Sally-Anne, BSc.	LT CDR(MCC)	Q		01.10.04	RCDM
Bagshaw, James Richard William, BA.	LT(CC)	X	MW	01.09.98	FOST MPV SEA
Bailes, Kenneth Peter, BA	LT(CC)	X	FC	01.09.00	MWS COLLINGWOOD
Bailey, Daniel Standfast,	MAJ(FTC)	-		01.09.02	FPGRM
Bailey, Ian John, BEng, AMIEE.	LT(FTC)	E	WE	01.09.03	JFCHQ BRUNSSUM
Bailey, Jeremy James, BEng, MSc, CEng, MIMarEST	LT CDR(FTC)	E	ME	01.10.02	FWO PORTS SEA
Bailey, Michael,	LT(IC)	X	EW	01.07.04	JARIC
Bailey, Sian, BSc, PGCE.	LT(CC)	E	TM	01.08.99	DARTMOUTH BRNC
Bailey, Simon Glenn,	LT(IC)	X		01.01.05	CHATHAM
Bailey, Timothy David,	LT(IC)	E	WE	01.01.03	DLO BRISTOL
Baillie, Robbie William, BSc, PGCE.	LT(IC)	E	TM	01.05.00	1 ASSAULT GP RM
Bainbridge, John,	LT(IC) (Act Lt Cdr)	X	MCD	30.06.98	MWS DEF DIV SCHL
Bainbridge, Paul Anthony,	LT(IC)	S		12.08.05	EDINBURGH
Bainbridge, Stuart Darryl,	LT(FTC)	X	P	01.03.95	824 SQN
Baines, Andrew Richard, BSc.	LT(FTC)	X	P	01.07.97	EXCHANGE USA
Baines, David Michael Llewellyn, MSc.	LT CDR(FTC)	E	IS	01.10.01	FLEET COSCAP
Baines, Gary Anthony,	CAPT RM(FTC)	-	SO(LE)	01.01.01	RMR LONDON
Bains, Baldeep Singh, MB, ChB	SURG LT(SCC)	-		01.08.01	NELSON (PAY)
Baird, Elaine Harper, BSc	LT CDR(SCC)	Q		11.03.01	UKNSU NAPLES
Baird, George Mitchell,	LT(IC)	X	P	01.09.03	846 SQN
Baker, Adrian Bruce, MB, CHB, MSc, MFOM, DipAvMed, MRAeS	SURG CDR(FCC)	-	(CO/M)	30.06.94	FLEET AV SULTAN
Baker, Adrian Paul, BEng, pcea	LT CDR(FTC)	X	O	01.11.99	FLEET COSCAP
Baker, Alasdair,	CAPT RM(IC)	-	C	01.07.01	SFSG
Baker, Helen Mary Hartley, BEd	LT(IC)	S		01.05.04	JSCSC
Baker, James Edward Gunn, BA, MPhil	LT(IC)	X		01.09.02	MWS COLLINGWOOD
Baker, James Kieron, MSc.	SLT(IC)	X	P U/T	01.05.03	RNAS YEOVILTON
Baker, Michael Benson, BA.	MAJ(CC)	-	P	01.10.05	847 SQN
Baker, Michael John, BEng, CEng, MIEE.	LT CDR(FTC)	E	WE	01.06.98	DGMC SEA
Bakewell, Robert Andrew,	SLT(IC)	X		01.01.04	OCEAN
Bakewell, Timothy David, psc(j)	MAJ(FTC)	-		01.09.00	42 CDO RM
Baldie, Steven Anthony Hamilton, BEng	LT(CC)	X	P	15.11.98	848 SQN HERON
Baldwin, Christopher Martin, BA, pce, MSc.	LT CDR(FTC)	X	MCD	01.03.95	MANCHESTER
Baldwin, Simon Frederic, BSc, psc	CDRE(FTC)	E	AE	01.07.04	MERLIN IPT
Balfour, Ross Donald,	LT(IC)	X		01.07.04	MWS DEF DIV SCHL
Balhetchet, Adrian Stephen, BEng, CEng, MRAeS, Eur Ing	LT CDR(FTC)	E	AE	01.03.00	JSCSC
Ball, Andrew David, n, SM(n)	LT(FTC)	X	PWO(U)	01.01.99	CHATHAM
Ball, Matthew Peter, BEng, PGDip	LT(CC)	E	MESM	01.12.99	FWO FASLANE
Ball, Michael Peter, BSc, MIEE, CEng.	CDR(FTC)	E	WESM	30.06.04	HQ DCSA
Ball, Stephen James,	LT CDR(FTC)	E	ME	01.10.02	DRAKE SFM
Ball, William John Edgar,	LT(IC)	E	ME	01.05.03	FLEET COSCAP
Ballantyne, Craig, SM(n).	LT(CC)	X	SM	01.05.02	TALENT
Ballard, Adam Paul Vince,	LT(CC)	X		01.09.04	IRON DUKE
Ballard, Mark Lewis, BEng, MIEE, CEng	LT CDR(FTC)	E	WESM	01.12.00	VIGILANT(PORT)
Balletta, Rene James, n	LT CDR(FTC)	X	PWO(C)	01.11.04	EXCHANGE CANADA
Ballinger, Alexander,	2LT(IC)	-		01.08.02	CTCRM LYMPSTONE
Balm, Stephen Victor, psc(a)	LT COL(FTC)	-	LC	30.06.92	RMB STONEHOUSE
Balmer, Guy Austin,	MAJ(FTC)	-		24.04.02	DARTMOUTH BRNC
Balston, David Charles William, BA, pce, pce(sm), psc	CDR(FTC)	X	SM	30.06.97	MOD (LONDON)
Barnforth, Christian John Milton, BEng, CEng, MIEE	LT CDR(FTC)	E	WESM	01.12.05	MOD (LONDON)
Bance, Nicholas David, BSc.	LT CDR(FTC)	X	P	01.10.04	750 SQN HERON
Band, James Wright, BEng, MA, psc(j)	CDR(FTC)	E	AE	30.06.04	DLO YEO
Band, Sir Jonathon, KCB, ADC, BA, jsdc, pce, hcsc	ADM	-	PWO	02.08.02	MOD (LONDON)

(CHIEF OF NAVAL STAFF AND FIRST SEA LORD FEB 06)

Name	Rank	Branch	Spec	Seniority	Where Serving
Bane, Nicholas St John, BEng	LT(CC)	X	P	01.07.00	848 SQN HERON
Banfield, Steven David, BA	LT(IC)	X		01.09.04	CUMBERLAND
Bankier, Stewart,	LT CDR(FTC)	X		19.02.96	FLEET FOSNNI
Banks, Morven Janet, BSc	LT(IC)	X		01.01.04	RICHMOND
Bannister, Andrew Neil, BSc	LT CDR(FTC)	E	WE	01.10.01	CAPT MCTA
Bannister, Jonathan,	LT(CC)	X		01.02.03	MONTROSE
Bannon, William John Joseph, BA	SLT(IC)	X		01.11.04	DARTMOUTH BRNC
Barber, Alexander Stewart Leslie, BSc	LT(IC)	X		01.01.05	CHATHAM
Barber, Christopher James Harrison, BA	LT(FTC)	X	O	01.02.95	RNAS CULDROSE
Barber, Mark, BSc	LT(IC)	X	P	01.09.03	771 SQN
Barden, Paul Edward,	CAPT RM(IC)	-	SO(LE)	01.07.04	40 CDO RM
Barfoot, Peter Michael, BSc	LT(IC)	X	FC	01.09.03	NOTTINGHAM
Barham, Edward James, BA	SLT(IC)	X	O U/T	01.09.03	RNAS CULDROSE
Bark, James Spencer, pce(sm), SM	LT CDR(FTC)	X	SM	01.09.96	FOST FAS SHORE
Barker, David Charles Kingston, pce, pcea	CDR(FTC)	X	O	30.06.01	BDS WASHINGTON
Barker, Helen Anne,	SLT(IC)	S		01.09.04	MONTROSE
Barker, John Wilson, MBE, pcea	LT CDR(FTC)	X	O	01.10.99	EXCHANGE N ZLAND
Barker, Nicholas James, MA, pce, pcea, psc	LT CDR(FTC)	X	P	01.05.90	LAIPT
Barker, Paul David, BEng	LT(FTC)	E	P	01.04.00	820 SQN
Barker, Peter Roy, BSc	SLT(IC)	S		01.01.04	CUMBERLAND
Barker, Piers Thomas, BSc, pce(sm), SM	CDR(FTC)	X	SM	30.06.05	FLEET COMOPS NWD
Barker, Richard Demetrious John, OBE, MA, pce, pce(sm), psc(j)	CDR(FTC)	X	SM	30.06.97	PJHQ
Barker, Ruth,	SURG LT(SC(MD)	-		01.08.05	DARTMOUTH BRNC
Barker, Timothy John,	LT(CC)	X	O	16.10.99	771 SQN
Barker, Victoria Susan, BM, BS, BMS	SURG LT(MC(MD)	-		07.08.02	MDHU DERRIFORD
Barlow, David, MA	CHAPLAIN	CE		04.04.78	AFCC
Barlow, Matthew,	2LT(IC)	-		01.08.02	CTCRM LYMPSTONE
Barnard, Edward Benjamin Graham, BM, BS, BMS	SURG LT(SCC)	-		04.08.04	CDO LOG REGT RM
Barnard, Toby James, BEng	LT(IC)	E	TM	01.08.01	RMB STONEHOUSE
Barnbrook, Jeremy Charles, pcea	LT CDR(FTC)	X	P	16.12.96	771 SQN
Barnes, James Richard,	LT CDR(FTC)	X	AAWO	01.08.99	CATTISTOCK
Barnes, Nicholas John,	LT(IC)	S		01.05.03	NAVSEC
Barnes, Patrick Alan Lambeth, BSc	LT(CC)	X	P	01.04.94	FLEET AV VL
Barnes, Rex Warwick, MA, psc	LT COL(FTC)	-	LC	31.12.00	ALBION
Barnes-Yallowley, Jonathan James Hugh, pce, pcea	LT CDR(FTC)	X	P	16.07.92	CV(F) IPT
Barnett, Alan Clive, BA, MSc	LT CDR(FTC)	E	AE	01.02.02	EXCHANGE RAF UK
Barnwell, Alan,	CAPT RM(CC)	-	SO(LE)	21.07.01	COMATG SEA
Barr, David Jonathan,	LT(IC)	X	SM	01.09.05	RALEIGH
Barr, Derek Desmond,	LT(IC)	E	AE	01.04.02	849 SQN A FLT
Barr, Simon Peter, BSc	LT(CC)	X	P	01.09.99	EXCHANGE ARMY UK
Barrand, Stuart Martin, pce	CDR(FTC)	X	AAWO	30.06.02	FLEET COSP&S
Barratt, Stephen Mitchell,	LT CDR(FTC)	S	(W)	01.10.02	RNAS CULDROSE
Barrett, Benjamin Thomas, BA	LT(IC)	X		01.08.04	MWS HM TG (D)
Barrett, David Leonard, IEng, MIIE	LT CDR(FTC)	E	AE	01.10.01	JCA IPT UK
Barrett, Scott,	LT(IC)	X	SM	01.01.04	VANGUARD(PORT)
Barrett, Stephen James,	LT CDR(FTC)	E	WE	01.10.99	MOD (LONDON)
Barrick, Paul Vincent,	LT CDR(FTC)	E	EW	01.10.98	SCU SHORE
Barrie, Stuart, BEng	LT(IC)	E	WESM	01.09.04	VIGILANT(PORT)
Barritt, Olivier David, BA	LT(IC)	X	H2	01.04.00	SCOTT
Barron, Jeremy Mark,	LT(IC)	E	WESM	01.05.01	TORBAY
Barron, Patrick Joseph, BSc	LT CDR(FTC)	X	C	01.10.00	EAGLET
Barron, Philip Robert,	LT(CC)	X	O	01.01.04	815 FLT 215
Barron-Robinson, David Paul,	LT(FTC)	E	WESM	01.04.01	FOST DSTF
Barrow, Charles Michael,	LT(CC)	X	FC	01.01.02	JSCSC
Barrow, Jamie,	2LT(IC)	-		01.08.01	FPGRM
Barrow, Marc,	2LT(IC)	-		01.08.02	CTCRM LYMPSTONE
Barrows, David Malcolm, BEng, MSc, MIEE	LT CDR(FTC)	E	WE	01.10.03	ILLUSTRIOUS
Barrows, Susan Mary, BEng	LT CDR(FTC)	E	WE	01.10.03	MWS COLLINGWOOD
Barry, John Peter,	LT CDR(FTC)	X	PWO(U)	01.10.02	MHRF(F)
Barter, Emma Charlotte, BEng	SLT(IC)	E	ME U/T	01.01.04	SULTAN
Bartholomew, David John, BSc	LT(IC)	E	TM	01.05.00	SULTAN
Bartholomew, Ian Munro, ARICS, psc	CDR(FTC)	X	H CH	31.12.92	FLEET CMR

Name	Rank	Branch	Spec	Seniority	Where Serving
Bartlett, David Leslie, MEng	SLT(IC)	E	AE U/T	01.09.04	ILLUSTRIOUS
Bartlett, David Stephen George, BSc	CDR(FTC)	E	AE	30.06.04	AH IPT
Bartlett, Ian David, BEng, MSc	LT CDR(FTC)	E	MESM	01.01.98	SULTAN
Barton, Keith Jeffrey Atkinson, BEng, MSc, MRAeS	LT(CC)	E	AE	01.03.99	JSCSC
Barton, Mark Alfred, BEng, CEng, MIMechE, MRINA	LT CDR(FTC)	E	ME	01.07.00	NP IRAQ
Barton, Peter Glenn, MSc	CDR(FTC)	E	WE	30.06.99	HQ DCSA
Barton, Sarah Jane, MB, BS	SURG LTCDR(MCC)	-		04.08.04	NELSON (PAY)
Bartram, Gregory James,	LT(IC)	E	WE	01.05.02	NOTTINGHAM
Bartram, Richard James,	LT(CC)	X	P	01.11.00	NP AFGHANISTAN
Bass, Emma Margaret, BEng	LT(CC)	E	WE	01.09.01	DLO BRISTOL
Bass, Paul William,	LT(CC)	E	WESM	01.01.03	TORPEDO IPT
Bassett, Dean Anthony, BA, MNI, AMNI, pce, n	LT CDR(FTC)	X	PWO(A)	01.10.02	PJHQ
Bassett, Neil Edward,	LT CDR(FTC)	E	WE	01.10.99	JSSU CYPRUS
Bassett, Nicole, BSc	SLT(IC)	S		01.05.04	WESTMINSTER
Basson, Andrew Paul, MSc, FCIPD, MDA, psc	CDR(FTC)	E	TM	30.06.00	FLEET HQ WI
Bastiaens, Paul Alexander, BEng, MIEE, MRAeS	LT(IC)	E	AE	01.05.02	846 SQN
Bate, David Ian George,	LT CDR(FTC)	X	MCD	01.10.95	MWS EXCELLENT
Bate, Rohan Christopher, BSc	SLT(IC)	X		01.06.03	ROEBUCK
Bateman, Richard Michael, MB, CHB, FFARCSI	SURG LTCDR(MCC)	-		02.08.00	NELSON (PAY)
Bateman, Stephen John Francis,	CDR(FTC)	X	AAWO	30.06.93	RNLO GULF
Bates, Andrew James, BSc	LT(CC)	X	P	16.04.98	824 SQN
Bates, Nicholas Stuart, BSc	LT(CC)	X	O	01.04.00	824 SQN
Bath, Edward George,	LT CDR(FTC)	X	AAWO	27.12.95	MWS COLLINGWOOD
Bath, Michael Anthony William, BSc, psc(j)	CDR(FTC)	S	SM	30.06.00	MOD (LONDON)
Batham, Donald, MB, BS, DObstRCOG, Dip FFP, MRCGP	SURG CDR(SC(MD)	-	GMPP	01.09.04	JSU NORTHWOOD
Batho, William Guy Pakenham, BSc	LT(IC)	X	P U/T	01.07.05	DHFS
Bathurst, Sir (David) Benjamin, GCB, DL, rcds	ADM OF FLEET	-	P	10.07.95	
Batley, Jonathan Taylor, BMus	SLT(IC)	X	P U/T	01.06.03	RNAS YEOVILTON
Battrick, Richard Robert,	LT CDR(FTC)	X	AAWO	01.04.04	GLOUCESTER
Baudains, Terence John, BSc, pce	LT CDR(FTC) (Act Cdr)	X	CMA	01.04.89	FLEET FOTR
Baugh, Adrian Joseph Edward, MA	LT(IC)	E	WESM	01.02.06	RALEIGH
Baum, Stuart Richard, BSc, pce, pce(sm)	CAPT(FTC)	X	SM	30.06.06	FWO FASLANE SEA
Baverstock, Andrew Peter,	LT(CC)	X	AV	01.10.02	800 NAS (GR7)
Baxendale, Robert Fred, BSc, MA, psc(j)	MAJ(FTC)	-		01.09.99	MOD (BATH)
Baxter, Arran Charles,	LT(IC)	E	MESM	01.05.02	DRAKE CBS
Baxter, Frederick Joseph,	LT(IC)	E	AE	01.04.01	SULTAN
Baxter, Iain Menzies, BEng, CEng, MRAeS	LT CDR(FTC)	E	AE	01.01.00	DLO YEO
Baxter, John Charles, SM	LT(FTC) (Act Lt Cdr)	X	SM	27.09.95	CC MAR AGRIPPA
Bayliss, James Edward Lindley, BSc	SLT(IC)	X	P U/T	01.01.05	DARTMOUTH BRNC
Bayliss, Richard,	LT(IC)	X	EW	01.07.04	FLEET HQ NWD
Beacham, Philip Robert, BA	LT CDR(FTC)	X	P	01.07.03	FOST SEA
Beadle, John Thomas,	CHAPLAIN	SF		30.03.95	DARTMOUTH BRNC
Beadling, David John,	LT(CC)	E	MESM	01.09.01	OCLC MANCH
Beadnell, Robert Mark, MSc	LT CDR(FTC)	E	TM	01.01.04	RALEIGH
Beadon, Colin John Alexander, MBE, psc(a)	LT COL(FTC)	-		30.06.94	RMR BRISTOL
Beale, Michael Dean,	LT(FTC)	X	MCD	23.07.98	MWS DEF DIV SCHL
Beales, Nicola Susan, BA	LT(IC)	S		01.01.03	NELSON
Beanland, Peter Louis, BSc	LT(CC)	X		01.06.00	OCLC MANCH
Beard, David John, MB, BCH	SURG LT(SCC)	-		01.08.01	MDHU DERRIFORD
Beard, Graham Thomas Charles, BA, psc	CDR(FTC)	S		31.12.98	FLEET COSP&S
Beard, Hugh Dominic, pce, pce(sm), psc(j), SM(n), SM, MA	CDR(FTC)	X	SM	30.06.05	TRENCHANT
Beard, Richard Geoffrey,	LT(FTC) (Act Lt Cdr)	X	C	10.12.98	LOAN DSTL
Beard, Stephen Anthony,	LT(IC)	X		01.01.04	MWS COLLINGWOOD
Beardall, Michael John Doodson, pce, psc(j), MA	CDR(FTC)	X	AAWO	30.06.03	FLEET COMOPS NWD
Beardsley, Nigel,	CHAPLAIN	CE		03.05.05	MWS COLLINGWOOD
Beats, Kevan Ashley, pce	LT CDR(FTC)	X	PWO(U)	16.02.90	FLEET COMOPS NWD
Beattie, Paul Spencer, pce, n	LT CDR(FTC)	X	AAWO	01.10.01	MWS COLLINGWOOD
Beaumont, David Mark,	CAPT RM(IC)	-	SO(LE)	19.07.05	UKLFCSG RM
Beaumont, Ian Hirst, pce, pcea	CAPT(FTC)	X	O	30.06.04	NELSON
Beaumont, Steven John, BSc	LT CDR(FTC)	X	C	01.10.00	FLEET COSCAP
Beautyman, Andrew John, BEng	LT CDR(FTC)	E	MESM	01.10.03	VIGILANT(STBD)
Beaver, Robert Mark Steven, BSc, AMIMechE	LT(FTC) (Act Lt Cdr)	E	ME	01.05.98	DLO BRISTOL

Name	Rank	Branch Spec	Seniority	Where Serving
Beavis, John Alexander, BSc	LT(CC)	X MCD	01.04.99	EXCHANGE CANADA
Beazley, Phillip, sq	MAJ(FTC)	- SO(LE)	01.10.99	RALEIGH
Bebbington, David Mark,	LT(IC)	X	17.02.06	MWS COLLINGWOOD
Beck, Andrew James, BA	SLT(IC)	X	01.05.04	ILLUSTRIOUS
Beck, Edward Alexander, MEng	SLT(IC)	E ME U/T	01.09.04	DARTMOUTH BRNC
Beck, Simon Kingsley, pce	LT CDR(FTC)	X PWO(A)	01.04.99	CUMBERLAND
Becker, Robert Keith, BA	LT(IC)	X	01.05.03	NORTHUMBERLAND
Beckett, Keith Andrew, BSc, MDA, rcds	CAPT(FTC)	E MESM	30.06.04	FLEET COSP&S
Bedding, Darren, BA	LT(CC)	X P	01.06.00	EXCHANGE RAF UK
Bedding, Simon William Edward, BEng, CEng, MIEE	LT CDR(FTC)	E WE	01.04.00	PJHQ
Bedelle, Stephen James,	LT CDR(FTC)	E WE	01.10.03	EXCHANGE CANADA
Beech, Christopher Martin, pce	LT CDR(FTC)	X PWO(C)	01.07.98	MHRF(F)
Beech, Daymion John, BSc	LT(FTC)	X P	16.03.98	RNAS YEOVILTON
Beeching, Lee Graham,	SLT(IC)	X	01.02.05	DARTMOUTH BRNC
Beedle, James Daniel Stephen,	LT(IC)	X	01.01.06	SOUTHAMPTON
Beegan, Clive Francis, SM	LT(IC)	X SM	01.01.02	RALEIGH
Beete, Jon,	2LT(IC)	-	01.08.02	CTCRM LYMPSTONE
Belcher, Darren Ronald,	LT(IC)	E WE	01.07.04	MANCHESTER
Bell, Adrian Scott, pce, psc, hcsc	CAPT(FTC)	X PWO(U)	30.06.02	MOD (LONDON)
Bell, Catriona Mary, BSc	LT(CC)	X	01.02.99	FOST MPV SEA
Bell, Charlotte,	SURG SLT(SCC) (Act Surg Lt)	-	12.07.05	DARTMOUTH BRNC
Bell, David John, BEng	LT(IC)	X P	01.05.04	RNAS CULDROSE
Bell, Fiona Jean,	LT(IC)	E ME	01.09.05	OCEAN
Bell, Jeffrey Mark, BEng, CEng, MRAeS, MDA	LT CDR(FTC)	E AE	01.05.04	CHINOOK IPT
Bell, Lewis George,	LT(IC)	X	01.02.06	MONMOUTH
Bell, Lucy Jane,	LT(CC)	S	01.08.02	FLEET HQ PORTSEA
Bell, Mark,	LT CDR(FTC)	S SM	01.10.00	MWS COLLINGWOOD
Bell, Nicholas Andrew Graham, BEng	LT(IC)	X P	01.05.04	RNAS CULDROSE
Bell, Reginald Paul William,	LT CDR(FTC)	X AAWO	01.10.90	MWC PORTSDOWN
Bell, Richard,	SLT(IC)	X O U/T	01.05.03	RNAS CULDROSE
Bell, Robert Douglas, pce	LT CDR(FTC)	X PWO(U)	01.03.97	DLO BRISTOL
Bell, Scott William, MinstAM	LT(FTC)	S SM	01.04.01	TORBAY
Bell-Davies, Richard William, BSc, pce, psc	CDR(FTC) (Act Capt)	X PWO(U)	30.06.93	JFC HQ AGRIPPA
Bellfield, Robert James Astley, MA, pce, psc(j)	CDR(FTC)	X PWO(U)	30.06.04	PORTLAND
Benarr, Christopher Michael,	LT(FTC)	X	01.02.03	RNAS CULDROSE
Benbow, James Alexander Kennedy,	LT(IC)	X	01.05.04	SULTAN
Bence, David Elliott, pce	LT CDR(FTC)	X MCD	01.02.98	JSCSC
Benn, Gordon Ian,	SLT(IC)	X	01.02.05	DARTMOUTH BRNC
Benn, Stephen William, BEng, MAPM, MSc, CEng, MRAeS	LT CDR(FTC)	E AE	01.10.02	824 SQN
Bennet, George Charters,	CAPT RM(CC)	-	01.09.03	UKLFCSG RM
Bennett, Alan Reginald Courtenay, DSC,	CDRE(FTC)	X P	15.07.03	BDS WASHINGTON
FRAeS, jsdc, pce, pcea, psc, hcsc				
Bennett, Anthony John, FCIPD	LT CDR(FTC)	S (W)	01.10.97	FLEET COSP&S
Bennett, Brian Cecil Harold, BSc	LT(IC)	E TM	01.11.01	SULTAN
Bennett, Christopher David, BSc	LT(CC)	X P	01.03.00	847 SQN
Bennett, Douglas Prasad, BEng	LT(IC)	E IS	01.05.97	AFPAA JPA
Bennett, Elizabeth Claire, BSc	SLT(IC)	X	01.01.05	DARTMOUTH BRNC
Bennett, Graham Lingley Nepean, pce	LT CDR(FTC)	X PWO(U)	01.07.93	FOST NWD (JMOTS)
Bennett, Ian James, BSc	SLT(IC)	X O U/T	01.09.04	DARTMOUTH BRNC
Bennett, Mark Anthony, BEng	LT(IC)	E WESM	01.01.04	VANGUARD(PORT)
Bennett, Neil Malcolm, BA, psc, psc(j)o	LT COL(FTC)	- C	30.06.04	LN BPST SAFRICA
Bennett, Paul Martin, BA, pce	CAPT(FTC)	X PWO(A)	30.06.04	FLEET COSCAP
Bennett, Stuart Albin Frances James, MB, BS	SURG LT(MC(MD)	-	01.08.01	MDHU DERRIFORD
Bennett, William Dean, SM	LT CDR(FTC)	X C	01.10.00	CC MAR AGRIPPA
Bennett, William Ellis, MEng	LT(CC)	E ME	01.01.00	DLO BRISTOL
Benstead, Neil William John, BEng, MSc	LT CDR(FTC)	E ME	01.10.04	DLO BRISTOL
Bent, Philip Michael, BEng	LT(IC)	E WE	01.02.06	UKMARBATSTAFF
Bentham-Green, Nicholas Richard Heriot, psc	MAJ(FTC) (Act Lt Col)	- LC	01.09.92	FLEET COSP&S
Bentley, Grant Stockford,	LT(IC)	X P U/T	01.05.03	RNAS YEOVILTON
Benton, Angus Michael, BSc	LT CDR(FTC)	X MCD	01.09.96	MWC PORTSDOWN
Benton, Peter John, MB, BCh, FFOM, CHB	SURG CDR(FCC)	- (CO/M)	31.12.93	DRAKE CBS
Benzie, Nichol James Emslie, BSc	LT(CC)	X P	01.10.98	EXCHANGE RAF UK

Name	Rank	Branch	Spec	Seniority	Where Serving
Beresford-Green, Paul Maxwell,	LT CDR(FTC)	S		16.12.00	FLEET COSP&S
Bernard, Alain Raymond, BA	LT(CC) (Act Lt Cdr)	X	HM2	01.04.97	FOST SEA
Bernau, Jeremy Charles, pce, pce(sm), SM	LT CDR(FTC)	X	SM	01.11.91	FOST FAS SHORE
Berry, David Hartwell, MA	SLT(IC)	X		01.06.04	DARTMOUTH BRNC
Berry, James Thomas, BSc	LT(IC)	X	P	01.09.03	846 SQN
Berry, Mark Gustav,	LT(IC)	X	EW	25.08.04	SCU SHORE
Berry, Steven Mark,	LT(CC)	E	WE	01.01.02	DLO TES
Berry, Timothy James, BSc, n	LT(FTC)	X		01.09.98	MWS COLLINGWOOD
Bessant, Matthew, BSc	LT(IC)	X		01.04.05	TYNE
Bessell, David Alexander, BA, SM(n), SM	LT CDR(FTC)	X	SM	01.06.01	VENGEANCE(STBD)
Best, Robert Michael, BSc	LT(CC)	E	MESM	01.09.02	SUPERB
Best, Russell Richard, OBE, BA, pce, psc	CAPT(FTC)	X	PWO(U)	30.06.01	D STRAT PLANS
Bestwick, Michael Charles, MA, psc(j)	LT COL(FTC)	-		30.06.06	40 CDO RM
Betchley, James William, MSc	LT(IC)	X		01.05.05	SUPERB
Betteridge, Jeremy Trevor, MCMI, pce, pcea, psc	CDR(FTC)	X	P	30.06.96	DNR RCHQ SOUTH
Bettles, John,	LT(IC)	X		01.12.03	WESTMINSTER
Betton, Andrew, MA, pce, pcea, psc(j)	CDR(FTC)	X	O	30.06.03	MOD (LONDON)
Betts, Andrew Thomas James,	SLT(IC)	E	AE U/T	01.09.03	SULTAN
Betts, Peter Richard,	SLT(IC)	E	WESMUT	01.09.03	MWS COLLINGWOOD
Bevan, Jeffrey Richard,	LT(CC)	X	P	16.12.99	824 SQN
Bevan, Noel Stuart, MB, BS, FRCGP, LRCP, MRCS..... SURG CAPT(FCC) (Commodore)		-	GMPP	31.12.99	DPMD
Bevan, Simon, BSc, MBA, jsdc, psc(j)	CAPT(FTC)	X	METOC	30.06.03	MOD (LONDON)
Beveridge, Simon Alexander Ronald, BA, CertTh	CHAPLAIN	CE		28.04.93	RNAS YEOVILTON
Beverley, Andrew Peter, BSc	LT(IC)	E	IS	01.02.03	AFPAA(CENTURION)
Beverstock, Mark Alistair, BSc, CEng, FIEE, rcds	CAPT(FTC)	E	WESM	30.06.03	MOD (LONDON)
Bevis, Timothy John, MA, psc(j)	COL(FTC)	-		30.06.04	MOD (LONDON)
Bewick, David John, pce, psc(j), MA	CDR(FTC)	X	PWO(U)	30.06.02	PJHQ
Bhattacharya, Debdash, BSc	LT CDR(FTC)	X	P	01.10.03	RNAS CULDROSE
Bibbey, Mark William, BA, psc(m)	COL(FTC)	-		31.12.00	PJHQ
Bickley, Gary Neil,	LT(IC)	X		01.01.03	PORTLAND
Biggs, David Michael, pcea, BSc	LT CDR(FTC)	X	O	01.10.96	849 SQN A FLT
Biggs, Peter,	LT(IC)	X		01.05.02	RALEIGH
Biggs, William Patrick Lowther, BEng, MA, MSc, CEng, MIEE, psc(j)	CDR(FTC)	E	WE	30.06.04	MOD (LONDON)
Bignell, Stephen, BEng	LT CDR(FTC)	E	WE	01.04.00	FLEET COMOPS NWD
Billings, Andrew,	LT(IC)	X	REG	25.06.05	FLEET COSP&S
Billington, Nigel Stephen, BA, MInstAM, MILT, psc	LT CDR(FTC)	S	SM	01.02.88	DLO/DG LOG (SC)
Billington, Tony John,	LT CDR(FTC)	X	EW	01.10.00	FLEET COSCAP
Bilson, John Michael Frederick, pce	LT CDR(FTC)	X	AAWO	01.01.93	EXCHANGE USA
Bingham, Alexander Anthony John, MEng	LT(IC)	E	ME	01.05.03	DFTE PORTSMOUTH
Bingham, David Spencer,	LT CDR(FTC)	X	AAWO	01.03.99	FOST SEA
Binns, James Barnaby, BEng	SLT(IC)	E	MESM	01.09.03	FWO DEVONPORT
Binns, John Richard,	LT(CC)	E	WE	01.01.02	SANS IPT
Binns, Jon Frank, BA	LT(CC)	X	HM	01.05.01	BULWARK
Birbeck, Keith,	LT CDR(FTC)	E	WESM	01.10.98	FWO DEVONPORT
Birch, Peter Laurence, BEng	LT(IC)	X	P	01.01.03	815 SQN HQ
Birchall, James Charles, BSc	LT(CC)	X	P	01.04.98	847 SQN
Birchall, Stephen John, BSc, CEng, MIMarEST	CDR(FTC)	E	MESM	30.06.02	MOD (BATH)
Bird, Andrew William,	LT(IC)	X	P	01.09.04	RNAS YEOVILTON
Bird, David Edward, pcea	LT CDR(FTC(A)	X	P	01.10.93	DHFS
Bird, Gary Michael, BA	CAPT RM(CC)	-		01.09.99	JCTTAT
Bird, Jonathan Michael, BEng, pcea, gdas, MSc	LT CDR(FTC)	X	O	01.10.03	829 FLT 01
Bird, Matthew Graham James, BEng, CEng, MRAeS	LT CDR(FTC)	E	AE	01.11.02	DEF SCH OF LANG
Bird, Michael Philip, BA	LT(IC)	X		01.01.06	EDINBURGH
Bird, Paul,	2LT(IC)	-		01.08.02	CTCRM LYMPSTONE
Bird, Richard Alexander James, PGDIP, pce, n	LT CDR(FTC)	X	H CH	01.07.98	MOD (LONDON)
Bird, Timothy Michael, BA	SLT(IC)	S		01.06.03	RALEIGH
Bird, Toby Samuel Varnam, MA	LT(IC)	E	TM	01.09.98	EXCHANGE RAF UK
Birkby, Christina, BSc	LT(IC)	X		01.12.04	ILLUSTRIOUS
Birkin, Kay, BSc	LT(IC)	MS		01.01.04	DDS HALTON
Birleson, Paul Denzil, BSc	LT(FTC)	X	H2	01.09.99	RFANSU
Birley, Jonathan Hugh, pce	LT CDR(FTC)	X	PWO(U)	01.05.95	EXCHANGE USA
Birrell, Gavin Craig, BSc, MA	LT CDR(FTC)	X	PWO(C)	01.07.05	ILLUSTRIOUS

Name	Rank	Branch	Spec	Seniority	Where Serving
Birrell, Stuart Martin, MA, psc(j)	LT COL(FTC)	-		30.06.03	HQ 3 CDO BDE RM
Birse, Gregor James, BA, MSc, PGDip	LT CDR(FTC)	X	METOC	01.10.02	ILLUSTRIOUS
Birt, David Jonathan, MB, BS, FRCA	SURG CDR(FCC)	-	(CA)	30.06.01	MDHU DERRIFORD
Bishop, George Charles,	LT(FTC)	X	AV	27.07.95	RNAS YEOVILTON
Bishop, Paul Richard, BSc, MIMechE, MRAeS, CEng	CAPT(FTC)	E	AE	30.06.03	HARRIER IPT
Bissett, Ian Michael,	LT CDR(FTC)	E	AE	01.10.00	MERLIN IPT
Bissett, Phillip Keith, BSc	LT CDR(FTC)	E	AE	01.10.00	JCA IPT UK
Bisson, Ian Jean Paul, MSc, CEng, MIEE, psc, gw	CDR(FTC)	E	WE	30.06.99	MOD (LONDON)
Black, Edward John, MA(CANTAB)	LT(IC)	X	MW	01.01.02	MWS COLLINGWOOD
Black, Joanna Mary, BSc	LT(IC)	X		15.05.03	DUMBARTON CASTLE
Black, Kenneth James, BSc	SLT(IC)	X	O U/T	01.01.04	RNAS CULDROSE
Black, Sarah Beth, MA	LT(CC) (Act Lt Cdr)	S		05.11.99	FLEET FOTR
Blackburn, Andrew Roland James, BEng, MSc gw, CEng, MRAeS	LT(FTC)	E	AE	01.12.98	FLEET COSP&S
Blackburn, Craig Jonathan,	LT(IC)	X		01.09.04	MONMOUTH
Blackburn, Emma Catherine, BEng, MSc	LT(CC)	E	AE	01.07.99	FLEET COSP&S
Blackburn, Lee Richard, BEng	LT(FTC)	E	ME	01.09.00	ILLUSTRIOUS
Blackburn, Stephen Anthony, BSc, CEng, MIMarEST	LT CDR(FTC)	E	ME	01.03.98	DLO BRISTOL
Blackburn, Stuart James, SM(n), SM	LT CDR(FTC)	X	SM	01.05.02	TRAFALGAR
Blackett, William Philip Harry,	SLT(IC)	X		01.09.03	MWS COLLINGWOOD
Blackford, Oliver,	2LT(IC)	-		01.08.02	CTCRM LYMPSTONE
Blackler, Steven, BSc	LT(IC)	E	IS	01.01.01	ARK ROYAL
Blackman, Nicholas Trevor, BSc, MA, CEng, MIEE, psc(j)	CDR(FTC)	E	AE	30.06.03	DLO YEO
Blackmore, Andrew Michael,	SLT(IC)	E	WESM	01.09.03	FWO DEVPT SEA
Blackmore, James, BSc	LT(FTC)	X	P	16.01.98	LOAN DSTL
Blackmore, Mark Stuart, pce, pcea, psc(j)	CDR(FTC)	X	O	30.06.02	MCM1 SEA
Blackwell, Richard Edward,	LT CDR(FTC)	S	SM	01.12.96	ARK ROYAL
Bladen, Christopher Samuel,	LT(IC)	X	P	01.05.04	845 SQN
Blair, Duncan Guy Sanderman, MB, BCh, MRCGP, Dip FFP	SURG CDR(FCC)	-	GMPP	30.06.03	HQ DMETA
Blair, Graeme John Livingston, BEng, CEng, MIMechE	LT CDR(FTC)	E	MESM	01.05.04	VIGILANT(PORT)
Blair, Lee David,	LT(IC)	X		01.05.04	SOVEREIGN
Blake, Gary Edmund, BSc	CDR(FTC)	E	WESM	30.06.00	PJHQ
Blake, Matthew George,	LT(IC)	X		01.05.05	750 SQN SEAHAWK
Blake, Sherwyn, BSc, PGDip	LT(IC)	E	MESM	01.09.04	SUPERB
Blakeley, Anne Louise,	LT(SCC)	Q	CC	17.11.98	MDHU DERRIFORD
Blanchford, Daniel, BEng	MAJ(FTC)	-		01.09.02	JSCSC
Bland, Christopher David, MEng, AMIEE	LT(CC)	E	WESM	01.05.01	DLO BRISTOL
Bland, Steven Aaron, MB, CHB, BSc, RCSEd	SURG LTCDR(MCC)	-		07.08.01	NELSON (PAY)
Blatcher, David John,	SLT(UCE)(IC)	E	MESMUT	01.09.04	DARTMOUTH BRNC
Blatchford, Timothy,	LT(IC)	E	AE U/T	08.04.05	824 SQN
Bleakley, Charles, BSc	SURG SLT(SCC)	-		02.07.03	DARTMOUTH BRNC
Bleasdale, Daniel Robert, BSc	LT(IC)	E	TM	01.04.01	FWO DEVPT SEA
Blenkinsop, Graham John, BA	SLT(IC)	X		01.05.04	LIVERPOOL
Blethyn, Hugh Phillip, MSc	LT(IC)	E	IS	01.01.00	CINCFLEET FIMU
Blick, Sarah Louise,	LT(IC)	S		01.01.02	FLEET COSP&S
Bligh, Sarah Louise,	LT(CC)	X	FC	01.05.04	GLOUCESTER
Block, Andrew William George, MA, MIEE, pce	LT CDR(FTC)	X	AAWO	01.07.02	CAMPBELTOWN
Blocke, Andrew David,	LT CDR(FTC)	MS	(AD)	01.10.04	RN GIBRALTAR
Blois, Simon Dudley, BSc, MIEE	LT(FTC)	E	WE	01.04.01	RMC OF SCIENCE
Blount, Derek Raymond, BSc, CEng, MIMechE, isc	CDR(FTC)	E	MESM	30.06.06	FOST SM SEA
Blount, Keith Edward, pce, pcea, psc(j)	CDR(FTC)	X	P	31.12.00	FOST SEA
Blowers, Michael David, pce, pcea, psc(a)	CDR(FTC)	X	O	31.12.00	RNAS CULDROSE
Blunden, Jeremy Jonathan Frank, LVO, BSc, pce	CAPT(FTC)	X	PWO(N)	30.06.05	MOD (LONDON)
Blunt, Carla Lisa,	SLT(IC)	X		01.02.05	KENT
Blythe, James,	LT(IC)	X		01.12.01	RANGER
Blythe, Paul Christopher, pce, pce(sm), SM	LT CDR(FTC)	X	SM	01.10.99	FLEET COMOPS NWD
Blythe, Tom Stuart, psc(j)	MAJ(FTC)	-	LC	01.09.00	EXCHANGE ARMY UK
Blythen, Richard,	CHAPLAIN	RC		06.09.05	FWO DEVPT SEA
Boakes, Philip John,	LT(CC)	E	ME	01.05.02	ECHO
Boardman, Sarah Jane, MA	LT(CC)	S		01.01.02	RAF COTTESMORE
Boddington, Jeremy Denis Leonard, BSc, MRAeS, MDA, pcea, tp	LT CDR(FTC)	X	P	16.12.95	700M MERLIN OEU
Boddy, Katherine Louise, MB, CHB	SURG LT(SC)(MD)	-		06.08.03	RNAS CULDROSE
Bodman, Simon Alexander, BEng	LT(CC)	X		01.04.00	MWS COLLINGWOOD

Name	Rank	Branch	Spec	Seniority	Where Serving
Boeckx, Thomas Julius Francis, MSc	LT(FTC)	X		01.01.00	PUNCHER
Boissier, Robin Paul, MA, MSc, pce, pce(sm), psc	RADM	-	SM	26.08.02	DLO BRISTOL
(DIRECTOR GENERAL LOGISTICS (FLEET) SEP 04)					
Bolam, Andrew Guy, BSc, CEng, MIMarEST	LT CDR(FTC)	E	ME	01.06.94	MWS EXCELLENT
Bollen, Johanna Michelle,	LT CDR(FTC)	S		01.10.03	JHCHQ
Bolton, Jonathan Praed, BEng, CEng, MIMarEST	LT CDR(FTC)	E	ME	01.09.99	CV(F) IPT
Bolton, Matthew Thomas William, BEng, MSc,	LT CDR(FTC)	E	ME	06.02.00	FLEET COSP&S
CEng, MIMarEST, MIMechE					
Bolton, Stephen Jack,	LT CDR(FTC)	X	P	01.10.04	815 SQN HQ
Bond, Jason Eric, BA	LT(IC)	X	H2	01.05.02	820 SQN
Bond, Nigel David,	CDR(FTC)	S		31.12.00	JHCHQ
Bond, Robert Douglas Acton,	LT(CC)	X	P	01.09.04	846 SQN
Bond, Robert James,	LT(IC)	X		01.04.06	CYPRUS PBS
Bone, Christopher John, AMRAeS	LT CDR(FTC)	E	AE	01.05.92	FS MASU
Bone, Darren Nigel, pce, psc(j)	CDR(FTC)	X	PWO(A)	31.12.99	FLEET HQ WI
Bone, Richard Charles, BSc, psc(j)	LT CDR(FTC)	E	TMSM	01.05.98	MOD (LONDON)
Bonnar, John Andrew, BEng, MIEE	LT CDR(FTC)	E	WE	01.06.01	ARGYLL
Bonnar, Susan Mary,	LT(CC)	X	ATC	01.11.96	RNAS YEOVILTON
Bonner, Timothy John, MB, ChB	SURG LT(MC(MD)	-		09.08.01	MDHU DERRIFORD
Bonney, James Edward, BSc	CAPT RM(CC)	-	LC	01.09.01	OCEAN
Boon, Gareth John,	LT(FTC)	X	METOC	19.09.00	MWC SOUTHWICK
Boon, Simon Edward, BSc	LT(IC)	S		01.09.03	SUPERB
Boot, Stephen,	LT(IC)	S		01.07.03	YORK
Booth, Alan Kevin, MSc	SLT(IC)	X	P U/T	01.09.04	DARTMOUTH BRNC
Booth, Diccon Philip Paul, BSc, PhD	LT(IC)	E	TM	01.09.01	SULTAN
Booth, Rachael,	SURG SLT(SCC) (Act Surg Lt)	-		02.08.05	DARTMOUTH BRNC
Booth, Thomas Oliver, BSc	SLT(IC)	X		01.09.03	ECHO
Booth, William Norman, BSc, Cert Ed, IEng, MIEE, AMIMarEST	LT(FTC) (Act Lt Cdr)	E	ME	02.09.99	CAMPBELTOWN
Bootland, Erich Gustav, psc	CAPT(FTC)	MS	(AD)	24.07.02	MOD (LONDON)
Boraston, Peter John, BSc, CEng, MIEE	LT CDR(FTC)	E	WE	01.04.90	NELSON (PAY)
Borbone, Nicholas, pce	LT CDR(FTC)	X	AAWO	01.02.03	FLEET COSCAP
Borland, Stuart Andrew, BSc, MA, CEng, MIEE, psc(j)	CDR(FTC)	E	WE	30.06.01	OCEAN
Borley, Kim John, MA, CEng, MIEE, rcds, jsdc	RADM	-	WESM	07.09.04	FLEET FOTR
(FOTR-FOTR PERSONAL APR 06)					
Borrett, John Edward, BSc	LT(IC)	X		01.07.05	GLOUCESTER
Boschi, Paul Hamilton, BA	MAJ(CC)	-		01.10.05	45 CDO RM
Bosley, Benjamin Daniel, n	LT(FTC)	X		01.10.03	MWS COLLINGWOOD
Bosshardt, Robert George, pce, jsdc, MCIPD, MSc	CDR(FTC)	X	AAWO	31.12.93	FLEET FOTR
Boston, Justin, BA, MSc	LT CDR(FTC)	E	TM	01.01.05	MWC SOUTHWICK
Bosustow, Antony Michael, BEng, CEng, MIEE	LT CDR(FTC)	E	WE	01.06.98	MWS COLLINGWOOD
Botham, Adrian,	LT(IC)	E	WE	16.12.05	MWS COLLINGWOOD
Botterill, Hugh Walter Scott,	LT(IC)	X		01.05.03	LANCASTER
Botting, Neil Andrew, BSc	LT(CC)	X	SM	01.09.02	TRENCHANT
Bottomley, Steven,	LT(FTC) (Act Lt Cdr)	E	AE	06.09.96	AH IPT
Botwood, Tudor, MBE, BD	CHAPLAIN	SF		09.09.02	ARK ROYAL
Boud, Colin Stanley, BEng, PGDip, AMIMechE	LT(IC)	E	MESM	01.01.04	SCEPTRE
Boughton, Jonathan Anthony Lee, BEng, MIEE	LT(IC)	E	WE	01.02.03	HQ DCSA
Boughton, Timothy Frederick,	LT(FTC) (Act Lt Cdr)	X	P	01.07.97	JHCHQ
Bougourd, Mark Anthony, BEng, MRAeS	LT CDR(FTC)	E	AE	01.10.99	MERLIN IPT
Boulind, Matthew Angus, LLB	LT(IC)	X	O	01.01.02	815 FLT 212
Boulton, Graham Russell, BSc,	LT(IC)	X		01.01.05	PENZANCE
Boulton, Neil Andrew, BSc	LT CDR(CC)	E	TM	20.11.98	NELSON
Bourn, Sebastian,	SURG SLT(SCC)	-		01.07.03	DARTMOUTH BRNC
Bourne, Christopher Michael, pce, psc(j)	CDR(FTC)	X	O	30.06.04	BDS WASHINGTON
Bourne, Donald Sidney,	LT CDR(FTC)	E	AE	01.10.98	DLO YEO
Bourne, Stephen William,	CAPT RM(CC)	-	SO(LE)	01.04.04	1 ASSAULT GP RM
Bouyac, David Roger Louis,	LT(CC)	X	P	01.11.00	RNAS YEOVILTON
Bowbrick, Richard Charles, MA, pce, psc(j)	CDR(FTC)	X	AAWO	30.06.05	MWC SOUTHWICK
Bowden, Matthew Thomas Edward, BEng	LT CDR(FTC)	X	PWO(C)	01.02.03	FLEET COSCAP
Bowen, Michael, ARRC, BA, MSc	CAPT(FCC)	Q	RNT	27.03.01	DPMD
Bowen, Nigel Timothy, MA, pce, pcea, psc(j)	CDR(FTC)	X	O	30.06.05	PJHQ
Bowen, Richard James,	LT(IC)	E	WE	01.09.05	MANCHESTER

Name	Rank	Branch	Spec	Seniority	Where Serving
Bower, Andrew John, BSc, SM(n), SM	LT CDR(FTC)	X	SM	01.08.01	VANGUARD(PORT)
Bower, John William,	LT CDR(FTC)	S	(S)	01.10.02	RNAS YEOVILTON
Bower, Nigel Scott, MA, pce(sm), psc(j)	CDR(FTC)	X	SM	30.06.05	TURBULENT
Bowers, John Paul, pcea	LT CDR(FTC)	X	O	01.10.01	702 SQN HERON
Bowers, Keith James, MEng	LT(IC)	E	WE	01.09.04	CORNWALL
Bowers, Mark,	LT(IC)	E	IS	01.08.03	DCCIS FAREHAM
Bowes, Nigel,	2LT(IC)	-		01.08.01	FPGRM
Bowhay, Simon, BSc,	LT CDR(FTC)	E	WESM	01.05.99	DLO BRISTOL
Bowie, Alan Niven, MB, BCh, MRCGP	SURG CDR(FCC)	-	GMPP	28.10.05	RN GIBRALTAR
Bowie, Richard,	LT(IC)	E	SM	01.05.02	VANGUARD(PORT)
Bowker, Geoffrey Neil,	LT CDR(FTC)	X	ATC	01.10.93	MOD (LONDON)
Bowker, Jane Mary, MA	LT(IC)	X		01.05.03	MWS COLLINGWOOD
Bowman, Dean Elliott, BEng	SLT(IC)	E	ME U/T	01.09.04	ILLUSTRIOUS
Bowman, Robert James, BEng	LT CDR(FTC)	E	AE	01.04.03	EXCHANGE USA
Bowman, Simon Kenneth James,	LT(IC)	X	ATCU/T	01.06.05	RAF COTTESMORE
Bowra, Mark Andrew,	MAJ(FTC)	-		01.10.03	MOD (LONDON)
Bowyer, Richard John,	CAPT RM(CC) (Act Maj)	-	MLDR	01.05.00	FLEET COSCAP
Boxall, Pauline, BEng, MSc	LT CDR(FTC)	E	ME	01.04.05	STG BRISTOL
Boyce, the Lord, GCB, OBE, DL, rcds, psc	ADM			25.05.95	
Boyd, Elaine Marie, BSc	LT(IC)	S		01.05.05	NORTHUMBERLAND
Boyd, Nicholas, MA, MSc, CEng, MIMechE, psc(j)	CDR(FTC)	E	ME	30.06.05	CAPT MCTA
Boyes, Martyn Richard, BEng, MSc, CEng, PGDip, MIMarEST	LT CDR(FTC)	E	MESM	01.02.03	TORBAY
Boyes, Richard Austen,	LT(FTC)	X	P	01.03.89	829 SQN HQ
Boyle, Jonathan Bartley, BEng, MSc, CEng	LT CDR(FTC)	E	MESM	01.10.02	SCEPTRE
Brace, Anna Frances, BA	LT(IC)	X	ATC	01.01.04	RNAS CULDROSE
Bracher, Hugh,	LT CDR(FTC)	E	WESM	01.10.96	DRAKE SFM
Bracken, Christopher David,	MID(IC)	X	P U/T	01.05.04	DARTMOUTH BRNC
Bradbury, Simon,	CHAPLAIN	RC		18.09.96	FWO DEVPT SEA
Bradford, Giles Job, MEng	LT(CC)	X	P	01.06.02	845 SQN
Bradford, Malcolm Henry,	CAPT RM(CC)	-		01.09.04	CHFHQ
Bradford, Terrance Horace Colin,	LT CDR(FTC)	MS	(AD)	01.10.02	MDHU DERRIFORD
Brading, Roland David,	CAPT RM(CC)	-		01.03.04	NP IRAQ
Bradley, Martin James, BSc	SLT(IC)	X	O U/T	01.01.04	RNAS CULDROSE
Bradley, Matthew Thomas, pce, n	LT CDR(FTC)	X	PWO(U)	01.05.02	MWS COLLINGWOOD
Bradley, Patrick Martin, BEng, CEng, MIEE	LT CDR(FTC)	E	WE	01.06.00	MOD (LONDON)
Bradley, Rupert Litherland, LLB	LT(CC)	X	P	01.11.96	849 SQN HQ
Bradley, Trevor Adrian, BEng	LT(CC)	E	WE	01.05.02	MWS COLLINGWOOD
Bradshaw, Kevin Thomas, BSc, MDA	LT CDR(FTC)	E	WE	01.10.02	EXCHANGE USA
Brady, Matthew Vincent, BA	LT(IC)	X	P U/T	01.02.06	RNAS YEOVILTON
Brady, Sean, BSc	MAJ(FTC)	-		01.10.04	FLEET COSCAP
Brady, Sean Edward, pce	LT CDR(FTC)	X	PWO(U)	01.09.96	CAPT IST STAFF
Brady, Thomas William,	LT(FTC)	S	(W)	01.04.01	MOD (BATH)
Braham, Stephen Wyn, MSc, CEng, FIMarEST, psc	CAPT(FTC)	E	ME	30.06.06	CAPT MCTA
Brain, William James Whitelaw, FHCIMA	CAPT RM(CC)	-		01.09.00	FLEET COSCAP
Braithwaite, Geoffrey Charles,	LT(IC)	E	ME	01.04.04	LIVERPOOL
Braithwaite, Jeremy Sean, n	LT CDR(FTC)	X	H2	01.01.03	FLEET COMOPS NWD
Bramley, Stephen, pce, pcea, psc,	CAPT(FTC)	X	P	30.06.03	NAVSEC
Bramwell, John Gerald,	LT(CC)	X	O	01.04.93	EXCHANGE RAF UK
Brand, Simon Martin, BSc, MA, pce, pcea, psc(j)	CDR(FTC)	X	P	30.06.97	D STRAT PLANS
Brann, Robert William,	LT(IC)	X		01.05.04	CAMPBELTOWN
Brannighan, Ian Derek, MEng	LT(IC)	X	P	01.09.04	RNAS YEOVILTON
Bratt, James Richard,	SLT(IC)	X		01.11.05	RALEIGH
Bravery, Martin Anthony Edward, pce, pcea	LT CDR(FTC)	X	P	01.05.99	FOST SEA
Bray, Andrew John,	SLT(IC)	S		01.09.04	847 SQN
Bray, Katherine Elizabeth, MB, BSc, BS, Dip SM	SURG LT(SCC)	-		01.08.01	NELSON (PAY)
Braycotton, Edward James,	SLT(IC)	X	P U/T	01.02.05	DARTMOUTH BRNC
Brazenall, Benjamin Crawford, BEng	LT(IC)	X	P	01.01.04	845 SQN
Brazier, Lars Frank, MA,	LT(IC)	X	P	01.01.99	GANNET SAR FLT
Breach, Charles Edward Marshall,	CAPT RM(CC)	-	MLDR	01.04.04	FPGRM
Breckenridge, Iain Galloway, MA, pce, pce(sm), psc(j)	CDR(FTC)	X	SM	30.06.04	TIRELESS
Breckenridge, Robert John MacKay, BSc	SLT(IC)	X	P U/T	01.06.04	DARTMOUTH BRNC
Bree, Stephen Edward Peter, MB, BCh, FRCA	SURG CDR(FCC)	-	(CA)	30.06.00	MDHU DERRIFORD

Name	Rank	Branch	Spec	Seniority	Where Serving
Breen, Deborah Ann, BA	LT(CC)	X		11.12.99	MWS COLLINGWOOD
Breen, John Edward, MEng, MSc, CEng, MRAeS	LT(CC)	E	AE	01.09.01	JCA IPT UK
Brember, Peter Bruce,	LT(FTC) (Act Lt Cdr)	X	AV	25.07.96	RFANSU (ARGUS)
Brenchley, Nigel Gerard,	LT CDR(FTC)	S		17.02.00	RNAS YEOVILTON
Brennan, John Paul,	LT(IC)	E	WE	12.08.05	ALBION
Brennan, Paul Anthony, BSc, PGDip, IEng, MIIE	LT(FTC)	E	MESM	02.09.99	TURBULENT
Brettell, Jeremy Donald,	LT(IC)	X		01.05.05	ATHERSTONE
Bretten, Nicholas John,	SLT(IC)	X		01.07.03	SEVERN
Brewer, Charles William Godfrey, BSc	SLT(IC)	X		01.11.04	DARTMOUTH BRNC
Brewer, Christopher Edward, BSc, SM(n), SM	LT(FTC)	X	SM	01.01.00	TALENT
Brewin, David John, BSc	LT(CC)	X	P	01.03.99	EXCHANGE RAF UK
Brian, Neil, pcea	LT CDR(FTC)	X	O	01.10.02	824 SQN
Brian, Stephen Alan,	SLT(IC)	X		01.09.04	DARTMOUTH BRNC
Briant-Evans, Tom Arthur Hugh, BA	LT(IC)	X		01.12.04	VANGUARD(PORT)
Bridger, David William, BSc, PGDip, HND	CDR(FTC)	E	TM	30.06.96	CMT SHRIVENHAM
Bridger, Richard John, MA, pcea, psc(j)	CDR(FTC)	X	O	30.06.04	FSAST IPT
Brierley, Simon Paul John, BEng	LT(CC)	E	AE	01.09.02	HARRIER IPT
Briers, Matthew Peter, MA, pce, pcea, psc(j)	CDR(FTC)	X	P	30.06.03	RNAS YEOVILTON
Briggs, Cathryn Sarah,	LT CDR(MCC)	Q	OTSPEC	01.10.04	RCDM
Briggs, Charmody Elizabeth, BSc	LT(IC)	X	FC	01.12.01	EXCHANGE RAF UK
Briggs, Mark David, BEng	LT(CC)	E	WE	01.06.97	DLO BRISTOL
Briggs-Mould, Timothy Paul,	LT CDR(FTC)	E	WE	16.03.99	MONMOUTH
Brighouse, Neil George,	MAJ(FTC)	-	P	24.04.02	845 SQN
Brimacombe, Louise Marie, BSc	LT(CC)	S		01.02.00	FLEET COSP&S
Brims, Fraser John Hall, MB, ChB, MRCP	SURG LTCDR(MCC)	-		05.08.03	NELSON (PAY)
Brindley, Mark William,	LT(CC)	E	WE	01.01.03	MWS COLLINGWOOD
Brinsden, Mark Dudley, MB, BS, FRCSTr&Orth, MRCS	SURG LTCDR(FCC) (Act Surg Cdr)	-		01.08.99	MDHU DERRIFORD
Brint, Ian,	LT(CC)	S	SM	29.04.01	CC MAR AGRIPPA
Briscoe, James William Austen, BEng, MAPM	LT(IC)	E	WE	01.05.03	DARTMOUTH BRNC
Bristow, Paul Christopher, BA	LT(IC)	E	TM	01.09.98	FLEET HQ WI
Bristowe, Paul Andrew, BSc, FRGS, pce, pcea	LT CDR(FTC)	X	P	01.03.01	UKMARBATSTAFF
Britchfield, Alison Esther Phyllis, MA, BD	CHAPLAIN	SF		01.10.92	AFCC
Britton, Nicholas John, MBE, BSc	LT CDR(FTC)	X		01.04.90	CSIS IPT
Broadbent, Peter Stephen, BSc, MEng, CEng, MIEE	LT CDR(FTC)	E	WE	01.03.02	EXETER
Broadbent, Sarah Elizabeth,	LT(CC)	S		01.03.01	NELSON
Broadhurst, Michael Robert, BA, pce	LT CDR(FTC)	X	AAWO	01.12.00	FOST SEA
Broadley, Kevin James, BSc, MA, MPhil, pce, pcea, psc	CDR(FTC)	X	P	30.06.00	SA RIYADH
Broadwith, Joanna Louise, BA	SLT(IC)	X		01.02.04	KENT
Brock, Mathew Jonathan,	LT(CC)	X	MCD	01.01.02	DEF SCH OF LANG
Brock, Raymond Frederick,	LT CDR(FTC)	S		01.03.02	FLEET COSP&S
Brocklebank, Benjamin Michael Charles, BA	SLT(IC)	S		01.01.05	DARTMOUTH BRNC
Brocklebank, Guy Philip, BSc, FRSA, MIMgt, pce	CAPT(FTC)	X	PWO(C)	30.06.06	MOD (LONDON)
Brocklehurst, Judith Elizabeth, BSc	LT(MC(MD)	Q	IC*	26.04.01	NELSON (PAY)
Brocklehurst, Kelly Paul, BA	CAPT RM(CC)	-		01.09.02	FLEET AV SUPPORT
Brodie, Duncan John, BEng	LT(CC)	E	AE	01.01.02	FLEET COSP&S
Brodie, Ross William James, pce, n	LT CDR(FTC)	X	PWO(U)	01.12.02	LANCASTER
Brodie, Stephen David,	LT(SC(MD)	Q		08.03.01	NELSON (PAY)
Brodier, Mark Ian,	LT(FTC)	E	AE	04.09.98	SULTAN
Brogden, Thomas, MB, CHB	SURG SLT(SCC) (Act Surg Lt)	-		02.08.05	DARTMOUTH BRNC
Brolls, George Gibson,	SLT(IC)	X		01.02.05	DARTMOUTH BRNC
Bromage, Kenneth Charles,	CHAPLAIN	CE		02.08.92	RN GIBRALTAR
Bromige, Timothy Robert James, pce	LT CDR(FTC)	X	AAWO	19.05.92	SACT USA (SEA)
Bromwell, Mark Steven, MEng, MIEE	LT(CC)	E	WE	01.09.02	MOD (LONDON)
Brooking, Richard Robert,	LT(IC)	E	WESM	01.05.02	VANGUARD(STBD)
Brooks, Gary Lee, pce, PGDip	LT CDR(FTC)	X	H CH	01.04.99	SCOTT
Brooks, Graeme Christian Gibbon,	LT CDR(FTC)	X	PWO(A)	01.04.05	RICHMOND
Brooks, Kirsten Mary Louise, BA	LT(IC)	E	TM	06.04.97	MWS COLLINGWOOD
Brooks, Nicholas Robert, BEng	LT(CC)	E	MESM	01.09.01	RMC OF SCIENCE
Brooks, Paul Neil, MSc gw	LT(CC)	E	WE	01.01.03	MWS COLLINGWOOD
Brooksbank, Richard,	LT(CC)	S		01.05.05	WESTMINSTER
Brooksbank, Richard James, BSc, pce, pcea	CDR(FTC)	X	P	31.12.97	MOD (LONDON)

Name	Rank	Branch	Spec	Seniority	Where Serving
Brosnan, Mark Anthony, pcea	LT(CC)	X	O	16.07.93	GANNET SAR FLT
Broster, Lee John,	LT(IC)	E	WE	01.07.04	GRAFTON
Brothers, Anthony Herbert George,	LT(FTC)	E	WE	18.02.94	FLEET COSP&S
Brotherton, John Darren, QCBA	LT CDR(FTC)	X	P	16.04.02	RAF SHAWBURY
Brotherton, Michael, MBE, BD	CHAPLAIN	CE		04.09.84	FOST SEA
Brotton, Peter James, BSc, n	LT CDR(FTC)	X		01.04.06	ALBION
Brough, Geoffrey Alan,	CDR(FTC)	E	WESM	31.12.94	FLEET FOTR
Browett, Jon James, BSc,	LT(IC)	X		01.09.04	WALNEY
Brown, Aaron Richard Andrew,	LT(CC)	X	O	01.03.00	849 SQN A FLT
Brown, Alastair David, BEng	LT(IC)	E	ME	01.09.04	SUTHERLAND
Brown, Andrew, BM, BCH, MA(OXON), Dip OM, Dip SM, MRCGP	SURG LTCDR(MCC)	-	GMPP	05.08.03	CDO LOG REGT RM
Brown, Andrew Martyn, BEng	LT CDR(FTC)	E	WE	01.12.04	T45 IPT
Brown, Andrew Paul,	LT CDR(FTC)	X	ATC	01.02.04	RNAS YEOVILTON
Brown, Andrew Paul,	SLT(IC)	X		01.09.02	ST ALBANS
Brown, Andrew Scott, MSc	LT(IC)	X		01.09.01	MWS COLLINGWOOD
Brown, Bernard Craig,	LT(MC)(MD)	Q		11.06.00	MDHU DERRIFORD
Brown, David Campbell, MSc, MB, CHB, LRCP, MRCS, MSRP, FFOMSURG	CAPT(FCC)	-	CPDATE	30.06.02	FLEET COSP&S
Brown, Emma Louise, BA	LT(IC)	S		01.01.05	JHCHQ
Brown, Howard Spencer, MBE, pce, pcea, psc(j)	CDR(FTC)	X	P	31.12.99	ILLUSTRIOUS
Brown, James Alexander, BSc	LT(CC)	X	H2	01.05.00	814 SQN
Brown, James Alexander, BEng, MSc	LT(IC)	E	WESM	01.01.03	SOVEREIGN
Brown, Leonard Anthony, BA	MAJ(FTC)	-	P	01.09.03	BDS WASHINGTON
Brown, Lynda Elizabeth Margaret,	LT(IC)	S		29.10.04	CORNWALL
Brown, Malcolm Keith, MBE, BSc, pce	CDR(FTC)	X	AAWO	20.09.94	FLEET COSP&S
Brown, Michael Andrew, BSc	LT(IC)	X	P U/T	01.09.05	DHFS
Brown, Neil Logan, LLB	CAPT(FTC) (Barrister)	S	BAR	30.06.06	MOD (LONDON)
Brown, Nigel Peter, BSc, MA, psc(m), psc(j),	COL(FTC)	-	C	30.06.06	NAVSEC
Brown, Paul Alexander Everett, BA, pce, psc(j), n	CDR(FTC)	X	AAWO	30.06.06	EXETER
Brown, Peter St John, BEng, CEng, MIMarEST	LT CDR(FTC)	E	MESM	01.06.95	TALENT
Brown, Rebecca Josephine,	SLT(UCE)(IC)	X		01.09.05	DARTMOUTH BRNC
Brown, Richard,	CAPT RM(IC)	-	P	24.07.04	727 NAS
Brown, Robert Andrew Mark, OBE, pce,	CAPT(FTC)	X	AAWO	30.06.02	FLEET COSP&S
Brown, Sarah Suzanne,	SLT(IC)	X		01.11.05	WESTMINSTER
Brown, Scott James, BD	CHAPLAIN	SF		20.04.93	FLEET HQ WI
Brown, Sharon Mary Jean, MBA, PGDip	LT(IC)	S		01.07.04	FLEET COSP&S
Brown, Simon David, pce, n	LT CDR(FTC)	X	PWO(N)	01.11.02	EXCHANGE CANADA
Brown, Stephen,	LT(IC)	S		01.07.03	MONMOUTH
Brown, Stephen Glynn,	LT(CC)	X	P	04.08.00	848 SQN HERON
Brown, Stephen Harry, pce	LT CDR(FTC)	X	PWO(U)	15.01.01	MCM2 SEA
Brown, William Henry, MBE	CDR(FTC)	X	AAWO	30.06.00	CC MAR AGRIPPA
Browning, Rowan Susannah, BSc, adp, PGDip	LT CDR(CC)	E	IS	01.01.02	CMT SHRIVENHAM
Bruce-Jones, Nicholas William, BSc, MA, psc(j)	LT COL(FTC)	-		31.12.00	MOD (LONDON)
Bruford, Robert Michael Charles, pce	LT CDR(FTC)	X	AAWO	01.04.00	FLEET COSCAP
Brundle, Paul Robert, MBE	LT CDR(FTC)	X	ATC	01.10.95	MOD (LONDON)
Brunell, Paul Jonathan,	LT CDR(FTC)	E	AE	01.10.04	SULTAN
Brunsden-Brown, Sebastian Edward, pcea	LT CDR(FTC)	X	P	01.10.01	824 SQN
Brunton, Steven Buchanan, MSc, CEng, FIEE, MCGI, mdtc	CDRE(FTC)	E	WESM	03.04.06	MOD (LONDON)
Brutton, Joseph Henry, BEng	LT(CC)	E	MESM	01.08.97	JSCSC
Bryan, Rory John Lockton, BA, pce	LT CDR(FTC)	X	PWO(U)	30.06.03	NAVSEC
Bryant, Daniel John Grenfell,	LT CDR(FTC)	S	SM	01.10.02	FLEET COSP&S
Bryars, Paul Murray,	CAPT RM(CC)	-	SO(LE)	01.04.03	CTCRM (SEA)
Bryce, Graeme Edward, BDS	SGLTCDR(D)(MC)(MD)	-		29.06.05	JSU NORTHWOOD
Bryce, Neville Anthony, MBE	LT CDR(FTC)	E	MESM	01.10.03	VICTORIOUS(PORT)
Bryce-Johnston, Fiona Lorraine Stirling, MA	LT(MC)(MD)	Q		16.07.01	SULTAN
Bryden, David Gaskell,	SLT(IC)	X		01.09.04	MIDDLETON
Bubb, Jonathan David,	MAJ(FTC)	-	C	01.05.05	COMAMPHIBFOR
Buchan, Lindsay Helen, BSc	SLT(IC)	S		01.06.03	RALEIGH
Buchanan, David,	LT(IC)	E	ME	01.05.03	DRAKE SFM
Buchanan, Robert Michael, BEng	LT(CC)	E	AE	01.05.01	FS MASU
Buchan-Steele, Mark Anthony, BSc, MA, psc(j)	CDR(FTC)	S	SM	31.12.00	NEPTUNE DLO
Buck, James Edward, PGDIPAN, pce, n	LT CDR(FTC)	X	PWO(N)	01.04.00	NELSON

Name	Rank	Branch	Spec	Seniority	Where Serving
Buck, Sarah Rachael, BSc, PGCE, PGDip	LT(CC)	E	TM	01.05.98	DCTS HALTON
Buckenham, Peter James, BEng, AMIMechE	LT(FTC)	E	ME	01.10.99	RMC OF SCIENCE
Buckingham, Guy, SM(n), SM	LT CDR(FTC)	X	SM	01.12.01	RALEIGH
Buckland, Richard John Francis, pce, pcea, psc(j)o	CDR(FTC)	X	O	31.12.99	NP IRAQ
Buckle, Iain Lawrence, BEng, MBA, CEng, MIMarEST	CDR(FTC)	E	WE	30.06.05	MOD (BATH)
Buckley, Dominic David George, BA	LT(CC)	X	H1	01.02.94	NELSON
Buckley, Phillip James Anthony, jsdc, pce(sm), pce	CAPT(FTC)	X	SM	30.06.05	JDCC
Bucknall, Robin James Woolcott,	MAJ(FTC)	-		01.05.00	JSCSC
Buczkiewicz, Mathew James,	CAPT RM(CC)	-		01.09.03	45 CDO RM
Bugg, Kevin John,	LT CDR(FTC)	E	AE	01.03.02	JCA IPT USA
Buggins, Brian, QGM	LT(CC)	X	AV	01.05.02	DHU SEA
Bukhory, Hamesh, BEng	LT(CC)	E	AE	01.01.02	LOAN DARA
Bulgin, Martin Ronald,	LT(IC)	X	ATCU/T	01.01.05	RNAS CULDROSE
Bull, Andrew John, pcea, psc	CDR(FTC)	X	O	01.10.95	HQ1GP HQSTC
Bull, Charlotte Vivienne Rachel, BA, MinstAM	LT CDR(FTC)	S		01.10.04	FLEET HQ WI
Bull, Christopher Martin Sefton, MA, CEng, MIEE, psc(j)	CDR(FTC)	E	WESM	30.06.04	NEPTUNE DLO
Bull, Geoffrey Charles, BEng, MSc, MIMarEST, CEng	LT CDR(FTC)	E	MESM	01.11.94	DLO TES
Bull, Louis Paul, BA, SM(n)	LT(CC)	X	SM	01.07.00	SUPERB
Bull, Michael Antony John, BSc, SM(n), SM	LT(CC)	X	SM	11.09.99	TRENCHANT
Bullock, James Richard,	LT(CC)	X	P	01.08.02	846 SQN
Bullock, John Barry,	LT(IC)	E	ME	01.07.03	EDINBURGH
Bullock, Michael Peter, MBE	CAPT(FTC)	S	SM	30.06.05	DLO/DG LOG (SC)
Bullock, Robert Arthur, BSc	LT(CC)	X		01.09.00	MWS COLLINGWOOD
Bulmer, Renny John,	MAJ(FTC)	-	SO(LE)	01.10.00	HQ 3 CDO BDE RM
Bulmer, William Elliot, MA	LT(IC)	S		01.01.03	NEPTUNE BNSL
Bunney, Graham, BSc	LT(CC)	X	P	01.02.94	849 SQN A FLT
Bunt, Kevin John,	LT CDR(FTC)	S	(S)	01.10.00	RN LOGS SCHOOL
Burbidge, Kay, pcea	LT(CC)	X	O	01.09.98	814 SQN
Burch, Matthew Harold, BA	SLT(CC)	X		01.05.04	OCEAN
Burcham, Jason Richard,	CAPT RM(CC)	BS	SO(LE)	01.04.03	FLEET HQ WI
Burcham, Veryan,	LT(IC)	MS		13.08.04	FLEET COSP&S
Burdett, Richard Wyndham, BSc, CEng, MIMechE, MDA	LT CDR(FTC)	E	MESM	01.06.92	NEPTUNE DLO
Burge, Roger George,	LT CDR(FTC)	E	WESM	01.10.00	FLEET COSP&S
Burgess, Andrew James, MB, BCH, BSc, FRCA, FFARCS, DA	SURG CDR(FCC)	-	(CA)	30.06.96	MDHU DERRIFORD
Burgess, Gary Thomas Myles, BEng, MSc, CEng, PGDip, MIMarEST	LT CDR(FTC)	E	MESM	01.02.00	NAVSEC
Burgess, Mark John,	CAPT RM(CC)	-	SO(LE)	01.04.03	CHFHQ
Burgess, Philip Gordon, BEng	LT(IC)	E	ME	01.09.04	CORNWALL
Burgess, Stanley, pcea	LT CDR(FTC(A)	X	P	01.10.90	RNAS CULDROSE
Burghall, Rebecca Clare, BSc	LT(CC)	X	H2	01.08.01	ROEBUCK
Burgoyne, William Lawrence, BA	SLT(IC)	X		01.05.03	DARTMOUTH BRNC
Burke, Michael Christopher, BSc	LT CDR(FTC)	X	SM	01.09.95	SPARTAN
Burke, Paul Dominic, OBE, BA, pce, pce(sm)	CDR(FTC)	X	SM	30.06.02	FOST SM SEA
Burkett, Janis Ann, MB, BCH, BAO, DObstRCOG, Dip FFP, MRCGP, JCPTGP	SURG CDR(SCC)	-	GMPP	01.07.00	MOD (LONDON)
Burley, Matthew Richard, BEng, MSc	LT CDR(FTC)	E	MESM	01.06.05	NP BRISTOL
Burlingham, Alexander Charles Rains, BSc, MA	LT(IC)	E	TM	01.08.03	CTCRM
Burlingham, Brett Limmer, BSc, MA, CEng, MIMarEST, psc(j)	CDR(FTC)	E	ME	30.06.03	DLO/DG LOG (SC)
Burnell, Jeremy Richard Jenner, fsc	LT COL(FTC)	-		31.12.00	RMR SCOTLAND
Burnell-Nugent, Sir James Michael, KCB, CBE, MA, jsdc, pce, pce(sm) (COMMANDER-IN-CHIEF FLEET NOV 05)	ADM	-	SM	15.11.05	FLEET COMOPS NWD
Burnett, Paul Henry,	LT(IC)	MS		01.05.03	FLEET COSP&S
Burningham, Michael Robert, BA, psc(j)	CDR(FTC)	S	SM	30.06.03	UKMARBATSTAFF
Burnip, John Matthew, BSc	LT CDR(FTC)	E	ME	01.08.93	EXCHANGE CANADA
Burns, Adrian Conleth,	LT CDR(FTC)	S	SM	04.03.02	RN LOGS SCHOOL
Burns, Andrew John, BEng	LT(IC)	X	P	01.01.03	846 SQN
Burns, Andrew Paul, BA, pce	CDR(FTC)	X	PWO(A)	30.06.05	JSCSC
Burns, David Ian, BSc, ARCS, pce, psc(j), MA	CDR(FTC)	X	PWO(C)	30.06.04	MOD (LONDON)
Burns, Euan Paterson, BEng, MSc gw, CEng, MIEE	LT(FTC) (Act Lt Cdr)	E	WE	01.08.98	MOD (LONDON)
Burns, James Edward, BEng	LT(FTC)	E	WE	01.02.99	DRAKE SFM
Burns, Robin Douglas James, MSc, PGDip	LT CDR(FTC)	X	METOC	01.03.99	UN AFRICA
Burr, Christopher,	2LT(IC)	-		01.08.01	42 CDO RM
Burrell, Aleck Michael George,	MAJ(FTC)	-	LC	01.04.04	FLEET COSP&S

Name	Rank	Branch Spec	Seniority	Where Serving
Burrell, David James, MEng, SM(n)	LT(IC)	X	SM	01.09.02	VENGEANCE(STBD)
Burrell, Philip Mark, BSc, FCIPD, psc	CAPT(FTC)	E	TM	30.06.02	NELSON
Burrows, John Campbell,	LT(FTC)	E	MESM	15.10.93	TRIUMPH
Burrows, Michael John,	LT CDR(FTC)	X	P	01.10.94	EXCHANGE USA
Burrows, Thomas George,	SLT(IC)	X	P U/T	01.09.05	RNAS YEOVILTON
Burstow, Richard Stanley, pce	LT CDR(FTC)	X	PWO(U)	01.05.99	SHOREHAM
Burt, Douglas James,	LT(CC)	E	MESM	01.10.02	NEPTUNE DLO
Burt, Michael Tim,	LT(IC)	S		28.10.05	RN LOGS SCHOOL
Burt, Paul Ronald, BA, ACIS	LT CDR(FTC)	S	(S)	01.10.93	AFPAA HQ
Burton, Alex, BSc	LT(FTC)	X	O	01.11.00	RNAS YEOVILTON
Burton, Alexander James, BSc, pce, psc(j)	CDR(FTC)	X	PWO(U)	30.06.01	MOD (LONDON)
Burton, David Stephen, MSc	CAPT(FTC)	E	IS	30.06.03	MOD (LONDON)
Burton, James Harry,	LT(IC)	X		01.01.06	MWS COLLINGWOOD
Burton, Paul Richard,	LT(FTC)	E	ME	02.05.00	NP 2021
Burvill, Justin Paul, BEng, MSc, CEng, MIMarE	LT CDR(FTC)	E	MESM	01.03.03	TIRELESS
Burwin, Harvey Lee, BEng	LT CDR(FTC)	E	WE	01.11.96	DLO TES
Bush, Alexander John Taylor, pce	LT CDR(FTC)	X	PWO(U)	01.06.99	CYPRUS PBS
Bush, David Jonathon, MEng, MIEE	LT(IC)	E	WESM	01.05.04	SPARTAN
Bushell, Gary Robert,	LT CDR(FTC) (Act Cdr)	X		09.07.99	2SL/CNH FOTR
Buston, David Christopher,	CAPT RM(IC)	-		01.04.04	1 ASSAULT GP RM
Butcher, David,	CAPT RM(CC)	-	C	01.04.03	FLEET CIS PORTS
Butcher, Mark William,	SLT(IC)	X		01.09.05	BANGOR
Butler, Ian Anthony, MAPM	LT CDR(FTC)	E	AE	01.10.04	RAF COTTESMORE
Butler, Jonathon Edward, MEng	LT(IC)	E	WESM	01.09.03	TRAFALGAR
Butler, Lee Peter, IEng, AMRAeS	LT CDR(FTC)	E	AE	01.10.03	OCLC MANCH
Butler, Nicholas Abraham Marsh, MBA, pce, pcea	CAPT(FTC)	X	P	31.12.97	SA PARIS
Butler, Philip Michael, BSc	LT(IC)	X	P	01.01.01	846 SQN
Butler, Robin Andrew, BSc, PGCE	LT(IC)	E	TM	01.01.02	FLEET FOTR
Butler, Simon, BA	CAPT RM(IC)	-		01.09.02	40 CDO RM
Butterfield, Neil Philip, MB, BS, DA, DipAvMed	SURG CAPT(FCC)	-	GMPP	30.06.03	NELSON
Butterworth, Charlotte Louise, BMus	LT CDR(FTC)	S		01.02.06	NAVSEC
Butterworth, Leslie,	LT(FS)(CAS)	FS		16.01.99	DRAKE COB(CNH)
Buxton, Peter John, OBE, BA, BM, BCh, FRCR	SURG CAPT(FCC)	-	CPDATE	03.10.05	FLEET COSP&S
Bye, Marc David, BEng, CEng, MIMarEST	LT CDR(FTC)	E	ME	01.05.00	DLO/DG LOG (SC)
Byers, Hannah Rebecca,	SLT(IC)	E	AE	01.09.02	SULTAN
Byne, Nicholas,	LT(IC)	X	ATC	01.05.04	EXCHANGE RAF UK
Byrd, Liam Bernard,	LT(IC)	S		17.03.05	RNAS CULDROSE
Byrne, Adrian Charles, IEng, MIPlantE	LT CDR(FTC)	E	ME	01.10.03	RALEIGH
Byrne, Terence Michael,	LT CDR(FTC)	X	REG	01.10.02	DRAKE COB(CNH)
Byron, Douglas Charles,	LT(IC)	S		01.09.03	MONTROSE
Byron, James David,	LT CDR(FTC)	X	PWO(U)	01.05.03	MONMOUTH
Bywater, Richard Lewis, BEng, MA, MSc, CEng, MIEE, psc(j), gw	LT CDR(FTC)	E	WE	01.03.99	DLO BRISTOL

C

Name	Rank	Branch Spec	Seniority	Where Serving
Cackett, Thomas Edward Robert,	SLT(IC)	X	P U/T	01.05.03	RNAS YEOVILTON
Caddick, Andrew, PGDip	LT(IC)	E	MESM	01.09.03	TRENCHANT
Caddick, Stephen Antony,	LT(IC)	E	WE	01.07.04	MONMOUTH
Cahill, Karen Ann, BA	LT CDR(FTC)	X	FC	01.08.03	MOD (LONDON)
Cain, Christopher William,	LT CDR(FTC)	E	WESM	01.10.04	VENGEANCE(STBD)
Caldwell, Daniel James,	CAPT RM(CC)	-		01.09.03	NP IRAQ
Calhaem, Richard Tahi, BEng	LT(CC)	X	P	15.03.98	STRIKFORNATO
Callaghan, Paul Fraser, MBE, BSc, pcea	LT CDR(FTC)	X	P	01.10.99	RNAS CULDROSE
Callis, Gregory James, BEng	LT(IC)	E	ME	01.09.02	MWS DEF DIV SCHL
Callister, David Roy, pcea	LT CDR(FTC)(A)	X	O	01.10.95	815 FLT 202
Callon, Andrew McMillan,	CHAPLAIN	CE		05.06.90	DRAKE COB(CNH)
Calvin, Aaron James, MB, BCH, BAO	SURG LT(SCC)	-		04.02.03	NELSON (PAY)
Cameron, Andrew John Brunt, MA, rcds, pce	CDRE(FTC)	X	PWO(U)	20.06.06	FWO PORTS SEA
Cameron, Fiona, BSc	LT(CC)	E	TM	24.04.98	MWS HM TG (D)
Cameron, Mark John, BEng, MDA, CEng, MIEE	CDR(FTC)	E	WE	30.06.05	FLEET FOTR
Cameron, Peter Stuart, OBE, MA, psc(j)	LT COL(FTC)	-		30.06.02	UKLFCSG RM
Campbell, Alastair, BEng	LT(IC)	X	P	01.05.04	846 SQN
Campbell, Andrew, MSc, MRCGP, MFOM	SURG CDR(SC(MD))	-	(CM)	03.08.03	INM ALVERSTOKE

Name	Rank	Branch	Spec	Seniority	Where Serving
Campbell, David John, MB, BS, MSc	SURG CDR(FCC)	-	GMPP	30.06.02	SULTAN
Campbell, Iain Angus,	LT(CC)	X	P	16.04.96	GANNET SAR FLT
Campbell, James Colin, Cert Ed, HNC	LT CDR(CC)	E	IS	01.09.01	AFPAA JPA
Campbell, James Kininmonth, MB, BS, LRCP, FRCS, FRCSEd	SURG CAPT(FCC)	-	(CGS)	30.06.02	RH HASLAR
Campbell, Jonathon Gordon, BA	SLT(IC)	X		01.09.04	DARTMOUTH BRNC
Campbell, Keith Reid,	CAPT RM(CC)	-	C	01.04.04	45 CDO RM
Campbell, Leslie Michael, BA	LT CDR(FTC)	X	MW	01.07.00	NEPTUNE DLO
Campbell, Mark Alan McMillian, BEng	LT(FTC) (Act Lt Cdr)	X	P	01.09.96	FOST SEA
Campbell, Robin David Hastings, BEng, CEng, MIEE	LT CDR(FTC)	E	WESM	01.02.95	EXCHANGE FRANCE
Campbell, Timothy Ross, BSc	LT(CC)	X		01.06.00	MERSEY
Campbell-Baldwin, James William, BA	LT(IC)	X		01.05.03	CUMBERLAND
Campbell-Wilson, Cameron James,	SLT(IC)	X		01.11.04	DARTMOUTH BRNC
Camplisson, Owen Gerard,	SLT(IC)	X	P U/T	01.07.03	DHFS
Cannell, Graham Martin, BA	LT(CC)	X	P	01.11.99	RNAS YEOVILTON
Canning, Christopher Paul, BSc, pcea	LT CDR(FTC)	X	O	01.10.02	771 SQN
Canning, William Andrew, OBE, psc(m)	LT COL(FTC)	-		30.06.93	SA OSLO
Cannon, Leslie Brian, MB, BS, BSc, FRCS	SURG CDR(FCC)	-	(CO/S)	30.06.04	MDHU PORTSMOUTH
Cantellow, Richard Barry,	LT(IC)	X		01.01.03	ILLUSTRIOUS
Cantellow, Stuart John, BEng, MRAeS	LT(FTC)	E		01.06.01	JSCSC
Cantrell, Simon Richard David,	LT(IC)	X	P U/T	01.07.05	DHFS
Cantrill, Richard John, BSc	MAJ(FTC)	-	MLDR	01.09.04	42 CDO RM
Canty, Nigel Robert, BSc	LT CDR(FTC)	E	MESM	01.09.91	NEPTUNE DSA
Canty, Thomas Alexander, BEng, AMIMechE	LT(FTC)	E	ME	01.02.02	MOD (LONDON)
Capes, Stuart George, SM(n), SM	LT CDR(FTC)	X	SM	01.10.02	FLEET COSCAP
Capewell, David Andrew, OBE, psc(m), fsc, hcsc	BRIG(FCC)	-		18.10.04	PJHQ
Capps, James Alan, BSc	LT(IC)	X	P	01.01.05	RNAS YEOVILTON
Carbery, Stephen James,	LT(CC)	E	WE	01.01.02	MWS COLLINGWOOD
Carcone, Paul Nicholas, BSc	LT(CC)	S		01.12.99	FLEET FOTR
Carden, Peter David, pce, pcea, psc(j)	CDR(FTC)	X	O	30.06.99	MOD (LONDON)
Carey, David Brian,	SURG LTCDR(SC(MD)	-		01.06.04	NELSON (PAY)
Carey, Trevor James,	LT(IC)	E	ME	01.05.02	PORTLAND
Cargen, Malcolm Robert, BSc, psc	CDR(FTC)	E	AE	31.12.00	DLO YEO
Carlton, Paul David, MEng	LT(IC)	E	MESM	01.05.06	FWO DEVONPORT
Carman, Felix Spencer Dylan, BSc	LT(IC)	X		01.12.04	CORNWALL
Carne, Richard James Power, BSc, MBA, pcea	LT(FTC)(A)	X	O	16.05.87	700M MERLIN OEU
Carnell, Gregory James, pcea	LT(CC)	X	O	01.09.91	RNAS YEOVILTON
Carnell, Richard Paul, BA, BSc	LT(MC(MD)	Q		06.11.98	FLEET FOTR
Carnew, Sean Frederick, BA	LT(IC)	X	O	01.09.03	820 SQN
Carnie, Manson John, BA	LT(FTC)	X	P	01.09.99	815 FLT 200
Carns, Alistair Steve,	CAPT RM(IC)	-	MLDR	01.09.04	29 CDO REGT RA
Carpenter, Bryony Helen, BSc, PGCE	LT CDR(CC)	E	TM	01.10.04	MOD (LONDON)
Carpenter, Gary John, BEng	LT(IC)	E	WESM	01.09.05	VENGEANCE(STBD)
Carpenter, George Edward, MEng	LT(FTC)	X		01.10.02	CAMPBELTOWN
Carr, David John,	LT(IC)	X		01.01.06	RNAS YEOVILTON
Carr, David Leslie, pcea	LT CDR(FTC)(A)	X	O	01.10.89	FSAST IPT
Carr, Julia,	SLT(IC)	S		01.06.03	NEPTUNE DLO
Carr, Peter, BSc	CAPT RM(IC) (Act Maj)	-	SO(LE)	01.07.03	DGES LAND
Carretta, Mark Vincent, BSc, pcea	CDR(FTC)	X	P	30.06.06	846 SQN
Carrick, Richard James, BEng, MBA, MSc, CEng, MIMechE	CDR(FTC)	E	MESM	30.06.06	NP BRISTOL
Carrigan, Jonathan Andrew, BSc	LT CDR(FTC)	S		01.10.04	LANCASTER
Carrington-Wood, Clive Gordon, pce, MSc	LT CDR(FTC) (Act Cdr)	X	AAWO	01.10.91	NP IRAQ
Carroll, Benjamin John, MA, n, pce, psc(j)	LT CDR(FTC)	X	PWO(U)	01.02.98	SOUTHAMPTON
Carroll, Paul Christopher, BEng, MSc, CEng, MIMarEST	LT CDR(FTC)	E	ME	01.03.02	CAPT MCTA
Carroll, Philip John, BSc	LT CDR(FTC)	X	H1	01.01.98	EXCHANGE GERMANY
Carroll, Stephen Laurence, BEng, MSc	LT(FTC)	E	AE	01.01.99	DNR N IRELAND
Carrott, Deborah Louise,	SLT(IC)	X		01.02.05	DARTMOUTH BRNC
Carter, Andrew John Michael, BA	SLT(IC)	X	O U/T	01.05.04	RNAS CULDROSE
Carter, Christopher Antony,	LT(IC)	X		18.02.05	OCEAN
Carter, Ian Paul, pce	CDR(FTC)	X	AAWO	30.06.00	FLEET COSP&S
Carter, Jonathon Mark, BSc, BA(OU), MIEE	LT CDR(FTC)	E	WESM	01.06.96	NEPTUNE SWS
Carter, Kendall, BSc, pce	CDR(FTC)	X	PWO(N)	30.06.95	NBC PORTSMOUTH
Carter, Kevin Stanley,	LT CDR(FTC)	X		27.08.02	DEF SCH OF LANG

Name	Rank	Branch	Spec	Seniority	Where Serving
Carter, Nigel Robin,	LT(CC)	X	AV	29.04.01	CHFHQ
Carter, Paul, BSc, BEng, CEng, MIEE	LT(FTC) (Act Lt Cdr)	E	WESM	01.04.01	FLEET COSP&S
Carter, Robert Ian,	LT CDR(FTC)	X	ATC	01.10.95	RNAS YEOVILTON
Carter, Simon Neil, GCIS, psc(j)	CDR(FTC)	S	SM	30.06.04	JSCSC
Carter, Simon Peter,	LT CDR(FTC)	S	CA	01.10.04	LANCASTER
Carthew, Richard James, BA	LT(IC)	S	SM	01.05.01	MOD (LONDON)
Cartwright, Darren, MA, pce, pcea, psc(j)	CDR(FTC)	X	O	30.06.05	FWO PORTS SEA
Carty, Michael Gareth,	CAPT RM(CC)	-	P	01.09.05	RNAS YEOVILTON
Carver, Anthony Graham, BSc, MIEE	LT CDR(FTC)	E	WESM	01.05.89	ASM IPT
Carver, Charles Alistair, BA	SLT(IC)	S		01.05.03	FOST NWD (JMOTS)
Carvosso-White, Anna-Louise, BEng	LT(IC)	E	ME	01.09.02	MOD (LONDON)
Case, Alexander Charles, BSc, psc(j)	LT COL(FTC)	-		30.06.06	LOAN ABU DHABI
Case, Anthony,	LT(FTC)	S	CA	26.04.99	TRIUMPH
Case, Paul, MILog	LT CDR(FTC)	S	(S)	01.10.98	RNAS YEOVILTON
Casey, Adam Mark,	SLT(IC)	X	P U/T	01.01.05	RAF CRANWELL EFS
Cassar, Adrian Peter Felix, MA, pce, psc(j)	CDR(FTC)	X	MCD	30.06.98	JSCSC
Cassidy, Mark James,	CHAPLAIN	RC		24.09.00	DARTMOUTH BRNC
Cassidy, Stuart Martin, BEng	LT(IC)	X	P	01.09.03	845 SQN
Casson, Neil Philip, BSc, MBA, psc(j)	LT CDR(FTC)	E	TMSM	01.03.99	SULTAN
Casson, Paul Richard, BEng, MBA, psc(j)	CDR(FTC)	E	ME	30.06.01	MOD (LONDON)
Casson, Roy Frederick, BEng	LT(CC)	E	ME	01.07.00	DLO BRISTOL
Castle, Alastair Stuart, BSc, pcea	LT CDR(FTC)	X	P	01.12.01	824 SQN
Castle, Colin David,	LT(FTC) (Act Lt Cdr)	X	AAWO	19.09.00	ILLUSTRIOUS
Castledine, Benjamin,	SURG SLT(SCC)	-		28.12.04	DARTMOUTH BRNC
Caswell, Neil Cameron,	LT(IC)	S		28.10.05	RN LOGS SCHOOL
Cattanach, James Ian,	SLT(IC)	X		01.02.05	DARTMOUTH BRNC
Catton, Innes C,	CAPT RM(CC)	-		01.09.04	SFSG
Cattroll, David,	LT CDR(FTC)	E	MESM	01.10.04	SOVEREIGN
Cattroll, Iain Murdo, BSc, MIEE	LT CDR(FTC)	E	WE	01.03.94	MOD (LONDON)
Causton, John Fraser,	LT(IC)	X		01.09.02	MWS COLLINGWOOD
Cave, Joanne, BMus	SLT(IC)	X		01.09.03	SCOTT
Cavill, Niki Richard Dalgliesh,	CAPT RM(FTC)	-		01.05.01	COMAMPHIBFOR
Cawthorne, Matthew William Southworth, MA, psc(m)	LT COL(FTC)	-	MLDR	30.06.00	JACIG
Cessford, Richard Ian, BEng	LT(CC)	E	WE	01.12.99	CMT SHRIVENHAM
Chacksfield, Edward Nicholas, BA	LT(IC)	X	HM2	01.11.98	DARTMOUTH BRNC
Chadfield, Laurence James, BA	LT CDR(FTC)	X	PWO(C)	01.10.04	MOD (LONDON)
Chadwick, Kara, BA	LT(CC)	S		01.01.02	2SL/CNH
Chalmers, Donald Peter, MA, pce, psc(j)	CDR(FTC)	X	PWO(U)	31.12.99	FOST NWD (JMOTS)
Chamberlain, Nicholas Richard Lawrence, BEng	LT CDR(FTC)	E	WE	01.11.01	HQ DCSA
Chambers, Christopher Paul, BSc	LT(CC)	X	P	01.12.99	815 FLT 206
Chambers, Nigel Maurice Christopher, OBE, BSc, pce	CAPT(FTC)	X	PWO(U)	30.06.04	FLEET COSCAP
Chambers, Paul David, BEng	LT(FTC)	E	WE	01.12.97	CAPT MCTA
Chambers, Richard, BSc	LT(CC)	X	H2	01.04.00	JSCSC
Chambers, Thomas George,	LT CDR(FTC)	X	MCD	01.10.88	FLEET COSCAP
Chambers, William John, pce	CDR(FTC) (Act Capt)	X	MCD	30.06.93	NP IRAQ
Chan, Andrea,	A/SG LT(D)(SCC)	-		25.06.04	DRAKE COB(CNH)
Chandler, Nigel James, pce, BSc	CDR(FTC)	X	PWO(C)	30.06.06	JSCSC
Chandler, Philip John, BEng	LT(IC)	X	O U/T	01.01.02	702 SQN HERON
Chandler, Stephen Arthur,	LT CDR(FTC)	X	PWO(U)	01.01.87	FOST DPORT SHORE
Chang, Christopher Joseph,	LT(IC)	X		01.05.03	NP IRAQ
Chang, Hon Weng, BEng	LT(IC)	E	TM	01.08.02	FLEET HQ WI
Channon, Karen Dawn,	LT(IC)	MS		01.11.02	MDHU DERRIFORD
Chapell, Andrew, BA, GCIS	CDR(FTC)	S	SM	30.06.05	MARS IPT
Chapman, Charles Leslie, BEng, MIEE, CEng	LT CDR(FTC)	E	WESM	29.11.99	FOST SM SEA
Chapman, Darren Andrew,	LT CDR(FTC)	X	P	01.10.98	847 SQN
Chapman, James Lawrence John, BSc	LT(CC) (Act Lt Cdr)	X	HM	01.01.02	FOST SM SEA
Chapman, Martin Stuart,	LT(CC)	S		01.09.01	OCLC MANCH
Chapman, Neil Jeffrey, BEng	SLT(IC)	E	ME U/T	01.09.04	SOUTHAMPTON
Chapman, Nicholas John, BA, MBA, pce(sm)	LT CDR(FTC)	X	SM	01.05.90	MDC GIBRALTAR
Chapman, Peter, BEng, MSc, CEng, MIEE	LT CDR(FTC)	E	WE	01.09.01	DLO BRISTOL
Chapman, Simon, MA, psc(j)	MAJ(FTC)	-		01.09.98	CDO LOG REGT RM
Chapman, Simon John, BSc, pce	LT CDR(FTC)	X	AAWO	01.04.98	SOMERSET

Name	Rank	Branch	Spec	Seniority	Where Serving
Chappell, Matthew William, BEd	LT(IC)	E	TM	01.07.03	RALEIGH
Chapple, Colin Peter, BSc, PGCE	LT CDR(FTC)	X	METOC	01.05.90	MWC PORTSDOWN
Chapple, Sean,	CAPT RM(CC)	-	SO(LE)	01.04.04	CTCRM
Charlesworth, Graham Keith, MSc, CEng, MIEE, MCGI	CDR(FTC)	E	WESM	30.06.01	FLEET COSP&S
Charlier, Simon Boyce, pce, pcea, psc.	CDRE(FTC)	X	P	16.11.04	FLEET COSCAP
Charlton, Christopher Robin Alistair MacGaw, BA	CDR(FTC)	S		31.12.97	COM MCC NWD
Charlton, Kevin William, BSc, M ED	LT CDR(MC)(MD)	Q		25.10.02	RN GIBRALTAR
Charnock, Simon James,	SLT(IC)	S		01.06.03	RALEIGH
Chartres, David,	LT CDR(HC)	X		01.10.93	FLEET HQ WI
Chaston, Stephen Paul, SM(n), SM,	LT CDR(FTC)	X	SM	01.03.01	RALEIGH
Chatfield-Smith, Richard David,	LT CDR(FTC)	X	PWO(U)	01.07.03	CUMBERLAND
Chatterjee, Shatadeep, BEng, PGDip	LT(CC)	E	ME	01.09.02	FDG
Chatterley, Dawn Alice,	SLT(IC)	S		01.01.04	RALEIGH
Chattin, Antony Paul, BEng, MSc, psc(j)	MAJ(FTC)	-	MLDR	01.05.00	MOD (LONDON)
Chatwin, Nicholas John, BSc, pce, pcea	CDR(FTC)	X	P	30.06.05	JHCHQ
Chaudhary, Rahul,	LT(IC)	E	WE	01.01.06	MWS COLLINGWOOD
Chawira, Denis Nyarono, BSc	LT(IC)	X	MCD	01.08.97	DEF EXP ORD SCHL
Cheal, Andrew James, BA	LT(IC)	E	TM	01.04.02	CTCRM
Cheater, Christopher John,	SLT(IC)	E	MESM	01.09.02	VIGILANT(PORT)
Cheema, Sukhdev Singh,	LT(IC)	E	WESM	01.07.04	TRENCHANT
Cheesman, Christopher John, BEng, MSc	CDR(FTC)	E	AE	30.06.02	JFCHQ BRUNSSUM
Cheesman, Daniel James Edward, BSc	MAJ(FTC)	-	C	01.09.04	PJHQ
Chelton, Simon Roger Lewis, BA, MIL, CDipAF, OCDS(JAP)	CAPT(FTC)	S	SM	30.06.03	SA TOKYO
Cheshire, Thomas Edward, BEng, MSc, CEng, MIMechE	LT CDR(FTC)	E	MESM	01.10.02	FLEET COMOPS NWD
Cheshire, Thomas Smith, BSc	SLT(IC)	X		01.01.04	ILLUSTRIOUS
Chesterman, Graham John, pce, pcea	LT CDR(FTC)	X	O	01.02.93	MOD (LONDON)
Chesters, David Martin Brandon,	LT(FTC)	S		01.01.02	FLEET HQ WI
Cheyne, Roger Duncan, BEng	LT(FTC)	E	AE	01.04.01	771 SQN
Chichester, Mark Arlington Raleigh, BSc, pce, pce(sm)	LT CDR(FTC)	X	SM	01.10.90	ASM IPT
Chick, Nicholas Stevens,	LT(FTC)	X	P	16.11.95	820 SQN
Chick, Stephen John, CBE, BSc, pce, hcsc.	CAPT(FTC)	X	PWO(A)	30.06.01	FOST SEA
Chicken, Simon Timothy, OBE, MA, psc	COL(FTC)	-	LC	31.12.00	BDS WASHINGTON
Chidley, Timothy James, BSc, MA, CEng, MIMarEST, psc(j)	CDR(FTC)	E	ME	31.12.98	ARK ROYAL
Childs, David Geoffrey, BSc, CEng	CDR(FTC)	E	AE	30.06.02	CV(F) IPT
Childs, John Richard,	LT CDR(FTC)	X	AAWO	01.04.02	ILLUSTRIOUS
Chilman, Peter,	LT CDR(FTC)	S	SM	01.03.93	DLO BRISTOL
Chilton, Denise June,	LT(FTC)	S	(S)	01.04.01	LAIPT
Chilton, Jerard, BEng, CEng, MIEE	LT(CC)	E	WE	01.07.98	MWS COLLINGWOOD
Chilvers, Leah Dion,	LT CDR(MC)(MD)	Q	ACCEM*	01.10.04	RCDM
Chisholm, David,	SLT(IC)	E		01.01.05	MWS COLLINGWOOD
Chisholm, David Thomas, BEng	LT(IC)	E	MESM	01.05.06	VIGILANT(PORT)
Chisholm, Philip James Hampden, BSc	LT(IC)	X		01.07.05	CUMBERLAND
Chittick, William Brian Oliver, BDS, MSc	SGLTCDR(D)(FC)(MD)	-		10.07.02	DDS HALTON
Chivers, Paul Austin, OBE, MA, pce, pcea, psc(j)	CDR(FTC)	X	O	30.06.00	MOD (LONDON)
Choules, Barrie, MEng	LT CDR(CC)	E	TMSM	01.09.02	RNICG
Chrishop, Timothy Ian, pce, pcea	CDR(FTC)	X	O	30.06.03	SHAPE BELGIUM
Christian, Johanna, GradInstPS.	LT(FTC)	S		01.07.99	FLEET HQ WI
Christie, Andrew Bell,	LT(CC)	S	(S)	29.04.01	UKSU SHAPE
Christie, Campbell Stuart, BEd, psc, psc(j)	CDRE(FTC)	E	TM	08.11.05	FLEET FOTR
Christie, Neil,	2LT(IC)	-		01.08.01	45 CDO RM
Christmas, Stephen Peter,	LT(FTC)	X	P	16.08.91	FLEET AV CU
Chudley, Ian Vernon,	LT(IC)	X	P	01.05.03	771 SQN
Church, Alan David,	CDR(FTC)	S		31.12.96	FLEET COSP&S
Church, Simon James, BEng	SLT(IC)	E	MESM	01.09.03	FWO DEVONPORT
Church, Stephen Cofield,	LT(CC)	X	P	16.07.96	RAF CRANWELL EFS
Churcher, Jeremy Edward, pce, n	CDR(FTC)	X	H CH	30.06.06	ECHO
Churchill, Timothy Charles, BA, pce	CDR(FTC)	X	PWO(N)	31.12.93	MOD (LONDON)
Churchward, Matthew James,	MAJ(FTC)	-	LC	01.10.04	COMAMPHIBFOR
Ciaravella, Timothy James, BEng	LT(IC)	E	ME	01.04.04	ILLUSTRIOUS
Clague, John Joseph, MEng, n	LT(FTC)	X	PWO(U)	15.01.97	PORTLAND
Clapham, Grantley Thom, BEng	LT(IC)	E	IS	01.04.01	ALBION
Clare, Jonathan Francis,	MAJ(FTC)	-	SO(LE)	01.10.04	STRIKFORNATO

Name	Rank	Branch	Spec	Seniority	Where Serving
Claridge, Alexander Melville,	LT(SC(MD)	Q		12.04.03	NELSON (PAY)
Clark, Alan Sutherland, SM	LT CDR(FTC)	X	SM	01.10.03	FLEET COMOPS NWD
Clark, Alastair William Charles, MA, pce, pcea, psc(j)	CDR(FTC)	X	O	31.12.98	BDS WASHINGTON
Clark, Andrew Nelham, BSc, CEng, MIMechE	LT CDR(FTC)	E	MESM	01.09.91	RNAS YEOVILTON
Clark, Caroline Louise,	LT(CC)	S		01.08.00	MOD (LONDON)
Clark, David,	2LT(IC)	-		01.08.02	CTCRM LYMPSTONE
Clark, Donald Kennedy, BSc, CEng, MIMarEST	CDR(FTC)	E	MESM	30.06.98	FWO FASLANE SEA
Clark, Gavin Richard,	SLT(SC(MD)	Q		01.11.02	RH HASLAR
Clark, Ian David, MSc, CEng, MIMarEST	CDR(FTC)	E	MESM	30.06.03	CMT SHRIVENHAM
Clark, Kenneth Ian MacDonald, pce(sm)	CDR(FTC)	X	SM	31.12.94	UKMARBATSTAFF
Clark, Kevin Charles, BEng, MSc, CEng, MIMarEST, MCGI	LT CDR(FTC)	E	ME	01.11.94	DLO BRISTOL
Clark, Matthew Thomas, MA, psc(j)	CDR(FTC)	S	SM	30.06.05	FLEET COMOPS NWD
Clark, Michael Howard, n	LT CDR(FTC)	X	AAWO	01.03.04	LIVERPOOL
Clark, Oliver Ramsey, BA	SLT(IC)	S		01.01.05	DARTMOUTH BRNC
Clark, Paul, BA	SLT(IC)	X	P U/T	01.05.04	DARTMOUTH BRNC
Clark, Paul Anthony, BSc	LT(IC)	E	TM	01.01.04	DARTMOUTH BRNC
Clark, Paul Anthony,	MAJ(FTC)	-	SO(LE)	01.10.04	40 CDO RM
Clark, Philip John, BSc	LT(IC)	X	O U/T	01.09.05	849 SQN HQ
Clark, Russell Anthony,	LT(FTC)	X	O	01.08.99	815 FLT 217
Clark, Simon Mansfield,	CDR(FTC)	S	CMA	30.06.05	FLEET FOTR
Clark, Simon Richard, BEng, adp, PGDip, CEng, MIEE	LT CDR(FTC)	E	IS	01.05.97	CSIS IPT
Clark, Stephen, BSc	LT(CC)	E	TM	01.09.97	SULTAN
Clark, Stephen Michael, BA(OU)	LT(IC)	S		01.01.04	LIVERPOOL
Clarke, Adam Gregory, BSc	LT(CC)	S		01.11.99	NAVSEC
Clarke, Andrew Patrick,	LT CDR(FTC)	X	P	01.10.00	CHFHQ
Clarke, Bernard Ronald, MA, FRGS	CHAPLAIN	CE		30.06.81	SULTAN
Clarke, Charles Maxwell Lorne, OBE, pce	CDR(FTC)	X	PWO(U)	30.06.95	NP AFGHANISTAN
Clarke, Daniel, pcea	LT CDR(FTC)	X	O	01.10.03	LYNX OEU
Clarke, Daniel, SM(n), SM	LT(FTC) (Act Lt Cdr)	X	SM	01.01.99	TURBULENT
Clarke, David,	2LT(IC)	-		01.08.01	45 CDO RM
Clarke, Ian Bruce, MSc, pce, n	LT CDR(FTC)	X	PWO(A)	01.10.01	MOD (LONDON)
Clarke, James,	LT CDR(FTC)	E	WE	01.10.98	FLEET FOTR
Clarke, James Pauk, BEng	SLT(IC)	E	WE U/T	01.09.04	EXETER
Clarke, John Martin, MB, BS, MRCGP, DObstRCOG, Dip FFP	SURG CDR(FCC)	-	GMPP	30.06.02	NELSON (PAY)
Clarke, Mark, LCGI, AMNI, MCMI, SM(n), SM, NDipM	LT(FTC)	X	SM	01.04.01	FLEET COSCAP
Clarke, Matthew,	LT(CC)	X		01.01.02	TYNE
Clarke, Matthew David, BSc	LT(CC)	E	TM	01.05.98	RNICG
Clarke, Nicholas John, pce, pcea	CDR(FTC)	X	P	30.06.99	FLEET COSP&S
Clarke, Peter Martin,	CAPT RM(CC)	-	SO(LE)	01.01.02	MWS COLLINGWOOD
Clarke, Richard, MA, MBA, psc(j)	LT CDR(FTC)	E	TM	01.10.96	MWS COLLINGWOOD
Clarke, Richard William, BEng	LT CDR(FTC)	E	AE	01.03.02	849 SQN HQ
Clarke, Robert,	LT(CC)	X	P	16.08.96	829 FLT 01
Clarkson, Andrew Mark,	LT(MC(MD)	Q		04.05.01	RN GIBRALTAR
Clarkson, Antony Michael, MSc	LT(CC)	E	WE	01.01.03	MWS COLLINGWOOD
Claxton, Andrew Geoffrey Douglas, BSc	LT(IC)	X		01.04.04	NOTTINGHAM
Claxton, Martin Geoffrey,	CDR(FTC)	E	MESM	30.06.03	NEPTUNE DSA
Clay, Jason Christopher, BSc, SM(n), SM	LT CDR(FTC)	X	SM	01.10.03	SCEPTRE
Clay, Toby Charles De Candole, BSc	LT(CC)	X	P	01.09.97	815 FLT 210
Clayton, Abby Leanne,	SLT(IC)	X	O U/T	01.01.06	DARTMOUTH BRNC
Clayton, Christopher Hugh Trevor, pce, psc, hcsc	RADM	-	P	30.08.04	IMS BRUSSELS
(ASSISTANT DIRECTOR INTELLIGENCE DIVISION AUG 04)					
Clear, Nichola Jane, BEng	LT(CC)	E	ME	01.11.99	DSFM PORTSMOUTH
Cleary, Christopher Mycroft,	LT(CC)	S		01.01.02	COMATG SEA
Cleary, Stephen Peter, pce	CDRE(FTC)	X	AAWO	09.07.05	SACT USA (SEA)
Clee, James Stefan,	LT(IC)	X	HM2	01.10.02	ILLUSTRIOUS
Clegg, Martin Leslie, BSc, FRGS	LT CDR(FTC)	X	H CH	01.06.90	SHERWOOD
Clements, Elizabeth Joanne,	LT(CC)	S		01.05.99	RNAS YEOVILTON
Cleminson, Mark David, BEng	LT CDR(FTC)	E	MESM	01.02.05	SUPERB
Clewes, Sarah,	LT(IC)	S		12.08.05	FLEET COSP&S
Clews, Alan,	2LT(IC)	-		01.08.01	CTCRM LYMPSTONE
Clifford, Timothy John, BEng, MSc, CEng, MRAeS	CDR(FTC)	E	AE	30.06.02	MERLIN IPT
Clink, Adam Duncan, BSc, pcea	LT CDR(FTC)	X	P	01.10.01	RNAS YEOVILTON

Name	Rank	Branch	Spec	Seniority	Where Serving
Clink, John Robert Hamilton, OBE, PGDIPAN, pce, FRIN	CAPT(FTC)	X	PWO(N)	30.06.05	MOD (LONDON)
Cloherty, Andrew,	LT(IC)	E	WESM	08.04.05	FWO FASLANE SEA
Cloney, Justin William John, BA	LT(IC)	X	SM	01.09.03	TURBULENT
Clough, Christopher Ralph, MA, MSc, CEng, MIEE, psc(j), gw	CDR(FTC)	E	WE	31.12.00	FLEET COSP&S
Clucas, Malcolm Richard, pcea	LT CDR(FTC)	X	P	01.10.97	HANDLING SQN
Clucas, Paul Richard,	LT(FTC) (Act Lt Cdr)	X		04.04.91	PRESIDENT
Cluett-Green, Stephen Mark, pce, pcea	CDR(FTC)	X	P	30.06.02	FLEET COSCAP
Coatalen-Hodgson, Ryan, BA	SLT(IC)	X		01.09.02	HURWORTH
Coates, Adam James, BEng	LT(IC)	E	WE	01.01.03	HQ DCSA
Coates, Philip James Barton, MB, BS, MRCS	SURG LTCDR(FC(MD)	-		04.08.04	NELSON (PAY)
Coats, Daniel Simon, LLB	CAPT RM(CC) (Act Maj)	-		01.09.98	NP IRAQ
Cobbett, James Frank, pcea	LT CDR(FTC)	X	P	01.10.03	ILLUSTRIOUS
Cochrane, Christopher Duncan, MEng	LT(IC)	E	MESM	01.09.05	SULTAN
Cochrane, David Smith, BA	LT(IC)	X		01.08.04	MWS COLLINGWOOD
Cochrane, Malcolm David,	CDR(FTC)	E	AE	30.06.03	FLEET COSP&S
Cochrane, Michael Charles Nicholas, OBE, pce	CAPT(FTC)	X	PWO(N)	30.06.02	MOD (LONDON)
Cockram, Alice Louise, BA, MB, BCH	SURG LT(SC(MD)	-		04.02.04	CFLT MED(SEA)
Cocks, Anthony Edward John, MEng	SLT(IC)	X	O U/T	01.01.04	RNAS CULDROSE
Coffey, Ralph Bruce Dobson, MA, MEng, LCIPD, AMIMechE	LT(IC)	E	MESM	01.01.05	SULTAN
Cogan, Robert Edward Charles, BSc, DipFM	LT CDR(FTC)	S		01.10.04	WESTMINSTER
Cole, Alan Charles, BA	CDR(FTC) (Barrister)	S	BAR	30.06.05	PJHQ
Cole, Claire Victoria, BChD, MFDS,RCS	SGLTCDR(D)(MC(MD)	-		29.06.05	NELSON
Cole, Simon Philip,	LT CDR(FTC)	E	WE	01.10.97	NAVSEC
Cole, Stephen Paul, BEng	LT(IC)	E	AE	01.09.05	829 SQN HQ
Coleman, Alexander Peter Grant,	SLT(IC)	X		01.07.04	DRAKE COB
Coleman, Gareth William, BSc	SLT(IC)	S		01.09.04	DARTMOUTH BRNC
Coleman, James Martyn Peter, BA	LT(IC)	X	P U/T	01.11.05	815 FLT 212
Coleman, Timothy John Anthony,	LT(IC)	X		01.05.04	CHATHAM
Coles, Adam John,	LT(IC)	X		01.05.04	RNAS YEOVILTON
Coles, Andrew Laurence, OBE, MA, pce, psc(j), pce(sm)	CDR(FTC)	X	SM	30.06.03	MOD (LONDON)
Coles, Christopher John, BEng	CDR(FTC)	E	MESM	30.06.06	EXCHANGE AUSTLIA
Coles, Christopher Paul, BEng	LT(FTC)	E	AE	01.05.00	DLO TES
Coles, Simon Phillip, BSc, PhD	LT(IC)	E	TM	01.09.98	DEF NBC CENTRE
Coles-Hendry, Frances Ann, BA	LT(IC)	S		01.05.05	KENT
Collen, Sara Jean, BEng	LT(CC)	E	ME	01.12.97	ALBION
Collett, Stuart Mark, BM	SURG LTCDR(MCC)	-	GMPP	05.08.03	1 ASSAULT GP RM
Colley, Ian Paul,	LT(IC)	E	WESM	01.09.04	TALENT
Colley, Robert,	LT(CC)	X	REG	01.09.01	FLEET COSCAP
Collie, James Alexander, BA	SLT(IC)	X		01.05.03	MWS COLLINGWOOD
Collier, Andrew Sheldon, BA, FRGS	LT CDR(FTC)	X		01.06.93	CALLIOPE
Collier, David Edward, MEng	SLT(IC)	E	ME U/T	01.09.04	SOUTHAMPTON
Collier, Michael John,	LT(IC)	E	WE	01.07.04	MWS COLLINGWOOD
Collighan, Giles Thomas, pce	LT CDR(FTC)	X	AAWO	01.04.99	MOD (LONDON)
Collin, Martin,	MAJ(FTC)	-		01.04.04	JSCSC
Collins, Andrew Charles,	LT(CC)	X	O	01.11.00	815 FLT 200
Collins, Charles Anthony, BSc	SLT(IC)	X		01.11.03	PEMBROKE
Collins, Dale Anthony,	LT(CC)	E		01.05.02	DLO TES
Collins, Darren, MSc, IEng, MIExpE, MIIE	LT(FTC)	E	WE	09.01.01	STG BRISTOL
Collins, David Andrew,	LT(FTC)	E	MESM	02.05.00	SCEPTRE
Collins, David Anthony, MSc, PGCE	CDR(FTC)	X	METOC	30.06.06	JSCSC
Collins, David Ivan,	LT(IC)	S		01.07.04	ARK ROYAL
Collins, David Rudolf, BSc, PhD	LT(CC)	E	TM	01.01.97	RNICG
Collins, Gary Vincent, IEng, MIIE	LT(IC)	E	ME	01.07.04	CV(F) IPT
Collins, Graham John Simon, pce	LT CDR(FTC)	X	PWO(U)	07.04.96	EXCHANGE NLANDS
Collins, John,	CAPT RM(FTC)	-	SO(LE)	01.01.01	1 ASSAULT GP RM
Collins, Lorna Jane, BSc	LT(IC)	E	TM	01.09.00	DCCIS BLANDFORD
Collins, Mark,	LT(IC)	E	TM	01.05.04	SULTAN
Collins, Mark Andrew, MBA, MSc, adp	LT(FTC)	E	WE	09.01.01	MOD (LONDON)
Collins, Mark Christopher,	LT CDR(FTC)	X		01.10.03	SCOTIA
Collins, Paul Nicholas, pce, pcea, psc	CAPT(FTC)	X	P	30.06.02	UKMILREP BRUSS
Collins, Paul Reginald, BSc, CEng, MIEE	LT CDR(FTC)	E	WESM	01.09.95	MOD (LONDON)
Collins, Sarah Jane, BSc, PGDip	LT CDR(FTC)	E	IS	01.10.03	FLEET ISS

Name	Rank	Branch	Spec	Seniority	Where Serving
Collins, Simon Jonathan Peter, BA	LT(CC)	X	O	16.01.01	702 SQN HERON
Collins, Stephen James,	SLT(IC)	X	P U/T	01.11.05	RNAS YEOVILTON
Collins, Tamar Louise, BEng, MSc, PhD	LT(IC)	E	IS	01.01.96	HQ DCSA
Collinson, Neal Paul,	CAPT RM(IC)	-	SO(LE)	01.07.04	CTCRM
Collis, Martin John, BEng	LT CDR(FTC)	E	ME	01.08.99	FLEET COSP&S
Coltman, Timothy Patrick, MB, BS	SURG LTCDR(FC(MD)	-		01.08.00	NELSON (PAY)
Colvin, Michael Andrew Thomas, BSc	LT(IC)	X		01.05.04	ST ALBANS
Compain, Bridget Frances,	LT(IC)	X	P	01.01.03	846 SQN
Compain, Craig Herbert,	LT(FTC)	X	P	21.03.97	FLEET AV VL
Concarr, David Terry,	LT(CS)(CAS)	-		19.09.99	DNR NEE 1
Congreve, Steven Chistopher, BSc	MAJ(FTC)	-		01.05.00	HQBF CYPRUS
Conlin, John Anthony, MA	LT(IC)	X		01.01.99	MWS COLLINGWOOD
Conneely, Steven Andrew, IEng, MIIE	LT(FTC)	E	WE	09.01.01	DLO BRISTOL
Connell, Martin John, pce	CDR(FTC)	X	O	30.06.04	MOD (LONDON)
Connolly, Christopher John, BSc, MA, pce, psc(j)	CDR(FTC)	X	PWO(A)	31.12.00	FLEET COMOPS NWD
Connor, Daniel James, BMS, BM, BS, FRCA	SURG CDR(MCC)	-	(CA)	30.06.04	HQBF CYPRUS
Conran, Nicholas William Douglas, BSc	LT(IC)	S	SM	01.01.03	VANGUARD(PORT)
Conroy, David Alexander, MA	CHAPLAIN	RC		24.09.00	MWS COLLINGWOOD
Considine, Keith John,	LT(CC)	X	P	01.02.00	846 SQN
Conway, Michael John,	LT CDR(FTC)	X	EW	01.10.04	COM MCC NWD
Conway, Suzy Helen, BA	LT(FTC)	S		01.03.99	PJHQ
Cooch, Timothy James, BEng	LT(IC)	E	TM	01.07.02	SULTAN
Coogan, Thomas,	SLT(IC)	E		01.02.05	SULTAN
Cook, Christopher Buchan, MSc, CEng, MBCS, CITP	LT CDR(FTC)	E	IS	01.10.00	CINCFLEET FTSU
Cook, David John, MSc, MCGI, pcea, gdas	LT CDR(FTC(A)	X	O	01.10.97	FLEET COSCAP
Cook, Gordon Edward,	LT CDR(FTC(A)	X	O	01.10.00	815 SQN HQ
Cook, Michael Colin, BEng	LT CDR(CC)	E	TM	01.07.02	FLEET COSP&S
Cook, Myles Fitzpatrick, BA, psc(j)	MAJ(FTC)	-	C	01.05.00	MOD (LONDON)
Cook, Neville John Hunter,	LT(IC)	S		01.05.02	ECHO
Cook, Paul Roger, pce	CDR(FTC)	X	AAWO	31.12.98	NAVSEC
Cook, Timothy Arnold, BA, psc(j)o	MAJ(FTC)	-	C	01.09.97	1 ASSAULT GP RM
Cooke, David John, MBE, pce, pce(sm), hcsc	RADM	-	SM	20.07.04	STRIKFORNATO
(DEPUTY COMMANDER STRIKE FORCE NATO JUL 04)					
Cooke, David Phillip, BSc	LT(IC)	X		01.05.05	RALEIGH
Cooke, Graham John,	LT CDR(FTC)	X		01.10.99	NELSON
Cooke, Graham Spencer, BSc, pcea	LT CDR(FTC)	X	O	01.10.01	FOST SEA
Cooke, Joanne Madeleine, MB, ChB	SURG LTCDR(MCC)	-		02.08.05	MDHU DERRIFORD
Cooke, Jonathan Edward, pce, n	LT CDR(FTC)	X	PWO(U)	01.02.03	FLEET HQ WI
Cooke, Michael John,	LT CDR(FTC)	E	AE	01.10.02	FS MASU
Cooke, Robert Neale, BA	LT(CC)	E	AE	29.04.01	EXCHANGE CANADA
Cooke, Stephen Neil, BEng	LT(IC)	X	P	01.01.02	815 FLT 211
Cooling, Benjamin,	2LT(IC)	-		01.08.04	CTCRM LYMPSTONE
Cooling, Robert George, BA, jsdc, pce, hcsc	CDRE(FTC)	X	PWO(N)	28.08.02	ILLUSTRIOUS
Coomber, Jonathan Martin, BA	MAJ(FTC)	-	MLDR	01.09.01	40 CDO RM
Coope, Philip James, BEng, MIEE	LT CDR(FTC)	E	WE	01.03.03	CORNWALL
Cooper, Adam, BEng, MIEE	LT(IC)	E	WE	01.03.03	DLO BRISTOL
Cooper, Darren Thomas, BSc	SLT(IC)	X		01.11.04	DARTMOUTH BRNC
Cooper, Edwin Sigurd, MEng	LT(IC)	X	O	01.05.04	820 SQN
Cooper, Jack William,	MID(UCE)(IC)	X		01.09.05	ILLUSTRIOUS
Cooper, Janette Lindsey,	LT(SC(MD)	Q		01.11.01	UKSU JHQ LISBON
Cooper, Kevin Philip, BSc	CDR(FTC)	E	WE	30.06.05	FWO DEVPT SEA
Cooper, Lorna Jane,	LT(IC)	S		01.05.04	FLEET COSP&S
Cooper, Mark Andrew, pce, pce(sm)	CDR(FTC)	X	SM	31.12.00	RALEIGH
Cooper, Neil,	MAJ(FTC)	-	SO(LE)	01.10.05	FLEET ISS
Cooper, Nicholas James Williams,	MID(NE)(IC)	S		01.01.06	DARTMOUTH BRNC
Cooper, Peter Frank, MBE, MSc, CEng, MIMechE	LT CDR(FTC)	E	MESM	21.04.89	DRAKE CBS
Cooper-Simpson, Roger John, MA, psc(j)	MAJ(FTC)	-	C	01.05.00	45 CDO RM
Copeland, Stephen Nicholas, BEng, psc(j)	LT CDR(FTC)	E	AE	01.02.99	PJHQ
Copinger-Symes, Rory Sandham, psc(j)	LT COL(FTC) (Act Col)	-		30.06.02	NP IRAQ
Coppin, Nigel James,	LT(IC)	S		01.01.03	TIRELESS
Copsey, Nicholas Robert Benham,	CAPT RM(CC)	-		01.09.03	CTCRM
Corbally, Margaret Louise,	LT(IC)	X		01.01.05	MWS COLLINGWOOD

Name	Rank	Branch	Spec	Seniority	Where Serving
Corbett, Andrew Scott, pce, pce(sm), psc(j), MA	CDR(FTC)	X	SM	30.06.03	VANGUARD(STBD)
Corbett, Gerard John,	LT CDR(FTC)	X	ATC	01.10.96	HQ STC
Corbett, William Roger, BSc, FRMS, psc(m)	CDR(FTC)	X	METOC	30.06.01	FLEET COMOPS NWD
Corbidge, Stephen John, MBE, sq	MAJ(FTC) (Act Lt Col)	-	SO(LE)	01.10.97	MOD (LONDON)
Corcoran, Robert Martin, BA	SLT(IC)	X		01.05.03	MWS COLLINGWOOD
Corder, Ian Fergus, MA, jsdc, pce, pce(sm), hcsc	CDRE(FTC)	X	SM	09.11.04	FLEET COSP&S
Corderoy, John Roger, BEng, MA, MSc, psc(j)	CDR(FTC)	E	MESM	30.06.01	MOD (LONDON)
Cordner, Katharine, BDS	SG LT(D)(SCC)	-		04.07.02	RALEIGH
Cordner, Michael Anthony, BSc, MB, CHB	SURG LT(MC(MD)	-		01.08.02	MDHU DERRIFORD
Corkett, Kerry Stephen,	LT CDR(FTC)	X	REG	01.10.04	NELSON
Cormack, Andrew James Ross, MB, BSc, MRCGP, CHB	SURG LTCDR(FCC)	-	GMPP	05.08.03	ALBION
Cornelio, Stuart Michael, BSc	LT(IC)	X		01.09.05	RALEIGH
Corner, Gordon Charles, pce	CDR(FTC)	X	PWO(C)	30.06.03	COM MCC NWD
Corness, Andrew Stuart, MA, PGCE	CHAPLAIN	CE		06.09.04	FWO PORTS SEA
Cornford, Marc, BEng	LT(CC)	X	P	01.10.99	848 SQN HERON
Cornick, Robin Michael,	LT CDR(FTC)	X	MCD	01.10.97	SACLANT ITALY
Cornish, Michael Christopher, pce	LT CDR(FTC)	X	AAWO	01.07.95	FLEET COMOPS NWD
Corps, Stephen David,	LT CDR(FTC)	E	WE	11.11.98	KENT
Corrigan, Niall Richard, BSc, pce	CAPT(FTC)	X	PWO(A)	30.06.06	IMS BRUSSELS
Corrin, Colby St John, LLB, jsdc, psc	MAJ(FTC)	-	MLDR	01.09.92	RMC OF SCIENCE
Corry, Simon Myles, BSc, MA, MIEE, psc(j)	CDR(FTC)	E	WE	31.12.00	DARING
Cory, Nicholas John,	LT(IC)	X	EW	01.05.04	JSSU CHELTENHAM
Coryton, Oliver Charles Wyndham Spencer,	CAPT RM(CC) (Act Maj)	-		01.09.03	FLEET COSP&S
Costain, Kathryn Ann, BA	LT(IC)	S		01.09.05	702 SQN HERON
Costello, Gerard Thomas, BSc, CEng, MIEE, MDA	CAPT(FTC)	E	WESM	30.06.03	STG BRISTOL
Cottee, Benjamin Richard John,	LT(FTC) (Act Lt Cdr)	X	ATC	01.09.94	RAF SHAWBURY
Cotterill, Bruce Maxwell, BEng, MSc, MIEE	LT CDR(FTC)	E	WESM	01.03.00	PJHQ
Cottis, Mathew Charles,	LT CDR(FTC)	S	SM	01.10.01	JSCSC
Cotton, Emma Louise,	LT(FTC)	S	CMA	01.04.01	MOD (LONDON)
Cottrell, Ralph,	2LT(IC)	-		01.08.01	40 CDO RM
Coughlan, Scott, BA	LT(IC)	X	SM	01.09.03	VENGEANCE(STBD)
Coughlin, Peter James Leonard, BSc	LT(IC)	X	O	01.01.05	824 SQN
Coulson, Peter, BEng, MA, MSc, CEng, psc(j)	CDR(FTC)	E	WE	30.06.04	MOD (LONDON)
Coulthard, Adrian John, BSc, C PHYS, MInstP, CMath, MIMA	LT CDR(FTC)	E	TM	11.05.03	DHFS
Coulthard, John Kinnear, MSc, CEng, MIMechE, jsdc	CAPT(FTC)	E	MESM	30.06.05	DRAKE CBS
Coulton, Ian Christopher, MA, MBA, psc(j)	CDR(FTC)	MS		30.06.01	RH HASLAR
Coulton, Jamie Robert Spencer,	LT(CC)	X	P	16.06.98	815 SQN HQ
Coulton, Samantha Leigh,	LT(CC)	X		01.08.00	ARCHER
Counter, Paul Richard, MB, BS, MRCS	SURG LTCDR(MCC)	-		01.08.99	NELSON (PAY)
Coupar, Dean Robert, BSc	SLT(IC)	X		01.11.04	DARTMOUTH BRNC
Course, Andrew James, MBE, MA, MSc, CEng, MIEE, psc(j), gw	CDR(FTC)	E	WE	30.06.02	MOD (LONDON)
Court, Matthew Richard, BA	SLT(IC)	X		01.11.04	DARTMOUTH BRNC
Courtney, Timothy Paul,	LT(IC)	E	MESM	01.05.03	VIGILANT(PORT)
Coverdale, Paul, BSc, PGDip	LT(CC)	X	HM2	01.03.00	OCEAN
Covington, William MacArtney, CBE, ADC, pce, pcea, psc	CAPT(FTC) (Commodore)	X	P	31.12.96	HQ1GP HQSTC
Cowan, Aidan Roland,	LT(FTC)	X	PWO(C)	19.09.00	MWS COLLINGWOOD
Cowan, Kenneth Gordon,	MAJ(CC)	-		01.10.05	FLEET COMOPS NWD
Cowdrey, Mervyn Charles,	CDR(FTC)	S		30.06.93	FLEET FOTR
Cowie, Andrew David, BSc	LT(CC)	E	WE	01.01.02	FLEET COMOPS NWD
Cowie, Kevin Michael,	LT CDR(FTC)	X	C	01.10.99	HQ DCSA
Cowin, Timothy James, BSc	LT(CC)	X	P	01.11.98	848 SQN HERON
Cowley, Richard Merlin, BSc	LT CDR(FTC)	X	MCD	01.04.97	OCLC MANCH
Cowlishaw, Nicholas David,	LT(CC)	X	ATC	01.07.04	FOST DPORT SHORE
Cowpe, Paul,	LT(IC)	X	AV	28.10.05	DISC
Cowper, Ian Robert, BSc, CEng, MIMarEST	LT CDR(FTC)	E	ME	01.10.00	DLO BRISTOL
Cox, Andrew David, BMus	LT(IC)	X		01.08.05	ATHERSTONE
Cox, David John, BEng, MSc, CEng, MIEE	LT CDR(FTC)	E	WE	01.10.01	NAVSEC
Cox, Mark Bamber,	LT CDR(FTC)	S		01.10.04	CORNWALL
Cox, Matthew John, BSc	SLT(IC)	E	WE U/T	01.09.03	MWS COLLINGWOOD
Cox, Michael Shaun,	LT(IC)	X		01.05.04	JFC HQ AGRIPPA
Cox, Pieter William Studley, BSc, CEng, MIEE	CDR(FTC)	E	WESM	30.06.93	NAVSEC
Cox, Rex John, n	LT CDR(FTC)	X	AAWO	01.03.01	SEVERN

Name	Rank	Branch	Spec	Seniority	Where Serving
Cox, Simon,	2LT(IC)	-		01.08.01	42 CDO RM
Cox, Simon James,	LT(IC)	X		01.05.05	GLOUCESTER
Coxon, Helen Elizabeth Mary,	LT(IC)	X		01.09.05	MERSEY
Cox-Tregale, Jamie, BSc,	LT(IC)	X		01.04.04	MWS HM TG (D)
Coyle, Gavin James, BSc, pce, n	LT CDR(FTC)	X	PWO(U)	01.08.01	MWS COLLINGWOOD
Coyle, Ross Daniel,	LT(IC)	E	WE	01.05.02	SOUTHAMPTON
Crabb, Antony John, MSc	LT CDR(FTC)	X	PWO(U)	01.10.04	JHQSW MADRID
Crabbe, Robert James, BSc,	LT(CC)	X		01.12.98	SEVERN
Crabtree, Ian Michael, BSc, pce	CDR(FTC)	X	AAWO	31.12.90	FLEET COSP&S
Cragg, Richard Darryl, BEng	LT CDR(FTC)	E	MESM	01.10.04	TRAFALGAR
Craggs, Stuart, BEng, CEng, MIMechE	LT CDR(FTC)	E	AE	01.10.03	MERLIN IPT
Crago, Philip Thomas, BSc, CEng, FIMarEST	CDR(FTC)	E	ME	30.06.02	FWO DEVPT SEA
Craib, Alfred George,	LT CDR(FTC)	E	WE	01.10.02	NC3 AGENCY
Craig, Alexander Paul,	MID(IC)	X	P U/T	01.05.04	RNAS YEOVILTON
Craig, John Antony, pce	LT CDR(FTC)	X	MCD	01.05.02	MWS COLLINGWOOD
Craig, Kenneth Mitchell, BSc,	MAJ(FTC)	-		01.05.01	RM WARMINSTER
Craig, Michael Jon, BSc,	LT(IC)	X	P	01.05.03	845 SQN
Cran, Barrie Charles, BEng, MA, CEng, MIMechE, psc(j)	CDR(FTC)	E	MESM	30.06.03	FLEET COSP&S
Crane, Oliver Richard, BSc,	LT(CC)	X	P	01.10.98	DHFS
Craner, Matthew John, MB, BCh, MRCP	SURG CDR(FCC)	-		30.06.04	NELSON (PAY)
Crascall, Stephen John,	LT CDR(FTC)	X	AV	01.10.03	FLEET COSCAP
Craven, Dale,	LT(CC)	E	WESM	01.01.03	DLO BRISTOL
Craven, John Arthur Graham, MIL, MCMI	LT CDR(FTC)	S		01.09.85	2SL/CNH FOTR
Craven, Martin William, BEng	LT(CC)	X	P	01.08.98	815 FLT 207
Craven, Oliver Edward,	LT(IC)	X		01.09.05	GRIMSBY
Crawford, Adam Timothy Stephen, BSc	MAJ(FTC)	-		01.05.04	HQ 3 CDO BDE RM
Crawford, Alistair Alwyn, BEng	SLT(IC)	X	P U/T	01.11.04	DARTMOUTH BRNC
Crawford, Richard Ian,	LT(IC)	S		12.08.05	DSDA
Crawford, Valerie Elizabeth, BA, LLB	LT(CC)	X		01.04.02	ENDURANCE
Crawley, David Anthony,	LT(FTC)	E	ME	01.04.01	MWS EXCELLENT
Cree, Andrew Martin, BEng, MA, MSc, FCIPD, psc(j)	CDR(FTC)	E	TM	30.06.04	FLEET HQ WI
Cree, Malcolm Charles, BA, pce, psc(j), fsc	CAPT(FTC)	X	AAWO	30.06.06	FLEET HQ WI
Creech, Richard David, gdas, MCGI, MRIN, FInstLM, MAPM	LT CDR(FTC)	X	O	01.10.96	MERLIN IPT
Creek, Stephen Brian,	LT(IC)	E	WESM	01.01.02	DRAKE SFM
Crew, Julian Maynard, BA	LT(CC)	X	P	01.01.00	815 SQN HQ
Crewdson, Robert Paul,	SLT(IC)	X	O U/T	01.02.06	DARTMOUTH BRNC
Crichton, Gary,	LT(IC)	X		29.10.04	LIVERPOOL
Criddle, Gary David James,	LT(FTC)	X	O	01.06.96	815 SQN HQ
Crimmen, David John, pcea	LT CDR(CC)	X	P	01.10.02	771 SQN
Cripps, Michael James, MEng, MRAeS	LT(CC)	E	AE	01.09.02	849 SQN B FLT
Cripps, Nicola Jane, BA	LT(IC)	E	TM	01.01.04	SULTAN
Crisp, Dominic John Delves,	CAPT RM(IC)	-		01.09.05	CDO LOG REGT RM
Crispin, Toby Alexander Baldwin, MSc, MRIN, pcea, gdas	LT CDR(FTC)	X	O	01.04.94	MERLIN IPT
Critchley, Ian Joseph,	SLT(IC)	X	SM	01.09.04	TRENCHANT
Crockatt, Stephen Richard James,	LT CDR(FTC)	X	P	01.10.03	EXCHANGE USA
Crocker, Dominic Thomas Alcard, BSc	SLT(IC)	X		01.02.04	ALBION
Crockett, Simon Keith,	LT(IC)	E	ME	01.05.04	OCLC ROSYTH
Croft, David Francis, MA	LT(CC)	X	H2	01.01.99	MWS HM TG (D)
Crofts, David Jeffrey, BEng, MSc, MIEE	LT CDR(FTC)	E	WE	01.02.99	MOD (LONDON)
Croke, Anthony, pce, pcea, psc, ocds(Can)	CAPT(FTC)	X	P	30.06.99	LOAN OMAN
Crombie, Stuart, BA,	LT(IC)	X	O U/T	01.09.05	702 SQN HERON
Cromie, John Martin, MSc	LT(CC)	X	FC	01.05.00	EXCHANGE FRANCE
Crompton, Andrew Paul James, BSc,	LT(CC)	X	ATC	01.09.02	RNAS YEOVILTON
Crompton, Philip John,	LT(CC)	X	P	01.11.00	815 FLT 229
Crook, Andrea Susan, BA, jsdc	CDR(FTC)	S		30.06.97	NBC PORTSMOUTH
Crook, Richard Frank, BEng	SLT(IC)	E	ME U/T	01.09.04	EDINBURGH
Cropley, Andrew, BSc, MA, MA(Ed), MCIPD, psc(j)	CDR(FTC)	E	TM	30.06.03	DEF SCH OF LANG
Cropper, Fraser Brunel Nicholas, BEng, MSc	LT CDR(FTC)	E	AE	24.06.01	JSCSC
Cropper, Martin Andrew Keith, BA	LT CDR(FTC)	S	SM	16.05.90	DRAKE CBS
Crosbie, Donald Ernest Frederick,	LT CDR(FTC)	X	PWO(U)	01.02.00	NAVSEC
Crosby, David William Malcolm,	LT(IC)	X	SM	01.05.04	VIGILANT(PORT)
Crosby, John Paul, psc	LT COL(FTC)	-		30.06.93	JHQ/CIS LISBON

Name	Rank	Branch	Spec	Seniority	Where Serving
Crosland, Stephen Andrew, ...LT(IC)	E	WE		01.01.04	FLEET ISS
Cross, Andrew George, ...CAPT RM(CC) (Act Maj)	-	SO(LE)		01.04.02	CTCRM
Cross, Eric John, ...CAPT RM(CC)	-	P		01.01.02	1 ASSAULT GP RM
Cross, Nicholas, BSc ....LT(IC)	E	IS		01.07.02	MOD (LONDON)
Crossey, Matthew Darren, BSc, PGCE...LT(IC)	E	TM		01.06.01	SULTAN
Crossley, Charles Crispin, BSc, MDA, CEng, MIMechE, MIMarEST...............CDR(FTC)	E	ME		31.12.99	FLEET HQ WI
Crouch, Matthew, BSc ....LT(IC)	X			01.05.01	MWS COLLINGWOOD
Crouden, Stephen Frederick, psc(j)...LT COL(FTC)	-	SO(LE)		30.06.06	FLEET COSP&S
Crowe, David Michael, n...LT(FTC)	X			01.08.99	MWS COLLINGWOOD
Crowe, Philip David, BA ....SLT(IC)	X			01.06.03	BANGOR
Crowson, Elizabeth, MB, CHB, MRCGP, Dip FFP ....SURG LTCDR(SC(MD)	-	GMPP		06.05.01	RN GIBRALTAR
Crowther, Kevin Wayne, BSc, pce..LT CDR(FTC)	X	AAWO		29.03.91	T45 IPT
Croxton, Damien Philip, BSc...LT(IC)	S			01.02.06	NEPTUNE DLO
Crozier, Stuart Ross McDonald, BA...............................CDR(FTC) (Barrister)	S	BAR		30.06.01	NAVSEC
Crudgington, Paul, AFC, pcea...LT CDR(FTC)	X	P		01.09.87	824 SQN
Crundell, Richard John, BEng, MSc, gw...LT CDR(FTC)	E	WE		01.07.00	YORK
Cryar, Timothy Martin Craven, pce, n..CDR(FTC)	X	AAWO		30.06.05	YORK
Cubbage, Jamie, BEng, MIEE ....LT CDR(FTC)	E	WE		01.04.02	IRON DUKE
Cull, Iain, PGDIPAN, pce, n..LT CDR(FTC)	X	PWO(N)		01.05.02	MWS COLLINGWOOD
Cullen, Nicola Leonie, BSc..LT(CC)	E	TM		01.09.95	DARTMOUTH BRNC
Cullis, Christopher John, sq...MAJ(FTC)	-	LC		25.04.96	CDO LOG REGT RM
Cullum, William Eric, ...SLT(IC)	X			01.01.04	LEDBURY
Culwick, Peter Francis, BDS, MSc, MGDS RCS, MA..........................SGCDR(D)(FCC)	-			31.12.96	MOD (LONDON)
Cumberland, Noel Stanley, ...SLT(IC)	X	P U/T		01.05.03	RNAS YEOVILTON
Cumming, Frazer Smith, MEng ....LT(IC)	X	O		01.09.03	849 SQN B FLT
Cumming, Robert Angus, BEng...LT(FTC)	E	MESM		01.04.97	DLO BRISTOL
Cummings, Alan Thomas, pce, pcea, ocds(USN)..........................LT CDR(FTC)	X	O		01.03.97	ILLUSTRIOUS
Cummings, David John, BEng, MSc...LT CDR(FTC)	E	WE		01.11.02	MONTROSE
Cunane, John Richard, MCIT, MILT..LT CDR(FTC)	S	SM		10.10.98	BDLS CANADA
Cundy, Robert Graham, MBE, psc(j)...LT COL(FTC)	-			30.06.04	NP IRAQ
Cunnane, Keith John, BEng, MA, MSc, CEng, MIEE, psc(j).....................LT CDR(FTC)	E	WESM		01.10.01	TRAFALGAR
Cunnell, Rachael Louise, BA, MSc ....LT(CC)	S			01.01.03	RNP TEAM
Cunningham, David Andrew, MA, MCMI, pcea, psc(j)..........................CDR(FTC)	X	O		30.06.05	FLEET COSCAP
Cunningham, David Brand, ...LT(CC)	E	MESM		01.09.01	DRAKE SFM
Cunningham, John Gavin, BA, pce, pcea, PSC(ONDC)..........................CDR(FTC)	X	O		30.06.03	NAVSEC
Cunningham, John Stewart, ...MAJ(FTC)	-	SO(LE)		01.10.98	FLEET COSP&S
Cunningham, Justin Thomas, MA, psc(j)...LT COL(FTC)	-			30.06.06	NP IRAQ
Cunningham, Nigel John Whitworth, ...LT CDR(FTC(A)	X	O		01.10.03	702 SQN HERON
Cunningham, Paul, FCIPD, CDipAF...CAPT(FTC)	S			30.06.05	DLO/DG LOG (SC)
Cunningham, Richard Alister, MBE, pce, pcea, psc ....CDR(FTC)	X	P		30.06.00	MOD (LONDON)
Cunningham, Stuart Iain, ...LT(IC)	X			01.04.05	ATHERSTONE
Cunningham, Thomas Anthony, pce, pcea, psc ....CDRE(FTC)	X	O		22.02.05	MOD (LONDON)
Curd, Michael Christopher, BA...LT(IC)	X	O		01.01.05	815 FLT 208
Curlewis, Andrew John, BEng, MSc...LT CDR(FTC)	E	ME		01.04.00	FOST SEA
Curnock, Timothy Charles Ross, BEng ....SLT(IC)	E	WE U/T		01.01.04	MWS COLLINGWOOD
Curnow, Michael David, BSc, CEng, MIMechE, psc........................CDR(FTC)	E	ME		31.12.98	MOD (BATH)
Currass, Timothy David, BEng, MSc..LT CDR(FTC)	E	WE		01.03.99	FWO PORTS SEA
Currie, David William, BSc, pce..LT CDR(FTC)	X	AAWO		01.04.90	MOD (LONDON)
Currie, Duncan Gordon, ...LT CDR(FTC)	X	P		16.12.01	771 SQN
Currie, Michael John, BSc, pcea ....LT(CC)	X	O		16.08.99	824 SQN
Currie, Stuart McGregor, BEng, CEng, PGDip, MIMarEST......................LT CDR(FTC)	E	MESM		01.08.99	SPARTAN
Curry, Benedict Rodney, MBE, psc..LT COL(FTC)	-	C		30.06.02	UN AFRICA
Curry, Paul Thomas, BSc...CAPT RM(IC) (Act Maj)	-	SO(LE)		01.04.04	LN SIERRA LEONE
Curry, Robert Edward, BSc, n...LT CDR(FTC)	X	PWO(C)		01.11.01	ARK ROYAL
Cursiter, John Douglas, BEng...LT(IC)	X	SM		12.06.05	RALEIGH
Curtis, David, ...LT CDR(FTC)	E	WESM		01.10.04	ASM IPT
Curtis, Peter John, ...CAPT RM(IC)	BS	SO(LE)		24.07.04	CTCRM BAND
Curtis, Suzannah Elizabeth Hayton, BMus ....LT(CC)	S			01.09.99	DRAKE COB
Curtiss, Charlotte Jane, BSc ....LT(IC)	E	IS U/T		01.03.04	FLEET FOTR
Curwood, Jenny Elizabeth, BSc ....LT(CC)	S			01.11.98	NELSON
Cusack, Nicholas James, MSc, jsdc ....LT COL(FTC)	-	C		30.06.99	FLEET COSCAP
Cuthbert, Glen, BSc ....LT(IC)	X			01.05.04	MWS COLLINGWOOD

Name	Rank	Branch	Spec	Seniority	Where Serving
Cutlan, Sarah Louise, BEng	SLT(IC)	E	WE U/T	01.09.03	MWS COLLINGWOOD
Cutler, Andrew, BSc, SM(n), SM	LT(FTC)	X	SM	01.10.99	RALEIGH
Cutler, David Terry,	LT(IC)	E	ME	01.05.04	DARTMOUTH BRNC
Cutler, Tristan Paul, BSc	LT(CC)	S		01.10.99	NAVSEC
Cutt, John James Douglas, pce(sm), psc	CDR(FTC)	X	SM	30.06.94	JHQ/CIS LISBON

D

Name	Rank	Branch	Spec	Seniority	Where Serving
Dabell, Guy Lester, BSc, MA, psc(j)	CDR(FTC)	E	MESM	30.06.02	DLO BRISTOL
Dacombe, Carl Andrew, BSc	LT(IC)	X	FC	01.09.04	EXETER
Dailey, Paul George Johnson, MA, MSc, CEng, MIEE, MCMI, psc(j), Eur Ing	CDR(FTC)	E	WESM	30.06.03	MOD (LONDON)
Dainton, Steven, MA, pce, psc(j), n	CDR(FTC)	X	PWO(C)	30.06.04	ST ALBANS
Dainty, Robin Christopher, SM(n), SM	LT(CC)	X	SM	29.04.01	TURBULENT
Dale, Alistair,	LT CDR(FTC)	X	ATC	01.02.04	RNAS CULDROSE
Dale, Jamie Richard,	SLT(IC)	X	ATCU/T	01.09.03	RNAS YEOVILTON
Dale, Nathan Andrew,	LT(IC)	X	P	01.09.04	846 SQN
Dale-Smith, Guy, BA, PGDIPAN, pce	LT CDR(FTC)	X	PWO(N)	01.12.97	ATHERSTONE
Dale-Smith, Victoria Grace,	LT CDR(FTC)	X	P	15.03.05	MOD (LONDON)
Dalgleish, Grant Alastair, BA,	LT(IC)	X		01.05.04	YORK
Dalglish, Kenneth Michael, BSc	LT(IC)	E	WE	01.09.04	CHATHAM
Dallas, Lewis Ian, BEng	LT(IC)	E	MESM	01.09.05	SULTAN
Dalton, Feargal John, BEng, CEng, MIEE	LT CDR(CC)	E	WESM	01.10.03	RALEIGH
Dalton, Mark, BD	CHAPLAIN	SF		12.01.03	FWO DEVPT SEA
Daly, Julie Margaret, BEd	LT CDR(CC)	E	TM	01.10.02	FLEET COSP&S
Daly, Michael Philip,	LT(IC)	E	WE	01.01.04	FLEET COSCAP
Daly, Paul,	LT(FTC)	X	PWO(U)	01.05.99	SUTHERLAND
Danbury, Ian Gerald, BSc, CEng, MIEE	CDR(FTC)	E	WE	30.06.98	FOST SEA
Dando, Benjamin John,	MID(IC)	X	O U/T	01.09.04	RNAS CULDROSE
Dando, Jonathon Neil, n	LT CDR(FTC)	X	PWO(A)	01.08.00	FLEET COMOPS NWD
Dane, Richard Martin Henry, MBE, pcea	CDR(FTC)	X	P	30.06.05	824 SQN
Daniel, Benjamin James Edward, BA	LT(IC)	X	P	01.01.04	846 SQN
Daniell, Christopher John, pcea	LT CDR(FTC)	X	O	01.10.95	750 SQN SEAHAWK
Daniels, Ian James Russell, BSc, pcea, gdas	LT CDR(FTC)	X	O	01.10.95	JSCSC
Daniels, Stephen Anthony, pcea, psc, tp	CDR(FTC) (Act Capt)	X	P	30.06.00	DPA BRISTOL
Daniels, Stuart Paul,	LT(IC)	X		01.04.01	DRAKE COB
Daniels, Timothy Nicholas, BA, psc(j)	LT COL(FTC)	-	C	30.06.03	MOD (LONDON)
Dannatt, Timothy Mark, MSc, CEng, MIMechE, jsdc	CAPT(FTC)	E	ME	30.06.03	DLO BRISTOL
Daramola, Olufunmilayo, BSc, MB, CHB, MRCOG, MRCGP	SURG CDR(MC(MD))	-	GMPP	30.06.06	ILLUSTRIOUS
Darcy, John David, BA	SLT(IC)	X	P U/T	01.11.04	DARTMOUTH BRNC
D'Arcy, Paul Andrew, pcea	LT CDR(FTC)	X	O	01.10.02	RNAS YEOVILTON
D'Arcy, Tara,	LT(SC(MD))	Q		14.07.02	NELSON (PAY)
Darley, Matthew Edward, BSc	CAPT RM(CC)	-	P	01.09.01	847 SQN
Darlington, Alan, BA	LT(IC)	X	P	01.09.04	RNAS YEOVILTON
Darlington, Mark Robinson, BSc, pce	CAPT(FTC)	X	AAWO	30.06.04	FLEET COSP&S
Darlow, Paul Raymond,	LT CDR(FTC)	S	CA	01.10.02	MWC SOUTHWICK
Dart, Duncan James,	LT(IC)	X	P	01.09.04	846 SQN
Dart, Michael Paul,	SLT(IC)	X	O U/T	01.09.05	DARTMOUTH BRNC
Darwent, Andrew, BSc, MDA, CEng, MIEE	CDR(FTC)	E	WE	30.06.99	MOD (LONDON)
Darwent, Sean Anthony, BSc	LT(CC)	X	O	01.03.93	GANNET SAR FLT
Dathan, Timothy James, BEng, MSc, psc(j)	LT CDR(FTC)	E	ME	01.03.95	MOD (LONDON)
Daukes, Nicholas Michael, BSc	MAJ(FTC)	-	C	01.09.01	FLEET COSCAP
Davenport, Nigel Jefferson, BDS	SGLTCDR(D)(MCC)	-		16.01.97	1 ASSLT GP RM
Davey, Christopher Stephen, BSc	LT(IC)	X	P	01.01.04	OCLC BIRM
Davey, Gary Stuart, BEng, MSc	LT(IC)	E	AE	30.06.05	CV(F) IPT
Davey, Kelly, MB, MSc, CHB	SURG LT(SCC)	-		02.08.05	DARTMOUTH BRNC
Davey, Paul John, MSc, CEng, FIMarEST	LT CDR(FTC)	E	ME	01.06.89	DRAKE SFM
Davey, Timothy James, BSc	LT(FTC)	X	MCD	01.10.97	CAMPBELTOWN
David, Simon Evan James, MA, psc(j)	CDR(FTC)	S		30.06.03	SULTAN
Davidson, Gregor John, BEng	SLT(IC)	E	ME U/T	01.01.05	DARTMOUTH BRNC
Davidson, Justin David,	LT(IC)	E	ME	01.07.04	WESTMINSTER
Davidson, Neil Richard,	LT CDR(FTC)	X	P	01.10.03	JHCHQ
Davidson, Serena Rachel, BSc	LT(IC)	X	O U/T	01.09.05	849 SQN HQ

Name	Rank	Branch	Spec	Seniority	Where Serving
Davies, Alex, BEng	SLT(IC)	E	ME U/T	01.01.05	DARTMOUTH BRNC
Davies, Andrew James Albert, gdas	LT(CC)	X	O	01.08.90	NELSON
Davies, Anthony Robin, MA, psc, pce	CAPT(FTC)	X	PWO(A)	30.06.04	SA THE HAGUE
Davies, Christopher John, BSc, MIExpE, ACMI, pce, isc	CDR(FTC)	X	MCD	30.06.02	MCM3 SEA
Davies, Christopher Ronald, BEd	MAJ(FTC)	-		01.10.04	JSCSC
Davies, Christopher Stanley, MA	LT CDR(FTC) (Act Cdr)	X	METOC	01.09.90	COM MCC NWD
Davies, Daniel Tudor, BPh	LT(IC)	X		01.04.05	MWS COLLINGWOOD
Davies, Darren James,	LT(IC)	S		01.01.05	ARGYLL
Davies, Gary,	LT(HC)	E	SM	15.06.90	NELSON
Davies, Geraint William Tudor,	LT(CC)	X	FC	01.12.97	MWS COLLINGWOOD
Davies, Henry George Alexander,	LT(CC)	X	P	01.07.96	829 FLT 05
Davies, Huan Charles Ayrton, BSc	MAJ(FTC)	-	MLDR	01.09.00	PJHQ
Davies, Ian Ellis, pce, n	LT CDR(FTC)	X	H CH	01.12.98	LOAN HYDROG
Davies, James Somerfield Ayrton, BEng	SLT(IC)	E	AE U/T	01.09.03	SULTAN
Davies, Jason John,	LT(CC)	X	P	12.12.97	EXCHANGE RAF UK
Davies, Jason Lee,	LT(CC) (Act Lt Cdr)	MS		01.09.01	MDHU PORTSMOUTH
Davies, John Huw, MA, MSc, psc(j)	CDR(FTC)	X	METOC	31.12.00	RMC OF SCIENCE
Davies, John Robert, osc(us)	LT COL(FTC)	-		31.12.98	RMR MERSEYSIDE
Davies, Lee, BEng	LT CDR(FTC)	E	AE	01.01.02	RNAS YEOVILTON
Davies, Luke Magnus Ayrton,	CAPT RM(IC)	-		01.09.05	CDO LOG REGT RM
Davies, Mark Bryan, MA, pce, pcea, psc(j)o	CDR(FTC)	X	O	30.06.06	MOD (LONDON)
Davies, Nicholas Mark Samuel, BSc	LT(CC) (Act Lt Cdr)	X	HM	01.09.98	MWS HM TG (D)
Davies, Paul Nicholas Michael, pce, psc(m)	CAPT(FTC)	X	AAWO	31.12.98	MOD (LONDON)
Davies, Richard,	CAPT RM(IC) (Act Maj)	-		01.09.00	CTCRM
Davies, Sarah Jane, MA	LT(IC)	X		01.09.04	MWS COLLINGWOOD
Davies, Stephen Philip,	LT CDR(FTC)	E	WESM	01.10.01	MOD (BATH)
Davies, Timothy Gordon, BSc, MRAeS, odc(Fr)	CDR(FTC)	E	AE	31.12.98	NAVSEC
Davies, Trevor Martin, BEng, MSc, MIExpE	LT CDR(FTC)	E	WE	01.10.97	LOAN OMAN
Davis, Bernard James, OBE, LLB, LLM	CAPT(FTC) (Barrister)	S	BAR	01.04.04	MOD (LONDON)
Davis, Christopher John,	LT COL(FTC)	BS	SO(LE)	30.06.02	HQ BAND SERVICE
Davis, Edward Grant Martin, OBE, MA, psc(m)	COL(FTC)	-		30.06.04	MOD (LONDON)
Davis, Gary,	LT(IC) (Act Lt Cdr)	X	EW	01.01.01	JSSU CHELTENHAM
Davis, Martin Philip, BSc, pce, pcea, psc	LT CDR(FTC)	X	O	01.07.88	SA MALAYSIA
Davis, Peter Haydn, BEng	LT(IC)	E	TM U/T	01.09.02	YORK
Davis, Peter Henry, BA	LT(IC)	X		01.09.04	NP IRAQ
Davis, Richard,	LT(IC)	E	WESM	16.12.05	MWS COLLINGWOOD
Davis-Marks, Michael Leigh, OBE, BSc, MA, pce, pce(sm), psc, MNI	CAPT(FTC)	X	SM	30.06.04	FLEET COSCAP
Davison, Andrew Paul, BSc, MA, PGCE, psc(j), CMarSci, FIMarEST	CDR(FTC)	X	METOC	30.06.04	JWC/CIS STAVANGR
Davison, Gregory James,	LT CDR(FTC)	X	P	01.10.02	LOAN JTEG BSC DN
Davison, Laura Marie,	SLT(IC)	S		01.09.03	800 NAS (GR7)
Davison, Warren Matthew,	SLT(IC)	X	P U/T	01.06.05	DARTMOUTH BRNC
Daw, Simon James, pcea	LT CDR(FTC)	X	O	01.10.97	750 SQN SEAHAWK
Dawe, Christopher John,	LT(IC)	X	SM	01.04.05	TIRELESS
Daws, Richard Patrick Anthony, MSc, CEng, MIEE	CDR(FTC)	E	WESM	30.06.99	NAVSEC
Dawson, Alan James, BTech	LT CDR(FTC)	E	WESM	01.10.03	TALENT
Dawson, Allan,	CAPT RM(CC)	-	SO(LE)	01.04.03	1 ASSAULT GP RM
Dawson, Graham Alexander Edward, BSc, BEng	LT(IC)	E	TM	01.09.00	ILLUSTRIOUS
Dawson, Nigel Julian Frederick, MSc, FRGS	LT CDR(FTC)	E	TM	01.10.03	MOD (LONDON)
Dawson, Paul,	LT(FTC)	E	MESM	01.04.01	SULTAN
Dawson, Peter John,	CDR(FTC)	X	ATC	30.06.04	FLEET COSCAP
Dawson, Phillip Mark David,	LT(IC)	X	SM	01.01.02	FLEET COMOPS NWD
Dawson, Stephen Lee, MA, PGCE, MDA, psc	CDR(FTC)	E	TM	30.06.02	MOD (LONDON)
Dawson, Stewart Neville, BEng, MSc, CEng, MIEE	LT CDR(FTC)	E	WE	01.10.98	CMT SHRIVENHAM
Dawson, William, pce	LT CDR(FTC)	X	AAWO	01.11.98	HQ BFSAI
Day, Anthony,	LT(CC)	X	REG	01.01.03	MWS COLLINGWOOD
Day, Benjamin Thomas, BA	LT(IC)	X		01.04.02	FWO DEVPT SEA
Day, Michael Kershaw, BSc	LT(FTC) (Act Lt Cdr)	X	P	15.06.95	846 SQN
Day, Simon Nicholas, BEng, MSc, CEng, MIMarEST	LT CDR(FTC)	E	ME	01.10.03	YORK
De Jonghe, Paul Trevor, IEng, HNC, MIIE	LT CDR(FTC)	E	WE	01.10.94	LOAN OMAN
De La Rue, Andrew Nicholas, BA	LT(CC)	S	SM	01.09.01	VANGUARD(STBD)
De Reya, Anthony Luciano, BA, psc(j)o	MAJ(FTC)	-		01.09.01	HQ 3 CDO BDE RM
Deacon, Stephen, pce, pcea	LT CDR(FTC)	X	O	01.06.98	829 SQN HQ

Name	Rank	Branch	Spec	Seniority	Where Serving
Deakin, Johanna, BEng	LT CDR(FTC)	E	AE	01.10.03	DLO YEO
Deakin, Scott,	LT(IC)	E	WE	08.04.05	LANCASTER
Deal, Charlotte, BEng, MIEE, MAPM	LT(FTC)	E	WE	01.06.99	MWS COLLINGWOOD
Dean, James Robert, BA	LT CDR(FTC)	S		01.10.02	NELSON
Dean, Joanna Patricia, LLB	LT(IC)	X		01.02.06	MWS COLLINGWOOD
Dean, Michael Robin, MB, BCH, FFOM, MRCGP, DObstRCOG	SURG CAPT(FCC)	-	(CO/M)	30.06.03	INM ALVERSTOKE
Dean, Simon Ian Robert,	CAPT RM(CC)	-		01.09.02	40 CDO RM
Dean, Timothy Charles, BDS	SGLTCDR(D)(MCC)	-		22.07.02	RMB STONEHOUSE
Dean, William Michael Henry, BSc, gdas	LT CDR(FTC) (Act Cdr)	X	P	01.10.95	RAF COTTESMORE
Deaney, Mark Nicholas, BSc, CEng, MRAeS	CDR(FTC)	E	AE	31.12.00	HUMS IPT
Dearden, Steven Roy, MSc, CEng, FIMechE	CAPT(FTC)	E	MESM	30.06.02	DLO BRISTOL
Deavin, Matthew James,	LT(FTC)	X	P	01.07.95	800 NAS (GR7)
Dechow, William Ernest, OBE, BSc, jsdc	COL(FTC)	-		30.06.06	HQ DSC)
Dedman, Nigel John Keith, pce, pcea, fsc	CAPT(FTC)	X	O	30.06.01	NELSON
Deeks, Peter, BEng, CEng, PGDip, MIMarEST	LT(CC)	E	MESM	01.07.96	NP IRAQ
Deighton, Derek Simpson, pce	LT CDR(FTC)	X	AAWO	01.05.92	FOST NWD (JMOTS)
Dekker, Barrie James, MB, BS, FRCA	SURG CDR(MCC)	-	(CA)	30.06.06	MDHU PORTSMOUTH
Delahay, Jonathon Edward, BSc	CAPT RM(CC)	-		01.09.02	JSCSC
Dell, Iain Martin, MSc	CDR(FTC)	MS	(AD)	30.06.06	DMSTC
Deller, Mark Gareth, pce, pcea, psc	CDR(FTC)	X	P	30.06.05	FLEET COSCAP
De'Maine, Robert James, BSc	SLT(IC)	X	P U/T	01.09.04	DARTMOUTH BRNC
Dempsey, Sean Patrick, n	LT CDR(FTC)	X	PWO(A)	01.02.06	COMATG SEA
Denby, William,	SURG SLT(SCC)	-		25.09.04	DARTMOUTH BRNC
Denham, Daniel John,	LT(FTC)	X	P	01.06.98	HANDLING SQN
Denham, Nigel John,	CDR(FTC)	X	SM	31.12.00	FLEET COSCAP
Denholm, Iain Glenwright, pce	LT CDR(FTC)	X	AAWO	13.08.94	DLO BRISTOL
Denholm, James Lovell, MB, ChB	SURG LTCDR(MCC)	-	GMPP	07.08.01	1 ASSAULT GP RM
Denise, Alexander,	2LT(IC)	-		01.08.01	40 CDO RM
Denison, Alan Rae Van Tiel, MSc, CEng, MIMechE	LT CDR(FTC)	E	ME	01.02.89	DLO/DG LOG (SC)
Dennard, Kieron John, BEng	LT(IC)	E	ME	01.09.04	MONTROSE
Denney, James Robert, BA	LT(CC)	X		01.02.99	JSCSC
Denning, Oliver,	2LT(IC)	-		31.08.04	FPGRM
Denning, Paul Richard, OBE, MA, psc(m)	COL(FTC)	-	P	30.06.03	FPGRM
Dennis, James Alexander, BSc	MAJ(CC)	-	C	01.10.05	BULWARK
Dennis, Matthew John, SM(n)	LT CDR(FTC)	X	SM	01.10.01	FLEET HQ WI
Dennis, Philip Edward, BSc	LT CDR(FTC)	X	PWO(A)	01.07.04	LANCASTER
Denovan, Paul Andrew, BSc, CEng, MIEE	CDR(FTC)	E	WESM	30.06.04	DLO BRISTOL
Densham, Martin Philip John, BA, BSc	LT(CC)	X	H2	01.10.98	EXCHANGE USA
Denyer, Alistair Charles,	MID(UCE)(IC)	X		01.09.05	LIVERPOOL
Derby, Byron Dylan, BEng, MSc, MSc gw, CEng, MIEE, gw, NDipM	LT CDR(FTC)	E	WE	01.04.02	SACT BELGIUM
Dermody, Ryan Thomas,	LT(CC)	X	FC	01.12.00	RNAS YEOVILTON
Derrick, Gareth Gwyn James, BSc, MPhil, Eur Ing, CEng, MIEE, psc(j)o	CAPT(FTC)	E	WESM	30.06.06	NELSON
Derrick, Matthew John George, BEng	LT(CC)	E	TM	01.12.99	RNSR BOVINGTON
De'Silva, Oliver Anura, BA	SLT(IC)	S		01.09.04	DARTMOUTH BRNC
Despres, Julian Peter, ARRC	LT(MC(MD)	Q		19.11.02	MDHU DERRIFORD
Devenney, David,	CHAPLAIN	SF		06.01.03	1 ASSAULT GP RM
Devereux, Michael Edwin, BA	MAJ(FTC)	-	P	01.09.03	JHCHQ
Deverson, Richard Timothy Mark, pcea	LT CDR(FTC)	X	P	01.10.01	702 SQN HERON
Devlin, Craig John, BSc	LT(IC)	E	IS	01.01.04	SULTAN
Dew, Anthony Michael, MB, BCh	SURG LTCDR(MCC)	-		02.08.05	JSU NORTHWOOD
Dewar, Duncan Andrew, BSc, MA, psc(j)	LT COL(FTC)	-		30.06.03	45 CDO RM
Dewar, Joanna Clare, BM	SURG LTCDR(SCC)	-	GMPP	30.04.02	RALEIGH
Dewar, Michael James, BSc	LT(IC)	X		01.01.04	MWS HM TG (D)
Dewhirst, Michael,	SLT(IC)	E		01.01.05	MWS COLLINGWOOD
Dewsnap, Michael David,	LT CDR(FTC)	E	WE	01.10.01	HQ SACT
Dewynter, Alison Mary, MA(CANTAB), PGCE, MB, BS	SURG LT(SC(MD)	-		06.08.03	MDHU DERRIFORD
Di Maio, Mark David, BSc	LT(CC)	S		01.01.03	DLO BRISTOL
Dible, James Hunter, pce, psc(j)	CDR(FTC)	X	P	30.06.04	FLEET HQ WI
Dick, Colin Michael, BEng	LT(CC)	E	TMSM	01.01.97	FOST FAS SHORE
Dickens, David James Rees, OBE, pce, psc	CAPT(FTC)	X	PWO(U)	30.06.02	FLEET COSP&S
Dickens, David Stephen, BEng, MSc	LT CDR(FTC)	E	WE	01.10.04	SULTAN
Dicker, Nicholas Martin,	LT(IC)	X	SM	01.08.04	TORBAY

Name	Rank	Branch	Spec	Seniority	Where Serving
Dickie, Andrew,	A/SURG LT(SCC)	-		01.08.05	DARTMOUTH BRNC
Dickins, Benjamin Russell, BA	LT CDR(FTC)	X	PWO(U)	01.10.04	WESTMINSTER
Dickinson, Pamela Hepple, BEng, MSc	LT(IC)	E	ME	01.07.00	SULTAN
Dickson, James Ian, BSc	LT CDR(FTC)	S	SM	01.08.02	SULTAN
Dickson, Kenneth George, BEng	LT(IC)	E	WESM	01.09.05	VICTORIOUS(PORT)
Dickson, Stuart James, MB, CHB, MRCP, DTM&H	SURG LTCDR(MCC)	-		02.08.00	LOAN FIELD HOSP
Dillon, Ben, BEng, MIEE	LT(IC)	E	WE	01.04.03	MWS COLLINGWOOD
Dilloway, Philip John, BSc, MA	LT(MC(MD)	Q	RMN	07.12.96	RCDM
Dimmock, Guy Neil, BEng	SLT(IC)	E	ME U/T	01.01.05	DARTMOUTH BRNC
Dineen, John Michael George, MA, pce	LT CDR(FTC)	X	AAWO	01.04.02	FOST SEA
Dingley, Paul Alexander,	LT(FTC)	X	O	01.01.01	ARK ROYAL
Dingwall, Nils,	2LT(IC)	-		01.08.01	FPGRM
Dinham, Alan Colin, BSc, PhD	LT CDR(FTC)	E	TM	01.10.88	MOD (LONDON)
Dinsmore, Simon,	2LT(IC)	-		01.08.01	45 CDO RM
Disney, Luke,	2LT(IC)	-		01.08.04	42 CDO RM
Disney, Peter William, pcea	LT CDR(FTC)	X	O	01.10.94	824 SQN
Diver, Paul Harry, HND	LT CDR(FTC)	E	TM	01.10.04	MWS COLLINGWOOD
Dix, Caroline Patrica, MEng	SLT(IC)	E	AE U/T	01.09.03	SULTAN
Dixon, Arthur Kenneth, BEng, MIMechE	LT(IC)	E	MESM	01.09.00	SPARTAN
Dixon, Mark Edward, BEng, PGDip	LT(IC)	E	MESM	01.01.04	VICTORIOUS(PORT)
Dixon, Richard Andrew,	LT(CC)	X	P	01.01.01	815 FLT 215
Dixon, Robert James,	LT(IC)	X		01.09.05	HQ BFSAI
Dixon, Simon James,	LT(IC)	X	P	01.01.05	RNAS YEOVILTON
Dixon, Simon Peter,	LT(IC)	X		01.05.04	FLEET HQ NWD
Dobson, Amy Clare,	LT(CC)	X	O	01.04.03	750 SQN SEAHAWK
Dobson, Richard Andrew, BSc	LT CDR(FTC) (Act Cdr)	X	H CH	01.04.91	LOAN OMAN
Dobson, Serena Caroline Sandcroft, BA	SLT(IC)	X		01.05.03	MWS COLLINGWOOD
Docherty, Paul Thomas, BA, FCIPD, MNI, pce, psc	CDRE(FTC)	X	AAWO	16.07.04	FLEET COSP&S
Dodd, Kevin Michael, pcea	LT CDR(FTC)	X	O	01.04.99	820 SQN
Dodd, Laura, BEng	LT(CC)	E	ME	01.04.01	OCLC BIRM
Dodd, Nicholas Charles, MA, psc(j)	LT CDR(FTC)	S	SM	01.04.99	DRAKE COB
Dodd, Peter Michael,	LT(IC)	X	EW	01.01.04	MOD (LONDON)
Dodd, Stuart Eric, SM(n), isc	LT(CC)	X	SM	01.10.00	SULTAN AIB
Dodds, Matthew Lewis, BSc	LT(FTC)	X	MW	01.04.99	MWS COLLINGWOOD
Dodds, Ralph Scott, pce, pcea	LT CDR(FTC)	X	O	01.05.93	FLEET COSCAP
Dodds, Stephen,	LT(IC)	E	WE	12.08.05	BULWARK
Doe, James Richard, BSc	LT(IC)	X	SM	01.10.02	MOD (LONDON)
Doherty, Kenneth, MBE	LT CDR(FTC(A)	X	P	01.10.93	LOAN OMAN
Doherty, Melanie, BDS, MBA, MFGDP(UK)	SGLTCDR(D)(SC(MD)	-		05.01.02	NP BOSNIA
Doig, Barry John, BSc	LT(FTC)	X		01.12.97	FLEET COSCAP
Dominy, David John Douglas, pce, n	CDR(FTC)	X	AAWO	30.06.06	UKMARBATSTAFF
Dominy, Victoria Leigh, BSc	LT(IC)	E	TM	01.09.00	RNICG
Donaghey, Mark,	CAPT RM(IC)	-	SO(LE)	19.07.05	BULWARK
Donaldson, Andrew Michael, IEng, MIIE	LT(FTC)	E	WE	09.01.01	DLO BRISTOL
Donaldson, Stuart Bruce, pce(sm)	LT CDR(FTC)	X	SM	01.09.91	EXCHANGE USA
Donnelly, James Stephen, BEng, CEng, MRAeS	LT CDR(FTC)	E	AE	22.11.98	ADAS BRISTOL
Donovan, Paul Anthony, MBA, FCMI, FRSA	CHAPLAIN	RC		22.04.85	ILLUSTRIOUS
Donovan, Robin John, BA	LT CDR(FTC)	S	SM	01.01.01	DLO TES
Donovan, Simon James, BA	LT(CC)	X	SM	01.08.02	TORBAY
Doolan, Martin, MA, pce, psc(j)	CDR(FTC)	X	PWO(U)	30.06.01	NAVSEC
Dooley, Martin Edward,	LT(IC)	E	WE	01.01.04	MWS COLLINGWOOD
Doran, Catherine Margaret Campbell, BA, MB, CHB, BAO, MRCS	SURG LTCDR(MC(MD)	-		07.08.03	NELSON (PAY)
Doran, Iain Arthur Gustav, BA	LT CDR(FTC)	X	PWO(U)	01.10.04	FOST SEA
Doran, Katie Elizabeth, BSc	LT(FTC)	X		01.11.00	ST ALBANS
Doran, Shane Edmund, BEng, MAPM, CEng, MIMarEST	LT CDR(FTC)	E	ME	01.07.02	FOST SEA
Dore, Christopher Lewis, BSc	SLT(IC)	X		01.09.04	DARTMOUTH BRNC
Dorricott, Alan Joseph,	CDR(FTC)	E	ME	30.06.02	DSFM PORTSMOUTH
Doubleday, Steven, pcea	LT(IC)	X	P	16.10.98	CHFHQ
Dougan, David Steven,	LT(IC)	X	AV	28.10.05	ARK ROYAL
Douglas, Patrick John,	LT CDR(FTC)	X	P	01.12.00	849 SQN B FLT
Douglas, Paul Gordon, SM(n), SM	LT CDR(FTC)	X	SM	03.12.00	MOD (LONDON)

Name	Rank	Branch	Spec	Seniority	Where Serving
Douglas-Riley, Timothy Roger, QHP, MB, BS, ... SURG CAPT(FCC) (Commodore) MRCS, LRCP, MRCGP, DA, jsdc	-		GMPP	31.12.96	RCDS
Douglass, Martin Colin Marc, BEng, CEng, MIMarEST ....LT CDR(FTC)	E		ME	01.03.99	SULTAN
Doull, Donald James Murray, BEng, MSc, CEng, MIMarEST...................LT CDR(FTC)	E		MESM	01.10.02	FOST SM SEA
Dow, Andrew James Royston, ...CAPT RM(CC)	-			01.09.05	40 CDO RM
Dow, Clive Stewart, ... LT CDR(FTC) (Barrister)	S		BAR	01.10.04	RN LOGS SCHOOL
Dow, William Allister McGowan, MB, ChB, FRCA......................SURG LTCDR(MCC)	-			06.08.02	LOAN FIELD HOSP
Dowd, Jonathan Wyn, BEng..MAJ(FTC)	-			01.09.01	FPGRM
Dowdell, Robert Edmund John, BSc, pcea .... LT CDR(FTC)(A)	X		P	01.10.94	FLEET AV VL
Dowell, Paul Henry Neil, BSc, MA, psc(j), MIEE ....CDR(FTC)	E		WE	30.06.05	MOD (BATH)
Dowlen, Henry, MB, BSc, BS...SURG SLT(MDC) (Act Surg Lt)	-			18.07.05	DARTMOUTH BRNC
Dowling, Andrew Jonathan, BA .... LT(CC)	X		O	01.03.01	815 FLT 221
Downes, Colin Henry, BSc... LT CDR(FTC)	X		PWO(A)	01.09.01	MWS COLLINGWOOD
Downie, Alan John, MSc, IEng, FIIE ....LT CDR(FTC)	E		WE	01.10.97	FLEET COSP&S
Downie, David Ross MacLennan, BEng..LT(IC)	E			01.09.04	NP AFGHANISTAN
Dowrick, Michael Paul, BA(OU), MA, MMus........................CAPT RM(IC)	BS		SO(LE)	01.04.03	HQ BAND SERVICE
Dowsett, Patrick Giles, pce, n..LT CDR(FTC)	X		PWO(C)	01.09.01	CHATHAM
Doyle, Gary Lawrence, pce, pcea, psc(j) ....CDR(FTC)	X		O	31.12.99	COMATG SEA
Doyle, Nicholas Patrick, ...LT CDR(FTC)	X			01.08.02	EXCHANGE AUSTLIA
Dransfield, Joseph Asa James, BSc.. LT(CC)	X		O	01.05.99	815 SQN HQ
Draper, Stephen Perry, pce ....LT CDR(FTC)	X		AAWO	26.02.96	MWS COLLINGWOOD
Dray, Jake Michael, ...LT(IC)	X		PWO(U)	01.05.03	GLOUCESTER
Dreelan, Michael Joseph, MSc, pce ....LT CDR(FTC)	X		PWO(U)	01.08.99	JSCSC
Drennan, David Gordon, BA... SLT(IC)	X		P U/T	01.09.04	DARTMOUTH BRNC
Dresner, Rupert James, ...MAJ(FTC)	-		P	24.04.02	EXCHANGE USA
Drew, Christopher, BSc, MEng, MIEE ....LT(IC)	E		IS	01.05.01	AFPAA(CENTURION)
Drewett, Brian John Howard, MSc... SLT(IC)	X			01.06.03	CHIDDINGFOLD
Drewett, Colin Edward, BEM... LT(CS)(CAS)	-			19.09.98	2SL/CNH FOTR
Drewett, Robin Edward, MBE, pce, pcea ....CDR(FTC)	X		O	30.06.99	SULTAN AIB
Drinkwater, Ross, ...CAPT RM(IC)	-			01.09.05	45 CDO RM
Driscoll, Mark Sinclair, MIL, MA...LT(IC)	X			01.07.05	SCEPTRE
Drodge, Andrew Paul Frank, pcea ....LT CDR(FTC)	X		O	01.10.02	FLEET COSCAP
Drodge, Kevin Nigel, BSc.. LT(CC)	X		P	01.10.98	771 SQN
Droog, Sarah, ...SURG SLT(SCC) (Act Surg Lt)	-			19.06.05	DARTMOUTH BRNC
Drummond, Anthony Stanley, ...SLT(IC)	X			01.02.05	DARTMOUTH BRNC
Drummond, Karl Bruce, BDS ....SGLTCDR(D)(MCC)	-			13.07.03	LOAN BRUNEI
Dry, Ian, BSc..LT(IC)	E		IS	31.01.99	JHCHQ
Drylie, Andrew John, BSc ....LT CDR(FTC)	X		SM	01.02.92	CC MAR AGRIPPA
Drysdale, Steven Ronald, pce(sm), SM ....CDR(FTC)	X		SM	30.06.06	SOVEREIGN
Drywood, Tobias, BEng, MSc, MIMarEST ....LT CDR(FTC)	E		ME	01.04.01	FWO DEVPT SEA
D'Silva, Daniel Mark, BEng, CEng, MIEE .... LT(FTC)	E		WE	01.02.98	CMT SHRIVENHAM
Duby, Alon, MB, BCH, FRCS(ED)A&E, FFAEM..........................SURG LTCDR(SC(MD)	-		(CEM)	23.04.99	RCDM
Duce, Matthew,..LT(IC)	X			01.05.01	MONTROSE
Duckitt, Jack Nathan, ...CAPT RM(IC)	-			01.09.05	42 CDO RM
Dudley, Stephen Mark Terence, MA................................LT CDR(FTC)	S			01.01.99	MWS EXCELLENT
Duff, Alistair John, ...SLT(IC)	X			01.03.06	MWS COLLINGWOOD
Duff, Andrew, ...CHAPLAIN	CE			04.10.04	OCEAN
Duff, Andrew Patrick, pce ....LT CDR(FTC)	X		PWO(U)	01.09.00	NELSON
Duffy, Henry, MA, pce, psc(j) ....CDR(FTC)	X		PWO(C)	30.06.05	LIVERPOOL
Duffy, James Christopher, ...LT(IC)	X			01.12.04	VIGILANT(PORT)
Duffy, Mari Louise, MA ....LT(IC)	X			01.04.03	HQ BFSAI
Dufosee, Sean William, MBE, pcea ....LT CDR(FTC)	X		P	01.10.00	EXCHANGE ARMY UK
Duke, Adam John, BEng ....LT(IC)	X		SM	01.09.04	RALEIGH
Duke, Ronald Michael, MCMI..CDR(FC(MD)	Q		CPN	30.06.04	MOD (LONDON)
Dumbell, Phillip, BSc, MA, CEng, MIEE, psc................................CDR(FTC)	E		WESM	30.06.02	NW IPT
Dumbleton, David William, ...LT(FTC)	E		WE	01.04.01	DRAKE SFM
Dunbar, Samantha, BSc, PGCE, HND.. LT(CC)	E		TM	17.09.96	DCTS HALTON
Duncan, Colin John, ...LT(FTC)	X		P	01.09.93	RAF SHAWBURY
Duncan, Euan Maver, MA ....SLT(IC)	X			01.09.04	DARTMOUTH BRNC
Duncan, Giles Spencer, BSc ....MAJ(FTC)	-			01.05.04	HQ 3 CDO BDE RM
Duncan, Ian Stewart, BSc..CDR(FTC)	E		MESM	30.06.05	DLO BRISTOL
Duncan, Jeremy, ... LT CDR(FTC)(A)	X		P	01.10.01	820 SQN

Name	Rank	Branch	Spec	Seniority	Where Serving
Duncan, John Ernst, LLM	SLT(IC)	X		01.06.03	CHIDDINGFOLD
Dunham, Mark William, BSc, psc(m)	COL(FTC)	-		30.06.02	COMAMPHIBFOR
Dunkley, Simon Charles,	LT(FTC)	X	AV	26.04.99	RFANSU
Dunlop, Peter Francis, BSc, pce	LT CDR(FTC)	X	PWO(U)	01.04.91	FLEET COSCAP
Dunn, Andrew,	LT CDR(FTC)	E	AE	07.11.05	FLEET COSP&S
Dunn, Anthony,	LT(FTC)	X	AV	01.04.01	OCEAN
Dunn, Gary Russell, BEng, MSc, CEng, FInstLM, Eur Ing	LT CDR(FTC)	E	WESM	01.05.98	RALEIGH
Dunn, Nicholas Geoffrey, BSc, pcea	CDR(FTC)	X	P	30.06.06	MOD (LONDON)
Dunn, Paul Edward, SM, SM(n), pce(sm)	CDR(FTC)	X	SM	30.06.06	FOST SM SEA
Dunn, Robert Paul, MA, pce(sm), psc(j)	CDR(FTC)	X	SM	30.06.04	PJHQ
Dunne, James, BA	LT(IC)	X	SM	01.12.04	VIGILANT(PORT)
Dunne, Michael Gerard, BEM	LT CDR(FTC)	X	AV	01.10.02	FLEET AV SUPPORT
Dunsby, Nicholas Byron, PGDip	LT CDR(FTC)	E	MESM	01.10.01	FWO DEVONPORT
Dunt, Peter Arthur, CB, rcds	VADM	-	(S)	30.04.02	MOD (LONDON)
(CHIEF EXECUTIVE DEFENCE ESTATE AGENCY APR 02)					
Durham, Paul Christopher Langton, BEng, MRAeS, n	LT CDR(FTC)	E		18.05.03	AH IPT
Durkin, Jane, MB, BA, BS	SURG LT(SCC)	-		02.08.05	DARTMOUTH BRNC
Durkin, Mark Thomas Gilchrist, BSc, pce, psc(j)	CDR(FTC)	X	MCD	31.12.00	MOD (LONDON)
Durning, William Munro,	CDR(FTC)	MS		30.06.04	MDHU PORTSMOUTH
Durston, Andrew Philip,	SLT(IC)	X	P U/T	01.05.04	DARTMOUTH BRNC
Durston, David Howard, MBA, pce, pcea, psc, psc(j)	CAPT(FTC)	X	P	30.06.03	MOD (LONDON)
Durup, Jason Michael Stanley,	CAPT RM(CC) (Act Maj)	-	LC	01.09.00	1 ASSLT GP RM
Dustan, Andrew John,	CDR(FTC)	E	AE	30.06.03	DLO YEO
Duthie, Andrew George,	LT(IC)	E	AE U/T	08.04.05	RNAS CULDROSE
Dutton, Andrew Colin,	LT CDR(FTC)	S	SM	01.02.03	EXCHANGE USA
Dutton, David, MA, pce, psc(j)	CDR(FTC)	X	PWO(C)	31.12.00	MOD (LONDON)
Dutton, James Benjamin, CBE, BSc, rcds, psc(m)	MAJ GEN	-	C	04.05.04	CGRM/COMAMPHIBFOR
Dutton, Philip John,	LT CDR(FTC)	E	WESM	01.10.99	DLO BRISTOL
Dyer, Graham Richard,	LT CDR(FTC)	E	WE	01.10.04	FLEET FOTR
Dyer, Jonathan David Thomas, BTech, MSc, MBCS	LT CDR(FTC)	E	IS	01.09.99	IMS BRUSSELS
Dyer, Michael David James, BEng, MSc, CEng, MIEE	CDR(FTC)	E	WESM	30.06.00	NAVSEC
Dyer, Shani Danyell,	SLT(IC)	X		01.09.03	MERSEY
Dyke, Christopher Leonard, MA, pce, psc(j)	CDR(FTC)	X	PWO(C)	30.06.03	MWC SOUTHWICK
Dyke, Kenneth Andrew, BEng	LT CDR(FTC)	E	MESM	01.10.00	DLO BRISTOL
Dymock, Anthony Knox, CB, BA, pce, psc	VADM	-	AWO(C)	30.03.06	UKMILREP BRUSS
(UK MILITARY REPRESENTATIVE BRUSSELS. MILREP 01 MAR 06)					
Dymond, Justin Roy Melville, BEng	LT(IC)	E	WE	01.09.03	HQ DCSA
Dyter, Ross Courtney, MEng	LT(FTC)	E	ME	01.02.03	DRAKE SFM

E

Name	Rank	Branch	Spec	Seniority	Where Serving
Eacock, Jason,	LT(IC)	X		29.10.04	BROCKLESBY
Eaglestone, Stephen,	LT(IC)	E	MESM	01.02.01	SULTAN
Ealey, Nicholas James, BA	LT(IC)	X	SM	01.12.04	TORBAY
Earle-Payne, Gareth Ellis, BEng, PGDip	LT(IC)	E	MESM	01.09.03	SCEPTRE
Eastaugh, Andrew Charles, MSc, adp	CDR(FTC)	E	IS	30.06.06	FLEET COSCAP
Easterbrook, Christopher, BSc	LT(IC)	X		01.09.04	727 NAS
Easterbrook, Kevin Ivor Edgar, BEng, CEng, MIEE	LT CDR(FTC)	E	WE	01.12.99	FOST SEA
Easton, Derek William,	LT CDR(FTC)	X		01.10.02	TEMERAIRE
Eastwood, Richard Noah, MEng	LT(CC)	X	P	15.02.98	JATEBRIZENORTON
Eaton, Daniel,	2LT(IC)	-		01.08.02	CTCRM LYMPSTONE
Eaton, David Charles, BA	LT(CC)	X	ATC	01.01.02	RNAS CULDROSE
Eaton, Paul Graham, BSc	LT CDR(FTC)	X	METOC	01.06.94	OCEAN
Ebbens, Andrew John, sq	MAJ(FTC) (Act Lt Col)	-		01.09.87	STRIKFORNATO
Ebbern, Gareth John, BSc	SLT(IC)	X		01.09.03	BLYTH
Eddie, Alan George Watt, BTech	LT CDR(FTC)	E	WE	01.10.03	CAMPBELTOWN
Eden, Christopher,	2LT(IC)	-		01.08.01	45 CDO RM
Eden, Jeremy Rodney Hugh,	LT(IC)	MS		08.04.05	DPMD
Edey, Michael John, BSc, pce, n	LT CDR(FTC)	X	PWO(U)	01.12.01	MWS COLLINGWOOD
Edgar, Iain,	SURG SLT(SCC)	-		31.08.04	DARTMOUTH BRNC
Edge, Helen Ruth, BEng	LT(IC)	E	AE	01.07.02	847 SQN
Edge, John Howard, MA, MILT, MCIPD, psc(j)	CDR(FTC)	S	SM	30.06.04	DLO/DG LOG (SC)
Edge, Thomas William,	MID(IC)	X	P U/T	01.05.04	DARTMOUTH BRNC

Name	Rank	Branch	Spec	Seniority	Where Serving
Edgell, John Nicholas, OBE, pce, pce(sm), psc	CAPT(FTC)	X	SM	30.06.03	MOD (LONDON)
Edinburgh, His Royal Highness The Prince Philip, Duke of,	ADM OF FLEET	-		15.01.53	
KG, KT, OM, GBE, AC, QSO					
Edmondson, James Andrew,	LT(FTC)	X		01.04.01	CHATHAM
Edmondson, Mark,	LT(IC)	X		01.07.04	VIGILANT(PORT)
Edmondson, Simon, BA	MAJ(FTC)	-	P	01.10.05	COMAMPHIBFOR
Edney, Andrew Ralph, MBE, BEng, pce, pcea, psc	CDR(FTC)	X	P	31.12.96	RNAS YEOVILTON
Edson, Mark Andrew, HNC	LT(FTC)	E	WE	22.02.93	DRAKE SFM
Edward, Amanda Michelle, MB, CHB	SURG LT(SCC)			07.08.02	MDHU PORTSMOUTH
Edward, Gavin James, BEng, MSc gw, CEng, MIEE, psc(j)	LT CDR(FTC)	E	WE	01.07.03	RICHMOND
Edwards, Andrew Donald Pryce, MBE, BSc	LT CDR(FTC)	E	MESM	01.02.88	DRAKE DIS
Edwards, Andrew George, BEng, CEng, MRAeS	LT CDR(FTC)	E	AE	01.09.03	RNAS CULDROSE
Edwards, Charles John Albert, MB, BS, FRCA	SURG CDR(FCC)	-	(CA)	31.12.97	MDHU PORTSMOUTH
Edwards, David, PGDRP	LT(IC)	MS		01.01.02	DRAKE SFM
Edwards, Gavin Robert, BEng	SLT(IC)	E	AE U/T	01.09.04	OCEAN
Edwards, James, BSc, PGCE	LT(IC)	E	TM	01.09.96	DISC
Edwards, John David,	MID(IC)	X	P U/T	01.09.04	RNAS YEOVILTON
Edwards, Luke,	SLT(IC)	X	P U/T	01.09.05	RNAS YEOVILTON
Edwards, Michal Ian, BSc	SLT(IC)	X		01.11.03	BULWARK
Edwards, Richard Peter, BSc	LT(IC)	E	TM	01.04.02	FOST FAS SHORE
Edwards, Sharon,	LT(SC(MD)	Q		01.11.03	MDHU DERRIFORD
Edwards, Thomas Hugh Hamish, MPhil	LT(IC)	X		01.05.03	GLOUCESTER
Edwins, Mark Richard, MSc	LT(FTC)	E	ME	02.05.00	CAPT MCTA
Edye, Robin Francis,	CAPT RM(CC)	-		01.05.00	HQ 3 CDO BDE RM
Eedle, Richard John, BA, psc(j)o	LT CDR(FTC)	X	N	01.03.91	VANGUARD(STBD)
Egeland-Jensen, Finn Adam, MBE, PGDIPAN, pce	LT CDR(FTC)	X	PWO(N)	01.04.95	FLEET COSCAP
Egerton, Stephen Brian,	LT(FTC)	X	C	10.12.98	SHAPE BELGIUM
Eglin, Caroline Anne, BA	CHAPLAIN	SF		10.09.90	RALEIGH
Elborn, Teresa Kathleen, MHCIMA	LT CDR(FTC)	W	S	01.12.04	RALEIGH
Eldridge, James William Charles,	SLT(IC)	E		01.01.05	DARTMOUTH BRNC
Eldridge, Stephen J, BSc	LT(IC)	E	TM	01.02.03	SULTAN
Elesmore, John Douglas,	LT(IC)	X	C	29.10.04	BATCIS IPT
Elford, David Graham, MA, MSc, CEng, MIEE, MRAeS, psc(j)	CDR(FTC)	E	AE	30.06.98	MOD (LONDON)
Elkins, Stuart Spencer,	LT(IC)	S		01.05.02	CALEDONIA DLO
Ellerton, Paul,	LT(FTC)	X	P	16.10.94	815 FLT 219
Ellicott, Matthew James, BSc	SLT(IC)	X		01.05.03	MWS COLLINGWOOD
Elliman, Simon Mark, pce, psc(j)o	LT CDR(FTC)	X	PWO(U)	01.10.94	FOST SEA
Ellingham, Richard Edwin,	CHAPLAIN	SF		17.04.00	FWO PORTS SEA
Elliot-Smith, Teilo John, BA	LT(CC)	X	FC	01.09.02	MANCHESTER
Elliott, Jamie Alistair,	LT(CC)	E	AE	01.07.00	DLO YEO
Elliott, Mark Ferguson,	CAPT RM(CC)	-		01.09.03	OPTAG
Elliott, Michael Edward, MBE	LT(IC)	X	C	25.06.04	MWS COLLINGWOOD
Elliott, Oliver Luke, BSc	SLT(IC)	X		01.11.02	RAF SHAWBURY
Elliott, Stephen Peter,	LT(IC)	E	WE	01.01.04	MWS COLLINGWOOD
Elliott, Timothy Douglas,	LT(IC)	X		01.09.04	RNAS CULDROSE
Ellis, Andrew Christopher, BA	LT(CC)	X	P	01.05.99	849 SQN HQ
Ellis, Charles Richard, BEng, MIEE	LT(FTC)	E	WESM	01.03.00	MOD DIS SEA
Ellis, David Robert, BEng	LT(IC)	E	AE	01.09.02	824 SQN
Ellis, James Paul, BEng, MSc	LT CDR(FTC)	E	ME	01.10.04	ARGYLL
Ellis, Michael Philip, OBE, psc(a)	COL(FTC)	-	P	30.06.06	JHCHQ
Ellis, Nicholas Mark,	LT CDR(FTC)	X		18.07.97	DARTMOUTH BRNC
Ellis, Richard William, BSc	CDR(FTC)	E	AE	30.06.99	EUMS
Ellis-Morgan, Roger Terrence, MBE	LT(IC)	X	EW	01.05.02	PJHQ
Ellison, Peter John Patrick,	LT(IC)	X		01.01.06	PORTLAND
Ellison, Toby George, pce	LT CDR(FTC)	X	PWO(A)	01.10.03	WESTMINSTER
Ellwood, Peter George, SM	LT CDR(FTC)	X	SM	01.10.03	PJHQ
Elmer, Timothy Brendan, BDS, MFGDP(UK)	SGCDR(D)(FCC)	-	GDP UT	30.06.02	SULTAN
Elmore, Graeme Martin,	CHAPLAIN	CE		30.09.86	NEPTUNE 2SL/CNH
Elston, Adrian John,	LT CDR(FTC)	X	REG	01.10.03	FLEET COSP&S
Elvin, Andrew James, pce	CDR(FTC)	X	MCD	30.06.06	EXCHANGE USA
Elwell-Deighton, Dean Carl, pcea	LT(FTC) (Act Lt Cdr)	X	P	16.09.93	MOD (LONDON)
Emerson, Martin John,	LT(IC)	X		01.01.05	MWS COLLINGWOOD

Name	Rank	Branch	Spec	Seniority	Where Serving
Emery, Christian Stanley, ...LT(IC)	E	WE		01.05.03	SOUTHAMPTON
Emmerson, Debra Marie, ARRC, BSc ....LT(MC(MD)	Q	ONC		22.06.00	RFANSU (ARGUS)
Enever, Shaun Andrew, pcea .... LT(FTC)	X	O		01.09.96	702 SQN HERON
England, Lorraine, BSc ....LT CDR(FC(MD)	Q	REGM		01.10.04	RALEIGH
England, Philip Morgan, MSc ....LT(IC)	E	TM		01.04.00	1 ASSLT GP RM
Ennis, John Lee, ...LT(CC)	X	ATC		01.07.04	RNAS YEOVILTON
Enticknap, Kenneth, QGM, BSc..CDR(FTC)	E	ME		30.06.98	FLEET COSP&S
Entwisle, William Nicholas, OBE, MVO, MA, pcea, psc(j)..........CDR(FTC)	X	P		30.06.02	815 SQN HQ
Entwistle, Stephen Charles, pce, psc(j), MA, MNI........................CDR(FTC)	X	AAWO		30.06.00	SACT BELGIUM
Epps, Matthew Paul, BSc, PGCE, MBCS....................................LT(CC)	E	IS		17.07.99	BULWARK
Epsom, Oliver, BEng .... SLT(IC)	E	ME U/T		01.01.05	DARTMOUTH BRNC
Erhahiemen, Peter Ehimen, ...LT(IC)	E	TM U/T		01.05.04	RNICG
Errington, Ridley James Bentley, ...SLT(IC)	E	ME		01.09.02	YORK
Erskine, Peter Anthony, BA, MSc, MIMechE, psc............................CDR(FTC)	E	ME		30.06.96	DLO BRISTOL
Essenhigh, Angus Nigel Patrick, BA ....LT CDR(FTC)	X	PWO(A)		01.10.04	KENT
Essenhigh, Sir Nigel (Richard), GCB, rcds, pce, psc, hcsc .... ADM		PWO(N)		11.09.98	
Etchells, Stephen Barrie, BEng, CEng, MIEE ....LT CDR(FTC)	E	WESM		03.07.00	FOST SM SEA
Ethell, David Ross, BEng..MAJ(FTC)	-	LC		01.10.03	FPGRM
Euden, Christopher Peter, BA, n ....LT CDR(FTC)	X	PWO(A)		01.06.03	GLOUCESTER
Evans, Andrew, ...LT(IC)	S			01.07.04	ENDURANCE
Evans, Andrew William, ...LT CDR(FTC)	X	SM		01.10.95	MWC PORTSDOWN
Evans, Benjimin Gwynn, BSc ....LT(IC)	X			01.01.04	RNAS YEOVILTON
Evans, Charles Alexander, BA ....LT CDR(FTC)	S	SM		01.10.03	PJHQ
Evans, Charlotte, ...SURG SLT(SCC)	-			01.07.03	DARTMOUTH BRNC
Evans, Christian Peter, BA..LT(IC)	E	TM U/T		01.01.03	YORK
Evans, Christopher Anthony, BSc...LT(IC)	X	SM		01.05.03	RALEIGH
Evans, Christopher Charles, ...LT(IC)	E	MESM		01.07.04	VIGILANT(PORT)
Evans, David Anthony, ...LT(FTC) (Act Lt Cdr)	X	ATC		20.12.95	ARK ROYAL
Evans, David John, BSc, CEng, MIEE, MRAeS, psc ....CAPT(FTC)	E	AE		30.06.03	DLO YEO
Evans, David Mark Mortimer, psc(m) ....LT COL(FTC)	-	C		30.06.01	COMATG SEA
Evans, Edward Michael, MinstAM, MCIT, MILT ....CDR(FTC)	S	SM		30.06.06	FLEET COSP&S
Evans, Gareth Charles, BA, MB, ChB ....SURG LTCDR(MCC)	-			05.08.03	NELSON (PAY)
Evans, Geraint, BEng, MSc, MIEE..LT CDR(FTC)	E	WE		01.06.98	DOSG BRISTOL
Evans, Geraint, MB, CHB, FRCS, FFAEM ....SURG CDR(SC(MD)	-	(CEM)		17.10.05	RCDM
Evans, Giles, SM(n)..LT(FTC)	X	SM		01.05.94	FLEET COMOPS NWD
Evans, Graham Roy, BSc, pce......................................LT CDR(FTC) (Act Cdr)	X	PWO(U)		01.12.90	SHAPE BELGIUM
Evans, Helen Jane, MB, BSc, BCH ....SURG LT(SC(MD)	-			01.08.05	MDHU PORTSMOUTH
Evans, Jonathan, ...SURG SLT(SCC)	-			01.07.03	DARTMOUTH BRNC
Evans, Karl Nicholas Meredith, OBE, pce, pce(sm), psc(j), MA ....CDR(FTC)	X	SM		31.12.98	MOD (LONDON)
Evans, Kenneth, ...LT(IC)	X	AV		29.10.04	RFANSU (ARGUS)
Evans, Laura-Jane, BSc ....LT(CC)	X	O		01.09.02	849 SQN B FLT
Evans, Lee Stewart, ...LT(CC)	X	P		01.05.01	815 FLT 212
Evans, Marc David, MILDM, AMIAM ....LT CDR(FTC)	S			16.05.98	DLO/DG LOG (SC)
Evans, Martin Joseph, BSc, MA, pce, psc(j) ....CDR(FTC)	X	PWO(U)		30.06.06	STRIKFORNATO
Evans, Martin Lonsdale, ...CHAPLAIN	CE			01.09.98	1 ASSLT GP RM
Evans, Michael Clive, BSc, MA, MNI, MCMI, pce, pcea, psc ....CAPT(FTC)	X	P		30.06.04	DASC
Evans, Michael Edward, BEng, MSc, CEng, PGDip, MINucE ....LT(FTC)	E	MESM		01.08.97	SULTAN
Evans, Michael Russell, ...MID(IC)	X			01.01.04	DRAKE COB
Evans, Paul John, ...LT(IC)	E	WE		01.07.04	FOST SEA
Evans, Peter Alexander, MSc..SLT(IC)	X			01.05.04	CUMBERLAND
Evans, Peter Colin, MA, MSc, MBCS..LT(CC)	E	IS		01.05.96	MOD (LONDON)
Evans, Peter John, BSc, MA, psc(j), mdtc ....LT COL(FTC)	-	LC		30.06.05	BDS WASHINGTON
Evans, Robert, ...LT(IC)	E	AE		08.04.05	DARTMOUTH BRNC
Evans, Robert Paul, ...LT(IC)	E	WE		01.01.04	RALEIGH
Evans, Stephen, BSc, BTech ....LT CDR(FTC)	E	WESM		01.10.01	MOD (LONDON)
Evans, Thomas Edward, MB, CHB ....SURG LT(SCC)	-			07.08.02	MDHU PETERBRGH
Evans, Thomas William, ...SLT(IC)	S			01.09.03	RALEIGH
Evans, William Quennell Frankis, MNI, pce ....CDR(FTC)	X	PWO(N)		30.06.02	MANCHESTER
Evans-Jones, Thomas Matthew, ...CAPT RM(IC)	-			01.09.05	UKLFCSG RM
Eve, Laurie, ...CAPT RM(CC)	-	LC		01.09.03	539 ASSLT SQN RM
Eveling, Rachel Jane, BSc, PGCE ....LT(IC)	E	TM		01.05.98	DCTS PORTS
Evered, Jonathan Francis, BSc..SLT(IC)	X	P U/T		01.05.03	RNAS YEOVILTON

Name	Rank	Branch	Spec	Seniority	Where Serving
Everitt, Claire Julia, BDS, LDS RCS(Eng), MFGDP(UK) ....SGLTCDR(D)(MCC)	-			11.03.97	ILLUSTRIOUS
Everritt, Richard, MBE, BSc, MA, psc(j)..LT COL(FTC)	-	SO(LE)		30.06.04	MOD (BATH)
Evershed, Marcus Charles, MB, BCh, MRCGP, Dip FFP .... SURG CDR(FCC)	-	GMPP		30.06.02	DRAKE COB
Evison, Toby, MSc..LT(IC) (Act Lt Cdr)	E	IS		27.07.93	ILLUSTRIOUS
Ewen, Andrew Philip, BEng, MSc ....CDR(FTC)	E	AE		30.06.06	MOD (LONDON)
Ewence, Martin William, OBE, MA, pce, psc(j)...CDR(FTC)	X	AAWO		30.06.98	MWC PORTSDOWN
Exworthy, Damian Andrew Giles, BSc, MA ....LT CDR(FTC)	S			01.10.04	FLEET COSP&S

F

Name	Rank	Branch	Spec	Seniority	Where Serving
Fabik, Andre Nicholas, BA.. LT(CC)	X	HM2		01.05.01	ECHO
Fairclough-Kay, Matthew, BA ....LT(IC)	X			01.05.03	MOD (LONDON)
Falconer, Lisa Marie, ...LT(MC(MD)	Q			16.09.01	MDHU DERRIFORD
Falk, Benedict Hakan Geoffrey, MA, MNI, pce, psc(j) ....CDR(FTC)	X	PWO(A)		30.06.02	EXCHANGE USA
Fallowfield, Jonathan Paul, BTech...LT(FTC) (Act Lt Cdr)	E	WE		24.02.95	MOD (LONDON)
Fancy, Robert, OBE, pce, pce(sm)..CDR(FTC)	X	SM		31.12.00	PJHQ
Fanshawe, Edward Leo, ...LT(IC)	E	SM		01.05.03	RALEIGH
Farquharson-Roberts, Michael Atholl, CBE, QHS, ...SURG RADM	-	(CO/S)		09.12.03	FLEET COSP&S
MB, BS, MA, LRCP, FRCS (MDGN-PERSONAL APR 06)					
Farr, Ian Raymond, ... LT(CC)	X	P		16.08.00	829 FLT 01
Farrage, Michael Edward, BSc, psc .... CAPT(FTC)	E	TM		30.06.05	2SL/CNH FOTR
Farrant, James Derek, ... LT(FTC)	S			01.02.03	BULWARK
Farrant, Sam, BEng ....LT(IC)	E	WE		01.11.05	YORK
Farrington, John Lewis, BEng, MSc, CEng, MIEE, psc, psc(j)o ....LT CDR(FTC)	E	WESM		01.10.01	TURBULENT
Farrington, Richard, OBE, BA, jsdc, pce ....CDR(FTC)	X	PWO(C)		30.06.96	COMAMPHIBFOR
Farrow, Richard Dunstan, BA.. SLT(IC)	X			01.05.03	ATHERSTONE
Farr-Voller, Emma Marie, BSc...LT(IC)	E	TM		01.05.01	RALEIGH
Faulconbridge, David, MSc, CEng, MIEE, MIMarEST, psc..........................CDR(FTC)	E	MESM		31.12.94	MOD (BATH)
Faulkner, Daniel William, BEng, CEng, MRAeS.....................................LT CDR(FTC)	E	AE		29.11.97	JF HARROLE OFF
Faulkner, Jeffrey James, ARICS ....CDR(FTC)	X	H CH		30.06.01	LOAN HYDROG
Faulkner, Richard Ian, BSc...LT CDR(FTC)	E	ME		01.08.89	SULTAN
Faulkner, Stuart Glen, BEng, MRAeS.. LT(FTC)	E	AE		01.09.03	FS MASU
Faulks, David John, ...CDR(FTC)	S			30.06.02	MWC SOUTHWICK
Fawcett, Fiona Patricia, MA, psc(j)..LT CDR(FTC)	E	TM		01.05.98	FLEET COSP&S
Fear, Richard Keith, BSc, MIEE, MDA ....CDR(FTC)	E	WESM		30.06.99	CSIS IPT
Fearn, Daniel Colin Tyler, ...MID(IC)	X			01.02.05	DARTMOUTH BRNC
Fearn, Samual Richard, ... LT RM(IC) (Act Capt Rm)	-			01.09.04	FPGRM
Fearon, David John, BEng..LT(IC)	E	WE		01.09.03	CENTCOM USA
Feasey, Ian David, BA .... LT(CC)	X			01.09.02	MWS COLLINGWOOD
Feeney, Matthew Blake, BA .... LT(FTC)	X			01.04.00	PJHQ
Feeney, Michael Leonard, BEng, CEng, MIMarEST ....LT CDR(FTC)	E	ME		01.05.97	NELSON
Fellows, Christopher Richard, MEng..SLT(IC)	X	O U/T		01.01.04	RNAS CULDROSE
Fennell, Charles Benjamin, BSc.. LT(CC)	X	MCD		01.07.99	EXCHANGE AUSTLIA
Fenton, Gregory Morris, ...CAPT RM(IC)	-	SO(LE)		01.07.04	CTCRM
Fenwick, Julie Cheryl, BDS...SGCDR(D)(MC(MD)	-			30.06.05	MWS COLLINGWOOD
Fenwick, Robin John, BSc...MAJ(FTC)	-	P		01.10.04	800 NAS (GR7)
Fenwick, Steven Graham, BEng..SLT(IC)	E			01.09.04	DARTMOUTH BRNC
Ferguson, Christopher, ...CAPT RM(IC)	-	SO(LE)		19.07.05	40 CDO RM
Ferguson, Gordon Henry, IEng...LT CDR(FTC)	E	MESM		01.10.98	FOST SM SEA
Ferguson, Ian, ...SLT(IC)	X	O U/T		01.09.03	RNAS CULDROSE
Ferguson, Julian Norman, OBE, BA, BSc, pce, pce(sm) ....CDR(FTC)	X	SM		30.06.91	QHM CLYDE
Ferguson, Vikki Sara,...LT CDR(FC(MD)	Q	CC		01.10.02	MDHU DERRIFORD
Fergusson, Andrew Christopher, BSc...MAJ(FTC)	-			01.05.99	1 ASSAULT GP RM
Fergusson, Houston James, ...CDR(FTC)	S	SM		30.06.00	FLEET COSP&S
Fergusson, Iain Buchan, ... LT(CC)	X	SM		01.05.02	EXCHANGE NLANDS
Fergusson, Nigel Andrew, MSc, CEng, MIEE ....LT CDR(FTC)	E	WE		01.02.99	FLEET COSP&S
Ferns, Timothy David, LLB ....LT CDR(FTC)	S			01.06.99	JSCSC
Ferrey, Robert Michael, ...CAPT RM(IC)	-			01.09.03	CTCRM
Ferris, Daniel Peter Sefton, BEng, MA, MSc, CEng, MIEE, psc(j), gw............CDR(FTC)	E	WE		30.06.04	MOD (LONDON)
Ferris, Nathan, ...SLT(IC)	X			01.05.05	MONMOUTH
Ffoulkes, Wayne Martin, BSc, MIEE ....LT(IC)	E	TM		01.02.03	MWS COLLINGWOOD
Fiander, Peter John, BSc ....LT CDR(FTC)	E	MESM		01.02.87	ASM IPT
Fickling, James William Angus, BEng..LT(IC)	E	WE		01.09.04	EDINBURGH

Name	Rank	Branch	Spec	Seniority	Where Serving
Fiddock, Matthew Lee, BEng	LT(IC)	E	ME	01.07.03	SCOTT
Fidler, John Quentin, BSc	CAPT RM(CC)	-	LC	01.09.02	BULWARK
Fidler, Marcel Malcolm Graham,	LT(IC)	E	WE	01.07.04	OCLC BIRM
Field, Charles Richard Howard, BEng, CEng, FIMechE, MIMechE	LT CDR(FTC)	E	ME	01.01.04	GLOUCESTER
Fields, David Graham, MA, pce, psc(j)	CDR(FTC)	X	PWO(A)	30.06.03	WESTMINSTER
Fieldsend, Mark Andrew, BEng, fsc	CDR(FTC)	E	ME	30.06.03	AFPAA JPA
Fillmore, Raymond Jeffrey, SM(n)	LT(CC)	X	SM	01.12.00	VIGILANT(STBD)
Filshie, Sarah Jane, BA	LT(CC)	X	ATC	01.01.02	EXCHANGE RAF UK
Filtness, David Mark, BSc, SM(n)	LT(FTC)	X	SM	01.10.00	RALEIGH
Finch, Bruce Andrew, BA, MinstAM, MIL, MInsD, MCIPD, ADIPM	LT CDR(FTC)	S		01.08.01	FLEET COSP&S
Finch, Iain Robert,	LT(CC)	X		01.11.99	LOAN SAUDI ARAB
Finch, Robert Leonard, BEng, MSc, CEng, MIMarEST, AMIMechE	LT CDR(FTC)	E	ME	01.05.97	FLEET HQ WI
Finch, Steven,	LT(CC)	E	AE	29.04.01	RNAS CULDROSE
Finch, Timothy Stuart Aubrey, MILT, MCMI	LT CDR(FTC)	S	CA	01.10.97	FLEET COSP&S
Fincher, Kevin John, pce	LT CDR(FTC)	X	PWO(C)	01.10.95	T45 IPT
Finlayson, Alasdair Grant, MA, fsc	CAPT(FTC)	S		30.06.06	DLO/DG LOG (SC)
Finn, David William, MSc	LT CDR(FTC)	MS	(AD)	01.10.03	FLEET COSP&S
Finn, Graham John, MA, pcea, psc(j)	LT CDR(FTC)	X	P	01.10.00	UKMARBATSTAFF
Finn, Ivan Richard, BEng	LT CDR(FTC)	E	AE	01.10.00	MOD (LONDON)
Finn, James Sutherland, BSc	LT(CC)	X	P	01.01.01	829 FLT 05
Finn, Stuart Andrew, BSc	LT(FTC)	X	O	01.09.00	814 SQN
Finn, Tristan Alec,	CAPT RM(CC)	-		01.09.04	CTCRM
Finnemore, Richard Andrew, AMBIM, pce	CDR(FTC)	X	PWO(U)	30.06.05	DLO BRISTOL
Finney, Michael Edwin, pce, pce(sm)	CAPT(FTC)	X	SM	30.06.03	MOD (LONDON)
Firth, John Simon, BSc	LT(CC)	X		01.05.00	MWS COLLINGWOOD
Firth, Nigel Richard, pce, pce(sm)	LT CDR(FTC)	X	SM	01.03.95	FWO DEVONPORT
Firth, Rachel Jane Gardner,	LT CDR(FTC)	X	ATC	08.04.00	RNAS YEOVILTON
Firth, Stephen Kenneth, OBE, MSc, CEng, MIEE	CDR(FTC) (Act Capt)	E	MESM	31.12.90	DRAKE SFM
Fisher, Aaron George, BSc	MAJ(FTC)	-	LC	01.10.05	HQ 3 CDO BDE RM
Fisher, Clayton Richard Allan, MA, psc(j)	CDR(FTC)	S		30.06.04	FLEET COSP&S
Fisher, Morleymor Alfred Leslie, MBE, BSc, CEng, FIMarEST, MIMechE, MCMI	CDR(FTC)	E	MESM	30.06.94	DNR RCHQ NORTH
Fisher, Nicholas Douglas, BEng	LT(IC)	E	WE	01.09.04	ALBION
Fisher, Nicholas Gorden, MB, BS, MD, MRCP	SURG CDR(MCC)	-	(CM)	30.06.03	MDHU FRIMLEY
Fisher, Robert,	LT(FTC)	E	WE	10.06.88	DLO BRISTOL
Fisher, Robert James,	LT(CC)	X	P	01.06.96	848 SQN HERON
Fisher, Rupert Vincent,	LT(CC)	X	ATC	01.01.04	RAF WEST DRAYTON
Fisher, Stephen John, BA	LT(CC)	X	P	01.03.99	845 SQN
Fitter, Ian Stuart Thain, BSc, pcea	CDR(FTC)	X	O	30.06.02	FLEET AV VL
Fitzgerald, Colin,	LT CDR(FTC)	E	AE	01.10.03	DLO YEO
Fitzgibbon, John, BSc	SLT(IC)	X		01.01.04	SEVERN
Fitzpatrick, John Aloysius Joseph, BA	LT CDR(FTC)	X	O	01.07.05	LANCASTER
Fitzpatrick, Neil James, BSc	LT(IC)	X	FC	01.05.03	LIVERPOOL
Fitzpatrick, Paul John,	CAPT RM(CC)	-	SO(LE)	19.07.02	1 ASSAULT GP RM
Fitzpatrick, Paul Stanley,	CAPT RM(FTC)	-	SO(LE)	01.01.01	COMAMPHIBFOR
Fitzsimmons, Mark Brown, pce	LT CDR(FTC)	X	PWO(A)	01.09.95	MWS COLLINGWOOD
Flaherty, Christopher Lynton, BSc	LT(CC)	X	MCD	01.05.02	WALNEY
Flannagan, Donna Louise, LLB	LT(IC)	S		01.01.04	ALBION
Flannigan, Aiden, BSc	SLT(IC)	E	MESM	01.09.03	VANGUARD(STBD)
Flatman, Timothy David, BSc	LT(CC)	X	P	16.05.99	800 NAS (GR7)
Flatt, Leslie Declan,	LT(FTC)	E	WE	02.09.99	MWS EXCELLENT
Flatt, Liam Barrie, BA	SLT(IC)	X		01.09.03	BROCKLESBY
Fleet, Russell,	2LT(IC)	-		01.08.02	CTCRM LYMPSTONE
Flegg, Kirsty Gayle, MA	LT(FTC)	S		01.09.00	DLO YEO
Flegg, Matthew James, BEng, MRAeS	LT(FTC)	E	AE	01.04.01	DLO TES
Flegg, William John, BSc	SLT(IC)	X		01.11.03	CATTISTOCK
Fleisher, Simon Matthew, MEng, CEng, MIMechE	LT CDR(FTC)	E	ME	01.06.00	MWS EXCELLENT
Fleming, David Peter, BSc	LT(IC)	X	P	01.09.04	815 FLT 210
Fleming, Kevin Patrick, BSc, MA, ARCS, pcea, psc(j)	CDR(FTC)	X	O	30.06.06	702 SQN HERON
Fleming, Stephen Anthony,	LT CDR(FTC)	X		30.09.94	FLEET FOSNNI
Fletcher, Andrew Stuart,	SLT(IC)	X		01.09.02	MWS COLLINGWOOD
Fletcher, Ian James, BSc	LT(CC)	X	HM2	01.10.98	FLEET COMOPS NWD

Name	Rank	Branch	Spec	Seniority	Where Serving
Fletcher, Jonathan Henry Gibbin, BSc	SLT(IC)	X		01.11.03	SHOREHAM
Fletcher, Nicholas Edgar, BA(OU), pce, psc, FCIPD	CAPT(FTC)	X	PWO(A)	30.06.05	MOD (LONDON)
Flinn, John Andrew,	CAPT RM(CC)	-	SO(LE)	01.04.03	JT CIMIC
Flint, Grahame Frank, BA	SLT(IC)	X		01.09.04	DARTMOUTH BRNC
Flint, Helen Anne, BSc, PGCE	LT CDR(FTC)	E	TM	01.05.02	RNIC G
Flintham, Jason Edward,	LT(FTC) (Act Lt Cdr)	X	P	16.03.96	HQ1GP HQSTC
Flinton, Alexandra Rachel,	SLT(IC)	S		01.02.04	UKMARBATSTAFF
Flitcroft, Michael,	LT(IC)	E	WESM	01.07.04	DRAKE SFM
Float, Roger Andrew, MA, MSc, MCGI, AMIEE, psc(j)	CDR(FTC)	E	WE	30.06.02	MOD (LONDON)
Flood, Liam James, BSc	SLT(IC)	X		01.11.04	DARTMOUTH BRNC
Flower, Neil,	CAPT RM(CC)	-	P	01.04.03	847 SQN
Floyd, Robert Edward, BSc	LT(IC)	E	TM	01.01.03	SULTAN
Floyer, Hugo George, BSc	SLT(IC)	X		01.11.04	DARTMOUTH BRNC
Flynn, Andrew, BEng, MSc, CEng, MIMechE	LT CDR(FTC)	E	AE	01.05.04	JCA IPT UK
Flynn, Christopher,	MID(IC)	X	O U/T	01.01.05	RNAS CULDROSE
Flynn, Mark Christopher, BSC(EH)	LT(IC)	MS		01.07.04	DRAKE CBS
Flynn, Michael Thomas, MCIPD	CDR(FTC)	S		30.06.03	FOST SEA
Flynn, Simon John,	LT(FTC)	X	O	09.01.01	EXCHANGE USA
Foers, Paul Stephen, BEng	LT(IC)	E	WESM	01.09.04	VENGEANCE(STBD)
Fogell, Andrew David,	LT CDR(FTC)	S	SM	01.10.03	FOST SEA
Fogg, Duncan Stuart, MA, MSc, CEng, MIEE, gw	LT CDR(FTC)	E	WE	01.04.93	FLEET ISS
Follington, Daniel Charles,	LT CDR(FTC)	MS		01.10.04	MED S IPT
Fomes, Christopher John Henry,	CAPT RM(CC)	-	LC	01.04.01	ALBION
Fooks-Bale, Matthew Edward,	LT(IC)	X	P	01.09.04	RNAS YEOVILTON
Foote, Andrew Steven, BEng	LT(CC)	E	ME	01.07.00	NP IRAQ
Forbes, Duncan Graham, LLB	CAPT RM(FTC)	-		01.09.01	RMR SCOTLAND
Forbes, Matthew Peter, BSc	SLT(IC)	S		01.01.04	CUMBERLAND
Forbes, Paul Thomas,	LT(IC)	X	P	16.07.96	849 SQN B FLT
Forbes, Reuben Glen,	LT(IC)	X	C	01.07.03	FOST SEA
Ford, Anthony John, SM(n), SM	LT(FTC)	X	SM	04.04.96	FLEET FOSNNI
Ford, Barry Emerson,	LT(CC)	E	MESM	01.10.02	SULTAN
Ford, Graham Ronald, MSc, CEng, PGDip, MIMarEST	LT CDR(FTC)	E	MESM	01.10.04	SULTAN
Ford, Jonathan Douglas, BEng, CEng, MIEE	LT CDR(FTC)	E	WE	01.12.01	LIVERPOOL
Ford, Martin John, AFC, pcea	LT CDR(FTC)	X	O	05.08.98	GANNET SAR FLT
Foreman, John Lewis Rutland, MA, pce, psc(j)	CDR(FTC)	X	PWO(C)	30.06.01	EXCHANGE USA
Foreman, Neil Andrew,	CAPT RM(IC)	-	SO(LE)	19.07.05	45 CDO RM
Foreman, Simon Michael, BEng, MSc gw, CEng, MIEE	LT CDR(FTC)	E	WE	01.04.05	MOD (LONDON)
Foreman, Susan Louise, BSc	LT CDR(FTC)	X		24.12.03	MWS COLLINGWOOD
Forer, Duncan Anthony, BSc, PGCE, M ED	CDR(FTC)	E	TM	30.06.05	FLEET COSP&S
Forester-Bennett, Rupert Michael William,	LT CDR(FTC)	X	H CH	24.07.97	LOAN HYDROG
Forge, Stephen Mieczyseaw, BSc	LT(FTC)	S		01.05.00	NEPTUNE DLO
Forrest, David John, MEng	SLT(IC)	X	P U/T	01.01.05	DARTMOUTH BRNC
Forrest, Ewan,	2LT(IC)	-		01.08.02	CTCRM LYMPSTONE
Forrest, Paul Matthew,	2LT(IC)	-		01.08.01	40 CDO RM
Forsey, Christopher Roy, MSc, MIEE	CAPT(FTC)	E	WE	30.06.05	DLO BRISTOL
Forshaw, David Roy,	LT(FTC)	E	ME	02.09.99	MOD (LONDON)
Forster, Raymond Adrian,	LT CDR(FTC)	X	ATC	01.10.01	RNAS CULDROSE
Forster, Robin Makepeace, MA, psc(j)	LT COL(FTC)	-		30.06.05	FLEET COSP&S
Fortescue, Robert Christopher, MA, pce, pcea, psc(j)	LT CDR(FTC) (Act Cdr)	X	O	01.03.93	HQ BFSAI
Fortt, Paul David John,	LT(IC)	E	TM	01.05.01	RALEIGH
Forward, David James,	LT CDR(FTC)	E	AE	01.10.04	792 NAS(SEA)
Forward, Kirsty Louise, MEng	SLT(IC)	E	AE U/T	01.09.03	SULTAN
Foster, Alan James,	LT(IC)	E	MESM	01.05.03	SULTAN
Foster, Benjamin,	CAPT RM(CC)	-		01.09.00	1 ASSAULT GP RM
Foster, Bruce Michael Trevor, BSc	LT CDR(FTC)	E	TM	07.12.98	PJHQ
Foster, Crawford Richard Muir, MSc, MB, CHB, MRCGP, MFOM, Dip FFP	SURG CDR(FCC)	-	(CO/M)	31.12.00	INM ALVERSTOKE
Foster, David Hugh, psc(j)o, MSc	LT CDR(FTC)	X	MCD	01.05.99	SUPT OF DIVING
Foster, Duncan Graeme Scott, BSc, MA, PGDIPAN, pce, psc(j)	LT CDR(FTC)	X	PWO(N)	01.07.95	BDLS INDIA
Foster, Graeme Russell, BSc, psc(m)	LT COL(FTC)	-	LC	31.12.97	NAVSEC
Foster, Graham James, BSc, AMIMechE	CDR(FTC)	E	MESM	30.06.05	NP BRISTOL
Foster, Nicholas Paul, BA	CAPT RM(FTC)	-		01.05.00	1 ASSAULT GP RM

Name	Rank	Branch Spec	Seniority	Where Serving
Foster, Simon James Harry, BEng, MSc, CEng, MIMarEST, MIMechE ....LT CDR(FTC)	E	MESM	01.04.99	JSCSC
Foster, Toby George, BSc...LT CDR(FTC)	X	H1	01.04.03	MOD (LONDON)
Foulger, Thomas Edward, BDS...SGLTCDR(D)(FC(MD)	-	GDP	11.06.04	FWO DEVONPORT
Foulis, Niall David Alexander, BSc ....LT CDR(FTC)	X	HM	01.03.03	FLEET COMOPS NWD
Fowler, Christopher Donald, ...LT(IC)	E	WE	16.12.05	MWS COLLINGWOOD
Fowler, James, ...LT(IC)	MS		13.08.04	CDO LOG REGT RM
Fowler, Peter James Shakespeare, MSc...LT CDR(FTC)	E	MESM	01.04.90	NEPTUNE DSA
Fowler, Peter John, MSc, MB, BS, MRCS, ...SURG LTCDR(SC(MD)	-	GMPP	03.08.96	JSU NORTHWOOD
LRCP, MRCGP, DRCOG				
Fowler, Remington, BEng... SLT(IC)	E	WESMUT	01.09.03	MWS COLLINGWOOD
Fox, David John, ...LT(IC)	X		01.01.04	TORBAY
Fox, Jonathan Paul, BA...LT(IC)	X		01.02.06	QUORN
Fox, Kevin Andrew, BSc, CEng, MIEE ....CDR(FTC)	E	AE	30.06.94	SULTAN
Fox, Richard George, pcea ....CDR(FTC)	X	P	30.06.05	CHFHQ
Fox, Trefor Morgan, ...LT(CC)	X	HM	01.07.96	SCOTT
Fox-Roberts, Patrick Kirk, MEng .... SLT(IC)	E	WE U/T	01.01.05	DARTMOUTH BRNC
France, Sean Charles, BSc ....LT(MC(MD)	Q		25.08.99	MDHU PORTSMOUTH
Francis, Derek Edward, ...LT(FTC) (Act Lt Cdr)	X	PWO(U)	10.01.00	JARIC
Francis, John, ...LT CDR(FTC)	X	AV	01.10.94	RNAS CULDROSE
Francis, Steven John, MA, psc(j) ....LT COL(FTC)	-		30.06.03	PJHQ
Francis, Thomas Dewolfe Hamlin, BA ....CAPT RM(CC)	-		01.09.01	1 ASSAULT GP RM
Frankham, Peter James, BEng, MDA, CEng, MIMarEST.............................CDR(FTC)	E	WE	31.12.00	DARTMOUTH BRNC
Franklin, Benjamin James, pcea, psc(j) ....LT CDR(FTC)	X	O	01.10.98	RNAS CULDROSE
Franklin, Ross William, BSc...LT(IC)	X	P	01.01.05	RNAS YEOVILTON
Franklyn-Miller, Andrew David, MB, BS, Dip SM .... SURG LTCDR(MC(MD)	-	GMPP	04.08.04	DARTMOUTH BRNC
Franks, Christopher Stephen, BSc, CEng, MIEE ....LT CDR(FTC)	E	WESM	01.02.98	MOD (LONDON)
Franks, Donald Ian, adp ....LT CDR(FTC)	E	IS	01.10.94	MOD (LONDON)
Franks, Peter Dennis, MSc..LT CDR(FTC)	E	IS	01.10.93	AFPAA(CENTURION)
Fraser, Donald Kennedy, pce, MRIN ....LT CDR(FTC)	X	PWO(U)	01.07.84	FLEET COMOPS NWD
Fraser, Eric, BSc, pce, psc...CAPT(FTC)	X	PWO(C)	30.06.02	FOST NWD (JMOTS)
Fraser, Graeme William, MA...MAJ(FTC)	-	LC	01.10.01	JSCSC
Fraser, Heather Lee, BEng...LT CDR(FTC)	E	WE	01.07.04	NELSON
Fraser, Ian David, MSc..LT CDR(FTC)	E	AE	01.07.02	848 SQN HERON
Fraser, Ian Edward, pcea...LT(CC)	X	P	16.04.96	824 SQN
Fraser, James Michael, BA ....LT(IC)	X	P	01.07.03	RNAS YEOVILTON
Fraser, Michael John, ...MID(NE)(IC)	X	O U/T	01.09.05	DARTMOUTH BRNC
Fraser, Michael John Simon, MSc, PGDip ....LT(CC)	X	H2	01.09.01	EXCHANGE N ZLAND
Fraser, Patrick, BEng..LT CDR(FTC)	E	AE	01.10.03	OCLC PETERBRGH
Fraser, Robert William, MVO, LLB, rcds................................CDRE(FTC) (Barrister)	S	BAR	11.01.05	NAVSEC
Fraser, Timothy Peter, pce..CAPT(FTC)	X	PWO(N)	31.12.00	MWS COLLINGWOOD
Fraser, Wilson Cameron, ...LT CDR(FTC)	E	WESM	01.10.96	FOST FAS SHORE
Fraser-Smith, Sharron, ...LT(SC(MD)	Q		23.11.02	NELSON (PAY)
Frazer, Hamish Forbes, ...LT(CC)	X	FC	01.08.99	EXCHANGE AUSTLIA
Fredrickson, Charlotte Ann, ... SLT(IC)	X	O U/T	01.09.03	RNAS CULDROSE
Free, Andrew Stuart, BSc, HNC, MIIE ....LT(IC)	E	IS	01.05.00	DLO BRISTOL
Freegard, Ian Paul, MBE ....LT CDR(FTC)	S	(W)	01.10.99	NELSON
Freeman, David Russel, pce, psc(j), MA.....................................LT CDR(FTC)	X	O	01.06.96	RNAS YEOVILTON
Freeman, Edmund Malcolm Roger, BA ....LT(IC)	X		01.02.06	MWS COLLINGWOOD
Freeman, Mark Edward, sq..MAJ(FTC)	-		01.09.96	CTCRM
Freeman, Martin John, MSc, AMIMarEST ....LT(FTC)	E	MESM	01.04.01	ASTUTE
Freer, James, ...SURG SLT(MDC)	-		10.09.05	DARTMOUTH BRNC
Freeth, David John, BEng .... SLT(IC)	X	P U/T	01.11.04	DARTMOUTH BRNC
French, James Thomas, ...CDR(FTC)	E	ME	30.06.02	JFC HQ AGRIPPA
French, Jeremy Hugh, BEng..LT(IC)	X	P	01.01.02	848 SQN HERON
French, Kevin Lawrence, pce...LT CDR(FTC)	X	AAWO	09.07.93	FLEET COSCAP
French, Paul, BSc...LT(IC)	X	AE	02.08.02	JCA IPT USA
French, Stephen Amos, OBE, BEng, MSc, CEng, MIMarEST, MCGI, psc(j) .. CAPT(FTC)	E	MESM	30.06.96	MOD (LONDON)
Freshwater, Dennis Andrew, MB, BS, MRCP ....SURG LTCDR(FCC)	-		09.08.98	NELSON (PAY)
Fries, Charles Anton, BA, MB, BCH, MRCS ....SURG LT(SCC)	-		02.02.05	42 CDO RM
Frisby, Paul, ...LT(IC)	X	C	01.05.04	HQ DCSA
Frith, Adele Marie, LLB...LT(IC)	S		01.02.06	ARK ROYAL
Frost, Laurence John, BSc, IEng ....LT(IC)	E	WE	01.07.04	MWS COLLINGWOOD

Name	Rank	Branch	Spec	Seniority	Where Serving
Frost, Mark Adrian, BSc..LT CDR(FTC)	E	TM		01.01.03	ARK ROYAL
Frost, Michael John, ...CAPT RM(FTC(A)	-	SO(LE)		01.01.01	845 SQN
Frost, Timothy Simon, BEng ....LT(IC)	X	P U/T		01.05.05	RNAS YEOVILTON
Frost, Ursula Elizabeth, ...LT(IC)	S			01.11.04	MARS IPT
Fry, Jonathan Mark Stewart, MSc, CDipAF, CEng, FIMarEST, MCGI, psc ......CDR(FTC)	E	ME		31.12.98	FLEET COSP&S
Fry, Rebecca, ...SURG SLT(SCC)	-			20.09.04	DARTMOUTH BRNC
Fry, Sir Robert (Allan), KCB, CBE, BSc, MA, psc(m) ......LT GEN	-			07.07.03	NP IRAQ (MAR 06)
Fry, Timothy Graham, ...LT(CC)	E	WESM		01.01.02	CAPT MCTA
Fryer, Adrian Clifford, BSc, pce ....LT CDR(FTC)	X	AAWO		01.02.02	FLEET COSCAP
Fulford, John Philip Henry, BSc, psc(m) ....CAPT(FTC)	E	WESM		30.06.04	DLO BRISTOL
Fulford, Robin Nicholas, IEng, MIIE ....LT CDR(FTC)	E	WE		01.10.03	FLEET COSP&S
Full, Richard John, ...LT(CC)	X	O		01.06.98	849 SQN A FLT
Fuller, Charles Edward, ...LT(FTC)	X	P		16.08.97	DHFS
Fuller, James Bruce, BSc..MAJ(CC)	-	LC		01.10.05	ALBION
Fuller, James Edward, ...LT(IC)	X	FC		01.03.02	HQ STC
Fuller, Richard, ...LT(IC)	S			01.07.03	DCL DEEPCUT
Fuller, Simon Roland, MA, psc(j) ....MAJ(FTC)	-			01.09.01	MOD (LONDON)
Fuller, Stephen Paul, ...LT(CC)	E			01.05.02	SULTAN
Fullman, Gemma, BSc..LT(IC)	X			01.09.02	DNR PRES TEAMS
Fulthorpe, Steven, ...LT(IC)	E	TM		01.05.04	RNICG
Fulton, Craig Robert, pce, pce(sm) ....CDR(FTC)	X	SM		31.12.00	MWC PORTSDOWN
Fulton, David Marc, PGDip ....LT(IC)	E	MESM		01.05.02	VENGEANCE(STBD)
Fulton, Sir Robert (Henry Gervase), KBE, BA, rcds, psc(m), hcsc......LT GEN	-	C		03.06.03	MOD (LONDON)
(DEP CHIEF OF DEFENCE STAFF (EQUIP CAPABILITY) JUN 03)					
Funnell, Nicholas Charles, BSc, pce, pcea, psc(m) ....CDR(FTC)	X	O		30.06.96	FLEET HQ PORTS 2
Furlong, Keith, pce..LT CDR(FTC) (Act Cdr)	X	AAWO		01.03.96	FOST MPV SEA
Furmston, Gareth Hadyn, BSc ....LT(IC)	X			01.12.04	TRAFALGAR
Furness, Stuart Brian, MSc, MPhil, MIMA, pce, pcea....................CDR(FTC)	X	O		30.06.96	RNLO USNAVCENT
Fyfe, Karen Sabrina, ...LT(CC)	X	H1		01.10.00	SCOTT

G

Name	Rank	Branch	Spec	Seniority	Where Serving
Gabb, John Harry, MB, BS ....SURG CAPT(FCC)	-	GMPP		31.12.00	DRAKE COB
Gadie, Philip Anthony, sq..MAJ(FTC)	-			01.05.97	45 CDO RM
Gaffney, Benjamin, ...CAPT RM(IC)	-			01.09.05	CTCRM
Gahan, Richard James, BEng ....LT(IC)	E	WESM		01.09.04	VIGILANT(PORT)
Gair, Simon David Henley, BEng, MSc, MIEE, adp ....LT CDR(FTC)	E	WE		01.02.03	ARK ROYAL
Galbraith, Lee Andrew, ...CAPT RM(IC)	-			01.09.03	FLEET FOTR
Gale, Crystal Violet, ...LT CDR(FTC)	S			24.12.00	SULTAN
Gale, Mark Andrew, MA, MSc ....LT CDR(FTC)	E	MESM		01.02.00	NP BRISTOL
Gale, Simon Philip, MA, pce, psc(j) ....LT CDR(FTC)	X	PWO(U)		01.11.96	EDINBURGH
Gall, Michael Robert Carnegie, BDS, MSc, MGDS RCS........SGCDR(D)(FCC)	-			30.06.95	FLEET COSP&S
Gallimore, John Martin, ...LT(FTC)	X	EW		01.04.01	FOST SEA
Gallimore, Richard Myles, ...LT(IC)	X	P		01.10.00	RNAS YEOVILTON
Galvin, David, ...LT CDR(FTC) (Act Cdr)	E	WE		01.10.96	MOD (LONDON)
Gamble, Neil, ...LT(FTC)	X	P		01.11.93	RAF SHAWBURY
Gamble, Phillip, BSc..LT(CC)	X	O		15.05.93	849 SQN B FLT
Gamble, Stephen Boston, BA, BEng ....LT(CC)	X	P		01.06.97	815 SQN HQ
Game, Philip Gordon, BEng, MSc gw, CEng, MIEE......................LT CDR(FTC)	E	WE		01.10.00	WESTMINSTER
Gannon, Dominic Richard, ...CAPT RM(IC)	-	SO(LE)		24.07.04	1 ASSAULT GP RM
Garbutt, Helen Jane, LLB..LT(CC)	S			01.01.02	2SL/CNH
Gardiner, Dermot Richard Charles, MB, BCH, BAO ....SURG LT(SC(MD)	-			06.08.03	RFANSU (ARGUS)
Gardiner, Laura Marie, ...SLT(IC)	X			01.02.05	DARTMOUTH BRNC
Gardiner, Peter Fredrick David, ...LT CDR(FTC)	X	ATC		01.10.00	RNAS YEOVILTON
Gardner, Callum Brian, MB, ChB ....SURG LTCDR(MCC)	-			29.09.05	MDHU DERRIFORD
Gardner, Christopher Reginald Summers, LLB, DipFM, psc....................CAPT(FTC)	S	SM		30.06.06	FLEET COMOPS NWD
Gardner, Ewan Stephen Edward, BSc ....SLT(IC)	X			01.02.04	ALBION
Gardner, John Edward, BA, pce..LT CDR(FTC)	X	PWO(A)		01.07.00	MWC PORTSDOWN
Gardner, Louis Philip, ...LT(IC)	X	SM		01.05.04	TURBULENT
Gardner, Michael Peter, BSc..LT(CC)	X			01.05.00	MWS COLLINGWOOD
Gardner-Clark, Suzanne Lorraine, MSc..................................LT(MCC)	Q			05.11.98	CTCRM
Gare, Christopher James, n ....LT(CC)	X			01.07.00	MWS COLLINGWOOD
Garey, Emma Jayne, ...LT(IC)	X			01.01.05	LANCASTER

Name	Rank	Branch	Spec	Seniority	Where Serving
Garland, Andrew Neil,	MAJ(FTC)	-	SO(LE)	01.10.05	HQ 3 CDO BDE RM
Garner, Michael Edward,	LT(IC)	X		01.09.02	CORNWALL
Garner, Robert John,	MID(IC)	X		01.09.04	ENTERPRISE
Garner, Sean Martin, BA	LT(FTC) (Act Lt Cdr)	X	ATC	01.08.94	JSCSC
Garratt, John Kenneth, BA, pce, n	LT CDR(FTC)	X	AAWO	01.05.99	JSCSC
Garratt, Mark David, pce, pcea, psc(j)	CDR(FTC)	X	P	30.06.97	JSCSC
Garreta, Carlos Eduardo, BSc	LT(CC)	X	FC	01.05.01	YORK
Garrett, Stephen Walter, OBE, pce, pce(sm), psc(j)	CAPT(FTC)	X	SM	30.06.05	DRAKE COB
Gaskell, Harvey David, BEng	LT(CC)	X	P	16.10.98	EXCHANGE RAF UK
Gaskin, Daniel Edward,	LT(CC)	X		01.09.03	PJHQ
Gaskin, Simon Edward, MNI, MRIN, pce	LT CDR(FTC)	X		01.11.87	STG BRISTOL
Gass, Colin Joseph, BSc, psc, pce	CAPT(FTC) (Commodore)	X	AAWO	30.06.97	BDS WASHINGTON
Gasson, Nicholas Simon Charles, pce, ocds(USN), MA	CDR(FTC) (Act Capt)	X	PWO(U)	30.06.95	CMT SHRIVENHAM
Gatenby, Daniel, BSc	SLT(IC)	X		01.05.04	EDINBURGH
Gater, James Clive, BSc	LT(IC)	X		01.01.03	FOST DPORT SHORE
Gates, Nigel Sinclair, BEng	LT CDR(FTC)	X	P	16.03.93	MWC PORTSDOWN
Gates, William,	CHAPLAIN	SF		06.09.05	CTCRM
Gaunt, Amy Victoria, BA	LT(IC)	X	O	01.09.04	820 SQN
Gaunt, Neville Raymond, pce, pcea, psc, psc(j)	CDR(FTC)	X	O	30.06.98	2SL/CNH FOTR
Gay, David Allan Thomas, MB, BS	SURG LTCDR(MCC)	-		05.08.03	NELSON (PAY)
Gayfer, Mark Ewan, MA, MSc, CEng, MIEE	LT CDR(FTC)	E	WESM	01.12.99	FOST SM SEA
Gaytano, Ronald Troy McDonald, BEng, MSc	LT(CC)	E	AE	01.04.02	RNAS YEOVILTON
Gazard, Philip Neil, BEng, MBCS	LT CDR(FTC)	E	WE	01.10.99	SOMERSET
Gazzard, Julian Henry, PGDIPAN, pce	LT CDR(FTC)	X	PWO(N)	01.06.96	MWS COLLINGWOOD
Gearing, Richard Malcolm, BEng, AMRAeS	LT(IC)	E	AE U/T	01.09.05	820 SQN
Geary, Timothy William, BEng	CDR(FTC)	E	ME	30.06.05	DLO BRISTOL
Geddis, Richard Duncan, BEng, MIEE, CDipAF	LT CDR(FTC)	E	WESM	01.09.96	ASM IPT
Geldard, Michael Andrew, sq	MAJ(FTC)	-		01.05.01	UKLFCSG RM
Gelder, George Arthur, psc	LT COL(FTC)	-		31.12.93	LOAN DSTL
Gellender, Paul Scott,	CAPT RM(IC)	-	SO(LE)	24.07.03	FLEET COSP&S
Geneux, Nicholas Steven, BSc	LT(IC)	E	TM	01.09.00	FLEET FOTR
Gennard, Anthony, BA	LT CDR(FTC)	S		01.03.03	NORTHUMBERLAND
George, Alan Peter, pcea	CDR(FTC)	X	O	30.06.05	HQ STC
George, Christopher Alan, BSc	LT(IC)	X	SM	01.11.03	VICTORIOUS(PORT)
George, David Mark, pce	LT CDR(FTC)	X	PWO(A)	13.03.01	FOST SEA
George, James Andrew, BSc	SLT(IC)	X		13.02.06	DARTMOUTH BRNC
George, Nicholas David, BSc	CAPT RM(IC)	-		01.09.04	FPGRM
George, Seth Duncan, BSc, PGCE	LT(CC)	E	TM	01.06.00	FLEET FOTR
Geraghty, Felicity, BSc	LT(MC(MD)) (Act Lt Cdr)	Q		01.09.00	MDHU DERRIFORD
Gerrell, Frederick John, MBA	LT CDR(FTC)	MS		01.10.00	MOD (LONDON)
Gershater, Stefan Craig, BSc	LT(IC)	S		01.01.04	RNAS CULDROSE
Gething, Jonathan Blair, pce(sm)	CDR(FTC)	X	SM	30.06.02	FLEET COMOPS NWD
Gibb, Alexander,	CAPT RM(CC)	-	SO(LE)	01.04.03	1 ASSAULT GP RM
Gibbens, Carolyn Jane, MB, BS	SURG LT(SC(MD))	-		02.08.05	MDHU PORTSMOUTH
Gibbins, Paul,	CAPT RM(IC)	-	C	01.04.04	RMB STONEHOUSE
Gibbon, Lynne, ARRC, QHNS	CAPT(FCC)	Q	ONC	28.07.03	FLEET COSP&S
Gibbons, Nicholas Philip,	LT CDR(FTC)	X	O	01.10.02	750 SQN SEAHAWK
Gibbs, Adam Peter, BSc	SLT(IC)	X	O U/T	01.01.05	DARTMOUTH BRNC
Gibbs, Anthony Edward,	LT(IC)	X	ATC	08.04.01	DISC SEA
Gibbs, Anthony Maurice,	LT(CC)	X	P	01.03.99	702 SQN HERON
Gibbs, David John Edward, BEng	LT(CC)	X	P	01.02.98	771 SQN
Gibbs, Mark Peter, BEng	LT(FTC)	E	ME	01.04.02	SULTAN
Gibbs, Neil David, BSc, psc(j)o	CDR(FTC)	E	ME	30.06.06	MOD (BATH)
Gibbs, Philip Norman Charles, MSc, FRSA	LT CDR(FTC)	X	PWO(U)	01.02.89	EXCHANGE USA
Gibson, Adrian,	LT(IC)	E	WE	01.01.04	HQ DCSA
Gibson, Alastair David, MBE, MA	CDR(FTC)	S		30.06.06	PJHQ
Gibson, Alexander James, BSc	MAJ(FTC)	-	LC	01.05.05	COMATG SEA
Gibson, Andrew,	CDR(FTC)	E	AE	30.06.04	DLO YEO
Gibson, Andrew Richard, MB, BS, MRCS	SURG LTCDR(FCC)	-		01.08.99	NELSON (PAY)
Gibson, David Thomas, BSc	LT CDR(FTC)	E	AE	01.06.91	COS 2SL/CNH
Gibson, Ian Alexander, pce, psc(j)	CDR(FTC)	X	PWO(A)	31.12.92	DRAKE COB
Gibson, Mark James,	SLT(UCE)(IC)	X		01.09.05	DARTMOUTH BRNC

Name	Rank	Branch	Spec	Seniority	Where Serving
Gibson, Martin Jonathan Stuart, IEng, AMRAeS	LT(FTC)	E	AE	01.04.01	700M MERLIN OEU
Gibson, Sarah Jane, BA, MSc	LT(CC)	E	IS	01.01.99	MOD (LONDON)
Gibson, Terence Anthony,	LT(CC)	E	WE	01.01.02	JSCSC
Gilbert, Jamie Stuart Davidson,	MID(IC)	X	P U/T	01.11.04	RNAS YEOVILTON
Gilbert, Mark Ashley,	SLT(IC)	X	O	01.09.04	GANNET SAR FLT
Gilbert, Peter David, BEng, MA, MSc, CEng, FIMechE,	CDR(FTC)	E	ME	30.06.03	MOD (LONDON)
FIMarEST, FInstLM, MCGI, ACGI					
Gilbert, Ross Grant, LLB	LT(FTC) (Act Lt Cdr)	S	BAR	01.06.98	FLEET FOSNNI
Gilbertson, Cheryl Jane, BA	SLT(IC)	X	O U/T	01.09.03	RNAS CULDROSE
Gilding, Douglas Robert, BSc	MAJ(FTC) (Act Lt Col)	-		01.09.98	CTCRM
Giles, Andrew Robert,	CDR(FTC)	S	(S)	30.06.04	COM MCC NWD
Giles, David William, MBE, MSc, CEng, MIEE, psc(j)	CDR(FTC)	E	WE	30.06.04	STG BRISTOL
Giles, Gary John,	CAPT RM(FTC)	-	SO(LE)	01.01.01	RMR SCOTLAND
Giles, Kevin David Lindsay, BSc, pce	LT CDR(FTC)	X	MCD	01.05.92	FLEET COSCAP
Giles, Peter Anthony Illson, BSc	SLT(IC)	X		01.02.04	CUMBERLAND
Giles, Robert Keith, BEng, pce	LT CDR(FTC)	X	MCD	01.03.01	MCM1 SEA
Giles, Simon,	CAPT RM(IC)	-	SO(LE)	24.07.04	45 CDO RM
Gill, Alastair Brennan, BEng	LT(IC)	X	O U/T	01.01.06	824 SQN
Gill, Christopher David, SM(n), SM	LT(FTC)	X	SM	01.01.00	RALEIGH
Gill, Mark Hansen, BEng, pcea	LT CDR(FTC)	X	PWO(A)	01.07.02	849 SQN HQ
Gill, Martin Robert, BEng, MSc, CEng, MIMarEST, psc(j)	LT CDR(FTC)	E	MESM	01.04.95	MOD (LONDON)
Gill, Paul Simon, MA	LT(IC)	E	TM	01.01.00	MWS COLLINGWOOD
Gill, Steven Clark,	LT(FTC)	S	(S)	12.12.91	AFPAA(CENTURION)
Gillard, Katharine Ellen, BSc	LT(IC)	X		01.05.04	PENZANCE
Gillard, Victoria Anne,	LT(FTC)	X	HM	01.07.99	FWO DEVPT SEA
Gillett, David Alexander,	LT(FTC)	X	O	01.11.98	815 FLT 203
Gillett, Nathan David,	LT(IC)	X	AV	01.01.04	ILLUSTRIOUS
Gillham, Paul Robert,	LT CDR(FTC)	E	WE	02.03.95	CV(F) IPT
Gilliland, Samuel Saunderson,	LT(FTC)	E	WE	13.06.91	MWS COLLINGWOOD
Gillingham, George,	SLT(IC)	X	O	01.01.04	814 SQN
Gilmartin, Kieran Peter, BM	SURG LT(SC(MD)	-		06.08.03	CFLT MED(SEA)
Gilmore, Jeremy Edward,	LT(CC)	X	P	01.09.03	846 SQN
Gilmore, Martin Paul,	LT(CC)	X	P	01.06.96	750 SQN SEAHAWK
Gilmore, Steven John, BEng, CEng, MIEE	LT(CC)	E	WE	01.04.00	MOD (LONDON)
Gilmour, Craig James Murray, MNI, pce	CDR(FTC)	X	PWO(A)	30.06.02	UKMARBATSTAFF
Ginn, Robert Danny,	LT RM(IC) (Act Capt Rm)	-		01.09.03	FPGRM
Ginn, Robert Nigel,	CAPT RM(FTC) (Act Maj)	-	SO(LE)	01.01.95	1 ASSAULT GP RM
Gittoes, Mark Anthony Warren,	MAJ(FTC)	-		01.09.90	MOD (LONDON)
Gladwell, Trevor John, SM, BSc	LT CDR(FTC)	X	SM	01.12.93	CC MAR AGRIPPA
Gladwin, Michael David, BSc	LT(FTC)	X	ATC	01.01.01	OCEAN
Glancy, James Alexander,	2LT(IC)	-		01.09.01	40 CDO RM
Glass, Jonathon Eric, BSc	LT CDR(FTC)	X		01.09.94	MWS COLLINGWOOD
Gleave, Robert David, BSc	SLT(IC)	X	P U/T	01.11.04	DARTMOUTH BRNC
Glendinning, Andreana Sarah, MSc	LT(SC(MD)	Q		12.01.01	MDHU DERRIFORD
Glendinning, Christopher James Alexander,	LT(IC)	X		01.05.03	CLYDE
Glennie, Andrew Michael Gordon, BSc, CEng, MIMarEST, psc(j)	CDR(FTC)	E	ME	31.12.00	FLEET HQ WI
Glennie, Brian William, MBA	LT CDR(FTC)	E	WE	01.10.99	CV(F) IPT
Glennie, John,	SURG SLT(SCC)	-		14.09.05	DARTMOUTH BRNC
Gloak, James,	2LT(IC)	-		01.08.02	CTCRM LYMPSTONE
Glover, Thomas Fergusson,	SLT(IC)	X		01.05.05	ILLUSTRIOUS
Goddard, David Jonathan Sinclair, MBE, BSc, pce, FRIN	LT CDR(FTC)	X	PWO(N)	01.10.87	MWS COLLINGWOOD
Goddard, David Simon, BA	LT(IC)	S		01.05.04	VIGILANT(STBD)
Goddard, Ian Aleksis, BSc	LT(IC)	X	FC	16.11.01	YORK
Goddard, Paul, BSc	LT(IC)	E	WESM	01.05.02	FOST FAS SHORE
Godfrey, Kim Richard, BSc, pce	LT CDR(FTC)	X	MCD	01.09.93	FDG
Godfrey, Simeon David William, SM(n), SM	LT(FTC)	X	SM	01.04.01	RALEIGH
Godley, David John,	LT(CC)	E	WE	01.01.02	DLO BRISTOL
Godwin, Christopher Anthony, pcea	LT CDR(FTC)	X	P	01.02.99	771 SQN
Godwin, Lee Darren,	SLT(IC)	X		01.03.05	ILLUSTRIOUS
Gokhale, Stephen George, MB, CHB, BSc	SURG LT(SCC)	-		04.08.04	CDO LOG REGT RM
Gold, John William,	LT CDR(FTC)	X	EW	01.10.03	NELSON
Golden, Charles Alexander,	LT(IC)	E	ME	01.09.05	YORK

Name	Rank	Branch	Spec	Seniority	Where Serving
Golden, Dominic St Clair,	LT CDR(FTC)	X	FC	01.06.99	MWS COLLINGWOOD
Goldman, Paul Henry Louis, BEng, MSc, CEng, MIEE	LT CDR(FTC)	E	WE	01.04.99	FLEET HQ WI
Goldsmith, Darran, pcea	LT CDR(FTC)	X	O	01.10.99	RNAS CULDROSE
Goldsmith, David Thomas, BEng, MSc, CEng, MIEE	LT CDR(FTC)	E	WE	01.01.02	NORTHUMBERLAND
Goldsmith, Simon Victor William, BSc, pce	LT CDR(FTC)	X	PWO(C)	01.05.95	MOD (LONDON)
Goldstone, Richard Samuel, BA, n	LT CDR(FTC)	X	AAWO	01.08.02	EDINBURGH
Goldsworthy, Elaine Tania,	LT CDR(FTC)	S		01.10.04	MONTROSE
Goldthorpe, Michael, MCIPD	CDR(FTC)	S		30.06.05	MOD (LONDON)
Gomm, Kevin, BSc, pce, pce(sm)	LT CDR(FTC)	X	SM	01.06.91	FOST DSTF
Gooch, Michael David, BEng, PGDip	LT(IC)	E	MESM	01.09.02	DLO BRISTOL
Goodacre, Ian Royston, pce	LT CDR(FTC)	X	PWO(U)	01.05.98	CORNWALL
Goodall, Joanne Claire, BA	LT(IC)	E	TM	01.05.00	FWO DEVPT SEA
Goodall, Michael Antony, BEng, MSc	LT CDR(FTC)	E	ME	01.05.06	DLO BRISTOL
Goode, Alun Nicholas,	LT CDR(FTC)	X	PWO(A)	01.09.99	FOST DPORT SHORE
Goodenough, Raegan Elizabeth,	LT(IC)	E	ME	01.09.05	ALBION
Goodenough, Robert Henry, BEng	LT(FTC)	E	MESM	01.09.02	TURBULENT
Gooding, David Christopher,	SLT(IC)	X		01.01.04	MWS COLLINGWOOD
Goodman, Andrew Theodore, BSc, pce, n	LT CDR(FTC)	X	PWO(U)	01.03.98	MONTROSE
Goodman, David Frederick, SM(n), SM	LT(FTC)	X	SM	09.05.01	FWO FASLANE
Goodman, William,	2LT(IC)	-		01.08.03	40 CDO RM
Goodridge, Terence James,	MAJ(FTC)	-	SO(LE)	01.10.02	RM BICKLEIGH
Goodsell, Christopher David, MNI, pce, pce(sm)	CDR(FTC)	X	SM	30.06.06	MWS COLLINGWOOD
Goodsell, David Lee,	LT(CC)	E	WE	01.01.03	HQ DCSA
Goodship, Joanna Sophie, BEng, AMIMechE	LT(CC)	E	ME	01.07.99	SULTAN
Goodship, Mark Thomas, BEng	LT(FTC)	E	ME	01.01.98	MWS COLLINGWOOD
Goodwin, David Robert, pce	CDR(FTC)	X	PWO(U)	31.12.93	FLEET FOTR
Goodwin, Thomas, MBE	CHAPLAIN	SF		05.05.02	NEPTUNE 2SL/CNH
Goose, Samuel Jacob, MSc	SLT(IC)	X		01.11.04	DARTMOUTH BRNC
Goosen, Richard Davidson,	LT(IC)	X		01.05.04	MWS HM TG (D)
Gordon, Andrew Jon,	LT(IC)	E	ME	01.09.05	ILLUSTRIOUS
Gordon, David, BSc, psc	CDR(FTC)	E	TM	30.06.01	MWS COLLINGWOOD
Gordon, David,	LT(IC)	E	AE	01.05.04	RNAS YEOVILTON
Gordon, David Iain, BSc	LT(IC)	X	H2	01.05.01	EXCHANGE NLANDS
Gordon, Duncan Alexander, MB, CHB	SURG LT(SC)(MD)	-		06.08.03	CFLT MED(SEA)
Gordon, John,	LT(IC)	X	C	01.05.03	FLEET COSCAP
Gordon, Neil Leslie, BSc	LT CDR(CC)	E	ME	01.11.04	JSCSC
Gordon, Robert Stewart,	CAPT RM(CC)	-	C	01.04.03	UKLFCSG RM
Gordon, Stuart Ross, MA, pce, pcea, psc	CDR(FTC)	X	P	30.06.02	RN GIBRALTAR
Gorman, Darren Ashley, BSc	LT(CC)	X	P	01.09.02	845 SQN
Gorman, Glenn Kieran,	LT(IC)	X		15.01.04	BROCKLESBY
Goscomb, Paul Andrew, BA	LT(IC)	S		01.01.04	ARK ROYAL
Gosden, Stephen Richard, MSc, CEng, FIMarEST, pce	CAPT(FTC)	E	ME	30.06.02	SA BERLIN
Gosling, Darren John, MHCIMA, AMIAM	LT(CC)	S		01.04.01	ILLUSTRIOUS
Gosney, Christopher,	MAJ(FTC)	-	SO(LE)	01.10.05	42 CDO RM
Goss, Jonathan Renton Charles,	CAPT RM(IC)	-		01.09.05	45 CDO RM
Gothard, Andrew Mark, BEng, CEng, MIMarEST	LT(FTC)	E	ME	01.11.96	MWS COLLINGWOOD
Gotke, Christopher Torben, BEng	LT(FTC)	X	P	16.01.94	LOAN JTEG BSC DN
Gott, Stephen Bruce,	LT(IC)	S		01.05.03	FLEET COSP&S
Goudge, Simon David Philip, BA	LT CDR(FTC)	S		01.04.02	MOD (BATH)
Gough, Martyn John,	CHAPLAIN	CE		01.09.98	RNAS CULDROSE
Gough, Steven Roy,	LT CDR(FTC)	X		01.10.01	CAMBRIA
Gould, Amelia Alice, MEng, CEng, MIEE	LT(FTC)	E	WE	01.10.00	DLO BRISTOL
Gould, Ian,	LT(IC)	E	AE	01.05.03	DLO TES
Gould, James Davin,	LT(FTC)	X	PWO(A)	01.10.98	LIVERPOOL
Goulder, Jonathan David, BEng, n	LT(CC)	X		01.11.97	FOST MPV SEA
Goulding, Jonathan Paul, BA, ACMI, pce, n	LT CDR(FTC)	X	PWO(N)	01.03.03	MWC PORTSDOWN
Gourlay, James Stewart, BSc, psc	CDR(FTC) (Act Capt)	E	AE	30.06.96	AFPAA JPA
Gower, John Howard James, OBE, BSc, MNI, pce, pce(sm)	CAPT(FTC)	X	SM(N)	31.12.99	JSCSC
Goy, Sally Elizabeth, LLB	SLT(IC)	S		01.01.05	DARTMOUTH BRNC
Grace, Nicholas John, pdm	MAJ(FTC)	BS	SO(LE)	01.10.05	MWS RM SCH MUSIC
Grace, Trevor Paul,	LT CDR(FTC)	E	WE	01.10.98	HQ DCSA
Graddon, Giles John, BA	SLT(IC)	X		01.01.05	DARTMOUTH BRNC

Name	Rank	Branch	Spec	Seniority	Where Serving
Graham, Alastair Neil Spencer, MVO, BSc, AMIEE	LT CDR(FTC)	E	WESM	01.08.01	VENGEANCE(STBD)
Graham, Benjamin Robert, MA	SLT(IC)	S		01.09.04	DARTMOUTH BRNC
Graham, David Edward, MBE, pce	LT CDR(FTC)	X	AAWO	01.10.91	FLEET COSCAP
Graham, David Winston Stuart, BEng, MA, CEng, MIMechE, psc(j)	CDR(FTC)	E	MESM	30.06.03	FLEET HQ WI
Graham, Gordon Russell, BSc, psc(m)	CDR(FTC)	E	WE	30.06.97	FLEET COSP&S
Graham, Ian Edmund, pce, psc(j), n, MA	CDR(FTC)	X	PWO(A)	30.06.04	MOD (LONDON)
Graham, Mark Alexander, pcea	LT CDR(FTC)	X	O	01.10.01	LOAN OTHER SVCE
Graham, Penelope Jane, BA	LT CDR(FTC)	W	S	22.10.99	MOD (LONDON)
Grainge, Christopher Leonard, MB, BSc, BS, MRCP	SURG LTCDR(MC(MD)	-		04.08.04	NELSON (PAY)
Grant, Alan Kenneth, OBE, MA, pcea, pce	CDR(FTC)	X	O	30.06.93	DRAKE NBC/DBUS
Grant, David James,	LT CDR(FTC)	E	MESM	01.10.03	FOST SM SEA
Grant, Ian William, MA, psc(m), psc(j)	LT COL(FTC)	-	LC	30.06.91	FLEET COSCAP
Grant, Richard,	LT(IC)	E	ME	01.07.04	GRAFTON
Grant, Wayne Graham, BEng	LT(FTC)	E	AE	01.06.00	HARRIER IPT
Grantham, Guy James, BA	LT(IC)	E	IS	01.11.00	AFPAA JPA
Grantham, Stephen Jane, MSc, MA, CEng, MIMechE, MCGI, psc(j)	CDR(FTC)	E	MESM	30.06.01	MOD (LONDON)
Graves, Michael Edward Linsan, BSc	CDRE(FTC)	E	WESM	11.11.03	NELSON
Gray, Anthony James, MA, CEng, MRAeS, psc(j)	CDR(FTC)	E	AE	31.12.98	MERLIN IPT
Gray, Anthony John, MSc, CEng, MIMechE, psc(j)	CDR(FTC)	E	MESM	30.06.02	NP BRISTOL
Gray, David Kingston, BEng, MIEE	LT CDR(FTC)	E	WE	01.04.95	DSFM PORTSMOUTH
Gray, Emma Jane, BA	LT(CC)	S		01.09.01	DLO BRISTOL
Gray, James Alan, MA, psc(j)	MAJ(FTC)	-		01.05.03	45 CDO RM
Gray, James Michael, MEng	LT(IC)	E	AE U/T	01.09.03	JCA IPT UK
Gray, James Nelson Stephen,	LT(CC)	X	O	01.04.95	702 SQN HERON
Gray, John Allan, BEng, pce	CDR(FTC)	X	AAWO	30.06.06	JSCSC
Gray, John Arthur, BSc, SM(n)	LT(FTC)	X	SM	01.03.98	VIGILANT(PORT)
Gray, Karl Daniel, BSc	CAPT RM(FTC)	-	C	01.05.00	CTCRM
Gray, Mark Nicholas, MBE, MA, osc(us)	LT COL(FTC)	-		30.06.02	PJHQ
Gray, Michael John Henry,	LT(FTC)	X	AV	09.01.01	CHFHQ
Gray, Nathan John, BEng	LT(CC)	X	P	01.12.99	800 NAS (GR7)
Gray, Oliver William John,	2LT(IC)	-		01.08.01	40 CDO RM
Gray, Paul Reginald,	LT CDR(FTC)	X	P	01.10.02	EXCHANGE USA
Gray, Richard Laurence,	LT(IC)	X		01.09.03	CAMPBELTOWN
Gray, Robert Stanley, BSc	CDR(FTC) (Barrister)	S	BAR	31.12.99	OCEAN
Gray, Samuel Dennis,	LT(IC)	X		01.08.04	ARGYLL
Gray, Sarah Elizabeth,	LT(MC(MD)	Q		20.02.03	MDHU DERRIFORD
Gray, Simon Anthony Neatham, BSc	CAPT RM(CC)	-	C	01.09.02	18 (UKSF) SR
Gray, Timothy,	CAPT RM(IC)	-	SO(LE)	01.07.04	RAF CRANWELL EFS
Gray, Yvonne Michelle, BEd	LT CDR(FTC)	X	PWO(U)	01.02.03	ARK ROYAL
Grayson, Stephen,	LT(IC)	S	SM	01.07.04	TRENCHANT
Grears, Jonathan, MSc	LT CDR(FTC)	E	IS	01.09.99	RNEAWC
Greatwood, Ian Mark, BEng, MSc	LT CDR(FTC)	E	WESM	01.01.99	TORPEDO IPT
Greaves, Martin Richard,	LT(IC)	X	SM	01.08.04	FLEET COMOPS NWD
Greaves, Timoth Michal,	SLT(IC)	X		01.09.03	RNAS CULDROSE
Greedus, David Arthur, MA, psc(j)	LT COL(FTC)	-	SO(LE)	30.06.05	CTCRM
Green, Adam James, MEng	LT(IC)	X		01.12.04	MIDDLETON
Green, Adrian Richard, MSc, CEng, MIMechE, MCGI	CDR(FTC)	E	MESM	31.12.98	SULTAN
Green, Andrew John, MA, psc(j)	LT CDR(FTC)	E	TMSM	01.05.98	FLEET COSP&S
Green, Andrew Michael, BSc	LT CDR(FTC)	E	ME	01.07.01	NAVSEC
Green, David Patrick Savage, BEng, MA, MSc, CEng, MIEE, psc(j)	CDR(FTC)	E	WESM	30.06.03	MOD (LONDON)
Green, David Paul, SM	LT CDR(FTC)	X	SM	13.08.93	NAVSEC
Green, Gareth Mark, BA, psc(j)	MAJ(FTC)	-		01.09.98	FLEET COSCAP
Green, Gary Edward, psc(j)	LT COL(FTC)	-	SO(LE)	30.06.06	MOD (LONDON)
Green, Ian Andrew,	LT(FTC)	X	ATC	01.04.97	RNAS YEOVILTON
Green, Janette Lesley,	LT CDR(FTC)	W	AV	01.10.03	DISC
Green, Jayne Hannah, BSc	LT(CC)	X	O	01.09.99	815 FLT 210
Green, John, QHC	PR CHAPLAIN	CE		04.06.91	FLEET HQ WI
(DGNCS-PERSONAL APR 06)					
Green, John Anthony, BSc, CEng, MIEE, AMInstP, CDipAF, rcds, jsdc	CAPT(FTC)	E	WESM	31.12.97	FLEET COSCAP
Green, Jonathan,	LT(CC)	X	P	16.11.02	849 SQN HQ
Green, Leslie David, PGDip	LT(IC)	E	MESM	01.05.03	FOST SM SEA
Green, Michael Gerald Hamilton, MA, psc(j)	LT COL(FTC)	-	LC	30.06.04	539 ASSLT SQN RM

Name	Rank	Branch	Spec	Seniority	Where Serving
Green, Patrick George,	LT(IC)	MS		01.10.02	FLEET COSP&S
Green, Peter James, pce(sm), SM	CDR(FTC)	X	SM	30.06.05	TRAFALGAR
Green, Roger Richard, BA	LT(IC)	E	TM	08.01.00	JSCSC
Green, Stephen Noel, BSc, MA, CEng, MIEE, psc(j)	CDR(FTC)	E	WE	31.12.98	DRAKE SFM
Green, Timothy Cooper, BA, pce, SM(n), SM	LT CDR(FTC)	X	PWO(U)	01.10.01	ILLUSTRIOUS
Green, Timothy John, pce(sm), psc(a)	CDR(FTC)	X	SM	31.12.98	UKMILREP BRUSS
Green, William,	LT(IC)	E	WESM	01.07.04	NEPTUNE DLO
Greenaway, Nicholas Mark, pce	LT CDR(FTC)	X	AAWO	01.08.95	CV(F) IPT
Greenberg, Neil, BM, BSc, Dip OM, MRCPsych, MMedSci	SURG CDR(FCC)	-	(CN/P)	30.06.06	FLEET COSP&S
Greene, Michael John, BEd, MSc, psc	CDR(FTC)	E	TM	31.12.99	LOAN OMAN
Greener, Carl, MEng, MSc, CEng, MIEE	LT CDR(FTC)	E	WE	01.09.99	JSCSC
Greenhill, Matthew Charles, BA	LT(IC)	X		01.05.04	LEDBURY
Greenland, Michael Richard, pce, pcea	LT CDR(FTC)	X	P	16.04.95	JSCSC
Greenlees, Iain Wallace, OBE, BSc, pce	CAPT(FTC)	X	PWO(A)	30.06.05	NBC PORTSMOUTH
Greenway, Stephen Anthony, BEng, CEng, MIMarEST, MIMechE, CDipAFLT	CDR(FTC)	E	ME	01.02.00	CAPT MCTA
Greenwood, Antony Wyn, BSc	LT(CC)	X	HM	01.02.99	ECHO
Greenwood, Peter, pce	CDR(FTC)	X	MCD	30.06.01	BDS WASHINGTON
Greenwood, Peter Adam,	LT(CC)	X	P	16.10.99	820 SQN
Greenwood, Stephen, BSc, CEng, MRAeS, MDA	CDR(FTC) (Act Capt)	E	AE	31.12.97	DLO WYTON
Greenwood, Stephen James, BA	LT(IC)	X		01.05.05	TURBULENT
Gregan, David Carl, psc	CDR(FTC)	X	H CH	30.06.92	NS OBERAMMERGAU
Gregory, Alastair Stuart, BEng, MSc, CEng, MIMarEST, MRINA	CDR(FTC)	E	ME	30.06.06	JSCSC
Gregory, Anthony Edward, MB, CHB	SURG LT(SC(MD)	-		01.09.02	MDHU PORTSMOUTH
Gregory, Jonathan Edward, MA	LT(IC)	E	TM U/T	01.01.05	DARTMOUTH BRNC
Greig, Judith Anne, BEng	LT(IC)	E	TM	27.11.98	NELSON
Grenfell-Shaw, Mark Christopher, MA, MSc, CEng, MIEE	CDR(FTC)	E	WESM	30.06.05	DLO BRISTOL
Grennan, Eamonn Fergal, BEng, MSc	LT(CC) (Act Lt Cdr)	E	AE	01.05.98	SA MOSCOW
Grey, Christopher Sidney, BSc	LT(CC)	X	O	01.01.02	815 FLT 218
Grey, Edward John William, BA	LT(IC)	E	TM	03.04.99	JFC HQ AGRIPPA
Grice, Matthew Gordon, BEng	LT(IC)	E	AE	01.04.03	DLO TES
Grierson, Andrew Douglas, MEng	LT(IC)	E	TM	01.11.01	SULTAN
Grieve, Lynne Helen, BEng	LT CDR(FTC)	X	PWO(C)	01.10.04	CAMPBELTOWN
Grieve, Steven Harry, BSc, MA, CEng, MRAeS, psc	CDR(FTC)	E	AE	30.06.01	RNAS CULDROSE
Griffen, David John, BSc	LT(IC)	X	MW	01.04.00	BROCKLESBY
Griffin, Niall Robert, pcea	LT(IC)	X	P	01.10.01	CHFHQ
Griffin, Stephen,	LT(CC)	X	AV	01.09.01	RNAS CULDROSE
Griffiths, Alan Richard,	LT(FTC)	E	WE	09.06.89	MWS COLLINGWOOD
Griffiths, Andrew John, MSc, psc(j)	LT CDR(FTC)	E	TM	26.07.94	MWS COLLINGWOOD
Griffiths, Anthony,	LT CDR(FTC)	X	MW	01.10.97	MOD (LONDON)
Griffiths, Christopher John James,	LT(CC)	E	ME	29.04.01	1 ASSAULT GP RM
Griffiths, Colin Stuart Henry, BSc	LT(CC)	X	P	01.12.99	846 SQN
Griffiths, David Thomas, BSc, pce	LT CDR(FTC)	X	MCD	01.04.90	MOD (LONDON)
Griffiths, Francis Mark,	SLT(UCE)(IC)	E	ME U/T	01.09.03	DARTMOUTH BRNC
Griffiths, Glyn,	LT(IC)	E	WESM	01.01.03	TURBULENT
Griffiths, Michael Owen John,	LT CDR(FTC)	X	PWO(U)	16.01.00	FLEET COSP&S
Griffiths, Neil, BA	LT(CC)	X	MW	01.09.98	MWS COLLINGWOOD
Griffiths, Nicholas Alan,	CAPT RM(FTC) (Act Maj)	-		01.05.00	42 CDO RM
Griffiths, Nigel Colin,	LT(CC)	E	WE	01.01.03	JSCSC
Griffiths, Nigel Mills, QGM	LT(IC)	X	C	01.01.04	DCSA GIBRALTAR
Griffiths, Richard Hywel, SM(n), SM	LT CDR(FTC)	X	SM	01.06.04	TALENT
Grigg, Shelton Kent,	LT(IC) (Act Lt Cdr)	S	(W)	08.01.01	RALEIGH
Grimley, Daemon Marcus John, pce, pce(sm), BSc	LT CDR(FTC)	X	SM	01.11.89	FLEET FOSNNI
Grimley, Timothy Paul, BSc	SLT(IC)	S		01.04.03	814 SQN
Grimshaw, Ernest,	CHAPLAIN	SF		02.05.00	FWO PORTS SEA
Grindel, David John Stuart, BEd, MSc, psc(j)	CDR(FTC)	E	TM	30.06.02	FLEET COSP&S
Grindon, Matthew Guy, BEng	LT CDR(FTC)	X	P	01.10.00	848 SQN HERON
Grinnell, Jason, BSc, HND	LT(CC)	E	IS	01.10.01	AFPAA JPA
Gritt, Louisa Ann, BSc, PGDip	LT CDR(FTC)	X	H1	17.12.01	FLEET COSCAP
Grixoni, Martin Reynold Roberto,	MAJ(FTC)	-		01.09.90	NP IRAQ
Grocott, Peter Clark,	LT CDR(FTC)	S	(W)	01.10.00	JFCHQ BRUNSSUM
Groom, Ian Stuart, MBE, BEng, CEng, FIMarEST, MIMarEST	LT CDR(FTC)	E	ME	01.03.99	MOD (LONDON)

Name	Rank	Branch	Spec	Seniority	Where Serving
Groom, Mark Richard, MB, ChB, DipAvMed, ...SURG CDR(FCC)	-	(CO/M)		30.06.00	MOD (LONDON)
MRAeS, MFOM, MRCGP, AFOM, aws					
Grossett, Kelly Mary, BSc..SLT(IC)	X			01.01.05	DARTMOUTH BRNC
Grove, Jeremy John, ...LT(IC)	X	H2		01.07.04	ROEBUCK
Groves, Christopher Keith, pce(sm), SM(n) ....CDR(FTC)	X	SM		30.06.04	TORBAY
Groves, Richard, BEng, PGDip ....LT(IC)	E	MESM		01.09.04	VANGUARD(PORT)
Gubby, Adrian William, BEng ....LT(FTC)	E	WE		01.05.02	FLEET ISS
Guest, Craig Alan, ...SLT(IC)	X			01.01.05	DARTMOUTH BRNC
Guild, Ian William, ...SLT(IC)	E	WE U/T		01.09.03	MWS COLLINGWOOD
Guild, Nigel Charles Forbes, CB, BA, PhD, FIEE, MIMA, jsdc..........RADM	-	WE		06.01.00	MOD (LONDON)
(DIRECTOR GENERAL CAPABILITY (CS) DEC 03)					
Guilfoyle, Victoria Marion, ...LT(CC)	S			15.05.01	OCEAN
Gullett, Humphrey Richard, MA ....LT CDR(FTC)	S	SM		01.10.03	YORK
Gulley, Trevor James, MSc, CEng, MCGI ....CDR(FTC)	E	ME		30.06.98	RALEIGH
Gulliver, Jeffrey William, BEng ....LT(CC)	X			01.09.02	MWS COLLINGWOOD
Gunn, William John Simpson, BSc, PGDip ....LT CDR(FTC)	X	METOC		01.11.94	FOST SEA
Gunter, John Jeffrey, ...LT(IC)	X			01.07.04	WESTMINSTER
Gunther, Paul Thomas, ...LT CDR(FTC)	E	WESM		01.10.99	NAVSEC
Gurmin, Stephen John Albert, pce ....CDR(FTC)	X	PWO(C)		30.06.03	RNLO JTF4
Gurr, Andrew William George, pce.............................LT CDR(FTC)	X	AAWO		01.05.00	IRON DUKE
Guy, Charles Richard, BA, n..LT(FTC)	X	PWO(A)		01.03.98	MWS COLLINGWOOD
Guy, Frances Louisa, ...SLT(IC)	X			01.01.04	MWS COLLINGWOOD
Guy, Mark Andrew, MBE, BEng, MSc, MIEE...............CDR(FTC)	E	WE		30.06.06	DLO BRISTOL
Guy, Richard John, ...SLT(IC)	E	ME U/T		01.09.04	LANCASTER
Guy, Thomas Justin, MA, pce, psc(j), n ....CDR(FTC)	X	PWO(U)		30.06.05	NORTHUMBERLAND
Guyer, Simon Thomas Glode, psc(m).........................LT COL(FTC)	-	LC		30.06.95	LOAN ABU DHABI
Guyver, Paul Michael, MB, BS....................SURG LTCDR(MC(MD))	-			04.08.05	MDHU DERRIFORD
Gwatkin, Nicholas John, ...LT(CC)	X	MCD		29.04.01	HURWORTH
Gwilliam, Elizabeth Kate, BSc.......................................LT(IC)	E	TM		01.07.02	SULTAN
Gwillim, Vivian George, ...MAJ(FTC)	-	ML2@		01.09.93	DEF NBC CENTRE

H

Name	Rank	Branch	Spec	Seniority	Where Serving
Hackland, Andrew Stuart, ...LT(IC)	X	ATCU/T		01.04.03	RNAS YEOVILTON
Hackman, James David, BA ....LT(IC)	S			01.05.04	VANGUARD(STBD)
Hadden, David William, ...LT(IC)	X	C		16.12.05	FLEET COSCAP
Haddon, Richard William James, MB, BS, FRCA, ...SURG CDR(FCC)	-	(CA)		01.04.03	MDH
MRAeS, MRCGP, MRCS, LRCP, AFOM, DipAvMed					
Haddow, Fraser, psc ....COL(FTC)	-	MLDR		30.06.00	UKMILREP BRUSS
Haddow, Timothy Rowat, BEng, CEng, MIEE...............LT CDR(FTC)	E	PWO(C)		01.03.05	CV(F) IPT
Hadfield, David, MSc, CEng, MIMarEST......................CDR(FTC)	E	MESM		30.06.99	FLEET COSP&S
Hadland, Giles Vincent, ...LT(CC)	X			01.10.00	PJHQ
Hadley, Clive, ...LT(IC)	E	WESM		08.04.05	RALEIGH
Haggard, Amanda, BA ....LT(FTC) (Act Lt Cdr)	S			01.03.98	RH HASLAR
Hagger, Michael John, BSc ....LT(IC)	X			01.09.05	IRON DUKE
Haggo, Jamie Robert, BSc ....LT(CC)	X	P		16.04.98	702 SQN HERON
Haigh, Alastair James, BSc, pcea ....LT CDR(FTC)	X	P		01.10.03	815 FLT 203
Haines, Paul Roger, ...CDR(FTC)	E	WE		30.06.01	MOD (LONDON)
Haines, Russell James, MBA ....LT(CC)	S			01.02.99	NP IRAQ
Hains, Justin, BSc ....LT CDR(FTC)	X	MCD		01.04.04	MWS COLLINGWOOD
Hairsine, William, BA ....LT(IC)	X			01.07.05	YORK
Hale, Alexandra, ...SURG SLT(SCC)	-			20.11.04	DARTMOUTH BRNC
Hale, Amanda Diane, BSc..LT(IC)	E	TM		01.11.04	NEPTUNE 2SL/CNH
Hale, Bradley William, BEng, IEng, MIPlantE ....LT(IC)	E	TM		01.05.02	CTCRM
Hale, John Nathan, BSc...MAJ(FTC)	-	LC		27.04.02	539 ASSLT SQN RM
Hale, Stuart Dennis, ...LT(SC(MD))	Q			01.04.05	MDHU PORTSMOUTH
Haley, Christopher, ...LT(IC)	X	EW		13.08.04	FLEET FOSNNI
Haley, Colin William, MA, pce, psc(a) ....CDR(FTC)	X	AAWO		30.06.99	MOD (LONDON)
Haley, Timothy John, MSc, CEng, FIMarEST ....LT CDR(FTC)	E	ME		30.06.96	FOST SEA
Hall, Alexander Peter, BSc, MDA, pce, pcea, ARCS ....LT CDR(FTC)	X	O		01.03.93	LOAN OTHER SVCE
Hall, Andrew Jeremy, BSc ....LT CDR(FTC)	E	AE		01.08.98	DLO TES
Hall, Barry James, BEng, MAPM, MSc, CEng, MIMechE ....CDR(FTC)	E	MESM		30.06.06	FLEET COSP&S
Hall, Christopher John, ...LT(CC)	X			01.12.00	MWS COLLINGWOOD

Name	Rank	Branch	Spec	Seniority	Where Serving
Hall, Christopher Langford, BEng, PGDip, AMIMechE	LT(IC)	E	MESM	01.09.02	SUPERB
Hall, Christopher Mark Ian, MBE	CAPT RM(CC)	-		01.04.01	FLEET AV SUPPORT
Hall, Darren,	LT(FTC)	X	P	16.08.96	727 NAS
Hall, David James, BDS, MSc, MGDS RCSEd	SGCDR(D)(FCC)	-		31.12.99	DRAKE COB(CNH)
Hall, Derek Alexander,	LT CDR(FTC)	S	(W)	01.10.00	DARTMOUTH BRNC
Hall, Edward Charles Malet,	CAPT RM(IC)	-		01.09.05	42 CDO RM
Hall, Elizabeth Clair, BSc, MBA, PGCE	CDR(FTC)	S		30.06.02	NAVSEC
Hall, Graham William Russell, BSc	LT(IC)	X	H2	01.01.03	JSCSC
Hall, James Edward, BSc	LT(IC)	X	O	01.05.03	849 SQN A FLT
Hall, Jessica,	SG SLT(D)(SCC)	-		01.01.06	DARTMOUTH BRNC
Hall, Kilian John Darwin, BSc	LT(IC)	X	FC	01.05.01	RNAS YEOVILTON
Hall, Richard Mark, MA, psc	MAJ(FTC)	-		01.09.90	FOST SEA
Hall, Robert Langford, BSc, pce, CEng, MIEE	CDR(FTC) (Act Capt)	X	PWO(C)	30.06.03	PJHQ
Hall, Ryan Stacy,	SLT(IC)	X		01.07.04	TYNE
Hall, Sasha Louise,	LT(CC)	X		01.05.02	FOSNNI
Hall, Simon Jeremy, OBE, MSc, psc	LT COL(FTC)	-	MLDR	31.12.99	MOD (LONDON)
Hallam, Stuart Peter, BA	CHAPLAIN	CE		05.05.02	45 CDO RM
Hallett, Daniel John, BA	LT(IC)	E		01.11.02	SULTAN
Hallett, Simon John, BA	LT CDR(FTC)	S		01.03.01	COMAMPHIBFOR
Halliday, David Alistair, BA, jsdc, pce	CAPT(FTC)	X	AAWO	30.06.00	FLEET COSP&S
Halliwell, David Colin, BEng, MSc, psc(j)	LT(IC)	E	MESM	30.06.04	FLEET COMOPS NWD
Hally, Philip John, BSc	LT CDR(FTC)	S	CMA	01.11.00	MOD (LONDON)
Halpin, Andrew, MB, CHB	SURG LT(SC(MD)	-		02.08.05	INM ALVERSTOKE
Halsey, Karen Elizabeth, BSc	LT(CC) (Act Lt Cdr)	S		01.05.00	NP BOSNIA
Halsted, Benjamin Erik, MA	CAPT RM(IC)	-		01.09.01	FLEET AV SUPPORT
Halton, Paul Vincent, pce, pce(sm)	CDR(FTC)	X	SM	30.06.04	FOST SM SEA
Hamblin, Paul Anthony,	LT(IC)	X		01.02.06	MWS COLLINGWOOD
Hambly, Brian John, BEng, CEng, MIEE	LT(FTC)	E	WESM	01.09.95	FLEET COSP&S
Hamiduddin, Iqbal, BA	LT(IC)	X	SM	01.05.02	NP IRAQ
Hamilton, Graham Douglas, MSc	LT(CC)	X	AE	29.04.01	MERLIN IPT
Hamilton, Gregory Robert,	LT CDR(FTC)	X		01.10.94	MOD (LONDON)
Hamilton, Mark Ian, BEng, CEng, MIMarEST	LT(FTC)	E	ME	01.12.99	FWO PORTS SEA
Hamilton, Matthew Sean, BDS, MFGDP(UK)	SGLTCDR(D)(SCC)	-		30.08.05	RNAS CULDROSE
Hamilton, Richard Alexander, MSc, CEng, MBCS	LT CDR(FTC)	E	IS	01.10.93	CINCFLEET FIMU
Hamilton, Sarah Catherine, MB, ChB	SURG LT(MC(MD)	-		01.08.01	LOAN FIELD HOSP
Hamilton, Stuart John David,	CAPT RM(IC)	-		01.09.05	45 CDO RM
Hamilton, Susanna Mary, BEng	LT CDR(FTC)	E	ME	01.10.03	FLEET COSP&S
Hamlet, Max Clayton, BEng	SLT(IC)	E	AE U/T	01.09.04	OCEAN
Hammett, Barry Keith, CB, QHC, MA	DGNCS CE	CE		11.07.77	NELSON (MAR 06)
Hammock, Edward Richard Frederick, BEng	LT(IC)	E	MESM	01.09.05	SULTAN
Hammock, Simon George, BEng	LT(CC)	X	P	16.08.98	846 SQN
Hammon, Mark Alexander, BSc	LT(IC)	X		01.10.99	EXETER
Hammond, Christopher Robert, BA	SLT(IC)	S		01.01.04	MANCHESTER
Hammond, David Evan, BSc	MAJ(FTC)	-		01.09.02	2SL/CNH
Hammond, Mark Christopher,	MAJ(FTC)	-	P	01.05.00	LOAN OTHER SVCE
Hammond, Matthew,	2LT(IC)	-		01.08.02	CTCRM LYMPSTONE
Hammond, Meirion Mark Vivian, BSc	LT(CC)	X	P	01.04.00	849 SQN B FLT
Hammond, Paul Adrian, BEng, MSc, FIEE, gw	CAPT(FTC)	E	AE	30.06.06	DLO YEO
Hammond, Paul John, n	LT CDR(FTC)	X	PWO(U)	01.05.04	FOST SEA
Hamp, Colin John, BSc, pce, pcea, psc	CAPT(FTC)	X	O	30.06.04	FWO DEVPT SEA
Hampshire, Tony,	LT(CC)	X	MCD	01.10.00	DARTMOUTH BRNC
Hampson, Alexander Glendinning,	LT(IC)	X	P U/T	01.01.05	RNAS YEOVILTON
Hancock, Andrew Philip, pce, psc(j), MA	CDR(FTC)	X	PWO(U)	30.06.06	JHQSW MADRID
Hancock, James Henry, BA	LT(IC)	X		01.10.00	DEF SCH OF LANG
Hancock, Robert Thomas Alexander, BEng, MSc, MIEE	LT CDR(FTC)	E	WE	01.10.01	BULWARK
Hancock, Zena Marie Alexandra,	LT(CC)	X		01.11.97	RNP TEAM
Hancox, Jamie,	SLT(IC)	X		01.09.03	VIGILANT(STBD)
Hancox, Michael John, BEng, CEng, PGDip, MIMarEST	LT CDR(FTC)	E	MESM	01.02.99	TURBULENT
Hand, Christopher John, MB, CHB, FRCS, FRCSTr&Orth	SURG CDR(FCC)	-	(CO/S)	30.06.03	MDHU PORTSMOUTH
Handley, Jonathan Mark, MA, jsdc, pce, psc(j)	CAPT(FTC)	X	PWO(U)	30.06.05	PJHQ
Handoll, Guy Nicholas George, MEng, PGDip, AMIMechE	LT(FTC)	E	MESM	01.09.02	TORBAY
Hands, Adrian Peter, pcea	LT CDR(FTC(A)	X	P	01.10.94	FLEET COSCAP

Name	Rank	Branch	Spec	Seniority	Where Serving
Hands, Anthony James, BDS	SGLTCDR(D)(MCC)	-		26.06.02	LOAN BRUNEI
Hands, Edward,	2LT(IC)	-		01.08.01	42 CDO RM
Hankin, Robert Simon, MEng	LT(IC)	E	WESM	01.11.05	VICTORIOUS(PORT)
Hanks, Oliver Thomas,	LT(IC)	S		01.05.05	SUTHERLAND
Hannaby, Philippa Barbara, BA	SLT(IC)	E	TM U/T	01.01.04	DARTMOUTH BRNC
Hannah, William Ferguson, MBE	MAJ(FTC)	-	SO(LE)	01.10.01	RMB STONEHOUSE
Hannam, Darrell Brett, BSc	LT(CC)	X	O	01.08.99	EXCHANGE RAF UK
Hannam, Samantha Jane, BA	LT(IC)	S		01.05.03	RAF COTTESMORE
Hannigan, Jason Dean,	LT(IC)	X		17.02.06	MERSEY
Hannigan, Paul Francis, pcea	LT CDR(FTC)	X	P	01.10.01	845 SQN
Hanson, Mark Nicholas, BA	LT CDR(FTC)	S		01.10.02	FLEET COMOPS NWD
Hanson, Nicholas Anthony, BEng, CEng, MIEE, MIMarEST	LT CDR(FTC)	E	WE	01.06.98	IA BRISTOL
Hanson, Steven Jon, BSc	LT(IC)	X		01.05.04	VANGUARD(STBD)
Hanson, Sven Christopher, BSc	CAPT RM(CC)	-		01.05.01	1 ASSAULT GP RM
Harcombe, Andrew, BSc	LT(CC)	X	P	16.07.00	847 SQN
Harcourt, Robert James, BSc, PGCE, PGDip, pce	LT CDR(FTC)	X	PWO(U)	01.01.00	ST ALBANS
Hardacre, Paul Vincent, BSc, SM	LT CDR(FTC)	X	SM	01.06.94	FOST DSTF
Hardern, Simon Paul, MNI, pce, psc(j), MA	CDR(FTC)	X	PWO(U)	30.06.01	FLEET COSCAP
Hardie, Mark John, BA	CAPT RM(CC)	-		01.09.00	FPGRM
Hardiman, Nicholas Anthony, BEng, MSc	LT CDR(FTC)	E	MESM	01.05.03	TRENCHANT
Harding, Carl Sinclair, BEng, MBA, Cert Ed	LT CDR(CC)	E	TM	01.09.04	MWS COLLINGWOOD
Harding, David Malcolm, BSc, MAPM, CEng	CDR(FTC)	E	AE	30.06.03	HARRIER IPT
Harding, David Victor, BEng	LT(CC)	E	WESM	01.09.02	FWO FASLANE
Harding, Ellen Louise,	LT(IC)	S		12.11.02	SULTAN AIB
Harding, Gary Alan, BEng, MIEE, psc	LT CDR(FTC)	E	WE	01.12.94	T45 IPT
Harding, Russell George, OBE, BSc, pce, pcea	CAPT(FTC)	X	O	30.06.03	FLEET COSCAP
Hardman, Douglas,	2LT(IC)	-		01.08.02	CTCRM LYMPSTONE
Hardman, Mathew James, BSc	LT(IC)	X		01.10.99	CAMPBELTOWN
Hardwick, Adam James, BSc	SLT(IC)	X	P U/T	01.09.04	DARTMOUTH BRNC
Hardy, Duncan Mark, psc(j)	MAJ(FTC)	-	C	24.04.02	COMAMPHIBFOR
Hardy, Jonathon,	SLT(IC)	X	ATCU/T	01.02.04	RAF SHAWBURY
Hardy, Lee Charles, pce	CDR(FTC)	X	AAWO	30.06.02	MOD (LONDON)
Hardy, Leslie Brian,	LT(FTC) (Act Lt Cdr)	X	PWO(U)	16.12.94	FLEET COSCAP
Hardy, Robert John,	LT(CC)	X	ME	29.04.01	DUMBARTON CASTLE
Hardy-Hodgson, David Nicholas,	LT(IC)	E	AE	01.07.04	800 NAS (GR7)
Hare, John Herbert, BA, PGDip	LT CDR(FTC)	X	METOC	01.09.97	MWS COLLINGWOOD
Hare, Nigel James, pce	CDR(FTC)	X	PWO(N)	30.06.02	JDCC
Harford-Cross, Peter James, MA, SM(n), SM	LT(IC)	X	SM	01.02.00	FLEET COMOPS NWD
Hargreaves, Neale, MBE, MCGI, gdas	LT CDR(FTC)	X	O	01.10.97	FLEET COSCAP
Harkin, James Paul,	SLT(IC)	X		01.02.05	DARTMOUTH BRNC
Harland, Nicholas Jonathan Godfrey, BSc, jsdc, pce, psc(j)	CDRE(FTC)	X	O	13.09.04	UKMILREP BRUSS
Harland, Stuart James,	SLT(IC)	X	O U/T	01.01.05	DARTMOUTH BRNC
Harman, Stephen John, BSc	LT(CC)	S		01.12.01	SOVEREIGN
Harper, Ian Lorimer,	LT CDR(FTC)	X	AV	01.10.02	STG BRISTOL
Harper, James Andrew,	LT CDR(FTC)	X	O	01.10.97	FLEET AV VL
Harper, Kevan James,	SLT(IC)	X		01.05.03	RNAS CULDROSE
Harper, Philip Robert, BA, n	LT CDR(FTC)	X	PWO(N)	01.10.04	FOST SEA
Harradine, Paul Anthony, psc(j)	LT COL(FTC)	-	SO(LE)	30.06.02	LOAN KUWAIT
Harrap, Nicholas Richard Edmund, OBE, MNI, jsdc, pce, pce(sm)	CAPT(FTC)	X	SM	30.06.04	FOST FAS SHORE
Harriman, Peter,	LT(FTC) (Act Lt Cdr)	X	C	26.04.99	JFC HQ AGRIPPA
Harrington, Jonathan Barratt Harley, BEng	LT CDR(FTC)	E	WE	01.10.03	T45 IPT
Harrington, Lee, BEng	LT CDR(FTC)	E	ME	01.03.06	OCLC BRISTOL
Harriott, Ceri Louise, BA	LT(IC)	S		01.05.04	ST ALBANS
Harris, Alastair Mark, BA	LT(IC)	X	SM	01.02.06	SEVERN
Harris, Andrew Gordon, BEng, MAPM, MIEE	LT CDR(FTC)	E	WE	12.04.97	CV(F) IPT
Harris, Andrew Ian, MA, pce, pcea, psc(j)	CDR(FTC)	X	O	31.12.99	OCEAN
Harris, Carl Christian, BA, psc(j)	MAJ(FTC)	-		01.09.01	HQ ARRC
Harris, Hugh James Leonard,	LT(IC)	X		01.05.05	CATTISTOCK
Harris, Keri John, BEng, pcea	CDR(FTC)	X	O	30.06.05	MOD (LONDON)
Harris, Michael Trevor,	LT CDR(FTC)	S	CA	01.10.99	NAVSEC
Harris, Richard Alun, BEng	LT(IC)	E	WE	01.09.04	IRON DUKE
Harris, Richard Paul, BA	LT CDR(FTC)	S		01.10.02	DARTMOUTH BRNC

Name	Rank	Branch	Spec	Seniority	Where Serving
Harris, Robert, BEng	LT(IC)	E	AE(L)	20.02.06	OCEAN
Harris, Timothy Ronald, pce	CDRE(FTC)	X	PWO(U)	24.06.04	DARTMOUTH BRNC
Harris, Tristan,	MAJ(FTC)	-		01.09.02	MOD (LONDON)
Harrison, Andrew David,	LT(CC)	E	AE	29.04.01	DLO TES
Harrison, Anthony Kenneth,	LT(IC)	X	AV	25.06.05	RFANSU
Harrison, David, BEng, MIEE	LT CDR(FTC)	E	WESM	05.01.97	DLO BRISTOL
Harrison, Ian,	LT(IC)	X	O	01.10.02	FOST SEA
Harrison, James Colin, MB, BS	SURG LTCDR(MCC)	-		02.08.05	2SL/CNH
Harrison, Leigh Elliot, BSc	LT(IC)	X	FC	01.04.03	NOTTINGHAM
Harrison, Matthew,	2LT(IC)	-		01.08.02	CTCRM LYMPSTONE
Harrison, Matthew Sean, BEng, MSc, CEng, MIEE, psc(j), gw	CDR(FTC)	E	WE	31.12.99	MOD (LONDON)
Harrison, Paul Dominic, MBA, gdas	LT CDR(FTC)	X	O	01.10.03	849 SQN A FLT
Harrison, Paul Geoffrey, BEng, MA, CEng, MRAeS, psc(j)	CDR(FTC)	E	AE	30.06.04	AH IPT
Harrison, Richard Anthony, MSc, MDA, CDipAF, psc, gw	CDR(FTC)	E	WESM	31.12.89	DLO BRISTOL
Harrison, Richard Simon, BA	LT CDR(FTC)	X	P	01.10.04	MWC PORTSDOWN
Harrison, Stuart, BSc	LT(IC)	E	TM	10.05.04	SULTAN
Harrison, Thomas Iain, BEng, MPhil	LT(CC)	E	TM	01.01.96	RNICG
Harrop, Ian, BEng, MSc, CEng, MIMarEST, psc(j)	CDR(FTC)	E	MESM	30.06.05	FLEET COSP&S
Hart, Jonathan, MSc, CEng, MIEE, rcds(fm), psc	CAPT(FTC)	E	WESM	31.12.99	DLO BRISTOL
Hart, Mark Alan, BSc, MA, pce, psc(j)	CDR(FTC)	X	AAWO	30.06.04	MOD (LONDON)
Hart, Neil Lawrence Whynden,	LT CDR(FTC)	S	SM	01.10.02	DRAKE COB
Hart, Paul Andrew, BSc, FRGS, MInsD	LT CDR(FTC)	E	TM	01.10.98	DRAKE COB(CNH)
Hart, Stephen John Eric, BA	MAJ(FTC)	-		01.09.05	40 CDO RM
Hart, Steven David,	LT(IC)	X		01.08.02	MWS COLLINGWOOD
Hart, Steven James,	LT(IC)	X	ATCU/T	01.05.04	RNAS YEOVILTON
Hart, Tobin Giles De Burgh,	LT CDR(FTC)	X	P	01.10.00	LOAN JTEG BSC DN
Hartley, Andrew Paul, BEng, CEng, MIMarEST	LT CDR(FTC)	E	ME	02.03.00	CAPT MCTA
Hartley, Benjamin Paul Iles, BSc	LT(CC)	X	P	01.12.98	814 SQN
Hartley, James Henry Dean, BSc, PhD	LT(IC)	E	TM	01.05.98	RALEIGH
Hartley, John Laurence, BSc	LT CDR(FTC)	X	P	01.10.99	DHFS
Hartnell, Stephen Thomas, OBE, MA, rcds, psc	COL(FTC)	-		30.06.98	1 ASSLT GP RM
Harvey, Anna, BEng	SLT(IC)	E	AE U/T	01.09.04	BULWARK
Harvey, Barrie, BEng	LT CDR(FTC)	E	ME	01.06.05	DLO BRISTOL
Harvey, Colin Ashton, BSc	CDR(FTC)	E	MESM	30.06.00	FLEET COSP&S
Harvey, Graham Anthony,	LT(CC)	E	WE	01.01.03	JFC HQ AGRIPPA
Harvey, Keith, pce	CDR(FTC)	X	MCD	30.06.93	MWS COLLINGWOOD
Harvey, Paul Anthony, BSc	CDR(FTC)	X	ATC	30.06.06	DASC
Harvey, Paul Geoffrey,	LT(IC)	E	WE	01.01.04	CAPT MCTA
Harvey, Paul John,	LT(IC)	S	CA	08.01.01	AFPAA WTHY DOWN
Harvey, Robert Matthew Malvern Jolyon, pce	CDR(FTC)	X	AAWO	30.06.03	PJHQ
Harwood, Alun,	SLT(IC)	S		01.08.03	RALEIGH
Harwood, Christopher George, HNC, BTech	LT CDR(FTC)	E	WE	01.10.02	DRAKE SFM
Haseldine, Stephen George,	LT CDR(FTC)	X	ATC	01.02.98	FLEET AV VL
Haskins, Benjamin Stuart, BA	LT(IC)	X	SM	01.01.05	TORBAY
Haslam, Philip James, pce	CDR(FTC)	X	PWO(A)	30.06.04	SUTHERLAND
Hasted, Daniel,	CAPT RM(FTC)	-	C	01.05.99	RMR MERSEYSIDE
Hastings, Craig Steven,	SLT(IC)	S		01.06.05	RALEIGH
Hastings, Stephen Brian, BSc	LT(IC)	X		01.12.04	ENDURANCE
Hatch, Giles William Hellesdon, pce	CDR(FTC)	X	PWO(A)	31.12.98	SACT BELGIUM
Hatchard, John Paul, FRGS	LT(FTC) (Act Lt Cdr)	X	P	04.03.92	846 SQN
Hatchard, Pollyanna, BEng	LT(CC)	E	AE	01.01.00	DLO YEO
Hatcher, Rhett Slade, MA, pce, psc(j)	CDR(FTC)	X	P	30.06.04	PJHQ
Hatcher, Timothy Robert,	LT CDR(FTC)	E	WESM	01.10.00	SOVEREIGN
Hattle, Prideaux McLeod,	LT(CC)	X	PWO(U)	29.04.01	RICHMOND
Hatton-Brown, Oliver Robin, BEng	LT(IC)	E	ME	01.09.04	ILLUSTRIOUS
Haughey, John Patrick, MCIEH	LT(FTC)	MS		01.04.01	MED S IPT
Havron, Paul Richard,	LT(FTC)	E	WE	01.04.01	DLO BRISTOL
Haw, Christopher Edward, MC, BSc	MAJ(FTC)	-	MLDR	01.10.04	FLEET HQ WI
Hawkins, James Seymour, pcea	CDR(FTC)	X	O	30.06.06	JHCHQ
Hawkins, Martin Adam Jeremy, MA, pce, pcea, psc(j)	CDR(FTC)	X	O	30.06.03	849 SQN HQ
Hawkins, Richard Culworth, BA, jsdc, pcea	CAPT(FTC)	X	P	30.06.01	PJHQ
Hawkins, Robert Henry, pce	LT CDR(FTC)	X	MCD	01.10.91	EXCHANGE USA

Name	Rank	Branch	Spec	Seniority	Where Serving
Hawkins, Shane Robert, BEng, CEng, MIEE	LT(FTC)	E	WE	01.12.97	DRAKE DIS
Hawkins, Stephen,	LT(IC)	X	REG	01.07.04	DCPPA
Hawkins, Stuart,	LT(CC)	E	WE	01.01.02	MWS COLLINGWOOD
Haworth, Christopher,	LT(CC)	X	O	01.09.91	815 FLT 214
Haworth, John, IEng, MIIE	CDR(FTC)	E	ME	30.06.99	SULTAN
Haworth, Jonathan Hywel Tristan, BEng, CEng, MIEE	LT CDR(FTC)	E	WE	01.10.04	RMC OF SCIENCE
Haworth, Kentigern, MRCGP, DRCOG, DTM&H, Dip FFP	SURG CDR(SC(MD)	-	GMPP	30.06.05	INM ALVERSTOKE
Hawthorne, Michael John, MA, pce(sm), psc(j), pce,	CAPT(FTC)	X	SM	30.06.05	HQ DCSA
Hay, James Donald, BSc	CAPT(FTC)	E	WE	30.06.05	HQ DCSA
Hay, Michael, BEng, MIEE	LT CDR(FTC)	E	WE	01.03.06	RMC OF SCIENCE
Hay, Richard Harvey Iain, BSc	LT(IC)	X		01.07.05	RICHMOND
Hayashi, Luke Ronald, BSc	LT(IC)	X		01.11.99	MERSEY
Haycock, Timothy Paul, BSc, pce, pcea, psc	CDR(FTC)	X	O	30.06.05	PJHQ
Hayde, Phillip John, BSc, MRAeS, pcea	CDR(FTC)	X	P	30.06.06	JCA IPT USA
Hayden, John Michael Leonard, BSc	LT(IC)	E	IS	01.05.01	DCCIS BLANDFORD
Hayden, Timothy William, BSc, pcea	LT(CC)	X	P	01.12.96	824 SQN
Hayes, Claire Louise, BSc	LT CDR(FTC)	S		01.09.05	BULWARK
Hayes, James Victor Buchanan, BSc, psc(j)	CDR(FTC)	E	WESM	31.12.98	MOD CSSE USA
Hayes, Jennifer Dawn, BEng	SLT(IC)	E		01.01.05	DARTMOUTH BRNC
Hayes, Mark Andrew,	LT(IC)	X		01.01.03	EXCHANGE NLANDS
Hayes, Stuart John, pce	CDR(FTC)	X	MCD	30.06.00	BDS WASHINGTON
Hayle, Elizabeth Anne, BA, MSc, isc	LT CDR(FTC)	W	X	01.10.98	MWC PORTSDOWN
Hayle, James Kenneth, MA, psc(j).	CDR(FTC)	S	SM	30.06.05	DLO/DG LOG (SC)
Haynes, John Graham,	LT(IC)	X		01.01.06	RFANSU
Haynes, John William,	LT CDR(FTC)	X		01.10.98	FLEET FOTR
Haynes, Zoe Elizabeth, BSc	SLT(IC)	X	O U/T	01.05.04	RNAS CULDROSE
Hayton, James Charles, BA, MB, ChB	SURG LTCDR(MC(MD)	-		02.08.05	MDHU NORTH
Hayward, Clive Edward William, BA, SM	LT CDR(FTC)	X	SM	01.06.96	MOD (LONDON)
Hayward, Geoffrey,	LT CDR(FTC)	X	O	01.10.03	MWS COLLINGWOOD
Haywood, Andrew James, BA	LT(IC)	X	ATCU/T	01.11.05	RNAS CULDROSE
Haywood, Guy, pce, pcea.	CDR(FTC)	X	P	30.06.02	PJHQ
Haywood, Peter James, BEng, pcea	LT CDR(FTC)	X	P	01.10.03	824 SQN
Haywood, Simon Anthony,	CDR(FTC)	E	WESM	30.06.02	HQ SACT
Hazard, Lee,	LT(IC)	MS		01.01.04	INM ALVERSTOKE
Hazell, Emma Victoria,	SLT(IC)	X		01.02.05	DARTMOUTH BRNC
Hazelwood, Christopher David,	CAPT RM(FTC) (Act Maj)	-	SO(LE)	01.01.00	FLEET COSP&S
Hazelwood, Steve,	SLT(IC)	X		01.02.05	HQ DCSA
Hazlehurst, Jody Alan, BEng	LT(IC)	X		01.05.05	MWS COLLINGWOOD
Head, Steven Andrew, BEng, MSc, CEng, MIEE	LT CDR(FTC)	E	WE	01.03.01	DLO BRISTOL
Headley, Mark James, BSc	LT(CC)	X		01.04.00	RAIDER
Heal, Jeremy Phillip Carlton, psc	COL(FTC)	-		31.12.99	FLEET HQ WI
Heal, Tristan Stephen, MEng, ACGI	LT(CC)	E	WESM	01.04.01	FLEET COMOPS NWD
Healey, Mark Jon,	LT(CC)	E	AE	01.09.99	DLO TES
Healy, Anthony John,	CDR(FTC)	X	EW	31.12.99	JSSU CHELTENHAM
Heames, Richard Mark, BM, FRCA	SURG CDR(MCC)	-	(CA)	30.06.06	MDHU PORTSMOUTH
Heaney, Martin Joseph, BSc, pcea	LT(CC)	X	O	16.04.97	824 SQN
Heap, Graham George,	LT(IC)	E	MESM	01.05.04	DRAKE SFM
Heap, Steven A,	LT(IC)	E	MESM	01.07.04	TORBAY
Hearn, Samuel Peter, BA	LT(IC)	X	SM	01.09.00	DRAKE COB
Hearty, Stephen Patrick,	LT(IC)	E	ME	11.04.03	ENTERPRISE
Heath, Stephen Philip Robert, MEng	LT(IC)	E	MESM	01.09.02	SCEPTRE
Heatly, Robert Johnston, MBE, osc(us)	LT COL(FTC)	-		31.12.95	HQ SACT
Heaton, Henry Gerald, BSc	LT(IC)	X	H2	01.05.02	ECHO
Heaver, David Gerard Verney, MA, psc(m)	COL(FTC)	-		30.06.96	SHAPE BELGIUM
Heaver, John,	2LT(IC)	-		01.08.04	CTCRM LYMPSTONE
Hecks, Ian James, BA	CAPT RM(CC)	-		01.09.02	RM WARMINSTER
Hedgecox, David Colin, BEng, MSc, CEng, MIEE	LT CDR(FTC)	E	WE	01.06.04	LOAN DSTL
Hedges, Justin William, BSc, psc(j)	MAJ(FTC)	-		01.09.01	1 ASSAULT GP RM
Hedworth, Anthony Joseph, BComm	LT(FTC)	X	P	01.06.94	702 SQN HERON
Heenan, Martyn,	CAPT RM(IC)	-	SO(LE)	01.04.05	UKLFCSG RM
Heighway, Martin Richard, MSc, PGCE, MA(Ed)	LT(IC)	E	TM	01.01.96	DCTS HALTON
Heirs, Gavin George, MA	LT(CC)	X	P	01.08.98	849 SQN HQ

Name	Rank	Branch	Spec	Seniority	Where Serving
Helby, Philip Faulder Hasler, MBE, BSc, MBA, AMIEE, CDipAF	LT CDR(FTC)	E	MESM	16.07.82	DRAKE CBS
Heley, David Nicholas, pce	CDR(FTC)	X	PWO(U)	30.06.00	ILLUSTRIOUS
Heley, Jonathan Mark, BEng, MSc, CEng, MIMarEST	CDR(FTC)	E	MESM	31.12.00	MOD (LONDON)
Helliwell, Michael Andrew, BEng, CEng, MRAeS	CDR(FTC)	E	AE	30.06.05	NELSON
Hellyn, David Robert,	CDR(FTC)	E	WE	30.06.06	DLO DEF MUN GP
Hember, Marcus James Christopher, n	LT(FTC)	X		01.05.00	MWS COLLINGWOOD
Hembrow, Terence,	MAJ(FTC)	-	SO(LE)	01.10.97	RMB STONEHOUSE
Hembury, Lawrence,	CAPT RM(CC)	-	C	01.04.03	EXCHANGE ARMY UK
Hemingway, Darren Graham, BSc	LT(IC)	E	TM	01.01.00	SULTAN
Hemingway, Ross, MB, CHB	SURG LT(SCC)	-		07.08.02	NELSON (PAY)
Hempsell, Adrian Michael, MSc, n	LT CDR(FTC)	X	PWO(A)	01.06.02	FOST SEA
Hemsworth, Kenneth John, BEng, CEng, MIMarEST	CDR(FTC)	E	ME	30.06.06	FLEET COSP&S
Henaghen, Stephen John,	LT(IC)	X	PWO(A)	13.07.01	BULWARK
Henderson, Andrew Graham, BSc	SLT(IC)	X	O U/T	01.01.04	RNAS CULDROSE
Henderson, Arthur,	SURG SLT(SCC)	-		20.09.04	DARTMOUTH BRNC
Henderson, Holly Anne, BSc	SLT(IC)	X	O U/T	01.09.04	DARTMOUTH BRNC
Henderson, Robert John,	LT CDR(FTC)	E	AE	01.10.04	702 SQN HERON
Henderson, Sam Charles, BA	LT(IC)	S		01.10.00	RALEIGH
Henderson, Stuart Philip, BEng, MSc, CEng, MIMarEST	LT CDR(FTC)	E	ME	01.03.99	FLEET COMOPS NWD
Henderson, Thomas Maxwell Philip, BSc, pce	LT CDR(FTC)	X	PWO(U)	01.04.91	CINCFLEET FIMU
Hendrickx, Christopher John, BEng	LT CDR(FTC)	E	WE	01.01.04	EDINBURGH
Hendy, Richard,	LT CDR(FTC)	S		01.10.04	RAF COTTESMORE
Henley, Simon Michael, MBE, BSc, CEng, MRAeS, jsdc	RADM	-	AE	30.01.06	DLO TES (TECHNICAL DIRECTOR APR 06)
Hennessey, Timothy Patrick David, BSc, pce, psc	CAPT(FTC)	X	O	30.06.03	RCDS
Henning, Daniel Clive Walker, MB, BCH, BAO	SURG LT(SC(MD))	-		19.09.03	MDHU PORTSMOUTH
Henry, Mark Frederick, MB, BCh, MSc, MRCS	SURG LTCDR(FCC)	-		06.08.02	MDHU DERRIFORD
Henry, Timothy Michael, pce, n	CDR(FTC)	X	PWO(U)	30.06.05	JSCSC
Henson, Andrew John,	LT(IC)	E	WESM	01.07.04	SPLENDID
Hepplewhite, Mark Barrie,	LT(CC)	E	AE	01.09.99	LOAN DSTL
Hepworth, Andrew William David, BEng, MSc	LT CDR(FTC)	E	IS	01.05.98	JSCSC
Herbert, Lara,	SURG LT(SCC)	-		03.08.05	DARTMOUTH BRNC
Herman, Thomas Rolf, OBE, BSc, pce(sm)	CDR(FTC)	X	SM	30.06.92	MOD (LONDON)
Hermer, Jeremy Peter, MBE	MAJ(FTC)	-		01.09.01	CTCRM
Herod, Thomas,	SURG SLT(SCC)	-		22.01.05	DARTMOUTH BRNC
Herridge, Daniel Jonathon,	LT(IC)	X		01.08.05	MWS COLLINGWOOD
Herring, Jonathan James Auriol, BSc, MA, psc	LT COL(FTC)	-		30.06.98	FLEET HQ WI
Herron, Richard Pater, BA	SLT(IC)	X	P U/T	01.02.05	DARTMOUTH BRNC
Herzberg, Mark,	LT(IC)	E	WE	08.04.05	EXETER
Hesketh, John James, BSc	LT(IC)	X	O U/T	01.11.01	702 SQN HERON
Hesketh, Michael,	SG SLT(D)(SCC) (Act Sg Lt(D))	-		25.06.04	40 CDO RM
Hesling, Gary, pce, n, PGDip	LT CDR(FTC)	X	H CH	28.02.02	ENDURANCE
Hester, James Francis William, BA	CAPT RM(CC)	-		01.09.01	40 CDO RM
Hetherington, Thomas Angus, BSc	LT(IC)	E	ME	01.12.03	NORTHUMBERLAND
Hett, David Anthony, BSc, FRCA, LRCP, MRCS, DA	SURG CAPT(FCC)	-	(CA)	01.06.05	RH HASLAR
Heward, Mark George,	LT(IC)	X		01.01.04	KENT
Hewitson, Jonathan George Austin, BSc	LT(CC)	X	MW	01.08.00	SHOREHAM
Hewitt, Antony, BEng, CEng, MIMarEST	LT CDR(FTC)	E	MESM	01.06.95	NEPTUNE BNSL
Hewitt, David Leslie, MA, pce, psc(j)	LT CDR(FTC)	X	AAWO	01.07.99	MOD (LONDON)
Hewitt, Lloyd Russell,	LT CDR(FTC)	S		16.11.97	AFPAA JPA
Hewitt, Mark John, MIIE	LT(CC)	E	ME	29.04.01	CLYDE
Hewitt, Nigel,	LT(IC)	E	AE U/T	08.04.05	RNAS CULDROSE
Hewitt, Richard Paul,	LT(IC)	X		01.01.04	MWS COLLINGWOOD
Hewlett, Philip James Edward, MEng	LT(IC)	E	WESM	01.11.05	SCEPTRE
Heywood, Robert Hugh, BEng	SLT(IC)	E	MESM	01.09.03	VANGUARD(PORT)
Hibberd, Nicholas James, pce, pce(sm), psc(j), MA	CDR(FTC)	X	SM	30.06.04	SUPERB
Hibbert, Martin Christopher,	LT CDR(FTC)	X		01.10.96	MWS COLLINGWOOD
Hibbert, Oswald Alphonso,	CAPT RM(CC)	-	SO(LE)	19.07.05	CHFHQ
Hickey, Ruth,	SG SLT(D)(SCC) (Act Sg Lt(D))	-		24.06.05	MWS COLLINGWOOD
Hicks, Nicholas John Ivatts, BSc, n, SM(n), SM	LT(CC)	X	SM	01.06.98	VANGUARD(PORT)
Hickson, Michael Stuart Harris, BEng, MRAeS	LT CDR(FTC)	E	(AE)	01.08.03	845 SQN
Higgins, Andrew John,	LT(CC)	X	FC	01.08.95	RAF COTTESMORE

Name	Rank	Branch	Spec	Seniority	Where Serving
Higgins, Damian James, BSc	LT(IC)	X	P U/T	01.07.05	DHFS
Higgins, Godfrey Nigel, BEng, CEng, MRAeS	CDR(FTC)	E	AE	30.06.04	DLO TES
Higgins, Peter Martin, BEng	LT(CC)	X	P	16.12.01	815 FLT 214
Higginson, Nicholas John, BEng	LT(IC)	X		01.06.00	OCLC MANCH
Higgs, Robert James,	LT CDR(FTC)	X	C	01.10.00	MWS COLLINGWOOD
Higgs, Thomas Arthur, BSc	LT CDR(FTC)	S		01.02.02	FLEET COMOPS NWD
Higham, Duncan John,	CAPT RM(IC)	-		01.09.04	CTCRM
Higham, James Godfrey, BEng, MA, MSc, MIEE, psc(j), gw	CDR(FTC)	E	WE	30.06.06	T45 IPT
Higham, Stephen William James Andrew, MA, LLM	LT CDR(FTC)	X	PWO(A)	01.10.04	MONTROSE
Hignett, Geraldine,	LT(IC)	E	TM	01.06.03	MWS COLLINGWOOD
Higson, Beverly Lynn, BSc, PGDip, MIMA, CMath	LT CDR(CC)	E	IS	01.10.03	SHAPE BELGIUM
Higson, Glenn Robert,	LT(IC)	X	AV	25.06.05	CHFHQ
Hill, Adrain Jason, BSc	LT(CC)	X	O	01.10.96	RNAS CULDROSE
Hill, Christopher John, BSc	LT(IC)	X		01.04.04	TRAFALGAR
Hill, Christopher Joseph,	CAPT RM(IC)	-	SO(LE)	19.07.05	CDO LOG REGT RM
Hill, David, BEng, CEng, MRAeS, MIL, psc(j)o	LT CDR(FTC)	E	AE	01.03.99	DLO YEO
Hill, George Alexander,	LT CDR(FTC)	E	WESM	01.10.98	NEPTUNE DLO
Hill, Giulian Francis, BEng, MSc, CEng, MCGI, MIMarEST, psc(j)	CDR(FTC)	E	ME	30.06.04	DLO BRISTOL
Hill, Graham Allen, MB, ChB, FRCS, FRCS(ORTH)	SURG CDR(FCC)	-	(CO/S)	31.12.00	MDHU PORTSMOUTH
Hill, John,	CHAPLAIN	CE		17.01.94	RH HASLAR
Hill, Jonathan Paul, BSc	MAJ(FTC)	-		01.05.05	EXCHANGE USA
Hill, Mark Robert, pce, pcea	LT CDR(FTC)	X	P	22.06.96	HQBF CYPRUS
Hill, Philip John, BEng, CEng, MIEE	CDR(FTC)	E	WESM	30.06.04	CMT SHRIVENHAM
Hill, Richard Andrew,	LT CDR(FTC)	X	MW	01.09.95	FLEET COSCAP
Hill, Roy Keith John, MA, ACMA, psc(j)	CDR(FTC)	S	CMA	30.06.03	MOD (LONDON)
Hill, Thomas Edward, BEng	LT(IC)	X	O	01.05.03	849 SQN B FLT
Hilliard, Robert Godfrey, MA, DipTh	CHAPLAIN	CE		01.08.80	FLEET COSP&S
Hillier, Andrew,	CHAPLAIN	CE		13.09.05	FWO PORTS SEA
Hillman, Christopher Mark, MB, BCH	SURG LT(SC(MD)	-		03.08.04	VIGILANT(STBD)
Hills, Anthony Alexander, pce, pcea	LT CDR(FTC)	X	P	01.12.94	RAF CRANWELL EFS
Hills, Matthew,	2LT(IC)	-		01.08.02	CTCRM LYMPSTONE
Hills, Michael John,	CHAPLAIN	CE		21.04.98	FPGRM
Hills, Richard Brian, MA, psc(j)	MAJ(FTC)	-		01.05.99	NAVSEC
Hilson, Steven Millar, MBA, pcea	LT CDR(FTC)	X	O	01.10.04	MWS COLLINGWOOD
Hilton, James N,	CAPT RM(CC)	-		01.09.03	NP BOSNIA
Hilton, Simon Thomas, BEng	LT(CC)	X	O	01.04.99	MWS COLLINGWOOD
Hinch, Neil Eric,	CDR(FTC)	X		30.06.03	2SL/CNH FOTR
Hinchcliffe, Alan, BSc	LT(CC)	X	P	01.03.94	GANNET SAR FLT
Hind, Kristian Nicholas,	LT(IC)	X	AV	01.07.04	RFANSU
Hindmarch, Stephen Andrew, BA	LT(CC)	X	P	01.09.96	RAF CRANWELL EFS
Hine, Michael Joseph,	LT(IC)	S		01.07.04	TURBULENT
Hine, Nicholas William, pce, pce(sm), psc(j), SM(n), MA, BSc	CDR(FTC)	X	SM	30.06.06	JSCSC
Hirons, Francis Durham, BSc, n	LT(CC)	X		01.02.99	BITER
Hirstwood, John Laurence,	LT(CC) (Act Lt Cdr)	X		01.09.01	BULWARK
Hiscock, Stephen Richard Blackler, BEng	LT(FTC)	E		01.02.99	PJHQ
Hitchcock, Beth, BEng	SLT(IC)	E	ME U/T	01.01.05	DARTMOUTH BRNC
Hitchings, Michael James, BEng	SLT(IC)	E	MESM	01.09.03	SUPERB
Hitchins, Edward Graham David,	CHAPLAIN	CE		06.01.03	CDO LOG REGT RM
Hoare, Peter Francis,	CAPT RM(CC)	-	SO(LE)	21.07.01	RMR MERSEYSIDE
Hoare, Peter James Edward, pcea	LT CDR(FTC)	X	O	01.10.04	OCEAN
Hobbs, Richard, MSc, IEng, FIIE	CDR(FTC)	E	WE	01.10.98	CAPT MCTA
Hobbs, Thomas Peter, BEng	LT(IC)	E	WE	01.09.04	KENT
Hobson, Ian Stuart, BTech	LT CDR(FTC)	E	WESM	01.10.00	FWO FASLANE
Hocking, Mark John Eldred, IEng, MIIE	LT(FTC)	E	WE	01.04.01	DLO BRISTOL
Hockley, Christopher John, MSc, CEng, MIMarEST, psc	CDRE(FTC)	E	ME	01.06.05	DPA TES
Hodder, Philip James,	LT(IC)	X	SM	01.09.03	TRENCHANT
Hodds, Sara,	LT(SC(MD)	Q		01.11.02	NELSON (PAY)
Hodge, Christopher Michael, MSc, BEng, MIMarEST	LT CDR(FTC)	E	MESM	01.10.04	VENGEANCE(STBD)
Hodges, Philip Robin, MSc	SLT(IC)	E	ME U/T	01.09.04	SOUTHAMPTON
Hodgkins, Jonathan Mark, pce, pcea, psc(j)	CDR(FTC)	X	O	30.06.02	MOD (LONDON)
Hodgkinson, Samuel Peter,	LT(IC)	X	P	01.09.04	848 SQN HERON
Hodgson, Jonathan Richard, IEng, MIIE	LT(FTC)	E	ME	02.05.00	CAPT MCTA

Name	Rank	Branch Spec	Seniority	Where Serving
Hodgson, Timothy Charles, MBE, MA, CEng, MIMarEST, MIMechE, psc(j)...CDR(FTC)	E	MESM	31.12.99	CNNRP BRISTOL
Hodkinson, Christopher Brian, pce, MA, psc(j).....................................CDR(FTC)	X	PWO(A)	30.06.02	MOD (LONDON)
Hofman, Alison Jayne, MSc..LT CDR(FC(MD))	Q	IC	01.10.04	NAVSEC
Hogben, Andrew Lade, pce..LT CDR(FTC)	X	AAWO	01.03.99	UKMARBATSTAFF
Hogben, Michael John, BEng, PGDip...LT(IC)	E	MESM	01.01.04	TRAFALGAR
Hogg, Adam James, ...LT(IC)	X	P	01.05.03	800 NAS (GR7)
Hogg, Christopher William, BSc ....LT CDR(FTC)	X	PWO(A)	01.03.97	EXCHANGE NLANDS
Hogg, Graham David, ...CAPT RM(IC)	-		01.09.05	CDO LOG REGT RM
Holberry, Anthony Paul, psc, psc(j)... CAPT(FTC)	E	WE	30.06.04	MOD (LONDON)
Holbrook, Simon James, ...SLT(IC)	X		01.02.05	DARTMOUTH BRNC
Holburt, Richard Michael, BSc ....SLT(IC)	S		01.11.03	RALEIGH
Holden, John Lloyd, BA, SM ....LT(IC)	X	SM	01.12.99	UNOMIG
Holden, Neil, ...LT CDR(FTC)	X	MCD	01.04.01	MWS COLLINGWOOD
Holden, Paul Andrew, ...LT CDR(FTC)	E	AE	01.10.02	DLO WYTON
Holden, Robert John, ...LT CDR(FTC(A))	X	O	01.10.99	849 SQN HQ
Holder, John Michael, BSc ....LT(CC)	X	P	01.08.97	824 SQN
Holder, Shaun, ...2LT(IC)	-		01.08.02	CTCRM LYMPSTONE
Holdsworth, Howard William, LLB, MSc ....CAPT(FTC)	E	AE	30.06.04	DPA BRISTOL
Holdsworth, Rachel Ann, BEng ....LT(IC)	E	WE	01.01.03	ST ALBANS
Holford, Stephen James, BEng ....LT(FTC)	E	MESM	01.05.01	FLEET COMOPS NWD
Holgate, James Alan, ...LT(CC)	E	WE	01.08.02	LANCASTER
Holihead, Philip Wedgwood, pce, psc(a)...........................CDR(FTC) (Act Capt)	X	AAWO	30.06.93	DA SANAA
Holland, Amanda Louise, ...LT CDR(MCC)	Q	IC	01.10.04	MDHU DERRIFORD
Holland, Charlotte Claire, BA ....LT(CC)	S		01.05.02	CHFHQ
Holland, Christopher, ...LT(IC)	E	AE	01.05.03	JSCSC
Holland, Nicholas Roy, BSc ....LT CDR(FTC)	S	(S)	01.10.99	AFPAA JPA
Holland, Rebecca Jane, ...LT(CC)	X		01.01.03	2SL/CNH
Holland, Richard, ...SLT(IC)	X		01.02.05	DARTMOUTH BRNC
Holland, Simon Martin Walkington, BSc...........................LT CDR(CC)	E	TM	01.05.01	NEPTUNE 2SL/CNH
Holland, Steven, ...LT(IC)	E	AE U/T	08.04.05	20(R) SQN (RN)
Holland, Toby, ...SURG SLT(SCC)	-		23.09.03	DARTMOUTH BRNC
Holliehead, Craig Lewis, BSc ....LT(CC)	X	O	01.01.02	815 SQN HQ
Hollingworth, Christopher Robert, ...SLT(IC)	X		01.02.04	EDINBURGH
Hollins, Rupert Patrick, MA ....CDR(FTC) (Barrister)	S	BAR	30.06.03	NAVSEC
Holloway, Benjamin Scott Vere, ...SLT(IC)	S		01.05.04	MWS COLLINGWOOD
Holloway, Jonathan Toby, MSc, CEng, MIMechE, jsdc ....CAPT(FTC)	E	MESM	30.06.02	RCDS
Holloway, Nicholas, BEM....................................CAPT RM(FTC) (Act Maj)	-	SO(LE)	01.01.98	RM CONDOR
Holloway, Steven Andrew, pce ....LT CDR(FTC)	X	PWO(U)	01.10.03	PJHQ
Hollyfield, Peter Richard, BSc..LT(IC)	E	IS	01.05.00	MOD (LONDON)
Holmes, Annabel Mary, ...LT(CC)	X	ATC	15.03.00	RNAS YEOVILTON
Holmes, Christopher, ...SLT(IC)	E		01.01.05	SULTAN
Holmes, Christopher John, psc(j)..LT COL(FTC)	S	C	30.06.06	FLEET COMOPS NWD
Holmes, Graham, pce(sm)..LT CDR(FTC)	X	SM	01.12.87	MWC PORTSDOWN
Holmes, Jonathan David, ...LT CDR(FTC)	X	H CH	04.02.99	BANGOR
Holmes, Matthew John, MA, psc(j)..LT COL(FTC)	-		30.06.03	42 CDO RM
Holmes, Patrick James Mitchell, BA, BSc..LT(IC)	X	P	01.05.02	820 SQN
Holmes, Paul Stewart, BDS......................................SGLTCDR(D)(SCC)	-		20.07.03	DRAKE COB(CNH)
Holmes, Rachel Mary, BA ....LT(IC)	E	IS	01.09.00	RMC OF SCIENCE
Holmes, Robert, pce, psc(a)..CDR(FTC)	X	PWO(A)	31.12.95	TEMERAIRE
Holmes, Rupert Womack, BEng..LT CDR(FTC)	E	AE	01.04.95	DLO YEO
Holmwood, Mark Alan Gresert, BEng..LT(CC)	E	ME	01.08.99	FOST MPV SEA
Holroyd, Jonathon Edward James, BSc ....LT(CC)	X	O	16.02.98	824 SQN
Holt, John David, BSc, BA, MIIE..LT(IC)	E	SM	01.05.00	NP IRAQ
Holt, Justin Sefton, MBE, MA, psc(j) ....LT COL(FTC)	-	LC	30.06.05	JSCSC
Holt, Roger James, ...LT(IC)	E	MESM	25.06.05	SULTAN
Holt, Steven, MA, PGDIPAN, pce, psc(j) ....CDR(FTC)	X	PWO(N)	30.06.03	MOD (LONDON)
Holt, Timothy David, MA ....SLT(IC)	X		03.01.06	DARTMOUTH BRNC
Holvey, Paul Jonathan, ...LT(FTC)	E	MESM	01.04.01	TRIUMPH
Holyer, Raymond John, MSc..CAPT(FTC)	MS	(P)	06.07.04	RCDM
Honey, John Philip, BSc, CEng, MIMarE, MIMechE......................................LT CDR(FTC)	E	MESM	01.03.88	DRAKE CBS
Honnoraty, Mark Robert, pce(sm), SM(n)......................................CDR(FTC)	X	SM	30.06.05	VIGILANT(STBD)
Hood, Kevin Christopher, MA, psc(j)..CDR(FTC)	S		30.06.03	ILLUSTRIOUS

Name	Rank	Branch	Spec	Seniority	Where Serving
Hood, Kevin Michael, BEng, MSc	LT CDR(FTC)	E	MESM	01.04.98	FLEET COSP&S
Hood, Matthew John,	MAJ(FTC)	-		25.04.96	EXCHANGE AUSTLIA
Hook, David Arnold, psc(m)	COL(FTC)	-	C	30.06.03	FLEET COSCAP
Hooper, Thomas,	LT(IC)	S		01.01.05	RALEIGH
Hooper, William Robert, MSc(Econ)	LT(IC)	X		01.01.06	RNAS YEOVILTON
Hope, Karl, BSc, CEng, PGDip, MBCS, adp	LT CDR(FTC)	E	IS	01.09.96	AFPAA(CENTURION)
Hope, Mark Roger, BEng	LT CDR(FTC)	E	AE	01.07.04	DLO WYTON
Hoper, Paul Roger, MCGI, pcea, gdas, BSc	LT CDR(FTC)	X	O	01.10.96	FLEET COSCAP
Hopkins, Anthony Edward Tobin, BSc	LT(IC)	X	H2	01.04.02	RFANSU
Hopkins, Catherine,	LT(CC)	X	ATC	01.05.01	ILLUSTRIOUS
Hopkins, Nicola Sari, BSc	LT(IC)	X		01.05.01	ARGYLL
Hopkins, Rhys, MA	CAPT RM(IC)	-		01.09.01	FPGRM
Hopkins, Richard Michael Edward,	CAPT RM(CC) (Act Maj)	-		01.09.00	NP AFGHANISTAN
Hopkins, Steven David,	LT CDR(FTC)	X	P	01.10.03	750 SQN SEAHAWK
Hopper, Gary,	LT(IC)	E	WESM	01.01.04	DLO BRISTOL
Hopper, Ian Michael,	LT CDR(FTC)	X	MW	09.04.02	MWS COLLINGWOOD
Hopper, Simon Mallam, BA, pce, n	LT CDR(FTC)	X	PWO(A)	01.02.01	JSCSC
Hopper, Stephen Owen, pce, psc(j), MA	CDR(FTC)	X	PWO(N)	31.12.99	JSCSC
Hopton, Matthew James, BA	LT(IC)	X		01.07.05	SUPERB
Hopwood, Adrian,	LT(IC)	X		17.12.04	ILLUSTRIOUS
Horlock, Andrew,	LT(IC)	MS		08.04.05	INM ALVERSTOKE
Horn, Neil Richard, BEng	SLT(IC)	X	P U/T	01.04.04	RNAS YEOVILTON
Horn, Peter Barrick, MBE, pce	CDR(FTC)	X	PWO(A)	30.06.99	FLEET COSCAP
Hornby, Simon, MB, CHB	SURG SLT(SCC) (Act Surg Lt)	-		27.07.05	DARTMOUTH BRNC
Horne, Archibald,	CDR(FTC)	X	C	30.06.06	IMS BRUSSELS
Horne, Jason Richard, pce, SM(n)	LT CDR(FTC)	X	PWO(U)	01.10.02	HURWORTH
Horne, Timothy George, MA, MSc, pce, psc, psc(j)	CDR(FTC)	X	PWO(A)	30.06.97	FLEET COSP&S
Horne, Trevor Kingsley, MA, PGDip, FRICS, FCMI, pce, psc	LT CDR(FTC)	X	H CH	31.12.94	LOAN HYDROG
Horner, Patrick Andrew, MBA, pce	LT CDR(FTC)	X	AAWO	01.08.94	PJHQ
Horsley, Alan Malcolm Ronald, MA, pce, psc(j)	LT CDR(FTC) (Act Cdr)	X	PWO(N)	01.07.94	LOAN BMATT GHANA
Horsted, James Alexander, MEng, PGDip, AMIMechE	LT(FTC)	E	MESM	01.09.02	VENGEANCE(STBD)
Horton, James Robert, BEng	LT(IC)	X	P	01.11.00	815 FLT 202
Horton, Mark Philip,	CAPT RM(IC)	-		19.07.05	1 ASSAULT GP RM
Horwell, Brian Bernard,	LT CDR(FTC)	E	WE	01.10.01	LOAN BRUNEI
Horwood, Neil Anthony,	LT(CC)	S		01.01.02	MOD (LONDON)
Hosker, Timothy James, MA(CANTAB), MCIPD, psc	CAPT(FTC)	S		30.06.04	MOD (LONDON)
Hosking, David Blaise, MBE, MA, pce, psc	CDR(FTC)	X	MCD	31.12.94	RCDS
Hough, Peter Jonathan, MEng	LT(IC)	X	SM	01.12.05	MWS COLLINGWOOD
Hougham, Thomas Neil,	LT(IC)	X	P	01.09.05	RNAS CULDROSE
Houghton, Philip John, MA, pce, MDA	LT CDR(FTC)	X	PWO(U)	01.07.94	LOAN DSTL
Houlberg, Kenneth Mark Torben, pce, n	LT CDR(FTC)	X	PWO(A)	01.11.97	FLEET COSCAP
Houlberg, Kristian Anthony Niels, BM, MRCP	SURG LTCDR(FCC)	-		01.08.99	NELSON (PAY)
Houlston, Ian James Edward, BEng	LT(IC)	X	P	01.01.05	RNAS YEOVILTON
Hounsom, Timothy Rogers, n	LT CDR(FTC)	X		01.04.05	MWS COLLINGWOOD
Hounsome, Jonathan Robert,	LT CDR(FTC)	X	O	01.04.04	771 SQN
Hourigan, Mark Peter,	LT CDR(FTC)	X	P	01.10.03	845 SQN
Houston, Darren John McCaw, pce, n	LT CDR(FTC)	X	PWO(N)	01.10.01	ILLUSTRIOUS
Houvenaghel, Ian Michael,	MAJ(FTC)	-		01.10.04	CTCRM
Howard, Charles William Wykeham,	CHAPLAIN	CE		28.09.82	FWO PORTS SEA
Howard, Daniel Gordon, MA, MBA, MIL, psc(j)o	CDR(FTC)	X	ATC	30.06.06	BF BIOT
Howard, James William,	SLT(IC)	X		01.02.06	CUMBERLAND
Howard, Keith Anthony, MSc, CEng, MIMarEST	LT CDR(FTC)	E	ME	01.07.90	DRAKE COB
Howard, Martin John, BSc	LT(IC)	X	O U/T	01.09.04	DARTMOUTH BRNC
Howard, Naomi Avice, BSc	LT(CC) (Act Lt Cdr)	X	H1	01.09.98	ENDURANCE
Howard, Neil, BEng, MRAeS, psc(j)o	LT CDR(FTC)	E	AE	31.10.94	JCA IPT UK
Howard, Nicholas Henry, BEng, CEng, MRAeS	LT CDR(FTC)	E	AE	01.06.00	CHFHQ(SHORE)
Howard, Oliver Melbourne, MB, BS, FRCP	SURG CAPT(FCC)	-	(CM)	31.12.94	HQ DMETA
Howard, Richard David, BEd	CAPT RM(IC)	-		01.05.00	COMAMPHIBFOR
Howarth, Dillon Wharton, MSc, pce, pcea, gdas	LT CDR(FTC(A) (Act Cdr)	X	O	01.06.90	LOAN JTEG BSC DN
Howarth, John,	MAJ(FTC)	-	SO(LE)	01.10.05	CHFHQ
Howarth, Michael Clifford,	LT(IC)	S		17.02.06	DARTMOUTH BRNC
Howarth, Stephen Joseph,	MAJ(FTC)	-		01.09.05	45 CDO RM

Name	Rank	Branch Spec		Seniority	Where Serving
Howe, Craig Michael, BEng... LT(CC)	X	P		01.07.98	RAF SHAWBURY
Howe, Johnathan Karl Alexander, MEng... SLT(IC)	E	AE		01.09.03	SULTAN
Howe, Julian Peter, BA, pce..LT CDR(FTC)	X	PWO(A)		01.10.01	MWS COLLINGWOOD
Howe, Sarah Elizabeth, BDS... SGCDR(D)(FCC)	-			31.12.98	DDS SCOTLAND
Howe, Scotty, ...CAPT RM(CC) (Act Maj)	-			01.04.01	LN BMATT (CEE)
Howe, Thomas, BSc, SM(n) ....LT CDR(FTC)	X	PWO(N)		01.11.05	RALEIGH
Howell, Henry Roderick Gwynn, MSc, PGDip...............................LT CDR(CC)	X	METOC		01.10.00	LOAN DSTL
Howell, Michael Alfred, MB, BS, MA, MA(CANTAB), ... SURG CDR(FCC)	-	(CEM)		30.06.99	NAVSEC
FRCS, FFAEM, psc(j)...					
Howell, Peter Charles Henry, ...LT(IC)	E	MESM		01.05.04	FWO FASLANE
Howell, Simon Brooke, pce, psc(j), MA...CDR(FTC)	X	PWO(A)		30.06.04	FLEET COSCAP
Howells, Simon Murray, ... LT(FTC)	X	EW		19.09.00	EXCHANGE USA
Howes, Francis Hedley Roberton, OBE, BSc, MA, rcds, psc.........................COL(FTC)	-	MLDR		30.06.02	JSCSC
Howes, Nicholas James, ...CDR(FC(MD)	Q	ACC/EM		30.06.04	MDHU PORTSMOUTH
Howes, Richard Jonathan, ...SURG SLT(SCC) (Act Surg Lt)	-			01.08.05	DARTMOUTH BRNC
Howie, Emma Jane, ... LT(CC)	X	O		01.01.01	JSCSC
Howorth, Keith, BSc, MNI, MCGI, pce, pcea.............................LT CDR(FTC)	X	O		01.12.92	UKMFTS IPT
Hubschmid, Spencer Raymond, BSc ....LT(CC)	E	WESM		01.11.99	MOD CSSE USA
Hucker, Oliver Charles, ...LT(IC)	X			01.02.06	EXETER
Hudson, Andrew, SM(n)..LT(IC)	X	SM		01.10.02	RALEIGH
Hudson, Jeremy David, MA, psc(j) ....LT COL(FTC)	-	MLDR		30.06.02	CTCRM
Hudson, Jonathan David Piers, MB, ChB, ...SURG LTCDR(SC(MD)	-	GMPP		02.08.00	1 ASSAULT GP RM
Dip FFP, MRCGP, JCPTGP					
Hudson, Melanie, BA .... LT(CC)	X	ATC		10.10.97	RNAS YEOVILTON
Hudson, Peter Derek, CBE, BSc, pce ....CDRE(FTC)	X	PWO(N)		31.12.04	MOD (LONDON)
Hudson, Philip Trevor, ...LT CDR(FTC)	X	AV		01.10.96	DLO WYTON
Hudson, Rachel Elizabeth, BA...LT(IC)	X	P		01.05.04	845 SQN
Hudson, Tom Alistair John, BEng..LT(IC)	E	TM U/T		01.05.04	RNICG
Huggins, Kathryn Elizabeth, BSc..LT(SC(MD)	Q			01.11.02	RN GIBRALTAR
Hughes, Andrew Simon, MB, BCh, MRCGP.......................SURG CAPT(FCC)	-	GMPP		30.06.04	NEPTUNE DLO
Hughes, Benjamin Frederick Mostyn, BA .... LT(CC)	S			01.01.03	GLOUCESTER
Hughes, Charlotte Louise, ...SURG LT(SC(MD)	-			02.08.05	DARTMOUTH BRNC
Hughes, Christopher Bryan, BSc..LT(CC)	X	O		01.06.99	849 SQN HQ
Hughes, David James, MB, ChB...SURG LTCDR(MCC)	-	SM		01.08.99	NELSON (PAY)
Hughes, Frank Charles, ...LT(IC)	E	WE		01.01.03	JARIC
Hughes, Gareth David, BEng ....LT(CC)	E	ME		01.01.02	SCOTT
Hughes, Gareth Llewelyn, psc ....CDR(FTC)	S			31.12.00	FLEET COSP&S
Hughes, Gary Edward, ...LT(CC)	X	AV		01.05.02	RFANSU
Hughes, Gary George Henry, ...CDR(FTC)	X	C		30.06.06	HQ DCSA
Hughes, Geoffrey Alan, BA ....LT(IC)	S			01.09.03	MONMOUTH
Hughes, John James, BEng ....LT(CC)	X	P		01.08.99	848 SQN HERON
Hughes, Jon-Paul Hudson, MA, psc(j) ....LT COL(FTC)	-	C		30.06.06	MOD (LONDON)
Hughes, Mark Jonathan, BSc, DipEcon ....MAJ(FTC)	-			01.09.01	RM WARMINSTER
Hughes, Nicholas Justin, pce, pce(sm) ....CDR(FTC)	X	SM		31.12.96	JDCC
Hughes, Paul Antony, MB, BS, FRCGP, DObstRCOG, Dip FFP, JCPTGPSURG CDR(FTC)	-	GMPP		30.06.98	JSCSC
Hughes, Richard, ...SURG SLT(SCC)	-			01.07.03	DARTMOUTH BRNC
Hughes, Robert Ian, BSc, CEng, MIEE, jsdc .... CAPT(FTC)	E	WESM		30.06.02	HQ DCSA
Hughes, Samuel, ...2LT(IC)	-			01.08.02	CTCRM LYMPSTONE
Hughes, Scott Maurice, BSc ....LT(CC)	X	P		16.07.97	849 SQN A FLT
Hughes, Stephen John, psc(m) ....LT COL(FTC)	-			30.06.94	SHAPE BELGIUM
Hughes, Thomas William, MEng, PGDip, AMIMechE ....LT(IC)	E	MESM		01.01.04	SOVEREIGN
Hughesdon, Mark Douglas, BEng, MSc, CEng, MIEE ....LT CDR(FTC)	E	WE		01.02.98	MOD (BATH)
Hugo, Ian David, pce, pce(sm), MNI ....CDR(FTC)	X	SM		31.12.96	DRAKE COB
Hulme, Timothy Mark, MA, pce, pcea, psc(j) ....LT CDR(FTC)	X	O		01.03.97	FLEET COSP&S
Hulse, Anthony William, ...CAPT RM(FTC) (Act Maj)	-	C		01.04.01	UKLFCSG RM
Hulse, Rebecca Jane, LLB...LT(IC)	S			01.05.05	FOST FAS SHORE
Hulse, Royston Matthew, BA...LT(IC)	X	FC		01.09.03	NP IRAQ
Hulston, Lauren Marie, BSc ....LT(CC)	X	O		01.09.01	820 SQN
Hume, Charles Bertram, BSc, CEng, MIMechE.............................CDR(FTC)	E	MESM		31.12.91	NP DNREAY
Hume, Kenneth John, BEng .... LT(CC)	X	HM		01.03.99	ENDURANCE
Humphery, Duncan, BEng ....LT(FTC)	E	ME		01.06.98	DLO BRISTOL
Humphrey, Darren, ...SLT(SC(MD)	Q			01.11.05	NELSON (PAY)

Name	Rank	Branch	Spec	Seniority	Where Serving
Humphrey, Ivor James,	LT CDR(FTC)	E	WE	17.09.98	FOST SEA
Humphreys, John Illingworth, MNI, pce(sm)	CDR(FTC)	X	SM	30.06.94	IMS BRUSSELS
Humphries, Graham David,	LT(CC)	X	P	01.05.01	845 SQN
Humphries, Mark, MSc	LT(IC)	X	P	01.07.00	LOAN OTHER SVCE
Humphrys, James Alan, BSc, MA, pce, psc	CAPT(FTC)	X	PWO(U)	30.06.04	FLEET COSP&S
Hunkin, David John, pce	LT CDR(FTC)	X	MCD	01.12.99	PJHQ
Hunnibell, John Richard,	LT(IC)	X		01.05.04	MWS COLLINGWOOD
Hunt, Andrew James,	LT(IC)	X	FC	01.05.04	SOUTHAMPTON
Hunt, Ben Paul, BSc	LT(IC)	X	P	01.09.03	RNAS CULDROSE
Hunt, Darren, MM	CAPT RM(CC)	-	P	01.01.01	CHFHQ
Hunt, Fraser Brain George, pcea	LT CDR(FTC)	X	P	01.10.03	829 SQN HQ
Hunt, Jeremy Simon Paul, BSc, PGDip	LT CDR(FTC)	X	METOC	05.02.95	MWS HM TG (D)
Hunt, Patrick Edward Robin David, HNC	LT CDR(FTC)	E	WE	01.10.03	FLEET COSP&S
Hunt, Patrick Simon, BEng, MIEE	LT(FTC)	E	WE	01.01.99	JSENS IPT
Hunt, Rachel Eleanor, MA	LT(IC)	X		01.01.03	FOST DPORT SHORE
Hunt, Robert James Campbell, LLB	LT(CC)	S		01.09.02	NP AFGHANISTAN
Hunt, Stephen Christopher,	LT CDR(FTC)	X	AAWO	01.10.03	LIVERPOOL
Hunter, Clare Roberta, BSc, MB, BS, DipAvMed	SURG LT(SCC)	-		07.08.02	MDHU DERRIFORD
Hunter, Darran James, BEng	SLT(IC)	E	ME U/T	01.09.04	ILLUSTRIOUS
Hunter, Deryk John Clark, BSc	SLT(IC)	X	ATCU/T	01.02.05	DARTMOUTH BRNC
Hunter, Neil Mitchell, BSc, pce, pcea, psc(j)o	CDR(FTC)	X	P	30.06.04	DPA BRISTOL
Huntingford, Damian Jon, BA	CAPT RM(CC)	-		01.09.00	1 ASSAULT GP RM
Huntington, Simon Peter, BSc, MA, pce, psc(j), n	CDR(FTC)	X	PWO(U)	30.06.05	MOD (LONDON)
Huntley, Ian Philip, BA, psc(m), psc(j)	COL(FTC)	-		30.06.02	HQ 3 CDO BDE RM
Hurley, Christopher, BSc	LT CDR(FTC)	X	PWO(A)	01.06.02	PJHQ
Hurley, Karl Antony,	LT(MCC)	Q	ACC/EM	26.05.99	NELSON (PAY)
Hurman, Richard Nicholas,	LT(IC)	X		01.09.05	SEVERN
Hurrell, Piers Richard, MA, pce, psc(j), n	CDR(FTC)	X	AAWO	30.06.05	RICHMOND
Hurry, Andrew Patridge, pcea	LT CDR(FTC)	X	P	01.11.94	FLEET HQ PORTS 2
Hurst, Charles Nicholas Somerville,	LT(IC)	X	SM	01.02.01	FLEET COMOPS NWD
Husband, James, MEng	LT(IC)	E	MESM	01.01.05	SULTAN
Hussain, Amjad Mazhar, MSc, CEng, MIEE, jsdc	CDRE(FTC)	E	WE	09.07.02	RCDS
Hussain, Shayne, MBE, BSc, PhD, PGDip	LT CDR(FTC)	X	METOC	01.03.99	JSCSC
Hussey, Steven John, BSc, MA, psc(j)	MAJ(FTC)	-	P	01.09.99	847 SQN
Hutchings, James Stewart,	LT CDR(FTC)	E	AE	01.10.00	FLEET AV VL
Hutchings, Justin Robert, MA, SM(n), SM	LT(CC)	X	SM	01.04.99	TORBAY
Hutchings, Richard Peter Hugh, MA, SM(n)	LT(CC)	X	SM	01.12.05	JSCSC
Hutchings, Sam David, BM, DipIMC RCSED, MRCS	SURG LTCDR(FCC)	-		06.08.02	NELSON (PAY)
Hutchins, Iain David MacKenzie, n	LT(FTC)	X	PWO(A)	01.09.98	MONMOUTH
Hutchins, Richard Frank, BEng, MSc	LT CDR(FTC)	E	MESM	01.06.01	FOST SM SEA
Hutchinson, Christopher John, BSc, PGDip	LT CDR(FTC)	X	METOC	01.09.00	JHQ/CIS LISBON
Hutchinson, Michael Robert,	LT(IC)	X	FC	01.01.05	ILLUSTRIOUS
Hutchinson, Nicholas James, BA	LT(CC)	X		01.01.02	EXCHANGE ITALY
Hutchinson, Oliver James Procter, pce	CDR(FTC)	X	AAWO	30.06.06	JSCSC
Hutchinson, Peter, IEng, AMIMarEST	LT(FTC)	E	ME	14.06.96	DSFM PORTSMOUTH
Hutchison, George Bruce, pcea, psc(j)	CDR(FTC)	X	O	30.06.03	HQ SACT
Hutchison, Paul Gordon, BEng, MSc, MIMarEST, CEng	LT CDR(FTC)	E	MESM	01.05.98	DRAKE SFM
Hutton, Graham, pcea	LT CDR(FTC)	X	O	01.10.04	MWC SOUTHWICK
Hutton, James Kyle, psc(m)	LT COL(FTC) (Act Col)	-		30.06.97	STRIKFORNATO
Hutton, Katharine Denise, BEd, LCIPD	LT CDR(FTC)	E	TM	21.01.02	FLEET COSP&S
Huynh, Cuong Chuong, BA	LT(CC)	S		01.03.02	UKLFCSG RM
Hyde, James William, MEng	LT(CC)	E	WE	01.09.02	DLO BRISTOL
Hygate, Alison Margaret, BEng	LT CDR(FTC)	X		01.05.02	OCLC BIRM
Hyldon, Christopher John, BSc, FRAeS, jsdc, sondc	CAPT(FTC)	E	AE	30.06.99	SA BUENOS AIRES
Hynde, Claire Louise, BSc	LT(CC)	S		22.04.05	MOD (LONDON)

I

Ibbotson, Richard Jeffery, DSC, MSc, CGIA, pce	RADM	-	PWO(U)	23.06.05	NAVSEC
(NAVAL SECRETARY JUN 05)					
Iliffe, David Ian, BD, MLITT	LT(IC)	X		16.11.98	BDS WASHINGTON
Imm, Nicholas David Harvey, BM, DRCOG, MRCGP	SURG LTCDR(SC(MD))	-	GMPP	23.11.01	OCEAN
Imrie, Peter Blain, DSM	LT CDR(FTC)	X	AV	01.10.04	NELSON

Name	Rank	Branch	Spec	Seniority	Where Serving
Imrie, Samantha Jane, BA	LT(IC)	S		01.09.03	DLO/DG LOG (SC)
Ince, David Peter,	LT CDR(FTC)	X	MCD	01.12.97	EXCHANGE USA
Ingamells, Stephen David, BSc	LT(IC)	X	P	01.01.04	846 SQN
Inge, Daniel Jon,	LT(FTC) (Act Lt Cdr)	X	ATC	01.05.95	ILLUSTRIOUS
Ingham, Andrew Richard, BEng, n	LT(FTC)	X	PWO(A)	01.09.98	CHATHAM
Ingham, Lee-Anne, LLB	LT(IC)	X		01.09.01	MWS HM TG (D)
Ingham, Nicholas Hampshire,	LT(CC)	X		01.09.04	QHM CLYDE
Inglis, David John, BSc	LT(IC)	X	P	01.01.02	846 SQN
Inglis, Graham Douglas, BSc	LT(IC)	X		01.05.04	IRON DUKE
Inglis, William Sinclair,	SLT(IC)	X		01.01.04	VIGILANT(STBD)
Ingram, Dean Daniel,	SLT(IC)	X		01.02.05	DARTMOUTH BRNC
Ingram, Gareth John, BSc	LT CDR(FTC)	X	O	01.12.03	702 SQN HERON
Ingram, Richard Gordon, pce, psc(a)	CDR(FTC)	X	AAWO	30.06.98	MOD (LONDON)
Inness, Matthew John, BEng, PGDip	LT(IC)	E	MESM	01.10.02	SPARTAN
Insley, Andrew David, BSc	LT(IC)	X		01.09.05	HURWORTH
Instone, Malcolm John, BA, n	LT(CC)	X		01.11.98	DARTMOUTH BRNC
Instrell, Christopher Bryce, MEng	SLT(IC)	X	P U/T	01.02.05	DARTMOUTH BRNC
Ireland, Alasdair Robbie, MNI, pce, psc(j), MA	CDR(FTC)	X	AAWO	30.06.99	COS 2SL/CNH
Ireland, John Mitchell,	LT CDR(FTC)	E	MESM	01.10.02	MOD (BATH)
Ireland, Philip Charles, DSC, pce	CDR(FTC)	X	MCD	30.06.04	STRIKFORNATO
Ireland, Roger Charles, MBE, MILT, ACIS	CDR(FTC)	S	SM	31.12.95	FLEET COSP&S
Irons, Paul Andrew,	LT CDR(FTC)	X		01.07.97	MOD (LONDON)
Irons, Rupert Charles St John, BSc, n	LT CDR(FTC)	X	PWO(C)	01.10.03	COMATG SEA
Irving, Paul John, BA, AMInstP	LT(IC)	X	P U/T	01.09.05	RNAS YEOVILTON
Irving, Thomas Charles, BA	LT(IC)	S		01.05.03	NELSON
Irwin, Mark Andrew, BEng, MSc, CEng, MIMechE	LT CDR(FTC)	E	ME	09.01.97	DLO BRISTOL
Irwin, Stuart Gordon,	LT(CC)	X	P	01.06.00	JSCSC
Isaac, Philip, FCIS, ACIS	CDR(FTC)	S		31.12.99	FLEET HQ PORTS 2
Isaac, Stella Monica, BEd	LT(IC)	X	TM	01.09.03	DFTE PORTSMOUTH
Isaacs, Nathan James, BSc	LT(IC)	X		01.05.04	IRON DUKE
Isbister, Elspeth Joy, MB, CHB	SURG LT(SC(MD)	-		06.08.03	CFLT MED(SEA)
Isherwood, Carl Richard, BD	LT(IC)	X		01.05.04	MWS COLLINGWOOD
Issitt, Barry David,	LT(IC)	X	P	01.01.02	LOAN OTHER SVCE
Isted, Lee Raymond, MPhil	SLT(IC)	S		01.09.04	DARTMOUTH BRNC
Ives, David Jonathan, BSc	LT(CC)	X	HM	01.06.00	FWO DEVPT SEA
Ivill, Stephen, QCBA	LT(IC)	X	O	01.07.04	814 SQN
Ivory, Thomas Joel, BEng	LT(IC)	E	WE	01.11.05	CUMBERLAND

J

Name	Rank	Branch	Spec	Seniority	Where Serving
Jackman, Andrew Warren, pce	CDR(FTC)	X	PWO(C)	30.06.98	MOD (LONDON)
Jackman, Richard William, BSc, MIEE, psc, FIEE, CEng	CDRE(FTC)	E	WE	26.08.03	NC3 AGENCY
Jackson, Amie Ruth, BA	SLT(IC)	X		01.01.05	DARTMOUTH BRNC
Jackson, Andrew Stephen, MA, MSc, psc(j)	CDR(FTC)	E	MESM	30.06.05	MOD (LONDON)
Jackson, Anthony,	LT(IC)	S		21.12.01	DRAKE COB
Jackson, David John, BEng, MSc	LT CDR(FTC)	E	AE	01.03.00	DLO YEO
Jackson, Howard Charles, BEng	LT(CC)	X	P	01.05.01	845 SQN
Jackson, Ian, SM	LT(CC)	X	H2	01.03.97	MWS HM TG (D)
Jackson, Ian Anthony, MSc, psc(j)o	LT CDR(FTC)	E	ME	01.04.96	FLEET COSP&S
Jackson, John Charles Alan, BA	SLT(IC)	X		01.09.04	DARTMOUTH BRNC
Jackson, Mark Harding, MA, Cert Ed	CHAPLAIN	CE		19.04.83	CMT SHRIVENHAM
Jackson, Matthew John Andrew, MA, psc(j)	MAJ(FTC)	-		01.09.02	PJHQ
Jackson, Pamela, BSc	LT(CC)	X	ATCU/T	01.02.00	EXCHANGE RAF UK
Jackson, Paul Anthony, MILT	LT CDR(FTC)	S	(W)	01.10.01	FLEET COSP&S
Jackson, Peter Neil, BA, BEng, CEng, MIEE, LLB, LLM	LT CDR(FTC)	E	AE	01.02.99	DLO TES
Jackson, Stevan Kenneth, FRGS, FInstLM, MCIPD	CAPT(FTC)	MS		31.08.04	MOD (LONDON)
Jackson, Stuart Harry, BSc, MBA, MRAeS	LT CDR(FTC) (Act Cdr)	E	AE	01.07.89	MOD (BATH)
Jacob, Andrew William, BA	LT(CC)	X	H2	01.07.00	RNAS CULDROSE
Jacques, Karen Michelle, BA, n	LT CDR(FTC)	X		01.05.05	2SL/CNH
Jacques, Marcus James,	LT CDR(FTC)	X	AAWO	01.07.02	UKMARBATSTAFF
Jacques, Nicholas Adrian,	LT CDR(FTC)	X	O	01.10.02	MWC PORTSDOWN
Jagger, Paul Richard Albert, MSc, AMIEE	CAPT(FTC)	E	WESM	30.06.05	ASM IPT
Jaggers, Gary George, pcea	LT CDR(FTC(A)	X	O	01.10.01	820 SQN

Name	Rank	Branch	Spec	Seniority	Where Serving
James, Adam Jon, pce	LT CDR(FTC)	X	H CH	01.10.97	DARTMOUTH BRNC
James, Andrew George, BEng, PGDip, AMIMechE	LT(FTC)	E	MESM	01.09.02	TALENT
James, Christopher, BSc, CEng, MIMarEST, MIMechE	LT CDR(FTC)	E	MESM	01.06.91	ASM IPT
James, Christopher William, pce	LT CDR(FTC)	X	AAWO	27.10.93	SA MALAYSIA
James, David Russell, pce, pcea, psc	CAPT(FTC)	X	O	30.06.04	NP IRAQ
James, Gareth Clark Miguel,	LT(IC)	S		01.05.03	SCOTT
James, Ian, BChD, MA, MFGDP(UK), MCMI, psc(j)	SGCDR(D)(FCC)	-		30.06.05	DDS HALTON
James, Katherine Jeanette,	LT(FC(MD) (Act Lt Cdr)	Q	CC	26.11.96	RCDM
James, Mark,	LT(FTC)	E	WE	01.04.01	FOST SEA
James, Paul Melvyn, MA, psc(j)	LT COL(FTC)	-		30.06.06	FLEET HQ PORTS 2
James, Richard Michael, BSc	LT(CC)	X	SM	01.11.01	VANGUARD(PORT)
James, Robert,	LT(IC)	X	AV	01.07.04	RFANSU
James, Victoria Helen,	SLT(MD)	Q		01.08.02	MDHU PORTSMOUTH
Jameson, Andrew Charles, LLB, psc(j)	CDR(FTC) (Act Capt) (Barrister)	S	BAR	31.12.98	FLEET COSP&S
Jameson, Andrew John, BA	LT(IC)	E	TM	01.09.98	RNICG
Jameson, Roger Mark, BSc	LT(FTC)	X	P	16.07.92	NELSON
Jamieson, Paul Andrew,	LT(IC)	X	SM	01.01.06	RALEIGH
Jamieson, Scott,	SURG SLT(SCC)	-		13.09.04	DARTMOUTH BRNC
Jamison, James Scott,	CAPT RM(IC)	-		01.09.04	OCLC ROSYTH
Janaway, Paul, BSc, CEng, MIEE	CDR(FTC)	E	WE	30.06.05	HQ DCSA
Jane, Samuel Charles, BSc	LT(IC)	X		01.07.05	PEMBROKE
Janzen, Alexander, BA	MAJ(FTC)	-	C	01.10.04	42 CDO RM
Jaques, David Anthony,	LT(CC) (Act Lt Cdr)	X		16.08.92	PJHQ
Jaques, Simon Christopher David, MB, BS, MSc	SURG LT(SC(MD)	-		06.08.03	ENDURANCE
Jardine, Darren Scott, MRIN, n, MSc	LT CDR(FTC)	X	AAWO	01.10.03	EXCHANGE CANADA
Jardine, Graham Andrew, pce, pcea, psc(j)	CDR(FTC)	X	O	30.06.98	MOD (LONDON)
Jardine, Iain, BEng	LT(IC)	X	P	01.05.04	848 SQN HERON
Jarman, Paul Richard,	LT(CC)	E	WESM	01.01.02	RALEIGH
Jarvis, David John, BSc, CEng, MIEE, psc	CDRE	E	WESM	25.04.06	DLO BRISTOL
Jarvis, Laurence Richard, BSc, psc(j)	CDR(FTC)	E	ME	30.06.02	ALBION
Jarvis, Lionel John, MB, BS, LRCP, FRCR, MIEE, MRCS, rcds	SURG CAPT(FCC) (Commodore)	-	CPDATE	31.12.99	MOD (LONDON)
Jayes, Neil John,	LT(FTC)	X	REG	01.04.01	BFPO AGENCY DLO
Jefferis, Briony Angharad,	LT(SC(MD)	Q		01.09.04	RN GIBRALTAR
Jefferson, Peter Mark, pcea	LT CDR(FTC)	X	O	01.10.96	849 SQN B FLT
Jefferson, Toby Simon, BEng	LT CDR(FTC)	E	AE	01.10.04	RNAS YEOVILTON
Jeffery, Samuel,	SURG SLT(SCC)	-		30.06.04	DARTMOUTH BRNC
Jeffs, Samuel George,	MID(IC)	X		01.11.04	MIDDLETON
Jemmeson, Susannah Hazel, BA, MSc	LT(IC)	S		01.05.03	UKMCC BAHRAIN
Jemmett, Simeon,	2LT(IC)	-		01.08.02	CTCRM LYMPSTONE
Jenkin, Alastair Michael Hugh, BSc, MA, CEng, MIEE, psc(m)	CDR(FTC)	E	WE	31.12.96	CV(F) IPT
Jenkin, James Richard Saint Lawrence,	LT CDR(FTC)	X	SM	01.05.92	FORWARD
Jenkins, Alastair Rodney, BSc	LT(CC)	X	P	16.06.98	RAF CRANWELL EFS
Jenkins, David Gareth, BSc, SM(n)	LT(CC)	X	SM	01.09.01	RALEIGH
Jenkins, Gari Wyn, BEng, MBA, MSc, gw	CDR(FTC)	E	WE	30.06.03	HQ DCSA
Jenkins, Gwyn, psc(j)	MAJ(FTC)	-		01.09.01	1 ASSAULT GP RM
Jenkins, Ian Lawrence, CB, CVO, MB, BCH, FRCS (SURGEON GENERAL (SL 01) OCT 02)	SURG VADM	-	CPDATE	21.10.02	MOD (LONDON)
Jenkins, Robert Christopher, BSc	LT(IC)	E	TM	01.12.99	JSCSC
Jenkins, Thomas Richard,	LT(IC)	X		01.09.05	EXCHANGE USA
Jenks, Anthony William Jervis, FIMarEST, CMarSci	LT CDR(FTC)	X	H CH	16.04.87	SCOTT
Jenks, Jennifer Claire Belinda, BSc, BDS, MFGDP(UK)	SGLTCDR(D)(MC(MD)	-		24.09.05	JSU NORTHWOOD
Jenner, Andrew Christopher, BEng	LT(IC)	E	TM	16.09.97	SULTAN
Jennings, Christian Rubin, MBE	LT(IC)	S		01.01.04	AFPAA(CENTURION)
Jennings, William, BEng	LT CDR(FTC)	E	ME	01.03.03	IRON DUKE
Jepson, Nicholas Henry Martin,	MAJ(FTC)	-	C	01.09.03	HQ 3 CDO BDE RM
Jermy, Stephen Charles, BSc, MPhil, pce, pcea	CDRE(FTC)	X	O	10.09.02	MOD (LONDON)
Jermyn, Nicholas Charles, BA	MAJ(FTC)	-	LC	01.09.00	JSCSC
Jerrold, William Harry, MEng	LT(IC)	E	ME	01.09.03	GLOUCESTER
Jervis, Neil David, pce(sm)	CDR(FTC)	X	SM	30.06.99	SACT BELGIUM
Jess, Aran Ernest Kingston, BSc, MPhil	MAJ(FTC)	-	MLDR	01.10.04	45 CDO RM
Jess, Ian Michael, MA, MSc, CEng, MIMarEST, psc	CDRE(FTC)	E	ME	15.12.05	DLO BRISTOL

Name	Rank	Branch	Spec	Seniority	Where Serving
Jessiman, Sarah Irene, BDS	SGLTCDR(D)(MCC)	-		20.06.02	FORT BLOCKHOUSE
Jessop, Paul Edward, MBE, BEng, MSc, CEng, MIMechE	CDR(FTC)	E	MESM	31.12.00	NP BRISTOL
Jewson, Benjamin David, BEng	LT(IC)	X	O	01.05.04	815 FLT 211
Johansen, Stephen Paul,	LT(IC)	E	ME	01.05.04	SULTAN
John, Gareth David, MBE, BSc, PGDip, CEng, MIEE	LT CDR(FTC)	E	WE	01.09.92	JFC HQ AGRIPPA
Johns, Adrian James, CBE, ADC, BSc, pce, pcea, psc, hcsc	VADM	-	P	25.10.05	FLEET HQ WI
(SECOND SEA LORD/COMMANDER-IN-CHIEF NAVAL HOME COMMAND OCT 05)					
Johns, Leslie Ernest,	LT(FTC)	X	REG	23.07.98	CALEDONIA DLO
Johns, Michael Glynn, BSc, pcea	LT CDR(FTC)	X	O	01.10.99	MERLIN IPT
Johns, Sarah Alice Bedford, MSc, MCIPD	LT CDR(FTC)	E	TM	01.10.96	FLEET COSP&S
Johns, Tony, MSc, rcds, psc	CDRE(FTC)	E	MESM	06.04.06	NP BRISTOL
Johnson, Alex David, BSc	LT(CC)	X	P	01.01.99	DHFS
Johnson, Amanda Constance,	LT(CC)	S		01.09.00	NAVSEC
Johnson, Andrew Martin,	LT(IC)	X		01.10.05	MWS COLLINGWOOD
Johnson, Andrew Stephen, pce	CDR(FTC)	X	AAWO	31.12.99	MOD (LONDON)
Johnson, Bryan, BSc, pce	LT CDR(FTC)	X	PWO(U)	01.05.88	MWS COLLINGWOOD
Johnson, Chad Colin Burnett, BEng, CEng, MRAeS	LT CDR(FTC)	E	AE	01.04.02	815 SQN HQ
Johnson, Christopher J, BSc	SLT(IC)	X	O U/T	01.09.04	DARTMOUTH BRNC
Johnson, Grenville Philip, MBE, jsdc, pce	CDR(FTC) (Act Capt)	X	MCD	31.12.91	SAUDI AFPS SAUDI
Johnson, James Charles, MBE, BEng, MBA, CEng, MIEE	CDR(FTC) (Act Capt)	E	WESM	31.12.99	DPA BRISTOL
Johnson, Kevin, MBE	LT(FTC)	S	(S)	09.01.01	DLO BRISTOL
Johnson, Mark,	MAJ(CC)	-	P	01.10.05	846 SQN
Johnson, Mark Ralph Edward, BSc	LT(FTC)	X		01.07.98	EXPLOIT
Johnson, Mark William, BSc	LT(IC)	X	H2	01.09.02	ROEBUCK
Johnson, Matthew David, BSc	SLT(IC)	X	P U/T	01.06.04	DARTMOUTH BRNC
Johnson, Michael David, ACMI	LT CDR(FTC)	S	(W)	01.10.03	CC MAR AGRIPPA
Johnson, Paul Raymond, BEng	LT(CC)	E	AE	01.02.99	RNAS YEOVILTON
Johnson, Scott, SM(n), SM	LT(FTC)	X	SM	01.09.99	TRAFALGAR
Johnson, Sharon Valerie,	LT(SC(MD)	Q		01.09.03	NELSON (PAY)
Johnson, Symon,	LT(CC)	X	P	16.01.97	AACC MID WALLOP
Johnson, Thomas,	SLT(UCE)(IC)	E	WE U/T	01.09.05	DARTMOUTH BRNC
Johnson, Tim Paul,	LT(IC)	X		01.07.05	QUORN
Johnson, Voirrey,	LT(FC(MD) (Act Lt Cdr)	Q		25.01.96	MOD (LONDON)
Johnston, Andrew Iain, BA	LT(IC)	X	P	01.05.04	845 SQN
Johnston, Charles Gardner, MB, BCh, BAO, FFARCSI	SURG CAPT(FCC)	-	(CA)	31.12.00	MDHU DERRIFORD
Johnston, David Raymond,	LT(CC)	S		01.05.02	TRAFALGAR
Johnston, Gavin Stewart, MA	LT(CC)	X	P	01.12.98	DHFS
Johnston, Karl George,	CAPT RM(CC)	-		01.09.03	CTCRM
Johnston, Kirsten Iona, MSc	LT(IC)	E	TM	01.05.99	NELSON
Johnston, Richard Patrick, MB, BS, MRCP, MFOM, DipAvMed	SURG CAPT(FCC)	-	(CO/M)	19.08.05	MOD (LONDON)
Johnston, Timothy Alan, pce, pcea, psc(j)	CDR(FTC)	X	P	30.06.03	MOD (LONDON)
Johnstone, Clive Charles Carruthers, BSc, pce	CAPT(FTC)	X	PWO(A)	30.06.03	BULWARK
Johnstone-Burt, Charles Anthony, OBE, MA, FCIPD, pce, pcea, hcsc	CDRE(FTC)	X	P	10.01.02	JHCHQ
Joll, Simon Mark, BA, MInstAM, AMIAM	LT CDR(FTC)	S	SM	01.10.01	DLO/DG LOG (SC)
Jones, Adam Edward, BEng, pcea	LT CDR(FTC)	X	PWO(A)	01.11.02	846 SQN
Jones, Aled Lewis, MB, CHB, BSc	SURG LT(SCC)	-		06.08.03	CFLT MED(SEA)
Jones, Alun David, BA, pce, pcea	LT CDR(FTC)	X	P	01.11.97	JSCSC
Jones, Anna Louise, BA	LT(IC)	S		01.11.04	RN LOGS SCHOOL
Jones, Christopher,	SLT(IC)	E		01.01.05	SULTAN
Jones, Christopher,	MID(NE)(IC)	X	O U/T	01.09.05	DARTMOUTH BRNC
Jones, Christopher David, MSc	LT(CC)	E	WE	01.01.02	MWS COLLINGWOOD
Jones, Collin Raymond,	LT(CS)(CAS)	-		08.01.99	DNR NWE 2
Jones, Craig Antony, MBE, n	LT CDR(FTC)	X	PWO(C)	01.11.99	MOD (LONDON)
Jones, Darren Paul, MEng	SLT(IC)	E	AE U/T	01.09.03	SULTAN
Jones, David Allen, MSc	LT CDR(FTC)	E	MESM	01.10.99	FWO DEVONPORT
Jones, David Bryan, BEng, MSc, AMIMechE	LT CDR(FTC)	E	MESM	01.07.99	NP DNREAY
Jones, David Kenneth,	LT(IC)	S		01.05.03	RALEIGH
Jones, David Lloyd, BTech	LT CDR(FTC)	E	WE	01.10.02	FWO DEVONPORT
Jones, David Michael, BEng, MIEE	LT CDR(FTC)	E	WE	01.07.04	MWS COLLINGWOOD
Jones, Emmanuel Nelson Lomotetteh,	LT(IC)	X		01.01.03	TYNE
Jones, Gareth David, BSc, PGCE	LT CDR(FTC)	E	TM	01.09.03	RNICG
Jones, Gillian Anne, BEng, PhD	LT(IC)	E	TM U/T	01.05.02	RNICG

Name	Rank	Branch Spec	Seniority	Where Serving
Jones, Glyn Robert, MA(CANTAB), MA, pce, psc(j)	CDR(FTC)	X	METOC	30.06.05	MOD (LONDON)
Jones, Gordon James Lyn, BSc	LT(IC)	X		01.09.03	RFANSU
Jones, Hayley, BEng	SLT(IC)	E	WE U/T	01.03.04	MWS COLLINGWOOD
Jones, Huw Ashton, MSc	CDR(FTC)	E	MESM	31.12.00	ASM IPT
Jones, Ian Michael, BEng	LT(FTC)	E	AE	01.11.99	ILLUSTRIOUS
Jones, Lyndsey Helan, BEng	LT(IC)	E	TM	13.02.00	SULTAN AIB
Jones, Marc Robert,	SLT(IC)	S		01.01.04	CAMPBELTOWN
Jones, Mark Douglas, BEng	LT(CC)	X	O	16.01.95	702 SQN HERON
Jones, Mark Robert,	LT(IC)	E	WE	01.07.04	DLO BRISTOL
Jones, Mark Roger, BEng	LT(FTC)	E	WE	01.06.00	NELSON (PAY)
Jones, Martin Clifford, BSc, FIMarEST, pce, psc(j), n	CDR(FTC)	X	H CH	30.06.01	MOD (LONDON)
Jones, Martin David, BA	LT CDR(FTC)	X	PWO(A)	01.01.03	CAPT MCTA
Jones, Martyn Aubrey, BA, IEng, MIPlantE, MSE	LT(FTC) (Act Lt Cdr)	E	ME	13.06.97	NOTTINGHAM
Jones, Matthew Russell, MBE, BA	MAJ(FTC)	-		01.09.98	45 CDO RM
Jones, Michael, pce	LT CDR(FTC)	X	AAWO	01.03.95	FOST SEA
Jones, Nicholas Howard, BSc, PhD	LT(IC)	E	IS U/T	01.05.02	RNICG
Jones, Nigel Patrick, pce, SM(n), SM	LT CDR(FTC)	X	PWO(U)	01.02.99	UKMARBATSTAFF
Jones, Paul, pce, psc(j), MA	CDR(FTC)	X	MCD	30.06.04	FLEET COSCAP
Jones, Paul David, SM(n), SM	LT CDR(FTC)	X	SM	01.10.04	TORBAY
Jones, Philip Andrew, MA, jsdc, pce	CDRE(FTC)	X	PWO(C)	13.12.04	FLEET COSCAP
Jones, Richard William, MA, MSc, CEng, MIMarEST, psc(j)	CDR(FTC)	E	ME	30.06.02	MOD (LONDON)
Jones, Robert Peter Martyn, BA	CAPT RM(FTC)	-		01.09.03	RM WARMINSTER
Jones, Russell Keenan, PGDip, IEng, MIEE	LT(FTC)	E	MESM	19.06.98	SOVEREIGN
Jones, Simon Sean,	LT(IC)	X	AV	01.04.01	DLO TES
Jones, Stephen,	LT(IC)	E	ME	01.05.03	RNAS CULDROSE
Jones, Timothy Mark, BSc, DIPRP	LT(FTC)	MS		01.04.01	FLEET COSP&S
Jones, Toby, BA	SLT(IC)	X		01.02.04	ARGYLL
Jones, William Colston,	SLT(IC)	X		01.02.04	RNAS CULDROSE
Jones-Thompson, Michael John,	LT(FTC) (Act Lt Cdr)	X	AAWO	01.04.01	MWC PORTSDOWN
Jordan, Adrian Mark, BDS, MSc, LDS RCS(Eng)	SGCDR(D)(FCC)	-	GDP UT	31.12.98	NELSON
Jordan, Andrew Aidan, MA, pce, psc(j), n	CDR(FTC)	X	PWO(U)	30.06.05	IRON DUKE
Jordan, Anna Frances, LLB	LT(IC)	X		01.09.99	RNP TEAM
Jordan, Mark David, BSc, BEng	LT(CC)	E	WE	01.05.01	NP IRAQ
Jordan, Nicholas Stuart,	LT CDR(FTC)	E	WE	01.10.98	FLEET COSCAP
Jose, Steven, BA	LT CDR(FTC)	E	AE	01.03.02	LOAN JTEG BSC DN
Jowett, Adrian,	SURG SLT(SCC)			05.11.04	DARTMOUTH BRNC
Joyce, David Andrew, BEng, MSc, MPhil, CEng, MIEE	LT CDR(FTC)	E	WE	01.10.00	FLEET HQ WI
Joyce, David James, BEng	LT(IC)	E	ME	01.09.04	CAMPBELTOWN
Joyce, Philip, BSc, psc(j)	LT COL(FTC)	-		30.06.04	NP IRAQ
Joyce, Thomas Jeremy, pcea	LT CDR(FTC)	X	P	01.11.99	815 SQN HQ
Jubb, Clare Louise, MEng	LT(IC)	E	WE	01.09.05	LIVERPOOL
Juckes, Martin Anthony,	CDR(FTC)	E	AE	30.06.06	JSCSC
Julian, Timothy Mark,	LT CDR(FTC)	X	P	01.10.04	FLEET COSP&S

K

Kadinopoulos, Benjamin Alexander, BA	LT(FTC)	E	WE	01.09.03	DLO BRISTOL
Kantharia, Paul,	LT(IC)	E	MESM	25.06.05	SULTAN
Karsten, Thomas Michael, BA, jsdc, pce	CAPT(FTC)	X	PWO(U)	31.12.00	MWC SOUTHWICK
Kassapian, David Lee, BA, psc(j)	LT COL(FTC)	-		30.06.04	CTCRM
Kay, Paul Stuart, SM(n), SM	LT(IC)	X	SM	01.04.01	VANGUARD(PORT)
Kay, Victoria Joanne, MEng	SLT(IC)	E	WE	01.11.02	MWS COLLINGWOOD
Keam, Ian,	LT(IC)	E	AE U/T	13.08.04	LYNX OEU
Keane, Brendan Michael, BEng, MIEE	LT(IC)	E	WE	01.05.03	CORNWALL
Keane, Gillian Ann,	LT(IC)	X	ATC	01.05.03	FOST DPORT SHORE
Keane, Joseph Patrick,	SLT(IC)	X	O U/T	01.05.03	702 SQN HERON
Kearney, Paul Leonard, BDS, psc(j)o	MAJ(FTC)	-		27.04.02	SFSG
Kearsley, Iain P, BA	SLT(IC)	S		01.10.04	RALEIGH
Keay, Gordon McBain,	CAPT RM(IC)	-	SO(LE)	19.07.05	MOD (LONDON)
Keble, Kenneth Wayne Latimer, OBE, jsdc, pce, pcea	CAPT(FTC)	X	O	30.06.05	MOD (LONDON)
Keefe, Patrick Charles, BSc	CDR(FTC)	S		31.12.95	NELSON
Keegan, Amanda Claire, BSc	LT(IC)	X	P U/T	01.09.05	DHFS
Keegan, William John, BSc, CEng, MIEE, psc	CDRE(FTC)	E	WE	26.04.05	RALEIGH

Name	Rank	Branch	Spec	Seniority	Where Serving
Keeley, Stephen Peter, PGDip	LT CDR(FTC)	E	MESM	01.10.02	DRAKE SFM
Keen, Neil, BEng, MIEE	LT CDR(FTC)	E	WE	01.06.01	SOUTHAMPTON
Keenan, Benjamin F, BEng, MSc, PGDip, AMIMechE	LT(IC)	E	MESM	01.09.02	TIRELESS
Keenan, Douglas John, BSc	SLT(IC)	X	O U/T	01.05.04	RNAS CULDROSE
Kehoe, Anthony Desmond, MB, ChB	SURG LTCDR(FCC)	-		01.12.00	NELSON (PAY)
Keillor, Stuart James, SM(n)	LT(CC)	X	SM	01.09.04	SCEPTRE
Keith, Benjamin Charles, BSc	LT(CC)	X	P	01.05.00	815 FLT 226
Keith, Gary,	CHAPLAIN	CE		03.01.06	RE ENTRY(RN)
Kelbie, Ewan, MA, pce, pcea, psc(j)	CDR(FTC)	X	P	30.06.02	MOD (LONDON)
Kellett, Andrew, BEng, CEng, MIMarEST	LT CDR(FTC)	E	ME	01.10.03	FOST SEA
Kelley, Alexandra Louise, BSc	SLT(IC)	X	O U/T	01.01.04	RNAS CULDROSE
Kelley, Victoria Lee, MEng	SLT(IC)	E	AE U/T	01.09.04	BULWARK
Kelly, Anthony Paul,	MAJ(FTC)	-	SO(LE)	01.10.01	45 CDO RM
Kelly, Frank Aidan,	LT(SC(MD)	Q		01.02.02	RCDM
Kelly, Grant Jason, MA	LT(CC)	E	TM	01.09.96	ILLUSTRIOUS
Kelly, Howard Clifton, BEng	LT CDR(FTC)	E	MESM	01.04.02	ASTUTE
Kelly, John Anson, BEng	CDR(FTC)	E	ME	30.06.06	LOAN OMAN
Kelly, John Anthony, BMus, pdm	CAPT RM(CC) (Act Maj)	BS	SO(LE)	01.01.01	HQ BAND SERVICE
Kelly, Nigel James,	CHAPLAIN	CE		26.05.92	ALBION
Kelly, Patrick John,	SLT(IC)	X		01.06.04	OCEAN
Kelly, Philip Michael, BEng, MSc	MAJ(FTC)	-	P	01.09.02	800 NAS (GR7)
Kelly, Richard, pce(sm)	LT CDR(FTC)	X	SM	03.04.91	ASM IPT
Kelly, Simon Peter, BA	LT(FTC)	X	MCD	01.07.99	EXCHANGE FRANCE
Kelly, Stephen,	LT(IC)	X		01.01.03	FOST DPORT SHORE
Kelly, Thomas James, BA	CAPT RM(CC)	-	MLDR	01.09.00	EXCHANGE ARMY UK
Kelway, Jenna Rose, BEng	SLT(IC)	E	ME U/T	01.01.05	DARTMOUTH BRNC
Kemp, Alexander Charles,	CAPT RM(FTC)	-	LC	01.04.02	539 ASSLT SQN RM
Kemp, Peter,	SURG SLT(SCC)	-		20.09.04	DARTMOUTH BRNC
Kemp, Peter John, sq	MAJ(FTC)	-	MLDR	01.09.98	MOD (LONDON)
Kemp, Richard Lee, BA	LT(IC)	X		01.09.04	MERSEY
Kempsell, Ian, BSc, CEng, MIMarEST	LT CDR(FTC)	E	ME	26.06.96	VIVID
Kenchington, Robin Anthony Warwick,	MID(IC)	X	P U/T	01.11.04	RNAS CULDROSE
Kendall, Nick Robert, MEng	SLT(IC)	X	P U/T	01.02.05	DARTMOUTH BRNC
Kendall-Torry, Guyan Charles,	SLT(IC)	E	WESM	01.09.03	FWO FASLANE SEA
Kendrick, Alexander Michael, BEng	LT CDR(FTC)	E	WE	01.02.05	DLO BRISTOL
Kennan, Nicholas Paul, LLB	LT(IC) (Act Lt Cdr)	S		01.06.02	NP BOSNIA
Kenneally, Sean Joseph,	CAPT RM(FTC)	-	SO(LE)	01.01.00	1 ASSAULT GP RM
Kennedy, Catheryn Helena, BSc	LT(MC(MD)	Q	CC	07.05.98	MDHU DERRIFORD
Kennedy, Ian Christopher,	LT(SCC)	Q	RMN	26.05.02	DRAKE COB(CNH)
Kennedy, Ian James Andrew, BEng, MA, CEng, MIMarEST, psc(j)	CDR(FTC)	E	ME	30.06.03	OCEAN
Kennedy, Inga Jane, DipEd	CDR(MC(MD)	Q		30.06.05	MDHU DERRIFORD
Kennedy, Mark Paul,	SLT(IC)	X		01.11.04	DARTMOUTH BRNC
Kennedy, Nigel Henry, MSc, MIMarEST, psc	LT CDR(FTC)	E	ME	01.05.92	EXCHANGE CANADA
Kennedy, Roger John, BEng	LT(CC)	X	O	01.07.99	RNAS CULDROSE
Kennington, Lee Alexander, BSc	LT(FTC)	X	O	01.05.94	DARTMOUTH BRNC
Kennon, Stanley, BA, BD	CHAPLAIN	SF		17.09.00	FWO DEVPT SEA
Kenny, Luke E,	CAPT RM(IC)	-		01.09.04	42 CDO RM
Kenny, Stephen James, pce, MA	CAPT(FTC)	X	AAWO	30.06.05	HQ SACT
Kent, Isabel Maria, BEd	LT CDR(FTC)	W	X	20.02.99	DISC
Kent, Martin David, BSc, pce	LT CDR(FTC) (Act Cdr)	X	PWO(N)	01.05.89	2SL/CNH FOTR
Kent, Matthew John,	LT(CC)	E	ME	01.05.01	ST ALBANS
Kent, Robert Anthony John, MEng	SLT(IC)	E	WE U/T	01.01.05	DARTMOUTH BRNC
Kenward, Peter David, BSc, MA, DipFM, CEng, MRAeS, psc	CAPT(FTC)	E	AE	30.06.05	DLO YEO
Kenworthy, Leigh Keiron,	LT(MC(MD)	Q		01.04.99	MDHU PORTSMOUTH
Kenworthy, Richard Alan, BA, sq	MAJ(FTC)	-		30.04.98	DLO BRISTOL
Kerchey, Stephen John Victor, BSc, CEng, MIEE	CDR(FTC)	E	WE	31.12.00	MOD (LONDON)
Kerley, Benjamin John,	LT(IC)	X	P	01.05.03	RNAS YEOVILTON
Kern, Alastair Seymour,	MAJ(FTC)	-		01.09.00	STRIKFORNATO
Kerr, Adrian Nicholas, BEng, CEng, MIEE	LT CDR(FTC)	E	WESM	01.09.01	TORBAY
Kerr, Alan Thomas Frederick,	LT CDR(FTC)	X	PWO(U)	01.10.01	MWS COLLINGWOOD
Kerr, Jack,	LT CDR(FTC)	X		04.01.00	MWS COLLINGWOOD
Kerr, Martin,	SLT(IC)	X	P U/T	01.02.06	DARTMOUTH BRNC

Name	Rank	Branch Spec	Seniority	Where Serving
Kerr, Robert,	2LT(IC)	-	01.08.02	CTCRM LYMPSTONE
Kerr, William Malcolm McTaggart,	LT CDR(FTC)	X MCD	09.03.90	NAVSEC
Kershaw, Christopher Robert, MA, MB, BCh, FRCP, MRCS, DCH	SURG CAPT(FCC)	- (CC)	01.04.03	RH HASLAR
Kershaw, Richard James, BM	SURG LT(MC(MD)	-	07.08.02	NELSON (PAY)
Kershaw, Simon Henry Christopher, BDS, MFGDP(UK)	SG LT(D)(SCC)	-	18.07.01	NELSON
Kershaw, Steven, MA, MSc, CEng, MIEE, psc(j)	CDR(FTC)	E WESM	30.06.01	DLO BRISTOL
Kerslake, Richard William, pce, pcea	LT CDR(FTC)	X P	01.02.99	FLEET COSCAP
Kestle, Mark Edward,	LT(CC)	E ME	01.05.02	DLO BRISTOL
Kestle, Ryan,	2LT(IC)	-	01.08.01	40 CDO RM
Kettle, Richard Andrew, BA, psc(j)o	MAJ(FTC)	-	24.04.99	PJHQ
Kewley, Ian David, BA, n	LT(FTC)	X	01.08.98	LIVERPOOL
Key, Benjamin John, BSc, pce	CAPT(FTC)	X O	30.06.06	NP IRAQ
Khan, Mansoor Ali, MB, BS, MRCS	SURG LT(MC(MD)	-	01.08.01	NELSON (PAY)
Kidd, Andrew Nicholas, BSc	SLT(IC)	X	01.08.04	DARTMOUTH BRNC
Kidd, James Christian, MSc, CDipAF, psc, gw, MIEE, CEng	CDRE(FTC)	E WE	19.04.04	DPA BRISTOL
Kidd, Robert,	2LT(IC)	-	01.08.04	42 CDO RM
Kiernan, Colin Graham, BEng	LT(CC)	X P	01.05.02	815 FLT 221
Kiernan, Matthew Donal, BSc, DNE	LT(MC(MD) (Act Lt Cdr)	Q	30.05.97	FLEET COSP&S
Kierstan, Simon Janusz James, BEng	LT(IC)	E TM	01.01.01	RNICG
Kies, Lawrence Norman, BSc, PGCE	LT CDR(FTC)	E TM	01.10.03	RNICG
Kiff, Ian William,	LT(CC)	E WE	01.01.03	MWS COLLINGWOOD
Kilbane, Dominic Kevin John, BSc	LT(IC)	X SM	01.04.03	TIRELESS
Kilby, Stewart Edward, MA, pce, pcea, psc(j)	CDR(FTC)	X O	30.06.04	RNAS YEOVILTON
Kilmartin, Steven,	MAJ(IC)	-	01.10.05	FPGRM
Kimberley, Robert, BSc, n	LT CDR(FTC)	X PWO(U)	01.07.98	FLEET COMOPS NWD
Kimmons, Michael, BA, rcds	RADM	-	15.03.05	FLEET COSP&S
(FLEET-COS P AND S PERSONAL APR 06)				
King, Anthony Michael, BSc, CEng, MDA, MRAeS, MInstD	CAPT(FTC)	E AE	30.06.04	DCAE COSFORD
King, Charles Edward William, BA, FCIPD, jsdc, FCI/LOGT	CAPT(FTC)	S	30.06.04	FLEET FOTR
King, David Alexander, BA	LT(IC)	X	01.09.04	NOTTINGHAM
King, David Christopher Michael, BSc, MA, psc(j)	LT COL(FTC)	-	30.06.01	40 CDO RM
King, Edward Michael, MSc, CEng, MIEE, CDipAF, gw	CAPT(FTC)	E WE	30.06.03	JFC HQ AGRIPPA
King, Gordon Charles,	LT CDR(FTC)	E MESM	01.10.03	SUPERB
King, Iain Andrew, BSc	LT(IC)	X P	01.09.04	GANNET SAR FLT
King, Ian Jonathan, BEng	LT(IC)	E AE U/T	01.09.05	815 SQN HQ
King, Jason Matthew, PGDip	LT(IC)	E MESM	01.07.04	VENGEANCE(STBD)
King, Matthew,	MID(IC)	X P U/T	01.06.04	DARTMOUTH BRNC
King, Michael Andrew,	SLT(IC)	E WE	01.09.02	MWS COLLINGWOOD
King, Nicholas William, BEng, MSc	CDR(FTC)	E MESM	30.06.06	NEPTUNE DLO
King, Paul Christopher, MSc	LT CDR(FTC)	E ME	01.09.92	FLEET COSP&S
King, Richard Edward,	CAPT RM(IC)	- SO(LE)	19.07.05	FLEET HQ WI
King, Richard John, BSc, MA, psc(j)	MAJ(FTC)	-	01.05.01	EXCHANGE ARMY UK
King, Richard William, BSc, MPhil, pce, pcea	CDR(FTC)	X P	30.06.02	DARTMOUTH BRNC
King, Steven John,	LT CDR(FTC)	X P	01.10.04	771 SQN
King, William Robert Charles, BSc	LT(FTC)	X	01.10.00	MOD (LONDON)
King, William Thomas Poole, BEng, PGDip	LT(IC)	E MESM	01.09.01	TRAFALGAR
Kingdon, Simon Charles,	LT(IC)	S	01.01.02	RALEIGH
Kings, Simon John Nicholson, MBE, DipFM, FCMI, pce, pcea	CAPT(FTC)	X O	30.06.05	MOD (LONDON)
Kingston, Earl Anthony, BEng	LT(IC)	X P	01.09.02	814 SQN
Kingwell, John Matthew Leonard, pce, psc(j), MA	CAPT(FTC)	X PWO(U)	30.06.05	FLEET HQ WI
Kirby, Stephen Redvers, BSc, MA, pce, pcea, psc, ocds(USN), hcsc	CDRE(FTC)	X O	06.12.02	FLEET COSCAP
Kirk, Adrian Christopher, BEng	LT CDR(FTC)	E AE	01.05.05	AH IPT
Kirk, Kearney Robert,	CAPT RM(IC)	- SO(LE)	19.07.05	1 ASSAULT GP RM
Kirkby, Stephen James, BSc	LT(IC)	X	01.09.03	MWS COLLINGWOOD
Kirkham, Simon Philip, pcea	LT CDR(FTC)	X P	01.10.04	771 SQN
Kirkup, John Paul, BSc, MA, psc(j)	CDR(FTC)	E TM	30.06.03	JDCC
Kirkwood, Tristram Andrew Harry, BSc, pce	LT CDR(FTC)	X PWO(U)	01.11.02	UKMARBATSTAFF
Kirwan, John Anthony,	LT(CC)	S	07.04.02	AFPAA(CENTURION)
Kissane, Robert Edward Thomas, BEng, MSc	CDR(FTC)	E WE	30.06.03	CV(F) IPT
Kitchen, Bethan, BEng	LT(CC)	E AE	01.07.00	JF HARROLE OFF
Kitchen, Stephen Anthony, BEng	LT CDR(FTC)	E AE	01.01.98	LOAN DARA
Kitteridge, Daniel James, BA	LT(CC)	X P	01.01.00	848 SQN HERON

Name	Rank	Branch	Spec	Seniority	Where Serving
Klar, Phillip,	LT(IC)	MS	SM	01.07.04	FLEET COSP&S
Klidjian, Michael Jeffrey, BSc	LT(CC)	X	FC	01.05.01	RNAS YEOVILTON
Knapp, Victoria Elizabeth, BSc	SLT(IC)	X		01.11.04	DARTMOUTH BRNC
Knibbs, Mark, BA, pce, psc(j)	CDR(FTC)	X	PWO(U)	30.06.99	D STRAT PLANS
Knight, Alastair Cameron Fergus, BSc	LT(CC)	X	P	01.03.94	849 SQN A FLT
Knight, Alexander James,	SLT(IC)	X		01.11.05	BULWARK
Knight, Andrew James Luddington,	MID(IC)	X		01.02.05	DARTMOUTH BRNC
Knight, Andrew Robert, pcea	LT CDR(FTC)	X	P	01.10.01	814 SQN
Knight, Anthony William, MBE, BSc, pce	LT CDR(FTC)	X	PWO(C)	01.02.90	JFC HQ AGRIPPA
Knight, Damon Ashley, MBE, pce	CDR(FTC)	X	AAWO	30.06.01	JDCC
Knight, David William, BSc, pce	LT CDR(FTC)	X	AAWO	01.12.00	MWS COLLINGWOOD
Knight, Diane Joy,	LT CDR(FC(MD)	Q	IC	01.10.01	MDHU DERRIFORD
Knight, James,	2LT(IC)	-		01.08.04	LOAN OTHER SVCE
Knight, Jeremy Denis,	LT CDR(FTC)	X	EW	01.10.04	FLEET COSCAP
Knight, Jonathan Michael,	LT(IC)	X		01.01.06	RAF SHAWBURY
Knight, Keith John, MBE, BSc, BTech	LT CDR(FTC)	E	WESM	01.10.03	MTS IPT
Knight, Paul James, BSc, psc(j)	CDR(FTC)	E	AE	30.06.03	JHCHQ
Knight, Paul Richard, BSc, CEng, MIMarEST, psc	CDR(FTC)	E	MESM	30.06.03	ASM IPT
Knight, Robert Harry, PGDip	LT CDR(FTC)	E	MESM	01.10.03	FWO FASLANE
Knight, Stephen,	SLT(IC)	S		01.01.03	RNAS YEOVILTON
Knill, Robin Lloyd,	LT CDR(FTC)	S	(S)	01.10.97	MOD (BATH)
Knock, Gareth Paul,	LT CDR(FTC)	S	SM	01.10.01	NEPTUNE DLO
Knott, Michael Bruce, AMNI, pce	LT CDR(FTC)	X	PWO(N)	01.02.01	FOST SEA
Knott, Thomas Michael,	SLT(IC)	X		01.02.04	MWS COLLINGWOOD
Knowles, Christopher James, BSc	LT(IC)	X	P	01.03.01	814 SQN
Knowles, David,	LT(IC)	X		01.09.04	SUTHERLAND
Knowles, Gareth Robert,	CAPT RM(CC)	-	SO(LE)	01.04.04	42 CDO RM
Knowles, John Michael, OBE, rcds, pce, pcea, psc, FRAES, MA	CAPT(FTC)	X	P	30.06.99	SULTAN AIB
Knox, Graeme Peter, LLB, PGDipL	LT(FTC)	S		01.10.99	MOD (LONDON)
Koheeallee, Mohummed Cassim Rashid Charif, BEng	LT(IC)	X	P	01.05.04	848 SQN HERON
Kohler, Andrew Philip,	LT CDR(FTC)	X	PWO(A)	01.04.02	FLEET COSCAP
Kohn, Patricia Anne, n	LT(FTC)	X		01.07.00	MWS COLLINGWOOD
Kopsahilis, Alexandros,	SLT(IC)	X		01.05.05	MWS COLLINGWOOD
Kroon, Zoe,	LT(CC)	X	FC	01.10.00	CAPT IST STAFF
Krosnar-Clarke, Steven Matthew, MSc	LT CDR(FTC)	E	TM	01.10.98	MOD (LONDON)
Kyd, Jeremy Paul, PGDIPAN, pce, n, BSc	CDR(FTC)	X	PWO(N)	30.06.04	MOD (LONDON)
Kyle, Ryan,	CAPT RM(IC)	-		01.09.05	EXCHANGE NLANDS
Kyte, Andrew Jeffery, MA, psc(j)	CDR(FTC)	S		30.06.03	PJHQ

L

Name	Rank	Branch	Spec	Seniority	Where Serving
Lacey, Catherine Margaret, BEng	LT CDR(FTC)	E	WE	01.10.00	DPA BRISTOL
Lacey, Stephen Patrick, pcea	CDR(FTC)	X	O	30.06.02	HQ1GP HQSTC
Lade, Christopher John, BSc, pce	CDR(FTC)	X	MCD	30.06.98	MWS DEF DIV SCHL
Ladislaus, Cecil James, BEng	LT(CC)	X	SM	01.01.02	TURBULENT
Laidlaw, Jonathan Murray, BEng	LT(IC)	X	P	01.01.05	RNAS YEOVILTON
Laidler, Paul James, MEng	LT(CC)	E	WE	01.12.01	CAPT IST STAFF
Lai-Hung, Jeremy Jean Paul,	LT(IC)	S	SM	01.07.03	DARTMOUTH BRNC
Laing, Iain, BEng, CEng, MIEE, NDipM	LT CDR(FTC)	E	WE	01.09.01	FLEET FOTR
Laing, Neil Andrew,	LT(IC)	X	O U/T	01.02.04	RNAS CULDROSE
Laird, Iain Alexander,	SLT(IC)	X		01.06.04	DARTMOUTH BRNC
Lake, Andrew, BA	SLT(IC)	X	P U/T	01.01.04	RNAS YEOVILTON
Lamb, Andrew Gordon, n	LT CDR(FTC)	X	PWO(A)	01.10.02	COMAMPHIBFOR
Lamb, Robert John Favell,	LT(IC)	X		01.01.06	SOUTHAMPTON
Lamb, Scott Innes,	CHAPLAIN	CE		06.01.03	DRAKE COB(CNH)
Lambert, Allison,	LT CDR(CC)	X	ATC	01.10.03	FLEET AV VL SEA
Lambert, Anthony Wayne, MB, BS, FRCS	SURG CDR(FCC)	-	(CGS)	30.06.99	MDHU DERRIFORD
Lambert, Nicholas Richard, BSc, pce	CAPT(FTC)	X	AAWO	30.06.00	ENDURANCE
Lambert, Paul, BSc, MPhil, DipFM, rcds, pce, pce(sm), hcsc	RADM	-	SM	29.06.04	FLEET COMOPS NWD
(COMOPS APR 06)					
Lambourn, Peter Neil, pce, pcea, psc	CDR(FTC)	X	O	31.12.96	EUMS
Lambourne, David John, BSc, pcea	LT CDR(FTC)	X	P	01.10.97	FLEET AV VL
L'Amie, Christopher Andrew, BA	LT(IC)	X		01.01.03	NORTHUMBERLAND

Name	Rank	Branch Spec	Seniority	Where Serving
Lamont, Samuel Neville James, MB, BSc, BCh, BAO, MRCP ....SURG LTCDR(MCC)	-		02.08.05	NELSON (PAY)
Lancashire, Antony Craig, MA..MAJ(CC)	-	LC	01.10.05	FLEET HQ WI
Lancaster, James Henry David, LLB...LT(IC)	X	SM	01.01.03	VANGUARD(PORT)
Lancaster, Rebecca Mary, BEng..LT CDR(FTC)	E	TM	01.11.99	RNICG
Lander, Martin Christopher, MA, MDA, pce, pcea, psc, psc(j)....................CDR(FTC)	X	O	30.06.95	LOAN DSTL
Landrock, Graham John, pce...LT CDR(FTC)	X	MCD	01.09.93	SAUDI AFPS SAUDI
Lane, Elizabeth Helen, ...SLT(IC)	X		01.08.05	TYNE
Lane, Matthew John,			01.01.05	SHOREHAM
Lane, Nicholas, BSc ....LT(IC)	S	SM	01.05.00	FLEET COMOPS NWD
Lane, Roger Guy Tyson, CBE, FCMI, rcds, jsdc, psc(m), fsc, hcsc..................MAJ GEN	-	WTO	06.11.03	CC MAR AGRIPPA
(DCOMHRF(L) NOV 03)				
Lane, Roland James, BEng ....SLT(IC)	E	AE U/T	01.09.04	DARTMOUTH BRNC
Lang, Alasdair John Mathieson, BA...LT(IC)	X	O	01.01.05	815 FLT 206
Lang, Andrew James Nicholas, BEng ....LT CDR(FTC)	E	AE	01.02.02	RNAS YEOVILTON
Lang, Justine Suzanne, BSc, DCHS, PGDip...LT(MCC)	Q		30.09.98	JSU NORTHWOOD
Langbridge, David Charles, MSc, CEng, MIMechE, MCGI, jsdc ....CAPT(FTC)	E	MESM	30.06.01	DLO BRISTOL
Langford, Timothy Duncan, BSc ....SLT(IC)	X	ATCU/T	01.03.04	LEDBURY
Langhorn, Nigel, ...CDR(FTC)	X	AAWO	30.06.96	FLEET COSP&S
Langley, Eric Steven, pce ....CDR(FTC)	X	AAWO	30.06.05	LOAN DSTL
Langmead, Ben, ...SLT(IC)	X	O U/T	01.05.03	RNAS CULDROSE
Langrill, Mark Philip, BEng, MSc, CEng, MRAeS..LT CDR(FTC)	E	AE	01.10.01	FLEET HQ PORTS
Langrill, Tracey Jane, MA...LT(IC)	E	TM	01.02.95	MWS COLLINGWOOD
Langrish, Gary James, ...LT CDR(CC)	X	P	01.10.02	750 SQN HERON
Lanigan, Ben Ryan, ...LT(IC)	S		01.12.02	MWS DEF DIV SCHL
Lankester, Peter, BTech, pce, pcea, psc ....CDR(FTC)	X	P	30.06.92	SA PRETORIA
Lanning, Kerry Anne, BA..LT(CC)	S		01.01.00	RN LOGS SCHOOL
Lanning, Roderick MacGregor, BSc...LT(CC)	X	FC	01.03.00	EXCHANGE RAF UK
Large, Stephen Andrew, BEng, MSc ....LT CDR(FTC)	E	ME	01.03.03	BULWARK
Latchem, Andrew James, BEng ....SLT(IC)	X	P U/T	01.01.04	RNAS YEOVILTON
Latham, Daniel Geoffrey, BSc ....SLT(IC)	X	P U/T	01.09.04	DARTMOUTH BRNC
Latham, Mark Anthony, ...CAPT RM(IC)	-	C	01.04.04	CTCRM
Latham, Neil Degge, MSc, CEng, Hf, MIMechE, jsdc............................RADM	-	ME	28.02.05	DCMT SHRIVENHAM
(DIRDEFAC FEB 05)				
Latus, Simon Harry, BSc..LT(CC)	X		01.01.02	FOST MPV SEA
Lauchlan, Robert Alexander, BSc ....LT CDR(FTC)	E	WESM	01.08.00	VANGUARD(PORT)
Laughton, Peter, MBE..LT CDR(FTC)	X	MCD	01.04.04	MWS COLLINGWOOD
Laurence, Simon Timothy, ...LT(CC)	X	O	16.01.01	824 SQN
Laurence, Timothy James Hamilton, MVO, BSc, Hf, pce, psc(j)....................RADM	-	PWO(U)	05.07.04	MOD (LONDON)
(ASST CHIEF OF DEF. STAFF(PROGRAMMES) JUL 04)				
Lauste, William Emile, BA, NDipM..LT CDR(FTC)	E	TM	01.03.99	FLEET HQ WI
Laverty, Robert Edwin, BA, SM(n)...LT CDR(FTC)	X	SM	01.02.03	MWS COLLINGWOOD
Lavery, John Patrick, MVO...CDR(FTC)	S		30.06.99	NAVSEC
Law, Duncan, ...2LT(IC)	-		01.08.02	CTCRM LYMPSTONE
Law, James Samuel, ...LT(IC)	E	MESM	01.05.03	FWO DEVONPORT
Law, John, ...LT CDR(FTC)	X	MCD	27.03.95	NORTH DIVING GRP
Law, Richard, BEng, CEng, MIEE..LT(FTC)	E	WE	01.01.00	JSCSC
Law, Samuel James, MA..LT(IC)	S		01.09.03	FOST SEA
Lawler, Jon Andrew, MBE..CDR(FTC)	X	P	30.06.05	BDS WASHINGTON
Lawrence, Linda Jane, BA...LT(CC)	X	HM	16.09.99	DARTMOUTH BRNC
Lawrence, Stephen Paul, n, CMarSci, MIMarEST......................................LT CDR(FTC)	X	H CH	01.10.93	MWS HM TG (D)
Lawrence, Stuart Peter, ...LT CDR(FTC)	S		14.01.01	FLEET COSP&S
Lawrence-Archer, Sally Elizabeth Sophia, ...SLT(IC)	X		01.06.04	DARTMOUTH BRNC
Lawrenson, Timothy Alfred Horace, MEng...LT(IC)	E	WE	01.07.05	ARK ROYAL
Laws, Philip Eric Arthur, LLB, FCMA..CDR(FTC)	S	CMA	30.06.02	DCL DEEPCUT
Lawson, Alexandra Florence, BA ....LT(CC)	S		01.01.03	FLEET COSP&S
Lawson, Geoffrey John, ...LT CDR(FTC)	X		01.10.03	EXCHANGE USA
Lawson, Stephen Jonathan, pce, pce(sm)..LT CDR(FTC)	X	SM	01.09.91	RN GIBRALTAR
Lawton, Peter, MBE...CAPT RM(FTC) (Act Maj)	-	SO(LE)	01.01.99	1 ASSAULT GP RM
Laycock, Antony, BSc, pcea...LT(FTC)	X	O	16.07.94	848 SQN HERON
Layland, Stephen, BSc, pce, psc(j), MA ....CDR(FTC)	X	PWO(N)	30.06.02	MWS EXCELLENT
Layton, Christopher, BEng..LT(CC)	E	MESM	01.05.01	DLO BRISTOL
Le Gassick, Peter James, BEng ....LT CDR(FTC)	E	TM	01.10.04	RNICG

Name	Rank	Branch	Spec	Seniority	Where Serving
Lea, John, pce, pcea, psc(j)	LT CDR(FTC)	X	O	01.01.98	MOD (LONDON)
Lea, Sebastian Augustine Pollard, n	LT CDR(FTC)	X	PWO(C)	01.11.03	FLEET FOSNNI
Leach, Sir Henry (Conyers), GCB, DL, jssc, psc	ADM OF FLEET	-		01.12.82	
Leach, Sarah Jane, BEng	LT CDR(FTC)	E	ME	01.10.03	CHATHAM
Leadbetter, Andrew John, BA	LT(CC)	X		01.11.97	2SL/CNH
Leaker, Daniel Thomas,	LT(IC)	X	P	01.05.04	RNAS YEOVILTON
Leaman, Richard Derek, OBE, pce, psc(j), hcsc	RADM	-	AAWO	06.09.05	CC MAR AGRIPPA
(COS TO CDR ALLIED NAVAL FORCES S.EUROPE SEP 05)					
Leaman, Thomas Peter,	SLT(IC)	X		01.05.04	MWS COLLINGWOOD
Leaney, Michael John, MBE, BSc	LT CDR(FTC)	X	MCD	01.03.90	SUPT OF DIVING
Leaning, David John, PGDip	LT CDR(FTC)	E	MESM	01.10.01	TRIUMPH
Leaning, Mark Vincent, BSc, MA, pcea, psc	CDR(FTC)	X	P	30.06.03	FLEET COSCAP
Leaphard, Daniel Paul,	SLT(IC)	X		01.06.03	TYNE
Lear, Stuart Francis, BA	LT(CC) (Act Lt Cdr)	S		01.09.00	NP BOSNIA
Leason, Joanna Mary Elizabeth, MB, BS	SURG LTCDR(FC(MD)	-		04.08.04	NELSON (PAY)
Leason, Nicholas Charles,	LT(CC)	X		01.05.01	PSYOPS TEAM
Leather, Nicholas William Fishwick, MSc, MB, BS	SURG LT(SC(MD)	-		07.04.03	MDHU DERRIFORD
Leaver, Ashley,	LT(IC)	E	WE	01.07.04	DLO BRISTOL
Leaver, Charmian Elizabeth Lucy, MA, MSc, PGDip	LT CDR(FTC)	X	HM2	01.07.03	FLEET COMOPS NWD
Leckey, Elizabeth Helen, BEng	LT(IC)	E	AE	01.05.05	771 SQN
Ledward, Karen Louise,	LT(CC)	S		01.01.01	DRAKE SFM
Lee, Adam,	2LT(IC)	-		01.08.02	CTCRM LYMPSTONE
Lee, Daniel John, MDA, pce, psc	CDR(FTC) (Act Capt)	X	AAWO	31.12.96	FLEET HQ PORTS 2
Lee, David Alexander, BSc	LT(IC)	E	IS	01.09.03	SULTAN
Lee, Jonathan Coling,	LT CDR(FTC)	X	MW	01.10.94	FLYING FOX
Lee, Nicholas Foden, BEng, MIMechE, pcea	LT CDR(FTC)	X	P	01.03.99	750 SQN SEAHAWK
Lee, Nigel David, pce	LT CDR(FTC)	X	AAWO	16.06.03	FLEET COSCAP
Lee, Oliver Andrew, MA	MAJ(FTC)	-		01.05.04	JSCSC
Lee, Peter Alan, BEng	LT CDR(FTC)	E	ME	01.08.99	FWO PORTSMOUTH
Lee, Philip Marsden, BSc	LT(FTC)	X	P	16.07.94	RNAS YEOVILTON
Lee, Raymond Andrew,	LT(IC)	E	WESM	01.01.04	RALEIGH
Lee, Robert,	SURG SLT(SCC)	-		15.09.04	DARTMOUTH BRNC
Lee, Steven Edward, MEng, MIEE	LT(FTC)	E	WE	01.11.99	HQ DCSA
Lee, Steven Patrick, MA, psc(j)	MAJ(FTC)	-		27.04.02	42 CDO RM
Lee, Steven Yiu Lam, BEng, CEng, MIEE	LT(FTC)	E	WE	01.12.95	DLO BRISTOL
Lee, Warren, BEng	LT CDR(FTC)	E	WE	01.06.05	MWS COLLINGWOOD
Leech, Sarah Louise, BA	LT(IC)	S		01.05.05	848 SQN HERON
Leeder, Timothy Rupert,	LT(CC)	X		01.05.02	EDINBURGH
Lee-Gallon, Timothy James,	CAPT RM(IC)	-	LC	01.09.05	NP YEMEN
Leeming, Robert John, BSc, CEng, MIMAREST	CAPT(FTC)	E	ME	30.06.00	MOD (BATH)
Leeper, James Stephen, BSc	LT(CC)	X		01.01.02	MWS COLLINGWOOD
Lees, Adrian Christopher Slater, MEng	SLT(IC)	E	ME U/T	01.01.05	SULTAN
Lees, Edward Charles, n	LT CDR(FTC)	X	PWO(C)	01.02.99	DARTMOUTH BRNC
Lees, Sarah Elizabeth,	SLT(SC(MD)	Q		01.09.02	MDHU PORTSMOUTH
Lees, Simon Neville, BEd	LT CDR(FTC)	E	TM	01.10.02	MWS COLLINGWOOD
Leese, James Frederick,	LT(IC)	E	AE(L)	01.05.02	MERLIN IPT
Leeson, Antony Richard,	LT(CC)	X	FC	01.08.02	ILLUSTRIOUS
Leigh, Clara Jane,	SLT(IC)	X		01.08.03	GLOUCESTER
Leigh, John, osc(us)	LT COL(FTC)	-	MLDR	31.12.96	SULTAN AIB
Leigh-Smith, Simon, BM, BCH, DObstRCOG,	SURG CDR(MCC)	-	GMPP	30.06.04	MDHU FRIMLEY
Dip FFP, FFAEM, FRCS(ED)A&E, MRCGP					
Leightley, Simon Mark,	LT(CC)	X	MCD	01.04.04	PENZANCE
Leighton, Matthew Richard, BA	LT(FTC)	X	P	01.06.97	848 SQN HERON
Leitch, Iain Robertson, BSc, pce	LT CDR(FTC)	X	AAWO	01.10.96	FLEET HQ PORTS 2
Leivers, Andrew James,	LT(CC)	E	ME	01.09.99	539 ASSLT SQN RM
Lemkes, Paul Douglas, pce	CAPT(FTC)	X	AAWO	30.06.05	FWO PORTS SEA
Lemon, Robert Gordon Arthur, BSc	LT CDR(FTC)	E	WESM	01.09.84	DLO BRISTOL
Leonard, Mark, BEng, MIEE	LT CDR(FTC)	E	WE	01.10.97	NELSON (PAY)
Leonard, Thomas Andrew,	SLT(IC)	X		01.07.04	RAMSEY
Leong, Melvin,	SURG SLT(SCC)	-		23.06.04	DARTMOUTH BRNC
Lerwill, Sean Simon Guy,	CAPT RM(IC)	-		01.09.04	CTCRM
Leslie, Bruce Duncan,	LT(IC)	X	O	01.05.03	849 SQN HQ

Name	Rank	Branch	Spec	Seniority	Where Serving
Lester, Rodney Leslie,	LT(FTC)	X		10.01.00	DISC
Lett, Jonathan David, n, BA	LT CDR(FTC)	X	PWO(U)	01.10.00	STANAVFORMED
Lettington, Paul David William, BEng	LT(IC)	E	TM	01.01.04	CDO LOG REGT RM
Letts, Andrew John, BEng, CEng, MIEE	LT CDR(FTC)	E	WE	01.08.03	SAT IPT
Lew-Gor, Simione Tomasi Warren, MB, CHB, MRCS	SURG LTCDR(MCC)	-		05.09.00	NELSON (PAY)
Lewins, Grant,	LT CDR(FTC)	S	(W)	01.10.04	NEPTUNE DLO
Lewis, Andrew James, BEng, CEng	LT CDR(FTC)	E	MESM	01.03.04	VANGUARD(STBD)
Lewis, Angela Bridget, BA	LT(CC)	X	O	01.09.01	GANNET SAR FLT
Lewis, Barry Morgan,	CAPT RM(IC)	-		01.09.04	40 CDO RM
Lewis, Benjamin Charles, BSc	LT(FTC)	X	P	16.05.97	LOAN OTHER SVCE
Lewis, Daniel, BEng	LT(IC)	E	P	01.12.01	848 SQN HERON
Lewis, David James,	LT CDR(FTC)	X	O	01.10.98	FLEET COSCAP
Lewis, David John, BEng, MIEE	LT CDR(FTC)	E	WE	01.09.01	PJHQ
Lewis, Gary David,	LT CDR(FTC)	S		01.09.89	DLO BRISTOL
Lewis, Guy David, BEng, CEng, MIMarEST	LT CDR(FTC)	E	ME	03.02.00	NAVSEC
Lewis, James A E,	CAPT RM(IC)	-		01.09.04	EXCHANGE ARMY UK
Lewis, John Keene, BEng, MDA, AMIEE	CDR(FTC)	E	WESM	30.06.99	MWS COLLINGWOOD
Lewis, Jonathan Munro,	LT(IC)	X	SM	25.02.05	VIGILANT(STBD)
Lewis, Kay Elisabeth,	LT(CC)	X	PWO(A)	01.07.00	OCEAN
Lewis, Keith Alan, MBA	LT CDR(FTC)	X	PWO(C)	01.10.03	RN GIBRALTAR
Lewis, Mark David, MEng	LT(CC)	E	AE	01.09.02	NP IRAQ
Lewis, Matthew Jon,	CAPT RM(IC)	-		01.09.05	SFSG
Lewis, Paul Leonard,	LT(IC)	X		08.01.01	FLEET COMOPS NWD
Lewis, Simon John, MSc, CEng, MBCS, CITP	LT CDR(CC)	E	IS	01.01.05	MWS COLLINGWOOD
Lewis, Timothy John, pce, psc(j)	LT CDR(FTC)	X	PWO(U)	05.02.95	FLEET COMOPS NWD
Lewis, Wesley Darren, BSc,	LT(IC)	X	ATCU/T	01.09.03	RNAS CULDROSE
Ley, Alastair Blevins, SM(n), SM	LT CDR(FTC)	X	SM	01.11.03	RALEIGH
Ley, Jonathan Ashley, pce, n	LT CDR(FTC)	X	PWO(A)	01.08.00	JSCSC
Leyden, Tristan Neil,	MAJ(FTC)	-		01.09.05	45 CDO RM
Leyshon, Robert John, BDS, MFGDP(UK)	SGLTCDR(D)(MCC)	-		09.01.99	JSCSC
Lias, Carl David, BSc, MEng	CDR(FTC)	E	MESM	30.06.06	JSCSC
Liddell, Matthew Lewis,	LT(FTC)	E	ME	02.05.00	ENDURANCE
Liddle, Morag Ross,	LT(IC)	X	C	16.12.05	FLEET ISS
Liddle, Richard David, BEng	LT(CC)	X	P	01.04.00	GANNET SAR FLT
Liddle, Stephen Johnstone, MA, psc(j)	MAJ(FTC)	-		01.09.01	42 CDO RM
Ligale, Eugene,	LT(IC)	X		01.01.03	NOTTINGHAM
Lightfoot, Charles David, BSc, pce, pce(sm), psc(j), MA	CDR(FTC)	X	SM	30.06.03	TALENT
Lightfoot, Richard Alan,	LT(CC)	X	O	16.02.01	RNAS CULDROSE
Lilley, David John, BSc, pce, pcea, psc(m), psc(j)	CDR(FTC)	X	O	31.12.96	UKMFTS IPT
Lilly, David Mark, BEng	LT(CC)	X	P	01.12.98	RAF SHAWBURY
Lim, Fong,	SURG LT(SCC)	-		01.09.05	DARTMOUTH BRNC
Lincoln, Keith James, BEng, MBA, CEng, MIEE	LT CDR(FTC)	E	WE	01.07.03	SUTHERLAND
Linderman, Ian Ronald, BSc, MBA	LT CDR(FTC)	E	TM	01.10.99	FLEET FOTR
Lindeyer, Matthew James, BSc	LT(CC)	X	HM	01.05.02	ENTERPRISE
Lindley, Jeannine, BSc	LT(IC)	X		01.05.04	IRON DUKE
Lindley, Nicholas Paul, BSc, MA, psc(m)	LT COL(FTC)	-		31.12.99	JSCSC
Lindsay, David Joseph, BEng	LT(IC)	X	P	01.10.03	20(R) SQN (RN)
Lindsay, Irvine Graham, MA, pce, pce(sm), psc(j)	CDR(FTC)	X	SM	30.06.06	MWS COLLINGWOOD
Lindsay, Jonathan Mark, BSc	CAPT RM(CC)	-	MLDR	01.05.01	42 CDO RM
Lindsay, Michael Henry, MB, BSc, BS	SURG LT(SC(MD))	-		06.08.03	VIGILANT(STBD)
Lindsey, Richard, pce(sm), SM(n)	LT CDR(FTC)	X	SM	30.04.00	WALNEY
Lines, James Micheal, FCIPD, MDA	CDR(FTC)	S		30.06.02	MOD (LONDON)
Ling, Christopher, MSc, MRAeS	LT CDR(FTC)	E	AE	01.03.04	FLEET COSP&S
Lintern, Robert David, BA, MSc, PGDIP, MRIN, n	LT CDR(FTC)	X	HM	01.10.01	UKMARBATSTAFF
Lipczynski, Benjamin James, BEng	LT(IC)	E	WESM	01.11.05	FOST FAS SHORE
Lippe, Peter William,	LT(IC)	X	C	02.08.02	HQ DCSA
Lippitt, Simon Thomas, BEng	LT(CC)	X	ATC	01.04.98	EXCHANGE RAF UK
Lipscomb, Paul, BSc, CEng, MIMarEST	LT CDR(FTC)	E	MESM	01.11.95	RN GIBRALTAR
Lipson, Christopher Nicholas,	LT(IC)	X		01.09.04	GRIMSBY
Lison, Andrew Christopher, BEng, MA, MSc, CEng, MIEE, psc(j)	CDR(FTC)	E	AE	30.06.04	ARK ROYAL
Lister, Mark, pce(sm)	CDR(FTC)	X	SM	30.06.04	VENGEANCE(STBD)
Lister, Matthew John Laurence, BEng	SLT(IC)	E	MESM	01.09.03	SCEPTRE

Name	Rank	Branch	Spec	Seniority	Where Serving
Lister, Shaun, BEng	SLT(IC)	E	WE U/T	01.09.04	CORNWALL
Lister, Simon, SM	LT(FTC)	X	SM	08.04.94	MOD DIS SEA
Lister, Simon Robert, OBE, MSc, AMIMechE	CDRE(FTC)	E	MESM	06.07.04	DRAKE NBC/DBUS
Lister, Stephen Richard	LT CDR(FTC)	S	SM	01.04.93	SHAPE BELGIUM
Litchfield, Julian Felix, FCIPD	CDR(FTC)	S		30.06.98	BDS WASHINGTON
Litster, Alan, MBE, BSc, psc(j)o	LT COL(FTC)	-	LC	30.06.06	MOD (LONDON)
Little, Charles Stewart Anderson, BSc, pce, pce(sm)	LT CDR(FTC)	X	SM	01.02.90	NSRS IPT
Little, Craig Martin,	LT(CC)	X	O	01.10.02	829 FLT 02
Little, George,	2LT(IC)	-		01.08.01	45 CDO RM
Little, Graeme Terence, OBE, BEng, MSc, psc(j), MCGI	CDR(FTC)	E	ME	30.06.00	ILLUSTRIOUS
Little, Jonathan Ian, BEng	SLT(IC)	E	WE U/T	01.09.04	CAMPBELTOWN
Little, Matthew Iain Graham, BSc	LT(IC)	X		01.05.01	DHU SEA
Little, Rhoderick McKeand, BSc, CDipAF, CEng, MIEE, psc	CAPT(FTC)	E	WESM	31.12.98	LOAN DSTL
Liva, Anthony, BSc	CAPT RM(CC)	-		01.09.01	45 CDO RM
Livingston, Martin Philip James, BEng	LT(IC)	E	AE	01.05.02	CHINOOK IPT
Livingstone, Alan James, MBE, ocds(No)	LT COL(FTC)	-		30.06.04	UKMILREP BRUSS
Livsey, Andrew Everard John, BA	LT(FTC)	X		01.09.99	MWS COLLINGWOOD
Llewellyn, Jonathan Gwyn,	LT(FTC)	X	AV	20.09.99	ILLUSTRIOUS
Llewelyn, Kevin,	LT CDR(FTC)	X	ATC	01.10.97	MOD (LONDON)
Lloyd, Bruce Jeremy, BSc	LT(CC)	X	P	01.04.00	815 FLT 234
Lloyd, Christopher John, NDipM	CDR(FTC)	MS		30.06.03	NAVSEC
Lloyd, David Philip John, MBCS, MCIT, MILT	LT CDR(FTC)	S		01.09.91	FLEET HQ PORTS
Lloyd, Matthew Rome,	LT(IC)	S		01.09.02	SCEPTRE
Lloyd, Paul Robert, pce, psc(j), MA	CAPT(FTC)	X	PWO(N)	30.06.06	JDCC
Lloyd, Stephen John, MSc, CEng, MIMarEST, rcds, psc	CDRE(FTC)	E	MESM	27.03.06	ASM IPT
Loadman, Dougal Richard,	LT(IC)	E	TM U/T	01.03.04	ILLUSTRIOUS
Loane, Michael MacAire,	LT CDR(CC)	X	MCD	01.06.05	SAUDI AFPS SAUDI
Lochrane, Alexandre Edmond Ross, pce, psc(j)(o)	CDR(FTC)	X	PWO(U)	30.06.04	MWC SOUTHWICK
Lock, Andrew Glenn David,	MAJ(FTC)	-		01.04.04	NELSON (PAY)
Lock, William James, BSc	LT(IC)	X	O	01.05.02	814 SQN
Locke, Katie-Jane Charlotte, BA	SLT(IC)	S		01.09.04	DARTMOUTH BRNC
Locke, Nicholas Michael, BEng, PGDip	LT(IC)	E	MESM	01.09.04	VENGEANCE(STBD)
Lockett, John Brian, n	LT CDR(FTC)	X	PWO(U)	01.04.04	EDINBURGH
Lockhart, John Brian,	LT(IC)	E	AE	01.07.04	FLEET COSP&S
Loewendahl, Sara, BA	SLT(IC)	X		01.06.04	DARTMOUTH BRNC
Lofthouse, Ian, MA	CAPT(FTC)	E	MESM	30.06.05	NEPTUNE DLO
Logan, John Gordon, BA, PGCE, MISM	LT(SC(MD))	Q	RNT	27.07.96	MDHU PORTSMOUTH
Logan, Joseph Majella,	LT CDR(FTC)	X	FC	01.10.03	RNAS YEOVILTON
London, Nicholas John,	SLT(IC)	E	WE	01.09.03	MWS COLLINGWOOD
Long, Adrian Montague, BEng, MA, MSc, CEng, MIEE, psc(j)	CDR(FTC)	E	WE	30.06.06	FLEET COSP&S
Long, Anthony Donald, pce, pcea, psc(j)	CDR(FTC)	X	O	30.06.04	PJHQ
Long, Hugh Andrew,	CAPT RM(IC)	-		01.09.05	42 CDO RM
Long, Michael Selden,	LT(FTC)	X	MW	01.04.96	PJHQ
Long, Richard Peter,	CAPT RM(CC)	BS	SO(LE)	01.04.04	BRNC BAND
Long, Stuart, BSc	LT(CC)	X		01.01.97	ECHO
Longman, Matthew Stephen, BEng	LT(IC)	E	ME	01.09.04	LANCASTER
Longmore, David, BM	SURG LT(SCC)	-		04.08.04	CFLT MED(SEA)
Lord, Andrew Stephen, BA, PGCE, M ED, MCIPD	LT CDR(FTC)	E	TM	01.09.87	SULTAN
Lord, Richard James,	LT(FTC)	X	P	01.10.94	EXCHANGE DENMARK
Lorenz, Rudi,	SLT(IC)	X	P U/T	01.06.03	RNAS YEOVILTON
Loring, Andrew, BSc, MA, CEng, MIMechE, psc(j)	LT CDR(FTC)	E	ME	01.03.93	DLO BRISTOL
Louden, Carl Alexander,	LT(FTC)	X	C	23.07.98	HQ SACT
Loughran, Oliver Alexander Grenville,	SLT(IC)	X		01.02.05	DARTMOUTH BRNC
Loughrey, Neil Charles,	LT(CC)	E	AE	29.04.01	ARK ROYAL
Louis, David Richard Anthony,	LT(FTC)	X		01.07.04	MONMOUTH
Louw, Len,	LT(IC)	E	WESM	01.01.02	VENGEANCE(STBD)
Lovatt, Graham John, pce	LT CDR(FTC)	X	AAWO	01.04.03	COMATG SEA
Love, John James,	LT(IC)	E	AE	01.05.03	SULTAN
Love, Julie Dawn,	LT(FTC)	X	(W)	19.09.00	DLO YEO
Love, Robert Thomas, OBE, BSc, CEng, FIMarEST, psc	CDRE(FTC)	E	ME	04.05.04	CV(F) IPT
Love, Tristram Simon Nicholas, BEng, MSc, CEng, MIEE	LT CDR(FTC)	E	WESM	01.10.00	TRENCHANT
Lovegrove, Raymond Anthony, MSc, CEng, MIEE, gw	CDR(FTC)	E	WE	30.06.04	MOD (BATH)

Name	Rank	Branch	Spec	Seniority	Where Serving
Lovell, Alistair, BDS	SG LT(D)(SC(MD)	-		25.06.03	42 CDO RM
Lovell, James Edward Charles, BA	LT(CC)	X		01.01.03	SEVERN
Lovelock, Richard Benjamin, psc(m)	LT COL(FTC)	-		30.06.94	UKMILREP BRUSS
Lovering, Tristan Timothy Alan, MBE, BSc, MA(CANTAB)	LT CDR(CC)	E	TM	01.10.04	SULTAN
Lovett, Andrew Robert,	LT(CC)	E	AE	01.06.00	SULTAN
Lovett, Michael John, BSc	CDR(FTC)	E	WE	30.06.96	SA CAIRO
Lovett, Stephen Andrew, SM	LT(FTC)	X	SM	26.04.99	COM MCC NWD
Low, Simeon Alexander Sava, BA	LT(IC)	X		01.11.05	DUMBARTON CASTLE
Lowe, Gavin James, BA	LT(IC)	X		01.05.04	MWS COLLINGWOOD
Lowe, Julian Charles, BEng, MSc, CEng, MIMarEST	LT CDR(FTC)	E	ME	01.08.99	FLEET COSP&S
Lowe, Stuart Michael, BEng, MSc, MIEE	LT CDR(FTC)	E	WE	01.12.00	FLEET COSCAP
Lowe, Timothy Miles, jsdc, pce	CAPT(FTC)	X	PWO(N)	30.06.03	MWS COLLINGWOOD
Lower, Iain Stuart, BSc, pce, n	LT CDR(FTC)	X	AAWO	01.10.99	NAVSEC
Lowson, Roderick Mark, pce	LT CDR(FTC)	X	AAWO	01.04.97	GLOUCESTER
Lowther, James Marcus, BA, PGDIPAN, pce, n	LT CDR(FTC)	X	PWO(N)	01.07.98	TYNE
Lucas, Darren Philip, BEng	LT(IC)	E	WE	01.05.02	WESTMINSTER
Lucas, Nicholas Hugh, BA	LT(IC)	X		01.05.04	MONMOUTH
Lucas, Simon Ulrick,	CAPT RM(FTC)	-	SO(LE)	01.01.01	CTCRM
Luckraft, Christopher John, BD, AKC	CHAPLAIN	CE		05.08.87	NELSON
Lucocq, Carolyn Marie, LLB	LT(CC)	S		01.05.01	2SL/CNH
Lucocq, Nicholas James, BSc, MRIN, n	LT CDR(FTC)	X	PWO(A)	01.10.04	STANAVFORLANT
Ludlow, Julian Andrew, SM(n)	LT(CC)	X	SM	01.01.02	DARTMOUTH BRNC
Lugg, John Charles,	MAJ(FTC)	-	SO(LE)	01.10.04	CDO LOG REGT RM
Luke, Christopher James,	SLT(IC)	X		01.01.05	NORTHUMBERLAND
Lumsden, Peter Imrie, BEng	LT CDR(FTC)	X	P	01.04.05	DASC
Lundie, Andrew,	SURG SLT(SCC)	-		14.10.05	DARTMOUTH BRNC
Lunn, Adam Christopher, pce, pcea	LT CDR(FTC)	X	P	01.06.94	LOAN OMAN
Lunn, David Vaughan, MB, CHB, FFARCS, DA	SURG CAPT(FTC)	-	(CA)	30.06.06	MDHU DERRIFORD
Lunn, James Francis Clive, BSc, CEng, MIMarEST, MIMechE, psc	CDR(FTC)	E	MESM	31.12.93	MOD (LONDON)
Lunn, Mark Henry Bernard, MSc, CEng, MIMarEST	LT CDR(FTC)	E	MESM	01.07.00	SUPERB
Lunn, Thomas Ramsay,	LT CDR(FTC)	X		01.01.03	DRAKE COB
Lupini, James Martin, BA	LT(IC)	X		01.10.02	CAMPBELTOWN
Luscombe, Michael David, pcea	LT CDR(FTC)	X	P	01.10.99	849 SQN HQ
Lustman, Arnold Marc, GCIS	CDR(FTC)	S	SM	30.06.02	RMC OF SCIENCE
Luxford, Charles Alexander, BA	LT(CC)	X		01.05.02	MONMOUTH
Lynas, Jonathan Francis Alistair,	LT(CC)	X	P	01.09.00	NELSON (PAY)
Lynch, Paul Patrick, MC, BA	MAJ(FTC)	-		01.10.04	BDS WASHINGTON
Lynch, Rory Denis Fenton, BA	LT CDR(FTC)	X	P	16.04.02	771 SQN
Lynch, Stephen, pcea	LT CDR(FTC)	X	O	01.10.00	FLEET COSCAP
Lynn, Henry William,	LT(FTC)	X	PWO(U)	19.09.00	BULWARK
Lynn, Ian Herbert, pce	LT CDR(FTC)	X	PWO(U)	30.06.03	MERSEY
Lynn, Sarah Louise, MSc	LT(CC)	X	O	01.02.03	814 SQN
Lynn, Steven Robert, BEng	LT CDR(FTC)	E	WE	01.04.98	JSENS IPT
Lyons, Alan Gordon, BEng	LT(CC)	E	MESM	01.03.98	NP DNREAY
Lyons, Michael John, BEng, MSc, CEng, MIMechE	LT CDR(FTC)	E	MESM	01.06.04	NP BRISTOL

M

Name	Rank	Branch	Spec	Seniority	Where Serving
Mabbott, Keith Ian, BSc	LT(CC)	X	MCD	01.01.00	RAMSEY
Macaulay, Scott Charles,	LT(IC)	X	SM	01.05.05	VANGUARD(STBD)
MacColl, Andrew Alexander James,	LT(FTC)	X	ATC	01.05.96	RNAS CULDROSE
MacCormick, James, BSc	LT(IC)	E	WESM	01.05.02	MOD (LONDON)
MacCorquodale, Mairi Ann, MA, MPhil	LT(CC)	E	IS	01.09.98	SULTAN
MacCrimmon, Stuart Stanwix, BEng	CAPT RM(IC)	-		01.09.05	COMAMPHIBFOR
MacDonald, Alasdair Iain, BSc, MDA, CEng, MIEE, MCMI	CDR(FTC)	E	WE	30.06.98	MOD (BATH)
MacDonald, Alastair James, BEng, MSc, CEng, MIEE	LT CDR(FTC)	E	WE	01.09.02	MOD (LONDON)
MacDonald, Douglas Hugh Lawson, BSc, MA, MNI, pce, ocds(US)	CDR(FTC)	X	MCD	30.06.91	FLEET FOTR
MacDonald, Fiona Jane, LLB	SLT(IC)	S		01.05.04	WESTMINSTER
MacDonald, George Ewen, LLB	CAPT(FTC)	S		30.06.00	NAVSEC
MacDonald, Glen Dey, BA	LT CDR(FTC)	X		01.05.91	JHQ/CIS LISBON
MacDonald, Ian Robert, MBE, sq	MAJ(FTC)	-		08.02.93	EXCHANGE NLANDS
MacDonald, John Robert, BEng, MA, MSc, psc(j), gw	CDR(FTC)	E	WESM	30.06.04	MOD (LONDON)
MacDonald, Katrina Louise,	LT(IC)	X		01.09.03	2SL/CNH

Name	Rank	Branch	Spec	Seniority	Where Serving
MacDonald, Michael John,	CAPT RM(IC)	-		01.09.04	CTCRM
MacDonald, Stuart Brewey,	LT(IC)	S		01.11.00	OCEAN
MacDonald-Robinson, Nicholas Ulric Spencer, pce, n	LT CDR(FTC)	X	AAWO	01.04.98	FWO PORTS SEA
MacDougall, Gavin Ross,	LT CDR(FTC)	S		01.10.98	RN LOGS SCHOOL
MacDougall, Stewart John,	LT CDR(FTC)	E	WESM	01.10.03	CAPT MCTA
Mace, Stephen Barry, BEng, CEng, MIEE, psc(j)	CDR(FTC)	E	WE	30.06.04	FLEET COSP&S
Macey, Kevin, MSc, PGCE	LT(IC)	MS		01.07.04	RCDM
MacFarlane, Gordon Thomas, BMS, MB, CHB	SURG LT(SC(MD)	-		08.10.03	VANGUARD(STBD)
MacFarlane, Iain Stuart David, BSc	LT(FTC)	X	P	01.11.93	700M MERLIN OEU
MacGillivray, Ian, BEng, CDipAF, psc(j)	CDR(FTC)	E	WE	30.06.06	MOD (LONDON)
MacIntyre, Ian Douglas,	LT(CC)	E	WESM	01.01.02	DLO BRISTOL
MacKay, Andrew Colin, BA	LT CDR(FTC)	S		01.02.04	DISC
MacKay, Colin Ross, MSc, adp	CDR(FTC)	E	IS	30.06.02	CMT SHRIVENHAM
MacKay, Graeme Angus, pce, pcea, ocds(Can)	CAPT(FTC)	X	O	30.06.06	FLEET COSCAP
MacKay, Peter, BEng	LT CDR(FTC)	E	WE	01.12.98	DLO BRISTOL
MacKay-Brown, Alan, MB, CHB, MRCGP, DRCOG, Dip FFP	SURG LTCDR(SC(MD)	-	GMPP	01.08.05	CTCRM
MacKenow, Helen Rebecca, LLB	LT(IC)	S		01.09.04	LANCASTER
MacKenzie-Green, William,	2LT(IC)	-		01.08.01	42 CDO RM
Mackey, Martin Christopher, pce	LT CDR(FTC)	X	PWO(U)	01.06.99	RAMSEY
Mackie, David Francis Sarsfield, BEng, MSc, gw, MIEE, CEng	LT CDR(FTC)	E	WE	01.03.99	FLEET COSP&S
Mackie, Simon John, MB, BS, MRCS	SURG LTCDR(FCC)	-		12.08.01	NELSON (PAY)
MacKinnon, Donald James, BEng, MPhil, pce	LT CDR(FTC)	X	PWO(U)	01.01.01	MWS COLLINGWOOD
MacLaughlin, Richard Adrian, BA	LT(CC)	X	P	01.08.98	849 SQN A FLT
MacLean, Graham Francis,	LT(IC)	X		01.09.03	FOST DPORT SHORE
MacLean, Juliet Anna, BA	LT(CC)	X		01.04.00	JSCSC
MacLean, Malcolm Thomas,	LT(FTC) (Act Lt Cdr)	E	ME	02.09.99	LIVERPOOL
MacLean, Richard Gregor,	CAPT RM(IC)	-		01.09.05	MOD (LONDON)
MacLean, Shamus MacFarlane,	LT(IC)	X	SM	01.09.04	PJHQ
Macleod, Alanna,	SG SLT(D)(SCC) (Act Sg Lt(D))	-		24.06.05	DDS SCOTLAND
Macleod, Alastair Murray, BSc	SLT(IC)	X	P U/T	01.06.04	DARTMOUTH BRNC
Macleod, James Norman, BEng, MA, MSc, CEng, MIEE, psc(j)	CDR(FTC)	E	WE	30.06.04	MOD (LONDON)
Macleod, Mark Stuart, BEng	LT CDR(FTC)	E	AE	01.02.02	LOAN JTEG BSC DN
MacMillan, Steven James,	LT(IC)	E	AE	01.07.04	846 SQN
MacNaughton, Francis George, MBE, BA, pce	LT CDR(FTC)	X	PWO(A)	01.05.87	STG BRISTOL
MacNeil, Stephen William, pcea	LT CDR(FTC)	X	P	01.10.04	824 SQN
MacPhail, Neil MacTaggart,	LT(IC)	MS		01.05.03	DRAKE SFM
MacPherson, Craig Alexander Cameron, BSc	LT(IC)	X		01.01.03	GLOUCESTER
MacPherson, William Gordon Clark,	CAPT RM(CC)	-	MLDR	01.04.02	1 ASSAULT GP RM
MacQuarrie, Gary, BEng	LT(IC)	E	ME	01.05.02	RMC OF SCIENCE
MacRae, Justin Russell,	CAPT RM(CC)	-		01.09.03	RMR BRISTOL
MacRae, Kirk, BSc	SLT(IC)	X		01.01.04	IRON DUKE
Madders, Brian Richard, MBE, QHC	PR CHAPLAIN	RC		09.09.85	FLEET HQ WI
(DGNCS-DNCS FD E PRCC N APR 06)					
Maddick, Mark Jeremy, MA, psc(j)	LT COL(FTC)	-	LC	30.06.02	FPGRM
Maddison, Hugh Richard, BEng	LT(IC)	E	ME	01.01.03	NP IRAQ
Maddison, John David,	MAJ(FTC)	-	SO(LE)	01.10.05	NAVSEC
Maddison, Paul,	LT(IC)	E	WE	01.07.04	ILLUSTRIOUS
Maden, Steven,	LT(IC)	E	WESM	08.04.05	FWO FASLANE SEA
Madgwick, Edward Charles Cowtan, BDS, MFDS,RCS	SGLTCDR(D)(FC(MD)	-		23.07.01	DDS SCOTLAND
Madigan, Lee, BA	LT(IC)	X	H2	01.03.00	FLEET FOSNNI
Maese, Philip Andrew,	MAJ(FTC)	-	SO(LE)	01.10.97	1 ASSAULT GP RM
Magan, Michael James Christopher, BEng,	CDR(FTC)	E	WE	30.06.02	PAAMS PARIS
MA, MSc, CEng, MIEE, psc(j), gw					
Magill, Alasdair Fraser,	SLT(IC)	X		01.07.04	MANCHESTER
Magowan, Robert Andrew, MBE, BSc, odc(US)	LT COL(FTC) (Act Col)	-		30.06.03	MOD (LONDON)
Magzoub, Mohayed Mohamed Mustafa,	SLT(IC)	E	ME	01.09.02	SUTHERLAND
Maher, Michael Patrick, pce	CDR(FTC)	X	AAWO	30.06.05	FLEET COSP&S
Mahoney, Andrew John,	LT(IC)	X		01.07.05	MWS COLLINGWOOD
Mahony, Christopher David Copinger, psc(j)	LT CDR(FTC)	X	P	03.04.99	RAF AWC
Mahony, David Grehan, pce, pcea	CDR(FTC)	X	O	30.06.03	MOD (LONDON)
Mailes, Ian Robert Arthur, pcea	LT CDR(FTC)	X	O	01.10.03	824 SQN
Main, Edward Stafford, BSc, CEng, MIMarEST	CDR(FTC)	E	ME	30.06.98	T45 IPT

Name	Rank	Branch Spec	Seniority	Where Serving
Main, Matthew George,	SLT(UCE)(IC)	E	WESM	01.09.04	DARTMOUTH BRNC
Mains, Graham,	LT(CC)	X	O	18.03.99	824 SQN
Mair, Brian, pce	CDR(FTC)	X	MCD	30.06.02	MOD (LONDON)
Mair, Emma Jane, MB, CHB, MRCGP, DRCOG	SURG LTCDR(MCC)	-	GMPP	06.08.02	RCDM
Malcolm, Paul Stuart, BA	LT(CC)	X	H2	01.09.02	ENTERPRISE
Malcolm, Stephen Robert, MA, FIMarEST, CMarSci, pce, psc(j)	CDR(FTC)	X	H CH	31.12.00	SCOTT
Malkin, Sharon Louise, MA	LT CDR(FTC)	E	AE	01.10.02	820 SQN
Mallabone, James John Kenneth, BSc, PGCE	LT(CC)	E	TM	01.08.97	ARK ROYAL
Mallen, David John, BEng	LT CDR(FTC)	E	AE	01.10.03	RNAS CULDROSE
Malley, Mark Paul, BEng	LT CDR(FTC)	E	WESM	01.01.01	VIGILANT(STBD)
Mallinson, Ian Paul,	LT(IC)	X		01.09.04	NORTHUMBERLAND
Mallinson, Laurence John, BSc	LT(IC)	S		01.05.03	LAIPT
Mallinson, Robert, BEng, MA, pcea, psc(j)	CDR(FTC)	E	AE	30.06.05	DLO YEO
Mallows, James Andrew,	2LT(IC)	-		01.08.04	LOAN OTHER SVCE
Malone, Martin Thomas,	LT(IC)	S		01.05.03	ROEBUCK
Malone, Mick,	LT(IC) (Act Lt Cdr)	X		29.07.01	MWS COLLINGWOOD
Malone, Roger William, BSc	LT(IC)	X	H2	01.01.03	MWS COLLINGWOOD
Malster, Dudley Andrew,	LT(IC)	X		01.05.05	ST ALBANS
Maltby, Michael Robert James, BSc, CEng, MIMarEST	CDR(FTC)	E	ME	31.12.99	DLO BRISTOL
Maltby, Richard James,	MAJ(FTC)	-		01.05.03	COMAMPHIBFOR
Mandley, Philip John, MSc	LT CDR(FTC)	E	TM	01.05.02	RNICG
Manger, Garth Stuart Cunningham, osc(us)	LT COL(FTC)	-	C	30.06.02	MOD (LONDON)
Mann, Andrew William, BSc	LT(CC)	E	WE	01.01.02	TDL IPT
Mann, Colin Andrew,	LT(CC)	E	AE	01.10.02	MERLIN IPT
Mann, David Michael, BEng	LT(CC)	X		01.06.99	JARIC
Manning, David Simon, BA	SLT(IC)	X	P U/T	01.06.04	DARTMOUTH BRNC
Manning, Duncan, MA	MAJ(FTC)	-		01.09.02	1 ASSAULT GP RM
Manning, Gary Paul,	LT(CC)	S		01.09.01	FLEET COSP&S
Mannion, Robert Victor, pce, SM	LT CDR(FTC)	X	SM	01.06.95	SETT GOSPORT
Mansergh, Andrew Christopher, BA	CAPT RM(FTC)	-	LC	01.09.01	1 ASSAULT GP RM
Mansergh, Francis Antonia, BA, n	LT(FTC)	X		01.08.98	2SL/CNH
Mansergh, Michael Peter, BA, pce, hcsc	CAPT(FTC)	X	PWO(C)	31.12.00	MWS COLLINGWOOD
Mansergh, Robert James, LLB, rcds, pce, pce(sm)	CAPT(FTC)	X	SM	30.06.00	MOD (LONDON)
Mansfield, James Alexander, BA, n	LT(FTC)	X	PWO(U)	01.10.97	YORK
Manson, Colin Robert, BSc, PGDip, MIMarEST	LT CDR(FTC)	X	METOC	01.10.98	FLEET HQ NWD
Manson, Peter Duncan, BSc	MAJ(FTC)	-	P	01.09.99	OCEAN
Manson, Thomas Edward, BSc, MA, psc(j)	CDR(FTC)	E	AE	30.06.05	CHINOOK IPT
Mant, James Nicholas, BSc, CEng, MIEE	LT CDR(FTC)	E	WE	01.10.89	FLEET COSCAP
Mantle, Mark, MB, BS	SURG LTCDR(MCC)	-		07.08.01	NELSON (PAY)
Mantri, Anand Harishankar, BEng	LT(IC)	E	TM	22.05.00	DGMC SEA
Manwaring, Roy Geoffrey,	LT CDR(FTC)	MS		01.10.04	INM ALVERSTOKE
Maples, Andrew Thomas, MB, ChB	SURG LT(MC(MD)	-		01.08.01	MDHU DERRIFORD
Marden, Tony, MEng	LT(CC)	E	WE	01.02.02	MWS COLLINGWOOD
Mardlin, Stephen Andrew, DipFM	LT CDR(FTC)	S		01.04.99	DLO/DG LOG (SC)
Mardon, Karl Fraser, MBE	LT CDR(FTC)	X	PWO(U)	02.09.92	SULTAN
Marjoribanks, Charlotte,	LT(IC)	X	P U/T	01.09.03	RNAS YEOVILTON
Mark, Robert Alan, MSc, FRIN, MNI, MInsD	RADM	-	H CH	06.01.05	RCDS
(SENIOR NAVAL MEMBER RCDS DIRECTING STAFF JAN 05)					
Markey, Adrian Philip, BEng	LT CDR(FTC)	X	PWO(U)	01.08.01	EXCHANGE USA
Markwick, Kenneth William, BSc	LT(IC)	E	AE	01.05.03	JCA IPT UK
Marland, Eunice Elizabeth, BSc	LT(CC)	S	S	01.01.02	2SL/CNH
Marlor, Andrew, MEng	SLT(IC)	E	WESMUT	01.09.03	MWS COLLINGWOOD
Marmont, Kerry Lewis, BSc, CEng, MIEE	CDR(FTC)	E	WESM	31.12.00	NEPTUNE DLO
Marok, Jani, BSc, MA, psc(j)	LT COL(FTC)	-		30.06.02	MOD (LONDON)
Marquis, Adrian Colin, BEng	LT(CC)	X	P	01.12.93	EXCHANGE GERMANY
Marratt, Richard James, BSc, MA, MCIPD	LT CDR(FTC)	E	TM	01.09.02	CTCRM
Marriott, Matthew James,	LT(FTC)	X	FC	01.09.02	LIVERPOOL
Marrison, Graham Richard, PGDip	LT(IC)	E	MESM	02.08.02	NEPTUNE DLO
Marsh, Brian Henry, MBE, BSc, pcea, psc(j)(o)	LT CDR(FTC)	X	O	01.10.99	JHQ/CIS LISBON
Marsh, David Julian, BSc, MCMI	CAPT(FTC)	S		30.06.03	FLEET COSP&S
Marsh, David Richard,	LT(IC)	S		01.01.04	HQ 3 CDO BDE RM
Marsh, Michael Peter Alan,	LT CDR(FTC)	X		01.10.02	FOST FAS SHORE

Name	Rank	Branch	Spec	Seniority	Where Serving
Marsh, Stephen William,	LT(IC)	S		01.01.04	JSCSC
Marsh, Stuart David, BA	LT(IC)	X	H2	01.05.02	SCOTT
Marshall, Alistair John, BA	LT(IC)	X	SM	01.12.99	RALEIGH
Marshall, Andrew, MEng	SLT(IC)	X	P U/T	01.05.03	RNAS YEOVILTON
Marshall, Colin George,	LT(FTC)	X		01.12.04	LOAN NEW ZEALAND
Marshall, Fleur Tiffany, MB, CHB, MRCGP, DObstRCOG, Dip FFP	SURG LTCDR(MCC)	-	GMPP	07.08.01	SULTAN
Marshall, Gavin Peter, MEng	LT(CC)	E	ME	01.01.02	DUMBARTON CASTLE
Marshall, Jason,	LT(IC)	X		01.01.04	SULTAN
Marshall, Leon,	2LT(IC)	-		01.08.01	FPGRM
Marshall, Nathan Kyle,	SLT(IC)	X	O U/T	01.01.06	DARTMOUTH BRNC
Marshall, Paul, BEng, MSc, psc(j)	CDR(FTC)	E	ME	30.06.06	MOD (LONDON)
Marshall, Richard Anthony, pce, psc(m)	CDR(FTC)	X	MCD	31.12.92	JHQ/CIS LISBON
Marshall, Richard George Carter, pce	LT CDR(FTC)	X	PWO(C)	01.05.95	JSCSC
Marson, Gary Michael,	LT CDR(FTC)	E	WE	14.10.96	RMC OF SCIENCE
Marston, Robert Matthew, BSc	SLT(IC)	X		01.11.04	DARTMOUTH BRNC
Martin, Antony John,	LT(FTC) (Act Lt Cdr)	X	C	10.12.98	NP BOSNIA
Martin, Ben Russell, BSc	SLT(IC)	X		01.05.04	EDINBURGH
Martin, Bruce Anthony, BSc, CEng, MIMechE	CDR(FTC)	E	MESM	30.06.05	JSCSC
Martin, David Charles Sarsfield, pce	LT(CC) (Act Lt Cdr)	X	PWO(U)	01.09.01	MWS COLLINGWOOD
Martin, David Leslie,	SLT(IC)	X		01.09.03	MWS COLLINGWOOD
Martin, Graham,	LT(IC)	E	ME	01.07.04	ARK ROYAL
Martin, James Nigel, BSc	LT(IC)	X		01.01.06	NOTTINGHAM
Martin, Lisa Claire, MB, BS	SURG LT(SC(MD)	-		02.08.05	MDHU PORTSMOUTH
Martin, Michael Peter, BSc, CEng, PGDIPAN, MRAeS, AMRAeS	CDR(FTC)	E	AE	30.06.01	LAIPT
Martin, Michael Terence, OBE, BEng, MA, psc	CDR(FTC)	E	ME	30.06.01	FLEET COMOPS NWD
Martin, Neil, MB, BSc, ChB, MRCP	SURG LTCDR(MC(MD)	-		04.08.04	NELSON (PAY)
Martin, Neil Douglas, BSc, pcea, psc, gdas	LT CDR(FTC(A)	X	O	01.06.87	LOAN JTEG BSC DN
Martin, Nicholas Peter, MB, BS	SURG LTCDR(SCC)	-		26.08.04	NEPTUNE DLO
Martin, Nigel, DipFD	LT(FTC) (Act Lt Cdr)	X	C	20.09.99	JHQ/CIS LISBON
Martin, Paul John, BSc, psc(m)	LT COL(FTC)	-	C	31.12.93	BDS WASHINGTON
Martin, Rebecca Jane Whitehead, BA, MA(OXON)	LT(IC)	X		01.09.04	MWS HM TG (D)
Martin, Rebecca Liane,	LT(IC)	X	O	01.09.04	815 FLT 239
Martin, Robert James, BEng	LT(CC)	E	AE	01.02.00	DLO YEO
Martin, Roger Graham, pce	LT CDR(FTC)	X	AAWO	01.09.95	LOAN DSTL
Martin, Ronald Charles John Richard, BA	CHAPLAIN	SF		03.09.96	EXCHANGE USA
Martin, Simon Charles, OBE, LVO, pce, pce(sm), psc	CAPT(FTC)	X	SM	30.06.98	FWO DEVPT SEA
Martin, Simon James, BEng, MSc, CEng, MIEE	LT CDR(FTC)	E	WESM	01.02.00	SCEPTRE
Martin, Stuart William, MSc	LT(CC)	E	AE	01.08.99	FS MASU
Martin, Timothy Frederick Wilkins, LLB, MA, rcds	CAPT(FTC) (Barrister)	S	BAR	31.12.98	NAVSEC
Martindale, Holly,	SLT(IC)	X	ATCU/T	01.04.06	RAF SHAWBURY
Martyn, Alan Wallace, MSc, CEng, MRAeS	CDR(FTC)	E	AE	31.12.00	FLEET HQ WI
Martyn, Daniel, BA, MSc, SM(n)	LT(CC)	X	SM	01.05.01	RALEIGH
Martyn, Julie Marie, BSc	LT(SC(MD)	Q		01.03.03	RNAS CULDROSE
Masilamani, Nithyanand Samuel, MB, BS, FRCS	SURG LTCDR(SCC)	-		14.01.98	MDHU PORTSMOUTH
Maskell, Bernard Malcolm, BEng	LT(IC)	E	WESM	01.05.04	VIGILANT(STBD)
Maskell-Bott, John Malcolm, adp	LT(FTC) (Act Lt Cdr)	E	MESM	16.02.84	HQ BFSAI
Mason, Andrew Clive, BSc	LT(CC)	X		01.07.98	EXPLORER
Mason, Andrew Harold, MSc	CDR(FTC)	E	AE	31.12.99	JCA IPT USA
Mason, Angus Edward, BSc	SLT(IC)	X	P U/T	01.01.04	RAF CRANWELL EFS
Mason, David, BSc	SLT(IC)	X		01.11.03	CATTISTOCK
Mason, Jeffrey Sinclair, MBE, psc	BRIG(FTC)	-	LC	01.07.05	DLO/DG LOG (SC)
Mason, Lindsay Colleen, MSc	LT CDR(FTC)	E	TM	01.10.02	MWS COLLINGWOOD
Mason, Mark John, BSc	LT(CC)	X	MCD	01.01.00	SHOREHAM
Mason, Martin,	LT CDR(FTC)	E	AE	01.10.99	DLO TES
Mason, Nicholas Hugh, BSc, MinstP, MIIT, C PHYS	CDR(FTC)	E	TM	31.12.98	NELSON
Mason, Richard James, BSc	LT(IC)	X	SM	01.05.04	SCEPTRE
Mason, Richard William, BSc, MA, DipFM, CEng, MIEE, psc	CAPT(FTC)	E	WE	30.06.01	DLO BRISTOL
Mason-Matthews, Angela,	LT(IC)	X		01.09.04	JARIC
Massey, Alan Michael, CBE, BA, PGCE, rcds, pce, psc (ACNS JUL 05)	RADM	-	AAWO	05.07.05	MOD (LONDON)
Massey, Paul,	LT CDR(FTC)	X	AV	01.10.04	SULTAN

Name	Rank	Branch	Spec	Seniority	Where Serving
Masson, Neil Graham, BSc, SM(n)	LT(IC)	X	SM	01.05.02	TRAFALGAR
Masterman, Andrew Paul, BA, MLITT	LT(CC)	X		01.09.02	ALBION
Masters, James Christopher, MA, pce, psc(j)	CDR(FTC)	X	AAWO	30.06.06	FLEET COSCAP
Masters, Richard Hilary, BTech, MA, MA(Ed), FCIPD, psc(j)	LT CDR(FTC)	E	TM	01.01.92	SHAPE BELGIUM
Mather, Graeme Philip,	CDR(FTC)	E	ME	30.06.04	CMT SHRIVENHAM
Mathews, Andrew David Hugh, MSc, CEng, MIMechE, rcds, psc	RADM	-	MESM	24.03.05	DLO BRISTOL
(DIRECTOR GENERAL NUCLEAR SEP 05)					
Mathias, Philip Bentley, MBE, rcds, pce, pce(sm), psc	CDRE(FTC)	X	SM	13.12.05	MOD (LONDON)
Mathieson, Christopher Michael, BSc	SLT(IC)	X		01.11.04	DARTMOUTH BRNC
Mathieson, Kevin Richard, pcea	CDR(FTC)	X	P	30.06.06	FSAST IPT
Mathieson, Neil Braid, BEng, isc	LT(FTC)	E	AE	01.03.00	HARRIER IPT
Matthew, Mark Jonathan,	LT(CC)	S	SM	01.09.99	DRAKE COB
Matthews, David William, BEng, MSc	CDR(FTC)	E	WESM	30.06.05	FOST SM SEA
Matthews, Gary Anthony, MB, BCH, MRCP, FRCA	SURG CDR(FCC)	-	(CA)	30.06.04	MDHU DERRIFORD
Matthews, George, psc	LT COL(FTC)	-	SO(LE)	31.12.00	RMR TYNE
Matthews, Jonathan James, MB, ChB, RCSEd	SURG LTCDR(MCC)	-		01.08.01	NELSON (PAY)
Matthews, Justin,	LT(FTC)	X	O	16.05.94	849 SQN HQ
Matthews, Paul Brian, BEng, PGDip	LT CDR(FTC)	E	TM	01.10.99	JSCSC
Matthews, Paul Kinley,	LT CDR(FTC)	S		01.10.03	FOST SEA
Matthews, Peter Ronald,	LT(FTC)	E	AE	01.04.01	MERLIN IPT
Mattin, Paul Roger,	MAJ(FTC)	-	MLDR	01.05.00	CTCRM
Mattock, Nicholas John,	LT(IC)	X	P	01.01.05	RNAS YEOVILTON
Maude, Christopher Philip, MRAeS, pcea	LT CDR(FTC) (Act Cdr)	X	P	01.10.92	LOAN JTEG BSC DN
Maude, Colin David, BEng	LT(IC)	E	AE U/T	01.03.03	HARRIER IPT
Maude, David Howard,	LT CDR(FTC)	E	AE	01.10.99	DLO YEO
Maumy, Jonathan Marc,	MID(IC)	X	P U/T	01.01.05	RAF CRANWELL EFS
Maunder, James Gilmore,	LT(IC)	E	AE	01.05.04	DLO TES
Maw, Martyn John, BSc, CEng, MIEE	LT CDR(FTC)	E	WESM	01.12.90	UDSC IPT
Mawdsley, Gareth Richard,	LT(FTC)	S		01.09.01	MOD (LONDON)
Mawdsley, Owen Rupert Tristan Charles, BSc	SLT(IC)	X	O U/T	01.09.04	DARTMOUTH BRNC
Mawer, Kieren Jon, BEng	LT(IC)	E	ME	01.09.04	MANCHESTER
Mawer, Paul Rutherford,	CAPT RM(IC)	-	SO(LE)	01.07.04	40 CDO RM
Mawer, Sarah Louise, BSc,	LT(IC)	S		01.09.04	NOTTINGHAM
Maxwell, Malcolm Scott, BSc	LT(IC)	E	IS	01.09.01	SULTAN
Maxwell, Rachel, MA, pce, psc(j), n	LT CDR(FTC)	X	PWO(U)	01.05.02	GIBRALTAR PBS
May, Colin,	LT CDR(FTC)	X		01.07.04	JFC HQ AGRIPPA
May, Damien John,	CAPT RM(CC)	-	P	01.04.02	771 SQN
May, David Mark,	LT(CC)	X	REG	01.10.02	NEPTUNE 2SL/CNH
May, Dominic Peter, MBE, MDA, sq	LT COL(FTC)	-	MLDR	30.06.05	NAVSEC
May, John William,	LT(CC)	X	P	01.07.95	RNAS YEOVILTON
May, Nigel Peter, pce, pcea	CDR(FTC)	X	P	30.06.06	GRIMSBY
May, Peter James,	LT(FTC) (Act Lt Cdr)	X	C	29.10.93	HQ DCSA
May, Steven Charles, BEng, MSc	LT CDR(FTC)	E	ME	01.07.03	EXETER
Mayberry, Peter James, MEng	LT(IC)	X	SM	01.09.04	VANGUARD(PORT)
Maybery, James Edward, psc(j)	LT COL(FTC)	-		30.06.05	FLEET HQ WI
May-Clingo, Martin Stephen,	LT(FTC) (Act Lt Cdr)	X	AV	04.04.91	FLEET COSCAP
Mayell, Julie Ann, BA	LT CDR(FTC)	W	S	01.10.02	JSU NORTHWOOD
Maynard, Andrew Thomas Westenborg, MA, osc(us)	LT COL(FTC)	-		30.06.02	COMAMPHIBFOR
Maynard, Charles Ian, BA, n	LT CDR(FTC)	X	PWO(A)	01.02.03	FOST SEA
Maynard, Paul Andrew, BSc	CAPT RM(CC)	-		01.09.01	RM WARMINSTER
Mc Allister, Steven Edward, SM(n)	LT(CC)	X	SM	01.01.02	RALEIGH
Mc Currach, Robert Henry,	LT(CC)	X	FC	01.08.00	RNAS YEOVILTON
Mc Laren, James Patrick, sq	MAJ(FTC)	-		30.04.98	FLEET HQ WI
McAllister, Andrew Wallace, BSc	SLT(IC)	E	IS U/T	01.01.04	DARTMOUTH BRNC
McAlpine, Paul Anthony, pce, psc(j)	CAPT(FTC)	X	MCD	30.06.06	FLEET HQ WI
McArdle, Martin James, BA	SLT(IC)	X	P U/T	01.02.04	RNAS YEOVILTON
McArthur, Calum James Gibb, BM, BCh, BAO, MRCGP, LRCP, DObstRCOG, Dip FFP	SURG CAPT(FCC)	-	GMPP	30.06.02	PJHQ
McAuslin, Thomas McDonald, MMedSci	CDR(FTC)	MS	SM	30.06.04	MDHU DERRIFORD
McBain, Mandy Sheila, MCIPD	LT CDR(FTC)	W	S	01.12.04	NELSON
McBarnet, Thomas Francis, BSc, pce, psc(j)	CAPT(FTC)	X	PWO(U)	30.06.06	SHAPE BELGIUM
McBeth, Gary, BEng	LT(IC)	E	MESM	01.09.05	SULTAN

Name	Rank	Branch Spec	Seniority	Where Serving
McBratney, James Alexander Grant, SM(n), SM	LT CDR(FTC) X	SM	01.11.04	TRAFALGAR
McBride, Andrew,	SLT(IC) E	ME U/T	01.09.04	YORK
McCabe, Joseph, OBE, BA, MCIPD, psc	LT COL(FTC) (Act Col) -		31.12.92	FLEET CMR
McCabe, Shane Edward Thomas, MB, BSc, BS, FRCA	SURG LTCDR(MCC) -		01.08.00	NELSON (PAY)
McCall, Gary, BA	LT(CC) X	P	01.11.98	702 SQN HERON
McCall, Iain Robert, PGDIPAN, pce	LT CDR(FTC) X	PWO(A)	01.07.96	EXETER
McCallum, Guy Peter, BSc	LT(IC) X	P	01.09.03	845 SQN
McCallum, Malcolm Donald, BA	LT(IC) X	H2	01.05.03	ENTERPRISE
McCallum, Neil Ritchie, BEng, MSc, CEng, MIMarEST, AMIMechE	LT CDR(FTC) E	ME	01.06.05	MANCHESTER
McCallum, Nicola,	LT(IC) X		01.05.05	CORNWALL
McCamphill, Paul Joseph, BEng	LT(CC) E	WE	01.01.02	DLO BRISTOL
McCann, Toby, BEng	LT(FTC) E	AE	01.12.98	829 FLT 04
McCardle, John Alexander, BSc, jsdc	LT COL(FTC) (Act Col) -	P	30.06.02	CHFHQ
McCartain, Michael Brendon William, OBE, BSc, pce, pcea, psc	CDR(FTC) X	O	31.12.98	MOD (LONDON)
McCarthy, Daniel John, BEng	LT(IC) E	ME	01.09.02	RMC OF SCIENCE
McCarthy, Steven James, BEng, MSc, CEng, MIMarEST	LT CDR(FTC) E	ME	01.10.02	OCEAN
McCavour, Bryan Darrell,	LT(IC) X		01.09.05	OCEAN
McClelland, Patrick,	SLT(IC) X		01.01.05	RNAS CULDROSE
McClement, Duncan Lewis, BEng, PGDip, AMIMechE	LT(FTC) E	MESM	01.01.99	SULTAN
McClement, Sir Timothy Pentreath, KCB, OBE, jsdc, pce, pce(sm), hcsc	VADM -	SM	07.06.04	FLEET HQ WI
(FLEET-DCINCPERSONAL APR 06)				
McCloskey, Ian Michael, BEng, CEng, MIMarEST	LT CDR(FTC) E	ME	01.10.04	ST ALBANS
McClurg, Robert James, BEng	LT(FTC) E	WE	01.03.02	MWS COLLINGWOOD
McCombe, John, MIMarEST	LT CDR(FTC) E	ME	01.09.04	SUTHERLAND
McConochie, Andrew David, BSc	LT CDR(FTC) S		16.04.96	DRAKE COB
McConville, Claire Wendy,	LT(MC(MD) Q		28.03.00	CTCRM
McCormack, Gary,	LT(FTC) E	ME	01.09.03	JSCSC
McCormack, Stuart,	SLT(IC) X	ATCU/T	01.01.04	RNAS YEOVILTON
McCormick, Peter Edward, MEng	LT(CC) X	P	15.03.98	702 SQN HERON
McCowen, Polly Anne Charlotte, BA	LT(IC) S		01.05.01	RNAS YEOVILTON
McCoy, Mark, BEng	LT(FTC) E	AE	01.11.98	DARTMOUTH BRNC
McCrea, Mark John, BEng	LT(IC) E	ME U/T	01.05.05	ST ALBANS
McCue, Duncan, MA, MSc, CEng, MIMarEST, psc(j)	CDR(FTC) E	ME	30.06.06	FLEET COSCAP
McCulley, Steven Cameron,	CAPT RM(CC) -	LC	01.04.01	40 CDO RM
McCulloch, Alen John Ronald, MA, BD	CHAPLAIN SF		12.06.04	FWO DEVPT SEA
McCullough, Karen Margaret,	LT(SC(MD) Q		01.11.04	MDHU DERRIFORD
McCutcheon, Graeme,	LT(FTC) X	P	01.02.95	DHFS
McDermott, Owen David, BEng	LT CDR(FTC) E	WE	01.10.99	HQ DCSA
McDermott-Evans, Rachel, BA	LT(IC) X	O	01.01.05	815 FLT 207
McDiarmid, Dale Ashley, BSc	LT(IC) E	IS U/T	01.01.05	DARTMOUTH BRNC
McDonald, Andrew, BEng	LT(FTC) (Act Lt Cdr) E	AE	01.03.00	HARRIER IPT
McDonald, Duncan James, BEng	LT(FTC) E	ME	01.09.98	DARTMOUTH BRNC
McDonald, Morgan James,	LT(IC) X		01.01.05	PEMBROKE
McDonnell, David Shaw, BEng, PGDIP	LT CDR(FTC) X	METOC	01.03.99	MOD (LONDON)
McDonnell, Peter William, pce, pce(sm)	CDR(FTC) X	SM	30.06.98	FWO DEVPT SEA
McDonough, Ambrose Gerrard, BSc, pce	LT CDR(FTC) X	PWO(U)	01.07.96	DARTMOUTH BRNC
McDougall, William, PGDip	LT(IC) E	MESM	01.07.04	VIGILANT(STBD)
McElwaine, Richard Ian, BSc, MDA	CAPT(FTC) E	AE	30.06.03	MOD (LONDON)
McEvoy, Lee Patrick,	LT CDR(FTC) E	EW	01.10.03	FLEET COSCAP
McEwan, Rory Daniel, BEng	LT(CC) E	WESM	01.09.02	MWS COLLINGWOOD
McEwen, Craig James,	SLT(IC) X		01.09.03	OCEAN
McFadden, Andrew,	CHAPLAIN RC		01.09.98	NELSON
McFarland, Noeleen, BSc, Dip ICN	LT(MC(MD) Q	REGM	14.01.99	JSCSC
McFarlane, Andrew Lennox, OBE, BSc, CEng, MIMechE, rcds	CDRE(FTC) E	MESM	05.01.04	CNNRP BRISTOL
McGannity, Colin Stephen, BEng	LT(CC) X	O	16.03.00	MWS COLLINGWOOD
McGannity, Sophie Elizabeth Kate,	LT(IC) X		01.09.03	NELSON
McGarel, David Francis,	CDR(FTC) S	CA	30.06.06	HQ DCSA
McGhee, Craig, BEng	MAJ(FTC) -	P	01.09.02	847 SQN
McGhie, Ian Andrew, pce, pce(sm)	CDR(FTC) X	SM	31.12.99	MOD (LONDON)
McGivern, Ryan Patrick, BSc	LT(IC) X	P	01.09.04	RNAS YEOVILTON
McGlone, Fergus Robert,	MID(IC) X		01.11.04	PENZANCE
McGlory, Stephen Joseph, BA, pce	LT CDR(FTC) X	PWO(A)	01.06.02	FLEET COMOPS NWD

Name	Rank	Branch	Spec	Seniority	Where Serving
McGrane, Richard John, pce	LT CDR(FTC)	X	C	01.10.03	MOD (LONDON)
McGrath, Wayne James,	LT(IC) (Act Lt Cdr)	S	(S)	08.01.01	HQBF CYPRUS
McGreal, Benjamin, BEng	LT(IC)	X	P U/T	01.01.03	848 SQN HERON
McGrenary, Andrew,	LT CDR(FTC)	X		01.01.94	MOD (LONDON)
McGuire, James, SM(n), SM	LT CDR(FTC)	X	SM	24.08.04	SOVEREIGN
McGuire, Michael Joseph, pce, n	LT CDR(FTC)	X	PWO(A)	31.08.98	EXCHANGE CANADA
McGunigall, Roy, MSc, PGDRP	LT CDR(FTC)	MS	(AD)	01.10.04	DRAKE SFM
McHale, Gareth John, BSc, pce, pcea	LT CDR(FTC)	X	O	01.12.91	MARS IPT
McHale, Kevan,	CDR(FTC)	E	AE	30.06.05	JHCHQ
McHugh, Richard Henry, BEng	LT CDR(FTC)	E	ME	01.03.05	NP IRAQ
McInerney, Andrew Jonathon, BSc, MA, MDA, psc(j)	LT COL(FTC)	-		30.06.06	PJHQ
McInerney, David Francis,	SLT(IC)	X		01.02.05	COM MCC NWD
McInnes, James Gerard Kenneth, BSc, MIEE	CDR(FTC)	E	WESM	30.06.05	FOST SM SEA
McIntosh, James Declan, BA, MB, BS, DRCOG, MRCGP	SURG LTCDR(MCC)	-	GMPP	26.08.02	BULWARK
McIntosh, Simon,	SURG SLT(SCC)	-		12.09.05	DARTMOUTH BRNC
McIntyre, Alastair William,	LT CDR(FTC)	X		01.10.04	MOD (LONDON)
McIntyre, Caroline,	SLT(IC)	S		01.06.03	RALEIGH
McIntyre, Louise, MA	LT(CC)	X	MW	01.01.00	PEMBROKE
McJarrow, Duncan James, BDS, MGDS RCS, LDS RCS(Eng)	SGCDR(D)(FCC)	-		30.06.00	RNAS YEOVILTON
McKay, Thomas Westley, LLB	LT(IC)	X		01.01.02	EDINBURGH
McKee, Hamish McLeod, BA, BComm	LT(CC)	X	O	01.07.97	824 SQN
McKee, Robert William,	LT(IC)	X	O	01.05.04	RNAS YEOVILTON
McKeen, Stephen Alexander, BSc	LT(IC)	X	P U/T	01.07.05	RNAS YEOVILTON
McKeever, Shaun Alexander,	LT(IC)	X	MCD	01.07.04	MWS COLLINGWOOD
McKendrick, Andrew Michael, OBE, pce, pce(sm), psc(j)	CDR(FTC)	X	N	31.12.98	MOD (LONDON)
McKenna, Danelle Rosanne,	LT(CC)	X		01.07.03	MWS COLLINGWOOD
McKenzie, David, BSc, CEng, MIMarEST	CDR(FTC)	E	ME	30.06.00	SHAPE BELGIUM
McKenzie, Hannah Kathryn,	SLT(IC)	S		01.02.04	DLO/DG LOG (SC)
McKenzie, Malcolm, MBE, pce, pcea	LT CDR(FTC)	X	O	03.03.98	HQ1GP HQSTC
McKie, Andrew, MBE, MA, pcea, psc	CDR(FTC)	X	P	31.12.00	DHFS
McKinlay, Jayne Alice Campbell, MB, BSc, BCH	SURG LT(SC(MD)	-		01.02.05	CFLT MED(SEA)
McKnight, Derek James Stewart, pce	LT CDR(FTC)	X	MCD	01.07.03	MWS COLLINGWOOD
McKnight, Nicholas William, MSc	LT CDR(FTC)	S		01.10.93	AFPAA JPA
McLachlan, Andrew Charles, BA	LT(IC)	E	TM	19.01.04	40 CDO RM
McLachlan, Jennifer Kim, MB, ChB, FRCA	SURG LTCDR(MCC)	-		17.08.00	NELSON (PAY)
McLachlan, Michael Paul, AMIMarE	LT CDR(FTC)	E	ME	01.10.02	DFTE PORTSMOUTH
McLaren, Stuart Caldwell,	CAPT RM(IC)	-		01.09.04	LN SIERRA LEONE
McLarnon, Christopher Patrick Charles, MSc	LT CDR(FTC)	E	IS	01.09.99	CSIS IPT
McLaughlan, Christopher Thomas, BSc	SLT(IC)	X	P U/T	01.05.04	DARTMOUTH BRNC
McLaughlin, Steven, MA, PGCE	LT(IC)	E	TM	01.12.98	SULTAN
McLaughlin, Vincent, BEng	LT(IC)	E	ME	01.09.04	BULWARK
McLean, Christopher Richard, MB, BS, MRCS, DP	SURG LTCDR(SCC)	-		07.08.01	NELSON (PAY)
McLean, Daniel James,	SLT(IC)	S		01.09.04	MANCHESTER
McLean, David, BSc, BD	CHAPLAIN	RC		18.09.96	RALEIGH
McLean, Rory Alistair Ian, CB, OBE, pce, hcsc	VADM	-	P	16.09.04	MOD (LONDON)
(DEPUTY CHIEF OF DEFENCE STAFF (HEALTH) SEP 04)					
McLennan, Andrew,	LT(FTC)	X	O	01.04.95	820 SQN
McLennan, Richard Glenn, BSc, fsc	CDR(FTC)	E	AE	30.06.98	JFC HQ AGRIPPA
McLeod, Katherine Yvonne Louise,	LT(IC)	X		01.12.03	CAMPBELTOWN
McLocklan, Lee Michael,	LT(FTC)	S		01.04.00	MWS COLLINGWOOD
McLone, Simon Peter, BSc	LT(IC)	X	P U/T	01.05.05	DHFS
McMahon, Daniel Steven, BSc	LT(IC)	X		01.01.04	MWS HM TG (D)
McManus, Aidan,	SLT(IC)	X		01.02.05	DARTMOUTH BRNC
McMeekin, Nicola Sarah, BDS, BSc	SGCDR(D)(MCC)	-		15.07.05	RALEIGH
McMenamin, Diarmaid Martin, MB, BS	SURG LT(SC(MD)	-	SM	06.08.03	FWO DEVPT SEA
McMichael-Phillips, Scott James, BSc, ARICS, pce	CDR(FTC)	X	H CH	31.12.99	MOD (LONDON)
McMillan, Nelson,	LT(CC)	X		01.09.04	2SL/CNH
McMorrow, Kevin Martin,	MID(IC)	X	ATCU/T	01.06.04	DARTMOUTH BRNC
McMullan, Neil Leslie, BA, MSc	LT CDR(FTC)	E	TM	01.01.01	MOD (LONDON)
McNab, Gillian Jane, BDS	SG LT(D)(SCC)	-	GDP	19.06.02	DDS SCOTLAND
McNair, Euan Alan, AFC, pce, pcea, psc	CDR(FTC)	X	P	30.06.95	DASC
McNair, Kenneth, BSc	SLT(IC)	X	P U/T	01.01.05	DARTMOUTH BRNC

Name	Rank	Branch	Spec	Seniority	Where Serving
McNally, Neville James,	LT CDR(FTC)	S		01.11.98	DLO/DG LOG (SC)
McNally, Nicholas Anthony,	LT(IC)	E	ME	01.07.04	EXETER
McNamara, Ian Martin, BEng	LT CDR(FTC)	E	WESM	01.08.04	RALEIGH
McNeill Love, Robin Michael Cox, MSc, MB, BS, MRCGP,	SURG CDR(FCC)	-	(CO/M)	30.06.96	RN GI
MFOM, DA, DRCOG, DipAvMed, Dip FFP					
McPhail, Thomas Cameron, BSc	LT(IC)	X		01.05.04	HURWORTH
McPherson, Alan,	LT(IC)	S		01.05.04	VENGEANCE(STBD)
McQuaid, Ivor Thomas,	LT(IC)	E	WESM	12.08.05	FWO DEVPT SEA
McQuaker, Stuart Ross, MSc, PGDIPAN, pce, psc(j)	CDR(FTC)	X	PWO(N)	31.12.98	RNP TEAM
McQueen, Jason Bedwell, BSc, n	LT CDR(CC)	E	TM	01.10.03	DCTS PORTS
McQueen, Patrick Graham, BSc	LT(IC)	X		01.09.04	MWS COLLINGWOOD
McQuire, Duncan Ewen Alexander, BEng, MSc, CEng, MIMechE	LT(IC)	E	ME	01.01.03	DLO BRISTOL
McRae, Philip Compton, BEng, CEng, MIEE	LT CDR(FTC)	E	WESM	01.12.99	DPA BRISTOL
McSavage, Robert Ian, BSc	LT(IC)	X	O U/T	01.12.05	702 SQN HERON
McTaggart, Douglas Alexander,	LT (FTC)	E	WE	07.02.97	JES IPT
McTear, Karen, MBE, BSc,	CDR(FTC)	E	TM	30.06.05	FLEET FOTR
McWilliams, Adrian Robert,	LT (CC)	X	O	01.05.98	815 FLT 211
McWilliams, Jacqueline Elizabeth, BA, MSc	LT CDR(FTC)	X	MW	01.09.03	ARK ROYAL
Meacher, Paul Graham, BA	LT(IC)	X	FC	01.04.03	SOUTHAMPTON
Meachin, Michael Charles,	CHAPLAIN	SF		07.07.97	RNAS CULDROSE
Meakin, Brian Richard, BSc, MBA, pcea, psc(j)	CDR(FTC)	X	O	30.06.03	MOD (LONDON)
Mealing, David William, BEng, MRAeS	LT CDR(FTC)	E	AE	01.10.04	DLO TES
Mearns, Craig McDonald, MA, psc(j)	CDR(FTC)	S		30.06.05	RN GIBRALTAR
Mears, Richard John, BSc	CAPT RM(FTC)	-	C	01.05.00	CTCRM
Medlicott, Nicholas,	LT(IC)	X	AV	28.10.05	RFANSU
Meeds, Kevin, pce, pcea, psc(j)	LT CDR(FTC)	X	O	16.12.95	FLEET COSP&S
Meek, Camilla Simpson, BEng, DIPH&S, CEng, MIMarEST, AIEMA	LT CDR(FTC)	E	ME	01.03.02	EDINBURGH
Mehlsen, Nigel Mark Nicholas,	SLT(IC)	X		01.01.04	BROCKLESBY
Mehta, Kim Louise, BEng	LT(CC) (Act Lt Cdr)	E	TM	01.09.95	RNICG
Meigh, Peter David, BSc	LT(IC)	X		01.09.04	EDINBURGH
Meikle, Robert,	LT(CC)	X		01.04.01	BULWARK
Meikle, Stuart Andrew, BSc, IEng, MIIE	LT (FTC)	E	AE	01.04.01	FLEET HQ PORTSEA
Melbourne, Steven,	CAPT RM(IC)	-	SO(LE)	15.04.02	DGMC SEA
Mellor, Adrian John, MB, BCh, FRCA	SURG CDR(FCC)	-	(CA)	30.06.03	MDHU NORTH
Mellor, Barry John, MA, FCMI, psc(j)	CDR(FTC)	S		30.06.04	NELSON
Mellor, Daniel Peter, BEng	LT(IC)	E	MESM	01.09.05	SULTAN
Mellor, Rex Geoffrey, MB, BS, BSc	SURG LT(SC(MD)	-		01.12.04	CFLT MED(SEA)
Melville-Brown, Martin Giles,	LT CDR(FTC)	S	CA	01.10.01	FLEET COSP&S
Mennecke-Jappy, Gavin William George, BA	LT(CC)	X		01.08.97	EXCHANGE GERMANY
Menzies, Bruce, BSc,	LT(CC)	X	P	01.07.01	702 SQN HERON
Menzies, Gregor Malcolm, BSc	CAPT RM(CC)	-	MLDR	01.09.02	NP AFGHANISTAN
Mercer, Andrew Jude, MB, CHB	SURG LT(MC(MD)	-		01.08.01	MDHU DERRIFORD
Mercer, Simon Jude, MB, ChB	SURG LTCDR(MCC)	-		02.08.05	NELSON (PAY)
Mercer, Stuart James, BM, BCh, MD, MRCS	SURG LTCDR(FC(MD)	-		03.08.00	NELSON (PAY)
Merchant, Ian Charles,	CDR(FTC)	S		31.12.00	DLO/DG LOG (SC)
Merchant, Jeremy Mark, CGC	MAJ(FTC)	-	SO(LE)	01.10.04	1 ASSAULT GP RM
Meredith, Nicholas, BSc, pce(sm)	LT CDR(FTC)	X	SM	01.04.94	EXCHANGE FRANCE
Merewether, Henry Alworth Hamilton, MA, pce, pcea, psc(j)	CDR(FTC)	X	O	30.06.04	FOST DPORT SHORE
Merriman, Peter Orrill, BSc, CEng, MIMechE	CDR(FTC) (Act Capt)	E	MESM	30.06.99	NEPTUNE DLO
Merritt, Jonathan James, BEng, MSc, CEng, MCGI, MIMarEST	CDR(FTC)	E	ME	30.06.05	DLO BRISTOL
Mervik, Christopher Fields, OBE, rcds, pce, pcea, ocds(Can)	CAPT(FTC)	X	P	31.12.99	NELSON
Messenger, Gordon Kenneth, DSO, OBE, BSc, psc	COL(FTC)	-	MLDR	30.06.02	PJHQ
Metcalf, Stephen William, IEng, AMIMarEST	LT (FTC)	E	MESM	01.04.01	OCLC ROSYTH
Metcalfe, Anthony Paul Warren, pce	LT CDR(FTC)	X	PWO(U)	01.12.91	FLEET COSCAP
Metcalfe, Liam Michael,	CAPT RM(CC)	-	LC	01.09.03	FPGRM
Metcalfe, Richard John,	LT (FTC)	E	WE	04.09.98	MCM3 SEA
Methven, Paul, BEng, MBA, MSc, CEng, MIMarEST	CDR(FTC)	E	MESM	30.06.04	DLO BRISTOL
Mettam, Samuel Richard, MA	LT CDR(FTC)	S		01.09.02	CUMBERLAND
Mewes, David Bruce,	CAPT RM(CC)	-	SO(LE)	01.04.02	CTCRM
Meyer, Alexander James, BA	LT(CC)	X	FC	01.12.98	MWS COLLINGWOOD
Miah, Jahangir Hussain, BSc	LT(IC)	E	IS	01.09.01	RNEAWC
Miall, Merlin Christopher, BSc	LT(IC)	X	SM	01.05.03	MWS COLLINGWOOD

Name	Rank	Branch Spec	Seniority	Where Serving
Middleditch, Thomas Clifford,	SLT(UCE)(IC)	E	ME U/T	01.09.05	DARTMOUTH BRNC
Middleton, Christopher Sydney, BEd.	MAJ(FTC)	-	LC	01.10.04	40 CDO RM
Middleton, Donna Marie, BA	LT(CC)	S		01.03.99	FLEET HQ WI
Middleton, Mark Anthony,	LT(IC)	MS		28.10.05	INM ALVERSTOKE
Middleton, Simon William Frederick, MB, BSc, BS	SURG LT(SC)(MD)	-		11.09.03	ENDURANCE
Middleton, Toby Patrick Windsor, BSc, psc(m)	LT COL(FTC)	-	LC	31.12.00	COMATG SEA
Middleton, Wayne Trevor,	LT(CC)	S		01.08.00	RN LOGS SCHOOL
Midmore, Martin Jonathan,	LT CDR(FTC)	E	AE	01.10.03	FLEET AV VL
Midwinter, Mark John, MD, MB, BS, BSc, FRCS	SURG CDR(FCC)	-	(CGS)	31.12.98	MDHU DERRIFORD
Mifflin, Michelle Jane,	LT(CC)	X		01.01.05	SEVERN
Miklinski, Anthony Stanley, BSc, DipEd, psc	CDRE(FTC)	E	TM	02.03.04	MOD (LONDON)
Milburn, Philip Kenneth, pce	CDR(FTC)	X	AAWO	31.12.00	OCEAN
Milburn, Victoria,	LT(FTC)	MS	(AD)	01.04.01	INM ALVERSTOKE
Miles, Graham John, BSc, BEng, MRAeS	LT CDR(FTC)	E	AE	07.08.00	20(R) SQN (RN)
Miles, Philip John, BA	LT(FTC)	S		01.08.98	DLO/DG LOG (SC)
Miles, Richard, MB, BS, FRCR, MRCP	SURG CDR(FCC)	-	(CX)	30.06.03	MDHU DERRIFORD
Miles, Sean Andrew,	SURG LT(SC)(MD)	-		17.05.02	VIGILANT(PORT)
Mileusnic, Christopher John, BA	SLT(IC)	X	P U/T	01.02.04	RNAS YEOVILTON
Millar, Gordon Craig, BEng	LT CDR(FTC)	E	AE	15.05.98	MOD (LONDON)
Millar, Jennifer,	SURG SLT(SCC)	-		22.04.05	DARTMOUTH BRNC
Millar, Kevin Ian, MIIE	LT(FTC)	E	MESM	02.09.99	NEPTUNE BNSL
Millar, Stuart William Sinclair, MB, BS, MRCGP, Dip FFP	SURG CDR(FCC)	-	GMPP	30.06.02	MOD (LONDON)
Millard, Andrew Robert,	LT CDR(FTC)	X		01.01.99	PJHQ
Millard, Jeremy Robert, BEng, CEng, MIMarEST, AMIEE	LT(FTC)	E	ME	01.02.98	1 ASSLT GP RM
Millen, Ian Stuart, psc(j), MA	CDR(FTC)	X	EW	30.06.05	MOD (LONDON)
Miller, Alexander David, BA	SLT(IC)	S		01.05.03	MWS COLLINGWOOD
Miller, Colin Robert, pcea	LT CDR(FTC)	X	O	01.10.99	FLEET COSCAP
Miller, David Edward,	LT CDR(FTC)	MS	(AD)	01.10.03	FLEET COSP&S
Miller, Gary,	LT CDR(FTC)	X	AV	01.10.02	FLEET COSP&S
Miller, Ian, MEng	LT(FTC)	E	MESM	01.01.00	DLO BRISTOL
Miller, Kevin Roy, BEng	LT(CC)	E	WE	01.05.01	SOUTHAMPTON
Miller, Mandy Catherine, BEng, MSc gw	LT CDR(FTC)	E	WE	01.10.04	MWS COLLINGWOOD
Miller, Paul David, pce	LT CDR(FTC)	X	AAWO	01.02.01	YORK
Milles, Olivia Kate, BA	LT(IC)	X	P	16.06.00	771 SQN
Milligan, Robert James Charles, pcea, NDipM	LT(FTC)	X	O	16.04.92	RNAS YEOVILTON
Mills, Andrew, BEng	LT CDR(FTC)	X	WESM	01.05.95	SETT GOSPORT
Mills, Gary Anthony,	LT(FTC) (Act Lt Cdr)	X		19.09.00	MWS COLLINGWOOD
Mills, Gordon William,	LT(FTC)	E	WE	01.10.98	AFPAA(CENTURION)
Mills, Ian, BEng, CEng, MIEE	LT CDR(FTC)	E	WE	01.10.01	MWS COLLINGWOOD
Mills, Sydney David Gareth,	LT(CC)	X	P	01.01.95	FLEET AV VL
Mills, Thomas Clark, BSc, MA, psc(j)	LT CDR(FTC)	E	TM	01.10.93	EXCHANGE ARMY UK
Millward, Jeremy, MBE, pcea	CDR(FTC) (Act Capt)	X	P	31.12.99	HQ1GP HQSTC
Milne, Andre Paul, MA	LT(CC)	X	P	16.12.00	847 SQN
Milne, Andrew Richard, BA	MAJ(FTC) (Act Lt Col)	-	MLDR	01.09.88	2SL/CNH FOTR
Milne, Jason Robert,	CAPT RM(IC)	-	SO(LE)	24.07.04	FLEET HQ WI
Milne, Peter Barkes, BEng	LT(FTC) (Act Lt Cdr)	X	P	16.09.91	LOAN OTHER SVCE
Milne, William John Connington, BEng, PGDip	LT(FTC)	E	MESM	01.03.00	JSCSC
Milner, Hugh Christopher, ocds(No)	MAJ(FTC)	-		01.09.89	MOD (LONDON)
Milner, Lisa Deni, BSc	LT(IC)	X	ATCU/T	01.03.06	RNAS CULDROSE
Milner, Robert Adrian, MB, BS, MRCP	SURG LTCDR(MCC)	-		07.08.01	NELSON (PAY)
Milsom, Jonathan, BEng	LT CDR(FTC)	E	AE	01.10.99	801 NAS (GR7)
Mimpriss, Graham Donald, PGDip, pce, n	LT CDR(FTC)	X	H CH	01.04.99	ROEBUCK
Minall, Mark Lee,	LT(CC)	X	PWO(C)	01.05.02	ALBION
Minall, Paul Alan, BDS, FDS,	SGLTCDR(D)(MC)(MD)	-		24.07.96	FWO DEVONPORT
Mincher, David Joseph Francis, BEng, PGDip, MIMarEST	LT CDR(FTC)	E	MESM	01.07.02	VIGILANT(PORT)
Minnikin, Stephen Barry, MSc	LT(IC)	X		01.01.05	MANCHESTER
Minshall, Darren,	SURG LT(SC)(MD)	-		02.08.05	MDHU PETERBRGH
Minty, Darren, MEng	LT(IC)	E	ME U/T	01.09.05	ARK ROYAL
Mitchell, Andrew James, BEng	SLT(IC)	X	O U/T	01.02.05	DARTMOUTH BRNC
Mitchell, Christopher David,	LT CDR(FTC)	X	MW	01.12.04	COM MCC NWD
Mitchell, Henry George Murray, pcea, psc(j)	CDR(FTC)	X	P	30.06.01	RNAS YEOVILTON
Mitchell, Jamie Dundas, SM(n)	LT(CC)	X	SM	01.09.01	RALEIGH

Name	Rank	Branch Spec		Seniority	Where Serving
Mitchell, Patrick, IEng, MIIE	LT CDR(FTC)	E	WESM	01.10.04	HQ DCSA
Mitchell, Paul Jeffrey,	LT(IC)	X	HM	01.05.03	MWS COLLINGWOOD
Mitchell, Shouna Elizabeth, BSc.	LT(IC)	S		01.01.05	DLO YEO
Mitchell, Stephen Derek, IEng, MIMarEST	LT CDR(FTC)	E	MESM	01.10.01	TRIUMPH
Mittins, Simon,	LT(IC)	X	ATC	01.05.03	RAF COTTESMORE
Mockford, James Arthur,	LT CDR(FTC)	E	AE	01.10.96	JCA IPT USA
Moffat, John William, BEng	CAPT RM(CC) (Act Maj)	-		23.04.99	JT CIMIC
Moffatt, Danny,	CAPT RM(CC)	-	MLDR	01.09.03	29 CDO REGT RA
Moffatt, Neil Robert, BSc, CEng, MIMarEST	CDR(FTC)	E	MESM	30.06.02	DLO BRISTOL
Moffatt, Roger, pcea, tp	LT CDR(FTC(A)	X	P	01.10.95	LOAN JTEG BSC DN
Mole, Andrew James, MEng, PGDip	LT(IC)	E	MESM	01.09.03	VANGUARD(PORT)
Molloy, Lynne, BSc	LT(CC)	X	ATC	01.09.02	RNAS CULDROSE
Molnar, Richard Mark,	LT(FTC)	X	PWO(A)	01.04.01	MANCHESTER
Moloney, Benjamin Gareth,	SLT(IC)	X		01.05.04	EDINBURGH
Molyneaux, Dean George, BSc, CEng, MIEE, psc	CAPT(FTC)	E	WE	30.06.04	DLO BRISTOL
Molyneux, Ian Thomas, BEng, CEng, MIEE, MCMI	LT(FTC)	E	WESM	01.08.99	FOST FAS SHORE
Moncrieff, Ian, BA, pce, hcsc	CDRE(FTC)	X	PWO(C)	10.11.03	HQ BFSAI
Money, Christopher John, BA	LT(CC)	X	H2	01.06.00	ECHO
Monger, Paul David, MSc, PGDip	LT CDR(FTC)	X	METOC	01.10.94	FLEET COMOPS NWD
Monk, Kevin Neil,	LT(CC)	X	O	01.10.02	815 FLT 246
Monk, Stephen, pce, n	LT CDR(FTC)	X	PWO(N)	01.10.04	ARK ROYAL
Monnox, Jill,	LT(CC)	X		01.09.01	MWS COLLINGWOOD
Montagu, Timothy Benjamin Edward Paulet, BSc	SLT(IC)	X		01.01.04	HURWORTH
Montague, Andrew David, BSc	LT(IC)	X		01.10.05	MCM1 SEA
Montgomery, Charles Percival Ross, CBE, BEng, rcds, pce, psc	CDRE(FTC)	X	PWO(U)	25.11.03	MWS COLLINGWOOD
Montgomery, Harvie Ellams, BSc	LT(IC)	E	TM	01.11.04	45 CDO RM
Montgomery, Michael Henry, BSc, SM	LT CDR(FTC)	X	SM	01.12.97	CNH(R)
Moody, Alistair Charles, BEng, MSc, CEng, MIMarEST	LT(FTC)	E	MESM	01.02.99	NP BRISTOL
Moody, David Christopher, BEng, CEng, MIEE	LT CDR(FTC)	E	WE	01.07.00	FLEET COSCAP
Moon, Bethany Jean, BSc	SLT(IC)	X		01.09.04	DARTMOUTH BRNC
Moon, Ian Langland, BEng	LT(CC)	E	ME	01.05.01	JSCSC
Moore, Alison Louise,	SLT(IC)	X		01.02.06	DARTMOUTH BRNC
Moore, Christopher, BA, MSc	LT CDR(FTC)	X		05.12.99	FLEET HQ WI
Moore, Christopher Ian, pce	CDR(FTC)	X	AAWO	30.06.99	FWO PORTS SEA
Moore, Christpher,	2LT(IC)	-		01.08.02	CTCRM LYMPSTONE
Moore, Jonathan Peter,	SLT(IC)	X	P U/T	01.06.03	RNAS YEOVILTON
Moore, Martin, BA	LT CDR(FTC)	X	PWO(U)	01.06.00	FOST SEA
Moore, Martin Nicholas, MBE	CDR(FTC)	E	WESM	31.12.00	MOD (LONDON)
Moore, Matthew James,	LT(CC)	X	MCD	01.04.01	TYNE
Moore, Nicholas Gerald Arthur,	LT(IC)	S		17.03.05	DLO YEO
Moore, Nicholas James,	LT(CC)	X	P	01.04.00	LOAN OTHER SVCE
Moore, Paul Grenville, BDS	SGLTCDR(D)(FCC)	-		31.12.98	FLEET COSP&S
Moore, Piers Henry George, MA, psc(j)	LT CDR(FTC)	X	SM	01.06.96	MOD (LONDON)
Moore, Richard,	2LT(IC)	-		01.08.04	FPGRM
Moore, Sara, BSc	LT(IC)	E		01.02.03	SULTAN
Moore, Sean, LLB	LT CDR(FTC) (Barrister)	S		01.09.02	FOST DPORT SHORE
Moore, Suzanne Kathryn, BEd, pce, n	LT CDR(FTC)	X	PWO(U)	01.11.01	FLEET COMOPS NWD
Moore, William Ian,	CAPT RM(IC)	-		01.09.04	FPGRM
Moores, John,	LT CDR(FTC)	S	(S)	01.10.03	FOST SEA
Moores, John Keith, BSc, pce, pce(sm)	CAPT(FTC)	X	SM	30.06.03	VANGUARD(PORT)
Moorey, Christopher George, pce, psc(j)	LT CDR(FTC) (Act Cdr)	X	PWO(A)	01.03.94	HQ BFSAI
Moorhouse, Edward James,	MAJ(FTC)	-		24.04.02	JSCSC
Moorhouse, Stephen Mark Richard, BSc, pce	LT CDR(FTC)	X	O	01.02.04	NAVSEC
Moorhouse, Suzanne Marie, BA	LT CDR(FTC)	X		29.06.02	FLEET COSP&S
Moran, Benjamin Michael,	LT(CC)	X	SM	01.01.02	VANGUARD(STBD)
Moran, Craig Andrew,	LT(FTC) (Act Lt Cdr)	X	REG	10.01.00	JFC HQ AGRIPPA
Moran, John-Paul,	SLT(IC)	E	MESMUT	01.09.03	SULTAN
Moran, Julian Toby,	CAPT RM(CC) (Act Maj)	-		28.04.99	CTCRM
Moran, Russell James,	LT(CC)	X		01.06.99	FOST MPV SEA
Moreby, Martin Francis,	LT(FTC)	X	AV	02.04.93	CHFHQ
Moreland, Michael John, BSc, CEng, MIMarEST, psc(m)	CDR(FTC)	E	MESM	30.06.00	ASTUTE
Morey, Kevin Norton,	LT(FTC)	X		01.09.02	WESTMINSTER

Name	Rank	Branch	Spec	Seniority	Where Serving
Morey, Roland George,	LT(IC)	E	ME	11.04.03	BULWARK
Morgan, Ashley Karl,	MID(NE)(IC)	X	O U/T	01.05.05	RNAS CULDROSE
Morgan, Benjamin Penoyre, BSc.	LT(IC)	X	P	01.01.02	814 SQN
Morgan, Christopher William, SM(n)	LT(IC)	X	SM	01.05.02	TIRELESS
Morgan, David,	LT(IC)	X	EW	01.05.02	MWS COLLINGWOOD
Morgan, David Henry, BSc, pce	LT CDR(FTC)	X	PWO(U)	01.10.02	FOST SEA
Morgan, Edward James Arthur,	LT(CC)	X	P	12.02.99	845 SQN
Morgan, Fiona Caroline Frances, BA	LT(IC)	X		01.07.05	CHATHAM
Morgan, Forbes Scott, BEng, MSc, MIMarEST	LT CDR(FTC)	E	ME	01.11.97	FOST SEA
Morgan, Gareth Lee,	LT(CC)	X	P	01.09.04	845 SQN
Morgan, Huw Lloyd, BSc.	CAPT RM(CC)	-		01.09.01	FLEET AV SUPPORT
Morgan, Nicholas Vaughan, MB, BS, FRCSEd, Dip SM, jsdc	SURG CAPT(FCC)	-	GMPP	30.06.00	MOD (LONDON)
Morgan, Peter Thomas, DSC, pce, psc.	CAPT(FTC)	X	PWO(A)	30.06.06	NP IRAQ
Morgan, Rachael,	SURG SLT(SCC)	-		12.01.06	DARTMOUTH BRNC
Morgan, Rachel Sara,	LT(MC)(MD)	Q	REGM	06.09.99	NELSON (PAY)
Morgan, Stephen Alexander, HNC.	LT CDR(FTC)	E	WE	01.10.97	LOAN DSTL
Morgan-Hosey, John Noel, BEng, CEng, MIMarEST	LT CDR(FTC)	E	MESM	01.10.01	NP BRISTOL
Morisetti, Neil, BSc, jsdc, pce, hcsc	RADM	-	PWO(A)	18.11.05	UKMARBATSTAFF
(COMMANDER UK MARITIME FORCES NOV 05)					
Morley, Adrian, BA.	MAJ(FTC)	-	LC	01.05.03	FLEET FOTR
Morley, James David, MA, pce, psc(j).	CDR(FTC)	X	PWO(A)	30.06.04	LANCASTER
Morley, James Ian, MSc, CEng, MIMechE	LT CDR(FTC)	E	ME	01.11.05	DLO BRISTOL
Morphet, Kathryn, BSc, MA	LT(IC)	E	TM	01.01.01	DCTS HALTON
Morrell, Andrew John,	LT CDR(FTC)	X	SM	01.10.04	1 ASSAULT GP RM
Morris, Alistair John, MB, BSc, BS.	SURG LT(SC)(MD)	-		03.08.04	45 CDO RM
Morris, Andrew Julian, BSc, MDA, CEng, MIEE, MInsD	CDR(FTC)	E	WESM	31.12.99	DLO BRISTOL
Morris, Anthony Martin,	LT(FTC)	X	P	01.07.93	829 FLT 04
Morris, Daniel Rowland,	LT(CC)	X		01.10.02	MIDDLETON
Morris, Daniel William, BEng	LT(CC)	E	ME	01.01.02	SULTAN
Morris, Harriet Sophie, BA.	LT(IC)	S		01.09.02	FWO PORTSMOUTH
Morris, James Andrew John, BSc, MA, psc(j)	LT COL(FTC)	-		30.06.05	COMAMPHIBFOR
Morris, James Edward Dallas,	CAPT RM(IC)	-		01.09.05	NP AFGHANISTAN
Morris, John Owen, BComm, MA	CHAPLAIN	CE		06.10.92	CTCRM
Morris, Kevin Ian,	LT CDR(FTC)	S	CA	01.10.03	CHATHAM
Morris, Louisa Elizabeth, MB, BS	SURG LT(SC)(MD)	-		06.08.03	SULTAN
Morris, Paul, BSc, MA(Ed), PGDip, PGCE	LT CDR(FTC)	E	TM	01.10.99	RN GIBRALTAR
Morris, Paul Edward Mannering, sq	MAJ(FTC)	-	P	01.05.97	MOD (LONDON)
Morris, Paul John, BA.	LT(IC)	X	FC	01.09.01	CAPT IST STAFF
Morris, Paul William,	LT(IC)	X	AV	01.05.04	RNAS CULDROSE
Morris, Peter John, BEng, CEng, MIEE, MDA	LT CDR(FTC)	E	WESM	10.06.92	DA SOFIA
Morris, Philip John,	LT CDR(FTC)	X	C	01.10.97	FLEET CMR
Morris, Richard Charles, BSc.	CAPT RM(CC)	-	LC	01.09.03	539 ASSLT SQN RM
Morris, Richard John, pce.	CDR(FTC)	X	PWO(A)	30.06.06	MWS COLLINGWOOD
Morris, Simon Timothy, BEng, CEng, MIEE	CDR(FTC)	E	WESM	30.06.06	JSCSC
Morrison, Graham Lindsay, BDS, ... SGCAPT(D)(FC(MD) (Commodore)	-			31.12.96	DDS HALTON
MBA, DRD, FDS RCSEdin, jsdc					
Morrison, Jurgen,	LT(IC)	S		01.05.04	MOD (BATH)
Morrison, Paul,	LT CDR(FTC)	X	O	01.10.02	EXCHANGE AUSTLIA
Morrison, Robert William, IEng, MIMarEST, MCMI	LT CDR(FTC)	E	ME	01.10.97	DFTE PORTSMOUTH
Morrison, Shaun,	LT(IC)	E	MESM	01.07.04	TALENT
Morritt, Dain Cameron, BEng, MA, MSc, psc	CDR(FTC)	E	WE	31.12.98	MOD (LONDON)
Morrow, Oliver James, BSc	SLT(IC)	X		01.01.04	SEVERN
Morse, Andrew Charles, pcea	LT CDR(FTC)	X	O	01.01.92	DLO YEO
Morse, James Anthony, BSc, pce, hcsc.	CAPT(FTC)	X	PWO(N)	30.06.03	CHATHAM
Morse, Jeremy, BSc	LT(CC)	X	P	01.12.99	845 SQN
Morshead, Christopher, BEng, CEng, MRAeS	LT CDR(FTC)	E	AE	14.05.98	LOAN JTEG BSC DN
Mortimer, Philip Robert,	LT(IC)	E	WESM	01.01.04	TRIUMPH
Mortlock, Philip Alun, BEng, MIEE	LT(CC)	E	WESM	01.01.00	MOD (LONDON)
Morton, Benjamin Alexander, BA	LT(IC)	X		01.08.04	MWS COLLINGWOOD
Morton, James Henry,	CAPT RM(IC)	-		01.09.05	OCLC BIRM
Morton, Justin Clarke,	CAPT RM(CC)	-	SO(LE)	01.04.02	CDO LOG REGT RM
Morton, Neil,	SLT(IC)	X		01.01.05	RNAS CULDROSE

Name	Rank	Branch	Spec	Seniority	Where Serving
Morton, Nigel Peter Bradshaw, BSc, MA, psc	CDR(FTC)	S		30.06.99	DLO BRISTOL
Moseley, Stephen Huw, BEng	LT(IC)	X	P	01.09.02	829 FLT 04
Moses, Christopher,	2LT(IC)	-		01.08.02	CTCRM LYMPSTONE
Moss, Jonathan Edward, MSc	SLT(IC)	X		01.06.04	DARTMOUTH BRNC
Moss, Patrick John, MIIE	LT CDR(FTC)	E	WESM	01.10.00	DLO BRISTOL
Moss, Peter, psc(m)	CDR(FTC)	X	O	30.06.04	SA MUSCAT
Moss, Richard Ashley, BSc, pce	CDR(FTC)	X	O	30.06.06	MWS COLLINGWOOD
Moss, Richard Marc, BSc	LT(IC)	E	TM	01.01.02	MWS COLLINGWOOD
Moss, Timothy Edward, MBE, CEng, IEng, FIIE, MIMarEST	LT CDR(FTC)	E	ME	01.10.97	DLO BRISTOL
Moss-Ward, Edward George,	SLT(IC)	X		01.09.03	MWS COLLINGWOOD
Mouatt, David Michael, MEng	SLT(IC)	E	AE U/T	01.09.04	CAMPBELTOWN
Mould, Christopher William,	MID(NE)(IC)	X	P U/T	01.01.06	DARTMOUTH BRNC
Mould, Philip,	LT CDR(FTC)	X	P	01.10.02	800 NAS (GR7)
Moules, Matthew Alexander John, BSc, SM(n)	LT CDR(FTC)	X	SM	01.08.04	FOST DSTF
Moulton, Simon John, BSc, pcea	LT(FTC)	X	O	01.01.92	771 SQN
Mounsey, Carl Anthony,	LT(IC)	E	TM U/T	01.01.05	DARTMOUTH BRNC
Mount, James Bruce,	LT(CC)	X	P	01.06.00	DHFS
Mountford, Penny Claire, BEng, MSc, CEng, MIMechE	LT CDR(FTC)	E	ME	01.04.06	SULTAN
Mountjoy, Brian John, MIOSH	LT CDR(FTC)	E	WESM	01.10.01	SHAPE BELGIUM
Mountjoy-Row, Robin Eric,	LT(IC)	E	AE	01.05.04	FLEET HQ PORTSEA
Mountney, Gemma Ann, BSc	LT(IC)	X	MW	01.04.02	BANGOR
Mowat, Andrew Duncan John, MA	LT(IC)	S		01.01.03	MWC PORTSDOWN
Mowatt, Patrick, PGDip	LT CDR(FTC)	X	H1	01.05.04	MWS HM TG (D)
Mowthorpe, Sarah Louise, BSc	SLT(IC)	X		01.01.05	DARTMOUTH BRNC
Moy, David Keith,	LT(FTC)	E	ME	02.05.00	DSFM PORTSMOUTH
Moys, Andrew John, MSc, FRMS	LT CDR(FTC)	X	METOC	01.10.97	FOST SEA
Muddiman, Andrew Robert, BA	MAJ(FTC)	-		01.09.03	DEF SCH OF LANG
Mudford, Hugh Christopher, psc	LT COL(FTC)	-		30.06.99	OCEAN
Mugridge, Anthony Robert, MB, ChB, FRCSEd	SURG CAPT(FCC)	-	(CGS)	30.06.98	HQBF CYPRUS
Mugridge, David Robert, MA, MSc, MNI, pce, psc(j), n	LT CDR(FTC)	X	PWO(C)	01.02.98	FLEET HQ WI
Muir, Andrew, MEng	LT(IC)	E	ME U/T	01.02.06	EDINBURGH
Muir, Katie Marie, BA, PGDipL	SLT(IC)	X		01.11.03	WALNEY
Muir, Keith, MA, pce, pcea, psc(j)	CDR(FTC)	X	O	31.12.98	ARK ROYAL
Muirhead, Barry George, BEng	LT(CC)	X	P	01.08.98	829 FLT 02
Mules, Anthony John, n	LT CDR(FTC)	X	H1	01.03.98	ENTERPRISE
Mullen, Jason John, BA	LT CDR(FTC)	X	PWO(A)	01.10.04	CORNWALL
Mullin, Peter, BSc, FIMarEST, FCMI	LT CDR(FTC)	E	MESM	01.07.93	SULTAN
Mullins, Andrew Dominic, BEng, CEng, MIMarEST	LT CDR(FTC)	E	MESM	01.12.04	SULTAN
Mullins, Natalie Elizabeth, BEng	LT(IC)	E	AE U/T	01.09.04	824 SQN
Mullis, Geoffrey, MEng	SLT(IC)	E	WESM	01.01.04	MWS COLLINGWOOD
Mullowney, Paul, BEng	LT(CC)	X	O	01.02.99	750 SQN SEAHAWK
Mulroy, Paul James,	LT(IC)	E	MESM	18.02.05	SULTAN
Mulvaney, Paul Andrew, BSc	LT CDR(FTC)	E	AE	01.06.00	SULTAN
Muncer, Richard A, BEng	CAPT RM(CC)	-		01.09.00	CDO LOG REGT RM
Munday, Stephen William, BSc	LT(IC)	E	WE	01.01.04	GLOUCESTER
Mundin, Adrian John, BSc, CEng, MIMechE	LT CDR(FTC)	E	ME	01.04.92	MOD (LONDON)
Mundy, Alan Richard,	LT(IC)	MS		01.05.02	HQ 3 CDO BDE RM
Munns, Andrew Robert, BEng, CEng, MIMarEST	CDR(FTC)	E	ME	30.06.03	JWC/CIS STAVANGR
Munns, Edward Neil,	SLT(IC)	X		01.09.03	DARTMOUTH BRNC
Munro, Helen Louise, BSc	LT(IC)	E	TM	01.09.02	SULTAN
Munro, Kenneth, BEng, CEng, MIMarEST	LT CDR(FTC)	E	ME	01.04.95	DLO BRISTOL
Munro, Michael,	LT(IC)	E	WE	01.07.04	DLO BRISTOL
Munro-Lott, Peter Robert John, pcea, psc(j)(o), MA	CDR(FTC)	X	O	30.06.06	814 SQN
Murchie, Alistair Duncan, BEng, MSc, CEng, MIMarEST	LT CDR(FTC)	E	ME	01.10.03	WESTMINSTER
Murchison, Ewen Alexander, BSc, MA, psc(j)	MAJ(FTC)	-		01.09.00	HQ 3 CDO BDE RM
Murdoch, Andrew Peter, BSc	LT CDR(FTC) (Barrister)	S	BAR	01.11.02	NAVSEC
Murdoch, Andrew William, MSc, MIEE, CEng	CDR(FTC)	E	WESM	30.06.05	MOD (LONDON)
Murdoch, Gillian Agnes, BDS	SGLTCDR(D)(MCC)	-		20.07.03	RH HASLAR
Murdoch, Stephen John, MBA	CDR(FTC) (Act Capt)	S		31.12.99	DLO/DG LOG (SC)
Murgatroyd, Andrew Clive, MBE, BSc, jsdc, pce	CDR(FTC)	X	AAWO	31.12.94	MOD (LONDON)
Murgatroyd, Kevin John, BEng, pcea	LT(CC)	X	O	01.04.00	824 SQN
Murphie, John Dermot Douglas, pce, psc(m)	CAPT(FTC)	X	MCD	30.06.04	FLEET FOTR

Name	Rank	Branch	Spec	Seniority	Where Serving
Murphy, Andrew, MSc, IEng, MIIE	LT(FTC)	E	WE	09.01.01	MWS COLLINGWOOD
Murphy, Anthony, MBA, FCIPD	CDR(FTC)	MS		30.06.02	FLEET COSP&S
Murphy, Christian John, MEng	LT(IC)	E	AE U/T	01.09.04	814 SQN
Murphy, Diccon Andrew, BSc	LT(CC)	X	P	01.04.92	RNAS YEOVILTON
Murphy, James, BSc	LT CDR(FTC)	S	SM	01.06.92	RALEIGH
Murphy, Kian Stuart, BA	MAJ(CC)	-		01.10.05	FLEET CMR
Murphy, Nicholas, MBE, MNI, pce, psc(j)	LT CDR(FTC)	X	PWO(U)	01.09.90	PJHQ
Murphy, Paul Anthony, BA, ACMA	LT CDR(FTC)	S	CMA	01.03.00	MWS COLLINGWOOD
Murphy, Peter William, MSc, BEng	LT CDR(FTC)	E	MESM	01.09.95	ASM IPT
Murphy, Stephen Mark, BEng	LT CDR(FTC)	E	ME	01.08.04	CORNWALL
Murphy, Steven Robert Anthony, BA, pce(sm)	LT CDR(FTC)	X	SM	01.09.98	FLEET COSCAP
Murphy, Vanessa Jane, BA	LT(CC)	S		01.07.99	IRON DUKE
Murray, Alexander Bruce, psc(j)	MAJ(FTC)	-		26.04.00	40 CDO RM
Murray, Alister,	LT(CC)	MS		01.09.01	HQ DMETA
Murray, Andrew Sidney,	LT CDR(FTC)	X	P	01.10.99	GANNET SAR FLT
Murray, Gillian Patricia, BA	SLT(IC)	X		01.06.04	DARTMOUTH BRNC
Murray, Grant McNiven, BEng	LT CDR(FTC)	E	WESM	01.06.98	FOST SM SEA
Murray, Greig Martin, BSc	LT(CC)	X		01.09.02	NOTTINGHAM
Murray, Jamie Cameron,	SLT(IC)	X	P U/T	01.05.04	RNAS YEOVILTON
Murray, Simon David,	CAPT RM(CC)	-		01.09.04	RNAS YEOVILTON
Murray, Stephen John, pcea, gdas	CDR(FTC)	X	O	30.06.03	RNAS CULDROSE
Murray, William Justin, BSc	LT(IC)	X	P	01.05.04	846 SQN
Murrison, Richard Anthony, MA, GCIS, ACIS, psc(j)	CDR(FTC)	S		30.06.04	NELSON
Musgrove, James,	2LT(IC)	-		01.08.02	CTCRM LYMPSTONE
Musto, Edward Charles, BA, psc(m)	LT COL(FTC)	-		31.12.96	EXCHANGE USA
Mutch, Jonathan Rocliffe, BSc, pcea	LT(FTC)	X	P	01.09.94	NELSON
Muyambo, Nomalanga Nosizo, BSc	LT(IC)	E	TM	01.01.00	MWS COLLINGWOOD
Myatt, Marie-Claire,	SLT(UCE)(IC)	E	WE U/T	01.09.04	DARTMOUTH BRNC

N

Name	Rank	Branch	Spec	Seniority	Where Serving
Naden, Andrew Charles Keith, BSc, CEng, MIMarEST, psc(j)	CDR(FTC)	E	ME	30.06.02	FLEET ROSYTH
Naden, James Ralph, MSc, BA, PGDip, Cert Ed	LT CDR(FTC)	E	IS	01.10.94	CMT SHRIVENHAM
Nail, Vaughan Anthony, MA, psc	CAPT(FTC)	X	H CH	30.06.06	LOAN HYDROG
Nairn, Alan Barclay, BSc	LT CDR(FTC)	S		01.02.99	PJHQ
Naismith, David Hamilton, BSc, pcea	LT CDR(FTC)(A)	X	O	01.05.91	824 SQN
Napier, Alexander Austin,	SLT(IC)	X	ATC U/T	01.11.04	DARTMOUTH BRNC
Napier, Graham Andrew,	LT CDR(FTC)	E	AE	01.07.01	JHCHQ
Nash, Philip David, BSc	LT CDR(FTC)	X	PWO(A)	01.10.02	FLEET COSCAP
Nash, Robin David Cory, BSc	LT(IC)	X	H2	01.01.02	ENDURANCE
Nash, Rubin Piero, BSc	LT(IC)	X		01.01.02	SUTHERLAND
Nash, Russell Frank Roger,	LT(IC)	E	WESM	01.01.04	DLO BRISTOL
Naylor, Andrew James,	LT(FTC)	X	P	16.06.94	829 FLT 03
Neal, Simon Matthew, pcea	LT CDR(FTC)	X	O	01.10.03	814 SQN
Neale, Daniel Frederick,	LT(IC)	X		01.09.05	RICHMOND
Neary, Joseph, MSc, MB, BCH, FRCGP, DCH, PGCE	SURG LTCDR(SC(MD) (Act Surg Cdr)	-	GMPP	01.10.96	FLEET COSP&S
Neave, Andrew Michael,	LT CDR(FTC)	X	ATC	01.10.98	FLEET HQ PORTS
Neave, Christopher Bryan, OBE, BSc, pcea	CAPT(FTC)	E	AE(L)	30.06.01	JSCSC
Neave, James Robert,	SLT(IC)	X		01.12.04	MWS COLLINGWOOD
Necker, Carl Dominic, PGDIPAN, pce	LT CDR(FTC)	X	PWO(N)	01.11.99	PORTLAND
Neil, David Alexander,	SLT(IC)	X		01.05.02	FLEET HQ PORTS
Neild, Timothy, n.	LT CDR(FTC)	X	PWO(C)	01.10.03	FLEET HQ NWD
Neil-Gallacher, Ed,	SURG SLT(SCC)	-		25.11.05	DARTMOUTH BRNC
Nekrews, Alan Neil Laurence Michael,	LT(IC)	X		01.01.04	MWS COLLINGWOOD
Nelson, Andrew,	LT CDR(FTC)	E	WESM	01.10.95	CAPT MCTA
Nelson, Christopher Stuart, BSc, pce, n	LT CDR(FTC)	X	PWO(N)	01.03.01	BULWARK
Nelson, David Lawrence,	LT CDR(FTC)(A)	X	P	01.10.92	DLO TES
Nelson, Digby Theodore, BSc, psc	CAPT(FTC)	S		30.06.05	FLEET COSP&S
Nelson, Lisa Marie, BEng	LT CDR(FTC)	E	ME	01.01.03	ILLUSTRIOUS
Nelson, Matthew Rodney,	LT(CC)	X	P	16.11.98	MWS COLLINGWOOD
Nelson, Victoria, BA	LT CDR(FTC)	S		01.10.03	CAMPBELTOWN

Name	Rank	Branch	Spec	Seniority	Where Serving
Nelstrop, Andrew Marcus, MB, BCH, ... SURG LTCDR(MC(MD) MA(CANTAB), DipSM, MRCGP	-			11.02.04	CTCRM
Netherwood, Lyndsey Dawn, BA, n .... LT(FTC)	X			15.09.99	MWS COLLINGWOOD
Neve, Piers Charles, pce(sm) .... LT CDR(FTC)	X	SM		11.02.94	EXCHANGE USA
New, Christopher Maxwell, BEng, MSc, CEng, MIMechE .... LT CDR(FTC)	E	ME		01.04.97	FLEET HQ PORTS 2
New, Richard Ashley, ... LT(CC)	S			01.02.01	NEPTUNE DLO
Newall, Jeremy Andrew, ... LT CDR(FTC)	X	ATC		01.03.94	RNAS YEOVILTON
Newall, Paul John, MA .... LT(IC)	E	TM		01.09.02	CTCRM
Newby, Christopher, ... LT(IC)	X	O U/T		01.01.05	824 SQN
Newby Stubbs, Rebecca Louise, ... LT CDR(MCC)	Q	IC		01.10.05	DRAKE COB
Newell, Gary David, ... LT(CC)	E	ME		29.04.01	DFTE PORTSMOUTH
Newell, Jonathan Michael, MBE, MSc, CEng, FIMarEST, MIL, fsc .... CAPT(FTC)	E	ME		30.06.05	MOD (BATH)
Newell, Phillip Russell, BEng .... LT CDR(FTC)	X	H CH		01.06.01	COS 2SL/CNH
Newing, Stephen Geoffrey, psc .... LT COL(FTC)	-	MOR		30.06.98	FLEET CMR
Newland, Mark Ian, BSc, MA, pce, psc(j) .... CDR(FTC)	X	PWO(U)		30.06.03	MWS COLLINGWOOD
Newman, Andrew Michael, BSc .... SLT(IC)	X			01.01.05	DARTMOUTH BRNC
Newman, Christopher Richard Spencer, ... LT(IC)	X	H2		01.05.02	RFANSU (ARGUS)
Newman, David, ... LT(CC)	E	AE		01.01.99	EXCHANGE ARMY UK
Newman, Paul Henry, MBE, BSc .... LT CDR(FTC)	X	METOC		01.05.89	RNAS CULDROSE
Newth, Christopher, BSc .... LT(CC)	E	IS		01.05.00	UKMARBATSTAFF
Newton, David John, pce, psc .... CDR(FTC)	X	P		31.12.98	FLEET AV CRANWEL
Newton, Garry Arnold, pce(sm) .... CDR(FTC)	X	SM		30.06.00	NELSON
Newton, James Lloyd, DFC .... LT CDR(FTC)	X	P		01.10.04	FLEET AV VL
Newton, Michael Ronald, FIEIE, FIIE .... LT CDR(FTC)	E	WE		22.09.87	MOD (BATH)
Newton, Nicholas John Patrick, BSc, MB, BS .... SURG LT(SC(MD)	-			06.08.03	VIGILANT(PORT)
Newton, Owen Robert Alan, ... SLT(IC)	X			01.02.05	CORNWALL
Newton, Robert William, ... CAPT RM(CC)	-			01.09.03	40 CDO RM
Neyland, David A, BEng .... LT(IC)	X	P		01.09.04	RNAS YEOVILTON
Nguyo, David Ngibuini, MEng .... LT(IC)	E	WE		01.09.02	DCCIS FAREHAM
Nicholas, Bryan John, BSc, pcea .... LT CDR(FTC)	X	P		01.10.01	771 SQN
Nicholas, Jeremy Richard, ... CAPT RM(CC)	-	SO(LE)		01.04.03	1 ASSAULT GP RM
Nicholas, Stephen Paul, BEng, CEng .... LT CDR(FTC)	E	MESM		01.04.06	NEPTUNE DSA
Nicholls, Barry Austin, ... MAJ(FTC)	-	SO(LE)		01.10.04	FLEET COSP&S
Nicholls, Guy Anthony, IEng, MIEE .... LT CDR(FTC)	E	WE		01.10.99	CAPT MCTA
Nicholls, Larry Roy, ... LT(IC)	E	WE		01.05.03	ST ALBANS
Nichols, Elizabeth Anne, MB, BS, MRCGP, DObstRCOG .... SURG CDR(FCC)	-	GMPP		27.05.01	RALEIGH
Nicholson, Brian Harold, ... LT(CC)	E	AE		29.04.01	JSCSC
Nicholson, David Andrew Gore, BEng .... LT(CC)	X			01.01.01	TYNE
Nicholson, David Peter, BSc .... MAJ(FTC)	-	LC		01.09.05	MOD (LONDON)
Nicholson, Graeme, MB, CHB, MFOM, MRCGP .... SURG CDR(FCC)	-	(CO/M)		31.12.00	INM ALVERSTOKE
Nicholson, Jonathan Craig, BSc .... LT(FTC)	E	WE		02.09.99	SANS IPT
Nicholson, Kristin James, BA .... LT CDR(FTC)	S			01.08.02	PJHQ
Nicholson, Simon Charles Lawrence, pce .... CDR(FTC)	X	MCD		30.06.96	MWC SOUTHWICK
Nicklas, Colin James, BEng, MSc, CEng, MIEE .... LT CDR(FTC)	E	WE		01.06.00	MOD (LONDON)
Nicklin, Gareth James Edward, BEng, CEng, PGDip, MIMechE .... LT(FTC)	E	MESM		01.01.00	RMC OF SCIENCE
Nickolls, Kevin Paul, BEng .... LT CDR(FTC)	E	AE		01.01.00	COS 2SL/CNH
Nicol, Allan MacKenzie, ... LT(IC)	E	MESM		01.09.05	SULTAN
Nicol, Peter James Stewart, MB, BS, LRCP, MRCS, JCPTGP .... SURG CDR(FCC)	-	GMPP		30.06.94	MOD (LONDON)
Nicoll, Andrew John, BEng, MIEE .... LT CDR(FTC)	E	AE		01.04.05	FLEET FOTR
Nicoll, Steve Kenneth, ... CAPT RM(FTC) (Act Maj)	-	SO(LE)		01.01.96	1 ASSAULT GP RM
Nielsen, Erik Michael, ... CAPT RM(IC)	-	SO(LE)		01.07.04	DARTMOUTH BRNC
Nightingale, Samuel David, BSc .... LT(IC)	X			01.01.05	WALNEY
Nisbet, James Henry Thomas, BSc, pce, psc(j), MA .... CDR(FTC)	X	PWO(U)		30.06.03	MOD (LONDON)
Nix, Christopher James, MSc, PhD .... LT(IC)	E	IS U/T		01.09.02	OCEAN
Nixon, Alexander, ... 2LT(IC)	-			01.08.03	40 CDO RM
Nixon, Neville Paul, ... CAPT RM(IC)	-	SO(LE)		19.07.05	ALBION
Nixon, Paul William, MSc, CEng, MIMechE, MInstPS .... CDR(FTC)	E	MESM		30.06.96	DRAKE SFM
Nixon, Sebastian, ... SURG SLT(SCC)	-			15.12.05	DARTMOUTH BRNC
Noakes, Kevin Massie, BEng, MSc, CEng, MIEE, gw .... LT CDR(FTC)	E	WE		01.05.02	DLO BRISTOL
Nobbs, Christopher, ... SURG SLT(MDC)	-			07.09.05	DARTMOUTH BRNC
Noble, Kevan Leslie, ... CAPT RM(CC)	-	SO(LE)		01.04.03	EXCH ARMY SC(G)
Noble, Mark Jonathan Dean, psc .... COL(FTC)	-	P		31.12.99	RCDS

Name	Rank	Branch	Spec	Seniority	Where Serving
Noble, Tom Mark Dean,	CAPT RM(IC)	-		01.09.05	40 CDO RM
Noblett, Peter Gordon Arthur, MNI, pce, pce(sm)	LT CDR(FTC)	X	SM	01.10.01	VANGUARD(STBD)
Nokes, Oliver,	SLT(IC)	X		01.09.03	RAMSEY
Nolan, Anthony Laurence,	CDR(FTC)	X	C	30.06.01	COM MCC NWD
Nolan, Paul Ernest,	CAPT RM(CC)	-	P	01.04.02	847 SQN
Noon, David, MBE	LT CDR(FTC)	S	CA	01.10.03	RN LOGS SCHOOL
Noonan, Charles Daniel, BA	LT(CC)	X		01.05.01	PEMBROKE
Norcott, William Richard,	CAPT RM(IC)	-		01.09.04	RM WARMINSTER
Norford, Michael,	LT(FTC) (Act Lt Cdr)	X		03.04.97	MOD (LONDON)
Norgan, David James, BA, pce, n	LT CDR(FTC)	X	PWO(C)	01.07.01	FOST SEA
Norgate, Andrew Thomas, BSc, PGDip, SM(n), SM	LT(FTC)	X	H2	01.11.98	NP IRAQ
Norman, Jaimie McCoy, BA	CAPT RM(CC)	-		01.09.02	1 ASSAULT GP RM
Norman, Phillip Douglas,	LT CDR(FTC)	E	WE	01.10.99	CAPT MCTA
Norman, Stuart John, BSc	SLT(IC)	X		01.11.04	DARTMOUTH BRNC
Norman, Toby Benjamin,	LT(IC)	X		01.04.03	SOUTHAMPTON
Norris, Guy Patrick,	LT(IC)	X	O	16.07.93	771 SQN
Norris, James Garnet, MA, psc(j)	LT CDR(FTC)	E	AE	01.11.00	DLO YEO
Norris, Richard Edward, BDS, MA, LDS RCS(Eng), MGDS RCS, psc(j)	SGCAPT(D)(FCC)	-		26.10.04	DDS PLYMOUTH
Norris, William Desmond, MB, BSc, PhD, MRCGP, CHB	SURG LTCDR(FCC)	-	GMPP	20.05.02	INM ALVERSTOKE
Norriss, Mark William,	LT(IC)	X	P	01.01.05	845 SQN
North, Adam Christopher, MEng	SLT(IC)	E	AE U/T	01.09.03	SULTAN
Northcote, Mark Richard,	LT(CC)	X	MCD	01.12.00	SDG PLYMOUTH
Northcott, Philip James, BEng, PGDip	LT(FTC)	E	MESM	01.09.02	SOVEREIGN
Northeast, Paul,	LT(FTC)	S	SM	01.04.01	RN LOGS SCHOOL
Northover, Adam Frederick, BSc, n	LT CDR(FTC)	X	PWO(U)	01.08.05	FOST SEA
Northwood, Gerard Rodney, pce	CDR(FTC)	X	AAWO	30.06.99	JSCSC
Norton, Alexandra Louise Elizabeth, MEng	LT(CC)	E	ME	01.09.02	NP IRAQ
Norton, Ian Andrew,	LT(IC)	E	AE	01.07.04	848 SQN HERON
Norton, Thomas Charles Horatio, MA(OXON)	CAPT RM(FTC)	-	C	01.09.03	CHFHQ
Norwood, James Kenneth, BSc	LT(IC)	X		01.01.04	SHOREHAM
Norwood, Jeffrey Michael, BA, MB, BCH, DCH	SURG CDR(SCC)	-	DPHC	01.03.97	FLEET COSP&S
Notley, Edward John, LLB	LT(CC)	X	SM	01.01.03	TRAFALGAR
Notley, Louis Paul, BSc, MDA	CDR(FTC)	S	SM	30.06.04	PJHQ
Nottingham, James Mark,	SLT(IC)	X	P U/T	01.02.05	DARTMOUTH BRNC
Nottley, Simon Matthew,	LT(FTC)	E	WESM	01.04.01	MOD DIS SEA
Noyce, Nigel Roderick, MLITT	LT CDR(FTC)	X		15.01.97	FLEET COMOPS NWD
Noyce, Roger Grenville, MBE, MRINA	LT CDR(FTC)	X		01.10.04	FLEET COSCAP
Noyce, Vincent Robert Amos, pce, MSc	LT CDR(FTC)	X	PWO(A)	01.11.01	NP IRAQ
Noyes, David James, MA, psc(j)	CDR(FTC)	S		30.06.01	MOD (LONDON)
Nugent, Helen Ann,	SLT(IC)	X	O	01.09.04	824 SQN
Nunn, Christopher John, OBE, nadc, psc(a)	LT COL(FTC)	-	P	30.06.88	DA TBILISI
Nunnen, Catherine Rebecca, MA	LT(CC)	X	O	01.05.01	815 FLT 226
Nurse, Michael Talbot, BSc, psc	LT CDR(FTC) (Act Cdr)	E	AE	01.06.88	IMS BRUSSELS
Nursey, Adrian Paul, IEng, MIIE	LT(FTC) (Act Lt Cdr)	E	MESM	02.09.99	TRAFALGAR

O

Name	Rank	Branch	Spec	Seniority	Where Serving
Oakes, Michael Carson,	LT(IC)	X		01.05.02	539 ASSLT SQN RM
Oakley, Andrew J, BSc	LT(IC)	E	TM	01.01.01	RNICG
Oakley, Claire Marie,	LT(CC)	X	HM	01.05.01	OCEAN
Oakley, Sarah Ellen, MA, n	LT CDR(FTC)	X		01.05.05	MWS COLLINGWOOD
O'Brien, David,	SURG SLT(SCC)	-		10.09.05	DARTMOUTH BRNC
O'Brien, Kieran John, BEng, MA, psc(j)	CDR(FTC)	E	AE	30.06.06	MERLIN IPT
O'Brien, Patrick Michael Christopher, BEng, MSc, CEng, MIEE	CDR(FTC)	E	IS	30.06.04	FLEET COSP&S
O'Brien, Peter Charles, BSc, PGCE, adp	LT CDR(FTC) (Act Cdr)	E	IS	23.04.88	AFPAA JPA
O'Brien, Thomas Patrick,	LT(IC)	E	WESM	01.01.04	RALEIGH
O'Byrne, Patrick Barry Mary, pce(sm), SM(n)	LT CDR(FTC)	X	SM	01.11.00	JSCSC
O'Callaghan, Patrick Francis,	LT(IC)	X		01.05.02	FOST MPV SEA
O'Callaghan, Philip Peter,	CAPT RM(IC)	-	SO(LE)	19.07.05	NAVSEC
O'Connor, David McPherson,	CAPT RM(IC)	-	C	01.07.04	CTCRM
O'Connor, David Paul,	LT(CC)	E	WESM	01.01.03	DLO BRISTOL
Oddy, David Mark, pcea	LT CDR(FTC)	X	P	01.10.00	COMATG SEA

Name	Rank	Branch	Spec	Seniority	Where Serving
O'Donnell, Ian Mark, MBE, MA, psc	LT COL(FTC)	-	P	30.06.03	FLEET HQ PORTS 2
Officer, Robert Lennie,	LT(CC)	X	MW	01.02.96	FLEET FOSNNI
Offord, Matthew Ronald,	LT CDR(FTC)	X	MCD	01.04.02	QHM CLYDE
Offord, Stephen John Joseph, BA	LT(IC)	E	AE U/T	01.05.06	SULTAN
O'Flaherty, Christopher Patrick John, pce	LT CDR(FTC)	X	PWO(U)	01.03.99	NORTHUMBERLAND
O'Flaherty, John Stephen, BEng, CEng, MIMarEST, psc(j)	LT CDR(FTC)	E	ME	03.10.97	SULTAN
O'Grady, Matthew James, fsc	CDR(FTC)	S	SM	30.06.01	ARK ROYAL
O'Hara, Gerard Connor,	MAJ(FTC)	-		01.09.03	EXCHANGE FRANCE
O'Herlihy, Simon Ian, MA	MAJ(FTC)	-		01.09.02	42 CDO RM
O'Kane, Robert James, BSc	LT(CC)	X	O	16.05.00	771 SQN
O'Keefe, Thomas Declan,	LT RM(IC) (Act Capt Rm)	-		01.09.03	CDO LOG REGT RM
Okell, Peter,	2LT(IC)	-		01.08.01	45 CDO RM
Okukenu, Dele, pcea	LT(FTC)	X	P	01.01.96	848 SQN HERON
Oldfield, Christian Adam William, BEng, MRAeS	LT(IC)	E	AE U/T	01.09.05	RNAS YEOVILTON
Oliphant, William, MA, psc(j)	CDR(FTC)	S		30.06.05	COMATG SEA
Olive, Peter Nicholas, pce, psc(j), n	CDR(FTC)	X	PWO(A)	30.06.05	JDCC
Oliver, Carlton James,	LT(IC)	X	AV	01.05.04	SULTAN
Oliver, Graeme John, BSc	LT(CC)	S		01.12.99	FLEET COSP&S
Oliver, Graham, PGDip, BSc	LT CDR(FTC)	X	METOC	01.05.03	DEF SCH OF LANG
Oliver, Kevin Brian, BEng, MA, MSc, psc(j), mdtc	LT COL(FTC)	-	MLDR	30.06.04	FLEET HQ WI
Olivey, Timothy Douglas,	LT(CC)	X	O	01.05.02	LYNX OEU
Ollerton, Justin Clive,	LT(CC)	X	P	16.11.96	771 SQN
Ollis, Victoria,	LT(CC)	S		01.05.01	DLO/DG LOG (SC)
Olliver, Adrian John, MILT	LT CDR(FTC)	S	O	01.10.96	PJHQ
O'Maoil-Mheana, Patrick John,	LT(MC(MD)	Q	OTSPEC	30.03.96	JCTS IPT
O'Neill, Conor Mark, BA	LT(IC)	X		01.09.05	LIVERPOOL
O'Neill, Henry Lawrence,	LT(IC)	X	P	01.01.03	845 SQN
O'Neill, James, BA	LT(CC)	X	H2	22.11.99	MWS HM TG (D)
O'Neill, Patrick John, MA, MSc	CAPT(FTC)	E	WESM	30.06.06	HQ DCSA
O'Neill, Paul Joseph, BEng	LT CDR(FTC)	E	MESM	01.10.03	TRENCHANT
O'Neill, Timothy James,	LT(CC)	X	MCD	01.01.02	RAMSEY
Onions, Judith Mary, ARRC	CDR(FC(MD)	Q	IC	30.06.02	FLEET COSP&S
Onyike, Chinyere Eme, NDipM, BEng, MSc, CEng, MIEE, MCMI	LT CDR(FTC)	E	WE	01.01.02	CUMBERLAND
O'Nyons, Yorick Ian, BA, MDA, SM(n)	LT CDR(FTC)	X	SM	01.07.02	NAVSEC
Oram, Cemal,	MID(NE)(IC)	X	O U/T	01.01.06	DARTMOUTH BRNC
Orchard, Adrian Paul, pcea, psc(j)	CDR(FTC)	X	P	30.06.05	800 NAS (GR7)
Ordway, Christopher Norman Maurice Patrick,	MAJ(FTC)	-		01.09.05	UKLFCSG RM
O'Reilly, Christopher Andrew,	LT(IC)	S		01.05.04	FLEET HQ WI
O'Reilly, Terence Michael, MRAeS, psc(j)	CDR(FTC) (Act Capt)	E	AE	31.12.98	MOD (BATH)
O'Riordan, Michael Patrick, BSc, pce, pcea	LT CDR(FTC)	X	P	01.04.89	UN AFRICA
Orme, William Benjamin,	LT(CC)	X	P	01.05.02	845 SQN
Ormshaw, Martin Andrew, BA	LT(IC)	X	O U/T	01.01.06	702 SQN HERON
O'Rourke, Richard Michael,	LT(CC)	S		01.05.02	JSCSC
Orr, Keith John, BEng	LT(CC)	E	MESM	01.11.99	NEPTUNE DLO
Orr, Simon David,	CAPT RM(CC)	-	SO(LE)	03.04.02	CHFHQ
Orton, David Michael, BSc, DPhil	LT CDR(FTC)	E	TMSM	01.10.00	FLEET FOTR
Orton, Trevor,	LT(IC)	X		01.10.04	LANCASTER
Osbaldestin, Richard Alan,	LT(FTC)	X	MCD	01.10.98	EXCHANGE USA
Osborn, Colvin Graeme, BSc, SM	LT CDR(FTC)	X	SM	01.06.02	PJHQ
Osborn, Richard Marcus, pce	LT CDR(FTC)	X	AAWO	01.02.99	KENT
Osborne, John Michael, BSc	LT(IC)	E	TM	01.10.99	RNICG
O'Shaughnessy, David John, BEng, CEng, MIMarEST	LT CDR(FTC)	E	ME	01.06.05	OCEAN
O'Shaughnessy, Paul Charles, BEng, MIEE	LT(FTC)	E	WE	01.01.99	RMC OF SCIENCE
O'Shea, Eamon Patrick, BEng	LT CDR(FTC) (Act Cdr)	E	AE	01.07.98	EUMS
O'Shea, Matthew Kent, MPhil, MB, CHB, BSc	SURG LT(SC(MD)	-		06.09.04	VANGUARD(PORT)
Osmond, Justin Bruce, BEng, MA, MSc, psc(j)	CDR(FTC)	E	AE	30.06.05	DCAE COSFORD
O'Sullivan, Barrie Oliver,	LT CDR(FTC)	X	P	01.10.00	MOD (LONDON)
O'Sullivan, Matthew Richard John,	CAPT RM(CC)	-	P	01.09.04	847 SQN
O'Sullivan, Michael Louis James, BSc, PGDipL	LT CDR(FTC)	X	HCH	01.08.01	ENTERPRISE
O'Sullivan, Nicholas,	2LT(IC)	-		01.08.02	CTCRM LYMPSTONE
O'Sullivan, Paul Benedict, BEng, PGDip	LT(IC)	E	MESM	01.05.03	TURBULENT
Oswald, Sir (John) Julian (Robertson), GCB, rcds, psc	ADM OF FLEET	-	G	02.03.93	

Name	Rank	Branch	Spec	Seniority	Where Serving
Ottaway, Thomas Arthur,	LT(IC)	X	SM	01.05.03	SPARTAN
Ottewell, Paul Steven, BSc, SM(n),	LT CDR(FTC)	X	SM	01.01.05	TURBULENT
Oulds, Keith Antony, BEng	LT CDR(FTC)	X	MCD	01.09.00	MWS COLLINGWOOD
Oura, Adrian Nicholas, BA	CAPT RM(FTC)	-		01.09.00	DHU SEA
Ouseley, Daniel,	2LT(IC)	-		01.09.02	CTCRM LYMPSTONE
Ouvry, Janet Elisabeth Delahaize, BSc	LT(MCC)	Q		25.03.97	NELSON
Ovenden, Neil Stephen Paul, pce	LT CDR(FTC)	X	PWO(U)	01.02.95	EXCHANGE CANADA
Ovens, Jeremy John, BSc, MBA, pce, pcea, psc	CDR(FTC)	X	O	31.12.99	MOD (LONDON)
Overington, Michelle Teresa, LCIPD	LT(IC)	S		01.05.04	RALEIGH
Owen, Douglas Philip Collinson,	LT(IC)	X		01.09.02	KENT
Owen, Glyn,	LT(FTC)	X	O	16.02.97	UKMILREP BRUSS
Owen, Samuel Thomas Louis, SM(n)	LT(CC)	X	SM	01.11.00	MWS COLLINGWOOD
Owen, Vincent Frederick,	LT(IC)	X		01.05.02	702 SQN HERON
Owens, Daniel Tudor, BEng, CEng, MIMechE	LT CDR(FTC)	E	ME	01.08.99	FLEET COSP&S
Owens, John Whittal, MA	LT(IC)	X		01.01.05	820 SQN
Oxlade, Andrew Thomas, BSc	SURG SLT(SCC)	-		01.07.03	DARTMOUTH BRNC
Oxley, James David,	SLT(IC)	X		01.02.05	EXETER

P

Name	Rank	Branch	Spec	Seniority	Where Serving
Packer, Robert Graham,	LT(IC)	X		01.07.04	RNAS CULDROSE
Packham, Craig Nicholas Ronald,	LT(CC)	X	P	01.03.96	LYNX OEU
Padget, Joanna Louise, BSc	LT(IC)	E	TM	01.05.00	1 ASSLT GP RM
Page, Carrie Ann, BA	LT(IC)	S		01.09.05	ILLUSTRIOUS
Page, David Michael, BSc, MDA, CEng, MIEE	CDR(FTC)	E	WE	30.06.97	DLO BRISTOL
Page, Durward Charles Millar, BSc, MA, psc(j)	MAJ(FTC)	-		01.09.01	UKMARBATSTAFF
Page, Mark Robert,	LT(CC)	X	O	01.05.00	702 SQN HERON
Page, Michael Christian, MA, MBA, psc	LT COL(FTC)	-	LC	30.06.99	NELSON
Paget, Simon James,	LT(FTC)	X		02.05.00	RALEIGH
Pakes, Danyel Tobias, BEng, CEng	LT CDR(FTC)	E	WESM	01.01.04	ASM IPT
Palethorpe, Nicholas, BSc	LT(CC)	X		01.09.97	ARK ROYAL
Pallett, Angela Julie, MA	LT(CC)	S		01.01.03	RN LOGS SCHOOL
Palmer, Alan Charles, MB, ChB, MRCGP	SURG LTCDR(FCC)	-	GMPP	01.03.97	SETT GOSPORT
Palmer, Christopher Laurence, BSc, MIMgt, pce, pcea, psc	CDRE(FTC)	X	O	24.11.05	RNAS YEOVILTON
Palmer, Christopher Richard, MSc, IEng, AMINucE	LT(CC)	E	MESM	01.09.01	NP BRISTOL
Palmer, James Ernest, MSc, CEng, MIEE, MBCS, MInsD	CDR(FTC)	E	WE	31.12.96	MOD (LONDON)
Palmer, John, MA, CEng, MIEE	LT CDR(FTC)	E	WE	01.10.03	ST ALBANS
Palmer, Martin David, BSc	LT(IC)	X	H2	01.01.03	RFANSU
Palmer, Michael Edward, BEng, MSc, CEng, MIEE	LT CDR(FTC)	E	WE	01.11.01	PORTLAND
Palmer, Phillip Alan, BA, SM	LT CDR(FTC)	X	SM	01.07.89	MOD (LONDON)
Pamphilon, Michael John, pcea, psc	LT CDR(FTC(A))	X	P	01.03.88	814 SQN
Panther, Andrew Mark, BEng, MSc, CEng, MIEE	LT CDR(FTC)	E	WE	01.07.00	JSCSC
Pardoe, Elton Ramsey, MB, CHB, BSc	SURG LTCDR(SC(MD))	-		06.08.05	SETT GOSPORT
Pariser, Andrew Maurice, BSc	SLT(IC)	X		01.05.03	MWS COLLINGWOOD
Park, Brian Campbell, BA	LT CDR(FTC)	S		01.10.03	DCL DEEPCUT
Park, Ian David, MA	LT(CC)	S		01.08.98	MOD (LONDON)
Park, Lindsay, BDS	SG LT(D)(SC(MD))	-		27.06.03	SULTAN
Parker, Anthony Richard,	LT(IC)	S	(W)	29.10.04	845 SQN
Parker, Daniel John,	LT(IC)	S		01.05.05	RALEIGH
Parker, Darren Stuart,	LT(IC)	MS		01.07.04	MED S IPT
Parker, Henry Hardyman, MA, PhD, CEng, MIEE, psc	CAPT(FTC)	E	WESM	30.06.02	BDS WASHINGTON
Parker, Ian Robert, BSc	CDR(FTC)	E	MESM	31.12.93	DLO BRISTOL
Parker, James Robert, BSc	SLT(IC)	X	O U/T	01.01.05	DARTMOUTH BRNC
Parker, Jonathan Donald, BEng, MIEE, NDipM	LT(IC)	E	WE	01.04.03	HQ DCSA
Parker, Mark Neal, BEng, MSc, CEng, FIMarEST, MAPM, MCGI	CDR(FTC)	E	ME	30.06.01	EXCHANGE USA
Parker, Matthew Charles, BA	CAPT RM(FTC)	-	C	01.09.02	42 CDO RM
Parker, Matthew James, BA	LT(IC)	X	H2	01.01.04	ROEBUCK
Parker, Timothy Stephen, BSc, MIMarEST, MBCS, CMath	LT(FTC)	E	IS	01.11.95	PJHQ
Parkin, Brett,	LT(IC)	E	WESM	08.04.05	RALEIGH
Parkin, Malcolm Ian, BEng	LT CDR(FTC)	E	ME	01.07.99	EXCHANGE NLANDS
Parkin, Matthew James, BA	SLT(IC)	X		01.05.03	MWS COLLINGWOOD
Parkinson, Andrew Philip,	LT(FTC)	X	AV	23.07.98	FLEET COSP&S
Parkinson, Henry Michael Larissa,	LT(FTC)	E	AE	01.09.04	RNAS YEOVILTON

Name	Rank	Branch	Spec	Seniority	Where Serving
Parkinson, James Hugh George, MEng, SM(n)	LT(FTC)	X	SM	01.09.02	CHARGER
Parkinson, Nicholas,	SLT(IC)	X		01.01.05	SULTAN
Parks, Edward Patrick, jsdc, psc	MAJ(FTC) (Act Lt Col)	-		01.09.90	MWC SOUTHWICK
Parmenter, Alan John,	LT(FTC)	E	AE	01.04.01	FLEET AV VL
Parnell, Adam David, BEng, pce	LT CDR(FTC)	X	AAWO	01.04.01	FOST NWD (JMOTS)
Parnell, Daniel Christian,	LT(IC)	E	ME U/T	08.04.05	NORTHUMBERLAND
Parr, Matthew John, BSc, pce, pce(sm)	CAPT(FTC)	X	SM	30.06.02	FLEET COMOPS NWD
Parr, Michael John Edward,	LT CDR(FTC)	X	HM	02.02.05	COMATG SEA
Parrock, Neil Graham,	LT(CC)	X	P	01.07.95	DHFS
Parrott, James Philip,	LT CDR(FTC)	X	PWO(A)	01.07.04	EXETER
Parrott, Stuart Steven,	LT(IC)	X		01.04.06	ST ALBANS
Parry, Alexander Keith Illiam, BSc, MA, psc(j)	S			30.06.05	MOD (BATH)
Parry, Christopher Adrian, MB, BS, BSc, MRCS	SURG LTCDR(FCC)			12.08.99	NELSON (PAY)
Parry, Christopher John, CBE, MA, rcds, pce, pcea, psc	RADM	-	O	25.01.05	JDCC
(DGJDC JAN 05)					
Parry, Gareth Richard,	LT(IC)	X		01.10.03	BULWARK
Parry, Jonathan Allan, BSc	MAJ(FTC)	-	P	01.10.04	JHCHQ
Parry, Jonathan David Frank, MRAeS, pcea	LT CDR(FTC)	X	P	01.05.00	815 SQN HQ
Parry, Mark Roderick Raymond, BEng, MSc	LT CDR(FTC)	E	AE	01.05.04	NAVSEC
Parry, Roger John,	LT(FTC)	E	AE	16.10.92	GANNET SAR FLT
Parry, Stephen Joseph, BSc	SLT(IC)	X	ATCU/T	01.07.03	RAF SHAWBURY
Parry, Stuart David, LLB	LT(CC)	S		05.03.02	HQ SACT
Parselle, Stephen,	CHAPLAIN	CE		30.08.05	FWO PORTS SEA
Parsons, Andrew David, BSc, pce, n	LT CDR(FTC)	X	PWO(C)	01.01.00	PJHQ
Parsons, Brian Robert, BSc, MBA	CDR(FTC)	E	AE	31.12.00	FLEET COSCAP
Parsons, Christopher Graham, BSc, MDA, CEng, MIEE	CDR(FTC)	E	WE	31.12.00	MOD (LONDON)
Parsons, Robert John, BSc	LT(IC)	X	MW	01.11.00	PENZANCE
Parsons, Robert Martin James,	LT(CC)	X	H2	01.01.02	ENTERPRISE
Parton, Alan,	LT(FTC)	X	MCD	19.09.00	MWS COLLINGWOOD
Partridge, Simon Christopher, BSc	LT(IC)	X	HM	01.12.00	FLEET COMOPS NWD
Parvin, Philip Stanley, BEng, MBA,	LT CDR(FTC)	E	MESM	01.02.97	MONTROSE
MSc, CEng, FIMarEST, MIMechE, MCMI					
Parvin, Richard Alan, MA, psc(j)	MAJ(FTC)	-		01.05.03	PJHQ
Pascoe, James Roderick Munro,	CAPT RM(CC)	-		01.09.03	UKLFCSG RM
Paston, William Alexander,	LT(CC)	X	FC	01.05.02	HQ1GP HQSTC
Pastouna, James,	2LT(IC)	-		01.08.02	CTCRM LYMPSTONE
Patch, Stirling John, MBE	LT(IC)	E	ME	02.08.02	DFTE PORTSMOUTH
Pate, Christopher Michael,	LT(CC)	X	MW	01.01.04	BANGOR
Patel, Devang Ramesh, MB, BSc, BS, DipIMC RCSED	SURG LT(SCC)	-		01.08.01	RN GIBRALTAR
Paterson, James Malcolm Alexander,	LT(IC)	X		01.01.06	TYNE
Paterson, Michael Paul, MA, PGDIPAN, pce, psc(j), n	CDR(FTC)	X	PWO(N)	30.06.05	GLOUCESTER
Paterson, Thomas John,	CAPT RM(CC)	-	MLDR	01.04.02	RMR TYNE
Paton, Alan John Malcolm,	LT(FTC)	E	ME	19.06.98	DLO BRISTOL
Paton, Christopher Mark, BEng	MAJ(FTC)	-		01.09.02	NELSON (PAY)
Paton, Martin Stirling,	LT(IC)	E	MESM	01.05.04	SULTAN
Patrick, James, MSc, rcds, psc	CDRE(FTC)	E	TM	08.02.05	FLEET FOTR
Patrick, John Andrew,	LT(IC)	X		01.01.06	MWS COLLINGWOOD
Patten, Michelle Louise, BEng	SLT(IC)	E	AE	01.09.03	RNAS YEOVILTON
Patterson, David, BEng	LT CDR(FTC)	E	WE	01.10.02	ALBION
Patterson, John David, BSc, n	LT CDR(FTC)	X	PWO(A)	01.08.04	FOST SEA
Patterson, Pascal Xavier, BSc	SLT(IC)	X	O U/T	01.01.04	RNAS CULDROSE
Patterson, Scott Douglas, BEng, CEng, MIEE	LT CDR(FTC)	E	WE	01.07.05	DLO DEF MUN GP
Patterson-Hollis, Christopher, BEng, MIEE	LT CDR(FTC)	E	WE	01.04.97	JES IPT
Pattinson, Ian Howard, MSc	CDR(FTC)	S		30.06.98	MOD (BATH)
Patton, Richard,	LT(IC)	MS		01.05.02	RCDM
Paul, Gillian Morag,	SLT(IC)	X		01.06.03	RAMSEY
Paul, Russell William Fordyce, MA, psc	LT COL(FTC)	-	LC	30.06.01	1 ASSLT GP RM
Paulet, Michael Raoul,	LT(CC)	X	P	01.02.01	GANNET SAR FLT
Paulson, Richard Brian, BEng, MSc, MIEE	LT CDR(FTC)	E	WE	01.08.03	NOTTINGHAM
Pawsey, Simon Peter James, BEng	LT(IC)	E	TM U/T	01.01.05	DARTMOUTH BRNC
Payne, Christopher,	2LT(IC)	-		01.08.02	RE ENTRY(ARMY)
Payne, John Durley, BSc, pce, psc(j), n	LT CDR(FTC)	X	PWO(U)	01.06.98	UKMARBATSTAFF

Name	Rank	Branch	Spec	Seniority	Where Serving
Payne, Joseph Oliver, BEng	SLT(IC)	E	MESM	01.09.03	FWO DEVONPORT
Payne, Matthew John,	LT CDR(FTC)	X	PWO(C)	01.10.03	MWS COLLINGWOOD
Payne, Michael Thomas,	CAPT RM(CC)	-		01.09.03	HQ 3 CDO BDE RM
Payne, Miranda, BSc	LT(IC)	X		01.05.03	DRAKE COB
Payne, Philip John, BA	LT CDR(FTC)	X	HM	01.07.02	FWO DEVONPORT
Payne, Richard Charles, pce, pcea	CDR(FTC)	X	P	30.06.01	ALBION
Payne, William Dudley,	LT(IC)	X		01.05.03	ARGYLL
Peace, Richard William, PGDip, IEng, MIMarEST	LT CDR(FTC)	E	MESM	02.07.97	DLO BRISTOL
Peach, Graham Leslie, BSc, psc	CAPT(FTC)	E	WE	30.06.00	NELSON
Peachey, Neil,	SLT(IC)	E		01.01.05	MWS COLLINGWOOD
Peachey, Richard Matthew, BSc	LT(CC)	X	P	01.11.94	847 SQN
Peacock, Joel David,	SLT(IC)	X		01.12.05	MWS COLLINGWOOD
Peacock, Laura Gillian Joan, BMus	SLT(IC)	X		01.05.03	MWS COLLINGWOOD
Peacock, Stephen, BSc, MDA, CEng, MIEE	CDR(FTC)	E	WESM	30.06.03	EXCHANGE AUSTLIA
Peacock, Timothy James, MA, pce, pcea	CDR(FTC)	X	P	30.06.06	MONMOUTH
Peak, Martyn,	LT(FTC) (Act Lt Cdr)	X		03.04.98	ALBION
Peake, Stephen Peter,	LT(IC)	MS		01.07.04	DMSTC
Pearce, Elizabeth Anne, MA	LT(IC)	X		09.04.02	DARTMOUTH BRNC
Pearce, Jonathan,	LT(IC)	E	WE	01.01.04	CAPT MCTA
Pearce, Robert James, BA	LT(CC)	X		01.01.02	ALBION
Pearch, Sean Michael,	LT(FTC)	X	ATC	26.04.99	CHFHQ
Pearey, Michael Scott, DSC, BSc, jsdc, pce, pcea	CDR(FTC)	X	O	31.12.96	MOD (LONDON)
Pearmain, Stephanie Rosina, BSc, ADipC	LT(IC)	E	TM	14.05.00	OCLC PETERBRGH
Pears, Ian James, MSc, adp	LT CDR(FTC)	E	IS	01.10.00	PJHQ
Pearsall, Michael John Stanhope,	SLT(IC)	X		01.09.03	DUMBARTON CASTLE
Pearson, Alan James, BSc	LT(IC)	X	O U/T	01.01.05	RNAS CULDROSE
Pearson, Charles Peter Bellamy, BEng, CEng, MIMarEST	LT CDR(FTC)	E	ME	01.10.00	FOST SEA
Pearson, Christopher Robert, MA, MBA, MB, BChir, FRCS, DLO	SURG CDR(FCC)	-	(CE)	30.06.02	MDHU PORTSMOUTH
Pearson, Ian Thomas, BA, MEng	LT(IC)	E	P U/T	01.09.04	RNAS YEOVILTON
Pearson, James Carden,	LT(CC)	X	MCD	01.12.00	MWC PORTSDOWN
Pearson, Michael Forbes,	LT CDR(FTC)	X	O	01.03.01	PJHQ
Pearson, Neil, BEng, MSc, CEng, MIMarEST	LT CDR(FTC)	E	ME	01.08.97	FOST SEA
Pearson, Robert James, BA	SLT(IC)	X		01.01.04	QUORN
Pearson, Sarah Isobel, BA	SLT(IC)	S		01.01.04	CORNWALL
Pearson, Stephen John, MA, pce, psc(j)	CDR(FTC)	X	O	30.06.00	FOST SEA
Pearson, Susan, BEd	LT(CC)	S		01.05.01	NELSON
Peasley, Helen Susan, BA, PGCE	LT(IC)	E	IS	01.04.02	MWS COLLINGWOOD
Peattie, Ian William, BSc	LT(CC)	S		01.05.02	RNICG
Peck, Ian John, BSc, CEng, MRAeS, MDA	CDR(FTC)	E	AE	31.12.97	MOD (LONDON)
Peck, Simon Russell, MEng	LT(FTC)	E	AE	01.03.02	SULTAN
Pedler, Mark David, BEng	LT(CC)	X	P	01.07.97	EXCHANGE USA
Pedre, Robert George, BSc, ARCS	LT CDR(FTC)	X		01.10.04	MWS COLLINGWOOD
Pegg, Russell Montfort, pce, fsc	CAPT(FTC)	X	PWO(U)	30.06.05	CC MAR AGRIPPA
Pegrum, Terrence Allen, pcea	LT CDR(FTC)	X	P	01.10.99	JSCSC
Peilow, Benjamin Francis, BA, MILT, psc	CDR(FTC)	S		31.12.92	FLEET COSP&S
Pellecchia, Daniel Nicholas, LLB	SLT(IC)	X		01.09.04	DARTMOUTH BRNC
Pelly, Gilbert Ralph,	MAJ(FTC)	-		25.04.96	CTCRM
Penalver, Warren Craig,	LT(IC)	X	SM	01.01.04	SCEPTRE
Pendle, Martin Erle John, BSc, CEng, MIMarEST, jsdc	CAPT(FTC)	E	ME	30.06.06	DRAKE SFM
Pengelley, Tristan Anthony Hastings,	CAPT RM(CC)	X	C	01.09.04	40 CDO RM
Pengelly, Steven Paul, MB, CHB	SURG LT(SCC)	-		06.08.03	CFLT MED(SEA)
Penketh, Mark Geoffrey,	LT(FTC)	E	ME	02.09.99	FWO PORTS SEA
Penkman, William Alfred Vincent, BSc	MAJ(FTC)	-	P	01.09.04	JHCNI
Penn-Barwell, Jowan George, MB, CHB	SURG LT(SC(MD))	-		07.10.03	UKLFCSG RM
Pennefather, Douglas Cameron John,	CAPT RM(CC)	-		01.09.04	CTCRM
Pennington, Charles Edmond, BSc	CAPT RM(CC)	-		01.09.01	EXCHANGE ARMY UK
Penny, Anthony David, MSc, CEng, MIEE	CAPT(FTC)	E	WE	31.12.00	T45 IPT
Pentreath, Jonathan Patrick, BSc, pce, pcea, psc(j)	CDR(FTC)	X	P	30.06.03	MOD (LONDON)
Peppe, Alasdair George,	LT CDR(FTC)	X	PWO(U)	01.06.03	PJHQ
Pepper, Martin Richard, BSc, pce, pcea, psc,	CDR(FTC)	X	O	31.12.92	JDCC
Pepper, Nicholas Richard, BSc	SLT(IC)	S		01.09.04	DARTMOUTH BRNC
Pepper, Thomas,	SG LT(D)(SC(MD))	-	DPHSR	13.07.04	DRAKE COB(CNH)

Name	Rank	Branch	Spec	Seniority	Where Serving
Percharde, Michael Robert, BSc, pce, psc(j)	CDR(FTC)	X	AAWO	31.12.98	FLEET COSP&S
Percival, Fiona,	LT CDR(FTC)	S		01.10.03	NP IRAQ
Percival, Michael Christopher, MSc	LT CDR(FTC)	S		01.07.99	UKMARBATSTAFF
Percival, Victoria Helen, MEng	SLT(IC)	E	ME U/T	01.01.04	SULTAN
Percy, Nicolas Andrew, BSc	LT(CC)	X	MCD	01.04.99	GRIMSBY
Perera-Stack, Elizabeth, BSc	SLT(IC)	X		01.09.04	DARTMOUTH BRNC
Perkins, Ben, BEng	LT(FTC)	E	P	01.07.01	DLO YEO
Perkins, Michael Jonathan, BA, MDA, pce	CDR(FTC) (Act Capt)	X	AAWO	30.06.96	MOD (LONDON)
Perks, Andrew Barry, MEng	LT(IC)	X		01.11.05	RALEIGH
Perks, James Le Seelleur, pce(sm), SM(n)	CDR(FTC)	X	SM	30.06.05	SCEPTRE
Perrin, Mark Stephen, BA	CAPT RM(CC)	-		01.09.01	1 ASSAULT GP RM
Perry, Carl Steven Leslie, BSc	LT(IC)	E	TM	01.03.05	MWS COLLINGWOOD
Perry, Jonathan Neil, MB, ChB, FRCR	SURG CDR(FCC)	-	(CX)	31.12.96	MDHU PETERBRGH
Perry, Richard, BSc, BA(OU), MA, psc	CDR(FTC)	E	MESM	30.06.06	JSCSC
Perry, Robert William, sq	MAJ(FTC)	-	SO(LE)	01.10.00	1 ASSLT GP RM
Perryman, Ian Thomas Charles, BSc	LT(IC)	E	TM	01.01.00	RNICG
Perryment, Claire Patricia,	LT(CC)	X		01.08.01	MWS COLLINGWOOD
Peschardt, Charles William Hagbarth, BA, MCIPD	LT(IC)	X	P U/T	01.07.05	DHFS
Peskett, Daniel Mark, BEng, AMIMechE	LT(IC)	E	ME	01.03.03	CHATHAM
Petch, Alan Napier, BEng	LT(IC)	X	P	01.09.03	845 SQN
Peters, Andrew Douglas,	CAPT RM(CC)	-	SO(LE)	01.04.03	1 ASSAULT GP RM
Peters, Matthew Keith, BEng	SLT(IC)	E	ME	01.07.02	SULTAN
Peters, William Richard, BA, n	LT CDR(FTC)	X	PWO(U)	01.03.04	SOUTHAMPTON
Peterson, Keith Andrew, BEng	LT(IC)	E	WESM	01.09.03	SCEPTRE
Petheram, Anthony John, pce	LT CDR(FTC)	X	PWO(C)	01.09.97	DARTMOUTH BRNC
Petheram, Michael John, MBE, MA, pce, psc(j)	CDR(FTC)	X	PWO(U)	30.06.02	SULTAN
Petherick, Jason Stewart, pce, psc(j)	LT CDR(FTC)	X	AAWO	01.04.98	COMATG SEA
Pethick, Jerome Findlay, BEng	SLT(IC)	E	AE U/T	01.09.04	YORK
Pethybridge, Richard Alan, PGDIPAN, pce, n	LT CDR(FTC)	X	PWO(N)	01.05.97	ATHERSTONE
Petitt, Simon Richard, BEng, MBA, CEng, MIEE	CDR(FTC)	E	WE	30.06.03	ARK ROYAL
Pett, Jeremy Graham, BSc, MinstP, C PHYS	CDR(FTC)	E	TM	30.06.99	MOD (LONDON)
Pettigrew, Thomas Robert, BEng, IEng, MIIE	LT(CC)	E	TM	01.09.97	FOST FAS SHORE
Pettit, Samuel Anthony,	MID(IC)	X		01.02.05	DARTMOUTH BRNC
Pettitt, Gary William, pce	CDR(FTC)	X	PWO(U)	31.12.97	MOD (LONDON)
Petzer, Garth Stephen, MBE, DipTh	CHAPLAIN	CE		01.08.04	ARK ROYAL
Peyman, Tracy Anne,	LT(CC)	S		01.09.00	MOD (BATH)
Pheasant, John Christian Stephen, BSc	LT CDR(FTC) (Barrister)	S	BAR	01.10.00	FLEET COSP&S
Phelan, Sean Cameron,	SLT(IC)	X		01.01.06	DARTMOUTH BRNC
Phenna, Andrew, BEng	CDR(FTC)	E	WE	30.06.01	FWO PORTS SEA
Phesse, John Paul Lloyd, IEng, AMRAeS	LT CDR(FTC)	E	AE(L)	01.10.00	RNAS CULDROSE
Philip, Alistair David, BSc, n	LT(CC)	X	HM2	01.03.97	MWS HM TG (D)
Philips, Thomas James, MEng	LT(IC)	E	ME	01.01.06	CHATHAM
Philipson, Matthew James,	SLT(IC)	E	WE U/T	01.09.03	MWS COLLINGWOOD
Phillippo, Duncan George, MEng, PGDip	LT(IC)	E	MESM	01.05.04	TIRELESS
Phillips, Andrew Graham, BSc, CertTh	CHAPLAIN	CE		14.02.00	NEPTUNE 2SL/CNH
Phillips, Andrew Ralph, BA, IEng, MIIE	LT CDR(FTC)	E	AE	01.10.01	DCAE COSFORD
Phillips, David George, pce, pce(sm)	CDR(FTC)	X	SM	30.06.95	SHAPE BELGIUM
Phillips, David Guy,	CAPT RM(CC)	-	SO(LE)	01.04.03	CTCRM
Phillips, Edward Henry Lloyd, BA	SLT(IC)	X		01.02.04	ARGYLL
Phillips, Ian Michael, MSc	CDR(FTC)	MS		30.06.06	MOD (LONDON)
Phillips, James Charles, MB, CHB	SURG LT(MC(MD)	-		01.08.02	MDHU DERRIFORD
Phillips, James Nicholas, BEng, MSc, CEng, MIEE	LT CDR(FTC)	E	WE	01.03.03	DLO BRISTOL
Phillips, Jason Peter, pcea	LT CDR(FTC)	X	O	01.10.00	814 SQN
Phillips, Laura Claire,	LT(CC)	X		01.09.04	EXCHANGE SPAIN
Phillips, Mark Christopher, MBE	MAJ(FTC)	-	SO(LE)	01.10.04	1 ASSAULT GP RM
Phillips, Matthew Rhys,	LT(IC)	S		01.09.04	TIRELESS
Phillips, Richard Edward,	LT(CC)	X	P	01.09.03	RNAS YEOVILTON
Phillips, Richard Mark, MSc	LT(CC)	X		01.01.00	MWS COLLINGWOOD
Phillips, Simon Miles, MB, BS, MRCGP, Dip OM	SURG LTCDR(SCC)	-	GMPP	03.09.02	NELSON (PAY)
Phillips, Stephen John, MA, psc	LT COL(FTC)	-		30.06.04	JWC/CIS STAVANGR
Philo, Julian Quentin, BEng, CEng	LT CDR(FTC)	E	ME	01.06.98	FLEET COSP&S
Philpot, David John, BEng, MIEE, CEng	LT CDR(FTC)	E	WESM	18.07.00	TIRELESS

OFFICERS - ACTIVE LIST

Name	Rank	Branch	Spec	Seniority	Where Serving
Philpott, Marcus Cornforth, MB, CHB, ...SURG LT(SC(MD) (Act Surg Ltcdr)	-	GMPP		04.01.05	RNAS YEOVILTON
MRCGP, DRCOG, DCH, Dip FFP					
Philpott, Nigel Edward, psc(j)..CDR(FTC)	S			30.06.04	DARTMOUTH BRNC
Piaggesi, Gareth Fiorenzo, ...LT(IC)	E	AE		01.09.04	RAF WITTERING
Pickard, Richard James, BM, RCSEd...SURG LTCDR(SC(MD)	-			23.04.02	NELSON (PAY)
Pickard, Stephen Richard, ... LT(CC)	E	AE		01.09.00	FLEET COSP&S
Picken, Christopher Robert, MB, BCH, BAO................................SURG LT(MC(MD)	-			07.08.02	MDHU DERRIFORD
Pickering, David Allan, ...LT(IC)	MS			01.05.04	MDHU DERRIFORD
Pickles, David Richard, ...LT(FTC)	X	ATC		01.01.01	DARTMOUTH BRNC
Pickles, Ian Seaton, pce, pce(sm) ....CDR(FTC)	X	SM		30.06.97	BDS WASHINGTON
Pickles, Martin Richard, BSc...LT(CC)	X	P		01.05.01	815 FLT 244
Pickthall, David Nicholas, BSc, CEng, MIEE ....CDR(FTC)	E	WE		31.12.97	JFCHQ BRUNSSUM
Pickup, Richard Allan, CBE, BSc, MA, psc(m), psc(j)o ....COL(FTC)	-			30.06.03	SFSG
Pierce, Adrian Kevern Maxwell, PGDIPAN, pce, n...................................LT CDR(FTC)	X	PWO(N)		01.02.00	BLYTH
Pierce, Sarah Louise, ...LT(IC)	X	MW		01.09.05	TEMERAIRE
Pierson, Matthew Fraser, odc(Fr)..LT COL(FTC)	-			30.06.04	MOD (LONDON)
Pike, Martin Stephen, BSc...LT CDR(FTC) (Act Cdr)	S			01.03.91	HQ RHINE/EURO SG
Pike, Robin Timothy, ...LT(IC)	E	WESM		01.01.04	ASM IPT
Pilkington, Alex Gregory Howarth, BSc...MAJ(IC)	-			01.10.04	CTCRM
Pilkington, Barry Mark, MEng...SLT(IC)	X	P U/T		01.02.04	RNAS YEOVILTON
Pilkington, William James, ...CAPT RM(CC)	-			01.09.04	EXCHANGE ARMY UK
Pillai, Sonia, ...SURG SLT(MDC)	-			20.09.04	DARTMOUTH BRNC
Pillar, Christopher David, pce...LT CDR(FTC)	X	PWO(U)		01.03.95	NELSON
Pilsworth, Dermod Scott, CGIA ....LT CDR(FTC)	E	WE		01.06.85	T45 IPT
Pimm, Anthony Richard, BSc...LT(IC)	X			01.09.04	PORTLAND
Pimpalnerkar, Ashvin Lakshman, MSc, MB, ...SURG CDR(MCC)	-	(CO/S)		30.06.04	RCDM
BS, MChOrth, FRCS(ORTH)					
Pinckney, Mathew Robert Nicholas, ...CAPT RM(IC)	-			01.09.04	FOST SEA
Pinder, Christopher David, BEng..LT CDR(CC)	E	TM		01.10.04	DCAE COSFORD
Pine, Paul Martin, BSc, PGCE...LT(CC)	E	TM		06.12.98	MWS COLLINGWOOD
Pinhey, Andrew David, ...LT(IC)	MS			01.01.02	NEPTUNE BNSL
Pink, Simon Edward, PGDIPAN, pce, n...LT CDR(FTC)	X	PWO(N)		01.01.02	ALBION
Pinney, Richard Francis, MSc..CAPT RM(IC)	-			01.09.05	DNR DISP TEAM
Pinnington, Adam John, ...SLT(IC)	X			01.01.04	MIDDLETON
Piper, Benjamin James, ...SLT(IC)	X			01.05.03	MWS COLLINGWOOD
Piper, Neale Derek, ARRC, BSc...LT CDR(FC(MD)	Q	IC		01.10.03	MOD (LONDON)
Pipkin, Christopher, MB, BS, FRCPath..SURG CAPT(FCC)	-	CPDATE		30.06.04	NELSON
Pipkin, Peter John, BEng, CEng, MIEE..LT(FTC)	E	WE		01.04.00	RMC OF SCIENCE
Pipkin, Simon Christian, pcea...LT CDR(FTC)	X	P		01.10.95	DHFS
Pirie, Ian Thomas, ...LT(IC)	X	C		01.07.04	MWS COLLINGWOOD
Pirrie, James Alexander, ...LT(FTC)	X	C		19.09.00	HQ DCSA
Pitcher, Paul, BA, pce ....LT CDR(FTC)	X	PWO(C)		01.10.02	NELSON
Pitchford, Sara, ...SLT(IC)	MS			01.02.05	DARTMOUTH BRNC
Pitman, Lisa Jill, BEd...LT(IC)	S			01.01.03	PORTLAND
Pitt, Jonathan Mark, SM(n), SM...LT CDR(FTC)	X	SM		17.02.99	MOD (LONDON)
Pitt, William Thomas, ...LT(IC)	X	EW		01.01.03	UKMARBATSTAFF
Plackett, Andrew John, BSc, MA ....LT CDR(FTC)	E	TM		01.10.03	MWC SOUTHWICK
Plant, Ian Robert, BSc..LT CDR(FTC)	E	AE		01.07.90	LOAN JTEG BSC DN
Plant, Jeremy Neil Melrose, BSc, MDA ....CDR(FTC)	E	AE		31.12.99	FS MASU
Platt, Jonathan Howard, BSc ....LT(CC)	X	P		16.06.96	849 SQN B FLT
Platt, Nicola, ...LT(FTC)	S	(W)		03.04.98	FORT BLOCKHOUSE
Pledger, David, ...LT CDR(FTC)	X	AV		01.10.02	RFANSU
Plenty, Andrew Justin, ...LT(IC)	X	ATC		01.09.03	RNAS CULDROSE
Plewes, Andrew Burns, BSc ....MAJ(FTC)	-			27.04.02	COMAMPHIBFOR
Plunkett, Gareth Neil, ...SLT(IC)	X	P		01.09.03	RNAS YEOVILTON
Pocock, David, ...LT CDR(FTC)	S			16.10.00	AFPAA HQ
Podger, Kevin Gordon Ray, BSc, psc...CDR(FTC)	E	MESM		30.06.95	FLEET COSP&S
Podmore, Anthony, BSc..CDR(FTC)	E	TM		30.06.01	FLEET FOTR
Pointon, Bryony Margaret, MB, CHB ....SURG LT(SCC)	-			04.05.02	NELSON (PAY)
Polding, Martin, BA..LT(FTC)	X	P		01.11.93	848 SQN HERON
Poll, Martin George, BA, DipTh ....CHAPLAIN	CE			14.06.90	FLEET COSP&S
Pollard, Alexandra Eleanor, BA ....LT(CC)	X	FC		01.08.98	BLAZER

Name	Rank	Branch	Spec	Seniority	Where Serving
Pollard, Andrew John,	LT(FTC)	E	ME	01.04.01	SULTAN
Pollard, Jonathan Richard, BEng, MSc gw, CEng, MIEE, NDipM	LT(FTC)	E	WE	01.12.99	MWS COLLINGWOOD
Pollitt, Alexander William,	SLT(IC)	X	P U/T	01.05.03	RNAS YEOVILTON
Pollitt, David Nigel Anthony, pce, pce(sm), psc	LT CDR(FTC)	X	SM	01.04.89	FLEET COMOPS NWD
Pollock, Barnaby James, BSc,	LT(IC)	X		01.11.05	RNAS YEOVILTON
Pollock, David John, BSc, pce, pce(sm)	CDR(FTC)	X	SM	30.06.99	JSCSC
Pollock, Malcolm Philip, MA, pce, pcea, psc(j)	CDR(FTC)	X	O	30.06.05	MWC PORTSDOWN
Pollock, Sir Michael (Patrick), GCB, LVO, DSC, psc	ADM OF FLEET	-		01.03.74	
Pomeroy, Mark Anthony,	CDR(FTC)	E	ME	30.06.03	FWO PORTS SEA
Pomeroy, Philippa Mary, BEd, psc(j)	CDR(FTC)	S		30.06.06	MOD (LONDON)
Pond, Robert James,	LT(IC)	E	MESM	01.05.03	DARTMOUTH BRNC
Ponsford, Philip Kevin, BSc, MInsD, pce	LT CDR(FTC)	X	PWO(U)	01.01.99	FOST SEA
Poole, Daniel Charles, BA	LT(IC)	S		01.09.05	DLO BRISTOL
Poole, Jason Lee, MA, pce, psc(j)	CDR(FTC)	X	MCD	30.06.04	MOD (LONDON)
Poole, Timothy James, MRAeS, MCGI, pcea, gdas, MSc	LT(FTC)	X	O	16.01.92	700M MERLIN OEU
Pooley, Steven William, BSc	LT CDR(FTC)	E	WESM	01.07.96	TORPEDO IPT
Pope, Catherine Manuela, MA, MSc, psc	CDR(FTC)	X	METOC	24.06.98	HQ DCSA
Pope, Kevin David,	LT(IC)	X	P	01.01.05	RNAS YEOVILTON
Porrett, Johnathan Anthony,	LT CDR(FTC)	S	SM	14.11.95	FLEET COSP&S
Porritt, Colin,	LT(IC)	E		01.05.02	EXCHANGE AUSTLIA
Porteous, Russell,	LT(IC)	E	ME U/T	08.04.05	ILLUSTRIOUS
Porter, Derek Lowry, BA	LT(CC)	S	SM	01.06.97	RAF COTTESMORE
Porter, Matthew Edward, MBE, BSc, psc(j)	LT COL(FTC)	-		30.06.04	1 ASSAULT GP RM
Porter, Simon Paul, pce, psc(j)	CDR(FTC)	X	AAWO	31.12.99	FLEET COSCAP
Porter, Suzanne, MB, BSc, ChB, Dip FFP, DRCOG, JCPTGP	SURG LTCDR(MCC)	-	GMPP	01.08.01	RALEIGH
Porter, Timothy Benedict, BA	LT CDR(FTC)	S		01.05.02	UKSU JHQ LISBON
Postgate, Michael Oliver,	CAPT RM(CC)	-		01.09.05	40 CDO RM
Potter, David John,	LT(FTC)	X	O	24.07.97	824 SQN
Potter, David Lloyd, MB, CHB	SURG LT(SC(MD)	-		04.08.04	CDO LOG REGT RM
Potter, Michael John, CBE, ADC, MA, MSc, CEng, MIMarEST, MINucE, MinstP, C PHYS, psc	CAPT(FTC) (Commodore)	E	TM	30.06.97	FLEET FOTR
Potts, Duncan Laurence, BSc, pce	CAPT(FTC)	X	PWO(U)	30.06.00	MOD (LONDON)
Potts, Kevin Maxwell, pcea	LT CDR(FTC(A)	X	P	01.02.92	727 NAS
Potts, Ruth Ernestine, BSc	LT(CC)	S		01.08.00	CNH(R)
Pounds, Alexander,	2LT(IC)	-		01.08.02	CTCRM LYMPSTONE
Powell, Alan,	SLT(IC)	E		01.01.05	MWC SOUTHWICK
Powell, David Charles, MSc, CEng, MIMarEST	CAPT(FTC)	E	ME	30.06.06	AFPAA(CENTURION)
Powell, Gregory Mark John,	SLT(IC)	X		01.01.04	MWS COLLINGWOOD
Powell, Richard Laurence, MA, pce, pcea, psc(j)	CDR(FTC)	X	P	31.12.00	UKMARBATSTAFF
Powell, Steven Richard, pce	LT CDR(FTC)	X	PWO(C)	01.07.98	RMC OF SCIENCE
Powell, William Glyn, pce, pcea	LT CDR(FTC)	X	O	16.12.98	JHQ/CIS LISBON
Power, Benjamin,	SLT(IC)	X		01.09.03	SHOREHAM
Powles, Derek Anthony, MEng	LT CDR(FTC)	E	ME	01.02.04	RICHMOND
Powne, Simon Philip Watts,	LT(IC)	E	ME	01.05.02	1 ASSLT GP RM
Poynton, Claire Marie Frances, BSc	SLT(IC)	S		01.05.04	CHATHAM
Precious, Angus P,	CAPT RM(IC)	-		01.09.04	CDO LOG REGT RM
Preece, David Graeme, BA	LT CDR(FTC)	S	SM	01.08.01	FOST SM SEA
Preece, Simon Edward, BSc	LT(IC)	X		01.09.04	LEDBURY
Prendergast, Sally Ann, MSc, PGDip, FCIPD, MCIPD	LT CDR(CC)	S		25.06.02	RNICG
Prentice, David Charles,	LT CDR(FTC) (Act Cdr)	X	PWO(C)	22.12.97	EXCHANGE USA
Prescott, Shaun, BEng, MA, CEng, MIEE, psc(j)	CDR(FTC)	E	WE	30.06.01	MOD (LONDON)
Pressdee, Simon John,	LT(FTC)	X	MCD	01.07.98	FDU3
Pressly, James Winchester, BSc, MA, psc(j)	LT COL(FTC)	-		30.06.05	MOD (LONDON)
Prest, Neal Andrew,	LT(FTC)	S	(W)	01.10.04	MANCHESTER
Prest, Stephen Frederick, MEng, MIEE	LT(CC)	E	WE	01.06.00	JSCSC
Preston, Jacqueline Natalie, BSc	SLT(IC)	X	O U/T	01.01.04	DARTMOUTH BRNC
Preston, Mark Richard, BEng, CEng, MIMechE	LT CDR(FTC)	E	ME	01.10.99	MOD (BATH)
Preston, Ross Walker, BSc	MAJ(FTC)	-		01.09.02	CTCRM
Preston, Thomas Edward, MA	CAPT RM(CC)	-		01.09.02	40 CDO RM
Price, Andrew Michael, sq	LT COL(FTC)	-	C	30.06.06	FLEET HQ WI
Price, David Glyn,	CAPT RM(FTC)	-	SO(LE)	01.01.01	EXCHANGE AUSTLIA
Price, David John, pce	LT CDR(FTC)	X	AAWO	01.04.93	MWC PORTSDOWN

Name	Rank	Branch Spec	Seniority	Where Serving
Price, David William, ...CDR(FTC)	X	REG	30.06.05	FLEET COSCAP
Price, Frederick Earle Francis, MBE, MA, MSc, ...CDR(FTC) (Act Capt)	E	TM	30.06.95	JSCSC
MBA, PhD, CEng, Eur Ing, MIOA, MInsD, psc				
Price, James Edward Owen, BA.....................................CAPT RM(CC)	-		01.09.02	HQ1GP HQSTC
Price, John Philip, MA, MInsD, psc...................................CDR(FTC)	E	ME	30.06.96	MOD (LONDON)
Price, Joseph Charles, BSc...LT(CC)	X	MCD	05.03.01	LEDBURY
Price, Martin John, MA, psc ....LT COL(FTC)	-	MLDR	31.12.98	CDO LOG REGT RM
Price, Matthew William, BSc...SLT(IC)	S		01.01.05	DARTMOUTH BRNC
Price, Raymond Terence, ...CAPT RM(CC)	-	SO(LE)	01.04.02	CTCRM
Price, Tania Lucille, BSc, MA(Ed), Cert Ed, MCIPD ....LT CDR(FTC)	W	TM	01.10.92	HQ SACT
Price, Terence Peter, MSc..LT CDR(FTC)	E	WE	01.10.97	CAPT MCTA
Price, Timothy Andrew, pce, n..LT CDR(FTC)	X	AAWO	01.07.98	JSCSC
Price, Tracie Evelyn, BSc...LT CDR(CC)	E	TM	01.10.02	NAVSEC
Price, Trevor William, BSc, MA, psc(j)....................................CDR(FTC)	X	METOC	30.06.05	FLEET COMOPS NWD
Price, Victoria Juliette, MB, ChB, BSc.........................SURG LTCDR(MCC)	-		04.08.04	NELSON (PAY)
Priddle, Alexandria C, BA ....LT(IC)	E	TM	01.01.02	DEF SCH OF LANG
Priddle, Steven Michael R, ...CAPT RM(IC)	-	P	01.04.04	845 SQN
Prideaux, Robert John, ...LT(IC)	E	MESM	01.07.04	VANGUARD(STBD)
Priest, James Edward, BEng ....LT(CC)	X	P	15.02.98	MWS COLLINGWOOD
Priestley, Catherine, BSc..LT(IC)	E	TM	01.01.00	RALEIGH
Prince, Mark Edward, BEng, CEng, MIMarE.........................LT CDR(FTC)	E	MESM	01.10.00	FLEET COSP&S
Pringle, Anthony, pce, pcea..LT CDR(FTC)	X	P	01.07.90	MOD (LONDON)
Prinsep, Timothy John, BEng, CEng, MIEE ....LT CDR(FTC)	E	WE	01.06.00	FLEET COSCAP
Prior, Grant Michael, IEng, FIIE...CDR(FTC)	E	WE	30.06.05	DLO TES
Prior, Iain Alexander, ...LT(FTC)	E	ME	01.04.01	MWS EXCELLENT
Prior, Kate Rebecca Edna Jane, MB, BS........................SURG LTCDR(MCC)	-		06.08.02	NELSON (PAY)
Prissick, Matthew Alexander, BSc ....SLT(IC)	S		01.05.04	GLOUCESTER
Pritchard, Gavin Scrimgeour, pce...CDR(FTC)	X	PWO(U)	30.06.01	KENT
Pritchard, Lloyd, ...2LT(IC)	-		01.08.00	45 CDO RM
Pritchard, Simon Andrew, MA, psc.......................................LT COL(FTC)	-		30.06.06	MWC SOUTHWICK
Procter, Jamie Edward, BEng, MA, MSc, Cert Ed, PGDip, psc(j) ....LT CDR(FTC)	E	TMSM	01.10.01	SULTAN
Proctor, Anna Rachael, BM, Dip FFP.........................SURG LT(MC(MD)	-		01.08.01	NELSON (PAY)
Proctor, Nicholas Stephen, ...LT(IC)	S	SM	01.05.03	UKSU JHQ NORTH
Proctor, William John Gibbon, BEng, CEng, MIEE, MSc.................LT CDR(FTC)	E	WE	01.03.02	MWS COLLINGWOOD
Prodger, Andrew Phillip, ...LT(IC)	E	WESM	01.01.03	DLO BRISTOL
Proffitt, Adrian, ...SURG LT(SCC)	-		16.09.05	DARTMOUTH BRNC
Prole, Nicholas Mark, ...LT(FTC)	X	P	16.09.97	846 SQN
Prollins, Mark Richard, ...MID(NE)(IC)	X		01.11.05	DARTMOUTH BRNC
Prosser, Matthew James, ...LT(CC)	X	MW	01.08.01	LEDBURY
Proud, Andrew Douglas, BEng ....LT CDR(FTC)	E	AE	11.06.99	MOD (LONDON)
Proudman, Michael Paul, ...SLT(IC)	X		01.08.03	MWS COLLINGWOOD
Prowse, David George, ...LT(FTC)	E	ME	01.04.01	ENTERPRISE
Pruden, Ian, BSc..MAJ(CC)	-		01.10.04	FLEET HQ WI
Pryce, Helen Claire, BEng ....LT(IC)	E	ME	01.09.04	SOMERSET
Pugh, Geoffrey Noel John, BEng..LT(IC)	X	ATCU/T	01.10.03	RNAS CULDROSE
Pugh, Jonathan, BEng, CEng, MIEE ....LT CDR(FTC)	E	WE	08.03.00	MWS COLLINGWOOD
Pullin, Kate Marise, ...MID(NE)(IC)	X	O U/T	01.01.06	DARTMOUTH BRNC
Pulvertaft, Rupert James, odc(Fr) ....LT COL(FTC)	-		30.06.03	EUMS
Punch, John Matthew, BSc...LT(CC)	X	P	01.01.01	MWS COLLINGWOOD
Punton, Ian Matthew, BEng, CEng, MRAeS, psc(j) ....CDR(FTC)	E	AE	30.06.06	JF HARROLE OFF
Purdy, Richard John, ...LT(IC)	E	AE	01.09.04	702 SQN HERON
Purser, Lloyd John, MBE ....CAPT RM(IC)	-	SO(LE)	19.07.05	1 ASSAULT GP RM
Purvis, David Mark, MEng ....LT CDR(FTC)	E	AE	16.10.04	LOAN JTEG BSC DN
Purvis, Stephen Graham, ...LT(IC)	X		01.05.05	RNAS YEOVILTON
Puxley, Michael Edward, BEng, CEng, MIEE ....LT CDR(FTC)	E	WESM	01.09.04	RALEIGH
Pyette, Marc Daniel Victor Crosby, BA, MSc.............................SLT(IC)	X		01.02.04	ALBION
Pyke, Danial, ...2LT(IC)	-		01.08.02	CTCRM LYMPSTONE
Pyne, Robert Leslie, BA, DipTh.......................................CHAPLAIN	CE		23.01.90	2SL/CNH FOTR

Q

Quaite, David Geoffrey, BSc ....LT(IC)	X		01.01.03	MWS COLLINGWOOD
Quaye, Duncan Thomas George, MSc, CEng, FIMarEST.................CDR(FTC)	E	ME	30.06.98	DFTE PORTSMOUTH

Name	Rank	Branch Spec	Seniority	Where Serving
Quekett, Ian Peter Scott, BEng, MSc, MIEE, psc(j)	LT CDR(FTC)	E	WE	01.08.99	AFPAA HQ
Quick, Benjamin Paul, BSc	SLT(IC)	X		01.06.03	ROEBUCK
Quick, Neville Hellins, BSc, CEng, MIEE	LT CDR(FTC)	E	WE	01.05.91	CAPT MCTA
Quine, Nicholas John, MA, MIEE, psc	LT CDR(FTC)	E	WE	01.12.88	MWS COLLINGWOOD
Quinn, Antony David, BSc, PGDip	LT(IC)	E	TM	01.07.00	FPGRM
Quinn, Mark Eugene, MSc	LT(IC)	E	IS	01.03.00	MWS COLLINGWOOD
Quinn, Michael Gerard, BA	LT(CC)	X	FC	01.01.02	FOST SEA
Quinn, Paul Anthony, OBE, BA, FCMI,	CAPT(FTC)	S	SM	30.06.00	FLEET COSP&S
FHCIMA, FCIPD, MInstPS, CDipAF, jsdc					
Quinn, Shaun Andrew, pcea	LT CDR(FTC)	X	O	01.10.04	FOST NWD (JMOTS)
Quinn, Thomas,	2LT(IC)	-		01.08.02	CTCRM LYMPSTONE
Quirk, Anthony Thomas, IEng, MIIE	LT(FTC)	E	WE	02.09.99	DSFM PORTSMOUTH

R

Name	Rank	Branch Spec	Seniority	Where Serving
Raby, Nigel John Francis, OBE, MSc, jsdc	RADM	-	WE	02.09.04	2SL/CNH FOTR
(MAR 06)					
Race, Nigel James, MA, pce, psc(j)	CDR(FTC)	X	PWO(C)	31.12.99	RN SINGAPORE
Rackham, Anthony David Henry, BSc, pce	LT CDR(FTC)	X	PWO(A)	01.10.02	MWS COLLINGWOOD
Rackham, Katharine, BSc, n	LT CDR(FTC)	X		01.03.05	NAVSEC
Radakin, Antony David, LLB, pce, psc(j), MA	CDR(FTC)	X	PWO(U)	30.06.02	MOD (LONDON)
Radbourne, Neville Ian,	LT CDR(FTC)	E	WE	01.10.02	HQ DCSA
Radford, Andrew James, BEng	LT(FTC)	X	P	01.06.92	848 SQN HERON
Rae, Alistair Lewis, BEng, CEng, MIEE	LT CDR(FTC)	E	WE	01.04.05	FLEET COSCAP
Rae, Anthony James William, BSc, pcea	LT CDR(FTC) (Act Cdr)	X	P	01.10.99	MOD (LONDON)
Rae, Derek Gordon, BSc, PGDip	LT CDR(FTC)	X	H1	01.03.04	GLEANER
Rae, Scott MacKenzie, MBE, QHC, BD	PR CHAPLAIN	SF		02.02.81	FLEET HQ WI
DGNCS-DNCS PPO PCSFCC N APR 06)					
Rae, Stephen Gordon, AGSM	LT CDR(FTC)	S		01.02.00	FLEET COSP&S
Raeburn, Craig, BSc, SM(n)	LT(FTC)	X	PWO(U)	01.09.96	MONTROSE
Raeburn, Mark, pce, n	LT CDR(FTC)	X	PWO(N)	01.07.02	MWS COLLINGWOOD
Raffaelli, Philip Iain, MSc, MB, BCH, MRCGP, FFOM, rcds, jsdc	SURG RADM	-	CPDATE	04.05.04	HQ DMETA
CHIEF EXECUTIVE MAY 04)					
Rainey, Owen Hamilton, MB, BCH, BAO	SURG LT(SC/MD)	-		02.08.05	NELSON (PAY)
Ralls, Damien William, BEng	LT(IC)	E	WESM	01.09.04	MWC PORTSDOWN
Ralph, Julian,	SURG LT(SCC)	-		16.03.04	DARTMOUTH BRNC
Ralston, William Archibald, BSc, LCIPD, PGCE	LT(IC)	E	TM	01.01.02	FOST FAS SHORE
Ramaswami, Ravi, MB, BS	SURG LTCDR(SC/MD) (Act Surg Cdr)	-	(CO/M)	27.07.96	INM ALVERSTOKE
Ramm, Steven Charles, pce, pce(sm), psc, psc(j)	CAPT(FTC)	X	SM	31.12.98	FWO FASLANE SEA
Ramsay, Alastair, BSc	LT(IC)	E	TM	01.07.02	RALEIGH
Ramsey, Jeremy Stephen, BSc	LT CDR(FTC)	S		16.04.89	AFPAA JPA
Ramsey, Ryan Trevor, pce(sm), SM(n)	LT CDR(FTC)	X	SM	01.11.00	EXCHANGE USA
Ramshaw, George William Lilwall, BSc, CEng, FCMI, MIEE, MDA, MCIPD	CDR(FTC)	E	WE	30.06.99	T45 IPT
Rance, Maxwell George William, MA, psc(j)	CDR(FTC)	S		31.12.99	MOD (BATH)
Rand, Marc James, BEng, MSc	LT CDR(FTC)	E	ME	01.05.01	MANCHESTER
Rand, Mark Andrew,	LT(CC)	E	WESM	01.01.02	FLEET COMOPS NWD
Rand, Mark Conrad,	CAPT RM(IC)	-		24.07.04	1 ASSAULT GP RM
Randall, David Frederick, BA, MSc	CDR(FTC)	S		30.06.02	AFPAA JPA
Randall, Richard David, BSc, MDA, CEng, MIMechE	CDR(FTC)	E	MESM	30.06.03	DLO BRISTOL
Randle, Martin Philip, MB, CHB, FRCSEd, MRCOG, JCPTGP	SURG CDR(SC/MD)	-	GMPP	01.09.05	RALEIGH
Randles, Steven, BA	LT(CC)	X		01.06.00	TRACKER
Rankin, Graham Johnathon,	LT(CC)	X	PWO(A)	01.09.01	UKMARBATSTAFF
Rankin, Suzanne Jayne,	LT CDR(FC/MD)	Q	ONC	01.10.03	JSCSC
Ransom, Benjamin Robert James,	LT(IC)	X		01.09.00	MANCHESTER
Ranson, Christopher David, MSc, DipFM, CEng, MIEE	CDR(FTC)	E	WE	30.06.99	HQ DCSA
Rasor, Andrew Martin, pcea	LT CDR(FTC)	X	P	01.10.04	845 SQN
Ratcliffe, John Paul, BSc, PGDip	CAPT(FTC)	E	TM	30.06.06	DISC
Raval, Vivek,	SLT(IC)	X		01.02.05	DARTMOUTH BRNC
Rawal, Krishna Mark, MB, BS, DObstRCOG, MRCGP	SURG CDR(MCC)	-	GMPP	30.06.05	UKSU JHQ LISBON
Rawles, Julian Roy,	LT(FTC) (Act Lt Cdr)	X	ATC	01.04.99	CHFHQ
Rawlings, Damian Paul, BEng, MDA	LT CDR(FTC)	E	ME	01.08.95	FLEET COSP&S
Rawlings, Gary Andrew,	LT(FTC)	E	ME	01.04.01	ECHO
Rawlins, Simon Terence,	LT(CC)	X	P	01.04.02	LOAN OTHER SVCE

Name	Rank	Branch	Spec	Seniority	Where Serving
Rawlinson, Kathryn Elizabeth,	SLT(IC)	X		01.05.03	BLYTH
Rawlinson, Stephen James, BEng, CEng, MIMarEST	LT CDR(FTC)	E	MESM	01.03.99	MANCHESTER
Rawson, Scott Michael, BEng, MSc	LT CDR(FTC)	E	MESM	01.04.03	SULTAN
Ray, Benjamin Timothy, BEng	SLT(IC)	E	ME	01.01.04	UKMFTS IPT
Ray, Louise Barbara, LLB	LT(IC)	X		01.08.04	MANCHESTER
Raybould, Adrian Glyn, MA, MSc, CEng, MIEE, psc(j)	CDR(FTC)	E	WESM	30.06.01	FLEET COSCAP
Rayner, Andrew, BEng, MSc, MIEE	LT CDR(FTC)	E	WE	01.12.00	FOST SEA
Rayner, Brett Nicholas, psc	CAPT(FTC)	S		30.06.99	HQ SACT
Raynes, Christopher, BSc	LT(CC)	X	P	16.09.98	EXCHANGE ARMY UK
Rea, Stephen Dennis,	LT(CC)	X		01.07.00	JSCSC
Read, Alun John,	LT CDR(FTC)(A)	X	P	01.10.04	DHFS
Read, Clinton Derek,	CAPT RM(FTC) (Act Maj)	-		01.05.00	NP AFGHANISTAN
Read, Jonathon Asher Jason Marcus, MB, BS	SURG LTCDR(MC(MD)	-	O U/T	04.08.04	MDHU DERRIFORD
Read, Paul Steven, BEng, MSc gw, CEng, MIEE	LT(FTC)	E	WE	01.03.97	DLO BRISTOL
Read, Richard John, BA	MAJ(FTC)	-	LC	01.09.02	FLEET COSCAP
Readwin, Roger Roy, BA	LT CDR(FTC)	X	PWO(A)	01.04.04	UKMARBATSTAFF
Reah, Stephen, BEng	LT CDR(FTC)	E	ME	02.05.00	FLEET COSP&S
Rearden, Richard Joseph,	MAJ(FTC)	-	SO(LE)	01.10.03	JSCSC
Reaves, Charles Edward, LLB	LT(CC)	S		01.01.04	MOD (LONDON)
Redding, Andrew Mark,	LT(IC)	MS		01.07.04	MDHU PORTSMOUTH
Redman, Charles Jeremy Rufus, pce, n	LT CDR(FTC)	X		23.11.98	OCEAN
Redman, Christopher Douglas Jeremy, BDS, MSc, SGCDR(D)(FCC)	-			31.12.00	EXCHANGE USA
LDS RCS(Eng), MGDS RCS, MFDS,RCS					
Redmayne, Mark Edward, BA	LT(CC)	X		01.06.99	GIBRALTAR PBS
Redmayne, Michael Julian, BSc	LT(IC)	X	H2	01.01.03	FWO DEVPT SEA
Redstone, Colin,	CDR(FTC)	S	SM	31.12.98	PJHQ
Reece, Nigel David, BEng, MSc, CEng, PGDip,	LT CDR(FTC)	E	MESM	01.03.00	CNNRP BRISTOL
MIEE, MIMechE, MIMarEST					
Reed, Andrew William, OBE, BSc, pce	CDR(FTC)	X	AAWO	31.12.00	MOD (LONDON)
Reed, Darren Keith, BA, PGDipl	LT CDR(FTC)	S	BAR	01.12.04	ENDURANCE
Reed, Edward Christopher Dominic,	CAPT RM(IC)	-		01.09.05	45 CDO RM
Reed, Frank, OBE, BA, MSc, psc	CDRE(FTC)	MS	(P)	12.06.02	FLEET COSP&S
Reed, James Hamilton, pce, pcea, psc(j)o	LT CDR(FTC)	X	P	01.04.95	JDCC
Reed, Jeremy Jameson, BSc	MAJ(CC)	-		01.01.01	JACIG
Reed, Jonathan Charles,	LT CDR(FTC)	E	AE	01.10.02	814 SQN
Reed, Mark, BSc, PGDip	LT CDR(FTC)	X	METOC	01.10.98	MOD (LONDON)
Reed, Nicholas,	LT CDR(FTC)	S	SM	01.10.04	NOTTINGHAM
Reed, Peter Kirby,	SLT(UCE)(IC)	E	ME	01.09.01	SULTAN
Rees, Adam Martin, BA, MSc	LT(CC)	E	TM	01.09.98	FLEET HQ PORTSEA
Rees, John Blain Minto, BSc, jsdc	CAPT(FTC)	E	TM	31.12.99	NAVSEC
Rees, John Patrick, MSc	CDR(FTC)	S		30.06.06	JDCC
Rees, Justin Harrington, BSc, MCIT, MILT, ACIS	CDR(FTC)	S		01.07.00	RALEIGH
Rees, Karen Margaret Mary, LLB	LT(CC)	S		01.10.99	DARTMOUTH BRNC
Rees, Paul Stuart Chadwick, MB, BS, MRCP, DiplMC RCSED	SURG LTCDR(MCC)	-		06.08.02	NELSON (PAY)
Rees, Richard Thomas, BEng, n	LT CDR(FTC)	X	PWO(U)	01.12.03	NORTHUMBERLAND
Rees, Simon Geoffrey,	LT(IC)	X	SM	01.12.05	RALEIGH
Reese, David Michael, BSc	LT CDR(FTC)	X	O	01.09.02	LOAN OTHER SVCE
Reeves, Andrew Philip, SM(n)	LT(CC)	X	SM	01.01.03	RALEIGH
Reeves, Paul Keith, PGDip	LT(CC)	E	MESM	01.08.00	TIRELESS
Reid, Benjamin William,	CAPT RM(IC)	-		01.09.05	45 CDO RM
Reid, Charles Ian, BSc, pce, pce(sm), psc(j)	CDR(FTC)	X	SM	31.12.99	MOD (LONDON)
Reid, Douglas Russell,	LT(IC)	X	AV	01.07.04	SULTAN
Reid, James Lyle, BSc	LT(IC)	X		01.05.00	DUMBARTON CASTLE
Reid, James Robert, BA	SLT(IC)	X		01.11.04	ALBION
Reid, Jason Charles James, BEng, CEng, MIEE	LT CDR(FTC)	E	WESM	01.04.01	MOD (LONDON)
Reid, Joseph Anthony William, MSc	LT(IC)	X	O U/T	01.12.05	702 SQN HERON
Reid, Martyn, pce, pcea, psc	CDR(FTC)	X	O	30.06.94	SHAPE BELGIUM
Reid, Martyn Richard,	LT(CC)	X		01.04.95	MWS COLLINGWOOD
Reidy, Paul Alan, pce(sm), SM	LT CDR(FTC)	X	SM	01.11.98	MOD (LONDON)
Reilly, John,	SURG SLT(SCC)	-		20.09.04	DARTMOUTH BRNC
Reilly, Paul, BA	LT(IC)	E		08.06.04	NELSON
Reindorp, David Peter, PGDIPAN, AFRIN, psc(j)o, pce	CDR(FTC)	X	PWO(N)	30.06.02	JSCSC

Name	Rank	Branch	Spec	Seniority	Where Serving
Relf, Elizabeth Mary, ...LT(IC)	X	O U/T		01.05.05	824 SQN
Relf, Kerry Marie, BA.................................LT(CC) (Act Lt Cdr)	S			01.07.99	FLEET COSP&S
Renaud, Gavin Andrew Richard, ...LT(CC)	X	O		16.10.01	CTCRM
Rennie, Richard Anthony, ...SURG SLT(SCC)	-			01.07.03	DARTMOUTH BRNC
Renshaw, Paul, ...CAPT RM(CC)	-			01.09.04	40 CDO RM
Renwick, John, ...CDR(FTC)	S	SM		30.06.02	MOD (LONDON)
Reston, Samuel Craig, MB, ChB .... SURG LTCDR(FCC)	-			07.08.01	NELSON (PAY)
Retter, Rachael Louise, BA ....LT(IC)	X	H2		01.07.00	GLEANER
Revell, Aaron Daniel, ...SLT(IC)	X			10.09.05	MONTROSE
Rex, Colin Antony, ...LT(CC)	X	P		01.10.99	848 SQN HERON
Reynolds, Andrew Charles James, BEng ....LT(CC)	E	ME		01.09.02	DNR PRES TEAMS
Reynolds, Andrew Graham, BEng, MSc, CEng, MIMechE, MCGI ....CDR(FTC)	E	ME		30.06.04	BDS WASHINGTON
Reynolds, Ben K M, ...CAPT RM(IC)	-			01.09.04	NP IRAQ
Reynolds, Darren Paul, ...LT(IC)	E	WE		08.04.05	RICHMOND
Reynolds, Huw Francis, BEng......................................LT(CC)	E	P		01.03.02	815 FLT 246
Reynolds, James, ...LT(CC)	X			01.01.03	CUMBERLAND
Reynolds, Mark Edward, BEng.....................................LT(FTC)	E	ME		01.09.03	NOTTINGHAM
Reynolds, Matthew Jowan, ...LT(CC)	X			01.05.01	ARGYLL
Reynolds, Timothy Edward, MA ....CDR(FTC)	X	METOC		30.06.98	SHAPE BELGIUM
Reynolds, Timothy Paul, BSc, MDA......................LT CDR(FTC)	E	IS		30.04.95	CTCRM
Reynolds, Zoe Anne, ...LT(IC)	X			01.12.03	TYNE
Rhodes, Andrew Gregory, BEng, psc(j)o.........................CDR(FTC)	E	WE		30.06.02	BDS WASHINGTON
Rhodes, Andrew William, ...LT(FTC)	E	WE		01.04.01	NCSA SECTOR NWD
Rhodes, Martin James, MSc, gdas ....LT CDR(FTC)	X	O		01.10.04	771 SQN
Rhodes, Paul Edwin, MCGI.........................CAPT RM(CC) (Act Maj)	-	SO(LE)		21.07.01	FPGRM
Rich, David Charles, pce(sm), pce.............................LT CDR(FTC)	X	SM		20.05.97	MWC PORTSDOWN
Rich, Duncan, BA..SLT(IC)	X			01.11.04	DARTMOUTH BRNC
Rich, Jonathan George, MA, MIPD, MCIPD, pcea, psc(j).........CDR(FTC)	X	P		30.06.04	FLEET COSP&S
Richards, Alan David, jsdc, pce, pcea........................CDRE(FTC)	X	P		24.06.02	BDS WASHINGTON
Richards, Anthony Jeremy, ...LT(CC)	S	SM		01.10.00	UKMARBATSTAFF
Richards, Christopher Martin, pce, psc ....CAPT(FTC)	X	AAWO		30.06.04	UKMARBATSTAFF
Richards, Fraser Charles, SM ....LT CDR(FTC)	X	SM		01.10.03	MOD DIS SEA
Richards, Guy Benjamin, ...LT(IC)	S			01.01.04	ARK ROYAL
Richards, James Ian Hanson, BEng, CEng ....LT CDR(FTC)	E	WESM		01.10.04	FOST FAS SHORE
Richards, Paul, BSc, MIIE ....LT(CC)	E	ME		29.04.01	RALEIGH
Richards, Robert David, BEng ....SLT(IC)	E	WESM		01.09.04	EXETER
Richards, Stephen William, psc(j).................................MAJ(FTC)	-	SO(LE)		01.10.99	COMAMPHIBFOR
Richards, Steven Charles Arthur, ...LT(CC)	E	WE		01.01.02	CSIS IPT
Richardson, Adrian Paul, BEng ....LT(CC)	E	WESM		01.01.01	VIGILANT(PORT)
Richardson, Benjamin, ...2LT(IC)	-			01.08.04	LOAN OTHER SVCE
Richardson, David MacBeth, ...MID(UCE)(IC)	X			01.09.04	DARTMOUTH BRNC
Richardson, Gary, ...LT(IC)	X			18.02.05	MWS HM TG (D)
Richardson, Gavin Andrew, BSc, pcea..................LT CDR(FTC)	X	O		01.10.01	824 SQN
Richardson, Geoffrey Leslie, BSc ....LT CDR(FTC)	X	P		01.10.02	848 SQN HERON
Richardson, George Nicholas, BA ....LT CDR(FTC)	S			01.07.01	MOD (BATH)
Richardson, Ian Hayden, ...LT(CC)	X	MCD		01.03.00	FOST MPV SEA
Richardson, John Francis, BEng ....LT(IC)	X			01.09.04	EDINBURGH
Richardson, Mark Anthony, BSc.........................LT CDR(FTC)	E	IS		01.09.97	AFPAA JPA
Richardson, Michael Colin, ...MAJ(FTC)	-	SO(LE)		01.10.05	RMDIV LECONFIELD
Richardson, Peter, ...LT CDR(FTC)	X	P		01.10.02	848 SQN HERON
Richardson, Peter Stephen Mark, BEng, CEng, MIEE...........LT CDR(FTC)	E	WE		01.08.99	FLEET COSP&S
Richardson, Philip Charles, BSc........................LT CDR(FTC)	X	P		01.03.06	815 FLT 239
Richardson, Simon Joseph, ...CAPT RM(IC)	-	SO(LE)		19.07.05	CDO LOG REGT RM
Richardson, Sophie Charlotte, BA ....LT(FTC)	S			01.09.03	ILLUSTRIOUS
Riches, Anthony Ian, BA..LT(IC)	X			01.05.03	HQ BFSAI
Riches, Ian Charles, OBE, pce(sm).................................CDR(FTC)	X	SM		30.06.04	DLO BRISTOL
Richmond, Iain James Martin, BA, pce, pcea ....CAPT(FTC)	X	P		30.06.04	MOD (LONDON)
Richter, Alwyn Stafford Byron, BEng, CEng, MIEE ....LT CDR(FTC)	E	WE		01.09.00	SCU SHORE
Rickard, Jack, BSc......................................LT(CC) (Act Lt Cdr)	S	SM		12.11.97	NP IRAQ
Rickard, Rory Frederick, MB, BCh, BAO, FRCSEd................. SURG CDR(FCC)	-			30.06.04	NELSON (PAY)
Riddett, Adam Owen, BSc..LT(CC)	X			01.09.02	ST ALBANS
Rider, John Charles Raymon, BSc, n, SM(n)........................LT(CC)	X	SM		01.01.02	MWS COLLINGWOOD

Name	Rank	Branch	Spec	Seniority	Where Serving
Ridge, Mervyn Henry,	LT CDR(FTC)	E	WESM	01.10.04	DLO BRISTOL
Ridgwell, Daniel Robert, BEng	LT(IC)	E	ME U/T	01.09.05	RICHMOND
Ridley, George Edward,	SLT(IC)	X	P U/T	01.04.06	RNAS YEOVILTON
Ridley, Jon, BMus, MMus	CAPT RM(IC)	-	SO(LE)	24.07.04	MWS RM SCH MUSIC
Rigby, Jeremy Conrad, MA, MILDM, psc(j)	CDR(FTC)	S		31.12.00	BULWARK
Riggall, Andrew Derek,	LT CDR(FTC)	X	P	01.10.03	FLEET COSCAP
Riggall, Linda Jean, BA	LT(CC)	X	PWO(C)	01.05.98	ILLUSTRIOUS
Riggs, Matthew George Winston, BA	LT(IC)	S		01.01.04	FLEET HQ WI
Riley, Michael Jaeger, BSc, jsdc, pce, psc(j)	CDR(FTC)	X	AAWO	31.12.93	JSCSC
Riley, Ralph Aidan, BA	LT(IC)	X	O	01.06.05	824 SQN
Rimington, Anthony Kingsmill, BA	LT CDR(FTC)	X	P	01.10.03	ILLUSTRIOUS
Rimmer, Heather Elizabeth, BA, psc(j)	LT CDR(FTC)	E	TM	22.07.96	FLEET HQ PORTSEA
Rimmer, Owen Francis, BA, SM(n)	LT(CC)	X	SM	01.01.02	VANGUARD(PORT)
Rimmer, Robin,	LT CDR(FTC)	E	WE	01.10.98	DFTE PORTSMOUTH
Riordan, Shaun Paul,	SLT(IC)	E	WE U/T	01.09.03	MWS COLLINGWOOD
Ripley, Benjamin Edward, pce, n	LT CDR(FTC)	X	PWO(U)	01.11.02	PENZANCE
Ripley, Stephen Lee,	LT(IC)	E	WE	01.07.04	GLOUCESTER
Rippingale, Stuart Nicholas, MSc, PGCE	CDR(FTC)	E	IS	30.06.05	AFPAA(CENTURION)
Risdall, Jane Elizabeth, MA, MB, BS, FFARCSI	SURG CDR(FCC)	-	(CA)	31.12.98	MDHU PETERBRGH
Risley, James Grant, BEng	LT(CC)	E	MESM	01.02.00	NP BRISTOL
Risley, Jonathan, BSc, MA, CEng, MBCS, CITP, CDipAF, adp	CDR(FTC)	E	IS	31.12.00	NELSON
Ritchie, Douglas Brian,	LT(CC)	E	MESM	01.09.01	SULTAN
Ritchie, Iain David, BSc	LT(CC)	X	HM	01.08.02	RAF WITTERING
Ritchie, John Noble, SM	LT CDR(FTC)	X	SM	01.04.02	BDS WASHINGTON
Ritchie, William James, MSc, sq	LT COL(FTC)	-	SO(LE)	30.06.06	FLEET ISS
Ritson, Jonathan,	SURG SLT(SCC)	-		19.10.03	DARTMOUTH BRNC
Ritsperis, Athos, MAPM, MSc, DIC, PGCE, MIEE, MBCS, MIL, ACGI, ARCS	LT(CC)	E	IS	01.01.92	DEF SCH OF LANG
Rix, Anthony John, ADC, pce, psc	CAPT(FTC) (Commodore)	X	PWO(U)	30.06.97	UKMARBATSTAFF
Robb, Michael Edward, BA	LT(CC)	S		01.08.97	FLEET COSP&S
Robbins, Harry Vincent,	CAPT RM(CC)	-	P	01.01.02	845 SQN
Robbins, Jeremy Matthew Francis, MBE, BSc, psc(m), hcsc	COL(FTC) (Act Brig)	-	C	30.06.99	RCDS
Robert, Iain Andrew,	LT(CC)	E	AE	29.04.01	MERLIN IPT
Roberts, Andrew Paul, BEng	LT(IC)	E	AE	01.05.02	814 SQN
Roberts, Benjamin, BA	LT(IC)	S		01.09.03	ARGYLL
Roberts, David Alan, pce	LT CDR(FTC)	X	PWO(A)	01.05.92	COM MCC NWD
Roberts, David Howard Wyn, BA, pce	LT CDR(FTC)	X	AAWO	01.04.91	DPA BRISTOL
Roberts, David Stephen, BSc	SLT(IC)	X		01.11.03	QUORN
Roberts, Dean, BEng	LT CDR(FTC)	E	WE	04.04.99	DLO BRISTOL
Roberts, Ellis William,	LT CDR(FTC)	E	AE	01.10.95	RNAS YEOVILTON
Roberts, George Edward, BA	SLT(IC)	X	O U/T	01.09.04	DARTMOUTH BRNC
Roberts, Iain Gordon, BSc, BEng	LT CDR(FTC)	E	WESM	01.10.03	DRAKE COB
Roberts, Ian Thomas, OBE, pce(sm), psc(j), MA	CDR(FTC)	X	SM	30.06.02	FLEET HQ WI
Roberts, Kenneth Eric, BEng, MSc, CEng, MIEE, gw	LT CDR(FTC)	E	WE	01.01.99	MOD (LONDON)
Roberts, Martin Alan,	LT(FTC)	X	O	01.11.94	EXCHANGE CANADA
Roberts, Martyn, BEng	LT CDR(FTC)	X	O	01.10.02	LOAN JTEG BSC DN
Roberts, Michael John, LLB	LT(IC)	S		01.09.04	824 SQN
Roberts, Michael Thomas, BSc	SLT(IC)	X		01.11.04	DARTMOUTH BRNC
Roberts, Nicholas Steven, BEng, MSc, Hf, psc(j)	CDR(FTC)	E	WE	30.06.99	JSCSC
Roberts, Nigel David,	LT(CC)	X	O	10.02.98	702 SQN HERON
Roberts, Peter Andrew,	CAPT RM(CC)	-	SO(LE)	01.04.04	1 ASSAULT GP RM
Roberts, Peter Stafford, pce	CDR(FTC)	X	AAWO	30.06.06	DUMBARTON CASTLE
Roberts, Selvin Clive, BEng	LT CDR(FTC)	E	MESM	01.10.99	NEPTUNE DLO
Roberts, Stephen David, BEng, MSc, CEng, MIEE, psc(j)	CDR(FTC)	E	WE	30.06.03	LOAN DSTL
Roberts, Stephen Mark,	LT(IC)	X	ATCU/T	01.02.06	RNAS CULDROSE
Roberts, Suzi,	LT(IC)	S		23.03.03	CAPT IST STAFF
Roberts, Timothy John, BEng, MSc	CDR(FTC)	E	MESM	30.06.03	DLO BRISTOL
Robertshaw, Ian Weston, BEng, CEng	LT CDR(FTC)	E	WESM	01.04.04	MWC PORTSDOWN
Robertson, Adam Joseph,	LT(IC)	E	WE	01.09.05	NOTTINGHAM
Robertson, David Cameron, BSc, MA, MRIN, pce, psc(j), n	CDR(FTC)	X	H CH	30.06.05	ENTERPRISE
Robertson, Douglas Malcolm, BSc	LT CDR(FTC)	X	ATC	01.10.93	CV(F) IPT
Robertson, Ian Wallace, BEng	LT(IC)	E	WE	01.08.03	HQ DCSA
Robertson, Kevin Francis, pce	CDR(FTC)	X	PWO(C)	30.06.98	SCU SHORE

Name	Rank	Branch Spec		Seniority	Where Serving
Robertson, Michael George, BSc, pce, psc(j)	CDR(FTC)	X	O	30.06.03	SULTAN AIB
Robertson, Neil Bannerman, psc(j)	MAJ(FTC)	-		01.05.00	MOD (LONDON)
Robertson, Paul Noel, LLB, pcea	LT CDR(FTC(A)	X	O	01.10.00	LOAN JTEG BSC DN
Robertson, Stuart Thomas, BA	LT(CC)	S	SM	01.03.99	HARRIER IPT
Robertson Gopffarth, Alexander Alistair John, BSc, SM(n)	LT CDR(FTC)	X	SM	01.02.05	NP IRAQ
Robey, James Christopher,	LT(CC)	X		01.10.00	LIVERPOOL
Robey, Stephanie Jane,	LT(IC)	X		01.08.01	MWS COLLINGWOOD
Robin, Christopher Charles Edward, pce, pcea, psc(j)	LT CDR(FTC)	X	P	01.09.94	FLEET HQ WI
Robin, Julie Isobel, MB, ChB	SURG LTCDR(MCC)	-		02.08.05	NELSON (PAY)
Robinson, Andrew, BSc, jsdc	CDR(FTC)	X	METOC	30.06.97	FLEET COSP&S
Robinson, Andrew,	LT(FTC) (Act Lt Cdr)	MS		01.04.01	MOD (LONDON)
Robinson, Charles Edward Thayne, pce, psc(j), MA	CDR(FTC)	X	PWO(U)	30.06.99	JFCHQ BRUNSSUM
Robinson, David,	LT(CC)	S		01.10.02	DLO BRISTOL
Robinson, Guy Antony, MA, pce, psc(j)	CDR(FTC)	X	PWO(A)	30.06.02	MOD (LONDON)
Robinson, Lee David,	LT(IC)	E	WESM	01.07.04	VICTORIOUS(PORT)
Robinson, Matthew Steven,	LT(IC)	X	P	01.05.04	820 SQN
Robinson, Michael,	SURG SLT(MDC)	-		16.09.04	DARTMOUTH BRNC
Robinson, Michael Peter, MA, MSc, CEng, MIMarEST, psc(j)	CDR(FTC)	E	MESM	30.06.02	DLO BRISTOL
Robinson, Paul Henry, pce, pce(sm)	CDRE(FTC)	X	SM	30.09.03	JSCSC
Robinson, Paul James, BA	LT(IC)	S		01.09.05	NBC PORTSMOUTH
Robinson, Philip James Owen, BSc	CAPT RM(CC)	-		01.09.01	1 ASSLT GP RM
Robinson, Richard John,	LT(FTC)	X	ATC	01.04.01	FOST DPORT SHORE
Robinson, Steven Leslie, BEng	LT(FTC)	E	WE	01.01.01	HQ DCSA
Robinson, Timothy George,	SURG LT(SC(MD)	-		02.08.05	DARTMOUTH BRNC
Robison, Garry Stuart, ADC, MPhil, psc(m), psc(j), hcsc	BRIG(FTC)	-		15.09.03	CTCRM
Robley, William Forster,	LT(FTC)	X	P	01.06.96	771 SQN
Robson, Christine Jane, ARRC	LT CDR(FC(MD)	Q	IC/CC	01.10.00	HQ DMETA
Rochester, Andrew David, BSc	CAPT RM(CC)	-		01.09.02	UKLFCSG RM
Rochester, Richard William,	MAJ(IC)	-	LC	01.10.04	CTCRM
Rock, James Andrew, BA	SLT(IC)	X	P U/T	01.06.04	DARTMOUTH BRNC
Roddy, Michael Patrick, MBE, BSc, psc(j)o	MAJ(FTC)	-		27.04.02	40 CDO RM
Rodgers, Beth Mary, BSc	SLT(IC)	X		01.05.04	BULWARK
Rodgers, Darren,	LT(IC)	X	P	01.07.93	848 SQN HERON
Rodgers, Steven,	CDR(FTC)	E	WE	30.06.04	MOD (BATH)
Roe, Roma Jane,	LT(IC)	E	AE	01.07.04	820 SQN
Rofe, Sion Anthony,	SLT(IC)	X	O U/T	01.01.05	DARTMOUTH BRNC
Roffey, Kevin David, BEng	LT(IC)	E	AE	01.09.04	846 SQN
Rogers, Alan,	LT CDR(FTC)	X	AV	01.10.01	792 NAS(SEA)
Rogers, Andrew Gavin, BEng, MDA, CEng, MIEE	LT CDR(FTC)	E	WE	01.02.98	HQ DCSA
Rogers, Christopher Mark, BEng, CEng, PGDip, MIEE, MCMI	LT CDR(FTC)	E	WE	01.06.00	FLEET COSP&S
Rogers, Julia Ann,	LT(IC)	X	P	01.08.99	845 SQN
Rogers, Julian Charles Everard, SM	LT CDR(FTC)	X	SM	01.03.03	FOST FAS SHORE
Rogers, Matthew Stideford, BA	LT(IC)	X		01.01.06	PORTLAND
Rogers, Orlando,	LT RM(IC)	-		01.09.05	CTCRM
Rogers, Philip Scott, BSc	LT(FTC) (Act Lt Cdr)	E	TM	01.01.95	DARTMOUTH BRNC
Rogers, Phillip Richard, MEng, PhD	LT(IC)	E	TM U/T	01.09.02	IRON DUKE
Rogers, Simon James Peter, BA	LT(FTC)	X		01.07.98	MWS COLLINGWOOD
Rogers, Simon Milward, BSc	CAPT RM(CC)	-		01.09.02	1 ASSAULT GP RM
Rogers, Timothy Hugh Goddard,	LT CDR(FTC)	X		04.12.98	NAVSEC
Rogerson, Alison Elizabeth, BMus	SLT(IC)	S		01.05.03	DRAKE NBC/DBUS
Roissetter, David,	CHAPLAIN	SF		03.01.06	FWO PORTS SEA
Rollason, Caroline Anne,	LT(CC)	S		01.11.00	CHFHQ
Rolls, Edward Christopher, BSc	SLT(IC)	X	ATCU/T	01.07.03	RNAS YEOVILTON
Rolph, Andrew Peter Mark, pce	CDR(FTC)	X	PWO(C)	30.06.04	FLEET COSP&S
Rom, Stephen Paul, IEng, MIIE	LT(FTC)	E	WE	02.09.99	DLO BRISTOL
Romney, Paul David, PGDIPAN, MRIN, pce	CDR(FTC)	X	PWO(U)	30.06.06	MWS COLLINGWOOD
Ronald, Euan Taylor, BSc	LT(IC)	X		01.05.03	NORTHUMBERLAND
Rook, Graeme Inglis, MSc, CEng, MIEE, MBCS	LT CDR(FTC)	E	WE	01.04.98	FLEET COSCAP
Rooke, Adam Edward, MEng	SLT(IC)	E	MESM	01.09.03	VANGUARD(PORT)
Rooke, Kate Elizabeth, MEng	SLT(IC)	E	AE U/T	01.09.03	SULTAN
Rooke, Zoe Selina, BA, MA(OXON)	LT(IC)	E	TM	01.01.02	DEF NBC CENTRE
Rooney, Michael, BEng, MIEE	LT(CC)	E	WE	01.09.00	CAPT MCTA

Name	Rank	Branch	Spec	Seniority	Where Serving
Rooney, Thomas, ...	LT(IC)	E	WE	08.04.05	PORTLAND
Roper, Martin, pcea...	CDR(FTC)	X	O	30.06.06	DLO BRISTOL
Roscoe, David, MB, CHB	SURG LT(SC(MD)	-		04.08.04	40 CDO RM
Roscoe, Robert David, BEng	LT CDR(FTC)	E	WE	01.04.99	FWO DEVPT SEA
Rose, Alan, BSc	LT(IC)	E	WESM	01.09.02	NEPTUNE BNSL
Rose, Andrew Donald, BA...	LT(FTC)	X	O	16.12.97	PJHQ
Rose, Caroline Mary, BEng, MSc, CEng, MIMechE, AMIMarE.................	LT CDR(FTC)	E	ME	30.08.02	FLEET FOTR
Rose, John Gordon, MBE, psc(m), hcsc...	MAJ GEN	-		06.02.06	MOD (LONDON)
(DGIC FEB 06)					
Rose, Marcus Edward, ...	SLT(IC)	E	WE U/T	01.09.03	MWS COLLINGWOOD
Rose, Michael Frederick, BEng, MSc, CEng, MIMarEST	LT CDR(FTC)	E	ME	28.12.99	NAVSEC
Rose, Simon Paul, BEng..	SLT(IC)	E	WE U/T	01.01.04	MWS COLLINGWOOD
Rose, Simone, BA...	LT(IC)	S		01.05.03	MOD (LONDON)
Roskilly, Martyn, MSc	CAPT RM(CC)	-	P	01.05.01	847 SQN
Ross, Sir Andrew Charles Paterson, Bt, BSc, ocds(No), psc	LT COL(FTC)	-		30.06.05	FLEET COSCAP
Ross, Angus Allan, BA, MSc	CAPT(FTC)	S		30.06.02	FLEET COSP&S
Ross, Gareth Donald Anthony, ...	LT(IC)	X	AV	01.05.03	ARK ROYAL
Ross, Gawain, ...	MAJ(FTC)	-	SO(LE)	01.10.05	1 ASSAULT GP RM
Ross, Ian, BEng, CEng, MIMarE	LT CDR(FTC)	E	ME	01.08.00	SAUDI AFPS SAUDI
Ross, Jonathan Hubert, BSc, MA, ACGI, psc(j)	LT COL(FTC)	-		30.06.02	MOD (LONDON)
Ross, Paul William, BSc, PGCE	LT(IC)	E	TM	01.01.02	JSCSC
Ross, Robert Alasdair, MB, BS, FRCS, Dip FFP............................	SURG CDR(FCC)	-	GMPP	31.12.99	HQ 3 CDO BDE RM
Roster, Shaun Patrick, ...	LT(FTC)	X	O	16.11.94	815 SQN HQ
Rostron, David William, BEng..	LT CDR(FTC)	E	MESM	01.01.04	SPARTAN
Rostron, John Harry, ...	LT(CC)	E	WESM	01.01.03	OCLC MANCH
Roue, James Llewellyn, BA	LT(IC)	S		01.01.03	EXETER
Roue, Kathryn Sian, MB, BCH, BSc..	SURG LT(SC(MD)	-		03.08.04	DRAKE COB
Round, Matthew James, BA, BSc, PGCE	LT(CC)	X	O	01.05.02	849 SQN HQ
Routledge, William David, ...	LT(FTC)	X		10.12.98	DHU SEA
Rowan, Nicholas Anthony, BEng..	LT CDR(FTC)	E	MESM	01.10.01	NEPTUNE DLO
Rowberry, Adrian Graham, BSc	LT(IC)	X	MW	01.01.02	MWS COLLINGWOOD
Rowe, Andrew James, ...	LT CDR(FTC)	E	WE	01.10.04	HQ DCSA
Rowe, Paula Elizabeth, MBA	LT CDR(FTC)	E	TM	01.10.97	COMAMPHIBFOR
Rowe, Richard Dudley, BD	CHAPLAIN	SF		24.09.00	NELSON
Rowell, Graham Edward, MSc...	CAPT(FTC)	E	AE	30.06.04	DLO WYTON
Rowland, Paul Nicholas, BEng, CEng, MIMarEST	LT CDR(FTC)	E	MESM	01.01.00	VIGILANT(STBD)
Rowlands, Andrew Richard, BEng, MSc gw	LT CDR(FTC)	E	WE	01.06.04	HQ DCSA
Rowlands, Kevin, BSc, MA, pce..	LT CDR(FTC)	X	PWO(A)	01.10.01	NOTTINGHAM
Rowley, Thomas Patrick, ...	LT(IC)	X		28.10.05	PENZANCE
Rowntree, Paul James, BA...	SLT(IC)	X		01.06.04	DARTMOUTH BRNC
Rowse, Mark Lawrence, BEng, CEng, MIMarEST, psc(j)........................	CDR(FTC)	E	WE	30.06.03	DLO BRISTOL
Rowson, Marcus Jonathan, BSc...	LT(CC)	X	P	16.11.99	845 SQN
Roy, Alexander Campbell, OBE, osc(us)...	LT COL(FTC)	-		31.12.90	LN BMATT (CEE)
Roy, Christopher Alan, ...	LT(CC)	X	P	01.01.04	JSCSC
Royce, Roderick Henry, BEng	LT(IC)	X	P U/T	01.02.06	RNAS YEOVILTON
Roylance, Jaimie Fraser, MA, psc(j)...	MAJ(FTC)	-	P	01.09.01	JHCHQ
Royle, Nigel Alexander, ...	LT(IC)	E	ME	01.05.03	CAPT MCTA
Royston, James Lawrence, MA	LT(IC)	X	SM	01.09.03	TORBAY
Royston, Stuart James, pce, n...	LT CDR(FTC)	X	PWO(C)	01.05.98	FLEET HQ PORTS
Rucinski, Peter Gerard, BEng	LT(IC)	E	WE	01.01.04	DHU SEA
Rudd, Philip, ...	CAPT RM(IC)	-	P	01.04.04	DHFS
Ruddock, Gordon William David, n	LT CDR(FTC)	X	AAWO	01.07.03	GLOUCESTER
Ruddock, Jane, MA..	LT(IC)	E	TM	01.01.99	MWS COLLINGWOOD
Rudkin, Adam Llywelyn, MEng..	LT(IC)	E	AE U/T	01.09.05	RNAS YEOVILTON
Rugg, Christopher Phillip, BSc	LT(IC)	X	P	01.09.04	RNAS YEOVILTON
Runchman, Phillip Charles, MA, BM, BCH, FRCS	SURG CAPT(FCC)	-	(CGS)	01.04.03	MDHU PORTSMOUTH
Rundle, Anthony Littlejohns, BEng, CEng, MIEE............................	LT CDR(FTC)	E	WE	01.10.00	GLOUCESTER
Rusbridger, Robert Charles, MSc, psc	CAPT(FTC)	E	ME	30.06.03	DLO BRISTOL
Rushworth, Andrew William Edward, BEng...	LT(IC)	E	ME U/T	01.09.05	MONMOUTH
Rushworth, Benjamin John, BSc, ARCS, n..	LT(FTC)	X	PWO(N)	01.05.98	NOTTINGHAM
Russell, Bruce, BEng, MA, CEng, MIEE, psc(j)...........................	LT CDR(FTC)	E	WESM	01.05.00	FLEET HQ WI
Russell, Colin, ...	LT(FTC)	E	AE	01.01.00	FS MASU

Name	Rank	Branch	Spec	Seniority	Where Serving
Russell, Gillian Spence, BEng	LT CDR(FTC)	S		01.08.03	FLEET COSP&S
Russell, Mark James,	LT(IC)	E	MESM	01.05.03	DRAKE CBS
Russell, Martin Simon, BA	LT(CC)	X	O	01.01.02	849 SQN HQ
Russell, Nigel Anthony David,	LT CDR(FTC)	X	PWO(A)	01.10.04	DARTMOUTH BRNC
Russell, Paul, MNI, pce	LT CDR(FTC)	X	AAWO	01.05.01	MWS COLLINGWOOD
Russell, Philip Robert, BTech, MA, MSc, CEng, FIMarEST, MRINA, psc(j)	CDR(FTC)	E	ME	30.06.05	MOD (LONDON)
Russell, Simon Jonathon, OBE, MSc, MInstPS, MILT, MRAeS, psc, psc(j)	CDR(FTC)	E	AE	30.06.98	DLO YEO
Russell, Thomas, pce, psc(j)	LT CDR(FTC)	X	MCD	01.07.93	SDG PLYMOUTH
Ruston, Mark Robert, BEng, MSc, CEng, MIEE	LT(FTC)	E	WE	01.01.99	DNR RCHQ NORTH
Rutherford, Adam Todd,	CAPT RM(IC)	-	MLDR	24.07.04	UKLFCSG RM
Rutherford, Kevin John, BSc	LT(CC)	X	P	01.10.93	771 SQN
Rutherford, Timothy James, BEng	LT CDR(FTC)	E	AE	30.12.00	848 SQN HERON
Rutter, John Charles, BA	SLT(IC)	X	P U/T	01.09.04	DARTMOUTH BRNC
Ryall, Tom Armstrong Scott, BA	CAPT RM(CC)	-		01.09.04	SFSG
Ryan, Dennis Graham, BSc	CDR(FTC)	E	AE	30.06.02	ILLUSTRIOUS
Ryan, John Peter,	LT(FTC)	E	MESM	02.05.00	DLO BRISTOL
Ryan, Nicholas, BEng, CEng, MIMarEST	LT CDR(FTC)	E	ME	01.07.03	CAMPBELTOWN
Ryan, Patrick Douglas Blackwood,	LT(FTC)	X	SM	01.09.02	RALEIGH
Ryan, Paul Justin, BEng	LT(IC)	X	P	01.09.02	814 SQN
Ryan, Richard Michael, BSc, pce, pcea	LT CDR(FTC)	X	O	01.04.97	JSCSC
Ryan, Sean Joseph, BA, pce(sm), SM(n)	LT CDR(FTC)	X	SM	01.04.01	PEMBROKE
Ryan, Stephen James, BEng	SLT(IC)	E	MESMUT	01.09.03	CORNWALL
Rycroft, Alan Edward, pce, pcea, psc(j)	CDR(FTC)	X	O	30.06.96	PJHQ
Ryder, Matthew Robert, BEng	LT(IC)	E	WE	01.02.06	SOMERSET
Ryder, Tony,	LT(IC)	X		13.07.04	MWS COLLINGWOOD
Rye, John Walter, MA, psc	MAJ(FTC)	-	C	01.09.84	RM WARMINSTER
Rymer, Alan Robert, BSc, CEng, MIMarEST, psc	CDRE(FTC)	E	ME	11.12.03	NAVSEC

S

Name	Rank	Branch	Spec	Seniority	Where Serving
Saddleton, Andrew David, psc(j)o	LT COL(FTC)	-	LC	30.06.05	BULWARK
Saffin, James,	SURG SLT(SCC)	-		16.12.05	DARTMOUTH BRNC
Saleh, Jenny, BSc	LT(IC)	E	TM	01.01.02	NELSON
Salim, Muttahir, BSc	LT(IC)	E	TM	01.09.98	NP IRAQ
Salisbury, David Peter, OBE, pce, pcea, psc(j)	CDR(FTC)	X	P	30.06.03	CC MAR AGRIPPA
Salmon, Andrew, OBE, MA, psc	BRIG(FTC)	-		13.04.04	FLEET HQ WI
Salmon, Michael Alan, pcea	CDR(FTC)	X	O	30.06.04	RAF AWC
Salter, Jeffrey Alan, BEng, MSc, CEng, MIEE, MIMarEST, psc(j)o	CDR(FTC)	E	WE	30.06.03	NELSON (PAY)
Saltonstall, Hugh Francis Rous, LLB	LT(CC)	X	P	01.05.02	815 FLT 217
Saltonstall, Philip James Rous, BA	LT(CC)	X	P	01.07.99	702 SQN HERON
Salzano, Gerard Mark, MBE, psc	COL(FTC)	-		30.06.06	MOD (LONDON)
Sambrooks, Richard John, BEng	LT(CC)	X	P	01.08.99	EXCHANGE RAF UK
Sampson, James Peter, BA, BSc	LT(IC)	E	IS	01.06.03	DCCIS FAREHAM
Sampson, Philip Henry, psc(m)	LT COL(FTC)	-		30.06.97	CTCRM
Samuel, Christopher David Robert, BSc	CAPT RM(CC)	-	C	01.05.01	UKLFCSG RM
Samuels, Nicholas,	LT(FTC)	X	SM	01.04.98	TIRELESS
Samways, Michael James,	LT(IC)	X		01.07.03	BROCKLESBY
Samwell, Michael Guy, BEng	LT(IC)	E	WESM	01.09.04	TIRELESS
Sanderson, Christopher Peter, MA, PGDip	LT(FTC)	X	H2	01.10.99	MWS COLLINGWOOD
Sanderson, Lee David, BEng, CEng, MIEE	LT CDR(FTC)	E	WE	01.10.04	T45 IPT
Sanderson, Robert Christopher, BDS, FDS RCPSGlas	SGCAPT(D)(FCC)	-	(COSM)	30.06.00	MDHU PORTSMOUTH
Sandle, Neil David, BEng, CEng, MIMarEST	LT CDR(FTC)	E	ME	01.08.03	DLO TES
Sandy, David John,	LT(IC)	X		17.12.04	ARK ROYAL
Sangha, Randeep Singh, BEng	LT(CC)	E	AE	01.12.98	700M MERLIN OEU
Sanguinetti, Hector Robert, MA, pce, psc(j)	CAPT(FTC)	X	PWO(C)	30.06.05	MOD (LONDON)
Sansford, Adrian James, BEng, MSc	LT CDR(FTC)	E	MESM	27.05.99	MOD (BATH)
Santry, Paul Matthew,	LT(FTC) (Act Lt Cdr)	X	C	01.04.01	MWS COLLINGWOOD
Sargent, David Reginald,	LT(CC)	S		01.01.02	PJHQ
Sargent, David Stuart, MB, BS, BSc	SURG LT(SC(MD)	-		06.08.03	CDO LOG REGT RM
Sargent, Lindsay, BSc, PGCE	LT CDR(IC)	E	TM	01.10.04	RNICG
Sargent, Philippa Mary, MA(OXON), n	LT CDR(FTC)	E	TM	01.10.04	JSCSC
Satterly, Robert James, BEng	LT(CC)	E	ME	01.01.01	RMC OF SCIENCE
Satterthwaite, Benjamin John, BA	LT(FTC)	X	PWO(A)	01.02.95	NORTHUMBERLAND

Name	Rank	Branch	Spec	Seniority	Where Serving
Sauer, Alexis Charlotte, BSc	LT(IC)	X		01.02.06	MWS COLLINGWOOD
Saunders, Christopher Edmund Maurice, MSc	LT CDR(FTC)	X	PWO(C)	01.06.05	BULWARK
Saunders, Jason Mervyn, BEng	LT(CC)	E	TM	01.09.94	RNIC G
Saunders, John Nicholas,	LT CDR(FTC)	X	PWO(N)	01.10.90	NBC PORTSMOUTH
Saunders, Timothy Mark, BSc, MA, psc(j)	CDR(FTC)	E	TMSM	30.06.04	FLEET COSP&S
Savage, Alexander Frederick, BSc	LT(IC)	S		01.01.05	FLEET COSCAP
Savage, Daniel Liam, BEng	LT(IC)	E	ME	01.01.03	ILLUSTRIOUS
Savage, Mark Roger, pce	LT CDR(FTC)	X	PWO(U)	01.09.98	FLEET COSCAP
Savage, Shane, BSc	LT CDR(FTC)	X	ATC	01.10.94	RNAS CULDROSE
Saward, Justin Robert Ernest, BEng, CEng, MRAeS	LT(FTC) (Act Lt Cdr)	E	AE	01.07.97	DASC
Sawford, Gavin Neil,	LT(CC)	E	WE	01.01.02	DLO BRISTOL
Sawicki, Andrew James, BEng	SLT(IC)	X	P U/T	01.11.04	DARTMOUTH BRNC
Sawyer, Jason Lyndon,	SLT(IC)	X		20.02.05	DARTMOUTH BRNC
Saxby, Christopher James, BEng, MSc, CEng, FIMarEST, MCGI, MIMarEST	CDR(FTC)	E	ME	30.06.03	DRAKE SFM
Saxby, Keith Alan,	LT CDR(FTC) (Act Cdr)	X	AAWO	24.02.94	JDLMO
Say, Russell G,	LT(IC)	E	WE	01.01.04	MWS COLLINGWOOD
Sayer, Russell Joe,	2LT(IC)	-		01.08.01	45 CDO RM
Saynor, Roger Michael, MBE	LT CDR(FTC)	X		01.10.96	MWS EXC BRISTOL
Saywell, James,	LT(IC)	E		01.06.02	801 SQN
Saywell-Hall, Stephen Eric,	LT(FTC)	E	AE	02.09.99	SULTAN
Scales, Dean Robert,	LT(IC)	X		18.02.05	CHIDDINGFOLD
Scandling, Rachel Jane,	LT CDR(FTC)	S		01.10.02	RICHMOND
Scanlon, Meredith Patricia, MSc	LT(IC)	X		01.04.04	MWS HM TG (D)
Scanlon, Michael, BSc	CAPT RM(CC) (Act Maj)	-		01.05.01	NAVSEC
Scarborough, David Colin, DMCMP	LT(IC)	MS		01.05.03	INM ALVERSTOKE
Scarlett, Christopher Joseph,	LT(IC)	E	WESM	01.01.04	MOD (LONDON)
Scarth, William, BSc, jsdc, pce, psc(j)	CDR(FTC)	X	MCD	30.06.97	LOAN KUWAIT
Schillemore, Paul Colin,	LT(FTC) (Act Lt Cdr)	E	WE	18.10.85	MWS COLLINGWOOD
Schleyer, Jonathan,	CAPT RM(IC)	-		01.09.02	BF BIOT
Schnadhorst, James Charles, pce	LT CDR(FTC)	X	PWO(U)	01.05.95	JACIG
Schofield, Julie Claire,	LT(CC)	X		01.09.04	EXCHANGE GERMANY
Schofield, Susan Ruth, MB, BS, MRCGP, JCPTGP	SURG LTCDR(MCC)	-	GMPP	08.08.01	UKNSU NAPLES
Scholes, Neil Andrew, MSc, CEng, MINucE, MIMarEST	LT(FTC)	E	MESM	02.09.99	DLO BRISTOL
Schwarz, Paul Michael Gunter,	CDR(FTC)	X	ATC	30.06.02	CC MAR AGRIPPA
Schwarz, Willam,	2LT(IC)	-		01.08.02	CTCRM LYMPSTONE
Scivier, John Stapleton, MCMI	LT CDR(FTC)	X	ATC	01.10.01	VICTORY
Scoles, Jonathon Charles, OBE, FCMI, pce, psc	CDR(FTC) (Act Capt)	X	PWO(U)	31.12.89	FLEET COSP&S
Scopes, David, BEng, MAPM, CEng, MRAeS	LT CDR(FTC)	E	AE	01.12.02	800 NAS (GR7)
Scorer, Andrew James, BA	LT(IC)	X		01.05.05	SEVERN
Scorer, Samuel James, nadc, jsdc, pce	CDRE(FTC)	X	PWO(U)	09.03.06	JDCC
Scorer, Thomas,	SURG SLT(SCC)	-		01.07.03	DARTMOUTH BRNC
Scott, Alexander James, BEng	LT(IC)	X		01.05.04	CHIDDINGFOLD
Scott, Catherine Roberta, BSc	LT(MC(MD))	Q		12.09.99	JSCSC
Scott, Christopher Ralph, OBE, MA, psc	COL(FTC)	-		30.06.05	PJHQ
Scott, James Baxter, BEng, CEng, MIMechE, psc(j)	CDR(FTC)	E	MESM	30.06.06	DRAKE CBS
Scott, Jason Andrew, BA, pce	CDR(FTC)	X	MCD	30.06.03	MOD (LONDON)
Scott, Julian Vivian,	LT(IC)	X	EW	01.07.04	FLEET FOSNNI
Scott, Mark Robert, pcea	LT CDR(FTC)	X	P	01.10.04	MOD (LONDON)
Scott, Michael, BEng, CEng, MIEE	CDR(FTC)	E	WESM	30.06.06	FWO FASLANE SEA
Scott, Michael, BEng	LT(IC)	X	P	16.08.97	771 SQN
Scott, Neil,	LT(CC)	X	HM	01.09.01	FLEET COMOPS NWD
Scott, Neil,	LT(IC)	X		01.05.03	UKMARBATSTAFF
Scott, Nigel Leonard James, BEng, CEng, MIEE, ACGI, psc(j)	CDR(FTC)	E	WESM	30.06.02	IA BRISTOL
Scott, Peter Darren,	SLT(IC)	X	ATCU/T	01.02.04	RAF SHAWBURY
Scott, Peter James Douglas Sefton, OBE, BD, FInstLM	CHAPLAIN	CE		03.09.91	DARTMOUTH BRNC
Scott, Richard Antony, BEng, MSc, CEng, MIEE	LT(FTC)	E	WE	01.08.94	T45 IPT
Scott, Robert John, pce, pcea	LT CDR(FTC)	X	O	02.03.98	RNAS YEOVILTON
Scott, Russell,	SLT(IC)	E		01.01.05	SULTAN
Scott, Simon John, MA, psc(j)	LT COL(FTC)	-	LC	30.06.05	JDCC
Scott, Stephen Charles,	MAJ(FTC)	-	SO(LE)	01.10.03	RM NORTON MANOR
Scott, Thomas,	2LT(IC)	-		01.08.01	42 CDO RM
Scott, Timothy Edward, MB, BS, MRCP	SURG LTCDR(MC(MD))	-		04.08.04	NELSON (PAY)

Name	Rank	Branch	Spec	Seniority	Where Serving
Scott, Wendy Ann, BDS	SGLTCDR(D)(SCC)	-		13.01.02	CDO LOG REGT RM
Scott-Dickins, Charles Angus, MSc	LT CDR(FTC)	X	METOC	01.10.94	GANNET SAR FLT
Scotter, Claire Marie, BSc	LT(IC)	E	IS	01.09.99	OCEAN
Screaton, Richard Michael, BEng, CEng, MIEE, MIMarEST	LT CDR(FTC)	E	ME	01.03.04	SOMERSET
Screen, James,	LT(IC)	E	WE	01.07.04	YORK
Scutt, Martin Jason, PhD, BM, BSc	SURG LT(SC(MD)	-		04.02.04	VENGEANCE(STBD)
Seagrave, Suzanna Jane, BEng	LT(FTC)	E	ME	01.11.00	NEPTUNE FD
Seal, Martin Richard,	LT(IC)	X		01.04.06	MWS COLLINGWOOD
Seal, Michael Owen, BA	LT(IC)	X	SM	01.09.04	SOVEREIGN
Sealey, Nicholas Peter, BSc, CEng, MIMarEST, psc	CAPT(FTC)	E	ME	30.06.02	DLO BRISTOL
Seaman, Alec,	2LT(IC)	-		01.08.01	CTCRM LYMPSTONE
Sear, Jonathan Jasper, MA, psc(j)	MAJ(FTC)	-		01.09.98	EXCHANGE ARMY UK
Searight, Mark Frederick Chamney, psc(j)	MAJ(FTC)	-		01.05.97	CTCRM
Searle, Andrew James Arthur, BEng	LT(IC)	E	WE	01.09.04	LIVERPOOL
Searle, Christopher Richard,	LT(IC)	S		01.07.04	SOUTHAMPTON
Searle, Emma Louise, BSc	LT(IC)	S		01.01.05	RNAS CULDROSE
Seatherton, Elliot Frazer Kingston, MBE, pce, psc(j)o	CDR(FTC)	X	PWO(N)	31.12.95	JDCC
Seddon, Jonathan David,	LT(IC)	X	FC	01.04.06	EXCHANGE RAF UK
Sedgwick, Hugo George, BSc	LT(IC)	X	SM	01.01.04	VENGEANCE(STBD)
Selden, John David Alan, BSc	LT(IC)	E	IS	01.11.03	JSCSC
Sellar, Trevor Jefferson,	CAPT RM(FTC)	-	SO(LE)	01.01.97	1 ASSAULT GP RM
Sellars, Scott John, BA, MinstAM	LT CDR(FTC)	S	CMA	01.10.04	EXETER
Sellers, Graham Donald, BEng, MSc, CEng, MIEE	LT CDR(FTC)	E	WE	01.02.01	CHATHAM
Selway, Mark Anthony, BEng	LT CDR(FTC)	E	AE	01.07.05	MOD (LONDON)
Selwood, Peter John, BSc	LT(MC(MD)	Q		26.02.01	MDHU PORTSMOUTH
Semple, Brian,	LT(IC)	X	P	01.01.03	800 NAS (GR7)
Sennett, Michael,	LT(IC)	E	TM	01.05.02	MWS COLLINGWOOD
Sennitt, John William, MBE, MSc, CEng, PGDip, MIEE, MBCS	LT CDR(FTC)	E	WE	01.08.92	DLO BRISTOL
Sephton, John Richard, BSc, FRMS, psc	CDR(FTC)	X	METOC	30.06.00	FLEET COSP&S
Sergeant, Nicholas Robin, CDipAF	LT CDR(FTC)	E	WE	01.10.99	FLEET COSP&S
Seton, James, BA	LT(IC)	X		01.01.04	ARGYLL
Seward, Stafford Allan, MBE	LT CDR(FTC) (Act Cdr)	X		01.10.02	NP YEMEN
Sewed, Michael Antony, BSc, pcea, gdas	LT CDR(FTC)	X	O	01.10.94	LYNX OEU
Sewell, Lynsey Elizabeth,	MID(NE)(IC)	X		01.01.06	DARTMOUTH BRNC
Sewry, Michael Ronald, BSc, CEng, MIEE, psc(a)	CDR(FTC)	E	AE	31.12.95	DLO WYTON
Seymour, Kevin William, pcea	CDR(FTC)	X	P	30.06.06	JSCSC
Shackleton, Scott James Sinclair, PhD, BA, BD	CHAPLAIN	SF		20.04.93	DRAKE COB(CNH)
Shadbolt, Simon Edward, MBE, BSc, psc(m), psc(j)	BRIG(FTC)	-	C	01.10.04	MOD (LONDON)
Shah, Rajesh Radhakrishna, MChOrth, FRCS	SURG LTCDR(SCC)	-		12.01.00	LOAN FIELD HOSP
Shakespeare, Benjamin, BSc	LT(IC)	X		01.04.05	MWS COLLINGWOOD
Shakespeare, Christopher Allan, BEng	LT(IC)	E	AE	01.09.04	DLO TES
Shallcroft, John Edward, pcea	LT CDR(FTC)	X	P	01.10.98	RAF CRANWELL EFS
Shanahan, Lloyd Anthony,	LT(IC)	X	P	01.05.03	845 SQN
Shanks, Diana Zoe, BSc	LT(IC)	X		01.01.03	MWS COLLINGWOOD
Sharkey, Elton Richard, BEng, MSc, PGDip	LT CDR(FTC)	E	MESM	01.06.03	TIRELESS
Sharkey, Michael,	CHAPLAIN	RC		01.10.90	42 CDO RM
Sharkey, Philip Joseph, BEng	LT(IC)	E	ME	01.09.03	ARK ROYAL
Sharland, Simon Patrick, BA, sq	MAJ(FTC)	-	LC	01.09.90	NAVSEC
Sharman, Max Christopher,	LT RM(IC) (Act Capt Rm)	-		01.09.03	FPGRM
Sharp, Andrew Peter,	LT(CC)	E	MESM	01.05.02	SETT GOSPORT
Sharp, Christopher,	LT(IC)	E	WE	12.04.02	FOST SEA
Sharp, John Vivian,	LT(CC)	X	P	01.07.03	DRAKE COB
Sharp, Richard,	2LT(IC)	-		01.08.02	CTCRM LYMPSTONE
Sharp, William,	SURG SLT(SCC)	-		01.06.05	DARTMOUTH BRNC
Sharpe, Gary Anthony,	CAPT RM(FTC)	-	SO(LE)	01.01.93	CTCRM
Sharpe, Grantley James, pce	LT CDR(FTC)	X	PWO(U)	01.02.88	MWS DEF DIV SCHL
Sharpe, Marcus Roger,	CAPT RM(CC)	-	SO(LE)	01.04.03	CTCRM
Sharpe, Thomas Grenville,	LT CDR(FTC)	X	AAWO	01.10.02	SOUTHAMPTON
Sharples, Joseph Henry, BA	LT(IC)	X	P U/T	01.11.05	RNAS YEOVILTON
Sharples, Mark James, BSc	SLT(IC)	X	O U/T	01.05.03	824 SQN
Sharpley, John Guy, MA, MB, BCh, MRCPsych	SURG CDR(FCC)	-	(CN/P)	30.06.02	FLEET COSP&S
Sharrott, Christopher, BSc	LT(IC)	X	P	01.09.03	815 FLT 207

Name	Rank	Branch	Spec	Seniority	Where Serving
Shattock, James Duncan, BEng	SLT(IC)	X	P U/T	01.11.04	DARTMOUTH BRNC
Shaughnessy, Sophie Louise, BEng, CEng, MIEE	LT CDR(FTC)	E	ME	01.10.02	CAPT MCTA
Shaves, Thomas Daniel Littlefield, BA	SLT(IC)	S		01.09.04	DARTMOUTH BRNC
Shaw, Alexander,	SURG SLT(SCC)	-		06.09.04	DARTMOUTH BRNC
Shaw, Andrew,	2LT(IC)	-		01.08.02	CTCRM LYMPSTONE
Shaw, Andrew Thomas,	CAPT RM(CC) (Act Maj)	-		01.09.03	CC MAR AGRIPPA
Shaw, Callum Roderick, BEng	LT(IC)	E	MESM	01.01.06	VANGUARD(STBD)
Shaw, Elizabeth,	SURG SLT(SCC)	-		05.09.05	DARTMOUTH BRNC
Shaw, Ian Brian, BEng	LT CDR(FTC)	E	WESM	15.09.91	ACDS(POL) USA
Shaw, Kevin Norman Graham, MA, PhD,	CDR(FTC)	E	WE	30.06.02	BDS WASHINGTON
CEng, MIEE, MRAeS, MRIN, psc(j)					
Shaw, Mark Alexander, BEng	LT(IC)	X		01.05.04	NP IRAQ
Shaw, Michael Leslie, BEng, CEng, MRAeS	LT CDR(FTC)	E	AE	11.02.00	847 SQN
Shaw, Neil Andrew,	LT(FTC)	E	WE	01.04.01	DFTE PORTSMOUTH
Shaw, Paul James, MBE	CDR(FTC)	S		30.06.04	EXCHANGE AUSTLIA
Shaw, Simon James, BA	LT(IC)	X		01.11.05	DUMBARTON CASTLE
Shaw, Steven Matthew, MA, psc(j)	CDR(FTC)	S		30.06.01	UKMARBATSTAFF
Shaw, Stewart Andrew,	LT(IC)	X	P	01.07.05	DHFS
Shawcross, Paul Kenneth, BSc, pcea	CDR(FTC)	X	P	30.06.03	MOD (LONDON)
Sheals, Emma Jane, BSc	LT(IC)	X		18.01.05	CUMBERLAND
Shearman, Alexander James, MB, CHB, BMedSc	SURG LT(SCC)	-		06.08.03	RNAS YEOVILTON
Shearn, Matthew Arthur, BA	LT(CC)	X	H2	01.04.00	ENTERPRISE
Shears, Gary Raymond, BSc	LT(IC)	X	ATCU/T	01.09.03	RNAS YEOVILTON
Sheehan, Mark Andrew, pce, pcea, psc	CDR(FTC)	X	O	30.06.01	MOD (LONDON)
Sheehan, Thomas John,	LT(IC)	E	WESM	01.01.04	RALEIGH
Sheikh, Nabil, BSc, PGDipL, CDipAF	LT CDR(FTC)	S	BAR	01.11.05	PJHQ
Sheils, Damian Edmund Tyrie,	LT(CC)	X	P	16.07.94	ARK ROYAL
Shepherd, Alan, IEng, MIIE	LT CDR(FTC)	E	WE	01.10.92	SAUDI AFPS SAUDI
Shepherd, Anya Clare, BSc	LT(IC)	X	FC	01.12.02	ARK ROYAL
Shepherd, Charles Scott, BSc, MA, pce(sm), psc(j)	LT CDR(FTC)	X	SM	01.01.97	FLEET COSCAP
Shepherd, Christopher Edward,	LT(IC)	E	WESM	01.09.05	TRAFALGAR
Shepherd, Martin Paul, pcea	LT CDR(FTC)	X	PWO(C)	01.04.04	MWS COLLINGWOOD
Shepherd, Oliver James,	MID(IC)	X		01.09.04	DUMBARTON CASTLE
Shepherd, Paul Rodney, pcea	LT CDR(FTC)	X	O	01.10.92	750 SQN SEAHAWK
Shepherd, Roger Guy, BEng, MIEE	LT CDR(FTC)	E	WESM	01.05.96	FLEET COMOPS NWD
Sheppard, Heidi Clare,	LT(IC)	X		01.04.06	EDINBURGH
Shergold, Paul James,	CAPT RM(FTC) (Act Maj)	-	SO(LE)	01.01.97	RM CHIVENOR
Sherriff, David Anthony, pce, pcea, psc(j)	CDR(FTC)	X	P	30.06.03	RNAS YEOVILTON
Sherwin, Antony John, BA	LT(IC)	X	O	01.01.05	771 SQN
Sherwood, Gideon Andrew Francis,	LT(CC)	X	FC	01.05.01	ARK ROYAL
Shield, Simon James, pce(sm), psc	CDR(FTC)	X	SM	31.12.98	ASM IPT
Shields, Kristofer Neil, BA	LT(IC)	X	SM	01.01.06	MWS COLLINGWOOD
Shipperley, Ian, BSc, CEng, MIMechE	CDR(FTC)	E	ME	30.06.98	DLO BRISTOL
Shirley, Andrew John, BEng, CEng, MIMechE	LT CDR(FTC)	E	MESM	01.08.01	MOD (BATH)
Shirley, Wayne Peter, MA, MBA, psc(j)	CDR(FTC)	E	WE	30.06.04	NEW IPT
Shirvill, Matthew John, MEng	SLT(IC)	E	ME U/T	01.09.04	OCEAN
Short, Gavin Conrad, BEng, MA, CEng, MIEE, psc(j)	CDR(FTC)	E	WESM	30.06.00	IMS BRUSSELS
Short, John Jeffrey, BEng, MA, AMIMechE, psc(j)	CDR(FTC)	E	ME	30.06.05	DLO BRISTOL
Short, Kevin James, BSc	SLT(IC)	X		01.11.04	DARTMOUTH BRNC
Shortall, James John, BSc	LT(IC)	X		01.05.05	CATTISTOCK
Shortland, Karen, BA	LT(IC)	S		01.01.04	NELSON
Shouler, Matthew Frederic, BA	SLT(IC)	X		01.06.04	DARTMOUTH BRNC
Shrestha, Shekhar, BEng	LT(IC)	E	ME	01.01.04	ARGYLL
Shrimpton, Helen Diane, MB, BCh, MA(CANTAB),	SURG CDR(MCC)	-	GMPP	30.06.06	RNAS CULDR
DObstRCOG, DipAvMed, Dip FFP, MRCGP					
Shrimpton, Matthew William, pcea	LT CDR(FTC)	X	P	01.10.03	771 SQN
Shrives, Michael Peter, MA, pce, pcea, psc, psc(j)	CDR(FTC)	X	P	30.06.95	JWC/CIS STAVANGR
Shropshall, Ian James,	LT(IC)	X	SM	01.09.03	TRENCHANT
Shropshall, Kelly Ann,	LT(IC)	X		01.08.05	RAF SHAWBURY
Shrubsole, Gareth Mark, BA	LT(IC)	X		01.09.05	QUORN
Shuttleworth, Stephen,	LT CDR(FTC)	E	ME	01.10.04	LANCASTER
Shutts, David, BEng, CEng, MIMarEST, psc(j)	CDR(FTC)	E	ME	30.06.05	DARING

Name	Rank	Branch	Spec	Seniority	Where Serving
Sibbit, Neil Thomas, pce, pcea, psc, psc(j)o	CDR(FTC)	X	O	30.06.96	SA LISBON
Sibley, Andrew Keith,	LT CDR(FTC)	E	ME	01.10.04	PORTLAND
Sidebotham, Simon Charles, BSc	LT(CC)	E	WE	01.01.03	HQ DCSA
Sidoli, Giovanni Eugenio, BDS, MSc, MGDS RCS	SGCAPT(D)(FCC)	-		01.01.05	DPMD
Sidoli, Luigi Tomasso Angelo, BSc	LT(IC)	X		01.02.06	MWS COLLINGWOOD
Sienkiewicz, Maryla Krystyna, LLB	LT(CC)	X		01.09.01	MWS COLLINGWOOD
Siggers, Benet Richard Charles, MB, CHB, DiplMC RCSED	SURG LTCDR(MCC)	-		02.08.00	NELSON (PAY)
Sillers, Barry, BSc, SM(n)	LT CDR(FTC)	X	SM	01.12.02	COM MCC NWD
Silver, Christina Kay,	LT CDR(FTC)	W	C	01.10.93	JSSU CHELTENHAM
Simm, Craig William, BEng	LT(FTC) (Act Lt Cdr)	E	AE	01.07.98	ARK ROYAL
Simmonds, Daniel Douglas Harold,	LT(CC)	X	SM	01.05.03	FLEET COMOPS NWD
Simmonds, Gary Fredrick,	LT CDR(FTC)	E	AE	01.10.98	FLEET COSCAP
Simmonds, Richard Michael, OBE, jsdc, pce, psc(a)	CDR(FTC) (Act Capt)	X	MCD	31.12.90	JFCHQ BRUNSSUM
Simmonite, Gavin Ian,	LT(CC)	X	P	16.11.00	846 SQN
Simmons, Nigel Douglas, MSc, CEng, FIEE	CDR(FTC)	E	WESM	30.06.99	MOD (LONDON)
Simmons, Robert Leigh,	CAPT RM(IC)	-	LC	01.09.03	1 ASSLT GP RM
Simms, David Martin,	LT(CC)	X	O	16.03.96	824 SQN
Simpson, Christopher John, BA	LT(IC)	X	P	01.01.04	RNAS CULDROSE
Simpson, Colin Chisholm,	LT CDR(FTC)	X	P	01.10.04	815 FLT 212
Simpson, David John,	CHAPLAIN	CE		07.03.05	FWO PORTS SEA
Simpson, Erin Leona,	SLT(IC)	E	WE	01.01.02	MWS COLLINGWOOD
Simpson, John,	LT(IC)	MS		12.08.05	NEPTUNE DLO
Simpson, Mark,	LT(IC)	E	ME	05.08.01	DLO BRISTOL
Simpson, Martin Joseph, PGDIPAN, pce	LT CDR(FTC)	X	PWO(N)	01.07.96	MWS COLLINGWOOD
Simpson, Matthew,	SURG SLT(SCC)	-		05.09.05	DARTMOUTH BRNC
Simpson, Paul Emmanuel, Dip ICN	LT(MCC)	Q		27.10.00	RCDM
Simpson, Robin Frank,	CAPT RM(IC)	-		01.09.05	42 CDO RM
Simpson, Scott Forsyth,	LT(CC)	X	O	01.02.01	JSCSC
Simpson, Thomas Westgarth, BA	CAPT RM(CC)	-		01.09.04	NP IRAQ
Simpson, William James Stuart, BEng	LT(CC)	E	MESM	01.01.02	VANGUARD(PORT)
Sims, Alexander Richard,	LT(CC)	X	O	15.06.00	JSCSC
Sims, Deborah Louise, BA	LT(CC)	X	FC	01.01.94	RNAS YEOVILTON
Sinclair, Andrew Bruce, odc(Aus)	LT CDR(FTC)(A)	X	P	01.02.84	RNAS YEOVILTON
Singleton, Mark Donald,	LT(FTC)	X	AV	10.12.98	FLEET PHOT PORTS
Sinha, Raman,	SLT(IC)	X	P U/T	01.08.04	RNAS YEOVILTON
Sisson, Christopher,	2LT(IC)	-		01.08.02	CTCRM LYMPSTONE
Skeer, Martyn Robert, MBE, pce, pcea	CDR(FTC)	X	P	30.06.02	JDCC
Skelley, Alasdair Neil Murdoch, MA, pce, n	LT CDR(FTC)	X	PWO(U)	01.03.03	MWS COLLINGWOOD
Skelley, Roger, BSc	SLT(IC)	X		01.11.04	DARTMOUTH BRNC
Skelton, John Steven, BEng, CEng, MIMarEST	LT CDR(FTC)	E	ME	01.10.04	DLO TES
Skelton, Richard Stuart, BEng	SLT(IC)	X		01.11.04	DARTMOUTH BRNC
Skidmore, Christopher Mark, BA, FCIS, FCMI, FCIPD, MILog	CDR(FTC) (Act Capt)	S	SM	31.12.98	MOD (LONDON)
Skinner, Amy Louise, BA	SLT(IC)	X		01.02.04	CUMBERLAND
Skinner, Jonathan Jeffery, BA	LT(IC)	X		01.02.06	MWS COLLINGWOOD
Skinner, Neil Daniel,	SLT(IC)	X		01.05.04	OCEAN
Skinsley, Terry John,	LT(IC)	X		01.05.03	RICHMOND
Skipper, James Alexander,	LT(FTC)	X		01.11.02	FLEET HQ NWD
Skittrall, Steven David, BEng	LT CDR(FTC)	E	AE	15.10.05	LOAN DARA
Skuse, Matthew, BSc, psc(j)o	MAJ(FTC)	-	MLDR	01.09.99	MOD (LONDON)
Skyrme, Laura,	SURG SLT(MDC)	-		01.07.03	DARTMOUTH BRNC
Slack, Jeremy Mark,	MAJ(FTC)	-	LC	01.05.97	11 (ATT) SQN
Slade, Christopher, pcea	LT CDR(FTC)(A)	X	P	01.10.90	RNAS CULDROSE
Slater, Sir Jock (John Cunningham Kirkwood), GCB, LVO, DL, rcde, pce	ADM	N		29.01.91	
Slattery, Damian John, BSc	LT(CC)	X	MCD	01.01.00	MIDDLETON
Slawson, James Mark, BSc, CEng, MIMarEST, psc	CAPT(FTC)	E	ME	30.06.04	NAVSEC
Slayman, Emily,	SLT(IC)	S		01.09.03	RALEIGH
Slight, Oliver William Lawrence,	LT(IC)	X	FC	11.09.05	EDINBURGH
Slimmon, Kevan William, MBA, NDipM	LT CDR(FTC)	E	WESM	01.10.04	VANGUARD(STBD)
Sloan, Graham Daniel,	LT(CC)	X	MW	01.10.02	CHIDDINGFOLD
Sloan, Ian Alexander, BEng	LT(FTC)	X	P	01.12.99	EXCHANGE RAF UK
Sloan, Mark Usherwood, BSc, pce, psc	CAPT(FTC)	X	PWO(U)	31.12.99	MOD (LONDON)
Slocombe, Christopher Alwyn, pcea, psc(j)	CDR(FTC)	X	P	30.06.06	845 SQN

Name	Rank	Branch	Spec	Seniority	Where Serving
Slocombe, Nicholas Richard, ...LT CDR(FTC)	X	ATC		01.10.02	FOST DPORT SHORE
Slowther, Stuart John, BEng, MSc...LT(CC)	E	WE		01.09.01	MWS COLLINGWOOD
Small, Richard James, BSc, SM(n) ....LT CDR(FTC)	X	SM		01.03.05	FOST DSTF
Smalley, Paul John, BEng ....SLT(IC)	X	P U/T		01.01.05	DARTMOUTH BRNC
Smallwood, Anthony John, ...CAPT RM(CC)	BS	SO(LE)		19.07.02	RM BAND SCOTLAND
Smallwood, Justin Patrick, BA, MBA, sq ....MAJ(FTC)	-			05.09.95	1 ASSLT GP RM
Smallwood, Rachel, BMus...LT(IC)	E	TM		01.04.02	FWO DEVPT SEA
Smallwood, Richard Iain, pce(sm), SM(n) ....LT CDR(FTC)	X	SM		12.10.01	EXCHANGE AUSTLIA
Smart, Caroline Rose, BSc ....LT(IC)	E	TM		01.07.03	SULTAN
Smart, Mark James, ...LT(FTC) (Act Lt Cdr)	E	AE		02.05.00	EXCHANGE GERMANY
Smart, Steven Joe, ...LT(FTC)	E	ME		23.02.90	SULTAN
Smedley, Rachel Laura, BA ....LT(IC)	S			01.05.05	FLEET COSCAP
Smerdon, Christopher David Edward, BA ....LT CDR(FTC)	S	SM		01.07.94	RNAS CULDROSE
Smith, Adam Hewitt, BSc...SURG SLT(SCC)	-			01.07.03	DARTMOUTH BRNC
Smith, Adrian Charles, BSc...LT CDR(FTC)	E	AE		16.03.84	CV(F) IPT
Smith, Adrian Gerard, BA, MA(CANTAB)..........................LT CDR(FTC)	E	WE		01.02.99	NBC PORTSMOUTH
Smith, Andrew John Edward, BA...LT(CC)	X			01.04.99	TRUMPETER
Smith, Andrew Paul, ...LT CDR(FTC)	X	PWO(A)		01.04.98	EXCHANGE USA
Smith, Anthony, MEng...LT(CC)	E	TM		09.01.99	CAPT IST STAFF
Smith, Ashley Mark, ...SLT(IC)	X	O U/T		01.09.05	824 SQN
Smith, Austin Bernard Dudley, ...LT CDR(FTC)	X	P		01.10.02	JSCSC
Smith, Barbara Carol, ...CDR(FC(MD)	Q	SCM		30.06.05	HQ DMETA
Smith, Benjamin, BA ....LT(IC)	X			01.05.05	TURBULENT
Smith, Brian Joseph, n, BA ....LT CDR(FTC)	X	AAWO		01.12.99	SOUTHAMPTON
Smith, Brian Stephen, BDS, MGDS RCSEd ....SGCDR(D)(FCC)	-			30.06.01	RN GIBRALTAR
Smith, Charles John, ...LT(IC)	X	C		01.05.03	COM MCC NWD
Smith, Christopher John Hilton, CEng, MIEE, BEng.............LT CDR(FTC)	E	WE		01.10.04	RMC OF SCIENCE
Smith, Christopher Julian, MA, FCIPD, psc(j)........................CDR(FTC)	S			30.06.06	FLEET FOSNNI
Smith, Clive Peter, pce..LT CDR(FTC)	X	PWO(U)		26.04.95	MWS COLLINGWOOD
Smith, Craig Adam, BEng...LT(IC)	E	WE		01.02.06	GLOUCESTER
Smith, David Jonathan, ...LT(IC)	X	SM		01.05.03	SUPERB
Smith, David Leslie, ...LT CDR(FTC)	X	AAWO		01.10.04	MWS COLLINGWOOD
Smith, David Munro, ...MAJ(FTC)	-	SO(LE)		01.10.04	45 CDO RM
Smith, Edward George Giles, BA ....LT(IC)	X	H2		01.08.02	SCOTT
Smith, Edwin Joseph, ...SLT(IC)	X			01.02.06	DARTMOUTH BRNC
Smith, Fiona, ...SURG SLT(SCC)	-			11.03.04	DARTMOUTH BRNC
Smith, Gordon Kenneth, ...CAPT RM(CC)	-	LC		01.10.00	FLEET COMOPS NWD
Smith, Graeme Douglas James, BSc...............................LT CDR(FTC)	X	PWO(C)		01.01.01	UKMARBATSTAFF
Smith, Gregory Charles Stanley, pce, pcea.....................LT CDR(FTC)	X	O		01.01.98	JSCSC
Smith, Gregory Kenneth, BSc, CEng, MIEE, MBCS, adp ....CDR(FTC)	E	IS		30.06.05	PJHQ
Smith, James Andrew, BSc...SLT(IC)	X			01.01.05	DARTMOUTH BRNC
Smith, Jason Edward, MB, BS, MSc, ...SURG CDR(FCC)	-	(CEM)		30.06.05	LOAN FIELD HOSP
DipIMC RCSED, Dip SM, FFAEM, MRCP					
Smith, Jason James, MB, BS, MRCS...............................SURG LTCDR(MCC)	-			07.08.01	NELSON (PAY)
Smith, Jennifer Clare, BEng..SLT(IC)	X			01.01.04	MERSEY
Smith, Kenneth Marshall, ...LT CDR(FTC)	X			16.11.88	FLEET COSP&S
Smith, Keven John, pcea ....LT CDR(FTC)(A)	X	P		01.10.95	JHCHQ
Smith, Kevin Alexander, BSc, CEng, MIMarEST ....CDR(FTC)	E	MESM		30.06.03	FWO DEVPT SEA
Smith, Kevin Donlan, MEng..LT(CC)	E	IS		01.02.97	DCCIS BLANDFORD
Smith, Kristian Mark, ...LT(IC)	X	P		01.05.04	RNAS YEOVILTON
Smith, Laurence Michael, ...MID(IC)	X	P U/T		01.09.04	RNAS YEOVILTON
Smith, Lesley Ann, BA, ...LT(IC)	X			01.01.05	RNAS YEOVILTON
Smith, Lynnette, ...LT(CC)	S			01.01.02	JSU NORTHWOOD
Smith, Malcolm, CDipAF ....CAPT(FTC)	S	SM		30.06.05	PJHQ
Smith, Mark MacFarlane, BEng, MAPM, CEng, MRAeS ....LT CDR(FTC)	E	AE		01.11.98	829 SQN HQ
Smith, Mark Peter, ...LT CDR(FTC)	MS			01.10.04	FLEET COSP&S
Smith, Mark Richard, BEng..LT CDR(FTC)	E	ME		14.07.95	DLO BRISTOL
Smith, Martin Linn, MBE, BSc, psc................................LT COL(FTC)	-			31.12.99	MOD (LONDON)
Smith, Martin Russell Kingsley, BA, PGDip, MDA ....CDR(FTC)	X	METOC		30.06.03	BDLS INDIA
Smith, Matthew David, MA...LT(IC)	S			01.09.04	SUPERB
Smith, Matthew Roy Thomas, BA...LT(IC)	X			01.10.05	KENT
Smith, Melvin Andrew, MSc, mdtc ....CDR(FTC)	E	WE		31.12.95	JFC HQ AGRIPPA

Name	Rank	Branch Spec	Seniority	Where Serving
Smith, Michael Daren,	LT CDR(FTC)	X	O	01.10.02	FLEET COMOPS NWD
Smith, Michael John, BEng, MIEE	LT CDR(FTC)	E	WESM	01.05.04	NEW IPT
Smith, Neil Dennis,	LT(IC)	E	MESM	25.06.05	SULTAN
Smith, Nigel John, pce	LT CDR(FTC)	X	PWO(U)	01.10.01	LIVERPOOL
Smith, Nigel Peter, BA, MSc, pce	LT CDR(FTC)	X	PWO(U)	01.07.91	SONAR 2087 IPT
Smith, Owen John,	LT(CC)	E	ME	01.04.02	ARK ROYAL
Smith, Paul,	LT(FTC)	X	MCD	01.04.01	BLYTH
Smith, Paul Martin, MEng	SLT(IC)	E	WE U/T	01.03.04	MWS COLLINGWOOD
Smith, Richard William Robertson,	LT CDR(FTC)	X	PWO(U)	01.05.93	DRAKE COB
Smith, Robert Charles Vernon, pcea	LT CDR(FTC)	X	O	01.10.00	JSCSC
Smith, Robert Edward,	LT(FTC)	X	O	10.12.98	FLEET COSCAP
Smith, Simon Ronald Frederick,	LT(IC) (Act Lt Cdr)	X	ATC	28.07.96	OCEAN
Smith, Stephen Clive,	LT(IC)	X	SM	01.05.04	FLEET COMOPS NWD
Smith, Stephen Frank,	MAJ(FTC)	-	SO(LE)	01.10.02	CTCRM
Smith, Steven Luigi, pce, MSc	CDR(FTC)	X	AAWO	30.06.05	JSENS IPT
Smith, Steven Rhodes Clifford, MB, ChB, FRCS, FRCSTr&Orth	SURG CDR(FCC)	-	(CO/S)	30.06.03	MDHU DERRIFORD
Smithson, Peter Edward, MSc, CEng, MRAeS	CDR(FTC)	E	AE	30.06.97	RNAS YEOVILTON
Smye, Malcolm Alexander, BEng	LT(CC)	E	AE	01.01.02	JSCSC
Smyth, Clive Robert,	LT(IC)	MS		01.05.02	DMSTC
Sneddon, Russell Neil,	LT CDR(FTC)	X	P	01.10.01	DASC
Snee, Paul,	LT(IC)	X		01.03.04	MWS COLLINGWOOD
Sneesby, Nicholas,	LT(IC)	E	AE	01.07.04	DLO YEO
Snel, Karen Elizabeth,	LT(IC)	X	O U/T	01.01.06	RNAS CULDROSE
Snell, Andrew James,	LT(CC)	E	ME	01.05.02	MOD (LONDON)
Snell, David Micheal,	LT(CC)	E	WE	01.01.02	MOD (LONDON)
Snelling, Paul Douglas, BEng, MSc	LT CDR(FTC)	E	MESM	01.10.02	DLO BRISTOL
Snelson, David George, CB, FCMI, MNI, pce, psc, hcsc	RADM	-	AWO(A)	05.11.02	FLEET COSCAP
(FLEET-COSCAP APR 06)					
Sneyd, Eric Patrick Bartholomew, MBE, BEng, MSc, MDA	CDR(FTC)	E	TM	30.06.06	MOD (LONDON)
Snook, Raymond Edward, pce, pcea, psc(j)	CDR(FTC)	X	O	30.06.98	SA ANKARA
Snow, Christopher Allen, CBE, BA, pce	CDRE(FTC)	X	SM	14.05.02	OCEAN
Snow, Maxwell Charles Peter, BSc, DipFM, pce, pcea, psc	CDR(FTC)	X	P	30.06.93	FLEET AV VL
Snow, Paul Frederick, BSc, CEng, MIMarEST	LT CDR(FTC)	X	ME	01.10.94	FLEET COSP&S
Snowball, Simon John, MA, psc	CDR(FTC)	X	PWO(N)	30.06.00	FLEET COSP&S
Snowden, Michael Brian Samuel, MB, CHB,	SURG LTCDR(MCC)	-	GMPP	01.08.99	NEPTUNE DL
MRCGP, DObstRCOG, Dip FFP					
Soar, Gary, pcea	LT CDR(FTC)	X	O	01.10.02	700M MERLIN OEU
Soar, Trevor Alan, OBE, pce, pce(sm)	RADM	-	SM	18.05.04	MOD (LONDON)
(CM(PA) MAY 04)					
Sobers, Scott, BEng, PGDip	LT(IC)	E	MESM	01.09.03	VIGILANT(PORT)
Solly, Matthew MacDonald, BSc, n	LT CDR(FTC)	E	TMSM	01.10.02	FLEET FOTR
Somerville, Nigel John Powell, MBE, MA	MAJ(FTC)	-		01.05.04	JSCSC
Somerville, Stuart James,	LT(FTC)	S	SM	01.04.01	RN LOGS SCHOOL
Soul, Nicholas John, BEng	LT CDR(FTC)	X	P	01.10.04	845 SQN
South, David John,	LT CDR(FTC)	X	AAWO	15.06.97	CC MAR AGRIPPA
Southall, Nicholas Christian Jeffrey, BSc	SLT(IC)	X		01.11.04	DARTMOUTH BRNC
Southall, Timothy Edward, BA	LT(IC)	X	O	01.09.05	SUTHERLAND
Southern, Mark John,	CAPT RM(CC)	-		01.09.03	42 CDO RM
Southern, Paul Jonathan, BSc, IEng, AMIMarEST	LT CDR(FTC)	E	ME	27.02.99	LOAN OMAN
Southern, Victoria,	MID(IC)	X		01.11.04	DARTMOUTH BRNC
Southorn, M, pce	LT CDR(FTC)	X	PWO(U)	21.07.99	ARGYLL
Southwood, Shaun Christopher,	LT(IC)	E	MESM	01.05.03	VICTORIOUS(PORT)
Southworth, Christopher, MEng	LT(IC)	X		01.01.06	RNAS CULDROSE
Southworth, Mika-John, BSc	LT(IC)	X		01.09.02	DEF SCH OF LANG
Sowden, Lesley Margaret, MB, CHB,	SURG LTCDR(MCC)	-	GMPP	02.08.00	FOST SEA
MRCGP, DObstRCOG, Dip FFP					
Spacey, Craig David, BEng	SLT(IC)	E	MESM	01.09.03	FWO DEVONPORT
Spackman, Lucy Charlotte,	SLT(IC)	X		01.01.05	DARTMOUTH BRNC
Spalding, Richard Edmund Howden, BSc, CEng, FIEE, FCMI, jsdc	CAPT(FTC)	E	WE	30.06.06	HQ DCSA
Spalding, Thomas Stephen, BA	SLT(IC)	X		01.05.04	DARTMOUTH BRNC
Spalton, Gary Marcus Sean, BSc, pce	CDR(FTC)	X	PWO(U)	31.12.92	SACT BELGIUM
Spanner, Paul,	MAJ(FTC)	-		01.05.01	FLEET COSP&S

Name	Rank	Branch	Spec	Seniority	Where Serving
Spark, Stephen Michael,	LT(IC)	X		01.05.03	VIGILANT(PORT)
Sparke, Philip Richard William, BA	LT CDR(FTC)	S		01.03.00	EXCHANGE FRANCE
Sparkes, Peter James, BSc, pce, n	CDR(FTC)	X	PWO(C)	30.06.04	MWS COLLINGWOOD
Sparkes, Simon Nicholas, BA(OU), pcea	LT CDR(FTC)	X	P	01.10.02	824 SQN
Sparks, Simon,	CAPT RM(CC)	-		01.09.04	CTCRM
Sparrow, Mark Jonathan, BSc	LT(CC)	X	P	16.04.99	LOAN OTHER SVCE
Spayne, Nicholas John, n	LT CDR(FTC)	X	PWO(U)	01.10.98	WILDFIRE
Spearpoint, Damon,	SLT(IC)	X		01.01.05	RAF COTTESMORE
Spears, Andrew Graeme, SM(n)	LT(CC)	X	SM	01.11.00	RALEIGH
Speedie, Alan Carrick,	CAPT RM(IC)	-		01.09.05	FPGRM
Speller, Nicholas Simon Ford, pce(sm), MDA, MCMI, MNI	LT CDR(FTC)	X	SM	01.05.88	FLEET HQ WI
Spence, Andrei Barry, BSc	CDR(FTC) (Barrister)	S	BAR	30.06.00	MOD (LONDON)
Spence, Nicholas Anthony, MA, pce	CDR(FTC)	X	PWO(U)	30.06.97	EUMS
Spence, Robert Graeme, BA	LT(FTC)	X	P	16.12.93	COMATG SEA
Spencer, Ashley Carver, BA	LT(CC)	X	MCD	01.05.01	QUORN
Spencer, Elizabeth Anne, BEd, MA, psc(j)	CDR(FTC)	X	METOC	30.06.99	FLEET COSCAP
Spencer, Jeremy Charles, BSc, PGDip	LT(FTC)	E	ME	02.09.99	FLEET COSP&S
Spencer, Richard Anthony Winchcombe, OBE, BA, psc(j)o	LT COL(FTC)	-	C	31.12.99	JSCSC
Spencer, Steven John,	LT CDR(FC(MD)	Q	CC	01.10.00	FLEET FOTR
Spicer, Clive Graham, BSc, CEng, MIMarEST	CDR(FTC)	E	ME	31.12.95	DA MANAMA
Spike, Adam James, BSc	LT(CC)	X	P	01.05.02	846 SQN
Spillane, Paul William,	LT(FTC)	X	O	01.07.96	ILLUSTRIOUS
Spiller, Michael Francis, BSc, psc	CDR(FTC)	S		31.12.98	PJHQ
Spiller, Stephen Nicholas, BEng, MSc gw	LT CDR(FTC)	E	WE	01.08.05	LOAN DSTL
Spiller, Vanessa Jane, pce, psc(j), MA	CDR(FTC)	X	PWO(U)	30.06.05	FLEET COMOPS NWD
Spink, David Andrew,	CAPT RM(CC)	-		01.09.02	40 CDO RM
Spinks, David William,	LT CDR(FTC)	X	PWO(A)	01.08.05	EXCHANGE FRANCE
Spinks, Robert John, BSc	LT(CC)	X	P	01.05.01	EXCH ARMY SC(G)
Spires, Trevor Allan, BSc, CDipAF, nadc	RADM	-	TM	21.10.03	AFPAA HQ
(CHIEF EXECUTIVE OCT 03)					
Spooner, Ross Sydney, BEng	LT CDR(FTC)	E	AE	01.04.04	RNAS CULDROSE
Spoors, Brendan Mark, BEng	LT(CC)	X	P	01.01.98	824 SQN
Springett, Simon Paul, LLB, CertTh	CHAPLAIN	CE		10.09.91	CTCRM
Squire, Paul Anthony, BSc, adp, CEng,	LT CDR(FTC)	E	WE	01.10.90	DCCIS FAREHAM
CITP, CDipAF, MIEE, MAPM, MBCS					
St Aubyn, John David Erskine, BSc	CDR(FTC)	E	WESM	30.06.01	MOD (LONDON)
Stace, Ivan Spencer, BEng, MA, MSc, CEng, MIEE, MCGI, psc(j), mdtc	CDR(FTC)	E	WESM	30.06.04	FWO DEVPT SEA
Stacey, Andrew Michael, BSc, pce	LT CDR(FTC)	X	PWO(A)	01.06.02	CHIDDINGFOLD
Stacey, Elizabeth,	LT(IC)	X		01.07.05	ALBION
Stacey, Hugo Alister,	LT CDR(FTC(A)	X	P	01.10.93	MERLIN IPT
Stack, Eleanor Frances,	LT(CC)	X		01.09.01	NELSON
Stackhouse, Martyn Carl,	SLT(IC)	X	P	01.01.04	824 SQN
Stafford, Benjamin Robert, MEng, CEng, MIMechE	LT(FTC)	E	MESM	01.02.00	DLO BRISTOL
Stafford, Derek Bryan,	MAJ(FTC)	-	P	01.10.03	846 SQN
Stafford, Wayne,	LT(FTC)	E	WESM	09.01.01	DLO BRISTOL
Stafford-Shaw, Damian Vaughan, BSc	SLT(IC)	E	TM U/T	01.09.03	LIVERPOOL
Stagg, Antony Robert, BEng, MSc	LT CDR(FTC)	E	AE	01.03.03	DARTMOUTH BRNC
Stait, Benjamin Geoffrey,	LT(FTC)	X	MCD	01.04.99	FDU1
Stait, Carolyn Jane, OBE, ADC, FCIPD, psc	CDRE(FTC)	W	S	22.06.04	NEPTUNE DLO
Stait, Emma Jane,	LT(CC)	S		01.04.99	NELSON
Staley, Simon Peter Lee, pce, pcea, psc(j)o	LT CDR(FTC)	X	O	01.02.99	NAVSEC
Stallion, Ian Michael, BA, pce, pce(sm)	CDR(FTC)	X	SM	31.12.94	MOD (LONDON)
Stamper, Jonathan Charles Henry, MSc	LT CDR(FTC)	E	IS	01.01.00	FLEET COSP&S
Stamper, Valerie Louise, BA	LT(IC)	S		01.03.06	RICHMOND
Stancliffe, Andrew Eden,	LT(IC)	E	AE	01.07.04	20(R) SQN (RN)
Standen, Colin Anthony,	CAPT RM(FTC)	-	SO(LE)	01.01.01	1 ASSLT GP RM
Standen, Gary David,	LT(CC)	E		01.05.02	815 SQN HQ
Stanford, Jeremy Hugh, BA, jsdc, pce	CAPT(FTC)	X	P	30.06.01	RNAS CULDROSE
Stangroom, Alastair, pce	CDR(FTC)	X	MCD	30.06.03	LOAN OMAN
Stanham, Christopher Mark,	LT CDR(FTC)	E	AE	01.10.01	846 SQN
Stanhope, Sir Mark, KCB, OBE, MA, MNI, rcds, pce, pce(sm), psc, hcsc	ADM	-	SM	10.07.04	HQ SACT
(DEPUTY SACT JUL 04)					

Name	Rank	Branch	Spec	Seniority	Where Serving
Stanistreet, Georgina Clare, BEng	LT(IC)	E	ME	01.05.04	IRON DUKE
Stanley, Andrew Brian,	LT(CC)	E	MESM	01.10.02	FWO DEVONPORT
Stanley, Nicholas Paul, MPhil, pce, psc	CAPT(FTC)	X	MCD	30.06.02	MOD (LONDON)
Stanley, Paul, BEd, jsdc, ODC(SWISS)	CDR(FTC)	E	TM	30.06.92	SULTAN
Stanley-Whyte, Berkeley John, BSc, MA, CEng, MIEE, psc(j)	CDR(FTC)	E	WESM	31.12.98	DLO BRISTOL
Stannard, Adam, MB, ChB, BSc	SURG LTCDR(MCC)	-		02.08.05	NELSON (PAY)
Stannard, Mark Philip,	LT CDR(FTC)	X		01.08.97	LOAN SAUDI ARAB
Stanning, Alastair,	SURG SLT(SCC)	-		02.02.06	DARTMOUTH BRNC
Stant, Mark Simon, BEng	LT(IC)	X	P U/T	01.11.05	RNAS YEOVILTON
Stanton, David Vernon, MBE, pcea, psc(j)	CDR(FTC)	X	O	30.06.03	RNAS CULDROSE
Stanton, Keith Victor,	CAPT RM(CC)	-	SO(LE)	01.04.03	CTCRM
Stanton, Paul Charles Maund, BSc, ACMA	LT CDR(FTC)	S	CMA	16.02.97	MOD (BATH)
Stanton-Brown, Peter James, BSc, SM(n)	LT CDR(FTC)	X	SM	01.02.01	FOST DPORT SHORE
Stanway, Charles Adrian, BSc, SM(n)	LT(FTC)	X	SM	01.09.00	SOVEREIGN
Stapley, Sarah Ann, MB, ChB, MD, FRCS, FRCSTr&Orth	SURG CDR(FCC)	-	(CO/S)	30.06.02	MDHU PORTSMOUTH
Starkey, David Samuel,	LT(IC)	X		01.02.06	MWS COLLINGWOOD
Starling, Christopher Michael,	CAPT RM(IC)	-	SO(LE)	19.07.05	42 CDO RM
Stead, Abigail, BSc	LT(IC)	X	P	01.01.04	RNAS YEOVILTON
Stead, Andrew Michael, BSc	LT(IC)	E	TM	01.07.99	RALEIGH
Stead, John Arthur, BSc	LT(IC)	E	WESM	02.09.99	CLYDE MIXMAN1
Stead, Richard Alexander, MBA	LT CDR(FTC)	MS	(AD)	01.10.01	JSCSC
Steadman, Rebecca Angharad Jane, BSc	LT(FTC)	X		01.04.02	BANGOR
Steadman, Robert Paul, BA	LT CDR(FTC)	X	AAWO	01.05.04	EDINBURGH
Stearns, Rupert Paul, MA, psc, psc(j)	COL(FTC)	-	LC	30.06.03	MOD (BATH)
Steeds, Sean Michael, pce, pcea, psc(j)	CDR(FTC)	X	P	30.06.98	SA ROME
Steel, Christopher Michael Howard, BSc, CEng, MIEE, MCMI, jsdc	CAPT(FTC)	E	WESM	30.06.04	RCDS
Steel, David George, ADC, BA, FCIPD, jsdc, FCILOGT	CDRE(FTC) (Barrister)	S	BAR	21.11.05	NBC PORTSMOUTH
Steel, Gareth,	2LT(IC)	-		01.08.02	CTCRM LYMPSTONE
Steel, Peter St Clair, BSc, jsdc, pce	CAPT(FTC)	X	P	30.06.01	NELSON
Steele, Matthew Stuart, BSc	LT(CC)	X	HM	01.05.02	SCOTT
Steele, Trevor Graeme,	LT(FTC)	X	O	11.12.92	MWS COLLINGWOOD
Steen, Kieron Malcolm, BSc	LT(FTC)	X	P	01.01.98	RAF LINTN/OUSE
Steer, Rebecca,	SURG SLT(SCC)	-		01.07.03	DARTMOUTH BRNC
Steiger, Robert Carl, BSc	LT(IC)	E	SM	01.11.03	FLEET COMOPS NWD
Stein, Graham Kenneth, BSc	LT(CC)	X	P	01.11.98	846 SQN
Stembridge, Daniel Patrick Trelawney,	LT CDR(FTC)	X	P	01.10.03	EXCHANGE USA
Stemp, Justin Edward, BA	MAJ(FTC)	-		01.09.04	FLEET COSP&S
Stenhouse, Nicholas John, BSc, MA, CEng, MIEE, psc	CDR(FTC)	E	WE	31.12.93	CALEDONIA DLO
Stephen, Barry Mark, BA, n	LT CDR(FTC)	X	PWO(U)	01.03.02	FOST MPV SEA
Stephen, Cameron Edward, BEng	SLT(IC)	E	AE U/T	01.09.04	ILLUSTRIOUS
Stephens, Christopher,	LT(IC)	E	WE	08.04.05	ILLUSTRIOUS
Stephens, Patrick George,	LT(IC)	X		01.07.05	TRAFALGAR
Stephens, Richard James, MBE, MA, psc(j)	LT COL(FTC)	-		30.06.03	FLEET AV SUPPORT
Stephens, Richard John, BSc, PGDip	LT CDR(CC)	X	METOC	01.09.02	FLEET COMOPS NWD
Stephens, Richard Philip,	LT CDR(FTC)	X	EW	01.10.99	FLEET COSCAP
Stephens, Samuel Jolyon Roderick, MSc	LT(IC)	X		01.01.06	CAMPBELTOWN
Stephenson, Christopher John, BSc	LT(IC)	X	MCD	01.04.03	CHIDDINGFOLD
Stephenson, David, BEng, MSc, CEng	LT CDR(FTC)	E	ME	22.11.95	CV(F) IPT
Stephenson, Keith James MacFarlane, BA, MSc	LT CDR(FTC)	E	IS	01.10.02	CINCFLEET FIMU
Stephenson, Philip George, BSc, MILog	LT CDR(FTC)	S	(S)	01.10.03	SOUTHAMPTON
Stephenson, Richard James Edgar,	LT(IC)	S		08.04.05	NP IRAQ
Sterry, Jasen Edward Baxter,	LT(CC)	X	REG	01.09.01	MCTC
Stevens, Andrew John,	LT(SC(MD)	Q		24.09.99	RH HASLAR
Stevens, Anthony, BA	LT(CC) (Act Lt Cdr)	E	TMSM	04.12.97	RALEIGH
Stevens, Christopher Kenneth,	MID(IC)	X		01.09.04	ST ALBANS
Stevens, Derek George,	LT(IC)	E	TM	01.01.02	CMT SHRIVENHAM
Stevens, Joseph Iain, BEng	LT(IC)	E	AE U/T	01.09.03	ILLUSTRIOUS
Stevens, Mark,	SLT(IC)	X		01.01.05	SULTAN
Stevenson, Adam Peter, BA	LT(IC)	X		01.09.04	SEVERN
Stevenson, Geoffrey Stewart, BDS, MFGDP(UK)	SGLTCDR(D)(MC(MD)	-		14.01.99	BULWARK
Stevenson, Julian Patrick, BEng	LT CDR(FTC)	E	MESM	01.11.05	NAVSEC
Stevenson, Laura Jane, BDS	SG LT(D)(SC(MD)	-		27.06.03	DRAKE COB(CNH)

Name	Rank	Branch	Spec	Seniority	Where Serving
Stevenson, Luke Lawrence,	SLT(IC)	E		01.02.06	PJHQ
Stevenson, Paul Michael, BEng, PGDip	LT(IC)	E	MESM	01.09.04	TURBULENT
Stevenson, Robert MacKinnon, BDS, MSc, MGDS RCS	SGCAPT(D)(FCC)	-		06.08.05	DDS PORTSMOUTH
Stevenson, Simon Richard,	LT(IC)	X	P	01.01.02	820 SQN
Stewart, Andrew Carnegie, MA, MIL, pce	CDR(FTC)	X	PWO(C)	30.06.00	MWS COLLINGWOOD
Stewart, Benjamin Christopher,	LT(IC)	X		01.05.03	MANCHESTER
Stewart, Charles Hardie, BSc	LT(IC)	X		01.09.01	DARTMOUTH BRNC
Stewart, David James, OBE, MC, BSc, MA, psc	COL(FTC)	-	C	30.06.05	CTCRM
Stewart, James Neil, BSc, MA, psc(j)	CDR(FTC)	E	TMSM	30.06.03	MOD (LONDON)
Stewart, Kenneth Currie, BSc	LT CDR(FTC)	E	TM	01.09.98	NEPTUNE 2SL/CNH
Stewart, Marcus Patrick Michael,	CHAPLAIN	CE		29.03.04	RNAS YEOVILTON
Stewart, Nicholas John, MSc	LT(IC)	X		01.05.04	MWS COLLINGWOOD
Stewart, Robert Gordon, BSc, psc	CAPT(FTC)	X	H CH	30.06.04	MOD (LONDON)
Stewart, Rory William, BSc	LT CDR(FTC)	E	MESM	01.07.91	DRAKE SFM
Stewart, Sean Thomas,	SLT(IC)	X		01.02.05	DARTMOUTH BRNC
Stickland, Charles Richard, BSc, MA, psc(j)	LT COL(FTC)	-	LC	30.06.04	COMAMPHIBFOR
Stidston, Ian James, BSc, MDA, MCIPD	CDR(FTC)	E	TM	31.12.00	NAVSEC
Stillwell-Cox, Andrew David Robert, MHCIMA, MCFA, MinstAM	LT CDR(FTC)	S	CA	01.10.00	RNAS CULDROSE
Stilwell, James Michael, BA, SM(n)	LT(CC)	X	SM	01.01.98	SCEPTRE
Stinton, Carol Ann,	LT CDR(FC(MD)	Q	OTSPEC	01.10.99	PJHQ
Stirzaker, Mark, BSc, MA, CEng, MINucE, AMIMechE	CDR(FTC)	E	MESM	30.06.05	FLEET COSP&S
Stitson, Paul,	CAPT RM(IC)	-		01.09.03	FPGRM
Stobie, Paul Lionel,	LT CDR(FTC)	E	AE	01.10.01	DLO WYTON
Stobo, Alexander,	LT(CC)	X	P U/T	01.10.00	845 SQN
Stock, Christopher Mark,	LT CDR(FTC)	X	O	01.10.04	MWC PORTSDOWN
Stocker, John Theodore, BA	SLT(IC)	X		01.01.05	DARTMOUTH BRNC
Stockings, Timothy Mark, BSc, pce, pcea, psc(j)	CDR(FTC)	X	P	30.06.00	ARK ROYAL
Stockton, Kevin Geoffrey, pce	LT CDR(FTC)	X	PWO(U)	19.11.00	LOAN OMAN
Stoffell, David Peter, GCIPD	LT CDR(FTC) (Act Cdr)	S	SM	27.11.98	FLEET FOTR
Stokes, Alan William,	LT CDR(FTC)	E	WESM	01.10.98	HQ DCSA
Stokes, Richard, BSc, MDA, DipFM, CEng, MIEE	CAPT(FTC)	E	WESM	30.06.06	MOD (LONDON)
Stone, Colin Robert Macleod, pce	LT CDR(FTC)	X	PWO(U)	01.05.85	FLEET COMOPS NWD
Stone, James William Gray, BSc	LT(CC)	X	O	01.05.02	849 SQN HQ
Stone, Nicholas Joseph John, BA	LT(CC)	S	SM	01.07.00	FLEET HQ WI
Stone, Nicholas Stuart,	SLT(UCE)(IC)	X		01.09.05	DARTMOUTH BRNC
Stone, Richard James, MBE	LT(FTC) (Act Lt Cdr)	E	ME	19.06.98	SOUTHAMPTON
Stoneman, Timothy John, BSc, MA, pce, psc	CDR(FTC)	X	AAWO	31.12.91	CAPT MCTA
Stonier, Paul Leslie,	CAPT RM(FTC) (Act Maj)	-	SO(LE)	01.01.01	CTCRM
Stonor, Philip Francis Andrew, pce, pcea, odc(Fr)	CDR(FTC)	X	P	31.12.95	UKMILREP BRUSS
Stopps, Gregory Alan Martin, BA	SLT(IC)	X		01.01.05	DARTMOUTH BRNC
Storey, Andrew Eric, SM(n)	LT(CC)	X	SM	01.05.02	TIRELESS
Storey, Anne-Louise, BSC(EH), MCIEH		MS		01.11.03	2SL/CNH
Storey, Ceri Leigh, BEng, MBA	LT CDR(FTC)	E	MESM	01.08.03	SCEPTRE
Storrs-Fox, Roderick Noble, BSc, MBA	CAPT(FTC)	S		30.06.06	MOD (BATH)
Storton, George Houston,	SLT(IC)	X		01.07.03	BLYTH
Story, Ruth Siobhan, BA	LT(IC)	X		01.01.06	SOUTHAMPTON
Stott, John Antony, MIEE	LT CDR(FTC)	E	WESM	26.05.91	BDS WASHINGTON
Stovin-Bradford, Matthew, psc(j)o	MAJ(FTC)	-	C	01.09.99	40 CDO RM
Stowell, Perry Ivan Mottram, pce, n	LT CDR(FTC)	X	PWO(U)	01.04.98	MONMOUTH
Stowell, Robin Barnaby Mottram, BEng, MSc, CEng	LT CDR(FTC)	E	ME	01.09.03	FLEET COSP&S
Strachan, Richard Parry, MB, CHB	SURG LT(SC(MD)	-		06.08.03	CFLT MED(SEA)
Stratford, Peter John,	LT(CC)	X	ATC	01.04.95	RAF SHAWBURY
Strathern, Roderick James, pce	LT CDR(FTC)	X	PWO(U)	01.10.98	FOST SEA
Strathie, Gavin Scott,	LT(CC)	X	ATC	01.06.96	NAIC NORTHOLT
Stratton, John Denniss, BSc, CEng, FRAeS, psc	CAPT(FTC)	E	AE	30.06.02	DLO YEO
Stratton, Matthew Paul, BEng, MSc	LT(FTC)	X	WE	01.05.99	MWS COLLINGWOOD
Stratton, Nicholas Charles, SM(n)	LT(CC)	X	SM	01.05.00	MWC PORTSDOWN
Stratton, Stuart John, PGDip	LT(IC)	E	MESM	01.05.01	VANGUARD(STBD)
Straughan, Christopher John, MBE, pce	LT CDR(FTC)	X	PWO(U)	01.12.90	FWO DEVPT SEA
Straughan, Harry, MSc, psc	CDR(FTC)	E	IS	31.12.97	DCCIS BLANDFORD
Straughan, Scott Richard, BSc, BEng	LT(CC)	E	IS	01.05.97	IMS BRUSSELS
Straw, Andrew Nicholas,	CDR(FTC)	S		30.06.03	FLEET COSP&S

Name	Rank	Branch	Spec	Seniority	Where Serving
Strawbridge, Chantal Marie, BA, BSc	LT(IC)	X		01.09.04	KENT
Street, Paul M,	LT(IC)	E	WESM	01.07.04	CAPT MCTA
Street, Sarah Caroline,	LT(IC)	S		01.05.04	NELSON
Streeten, Christopher Mark, BSc, CEng, MIEE, nadc	CDR(FTC)	E	WESM	30.06.02	MOD (LONDON)
Streets, Christopher George, MB, BSc, BCh, MD	SURG LTCDR(FCC)	-		01.08.98	NELSON (PAY)
Stretton, Darrell George,	LT(FTC)	X	AV	03.04.97	FLEET COSP&S
Strickland, Timothy John, BEng	SLT(IC)	X	P U/T	01.04.04	RNAS YEOVILTON
Stride, James Alan, BA, pce	LT CDR(FTC)	X	PWO(A)	01.10.03	EXETER
Stride, Jamieson Colin, pcea	LT CDR(FTC)	X	O	01.04.03	FOST SEA
Stringer, Graeme Ellis,	LT(FTC)	X	ATC	19.09.00	RNAS YEOVILTON
Stringer, Roger Andrew, pcea	LT CDR(FTC)	X	P	01.10.97	GANNET SAR FLT
Stroude, Paul Addison, BEng, n	LT CDR(FTC)	X	PWO(U)	01.08.04	CORNWALL
Strudwick, Russell,	LT CDR(FTC)	S	(W)	01.10.03	ST ALBANS
Strutt, Jason Fearnley, BEng, MSc	LT CDR(FTC)	E	WE	01.05.00	FOST SEA
Stuart, Euan Edward Andrew,	LT CDR(FTC)	X	PWO(A)	01.10.04	MWS COLLINGWOOD
Stuart, Simon Alexander, BSc	LT(IC)	X	O	01.09.04	815 FLT 229
Stubbings, Paul Richard,	CDR(FTC)	E	MESM	31.12.99	FWO DEVONPORT
Stubbs, Benjamin Duncan, BEng	LT(IC)	X	P	01.09.03	RNAS YEOVILTON
Stubbs, Ian,	LT(CC)	X	O	16.05.95	824 SQN
Stubbs, Ian,	LT(IC)	E	TM	01.02.03	MWS COLLINGWOOD
Stubbs, Martin Andrew,	LT CDR(FTC)	E	WESM	01.10.03	JSSU CHELTENHAM
Sturdy, Clive Charles Markus, pce	LT CDR(FTC)	X	PWO(U)	01.06.04	FDG
Sturgeon, David Marcus,	LT(IC)	S	SM	01.05.02	FWO DEVONPORT
Sturgeon, Mark, BEng	LT(IC)	E	WESM	01.09.02	SCU SHORE
Sturman, Richard William, BSc	LT(CC)	X	P	01.08.00	MWS COLLINGWOOD
Stuttard, Mark Christopher, pce	CDR(FTC)	X	PWO(A)	30.06.06	FLEET COSP&S
Stuttard, Stephen Eric,	LT CDR(FTC)	X	AV	01.10.97	HQ STC
Style, Charles Rodney, CBE, MA, rcds, pce, hcsc	VADM	-	PWO(U)	10.01.06	MOD (LONDON)
(DEP CHIEF OF DEFENCE STAFF (COMMITMENTS) JAN 06)					
Suchet, Robert,	CAPT RM(IC)	-		01.09.04	EXCHANGE ARMY UK
Suckling, Robin Leslie, pcea	LT CDR(FTC)	X	O	01.10.02	824 SQN
Suddes, Lesley Ann, BA, MA(CANTAB), psc(j)	CDR(FTC)	X	METOC	30.06.03	JSCSC
Sugden, Michael Rodney, BSc, MBA	LT CDR(FTC)	E	ME	01.10.94	DRAKE SFM
Sugden, Stephen Robert, HNC	LT CDR(FTC)	E	WE	01.10.99	FLEET HQ WI
Sullivan, Anne Gillian, BSc, MA, FRMS, psc(j)	CDR(FTC)	X	METOC	31.12.99	MOD (LONDON)
Sullivan, Colin, BA, psc	CDR(FTC)	X	METOC	31.12.96	MOD (LONDON)
Sullivan, Mark, BSc, BEng, CEng, MIEE	LT CDR(FTC)	E	WE	01.07.01	MANCHESTER
Summerfield, David Edward, osc(us)	LT COL(FTC)	-		30.06.00	RMR LONDON
Summers, Alastair John,	LT(CC)	X	P	01.12.00	849 SQN B FLT
Summers, James Alexander Edward, BEd	MAJ(FTC)	-		24.05.02	CTCRM
Sumner, Michael Dennis, MIIE	CDR(FTC)	E	WESM	30.06.03	MOD (LONDON)
Sunderland, John Dominic, MSc, CEng, MIEE	CDR(FTC)	E	WESM	31.12.97	MOD (LONDON)
Surgey, Ian, SM	LT CDR(FTC)	X	SM	26.10.97	FLEET COMOPS NWD
Sutcliff, Jonathan David, MEng	LT(IC)	E	WE	01.11.05	OCEAN
Sutcliffe, Edward Diccon, BA	LT(CC)	S	SM	01.05.98	CC MAR AGRIPPA
Sutcliffe, John, pce, pcea	CDR(FTC)	X	O	30.06.04	EXCHANGE USA
Sutcliffe, Paul Matthew, BA	LT(IC)	X	P	01.01.05	RNAS YEOVILTON
Suter, Francis Thomas,	LT(CC)	X	O	01.01.02	815 FLT 219
Sutherland, Gayl, BSc, Dip ICN	LT(FC(MD))	Q		25.10.00	MDHU DERRIFORD
Sutherland, Iain Duncan,	LT RM(CC) (Act Capt Rm)	-		01.09.03	FPGRM
Sutherland, Neil, MSc, psc(j)	MAJ(FTC)	-	C	24.04.02	42 CDO RM
Sutton, David, MBE	CAPT RM(CC)	-	P	01.04.01	847 SQN
Sutton, Gareth David, MSc, CEng, MIMarEST	LT CDR(FTC)	E	ME	01.06.93	DLO BRISTOL
Sutton, Gary Brian, pce	CAPT(FTC)	X	PWO(N)	30.06.05	DGMC SEA
Sutton, Richard Michael John,	LT CDR(FTC)	X	P	01.10.02	JHCHQ
Swain, Andrew Vincent, MBE, AFRIN, pce	CDR(FTC)	X	H CH	30.06.05	JSCSC
Swales, Richard, BSc	SLT(IC)	X	O U/T	01.01.05	DARTMOUTH BRNC
Swann, Adam Peter Drummond, BA	LT(IC)	X		01.03.06	MWS COLLINGWOOD
Swann, John Ivan, BSc	LT(FTC) (Act Lt Cdr)	X	EW	28.07.89	RNU RAF DIGBY
Swannick, Derek John, BSc, MA, FRMS, psc(j)	CDR(FTC)	X	METOC	30.06.02	MWS HM TG (D)
Swarbrick, Richard James, BA, pce, pcea, psc(j)	CDR(FTC)	X	P	30.06.04	JSCSC
Sweeney, Craig, BSc	LT(CC)	X	P	16.02.99	MWS COLLINGWOOD

Name	Rank	Branch	Spec	Seniority	Where Serving
Sweeney, Keith Patrick Michael, BEng	LT CDR(FTC)	E	ME	01.08.03	MOD (BATH)
Sweeney, Rachel Jane, BEng	LT(IC)	E	AE	01.01.04	849 SQN A FLT
Sweetman, David James,	LT(IC)	E	WE	01.11.05	MWS COLLINGWOOD
Sweny, Gordon,	2LT(IC)	-		01.08.01	42 CDO RM
Swift, Robert David,	LT(IC)	S		01.09.04	JSCSC
Swift, Robin David, pce	CDR(FTC)	X	PWO(U)	30.06.05	HQ SACT
Swindells, Mark, BEng	LT(CC)	X	P	16.07.99	EXCHANGE FRANCE
Swire, Barry John, BA	LT(SC(MD)	Q		26.07.02	RN GIBRALTAR
Sykes, Hannah Elizabeth, BA	SLT(IC)	X		01.01.04	PEMBROKE
Sykes, Jeremy James William, MSc, MB, CHB, FRCP, FFOM	SURG CAPT(FCC) (Commodore)	-	(CO/M)	31.12.98	INM ALVERSTOKE
Sykes, Malcolm, BEng, MSc, psc	CDR(FTC)	E	MESM	30.06.02	DRAKE SFM
Sykes, Matthew John,	LT(FTC)	X		01.09.02	ARK ROYAL
Sykes, Robert Alan, psc(j)o, BSc	LT CDR(FTC)	X	O	01.10.96	MOD (LONDON)
Sylvan, Christopher,	2LT(IC)	-		01.08.02	CTCRM LYMPSTONE
Symcox, Charles Michael,	SLT(IC)	X	P	01.01.05	RNAS YEOVILTON
Syrett, Matthew Edward, BSc, PGDip, PGDIPAN, PGDip, n, pce	LT CDR(FTC)	X	HM2	01.08.03	NAVSEC
Syson, Carl Frederick, MEng	LT(IC)	X	P	01.01.04	RNAS YEOVILTON
Syvret, Mark Edward Vibert, BSc, psc(j)o	LT COL(FTC)	-		30.06.01	MOD (LONDON)

T

Name	Rank	Branch	Spec	Seniority	Where Serving
Tabeart, George William, pce	LT CDR(FTC)	X	H CH	01.11.97	MWS COLLINGWOOD
Taberham, Hazel, BEng	SLT(IC)	E	AE U/T	01.09.03	SULTAN
Taborda, Matthew Anthony, BSc	LT(IC)	X		01.09.05	DUMBARTON CASTLE
Tacey, Richard Haydn,	LT(CC) (Act Lt Cdr)	X	PWO(A)	01.12.95	STRIKFORNATO
Tait, Martyn David, BEng	LT(CC)	E	TM	27.08.02	ASM IPT
Tait, Stacey Jane, BSc, MIEE	LT(CC)	E	WE	01.01.02	DLO BRISTOL
Talbot, Christopher Martin,	LT CDR(FTC)	X	C	01.10.99	FLEET FOSNNI
Talbot, Katherine Elizabeth Filshie, BSc	LT(IC)	X	FC	01.05.02	MWS COLLINGWOOD
Talbot, Richard John, BSc	LT(CC)	X		01.05.02	MWS COLLINGWOOD
Talbot, Richard Paul, MA, pce, psc(j)	CDR(FTC)	X	PWO(A)	30.06.00	MOD (LONDON)
Talbot, Simon James,	LT(IC)	X	FC	01.05.05	ARK ROYAL
Talbot, Stephen Edward, BSc	LT(IC)	X		01.05.05	WESTMINSTER
Talbott, Aidan Hugh,	CDR(FTC)	S		30.06.06	JSCSC
Tall, Iain Thomas George,	LT(IC)	E	WE	01.07.04	BULWARK
Tamayo, Brando Christian Craig, MB, ChB, DipIMC RCSED	SURG LTCDR(MCC)	-		01.08.99	NELSON (PAY)
Tamlyn, Stephen John, BSc	CAPT RM(FTC)	-		01.05.01	UKLFCSG RM
Tanner, Michael John, psc(j)	MAJ(FTC)	-		01.09.02	COMAMPHIBFOR
Tanner, Richard Carlisle, SM(n), SM	LT CDR(FTC)	X	SM	01.03.03	VIGILANT(STBD)
Tanser, Susan Jane, MB, BS, FRCA	SURG CDR(FCC)	-	(CA)	30.06.03	MDHU PORTSMOUTH
Tantam, Robert John Geoffrey, MEng, PGDip	LT(IC)	E	MESM	01.09.03	TORBAY
Tanzer, William,	SURG SLT(SCC)	-		08.10.05	DARTMOUTH BRNC
Tapp, Steven John,	CAPT RM(FTC)	-	SO(LE)	01.01.01	EXCHANGE ARMY UK
Tappin, Simon John, BEng	LT(CC)	X		01.01.02	GLOUCESTER
Targett, Edward Graeme,	MID(NE)(IC)	X	O U/T	01.09.05	DARTMOUTH BRNC
Tarnowski, Tomasz Adam, MSc, MIL	MAJ(IC)	-	LC	12.11.04	CTCRM
Tarr, Barry Stuart, BSc(Eng), MSc, CEng, MIMarEST	CDR(FTC)	E	MESM	30.06.02	NP BRISTOL
Tarr, Michael Douglas, OBE, BSc, pce, psc(a)	CAPT(FTC)	X	AAWO	30.06.02	MWS COLLINGWOOD
Tarr, Richard Nicholas Vaughan, BSc, CEng, MIMechE	CDR(FTC)	E	MESM	30.06.04	FLEET COSP&S
Tarrant, Robert Kenneth, pce, pce(sm)	CAPT(FTC)	X	SM	30.06.04	MOD (LONDON)
Tasker, Adam Murray, BA	LT(IC)	X	O U/T	01.05.05	RNAS CULDROSE
Tasker, Greg, psc(m)	LT COL(FTC)	-		31.12.95	UN AFRICA
Tate, Andrew John, BSc, MIEE, psc	CAPT(FTC)	E	WESM	30.06.02	NELSON
Tate, Nicholas Mark,	LT(IC)	E	ME	01.05.02	MWS EXCELLENT
Tate, Simon John, OBE, BSc, MA, CEng, MRAeS, psc(j)	CDR(FTC)	E	AE	31.12.99	JFCHQ BRUNSSUM
Tatham, Stephen Alan, BSc, MPhil	LT CDR(FTC)	E	TM	01.09.99	MWS COLLINGWOOD
Tattersall, Richard Brian,	LT CDR(FTC)	X	P	01.10.01	RAF AWC
Tatton-Brown, Hugh Trelawny,	LT(IC)	E	WE	01.09.05	EDINBURGH
Tawse, Lawrence Oliver John, BSc	LT(IC)	X	P	01.01.05	RNAS YEOVILTON
Tayal, Manish, MB, CHB, BSc	SURG LT(SCC)	-		01.08.04	FWO DEVPT SEA
Taylor, Alexander Ian,	MID(NE)(IC)	X	P U/T	01.09.05	DARTMOUTH BRNC
Taylor, Andrew,	LT(IC)	X		18.02.05	RALEIGH

Name	Rank	Branch Spec	Seniority	Where Serving
Taylor, Andrew Ian, BSc, SM(n), SM	LT(CC)	X	SM	01.12.99	FWO DEVPT SEA
Taylor, Andrew Lyndon, BA, MSc	LT CDR(CC)	E	IS	01.05.03	MWC SOUTHWICK
Taylor, Anna, HND, PGDip	LT CDR(CC)	E	IS	01.10.00	DNR N IRELAND
Taylor, Anthony Richard, BA, MA(CANTAB), pce, n, SM(n)	LT CDR(FTC)	X	PWO(N)	01.11.98	WESTMINSTER
Taylor, Brian David,	LT CDR(FTC)	X		01.07.96	FWO PORTS SEA
Taylor, Carl Richard,	LT CDR(FTC)	S		01.08.02	EXCHANGE USA
Taylor, Christopher Paul, BA	SLT(IC)	X		01.06.04	DARTMOUTH BRNC
Taylor, Christopher Simon, MSc	LT(CC)	E	TM	01.01.97	FWO FASLANE SEA
Taylor, Ian John, BEng	LT(CC)	E	TM	05.05.96	FOST DPORT SHORE
Taylor, Ian Kennedy, MSc	LT CDR(FTC)	S	(S)	01.10.01	COMAMPHIBFOR
Taylor, James Edward, BSc	LT(IC)	X	P	01.09.04	RNAS YEOVILTON
Taylor, James Edward Henry, BSc	LT(IC)	X		01.09.02	ILLUSTRIOUS
Taylor, James Tremayne, BSc	LT(IC)	X	O	01.09.04	849 SQN A FLT
Taylor, John Jeremy, MSc, CEng, FIMarEST	CAPT(FTC)	E	MESM	30.06.05	NP BRISTOL
Taylor, Jonathan Paul, SM(n), SM	LT CDR(FTC)	X	SM	01.10.03	MOD (LONDON)
Taylor, Keith Milbrun, BEng, MSc gw	LT(FTC)	E	WE	01.08.98	LOAN DSTL
Taylor, Kenneth Alistair, BSc, pce, pcea, psc	CDR(FTC)	X	O	31.12.97	CV(F) IPT
Taylor, Kenneth John,	LT CDR(FTC)	E	WESM	01.10.99	FLEET COSP&S
Taylor, Leslie, MBE, pcea	LT CDR(FTC(A))	X	P	01.10.94	RAF CRANWELL EFS
Taylor, Lisa Margaret,	LT(MC(MD))	Q		05.07.99	CFLT MED(SEA)
Taylor, Marc Glyn, BSc	SLT(IC)	X	P U/T	01.11.04	DARTMOUTH BRNC
Taylor, Marcus Anthony Beckett,	MAJ(FTC)	-	LC	01.09.01	JSCSC
Taylor, Mark Andrew, pce, pcea	LT CDR(FTC)	X	P	01.02.99	QUORN
Taylor, Mark Richard,	LT CDR(FTC)	X	C	01.10.00	HQ DCSA
Taylor, Martin Kenneth, OBE, osc	LT COL(FTC)	-	C	30.06.94	STRIKFORNATO
Taylor, Matthew Richard, MEng	SLT(IC)	X	P U/T	01.11.04	DARTMOUTH BRNC
Taylor, Neil John,	CAPT RM(CC)	-		01.09.02	CTCRM
Taylor, Neil Robert, BEng, AMIMechE	LT CDR(FTC)	E	ME	01.10.02	DRAKE SFM
Taylor, Neil Robert, BSc	SLT(IC)	X		01.02.04	CORNWALL
Taylor, Nicholas Frederick, MA, pce	LT CDR(FTC)	X	PWO(C)	16.02.87	HQ DCSA
Taylor, Nicholas Simon Charles, BA	LT(IC)	X		01.11.05	RALEIGH
Taylor, Peter George David, BSc, MA, psc(j)	LT COL(FTC)	-		30.06.03	HQ 3 CDO BDE RM
Taylor, Peter John, MB, BS, FRCS, DA, DTM&H	SURG CDR(FC(MD))	-	(CGS)	30.06.05	MDHU PETERBRGH
Taylor, Robert, BEng, MSc, CEng, MIEE, gw	LT CDR(FTC)	E	WE	01.09.99	DLO BRISTOL
Taylor, Robert,	2LT(IC)	-		01.08.05	CTCRM LYMPSTONE
Taylor, Robert Paul, BSc	LT(IC)	X	P	01.05.02	820 SQN
Taylor, Robert Scott, BSc, MB, BS	SURG LT(MC(MD))	-	SM	07.08.02	NELSON (PAY)
Taylor, Scott Andrew, BEng	SLT(IC)	X		01.06.03	ECHO
Taylor, Spencer Alan, MSc, CEng, MIEE	CDR(FTC)	E	IS	30.06.98	NAVSEC
Taylor, Stephen John, BEng, CEng, MIEE	LT CDR(FTC)	E	WE	01.10.01	PJHQ
Taylor, Stephen Mark,	LT CDR(FTC)	S		01.11.93	RNAS CULDROSE
Taylor, Stephen Robert, BEng	SLT(IC)	E	MESM	01.09.03	FWO DEVONPORT
Taylor, Stuart David, BSc	MAJ(FTC)	-		01.10.04	CTCRM
Taylor, William John, OBE, osc	COL(FTC)	-		30.06.04	CDO LOG REGT RM
Tazewell, Matthew Robert, BEng	LT(CC)	X	O	16.10.98	702 SQN HERON
Teasdale, James Paul, BEng, MIEE	LT(IC)	X	WE	01.11.05	CAMPBELTOWN
Teasdale, Robert Mark, BA	LT CDR(FTC)	S		16.01.93	RNAS CULDROSE
Tebbet, Paul Nicholas, pce	LT CDR(FTC)	X	PWO(U)	01.09.97	JSCSC
Teideman, Ian Charles, BEng, MIEE	LT CDR(FTC)	E	WE	01.03.00	JSCSC
Telfer, Duncan Deans,	LT(IC)	X	P U/T	01.11.05	RNAS YEOVILTON
Telford, Jonathan,	LT(IC)	E	TM U/T	01.01.05	DRAKE COB(CNH)
Temple, David Christopher,	LT(FTC)	E	WE	01.04.01	CAPT MCTA
Tennant, Michael Ian, MB, BS	SURG LTCDR(FC(MD))	-		14.09.00	NELSON (PAY)
Tennuci, Robert George, pce	LT CDR(FTC)	X	AAWO	01.12.99	NEW IPT
Terry, John Michael, MSc, CEng, MIMarEST	CDR(FTC)	E	ME	31.12.96	FLEET COSP&S
Terry, Judith Helen, BSc	LT(CC)	S		01.12.98	FOST NWD (JMOTS)
Terry, Michael Charles Gadesden, MB, BS, FRCS	SURG CDR(MCC)	-	(CGS)	30.06.03	MDHU PORTSMOUTH
Terry, Nigel Patrick,	LT(CC)	X	P	01.09.96	ILLUSTRIOUS
Tetchner, David James, BEng	LT(IC)	E	WE	01.11.05	SUTHERLAND
Tetley, Mark,	LT CDR(FTC)	X	O	01.10.03	824 SQN
Tetlow, Hamish Stuart Guy, BA	LT CDR(FTC)	X	SM	01.07.96	MOD (LONDON)
Thain-Smith, Julie Christina,	LT CDR(MC(MD))	Q		31.03.99	RCDM

Name	Rank	Branch	Spec	Seniority	Where Serving
Thicknesse, Philip John, MA, pce, pcea, psc	CAPT(FTC)	X	P	30.06.04	NP IRAQ
Thistlethwaite, Mark Halford, BSc, MCIPD, psc	CAPT(FTC)	E	AE	30.06.05	FLEET COSP&S
Thoburn, Ross, OBE, pce	CDR(FTC) (Act Capt)	X	O	30.06.92	DA BRUNEI
Thomas, Adam Joseph, BEng	LT(CC)	E	AE U/T	01.03.03	RNAS CULDROSE
Thomas, Andrew Giles,	SLT(IC)	E	ME	01.09.02	ST ALBANS
Thomas, Ann Louise, BEng	LT CDR(FTC)	E	TM	01.10.02	MOD (LONDON)
Thomas, Catherine Mary, MEng	SLT(IC)	X		01.01.05	DARTMOUTH BRNC
Thomas, Daniel Huw,	LT(FTC)	X	PWO(A)	01.07.99	SUTHERLAND
Thomas, David Jonathan,	LT CDR(FTC)	S	(S)	01.10.04	ARGYLL
Thomas, David Lynford, BDS, MSc, LDS RCS(Eng), MGDS RCS, MGDS RCSEd	SGCAPT(D)(FCC)	-		01.04.03	DDS SCOTLAND
Thomas, David William, BEng	LT(CC)	X	P	01.10.98	814 SQN
Thomas, David William Wallace, BA	CHAPLAIN	CE		18.10.88	CHFHQ
Thomas, Duncan James,	LT(IC)	X	O	01.05.05	815 FLT 202
Thomas, Francis Stephen,	CDR(FTC)	S	(SM)	30.06.99	DRAKE COB
Thomas, Jeffrey Evans,	CDR(FTC)	X	EW	30.06.04	MOD (LONDON)
Thomas, Jeffrey Graham,	CAPT RM(CC)	-		01.09.03	CTCRM
Thomas, Jeremy Huw, BEng, MPhil, MLITT	LT CDR(FTC)	E	WESM	01.02.98	DGMC SEA
Thomas, Jeremy Hywel, psc(m), hcsc	BRIG(FTC)	-	WTO	17.09.01	HQ 3 CDO BDE RM
Thomas, Joseph Maximilian, BSc	LT(IC)	X	P	01.05.04	RNAS YEOVILTON
Thomas, Kevin Ian, BSc	LT CDR(FTC)	X	METOC	01.10.92	CMT SHRIVENHAM
Thomas, Leslie, BSc	LT CDR(FTC)	X	C	01.10.99	FLEET COSCAP
Thomas, Lynn Marie, MB, BS, BSc, MRCP	SURG CDR(MCC)	-	(CM)	30.06.04	MDHU PORTSMOUTH
Thomas, Mark, BSc, PGDIPAN, AFRIN, n	LT(CC)	X	PWO(N)	01.09.98	MWS COLLINGWOOD
Thomas, Mark Anthony,	LT(IC)	E	WE	01.01.04	HQ DCSA
Thomas, Mark Peter,	SLT(IC)	X	O U/T	01.05.03	824 SQN
Thomas, Owen Hopkin, BSc	LT(CC)	X		16.10.99	PJHQ
Thomas, Patrick William, sq	MAJ(FTC) (Act Lt Col)	-	SO(LE)	01.10.96	FLEET ISS
Thomas, Richard Anthony Aubrey, MBE, MA, psc(j), pce	CDR(FTC)	X	PWO(U)	30.06.02	MOD (LONDON)
Thomas, Richard David,	SLT(IC)	S		01.09.05	RALEIGH
Thomas, Richard Kevin, BSc, pce, PSC(ONDC)	CDR(FTC)	X	PWO(U)	30.06.02	UKMARBATSTAFF
Thomas, Robert Paul, pce, pcea, psc	CDR(FTC) (Act Capt)	X	O	30.06.95	UKNMR SHAPE
Thomas, Ryan,	SURG SLT(SCC)	-		26.03.05	DARTMOUTH BRNC
Thomas, Sarah, BSc	SLT(IC)	X	O U/T	01.09.04	DARTMOUTH BRNC
Thomas, Simon Alan, MA, pce, pcea, psc(a)	CDR(FTC)	X	P	31.12.93	FLEET COSP&S
Thomas, Stephen Mark, BEng	LT CDR(FTC)	E	ME	01.01.01	DLO BRISTOL
Thomas, Stephen Michael,	LT(FTC)	X	P	16.02.96	814 SQN
Thomas, William Gwynne, BSc, pce, pcea	CDR(FTC)	X	O	31.12.00	CMT SHRIVENHAM
Thompson, Alastair James,	LT(IC)	X	P	01.01.04	815 FLT 219
Thompson, Andrew, BSc	CDR(FTC)	E	AE	30.06.02	RAF COTTESMORE
Thompson, Andrew Robert,	LT(CC)	X	O	01.02.92	815 SQN HQ
Thompson, Bernard Dominic, BA, pce	CDR(FTC)	X	MCD	30.06.02	FDG
Thompson, Claire Fiona, BSc	SLT(IC)	X		01.11.04	DARTMOUTH BRNC
Thompson, David Anthony, BSc	LT(CC)	X	P	16.04.99	MWS COLLINGWOOD
Thompson, David Huw,	MAJ(FTC)	-		01.09.05	MOD (LONDON)
Thompson, David Jess,	SLT(IC)	S		01.01.05	DARTMOUTH BRNC
Thompson, David John,	LT(IC)	X		20.02.04	EXETER
Thompson, Elizabeth Ellen, BEng	LT(IC)	E	ME(L)	01.05.04	CUMBERLAND
Thompson, Fiona,	LT CDR(MC(MD)	Q		01.10.05	NELSON (PAY)
Thompson, George Christopher,	SLT(IC)	X	P	01.09.03	815 FLT 208
Thompson, Graham Michael, BEM	MAJ(FTC)	-	SO(LE)	01.10.04	DISC
Thompson, James,	LT(CC)	X		01.05.04	LIVERPOOL
Thompson, Mark George, PGDIPAN, SM(n)	LT CDR(FTC)	X	SM	01.03.03	TRENCHANT
Thompson, Matthew,	SURG SLT(SCC)	-		08.09.05	DARTMOUTH BRNC
Thompson, Michael James, BEng, CEng, MIMarEST	LT CDR(FTC)	E	ME	01.10.03	KENT
Thompson, Neil James, pcea	CDR(FTC)	X	P	30.06.06	CHFHQ
Thompson, Paul Leslie, BSc	CAPT RM(CC)	-		01.09.01	SFSG
Thompson, Richard Charles, BEng, MA, psc(j)	CDR(FTC)	E	AE	30.06.02	JCA IPT UK
Thompson, Robert Anthony, BSc, pcea	LT CDR(FTC)	X	O	01.10.98	829 FLT 03
Thompson, Robert Joseph, BSc, jsdc	CAPT(FTC)	E	ME	30.06.03	FLEET COSP&S
Thompson, Sarah Kay, BSc	LT(SC(MD)	Q		01.11.03	MDHU PORTSMOUTH
Thompson, Sarah Leanne,	LT(IC)	X		01.05.03	SOMERSET

Name	Rank	Branch	Spec	Seniority	Where Serving
Thompson, Stephen John, MSc, CEng, MCGI, MIMarEST, psc(j)	CDR(FTC)	E	ME	31.12.99	T45 IPT
Thompson, William Alistair, BEng	LT(CC)	X	P	01.02.00	815 SQN HQ
Thomsen-Rayner, Lisa, BSc	LT(FTC)	X	PWO(C)	01.02.97	OCEAN
Thomsett, Harry Fergus James, BA	MAJ(FTC)	-	C	01.09.01	JSCSC
Thomson, Allan Brown, MBA, fsc, osc	COL(FTC)	-	MLDR	30.06.01	NELSON
Thomson, Colin Douglas, BSc, PGDip	LT CDR(FTC)	X	H CH	01.02.01	MOD (LONDON)
Thomson, David Forbes,	LT(FTC)	E	AE	01.04.01	JCA IPT USA
Thomson, Duncan, MA, pce, psc(j)	CDR(FTC)	X	PWO(U)	30.06.05	HQ SACT
Thomson, Iain Rodger, BSc	LT CDR(FTC)	E	WESM	22.05.97	MWS COLLINGWOOD
Thomson, Ian Wallace, MIIE	LT(FTC)	E	WESM	01.04.01	FLEET COSP&S
Thomson, James Christopher, BSc	LT(CC)	X	FC	01.01.99	MWS COLLINGWOOD
Thomson, Jane Margaret, BSc	LT(IC)	E	TM	01.01.01	DCTS PORTS
Thomson, Leighton George,	CAPT RM(CC)	-		01.09.04	CTCRM
Thomson, Luke,	2LT(IC)	-		01.08.02	CTCRM LYMPSTONE
Thomson, Michael Lee, BEng, MSc	LT(FTC)	E	ME	01.04.99	DLO BRISTOL
Thomson, Paul Allan, MEng	LT(IC)	E	AE U/T	01.09.05	IV (AC) SQN (RN)
Thomson, Paul Damian, BSc	LT(CC)	E	IS	24.02.97	FLEET ISS
Thomson, Roger Geoffrey, MB, BS, MRCGP, DCH	SURG CDR(MC(MD)	-	GMPP	05.11.03	CTCRM
Thomson, Steven, BSc, BD	CHAPLAIN	SF		13.09.04	FWO PORTS SEA
Thomson, Stewart McLean, BSc	LT(IC)	X		01.08.04	MWS COLLINGWOOD
Thorburn, Andrew,	CDR(FTC)	X	AV	30.06.04	CC MAR AGRIPPA
Thorley, Graham,	LT(IC)	X	SM	01.01.04	VIGILANT(PORT)
Thorne, Dain Jason, BEng, FRAeS	LT CDR(FTC)	E	AE	01.03.05	FLEET COSCAP
Thornhill, Andrew Philip, pdm	MAJ(FTC)	BS	SO(LE)	01.10.04	RM BAND PLYMOUTH
Thornhill, Stephen,	LT(IC)	MS		01.07.04	CDO LOG REGT RM
Thornley, Jeremy George Carter, BD	LT(IC)	X	SM	01.05.03	VANGUARD(STBD)
Thornton, Daniel Moss,	CAPT RM(CC)	-		01.09.05	45 CDO RM
Thornton, John,	2LT(IC)	-		01.08.03	LOAN OTHER SVCE
Thornton, Michael Crawford, pce, pcea, psc	LT CDR(FTC)	X	P	08.02.84	LOAN DARA
Thornton, Philip John, pcea	LT CDR(FTC(A)	X	P	01.10.93	RNAS YEOVILTON
Thorp, Benjamin Thomas, BEng, MSc	LT CDR(FTC)	E	ME	01.07.04	ARK ROYAL
Thorp, David Brian, BEng, MSc, MIEE	LT CDR(FTC)	E	WE	01.03.06	MOD (LONDON)
Thorpe, Elaine, BSc	LT(MC(MD)	Q		03.08.99	RCDM
Thorpe, Robert Michael, MA	CAPT RM(CC)	-		01.09.03	RM WARMINSTER
Thrippleton, Mark Graham, BEng	LT CDR(FTC)	E	AE	15.08.00	JCA IPT UK
Thurstan, Richard William Farnall, MA, psc(j)	MAJ(FTC)	-	LC	01.05.97	40 CDO RM
Thurston, Mark Stewart, BEM	LT(IC)	X	C	29.10.04	SAT IPT
Thwaites, Gerard James, ADC, BSc, CEng, MIMechE, psc	CDRE(FTC)	E	MESM	01.04.03	SULTAN
Thwaites, Lindsey William,	LT(IC)	E	WESM	01.07.04	ASTUTE
Tibballs, Laura Rosalind, BSc	LT(IC)	S		01.01.04	ENTERPRISE
Tibbitt, Ian Peter Gordon, MA, CEng, MIEE, jsdc	CDRE(FTC)	E	AE	15.04.02	DLO YEO
Tickle, Martin John, BSc	SLT(IC)	X		01.05.03	MWS COLLINGWOOD
Tidball, Ian Crofton, BEng	LT CDR(FTC)	X	P	01.10.04	FLEET AV VL
Tidman, Martin David,	CAPT RM(IC) (Act Maj)	-	SO(LE)	21.07.01	1 ASSAULT GP RM
Tiebosch, Nicola Kate, BSc	SLT(IC)	X		01.02.04	CUMBERLAND
Tilden, Philip James Edward, BA, ACMI, n	LT CDR(FTC)	X	PWO(U)	01.03.05	EXETER
Tilley, Duncan Scott Jamieson, pce	CDR(FTC)	X	H CH	30.06.00	NAVSEC
Tilsley, David, BSc	LT(IC)	E	IS	01.05.01	CINCFLEET FIMU
Tilson, David Richard, BEng	SLT(IC)	E		01.01.05	DARTMOUTH BRNC
Timbrell, Ian Philip James, BEng	LT(FTC)	E	ME	01.02.00	DLO BRISTOL
Tindal, Nicolas Henry Charles, MA, pce, pcea, psc(j)	CDR(FTC)	X	P	30.06.02	EXCHANGE USA
Tindall-Jones, Lee Douglas, BSc, MA, CEng, MIEE, psc	CDR(FTC)	E	WESM	31.12.99	MOD (LONDON)
Tinsley, Glenn Nigel, GCIS	CDR(FTC)	S		31.12.96	EXCHANGE AUSTLIA
Tinsley, Phillip,	CAPT RM(CC) (Act Maj)	-	SO(LE)	21.07.01	CTCRM
Titcomb, Andrew Charles, BEng, MA, MSc, psc(j)	CDR(FTC)	E	WESM	30.06.04	LAIPT
Titcomb, Mark Richard, BSc, pce, pce(sm), psc(j), MA	CDR(FTC)	X	SM	30.06.03	FLEET COSCAP
Titcombe, Adam James, BA	LT(CC) (Act Lt Cdr)	S		01.05.99	NP IRAQ
Tite, Anthony Damian,	LT CDR(FTC)	X	O	01.10.04	LOAN JTEG BSC DN
Titerickx, Andrew Terry,	CAPT RM(IC)	-	SO(LE)	01.07.04	40 CDO RM
Titmuss, Julian Francis, BA	LT CDR(FTC)	S	CMA	01.12.02	MOD (LONDON)
Titterton, Phillip James, OBE, pce, pce(sm)	CDR(FTC)	X	SM	30.06.99	MOD (LONDON)
Todd, Daniel Bevan, BA, CEng	LT(IC)	E	ME	01.03.99	JSSU CYPRUS

Name	Rank	Branch	Spec	Seniority	Where Serving
Todd, Geoffrey Alan,	LT(IC)	MS		01.05.03	MOD (BATH)
Todd, James William, BSc	CAPT RM(CC)	-	P	01.05.00	847 SQN
Todd, Michael Anthony,	MAJ(FTC)	-	SO(LE)	01.10.03	40 CDO RM
Todd, Oliver James, LLB	CAPT RM(CC)	-	MLDR	01.09.00	UKLFCSG RM
Toft, Michael David, BEng, CEng, MIEE	CDR(FTC)	E	WE	30.06.04	DLO BRISTOL
Tok, Chantelle Fen Lynne, BSc	LT(IC)	X	ATC	03.07.02	RNAS YEOVILTON
Toland, Martin James, BSc	LT(IC)	X		01.12.04	TALENT
Tolley, Peter Frederick Richmond, OBE, MB, BCh	SURG CAPT(FCC) (Commodore)	-	GMPP	31.12.95	FLEET COSP&S
Tomkins, Bradley Matthew, MB, BSc, BS	SURG SLT(SCC) (Act Surg Lt)	-		01.08.05	DARTMOUTH BRNC
Tomlin, Ian Stephen, BEng	LT(IC)	E	WESM	01.02.03	VENGEANCE(STBD)
Tomlinson, Amy Ruth, BA	LT(IC)	S		01.05.04	DRAKE COB
Tomlinson, David Charles,	LT(IC)	X	AV	03.04.97	RNAS YEOVILTON
Tonge, Malcolm,	LT(IC)	E	ME	01.05.03	DFTE PORTSMOUTH
Toomey, Nicholas John, BSc, MA, psc(j)	LT CDR(FTC)	S	SM	01.11.96	PJHQ
Toon, John Richard,	LT CDR(FTC)	E	AE	01.10.92	DLO TES
Toon, Paul Graham,	LT(FTC)	X	AV	26.04.99	ARK ROYAL
Toone, Stephen Anthony, BSc	LT(FTC)	E	WE	01.04.01	DLO BRISTOL
Toor, Jeevan Jyoti Singh, BSc, PGDip	LT CDR(FTC)	X	PWO(U)	01.09.98	IRON DUKE
Toothill, John Samuel, SM(n)	LT CDR(FTC)	X	SM	01.04.97	CC MAR AGRIPPA
Topham, Neil Edwin, BEng	LT(IC)	E	TM	01.02.01	SULTAN
Torbet, Linda, MEng	LT(IC)	E	AE U/T	01.01.04	845 SQN
Torney, Colin James,	LT(FTC)	E	MESM	02.09.99	VIGILANT(PORT)
Tothill, Nicholas Michael, MSc	CDR(FTC)	S		30.06.00	DPA BRISTOL
Tothill, Rachel Charlotte, MA	LT CDR(FTC)	S		17.08.00	NELSON
Totten, Philip Mark,	CAPT RM(CC)	-		01.09.00	UKLFCSG RM
Tottenham, Geoffry John,	SLT(UCE)(IC)	X		01.09.05	DARTMOUTH BRNC
Tottenham, Timothy William,	CAPT RM(IC)	-		01.09.03	FLEET HQ WI
Tough, Iain Shand, MEng	LT(IC)	E	WESM	01.09.03	VANGUARD(STBD)
Towell, Peter James,	CDR(FTC)	E	ME	30.06.06	JSCSC
Towler, Alison, BSc, PGDipL	CDR(FTC) (Barrister)	S	BAR	30.06.06	MOD (LONDON)
Towler, Perrin James Bryher, BSc, pce	LT CDR(FTC)	X	PWO(A)	01.06.94	FLEET COSCAP
Towner, Stephen,	SURG SLT(SCC)	-		13.09.04	DARTMOUTH BRNC
Townsend, Anna Mary,	SLT(IC)	X		01.02.05	DARTMOUTH BRNC
Townsend, Graham Peter,	LT(FTC)	X	O	01.05.94	771 SQN
Townsend, John Stafford, MB, BS, BSc, Dip FFP	SURG CDR(SCC)	-	GMPP	31.01.01	MWS COLLINGWOOD
Townshend, Jeremy John, BSc, MBA, FCIPD	CDR(FTC)	E	TMSM	30.06.04	FLEET COSP&S
Toy, Malcolm John, BEng, CEng, MRAeS	CAPT(FTC)	E	AE	30.06.05	DPA TES
Trafford, Michael,	LT RM(IC) (Act Capt Rm)	-		01.09.03	800 NAS (GR7)
Trasler, Mark Farnham, MSc	LT CDR(FTC)	MS	(LT)	01.10.00	FLEET COSP&S
Trathen, Neil Charles, BSc, pce	LT CDR(FTC)	X	PWO(N)	01.02.92	DRAKE COB
Treanor, Martin Andrew, MSc, psc	CDR(FTC)	E	AE	31.12.99	FLEET COSP&S
Tredray, Thomas Patrick, BA	LT CDR(FTC)	X	AAWO	01.02.01	MWS COLLINGWOOD
Tregunna, Gary Andrew, SM	LT CDR(FTC)	X	SM	08.08.03	PJHQ
Treharne, Mark Adrian, BEng, PGDip	LT(CC)	E	MESM	01.08.00	VENGEANCE(STBD)
Tremelling, Paul Nicholas, BEng	LT(FTC) (Act Lt Cdr)	X	P	16.04.98	HQ1GP HQSTC
Trent, Thomas, BEng, MPhil.	LT(IC)	X		01.09.03	LANCASTER
Tretton, Joseph Edward, BSc	LT(IC)	X		01.01.04	MWS HM TG (D)
Trevethan, Christopher John,	LT(IC)	X		28.10.05	LANCASTER
Trevithick, Andrew Richard, BSc, PGCE, MIMA, CMath	CDR(FTC) (Act Capt)	X	METOC	31.12.93	FLEET HQ WI
Trewhella, Graham Gilbey, BSc, MA, psc	LT CDR(FTC)	E	TM	01.05.91	MWS COLLINGWOOD
Trewinnard, Robin Michael, BEng	LT(CC)	E	AE	01.04.02	HARRIER IPT
Tribe, Jeremy David, BSc	LT(FTC)	X	P	16.10.87	DLO YEO
Trigwell, Simon,	LT(IC)	E	AE U/T	08.04.05	RNAS YEOVILTON
Trinder, Stephen John,	LT(FTC)	S	CA	30.01.96	DARTMOUTH BRNC
Tritschler, Edwin Lionel, BEng, BTech, MA, CEng, MRAeS, psc(j)	CDR(FTC)	E	AE	30.06.04	FLEET FOTR
Trosh, Nicholas, BEng	LT(IC)	E	WE	01.09.04	CAMPBELTOWN
Trotman, Stephen Peter, IEng, MIIE	LT(IC)	E	WESM	01.01.03	MWC PORTSDOWN
Trott, Edward Alan, BEng, MSc	LT CDR(FTC)	E	AE	01.12.02	FLEET COSP&S
Trotter, Steven, MSc, CEng, MIMarEST	LT CDR(FTC)	E	ME	01.12.87	FOST DPORT SHORE
Trubshaw, Christopher, pcea	LT CDR(FTC)	X	P	01.10.04	849 SQN A FLT
Truelove, Samantha,	LT(IC)	S		01.01.02	PJHQ
Trueman, Brian David,	LT(CC)	E	AE	01.05.00	DLO YEO

Name	Rank	Branch	Spec	Seniority	Where Serving
Trump, Nigel William, psc(j)	CDR(FTC)	S		30.06.03	ALBION
Trundle, Nicholas Reginald Edward, MA, pce, pcea, psc(j)	CDR(FTC)	X	O	31.12.98	MOD (LONDON)
Tucker, Philip James,	LT(IC)	X	P	01.09.04	RNAS YEOVILTON
Tucker, Simon James William, BA	CAPT RM(IC)	-	LC	01.09.02	RMR LONDON
Tuckett, Caroline Sybil Elizabeth, MA	SLT(IC)	S		01.01.05	DARTMOUTH BRNC
Tudor, Owen Jasper, BA	SLT(IC)	S		01.05.04	GLOUCESTER
Tuffin, Michael Graham,	LT(IC)	X	MW	01.01.05	MCM3 SEA
Tuhey, James Jonathan George, BEng	LT(IC)	E	WESM	01.09.05	TRENCHANT
Tulley, James Robert, BSc	CDR(FTC)	S		31.12.99	MWS COLLINGWOOD
Tulloch, Frederik Martin, BSc, CEng, MIEE	LT CDR(FTC)	E	WE	01.04.93	RMC OF SCIENCE
Tulloch, Stuart William,	MAJ(FTC)	-	SO(LE)	01.10.04	42 CDO RM
Tumilty, Kevin,	LT(IC)	E	WE	01.01.04	TDL IPT
Tuppen, Russell Mark, MNI, pce, pcea, psc, psc(j)o	CDR(FTC)	X	O	31.12.99	FLEET COSP&S
Turberville, Christopher Thomas Leslie, BA	LT(IC)	S		01.01.04	846 SQN
Turle, Paul James, IEng, MIIE	LT CDR(FTC)	E	ME	01.10.03	DFTE PORTSMOUTH
Turnbull, Graham David, pce, psc(j)	CDR(FTC)	X	H CH	30.06.02	HQ SACT
Turnbull, Nicholas Robin, BDS, MSc, FDS RCSEdin, MOrth	SGCDR(D)(FCC)	-	ORTHC	30.06.03	DDS PORTSMOUTH
Turnbull, Paul Sands, MB, BS, MFOM, AFOM	SURG CDR(FCC)	-	(CO/M)	30.06.01	EXCHANGE USA
Turnbull, Simon Jonathan Lawson, MA, MNI, pce, psc(j)	CDR(FTC)	X	PWO(U)	30.06.02	FLEET HQ WI
Turner, Allan James,	LT(FTC)	E	ME	01.04.01	SULTAN
Turner, Antony Richard, BA	CAPT RM(FTC)	-		01.09.00	1 ASSAULT GP RM
Turner, David James, LLB, PGDip	LT(FTC)	S	SM	01.04.00	FWO FASLANE
Turner, David Neil,	LT(CC)	X	P	01.06.95	702 SQN HERON
Turner, Derek Bayard, MBE, BSc, ARICS, pce	CDR(FTC)	X	H CH	30.06.02	MOD (LONDON)
Turner, Duncan Laurence,	LT(IC)	E	WE	01.01.06	MONTROSE
Turner, Ian, OBE, BSc, psc	CAPT(FTC)	X	H CH	30.06.02	FWO DEVONPORT
Turner, Jonathan Stephen, BA	LT(CC)	X	O	01.01.01	RNAS YEOVILTON
Turner, Joseph Seymour Hume, MA	CDR(FTC) (Barrister)	S	BAR	30.06.06	JDCC
Turner, Kerry Ann, BEng, PGDip	LT CDR(CC)	X	METOC	01.10.01	RNAS CULDROSE
Turner, Matthew, BEng	LT(IC)	E	ME	01.01.04	KENT
Turner, Matthew John, MB, BS, MRCGP, MRCS	SURG LTCDR(SC(MD)	-	GMPP	01.08.04	RNAS CULDROSE
Turner, Neil,	LT(IC)	E	AE	01.05.03	SULTAN
Turner, Phaedra Louise, BSc	LT(CC)	E	TM	01.02.99	MWS EXCELLENT
Turner, Robert Francis, BSc	LT CDR(FTC)	S	(W)	01.10.00	RALEIGH
Turner, Shaun Mark, jsdc, pce, pce(sm)	CDR(FTC) (Act Capt)	X	SM	30.06.90	MOD (BATH)
Turner, Simon Alexander, BSc	MAJ(FTC)	-		01.09.02	NAVSEC
Turner, Vicki Mary,	SLT(IC)	E	ME	01.09.02	ALBION
Tutchings, Andrew,	LT(FTC)	X		01.04.01	SHAPE BELGIUM
Tweed, Christopher James, MBE, BSc, MDA	LT CDR(FTC)	E	WE	01.02.89	FLEET HQ WI
Twigg, Katherine Louise, MSc	LT(CC)	X	HM	01.04.99	EXCHANGE USA
Twigg, Neil Robert, BEng	LT(CC)	X	P	16.03.01	800 NAS (GR7)
Twine, John Harold, MA, PGDip, psc(j)	LT CDR(FTC)	E	TM	01.01.99	NAVSEC
Twiselton, Matthew James,	LT(IC)	E	AE	01.05.03	SULTAN
Twiss, Paul Joshua, MEng	SLT(IC)	E	ME U/T	01.09.04	ILLUSTRIOUS
Twist, David Charles,	LT CDR(FTC)	S	(W)	01.10.99	CSSG (SEA)
Twist, Martin Thomas, BSc	MAJ(FTC)	-		01.09.01	LOAN JSOC SLOV
Tyack, Terence James, MA, pcea, psc(j)	LT CDR(FTC)	X	P	01.10.98	846 SQN
Tyacke, Richard Simon, BSc	SLT(IC)	X		01.05.03	MWS COLLINGWOOD
Tyce, David John,	MAJ(FTC)	-	SO(LE)	01.10.05	MWC PORTSDOWN
Tyler, Jeremy Charles,	LT CDR(FTC)	X	PWO(A)	01.07.04	MANCHESTER
Tyler, Peter Leslie,	LT CDR(FTC)	S		10.07.93	KING ALFRED
Tyrrell, Richard Kim,	MAJ(FTC)	-	LC	01.09.86	CTCRM

U

Name	Rank	Branch	Spec	Seniority	Where Serving
Ubaka, Philip Benizi Nnamabia,	CAPT RM(IC)	-	C	24.07.04	CDO LOG REGT RM
Ubhi, Wayne Gurdial, BEng, MSc	LT CDR(FTC)	E	ME	01.06.04	MONMOUTH
Udensi, Ernest Andrew Anene Anderson, BEng, MSc, CEng, MIEE	LT CDR(FTC)	E	WE	01.09.93	IA BRISTOL
Underwood, Nicholas John, BSc, psc(a)	MAJ(FTC) (Act Lt Col)	-		01.09.88	FLEET FOTR
Underwood, Richard Alexander Howard, BA	LT(IC)	S		01.08.01	UKMILREP BRUSS
Unsworth, Benjamin Matthew, BSc	SLT(IC)	X	O U/T	01.01.05	DARTMOUTH BRNC
Unwin, Nicholas Richard Forbes, BA	LT(CC)	X		01.08.02	UKMARBATSTAFF
Uprichard, Andrew James, BA	CAPT RM(CC)	-		01.09.04	45 CDO RM

Name	Rank	Branch	Spec	Seniority	Where Serving
Upright, Stephen William, BSc, pce, pce(sm)	CAPT(FTC)	X	SM	30.06.03	MOD (LONDON)
Upton, Iain David, BSc, CEng, MIEE	CDR(FTC)	E	WE	30.06.03	FLEET HQ WI
Urry, Simon Richard, MBE, BSc	MAJ(FTC)	-		01.10.04	NAVSEC
Urwin, Stuart James, BA	LT(CC)	X		01.06.00	LANCASTER
Usborne, Andre Christopher, BSc, FCMI, psc	CDR(FTC) (Act Capt)	E	WE	31.12.92	JSU NORTHWOOD
Usborne, Christopher Martin, BSc, CEng, MIEE	CAPT(FTC)	E	WE	30.06.04	FLEET COSP&S
Usher, Andrew Thomas,	CAPT RM(CC)	-	P	01.04.02	771 SQN
Usher, Brian,	CAPT RM(CC)	-	SO(LE)	01.04.02	539 ASSLT SQN RM
Ussher, Jeremy Howard David, BSc	LT(IC)	E	TM	01.05.00	FLEET HQ PORTSEA
Utley, Michael Keith, pce, n	CDR(FTC)	X	PWO(A)	30.06.06	MTS IPT
Utting, Roy Charles,	LT(IC)	E	WE	01.07.04	CAPT MCTA

V

Name	Rank	Branch	Spec	Seniority	Where Serving
Vale, Andrew John, MB, CHB	SURG LT(SCC)	-		07.08.02	MDHU PORTSMOUTH
Valender, Charles,	SG SLT(D)(SCC)	-		18.08.05	DARTMOUTH BRNC
Vallance, Michael Stefan, BSc	LT(CC)	X	P	01.05.98	AACC MID WALLOP
Van Beek, Luke, BSc, MBA, psc, psc(m)	CDRE(FTC)	E	WE	07.10.03	MOD (LONDON)
Van Duin, Martin Ivar Alexander, BSc	LT(IC)	X	P	01.01.02	815 FLT 203
Vanderpump, David John, BEng, psc(j)	CDR(FTC)	E	ME	30.06.00	BULWARK
Vandome, Andrew Michael, BSc, MIEE, psc(j)	CDR(FTC)	E	WE	30.06.99	HQ DCSA
Vardy, Kevin John, BSc	LT(IC)	E	WE	01.01.04	CSIS IPT
Varley, Ian Guy, BEng, pcea	LT CDR(FTC)	X	P	01.01.01	829 FLT 02
Varley, Peter George Sidney, BSc	LT(IC)	X		01.06.00	OCEAN
Vartan, Mark Richard, BSc	LT CDR(FTC)	X	H1	01.10.03	EXCHANGE AUSTLIA
Varty, Jason Alan, BSc	LT(CC)	X	H2	01.10.98	MWS HM TG (D)
Vaughan, David Michael, OBE, BA, MNI, pce, pce(sm), FRIN	CDR(FTC)	X	SM	31.12.90	CC MAR AGRIPPA
Vaughan, Edward Alexander, BSc	LT(IC)	X	P	01.09.04	RNAS YEOVILTON
Vaughan, James Richard, BEng, PGDip	LT(IC)	E	MESM	01.06.03	VICTORIOUS(PORT)
Veal, Alan Edward, BEng, CEng, MIEE	LT CDR(FTC)	E	WE	01.08.03	MWS COLLINGWOOD
Veal, Dominic Joseph,	LT(CC)	X		01.05.02	WESTMINSTER
Venables, Adrian Nicholas, MBCS, pce	LT CDR(FTC)	X	PWO(C)	01.12.97	RMC OF SCIENCE
Venables, Daniel Mark,	CAPT RM(CC)	-		01.09.02	40 CDO RM
Venn, Nicholas Spencer Collacott, BSc	MAJ(FTC)	-	P	30.09.01	847 SQN
Venner, Simon James, BSc	SLT(IC)	X		01.01.05	DARTMOUTH BRNC
Vereker, Richard John Prendergast, BEng	LT(IC)	X		01.01.06	MWS COLLINGWOOD
Verney, Kirsty Hilary, BDS, BSc	SGLTCDR(D)(SCC)	-		09.07.02	FLEET COSP&S
Verney, Peter Scott, pce, psc(j), MA	CDR(FTC)	X	PWO(A)	30.06.05	EDINBURGH
Verrecchia, Joseph Romano,	SLT(IC)	X		01.09.02	MWS COLLINGWOOD
Vessey, Lee Matthew,	LT(IC)	X		01.01.06	MERSEY
Veti, Mark Alister, LLB	LT(IC)	X		01.02.06	MWS COLLINGWOOD
Vickers, Charles H,	CAPT RM(IC)	-		01.09.04	OCLC MANCH
Vickers, John, BEng, MSc	CDR(FTC)	E	AE	30.06.06	JF HARROLE OFF
Vickery, Ben Robert, BA	LT(CC)	X	MCD	01.05.01	NORTHUMBERLAND
Vickery, Timothy Kenneth, BSc, MDA	LT CDR(FTC)	X	PWO(U)	01.11.95	T45 IPT
Vierow, Michael Keith,	LT(CC)	X		01.05.05	NORTHUMBERLAND
Vincent, Adrian, BEng, MPhil, CEng, MIMechE	LT CDR(CC)	E	TM	01.10.03	MOD (LONDON)
Vincent, Christopher, BSc	SLT(IC)	X		01.02.04	CHATHAM
Vincent, Daniel, BSc, PhD	LT CDR(CC)	E	TM	01.10.04	NP IRAQ
Vincent, Peter Hedley, MEng	LT(FTC)	X		01.01.04	BANGOR
Vines, Nicholas Owen, BSC(EH), MCIEH	LT(IC)	MS		01.12.02	FLEET COSP&S
Viney, Peter Michael,	LT(CC)	S	(W)	29.04.01	FLEET COSP&S
Visram, Adrian Haider, BA	LT(IC)	X		01.01.04	NOTTINGHAM
Vitali, Robert Charles, MA, pce, psc(j)	CDR(FTC)	X	AAWO	30.06.04	SOUTHAMPTON
Vivian, Philip,	LT(IC)	S		01.07.04	ILLUSTRIOUS
Vogel, Lanning David,	LT CDR(IC)	S	SM	01.10.04	CUMBERLAND
Voigt, Matthew Adam,	LT(IC)	X		01.12.03	RNAS YEOVILTON
Voke, Christen Alexander, BSc	LT(IC)	X	SM	01.08.02	TRENCHANT
Voke, Helen Louise, BA	LT(IC)	X		01.05.02	MONTROSE
Vollentine, Lucy,	LT CDR(FTC)	S		01.10.04	ILLUSTRIOUS
Vorley, Simon William, BSc	LT(FTC)	X	P	15.06.96	702 SQN HERON
Vout, Debra Kim,	LT(CC)	X	C	01.10.02	TEMERAIRE
Vowles, Austin Lewis Darlington, BSc	SLT(IC)	X	O U/T	01.09.04	DARTMOUTH BRNC

Name	Rank	Branch Spec	Seniority	Where Serving
Vowles, Iain Robert, MEng	SLT(IC)	E	WESM	01.09.02	FWO FASLANE SEA
Vowles, Mitchell John,	LT(FTC)	X		24.07.97	RALEIGH
Voyce, John Edington, BEng, MSc, MIMarEST	LT CDR(FTC)	E	ME	01.09.02	FLEET COSP&S

W

Name	Rank	Branch Spec	Seniority	Where Serving
Waddington, Andrew Kennneth, BSc, pce, psc(j)	CDR(FTC)	X	H CH	30.06.03	FWO DEVONPORT
Waddington, John, BSc	CDR(FTC)	E	WESM	30.06.02	NEPTUNE SWS
Wade, Andrew,	LT(IC)	MS		01.09.01	HQ DMETA
Wade, Jonathan Mark Robertson, BA	LT(IC)	X	P	01.02.99	814 SQN
Wade, Nicholas Charles, BSc	LT CDR(FTC) (Act Cdr)	X	PWO(C)	01.01.90	RNEAWC
Wadge, Guy David Ernest, BSc	LT(IC)	E	TM	08.05.01	DARTMOUTH BRNC
Wadsworth, Richard York, BEng	LT(CC)	E	ME	01.03.99	ARK ROYAL
Wagstaff, Andrew,	LT(CC)	S		01.05.02	FLEET COSP&S
Wagstaff, Neil,	LT CDR(FTC)	MS	(LT)	01.10.02	DMSTC
Wagstaff, Sally Elizabeth, Dip OHN	LT(SC(MD)	Q		01.01.03	MDHU PORTSMOUTH
Wain, Alexis William, MEng, MIEE	LT(IC)	E	WE	01.09.04	MONTROSE
Wainhouse, Michael James, pce	CDR(FTC)	X	PWO(A)	30.06.02	MOD (LONDON)
Waite, Matthew Temple, MA	CAPT RM(CC)	-		01.09.02	HQ 3 CDO BDE RM
Waite, Tobias Gerard, BSc	LT(CC)	X		01.05.01	GIBRALTAR PBS
Wake, Charlotte,	SURG SLT(SCC)	-		19.01.05	DARTMOUTH BRNC
Wakeling, Jonathan Lee, MA	CDR(FTC)	E	TM	31.12.94	RALEIGH
Waldmeyer, Edward,	CAPT RM(CC)	-		01.09.03	45 CDO RM
Wales, Benjamin David, BSc	LT CDR(FTC)	S	CMA	01.03.03	FLEET HQ WI
Walford, Lance Scott,	SLT(IC)	X	P U/T	01.02.05	RNAS YEOVILTON
Walker, Alasdair James, OBE, MB, ChB, FRCS	SURG CAPT(FCC)	-	(CGS)	30.06.04	MDHU DERRIFORD
Walker, Andrew John, BA, PGCE	MAJ(FTC)	-		01.05.01	SFSG
Walker, Clive Leslie,	CDR(FTC)	S		31.12.00	NAVSEC
Walker, Daniel Haydn, BSc	LT(IC)	X	O	01.01.04	849 SQN A FLT
Walker, Donald William Alexander, BA	LT CDR(FTC)	S		01.10.01	JSCSC
Walker, Graeme Hamish, BEng	SLT(IC)	E	AE U/T	01.09.04	CUMBERLAND
Walker, Ian Michael, BEng, PGDip	LT(IC)	E	MESM	01.01.03	SOVEREIGN
Walker, James John, MEng, ACGI	LT(CC)	X		01.01.04	RNAS CULDROSE
Walker, Jamie, BEng	LT(IC)	E	ME	01.01.03	OCEAN
Walker, Jamie Joseph,	LT(IC)	X	EW	01.07.04	JT CIMIC
Walker, John,	LT(IC)	X	EW	28.10.05	FLEET COMOPS NWD
Walker, Mark Christopher, pcea	LT CDR(FTC) (Act Cdr)	X	P	01.10.94	848 SQN HERON
Walker, Mark John, BMus	LT(IC)	X		01.02.06	MWS COLLINGWOOD
Walker, Mark Justin, BEng	LT CDR(FTC)	E	TM	01.10.02	RNSR BOVINGTON
Walker, Martin, BEng, MA, MSc, CEng, MIEE, psc(j)	CDR(FTC)	E	WE	30.06.00	MOD (BATH)
Walker, Martin Denis James, BA	LT(IC)	S		01.01.04	VIGILANT(PORT)
Walker, Matthew John Emrys, MSc	LT(IC)	E	TM	01.01.02	DCTS PORTS
Walker, Michael John,	LT CDR(FTC)	X		01.10.03	FLEET CMR
Walker, Nicholas John, MSc, psc(j)	CDR(FTC)	E	MESM	30.06.00	DLO BRISTOL
Walker, Nicholas Lee, pce	LT CDR(FTC)	X	PWO(U)	01.02.93	MOD (LONDON)
Walker, Nicholas MacLaren, BSc	LT CDR(FTC)	X	P	01.01.00	ALBION
Walker, Nicholas Michael Cleveland,	LT(CC)	X	P	01.08.02	GANNET SAR FLT
Walker, Nigel Albert,	LT CDR(FTC)	S	CA	01.10.00	PJHQ
Walker, Peter Richard, MBA, MSc	LT CDR(FTC)	E	IS	01.05.96	FLEET FOTR
Walker, Richard Eden, MA, psc	LT COL(FTC)	-	C	31.12.97	CTCRM
Walker, Richard Paul,	LT(IC)	X	O U/T	01.07.04	824 SQN
Walker, Robin Stuart,	LT(FTC)	X	MCD	19.09.00	WALNEY
Walker, Stephen James, BEng	LT(FTC)	E	WESM	01.04.02	SUPERB
Walker, Stephen Paul, SM, SM(n)	LT CDR(FTC)	X	SM	09.03.02	FLEET COMOPS NWD
Wall, Irene Joanne, BSc	LT(CC)	S		01.02.00	DRAKE COB
Wall, Karl,	LT(IC)	X	SM	01.07.04	RALEIGH
Wall, Steven Nicholas, BSc	LT(CC)	X	FC	01.02.99	MWS COLLINGWOOD
Wall, Thomas Christopher,	SLT(IC)	X	O U/T	01.02.05	DARTMOUTH BRNC
Wallace, Allan, BSc, PGDIPAN, pce	CDR(FTC)	X	PWO(N)	30.06.01	PJHQ
Wallace, Anthony Robert, BEng	LT(CC)	X	MW	01.01.02	HURWORTH
Wallace, David James, MSc	LT CDR(FTC)	E	IS	01.10.98	HQ DCSA
Wallace, George William Alexander, AFC, BSc, pce, pcea, ocds(Can), osc	CAPT(FTC)	X	P	30.06.04	BDLS CANADA
Wallace, Iain Stephen, BEng, PGDip	LT(IC)	E	IS	01.07.00	FLEET FOTR

Name	Rank	Branch	Spec	Seniority	Where Serving
Wallace, Michael Rupert Barry, BA, jsdc, pce, hcsc	CAPT(FTC)	X	PWO(U)	30.06.03	CAMPBELTOWN
Wallace, Richard Stuart, BSc	LT(IC)	X		01.09.02	NP BOSNIA
Wallace, Richard Stuart,	CAPT RM(CC)	-		01.04.01	HQ 3 CDO BDE RM
Wallace, Ryan Patrick, BSc	LT(IC)	E	IS	01.03.01	ILLUSTRIOUS
Wallace, Scott Peter, BSc	CAPT RM(CC) (Act Maj)	-		01.09.01	LN SIERRA LEONE
Wallace, Simon Jonathan, pce	LT CDR(FTC)	X	AAWO	01.03.02	FOST SEA
Wallace, Stewart Andrew, BSc	LT(FTC)	X	ATC	01.12.97	RAF COTTESMORE
Waller, Ramsay,	2LT(IC)	-		01.08.01	FPGRM
Waller, Steven Adrian, pce(sm), SM	LT CDR(FTC)	X	SM	01.03.99	NAVSEC
Walliker, Michael John Delane, OBE, BA, pce, pce(sm)	CDR(FTC)	X	SM	31.12.99	MOD (LONDON)
Wallington-Smith, James,	MID(UCE)(IC)	X		01.09.04	DARTMOUTH BRNC
Wallis, Adrian John, pce, pcea	CDR(FTC)	X	O	30.06.02	FLEET COSCAP
Wallis, Jonathan Spencer,	LT CDR(FTC)	X	P	01.10.02	750 SQN SEAHAWK
Walls, Kevin Finlay,	MAJ(FTC)	-	MLDR	01.05.00	CTCRM (SEA)
Walmsley, Elizabeth Ann, MA, ACIS, psc(j)	CDR(FTC)	S		30.06.05	FLEET HQ WI
Walpole, Peter Kenneth, ADC, BSc, pce	CDRE(FTC)	X	PWO(C)	07.07.03	FWO DEVPT SEA
Walsh, Andrew Harwood, BEng	LT(IC)	E		01.12.98	EXCHANGE ARMY UK
Walsh, David,	LT(IC)	S		01.02.01	DPA BRISTOL
Walsh, Dennis Gerard,	LT CDR(FTC)	E	AE	01.10.01	OCEAN
Walsh, Kevin Michael, BSc, n	LT CDR(FTC)	X	PWO(A)	01.11.04	SOUTHAMPTON
Walsh, Mark Anthony,	CDR(FTC)	S	CA	30.06.05	FOST DPORT SHORE
Walter, Stephen,	LT(IC)	E	ME	08.04.05	ENDURANCE
Walton, Andrew Paul,	LT CDR(FTC)	MS	(AD)	01.10.02	FLEET COSP&S
Walton, Colin Peter, BEng, CEng, MIEE	LT CDR(FTC)	E	WE	01.09.00	FLEET COSP&S
Walton, George James,	LT(IC)	X		01.05.03	MWS COLLINGWOOD
Walton, Jonathan Charles, MSc, MIEE, MCGI	LT CDR(FTC)	E	WE	01.12.90	NBC PORTSMOUTH
Walton, Simon Phillip,	LT(FTC)	X	SM	01.10.97	SOVEREIGN
Walton, Stephen David,	LT(FTC)	X	MW	01.10.98	QUORN
Walton, Stephen Paul,	LT CDR(FTC)	E	AE	01.10.01	CV(F) IPT
Wappner, Gary Dean, BA	LT(IC)	X	P	10.10.98	771 SQN
Warburton, Alison Mary, BSc	LT(SC)(MD)	Q		26.02.03	RN GIBRALTAR
Ward, Alexander James, MA	LT(CC)	S		01.09.02	FLEET HQ PORTSEA
Ward, Andrew James,	LT CDR(FTC)	X	MCD	01.06.03	EXCHANGE CANADA
Ward, Antony John,	SLT(IC)	X	O U/T	01.09.04	DARTMOUTH BRNC
Ward, Christopher James, MA	LT(SCC)	Q		01.05.04	RH HASLAR
Ward, Colin David, psc(j)	MAJ(FTC)	-	SO(LE)	01.10.03	HQ 3 CDO BDE RM
Ward, David Steven, BA	LT CDR(FTC)	X		01.10.97	DRAKE SFM
Ward, Douglas John, BSc	LT(IC)	S	SM	01.11.98	2SL/CNH
Ward, Jared Maurice,	LT(IC)	S		01.07.04	RNAS CULDROSE
Ward, Julie Anne, BA	SLT(IC)	X		01.01.05	DARTMOUTH BRNC
Ward, Matthew Bernard,	LT(CC)	X		01.10.02	846 SQN
Ward, Michelle Therese, MA	LT(CC)	X		01.04.99	EXCHANGE FRANCE
Ward, Nigel Anthony, BSc, MBA, IEng, MIIE, MCMI	LT(FTC)	E	WE	02.09.99	DSFM PORTSMOUTH
Ward, Rees Graham John, CB, MA, MSc, CEng, FIEE, rcds, jsdc, gw, hcsc	RADM	-	WE	27.04.99	HQ DCSA
(CHIEF EXECUTIVE DCSA JAN 02)					
Ward, Simon,	LT CDR(FTC)	X	PWO(A)	01.09.05	CUMBERLAND
Ward, Simon Ira, MA, pce, psc(j)	CDR(FTC)	X	AAWO	30.06.05	NOTTINGHAM
Ward, Stephen David, BEng	LT CDR(FTC)	E	ME	01.01.98	MOD (LONDON)
Warden, John Mitchell, MA, MBA, MSc, CEng, MinstP, C PHYS, psc(j)	CDR(FTC)	E	TMSM	30.06.02	FLEET COSP&S
Wardle, Mark,	LT(FTC) (Act Lt Cdr)	X	C	17.12.93	NP BOSNIA
Wardley, Harriet Diana Mary Porteous,	SLT(IC)	X		01.02.05	DARTMOUTH BRNC
Wardley, Thomas Edward,	LT(SC)(MD)	Q		01.03.05	MDHU DERRIFORD
Ware, Andrew Travis, BA	LT(IC)	X		01.05.02	849 SQN A FLT
Ware, Peter James, BSc	LT(IC)	X		01.01.05	TIRELESS
Wareham, Michael Paul, BEng, MSc	CAPT(FTC)	E	MESM	30.06.06	NEPTUNE DSA
Waring, John Robert, BSc, PhD	LT CDR(FTC)	E	TM	01.04.99	RALEIGH
Warn, Christopher John, SM	LT CDR(FTC)	X	SM	09.12.98	RNU ST MAWGAN
Warr, Caroline Helen,	LT(IC)	X		01.01.05	BULWARK
Warr, Richard Frank,	LT CDR(FTC)	E	WESM	01.10.02	FWO FASLANE
Warren, Anouchka Jane Lenham, BA	LT(IC)	X		01.12.05	MWS COLLINGWOOD
Warren, Brian Howard, OBE, BSc, pce	CAPT(FTC)	X	PWO(U)	30.06.05	MOD (LONDON)
Warren, Julian,	SURG SLT(SCC)	-		01.07.02	DARTMOUTH BRNC

Name	Rank	Branch	Spec	Seniority	Where Serving
Warren, Matthew James, BSc	LT(IC)	X		01.05.04	MWS HM TG (D)
Warren, Richard Alan, BSc	LT(IC)	X	P	01.09.03	RNAS CULDROSE
Warrender, William Jonathan, MA, pce, psc(j)	CDR(FTC)	X	PWO(A)	30.06.04	ARGYLL
Warrick, Mark, BEng	LT(IC)	E	WE	01.09.04	SOMERSET
Warwick, Philip David, pce, psc(j), MA	CDR(FTC)	X	PWO(U)	30.06.01	MOD (LONDON)
Washer, Nicholas Barry John, BSc, MA, pce, psc(j)	CDR(FTC)	X	PWO(C)	30.06.06	MWC PORTSDOWN
Waskett, Daniel, BEng	SLT(IC)	X	O U/T	01.01.04	RNAS CULDROSE
Wason, Jennifer Margaret, BEng	SLT(IC)	E	WE U/T	01.05.04	MWS COLLINGWOOD
Watchorn, James,	SURG SLT(SCC)	-		15.05.04	DARTMOUTH BRNC
Waterfield, Simon Jon, AMNI	LT CDR(FTC)	X		01.06.02	YORK
Waterhouse, Phillip, MA, MInstAM, MHCIMA, MILT	CDR(FTC)	S		30.06.06	RN LOGS SCHOOL
Waterman, John Henry, BSc, MA, CEng, MIMarEST, psc	CDR(FTC)	E	ME	31.12.97	FLEET COSP&S
Waters, Michael Rhodri, BSc	LT(IC)	X		01.01.05	RICHMOND
Waters, Nigel Roger, BSc	LT CDR(FTC)	S	SM	16.04.96	DLO/DG LOG (SC)
Watkins, Andrew Patrick Leonard, BSc	MAJ(FTC)	-		01.05.03	JSCSC
Watkins, Dean Thomas,	CAPT RM(CC)	-	SO(LE)	01.04.04	CTCRM
Watkins, Kevin John, BEng, MSc	LT(FTC)	E	ME	01.01.98	JSCSC
Watkins, Timothy Crispin, BSc, pcea	LT CDR(FTC)	X	P	01.10.00	845 SQN
Watson, Andrew Herbert, BEng, pcea	LT(FTC)	X	O	01.06.95	820 SQN
Watson, Anthony Peter,	LT(FTC)	E	MESM	02.09.99	DLO BRISTOL
Watson, Bradley Lawrence, BSc	LT(CC)	X	O	01.05.01	849 SQN HQ
Watson, Brian Robert,	CAPT RM(CC)	-	P	01.01.02	815 SQN HQ
Watson, Charles Robert, HNC	LT CDR(FTC)	E	WE	01.10.04	DCSA DHFCS FMR
Watson, Graham Brian,	CAPT RM(IC)	-	SO(LE)	24.07.04	CTCRM
Watson, Ian, n, BA	LT CDR(FTC)	X	PWO(A)	01.03.03	MWS COLLINGWOOD
Watson, James Richard, MEng	LT(IC)	E	ME U/T	01.09.05	KENT
Watson, Peter Gerald Charles, BEng, CEng, MIMarEST	LT CDR(FTC)	E	MESM	25.10.96	FOST SM SEA
Watson, Philip Frank,	MAJ(FTC)	BS	SO(LE)	01.10.00	RM BAND PTSMTH
Watson, Richard Douglas,	LT(IC)	X	MCD	01.10.02	MWS DEF DIV SCHL
Watson, Richard Ian,	MAJ(FTC)	-	SO(LE)	01.10.04	1 ASSAULT GP RM
Watson, Richard John, SM	LT CDR(FTC)	X	SM	01.08.89	FLEET COSP&S
Watson, Ross William,	SLT(IC)	X		01.02.05	DARTMOUTH BRNC
Watson, Simon Christopher,	LT(IC)	E	WE	01.09.05	ARK ROYAL
Watson, Stuart Benedict Cooper,	LT CDR(FTC)	S	SM	01.10.04	IRON DUKE
Watt, Anthony James Landon, pce	CDR(FTC)	X	PWO(U)	30.06.05	MONTROSE
Watts, Alun David,	CDR(FTC)	S	SM	30.06.02	FLEET FOTR
Watts, Andrew Peter, pcea	LT CDR(FTC)	X	O	01.10.93	RNAS CULDROSE
Watts, Graham Michael, BSc, CEng, FIMarEST, psc	CAPT(FTC)	E	ME	30.06.05	MOD (LONDON)
Watts, Jason Neil, BSc	LT(CC)	X	P	01.02.96	DHFS
Watts, Raymond Frederick, BSc, psc	CAPT(FTC)	E	WE	31.12.00	DLO DEF MUN GP
Watts, Richard Dennis, OBE, psc(m)	COL(FTC)	-	C	30.06.05	FLEET COMOPS NWD
Watts, Robert, pce(sm)	LT CDR(FTC)	X	SM	01.07.01	DARTMOUTH BRNC
Watts, Zoe Abigail, BSc	LT(CC)	X		01.01.99	SMITER
Waugh, Peter John, MA, MB, BCh, MFOM, LRCP, LRCS, DipAvMed	SURG CAPT(FCC)	-	(CO/M)	30.06.05	NBC PORTSMOUTH
Waugh, Richard Peter, BEng	LT(IC)	X	P	01.01.04	845 SQN
Way, Robert Andrew,	LT(IC)	X		01.01.01	UKMCC BAHRAIN
Weale, John Stuart, pce, pce(sm), BSc	CDR(FTC)	X	SM	30.06.99	UKMARBATSTAFF
Weale, Jonathan,	SURG SLT(SCC) (Act Surg Lt)	-		03.08.05	DARTMOUTH BRNC
Weare, Jonathan Bran, BA, MSc	LT(FTC)	S		01.09.99	2SL/CNH
Weaver, Neil, PGDip, IEng, MIMarEST	LT CDR(FTC)	E	MESM	01.10.02	ASM IPT
Weaver, Thomas Henry, BA	LT(CC)	X		01.01.03	IRON DUKE
Webb, Amy Francesca,	SLT(UCE)(IC)	X		01.09.04	DARTMOUTH BRNC
Webb, Andrew James, MBE, BSc, pce	CDR(FTC)	X	PWO(C)	30.06.03	FLEET HQ WI
Webb, Christopher McDonald, pcea	LT CDR(FTC(A)	X	O	01.10.96	FLEET AV CU
Webb, Eleanor Lucy, MA	LT(CC)	S		01.09.02	FLEET COSP&S
Webb, John Paul,	LT(IC)	X		01.10.02	VICTORY
Webber, Adam Andrew, MA	SLT(IC)	X		01.05.04	ILLUSTRIOUS
Webber, Christopher John, BEng, FRMS, MDA, MCIPD	LT CDR(FTC)	X	HM	26.08.97	RNAS YEOVILTON
Webber, Joanne Patricia, BA	LT(FTC)	X	O	01.09.94	829 FLT 05
Webber, Kerry Jane,	LT(CC)	X		01.11.96	OCLC MANCH
Webber, Richard James, MB, BS, Dip FFP, JCPTGP	SURG LTCDR(FCC)	-	GMPP	01.02.01	INM ALVERSTOKE

Name	Rank	Branch	Spec	Seniority	Where Serving
Webster, Andrew John, BSc	LT(IC)	E	TM	01.01.04	MWS COLLINGWOOD
Webster, Andrew Philip, BA	LT(CC) (Act Lt Cdr)	X	PWO(C)	01.11.94	MWS COLLINGWOOD
Webster, Mark,	SLT(IC)	X		01.04.04	LANCASTER
Webster, Richard James, BSc	LT(CC)	X	PWO(C)	01.12.98	NOTTINGHAM
Webster, Richard John, BA	LT CDR(FTC)	S		01.12.05	PORTLAND
Webster, Timothy John Cook, psc(m)	LT COL(FTC)	-	C	30.06.00	MOD (LONDON)
Weedon, Grant Antony,	LT(FTC)	E	ME	01.09.04	SOUTHAMPTON
Weightman, Nicholas Ellison,	LT CDR(FTC)	X	P	01.10.01	NAVSEC
Weil, Daniel Gerard, MEng	LT(IC)	E	AE	01.09.05	845 SQN
Weir, James Robertson,	CAPT RM(CC) (Act Maj)	-	SO(LE)	01.04.02	UKLFCSG RM
Weir, Scott Duncan, BEng	LT CDR(FTC)	E	WESM	01.10.99	VIGILANT(STBD)
Welborn, Colin George, FRGS, MDA, pce, psc(m)	CAPT(FTC)	X	MCD	30.06.03	FWO PORTS SEA
Welburn, Roy Stuart, BSc	CDR(FTC)	E	AE	31.12.00	RMC OF SCIENCE
Welch, Alan, MSc	LT(FTC)	MS	(AD)	20.09.99	MOD (LONDON)
Welch, Andrew, MBE	LT CDR(FTC)	X	O	13.10.95	DASC
Welch, James Fleming, MB, ChB, BMS	SURG LTCDR(FC(MD)	-		05.08.03	JSCSC
Welch, Katherine Alice,	LT CDR(CC)	S		01.10.04	MWS COLLINGWOOD
Welford, Robert Clive, BEng	LT CDR(FTC)	X	PWO(C)	01.02.99	PJHQ
Weller, Jamie Kevin, BEng	SLT(IC)	X	ATCU/T	01.06.04	DARTMOUTH BRNC
Wellesley, Richard Charles Robert, OBE, MDA, pce, pcea	CAPT(FTC)	X	O	30.06.03	MOD (LONDON)
Wellington, Stuart, HNC, BEng, MIEE	LT CDR(FTC)	E	WE	01.02.98	MOD (LONDON)
Wells, Barry Charles, BSc	LT CDR(FTC)	E	WESM	01.10.02	VICTORIOUS(PORT)
Wells, Jamie Duncan, BSc	LT(CC)	X		01.09.01	KENT
Wells, John Paul, BDS, MFGDP(UK)	SG LT(D)(SCC)	-	GDP	04.07.02	RH HASLAR
Wells, Jonathan,	LT CDR(FTC(A)	X	P	01.08.97	829 SQN HQ
Wells, Laura,	SURG SLT(SCC) (Act Surg Lt)	-		02.08.05	DARTMOUTH BRNC
Wells, Martin Neville,	LT(IC)	X		01.01.05	RNAS CULDROSE
Wells, Michael Peter, BSc, PGCE	LT CDR(FTC)	S		01.03.05	ALBION
Welsh, Georgina Louise, BA	LT(CC)	X	H2	01.05.02	ECHO
Welsh, John, BSc, CEng	LT(CC)	E	TM	15.10.95	MWS DEF DIV SCHL
Welsh, Michaela Penelope,	SLT(IC)	X		01.02.04	MWS COLLINGWOOD
Welsh, Richard Michael Karl,	LT(CC)	E	AE	01.02.01	RNAS CULDROSE
Wernham, William Frederick, MSc	LT(IC)	MS		01.04.04	NEPTUNE DLO
Wesson, Matthew,	LT(SC(MD)	Q		01.07.03	FLEET COSP&S
West, Sir Alan (William John), GCB, DSC, rcds, pce, psc, hcsc	ADM		AWO(A)	30.11.00	
West, Andrew William,	LT CDR(FTC)	S	(W)	01.10.01	UKNSU NAPLES
West, Anthony Bernard,	LT CDR(FTC)	X	REG	01.10.01	DCPPA
West, David John,	CAPT RM(IC)	-	P	19.07.02	845 SQN
West, Diana Michelle, BSc	SLT(IC)	X		01.02.04	CHATHAM
West, Graham George, BEng, CEng, MIMarEST	LT CDR(FTC)	E	ME	06.06.99	MOD (LONDON)
West, Michael Wallace, pce	LT CDR(FTC)	X	AAWO	05.08.92	LOAN OMAN
West, Nicholas Kingsley, BA	LT(CC)	S		01.04.00	FLEET HQ WI
West, Rory Julian, BSc, pcea	LT CDR(FTC)	X	PWO(U)	01.06.02	PJHQ
West, Timothy Lewis,	LT(IC)	S		01.09.05	COM MCC NWD
Westbrook, Jonathan Simon, MBE, pce(sm), pce	CAPT(FTC)	X	SM	30.06.02	PJHQ
Westbrook, Kevin, BEng	SLT(IC)	E	AE U/T	01.09.03	SULTAN
Westerman, Richard Warwick, MB, CHB	SURG LT(MC(MD)	-		13.08.02	RCDM
Westlake, Karly, BSc	SLT(IC)	X		01.04.03	RNAS YEOVILTON
Westlake, Simon Richard,	MAJ(FTC)	-	SO(LE)	01.10.05	CTCRM
Westley, Alexander James Rayner,	SLT(UCE)(IC)	E	WESM	01.09.03	DARTMOUTH BRNC
Westley, David Richard,	LT CDR(FTC)	X	P	01.10.01	EXCHANGE ARMY UK
Westoby, Guy Thomas Richard, BSc	LT(IC)	X		01.08.04	YORK
Weston, Graham Kenneth,	SLT(IC)	X	SM	01.09.03	SOVEREIGN
Weston, Helen Louise, BSc	LT(IC)	X		01.09.05	FLEET FOTR
Weston, Karl Nicholas Neville, BEng	LT(CC)	X	O	01.08.99	815 FLT 228
Weston, Mark William, BDS, MSc, MFGDP(UK)	SGCAPT(D)(FCC)	-		30.06.02	DDS HALTON
Westwood, Amanda,	SG SLT(D)(SCC)	-		26.07.05	DARTMOUTH BRNC
Westwood, Andrew James, BEng	LT(CC)	X	P	01.09.02	845 SQN
Westwood, Mark Robin Timothy, BEng, MA, MSc, CEng, MIMechE, MCGI, MIMarEST, psc(j), Eur In	LT CDR(FTC)	E	MESM	01.07.94	CNNRP BRISTOL
Westwood, Martin William, MA, pce, pcea, psc, psc(j)	CAPT(FTC)	X	P	30.06.02	NATO MEWSG VL
Westwood, Michelle Joy, BA	LT(IC)	S		01.09.04	CHATHAM

Name	Rank	Branch	Spec	Seniority	Where Serving
Westwood, Thomas Philip,	LT(IC)	X		01.01.04	SUTHERLAND
Whale, Victoria Alice,	LT(CC)	S		01.10.01	DLO/DG LOG (SC)
Whalley, Richard James,	LT CDR(FTC)	S	CMA	01.04.01	FLEET HQ WI
Whalley, Simon David, MILT, psc	CDRE(FTC)	S	SM	01.11.05	FLEET COSP&S
Wharrie, Craig George, BEng	LT(CC)	E	ME	01.12.00	OCLC MANCH
Wharrie, Ewan Killen Balnave, BSc	LT CDR(FTC)	E	TMSM	01.10.01	OCLC ROSYTH
Whatley, Mark,	SLT(IC)	S		01.07.05	RALEIGH
Wheal, Adrian Justin, BEng	LT CDR(FTC)	E	MESM	01.09.00	SULTAN
Wheatley, Ian James,	CHAPLAIN	CE		08.04.97	RALEIGH
Wheatley, Nicola Sian, BSc	LT(IC)	X	H2	01.01.03	MWS COLLINGWOOD
Wheaton, Bowden James Stewart, pcea, gdas	LT CDR(FTC)	X	O	01.10.98	LOAN JTEG BSC DN
Wheeler, Nicholas Jules, SM(n)	LT CDR(FTC)	X	SM	01.10.03	UKMARBATSTAFF
Wheen, Charles Jefferies David,	LT(IC)	X		01.01.04	MWS COLLINGWOOD
Whetter, Richard Scott, BSc	LT(IC)	E	TM	14.05.00	RNICG
Whetton, Julia Barbara Dawn,	LT CDR(FTC)	W	S	01.10.96	RNAS CULDROSE
Whitaker, Martin Jeffery, BEng	SLT(IC)	X	P U/T	01.01.04	RAF CRANWELL EFS
Whitaker, Michael John, BSc, CEng, MIMechE, MDA	CDR(FTC)	E	AE	30.06.97	MOD (LONDON)
Whitaker, Rachel Elizabeth,	LT(IC)	E	AE	01.09.05	848 SQN HERON
White, Alistair John McIntosh,	LT(IC)	X	P	01.05.04	RNAS YEOVILTON
White, Andrew Raymond, BSc, CEng, MIEE	CDR(FTC)	E	WESM	31.12.94	MOD (BATH)
White, Christopher Greville, BA,	SLT(IC)	X		01.09.04	DARTMOUTH BRNC
White, Daniel Julyan,	MID(IC)	X		01.11.04	DARTMOUTH BRNC
White, David John, BSc	LT(CC)	X	P	01.03.98	JSCSC
White, Douglas,	LT(IC)	E	WESM	01.01.04	VENGEANCE(STBD)
White, Haydn John, psc(j)o	LT COL(FTC)	-	LC	30.06.05	FLEET COSCAP
White, Ian Frank, SM(n), SM	LT CDR(FTC)	X	SM	18.11.99	MWC PORTSDOWN
White, Jason Paul,	LT(CC)	X	MCD	01.02.01	SDG PORTSMOUTH
White, Jonathan Andrew Paul, MA, pce(sm), psc(j)	CDR(FTC)	X	SM	30.06.03	MOD (LONDON)
White, Jonathan Eric, BSc	LT CDR(FTC)	S		01.11.02	JFC HQ AGRIPPA
White, Jonathan W,	LT RM(IC)	-		01.09.03	45 CDO RM
White, Katharine Jane, BSc	LT(CC)	X	ATC	01.01.04	RNAS YEOVILTON
White, Kevin Frederick, BEng	LT(FTC)	E	ME	01.07.97	DFTE PORTSMOUTH
White, Kristopher Trevor, BSc	SLT(IC)	X		01.11.04	DARTMOUTH BRNC
White, Mark William, OBE, BSc, MA, pce, psc	CDR(FTC)	X	PWO(U)	31.12.98	JSCSC
White, Paul Donald, BSc	LT(IC)	X	P	01.05.03	849 SQN A FLT
White, Paul Kennedy Lane,	MID(IC)	X		01.09.04	DARTMOUTH BRNC
White, Philip Alan, MSc, CEng, FIMarEST	LT CDR(FTC)	E	MESM	16.02.92	NEPTUNE DLO
White, Robert Fredrick,	CDR(FTC)	E	WE	30.06.05	FLEET FOTR
White, Robert Leonard,	LT CDR(FTC)	E	AE	01.10.04	FLEET AV VL
White, Ross Elliott, BEng	LT(IC)	X	P	01.05.04	824 SQN
White, Simon Henry Wilmot, BA, pcea	LT(FTC)	X	P	16.06.93	820 SQN
White, Stephen, BSc	LT(IC)	E	IS	01.01.00	AFPAA(CENTURION)
White, Stephen James,	LT(FTC)	X	C	09.01.01	DARTMOUTH BRNC
White, Stephen Noel, BA	CDR(FTC)	S		31.12.97	MOD (BATH)
White, Stephen Paul, IEng, MIIE	LT(FTC) (Act Lt Cdr)	E	WESM	10.06.88	FLEET COSCAP
White, Steven, BSc	LT(IC)	X		01.05.03	MWS COLLINGWOOD
Whitehall, Sally, BSc	LT(CC)	X		01.02.00	WESTMINSTER
Whitehead, Peter James,	LT(CC)	X	O	01.12.98	RNAS YEOVILTON
Whitehead, Robert John, BSc	LT(IC)	E	TM	01.01.02	MWS COLLINGWOOD
Whitehead, Steven John, BEng, CEng, MRAeS	LT CDR(FTC)	E	AE	01.03.00	RNAS CULDROSE
Whitehorn, Iain James, BSc, CEng, MIMarEST	CDR(FTC)	E	MESM	30.06.94	FLEET COSP&S
Whitehouse, Andrew Paul, MEng	LT(IC)	X	P U/T	01.09.05	DHFS
Whitehouse, David Spencer, SM(n), SM	LT(CC)	X	SM	01.04.00	SCEPTRE
Whitehouse, Dominic Patrick, MSc, MB, CHB, MRCP, AFOM, DCH, DTM&H	SURG CDR(FCC)	-	(CM)	01.04.03	NELSON (PAY)
Whitehouse, Marie Louise, BA	LT(IC)	X		01.11.05	RNAS YEOVILTON
Whitehouse, Niall Robert,	LT CDR(FTC)	E	AE	01.12.04	RNAS YEOVILTON
Whitehouse, Simon Robert, BSc, IEng, MIIE	LT(FTC)	E	WE	01.04.01	MCM2 SEA
Whiteman, John,	2LT(IC)	-		01.08.02	CTCRM LYMPSTONE
Whitfield, Joe Alexander,	LT CDR(FTC)	X	P	01.10.03	CHFHQ
Whitfield, Kenneth David, BEng	LT CDR(FTC)	E	AE	01.03.00	MERLIN IPT
Whitfield, Philip Mark, BSc	MAJ(FTC)	-		01.09.03	FLEET HQ WI

Name	Rank	Branch	Spec	Seniority	Where Serving
Whitfield, Robert Matthew Patrick, BSc	LT CDR(FTC)	X	P	01.05.03	RAF LINTN/OUSE
Whitlam, John, pce	LT CDR(FTC)	X	PWO(A)	01.10.00	LN MTU UKSAT(C)
Whitley, Ian Derek Brake, pce, n	LT CDR(FTC)	X	PWO(C)	01.06.99	SUTHERLAND
Whitlum, Andrew Colin, BEng, pcea	LT(CC)	X	P	16.08.96	DHFS
Whitmarsh, Adam Thomas,	CAPT RM(CC)	-		01.09.03	42 CDO RM
Whitson-Fay, Craig David,	LT(FTC)	X	O	15.02.01	849 SQN B FLT
Whittaker, Mark Adrian, BM, MRCPath	SURG CDR(FCC)	-	(CL)	30.06.05	MDHU PORTSMOUTH
Whittingham, Debra Jayne,	LT CDR(FTC)	W	X	01.10.98	CMT SHRIVENHAM
Whittington, Christopher Charles,	SLT(IC)	X	P U/T	01.11.05	RNAS YEOVILTON
Whittington, Rowland,	LT(IC)	E	WE	01.07.04	CORNWALL
Whittles, Gary Wayne,	LT(IC)	S		01.07.04	TALENT
Whitwell, Nicholas Shaun, n.	LT(FTC)	X	PWO(C)	01.07.99	BULWARK
Whitworth, Robert Maitland,	LT CDR(FTC)	X	PWO(U)	01.10.99	EXCHANGE AUSTLIA
Whybourn, Lesley Ann, MB, BSc,	SURG LTCDR(MCC)	-	GMPP	28.11.02	FLEET AV HENLOW
DipAvMed, Dip FFP, DRCOG, CHB					
Whyntie, Adrian, BSc, CEng, FIEE, jsdc	CDRE(FTC)	E	WE	01.04.05	HQ DCSA
Whyte, Gordon,	LT(IC)	E	WE	01.07.04	ARGYLL
Whyte, Iain Paul, MA, MSc, psc(j)	LT CDR(FTC)	E	TM	01.04.01	DARTMOUTH BRNC
Wick, Harry Mark Stephen,	LT(CC)	X		01.09.00	SUTHERLAND
Wickett, Richard James, BEng	LT(CC)	E	ME	01.03.02	FLEET FOTR
Wickham, Robert James, BEng	LT(IC)	X		01.05.01	ARK ROYAL
Wicking, Geoffrey Steven, BEng	LT CDR(FTC)	E	AE	01.10.03	LAIPT
Wielopolski, Mark Leszek Christopher Carpenter,	LT(IC)	X	P	01.05.01	845 SQN
Wightwick, Katherine Helen Torr, BA, BD	LT(IC)	X		01.08.01	FLEET HQ PORTS 2
Wilcocks, David Nicholas,	LT(IC)	X		01.07.05	CLYDE
Wilcocks, Philip Lawrence, DSC, BSc, AMRINA, pce, psc(a)	RADM	-	AAWO	19.04.04	FOSNNI
(FOSNNI/CINCFLEET COS MPS APR 06)					
Wilcockson, Roy,	LT(CS)RM(CAS)	-		07.05.99	DNR SWE 2
Wilcox, Christopher Raymond,	SLT(IC)	X	O	01.09.03	MWS COLLINGWOOD
Wilcox, Thomas Colin,	CAPT RM(CC)	-	P	01.04.01	847 SQN
Wild, Gareth, MB, CHB, BMS	SURG LT(MC(MD)	-		01.08.01	MDHU DERRIFORD
Wild, Richard James,	LT(CC)	S		01.01.02	NELSON
Wildin, Andrew, BEng, MSc, CEng, MIEE	LT CDR(FTC)	E	WE	01.10.04	JSSU CHELTENHAM
Wiles, Stephen John, MSc, CEng, MRAeS	CDR(FTC) (Act Capt)	E	AE	30.06.98	DLO WYTON
Wilkins, David Paul, SM(n)	LT(CC)	X	SM	01.05.01	VIGILANT(STBD)
Wilkins, Richard Ronald, BEng, CEng, PGDip, MIMechE	LT CDR(FTC)	E	MESM	01.10.03	VANGUARD(PORT)
Wilkins, Robert Lloyd, BEng, PGDip	LT(IC)	E	MESM	01.05.03	TRAFALGAR
Wilkinson, David Henry, n	LT CDR(FTC)	X	PWO(U)	01.06.00	FLEET COMOPS NWD
Wilkinson, Georgina,	LT(MCC)	Q	OTSPEC	06.10.97	MDHU DERRIFORD
Wilkinson, John Richard,	LT(IC)	X	AV	01.01.04	RNAS YEOVILTON
Wilkinson, Michael French,	LT(FTC) (Act Lt Cdr)	X	P	01.02.96	FLEET AV VALLEY
Wilkinson, Peter John, BA, FCIPD, pce, pce(sm)	RADM	-	SM	27.07.04	MOD (LONDON)
(DEFENCE SERVICES SECRETARY JUL 05)					
Wilkinson, Peter McConnell,	LT CDR(FTC)	X	P	01.10.96	771 SQN
Wilkinson, Richard Murray, BSc, PGCE, MDA, nadc, jsdc, FITD	CAPT(FTC)	E	TM	30.06.00	NATO DEF COL
Wilkinson, Robin Nicholas,	LT CDR(FTC)	X	P	01.10.98	FLEET AV VL
Wilkinson, Sarah Louise, MEng	SLT(IC)	E	ME U/T	01.01.04	SULTAN
Wilkinson, Timothy Lindow, BA	CHAPLAIN	SF		04.03.97	BULWARK
Williams, Amanda Charlotte,	LT(IC)	X	REG	01.07.04	NELSON
Williams, Anthony Michael,	LT(IC)	X		01.09.04	RAF SHAWBURY
Williams, Anthony Peter, DSC, MA, pce, psc(j)	CDR(FTC)	X	MCD	31.12.00	MCM2 SEA
Williams, Anthony Stephen,	LT(FTC)	X	FC	01.09.98	MWS COLLINGWOOD
Williams, Benjamin Ross, BDS	SGLTCDR(D)(SCC)	-		27.06.03	RALEIGH
Williams, Brett, MEng	LT(IC)	E	P	01.06.03	DHFS
Williams, Bruce Nicholas Bromley, OBE, BSc, pce, psc	CDRE(FTC)	X	PWO(U)	27.04.06	UKMARBATSTAFF
Williams, Caroline Mary Alexandra, PhD, BA	CDR(FCC)	Q	IC	30.06.05	RCDM
Williams, Cassandra Lyn, BEng	LT(CC)	E	AE	01.04.02	RAF COTTESMORE
Williams, Colin Nicholas Owen, BSc	LT CDR(FTC)	X	AAWO	01.06.01	YORK
Williams, Daniel Leslie, BA	LT(CC)	X	P	01.01.00	RAF SHAWBURY
Williams, David,	LT(CC)	X	P	08.06.00	847 SQN
Williams, David Ian, pce	LT CDR(FTC)	X	AAWO	29.05.92	TDL IPT
Williams, David Spencer, BEng, pce, psc(j)	CDR(FTC)	X	PWO(U)	30.06.05	DRAKE COB

Name	Rank	Branch	Spec	Seniority	Where Serving
Williams, Dean Ashley,	CAPT RM(IC)	-	SO(LE)	01.07.04	42 CDO RM
Williams, Dylan, BDS	SG LT(D)(SC(MD)	-		25.06.03	45 CDO RM
Williams, Gerwyn, ACMI, MinstAM	LT(IC) (Act Lt Cdr)	S		01.05.04	SAUDI AFPS SAUDI
Williams, James Laurence,	SLT(IC)	X		01.02.04	ALBION
Williams, James Phillip,	LT CDR(FTC)	X	AAWO	01.06.00	MWS COLLINGWOOD
Williams, Jemma Elizabeth, BSc	SLT(IC)	X	ATCU/T	01.11.04	DARTMOUTH BRNC
Williams, Lee John,	LT(IC)	E	WESM	01.07.04	TURBULENT
Williams, Luke Anthony John, BA	LT(IC)	X		01.04.05	VANGUARD(STBD)
Williams, Mark Adrian, pcea	LT CDR(FTC)	X	O	01.10.00	FLEET COMOPS NWD
Williams, Mark Henry, MA, pce, pce(sm), psc(j)	CDR(FTC)	X	SM	31.12.98	PJHQ
Williams, Mark Stuart, BSc	LT CDR(FTC)	S		29.03.97	NBC PORTSMOUTH
Williams, Martyn Jon, OBE, MA, CEng, MIEE, psc(j)	CDR(FTC)	E	WESM	30.06.00	ASM IPT
Williams, Matthew Charles,	CAPT RM(IC)	-		01.09.03	45 CDO RM
Williams, Nicola Marie,	SLT(IC)	X	P U/T	01.09.04	RNAS YEOVILTON
Williams, Nigel David Blackstone, BSc, jsdc, pce	CDR(FTC)	X	PWO(U)	31.12.91	STG BRISTOL
Williams, Nigel Lamplough, BSc, CEng, MIMarEST	CAPT(FTC)	E	ME	30.06.00	FLEET COSP&S
Williams, Oliver Charles Llewelyn, BSc	SLT(IC)	X		01.09.03	MWS COLLINGWOOD
Williams, Paul Allan, BEng	LT(CC)	E	ME	01.01.02	CAPT IST STAFF
Williams, Paul Glynn, BA	LT(IC)	X		01.05.01	NEPTUNE
Williams, Peter Mark, BEng, MBA	LT CDR(FTC)	E	TM	01.10.03	FLEET HQ WI
Williams, Peter Michael,	CAPT RM(IC)	-		01.09.03	FPGRM
Williams, Richard James,	SURG SLT(SCC) (Act Surg Lt)	-		01.08.05	DARTMOUTH BRNC
Williams, Robert Evan, OBE, LLB	CDR(FTC) (Barrister)	S	BAR	30.06.93	NAVSEC
Williams, Robert John Stirling, n	LT(FTC) (Act Lt Cdr)	X	PWO(C)	01.09.96	UKMARBATSTAFF
Williams, Roderick Charles, BSc	LT CDR(FTC)	E	ME	01.10.89	DSFM PORTSMOUTH
Williams, Simon Paul, BSc, pce	CAPT(FTC)	X	PWO(C)	30.06.03	CORNWALL
Williams, Simon Thomas, OBE, BSc, pce, pce(sm), hcsc	CDRE(FTC)	X	SM	03.05.05	UKMCC BAHRAIN
Williams, Stephen Wayne Leonard,	LT CDR(FTC)	S		01.04.01	MOD (BATH)
Williams, Thomas George Edward, BA	LT(IC)	X		01.06.04	MERSEY
Williams, Timothy Nicholas Edward, BSc, pce, pcea, psc	CDR(FTC) (Act Capt)	X	P	31.12.89	SA SEOUL
Williams-Allden, Lucy Alice, BEng	SLT(IC)	E	AE U/T	01.09.04	CAMPBELTOWN
Williamson, Alexander Karl, MSc	MAJ(FTC)	-	C	01.05.04	BDMT
Williamson, Peter James,	LT(IC)	X		01.10.02	CC MAR AGRIPPA
Williamson, Tobias Justin Lubbock, MVO, BEng, MA, pce, pcea, psc(j)	CDR(FTC)	X	O	31.12.00	NAVSEC
Willing, Nigel Phillip, BSc	LT(CC)	X	P	16.08.93	EXCHANGE FRANCE
Willis, Alistair James, MA, MBA, MILT, MCMI, psc(j)	CDR(FTC)	S		30.06.04	FLEET HQ WI
Willis, Andrew Stephen, n	LT(CC)	X		01.01.98	DARTMOUTH BRNC
Willis, Martyn Stephen,	LT CDR(FTC)	S	CA	02.05.95	MOD (LONDON)
Willmore, Simon,	SLT(UCE)(IC)	E	WE	01.01.03	DARTMOUTH BRNC
Wills, John Robert, BSc, CEng, MIMarEST	CAPT(FTC)	E	ME	31.12.97	SA ATHENS
Wills, Philip John, BSc	LT CDR(FTC)	X	O	01.01.01	ARK ROYAL
Wills, Robert Hartingdon, BEng, PGDip	LT(IC)	E	MESM	01.05.03	VIGILANT(STBD)
Willsmore, Stuart Andrew,	LT(IC)	X		01.07.05	MONTROSE
Willson, Neil, sq	MAJ(FTC)	-		01.09.96	CTCRM
Wilman, David Mark, BA	LT CDR(FTC) (Barrister)	S	BAR	01.10.01	FLEET COSP&S
Wilshaw, Gary,	LT(IC)	E	AE	01.05.03	OCLC BRISTOL
Wilshire, Nicholas,	LT(IC)	E	MESM	18.02.05	SULTAN
Wilson, Adrian Clive,	MAJ(FTC)	-	SO(LE)	01.10.03	42 CDO RM
Wilson, Alexander Charles, MA, psc, psc(j)o	LT COL(FTC)	-	LC	31.12.95	FLEET COSCAP
Wilson, Allan John, pce, n	LT CDR(FTC)	X	PWO(U)	01.10.03	UKMARBATSTAFF
Wilson, Charles Dominick, OBE, BSc, jsdc, pce	CDR(FTC)	X	MCD	30.06.95	SA COPENHAGEN
Wilson, Charles Kenneth, BA	SLT(IC)	S		01.09.03	RALEIGH
Wilson, Christopher Gordon Talbot, pce, pcea	LT CDR(FTC(A)	X	P	01.08.85	DLO YEO
Wilson, Christopher John, BEng, MBA, CEng, MIMarEST	LT CDR(FTC)	E	MESM	01.12.96	ASM IPT
Wilson, David John, MSc	LT(IC)	E	TM U/T	01.05.04	EXETER
Wilson, David Robert, pce, n	LT CDR(FTC)	X	AAWO	01.05.00	JSCSC
Wilson, David William Howard, psc(j)	LT COL(FTC)	-		30.06.03	DA ALGIERS
Wilson, Garth Henry Crawford, MEng	SLT(IC)	E	ME U/T	01.01.05	DARTMOUTH BRNC
Wilson, Gary Paul,	LT(IC)	X	SM	01.01.03	DEF SCH OF LANG
Wilson, Geoffrey John,	LT(FTC)	X	REG	19.09.00	SULTAN
Wilson, Graham John, MBE	LT CDR(FTC)	X	MCD	01.10.01	SUPT OF DIVING
Wilson, James Andrew,	LT(FTC)	E	ME	15.06.95	FLEET COSP&S

Name	Rank	Branch	Spec	Seniority	Where Serving
Wilson, John, BEng	LT(CC)	X	P	01.07.97	846 SQN
Wilson, Julian Graham, BA	MAJ(FTC)	-		01.09.04	UKLFCSG RM
Wilson, Kevin Paul, BSc, MDA, CEng, MIEE	CAPT(FTC)	E	WESM	30.06.05	HQ DCSA
Wilson, Michael George, BEng, PGDip	LT(IC)	E	MESM	01.01.03	SUPERB
Wilson, Neil Andrew, BA	LT(IC)	X	SM	01.05.03	RALEIGH
Wilson, Robert,	LT CDR(FTC)	X	PWO(A)	01.09.00	LEDBURY
Wilson, Simon Allistair,	LT(IC)	X	P	01.01.04	815 FLT 229
Wilson, Stephen Gordon, MNI, pce, psc	CAPT(FTC)	X	AAWO	30.06.03	DA BRIDGETOWN
Wilson, Stephen Richard, psc	LT COL(FTC)	-		30.06.94	FOST SEA
Wilson-Chalon, Louis Michael, BSc, pcea	LT CDR(FTC)	X	P	01.04.97	NAVSEC
Wilson-Smith, Rudi Adam,	LT(IC)	X	FC	01.09.01	UKMARBATSTAFF
Wiltcher, Ross Alexander, BA	LT CDR(FTC)	S		01.08.93	RALEIGH
Wilton, Mark, BSc	LT(IC)	X		01.12.04	ILLUSTRIOUS
Winand, Francis Michael John, BA, SM(n)	LT(CC)	X	SM	01.05.00	TALENT
Winbolt, Neil Irwin, BEng	LT(IC)	E	TM	01.04.00	FLEET HQ PORTSEA
Winborn, David John, BEng	LT(IC)	E	P	01.05.05	SULTAN
Winch, Emma Jane, BDS	SGLTCDR(D)(MCC)	-		24.01.99	MWS EXCELLENT
Winch, Joseph Adrian,	CAPT RM(CC)	-		01.09.04	UKLFCSG RM
Windebank, Stephen John, pcea	LT CDR(FTC)	X	P	01.10.02	750 SQN SEAHAWK
Windsar, Paul Andrew, BEng, CEng, MIEE	LT CDR(FTC)	E	WESM	27.11.98	DLO BRISTOL
Windsor, Mark, BSc, MA, MIMechE, psc	CAPT(FTC)	X	METOC	31.12.00	FLEET HQ WI
Wingfield, Melissa Helen, BDS	SGLTCDR(D)(MC(MD)	-		01.07.01	CTCRM
Wingfield, Michael James, BEng	LT(FTC) (Act Lt Cdr)	X	O	16.07.94	MWC PORTSDOWN
Winkle, Sean James, BA	CDR(FTC)	E	TM	30.06.05	SULTAN AIB
Winn, John Paul,	LT(CC)	X	HM2	01.10.00	SCOTT
Winskell, Thomas Robert,	MID(IC)	X		01.11.04	ALBION
Winsor, James, BSc	LT(CC)	X	H2	01.03.00	ALBION
Winstanley, Keith, MBE, pce, hcsc	CAPT(FTC)	X	PWO(N)	31.12.99	ALBION
Winstone, Nigel Patrick,	LT(IC)	E	MESM	25.06.05	SULTAN
Winter, Richard Jason, BEng, CEng, PGDip, MIEE, adp	LT CDR(FTC)	E	WE	01.08.01	FLEET COSP&S
Winter, Timothy McMahon, BEng, MA, CEng, MIMarEST, psc(j)	LT CDR(FTC)	E	ME	01.05.98	DLO BRISTOL
Winterbon, Andrew Richard,	LT(CC)	X	FC	01.05.01	800 NAS (GR7)
Winterton, Paul,	LT(CC)	X	O	01.05.04	820 SQN
Wintle, Geoffrey Lawrence, MSc, MCIT, MILT	CDR(FTC)	S	SM	30.06.03	RNAS CULDROSE
Wise, Graham John, BEng, MSc, CEng, MIEE, psc(j)	CDR(FTC)	E	WE	30.06.02	HQ DCSA
Wise, Simon David, BSc, MDA, CEng, FCMI, MIEE, CDipAF	CDR(FTC)	E	WE	31.12.96	DLO BRISTOL
Wiseman, George Richard,	MAJ(FTC)	-	SO(LE)	01.10.05	HQ 3 CDO BDE RM
Wiseman, Ian Carl, pce, n	LT CDR(FTC)	X	PWO(N)	01.02.03	ENDURANCE
Wiseman, Neil Christopher,	LT(CC)	X	O	16.06.96	750 SQN SEAHAWK
Withers, Daniel Michael,	MID(NE)(IC)	X	P U/T	01.01.06	DARTMOUTH BRNC
Withers, James Warren, BEng, CEng, MIEE	LT CDR(FTC)	E	WE	01.04.96	DLO BRISTOL
Witt, Alister Kevin,	LT(IC) (Act Lt Cdr)	MS		01.09.01	FLEET COSP&S
Witte, Richard Hugh, LLB, n	LT CDR(FTC)	X		01.12.05	GLOUCESTER
Witton, James William, pce	LT CDR(FTC)	X	PWO(U)	01.06.93	LOAN DSTL
Witton, Oliver Edward Nicholas John Charles,	SLT(UCE)(IC)	X		01.09.05	DARTMOUTH BRNC
Witts, Christopher Ian,	CAPT RM(IC)	-		01.09.03	CTCRM
Woad, Jonathan Patrick Rhys, BSc	LT(IC)	X		01.11.01	CORNWALL
Wolfe, David Edward, rcds, pce, pcea, fsc	CAPT(FTC)	X	O	30.06.02	SA MADRID
Wood, Alexander MacDonald, BSc, MB, CHB	SURG LT(SCC)	-		01.08.02	NELSON (PAY)
Wood, Andrew Graeme, BEng, MRAeS	LT(CC) (Act Lt Cdr)	E	AE	01.07.97	DLO WYTON
Wood, Christopher,	SLT(IC)	X		01.01.02	EXETER
Wood, Christopher Richard,	LT CDR(FTC)	X	P	01.01.05	MWS COLLINGWOOD
Wood, Christopher Taylor, BEng	LT(IC)	E	TM	01.01.00	NELSON
Wood, Craig, pce, n	LT CDR(FTC)	X	PWO(A)	01.08.01	RICHMOND
Wood, Gregory, MB, BS	SURG CDR(MCC)	-	GMPP	30.06.04	NELSON (PAY)
Wood, Iain,	SURG SLT(SCC) (Act Surg Lt)	-		01.08.05	DARTMOUTH BRNC
Wood, Iain Leslie, BA	LT(CC)	X	MW	01.01.99	CATTISTOCK
Wood, Joanne Tamar, BA	LT(IC)	X	ATCU/T	01.01.02	RNAS CULDROSE
Wood, John Lindsay, MSc, CEng, FIMarEST, MCGI, psc(j)	CDR(FTC)	E	ME	30.06.01	DPA BRISTOL
Wood, Jonathan Richard, BEng, MIEE	LT(IC)	E	WE	01.09.04	CUMBERLAND
Wood, Joseph Albert,	LT(FTC) (Act Lt Cdr)	X		03.04.98	TEMERAIRE
Wood, Julian,	SLT(IC)	E		01.04.04	SULTAN

Name	Rank	Branch	Spec	Seniority	Where Serving
Wood, Matthew David James, BSc	LT(IC)	E	TM	01.03.05	MWS COLLINGWOOD
Wood, Michael Leslie, BSc, MPhil, pce, n	LT CDR(FTC)	X	PWO(U)	01.12.04	FOST SEA
Wood, Michael William, BSc	LT(IC)	X		01.05.04	CORNWALL
Wood, Nicholas Robert,	LT(FTC)	X	PWO(U)	01.04.01	EXCHANGE AUSTLIA
Wood, Richard Ralph Thellusson, BA	LT(IC)	X	P	01.09.04	RNAS YEOVILTON
Wood, Robert,	CDR(FTC) (Barrister)	S	BAR	30.06.04	NAVSEC
Wood, Simon Andrew Hall, BEng	LT(CC)	X	P	01.05.00	846 SQN
Wood, Uvedale George Singleton, pcea	LT CDR(FTC)	X	P	01.04.99	LOAN OTHER SVCE
Woodard, Jolyon Robert Alban, BA, pcea	LT CDR(FTC)	X	P	01.10.03	CHFHQ
Woodard, Neil Antony, BSc, GCIPD	LT CDR(FTC)	S		01.10.04	UKMARBATSTAFF
Woodbridge, Richard George, BEng	LT CDR(FTC)	E	ME	01.08.04	CUMBERLAND
Woodcock, Simon Jonathan, BSc, CEng, MIMechE, psc(j)	CAPT(FTC)	E	ME	30.06.05	SULTAN
Woodford, Geoffrey Ian, MBE, BEng, CEng, MIEE	CDR(FTC)	E	WESM	30.06.06	FLEET COSP&S
Wooding, Graham Allen, BSc	LT(FTC)	E	WE	19.02.93	DCSA NWD REGION
Wooding, Steven,	LT(IC)	E	AE	01.05.04	MOD (LONDON)
Woodley, Stephen Leonard, BEng, MSc, PhD	LT(IC)	E	MESM	01.09.02	NP BRISTOL
Woodman, Daniel Peter, BEng	LT(IC)	E	ME	01.09.03	FWO PORTS SEA
Woodrow, Kevin, SM	LT CDR(FTC)	X	SM	01.10.03	FLEET COMOPS NWD
Woodruff, Anthony Desmond,	LT CDR(FTC)	X	PWO(U)	01.10.99	MWC PORTSDOWN
Woodruff, Dean Aaron, BEng, MSc	LT CDR(FTC)	E	ME	01.12.99	T45 IPT
Woods, James David, BSc	SLT(IC)	X	P U/T	01.01.05	DARTMOUTH BRNC
Woods, Jeremy Billing, pce, psc(j)	CDR(FTC)	X	AAWO	30.06.04	FLEET COSCAP
Woods, Michael James Peter, BEng	LT(FTC)	E	WESM	01.05.01	FOST FAS SHORE
Woods, Roland Philip, AMIAM, pce	CDR(FTC)	X	PWO(A)	31.12.98	BDS WASHINGTON
Woods, Timothy Christopher, MA, psc(j)	LT CDR(FTC)	E	TMSM	01.02.01	COM MCC NWD
Woodward, Alasdair James, LLB	SLT(IC)	X	P U/T	01.02.05	DARTMOUTH BRNC
Woodward, Darroch John, BA, BSc	LT CDR(FTC)	X	MCD	01.07.95	LOAN OMAN
Wookey, Mark,	LT(CC)	X	O	01.02.96	EXCHANGE BRAZIL
Woolfe, Kevin David,	LT(IC)	E		01.05.02	MERLIN IPT
Woolhead, Andrew Lyndon, BA, pce, n	LT CDR(FTC)	X	PWO(N)	01.10.03	OCEAN
Woolhead, Craig Morton, BA	LT(CC)	X		01.05.00	EXPRESS
Woollcombe-Gosson, David James, pce	LT CDR(FTC)	X	AAWO	01.06.97	MWS COLLINGWOOD
Wooller, Louise Frances Victoria, BA	LT(FTC)	X		01.02.00	ROEBUCK
Wooller, Mark Adrian Hudson, BA	LT CDR(FTC)	S	SM	01.10.01	JSCSC
Woolley, Martin James,	CDR(FTC)	X	MCD	30.06.06	LOAN OMAN
Woollven, Andrew Howard, pce	LT CDR(FTC)	X	PWO(U)	01.08.97	BROCKLESBY
Woollven, Christopher David, BSc	LT(CC)	X	O	01.08.99	815 FLT 206
Woolsey, Kevin Edward Keith,	LT(FTC) (Act Lt Cdr)	X	ATC	16.05.95	JSCSC
Woosey, David Alan, BA	LT(IC)	S		01.09.03	NEPTUNE DLO
Wordsworth, Jonathan David, BSc	LT(IC)	X		01.07.05	DUMBARTON CASTLE
Workman, Rayner John,	LT(IC)	X		01.09.03	ECHO
Worley, Thomas Frank, BA	LT(IC)	X		01.01.03	MWS COLLINGWOOD
Wormald, Robert Edward, MSc, CEng, FIMarEST, psc	CDR(FTC)	E	MESM	31.12.92	MOD (BATH)
Wort, Roland Stephen, BA, BSc	CHAPLAIN	SF		27.07.93	MWS COLLINGWOOD
Worthington, Jonathan Michael Francis, MA, psc(j)	CDR(FTC)	E	TM	30.06.06	JSCSC
Wotherspoon, Steven Robert, psc	LT COL(FTC)	-		30.06.94	NS OBERAMMERGAU
Wotton, Alan Christopher,	LT(IC)	X	P	01.07.04	AACC MID WALLOP
Wotton, Ryan John,	SLT(IC)	X	P	01.01.05	RNAS YEOVILTON
Woznicki, Stanley James,	LT CDR(FTC)	X	AAWO	16.06.88	MWS COLLINGWOOD
Wragg, Gareth Terence, SM(n)	LT(CC)	X	SM	01.01.01	VANGUARD(PORT)
Wragg, Helen Claire,	LT(IC)	S		01.06.03	FOST DPORT SHORE
Wraith, Neil,	MAJ(FTC)	-	LC	01.09.00	JSCSC
Wray, Arthur Douglas,	LT CDR(FTC)	E	WESM	01.10.01	NAVSEC
Wren, Stephen James,	LT(IC)	X		01.07.04	MONTROSE
Wrenn, Michael Reader William, FIIE, MIOSH	LT CDR(FTC)	E	WE	01.10.02	MOD (LONDON)
Wrennall, Eric Paul,	LT(CC)	E	ME	29.04.01	FOST SEA
Wrigglesworth, Stephen Mark,	LT(IC)	X	C	01.07.03	MWS COLLINGWOOD
Wright, Daniel James, LLB, SM	LT(IC)	X	SM	01.12.98	VENGEANCE(STBD)
Wright, David Anthony,	LT(FTC) (Act Lt Cdr)	X	MCD	29.07.94	ILLUSTRIOUS
Wright, David Ian, BEng, MSc, CEng, MIEE	LT CDR(FTC)	E	WE	01.09.04	LOAN DSTL
Wright, Douglas,	LT(IC)	E	AE	01.05.03	824 SQN
Wright, Gabriel Joseph Trevillian, MEng, DPhil	LT(IC)	E	WE	01.11.05	IRON DUKE

Name	Rank	Branch Spec	Seniority	Where Serving
Wright, Geoffrey Neil, MBE, BSc, CEng, MIMAREST .... CDR(FTC) (Act Capt)	E	MESM	30.06.93	DRAKE SFM
Wright, Helen Jane, ...LT(IC)	S		13.08.04	NELSON
Wright, James Andrew Humphrey, BA...SLT(IC)	X		01.01.05	DARTMOUTH BRNC
Wright, James Nicholas, ...SLT(IC)	S		01.05.03	HQ DCSA
Wright, Jeffrey Robert, ...LT(IC)	S	(W)	01.07.04	ECHO
Wright, Jennifer Sarah, BA...LT(IC)	S		01.09.04	CAMPBELTOWN
Wright, Jonathon Stuart, ...SLT(UCE)(IC)	S		01.09.04	DARTMOUTH BRNC
Wright, Martin Glenn, BEng ....SLT(IC)	E	ME U/T	01.01.04	SULTAN
Wright, Neil, MBE ....LT(IC)	E	AE	13.08.04	1 (F) SQN (RN)
Wright, Nigel Seymour, BEng, MSc, CEng, MIMarEST ....LT CDR(FTC)	E	ME	01.02.99	MOD (BATH)
Wright, Stuart Hugh, ... CDR(FTC) (Barrister)	S	BAR	30.06.05	DCPPA
Wright-Jones, Alexandra Elizabeth Megan, ...LT(SC(MD)	Q		29.11.02	NELSON (PAY)
Wrightson, Hugh Mawson, BSc, MA, CEng, MIEE, psc(j) ....CDR(FTC)	E	ME	31.12.97	FLEET COSP&S
Wrigley, Alexander John, MB, BS, BSc ....SURG LT(SCC)	-		03.08.04	CFLT MED(SEA)
Wroblewski, Jefferey Andre, ...LT CDR(FTC)	E	MESM	31.10.01	VICTORIOUS(PORT)
Wuidart-Gray, Spencer Richard, ...LT CDR(CC)	X	PWO(U)	01.03.02	OCEAN
Wunderle, Charles Albert, ...CDR(FTC)	S	(W)	30.06.00	DLO BRISTOL
Wyatt, Christopher, ...LT(FTC)	S	(S)	17.12.93	RNAS CULDROSE
Wyatt, David James, MCMI, pce, NDipM...LT CDR(FTC)	X	H CH	01.11.93	MWS HM TG (D)
Wyatt, Julian Michael, BSc, MDA, CEng, FIMarEST, MIMechE ....CDR(FTC)	E	MESM	30.06.03	FLEET FOTR
Wyatt, Steven Patrick, BSc...CDR(FTC)	E	WESM	31.12.95	DLO BRISTOL
Wykes, Thomas Edward Vernon, BEng, PGDip.......................................LT(IC)	E	MESM	01.01.05	TRENCHANT
Wylie, David, ...LT(IC)	X		02.08.02	RNAS YEOVILTON
Wylie, David Victor, ...CHAPLAIN	CE		01.12.98	40 CDO RM
Wylie, Ian Charles Henfrey, BEng, MBA, MIEE, CEng ....LT CDR(FTC)	E	WESM	01.11.00	ASTUTE
Wylie, Justin Joseph, BEng ....SLT(IC)	E	AE U/T	01.09.04	OCEAN
Wylie, Robert, MB, DipAvMed, Dip FFP, MRCGP, AFOM, CHB..........SURG CDR(FCC)	-	GMPP	01.04.03	RNAS YEOVILTON
Wyness, Caroline Jayne, BEng, n ....LT(FTC)	X		01.10.98	EXAMPLE
Wynn, Iain Andrew, ...SLT(IC)	S		01.01.05	DARTMOUTH BRNC
Wynn, Simon Raymond, PGDip, M ED, MSc....................................LT CDR(FTC)	X	METOC	01.09.97	MOD (LONDON)
Wynn Jones, Iago, BA ....LT(CC)	X	O	01.05.02	750 SQN SEAHAWK
Wyper, James Robert, BSc, SM(n) ....LT CDR(FTC)	X	SM	01.09.00	VIGILANT(PORT)
Wyper, John, ...LT(IC)	E	ME	08.04.05	ARGYLL

Y

Yapp, Roderic, ...2LT(IC)	-		01.08.02	CTCRM LYMPSTONE
Yarham, Nigel Peter, ...LT(IC)	X		01.01.04	MWS HM TG (D)
Yarker, Daniel Lawrence, MBA, pce, NDipM ....LT CDR(FTC) (Act Cdr)	X	AAWO	01.10.97	LN SIERRA LEONE
Yarker, Sam, ...MID(NE)(IC)	X	O U/T	01.01.06	DARTMOUTH BRNC
Yarnall, Nicholas John, MB, BCH, ...SURG LTCDR(FCC) (Act Surg Cdr)	-	(CO/M)	01.08.97	
DObstRCOG, MFOM, MRCGP, AFOM				
Yates, David Martin, ...CHAPLAIN	RC		01.09.98	SULTAN
Yates, Elizabeth Helen, MB, BS...SURG LT(SCC)	-		01.08.01	MDHU PORTSMOUTH
Yates, Lauren Olivia, BA...LT(IC)	S		01.09.03	FLEET COSP&S
Yates, Neal Peter, MBE, pce, pcea, psc ....LT CDR(FTC(A)	X	O	01.06.89	DLO YEO
Yates, Simon Peter, ...SLT(UCE)(IC)	X		01.09.04	DARTMOUTH BRNC
Yates, Stuart Edward, BSc, n ....LT(FTC)	X	PWO(A)	01.05.98	ALBION
Yelland, Christopher Brian, ...LT CDR(FTC)	X	O	01.10.01	702 SQN HERON
Yemm, Matthew Alvin, ...LT(IC)	X		01.02.06	MWS COLLINGWOOD
York, Gideon Rufus James, BEng...LT CDR(FTC)	E	MESM	01.05.04	DLO BRISTOL
Youldon, Louisa Jane, BSc ....LT(CC)	X	HM	01.05.01	SCOTT
Young, Angus, PGDIPAN, pce, n...LT CDR(FTC)	X	PWO(N)	01.06.99	YORK
Young, David Andrew, ...LT(IC)	E	AE	01.07.04	815 SQN HQ
Young, Gavin Lee, pce, psc(j), MA...CDR(FTC)	X	AAWO	30.06.04	MWC SOUTHWICK
Young, John Nicholas, ...LT(FTC)	X	AV	24.07.97	RNAS YEOVILTON
Young, Keith Hunter, ...LT(FTC)	E	ME	23.02.90	DRAKE SFM
Young, Martin Nicholas William, ...MID(NE)(IC)	X	O U/T	01.09.04	DARTMOUTH BRNC
Young, Michael Stephen, MBE, MA, MSc, PhD, FCIPD, ADipC, psc(j)..........CDR(FTC)	E	TM	30.06.06	FLEET HQ WI
Young, Rachel, BA, n ....LT(CC)	X		01.12.94	NAVSEC
Young, Stephen William, ...LT CDR(FTC)	S	SM	01.10.00	NAVSEC
Young, Stuart Sheldon, MSc, CEng, FIMarEST, MIMechE, jsdc...................CDR(FTC)	E	ME	30.06.95	CMT SHRIVENHAM
Youngman, Paul Glyn, ...LT(IC)	E	TM	01.02.04	42 CDO RM

Name	Rank	Branch	Spec	Seniority	Where Serving
Youp, Allan Thomas, BSc, PGCE, PGDip	LT CDR(CC)	E	TM	01.10.04	FWO PORTS SEA
Yuill, Ian Alexander, BSc, CDipAF, adp	CDR(FTC)	E	IS	01.10.96	FLEET ISS

Z

Name	Rank	Branch	Spec	Seniority	Where Serving
Zambellas, George Michael, DSC, BSc, pce, pcea, psc, hcsc	CDRE(FTC)	X	P	29.11.02	COMATG SEA
Ziolo, Jan Mathieson Christopher, BEng, PGDip	LT(IC)	E	MESM	01.01.05	VIGILANT(STBD)
Zipfell, Adam James, BSc	LT(IC)	X	P	01.09.02	AACC MID WALLOP
Zitkus, John James, BEng, MSc	SLT(IC)	E	WE U/T	01.05.04	MWS COLLINGWOOD

RFA OFFICERS

COMMODORE
R.C. THORNTON MDA

COMMODORE (ENGINEERS)
M.D. NORFOLK

Captains

R.H. Allan OBE	T.J. Iles	K.D. Rimell
R. Bennett	M.T. Jarvis	A.T. Roach OBE
D.J. Buck	I.E. Johnson	C.F. Simmons
S.H. Cant	N.A. Jones	J. Stones
R.W. Dorey	S.P. Jones	A.M. Swatridge
P.M. Farmer	D.P. Kehoe	W.G. Tait
C.J. Fell	D.L. Lamb	W.M. Walworth OBE
R.G. Ferris OBE	A.E. McNally	K. Watts
D.I. Gough	J. Murchie	P.S. Whyte MBE
P.T. Hanton	S.J. Norris	R.L. Williams
J.P. Huxley	I.N. Pilling	D.J.M. Worthington

Captain (Engineers)

P.J. Beer	C.L. Forrest	I. Schumacker
D.W. Birkett	R.S. Graham	R. Settle
A.C. Bowditch	A.J. Grant	D.S. Simpson
R.J. Brewer	P. Henney	A.G. Sinclair
C. Brown	R. Kirk	K. Smeaton
M.P. Cole	R.W. Langton	C.S. Smith
J.E. Collins	B.S. Layson	D.B. Smith
R.W. Cranstone	D.J. Moore	R.J. Smith
P.R. Daunton	J. J. Oakey	G.J. Stokes
I.Martin. Doolan-phillip	D.W.G. Phasey	G.T. Turner
I. Dunbar	D. Preston	A.D. Wills
A. Edworthy	E.M. Quigley	
I.W. Finlayson	J.W. Richardson	

SENIORITY LIST

ADMIRALS OF THE FLEET
(This rank is now held in abeyance in peacetime (1996))

Edinburgh, His Royal Highness The Prince Philip, Duke of, KG, KT, OM, GBE, AC, QSO.......15 Jan 53

Pollock, Sir Michael (Patrick), GCB, LVO, DSC, psc..1 Mar 74

Ashmore, Sir Edward (Beckwith), GCB, DSC, IRs, jssc, psc..9 Feb 77

Leach, Sir Henry (Conyers), GCB, DL, jssc, psc ....1 Dec 82

Oswald, Sir (John) Julian (Robertson), GCB, rcds, psc..2 Mar 93

Bathurst, Sir (David) Benjamin, GCB, DL, rcds ....10 Jul 95

ADMIRALS

FORMER CHIEF OF DEFENCE STAFF, FIRST SEA LORD OR VICE CHIEF OF DEFENCE STAFF WHO REMAIN ON THE ACTIVE LIST

Slater, Sir Jock (John Cunningham Kirkwood), GCB, LVO, rcds, pce ....29 Jan 91

Boyce, the Lord, GCB, OBE, DL, rcds, psc ....25 May 95

Abbott, Sir Peter (Charles) GBE, KCB, MA, rcds, pce.. 3 Oct 95

Essenhigh, Sir Nigel (Richard), GCB, rcds, pce, psc, hcsc ....11 Sep 98

West, Sir Alan (William John), GCB, DSC, rcds, pce, psc, hcsc...30 Nov 00

ADMIRALS

Band, Sir Jonathon, KCB, ADC, BA, jsdc, pce, hcsc... 02 Aug 02
(CHIEF OF NAVAL STAFF AND FIRST SEA LORD FEB 06)

Stanhope, Sir Mark, KCB, OBE, MA, MNI, rcds, pce, pce(sm), psc, hcsc ....10 Jul 04
(DEPUTY SACT JUL 04)

Burnell-Nugent, Sir James (Michael), KCB, CBE, MA, jsdc, pce, pce(sm)............................15 Nov 05
(COMMANDER-IN-CHIEF FLEET NOV 05)

VICE ADMIRALS

Dunt, Peter Arthur, CB, rcds .... 30 Apr 02
(CHIEF EXECUTIVE DEFENCE ESTATE AGENCY APR 02)

McClement, Sir Timothy (Pentreath), KCB, OBE, jsdc, pce, pce(sm), hcsc .... 07 Jun 04
(DEPUTY COMMANDER-IN-CHIEF FLEET/CHIEF NAVAL WARFARE OFFICER
(AS HEAD OF SPECIALISATION) JUN 04)

McLean, Rory (Alistair Ian), CB, OBE, pce, hcsc .... 16 Sep 04
(DEPUTY CHIEF OF DEFENCE STAFF (HEALTH) SEP 04)

Johns, Adrian (James), CBE, ADC, BSc, pce, pcea, psc, hcsc .... 25 Oct 05
(SECOND SEA LORD AND COMMANDER-IN-CHIEF NAVAL HOME COMMAND OCT 05,
REAR ADMIRAL FLEET AIR ARM (AS HEAD OF FIGHTING ARM) MAY 03)

Style, Charles Rodney, CBE, MA, rcds, pce, hcsc .... 10 Jan 06
(DEP CHIEF OF DEFENCE STAFF (COMMITMENTS) JAN 06)

Dymock, Anthony (Knox), CB, BA, pce, psc .... 30 Mar 06
(UNITED KINGDOM MILITARY REPRESENTATIVE TO NATO AND EUROPEAN UNION MAR 06)

REAR ADMIRALS

Ward, Rees Graham John, CB, MA, MSc, CEng, FIEE, rcds, jsdc, gw, hcsc .... 27 Apr 99
(CHIEF EXECUTIVE DCSA JAN 02)

Guild, Nigel Charles Forbes, CB, BA, PhD, FIEE, MIMA, jsdc .... 06 Jan 00
(DIRECTOR GENERAL CAPABILITY (CS) DEC 03)

Boissier, Robin Paul, MA, MSc, pce, pce(sm), psc .... 26 Aug 02
(DIRECTOR GENERAL LOGISTICS (FLEET) SEP 04)

Snelson, David George, CB, FCMI, MNI, pce, psc, hcsc .... 05 Nov 02
(CHIEF OF STAFF (CAPABILITY) TO COMMANDER-IN-CHIEF FLEET,
REAR ADMIRAL SURFACE SHIPS (AS HEAD OF FIGHTING ARM) JUN 04)

Spires, Trevor Allan, BSc, CDipAF, nadc .... 21 Oct 03
(CHIEF EXECUTIVE OCT 03)

Wilcocks, Philip Lawrence, DSC, BSc, AMRINA, pce, psc(a) .... 19 Apr 04
(FLAG OFFICER SCOTLAND, NORTHERN ENGLAND AND NORTHERN IRELAND,
FLAG OFFICER RESERVES APR 06)

Ainsley, Roger Stewart, MA, jsdc, pce, hcsc .... 27 Apr 04
(FLAG OFFICER SEA TRAINING APR 04)

Soar, Trevor Alan, OBE, pce, pce(sm) .... 18 May 04
(CM(PA) MAY 04)

Lambert, Paul, BSc, MPhil, DipFM, rcds, pce, pce(sm), hcsc .... 29 Jun 04
(COMMANDER (OPERATIONS) TO COMMANDER-IN-CHIEF FLEET, REAR ADMIRAL SUBMARINES
(AS HEAD OF FIGHTING ARM) JUN 04)

Laurence, Timothy James Hamilton, MVO, BSc, Hf, pce, psc(j)..05 Jul 04
(ASST CHIEF OF DEF. STAFF(PROGRAMMES) JUL 04)

Cooke, David John, MBE, pce, pce(sm), hcsc..20 Jul 04
(DEPUTY COMMANDER STRIKE FORCE NATO)

Wilkinson, Peter John, BA, FCIPD, pce, pce(sm)..27 Jul 04
(DEFENCE SERVICES SECRETARY JUL 05)

Clayton, Christopher Hugh Trevor, pce, psc, hcsc..30 Aug 04
(ASSISTANT DIRECTOR INTELLIGENCE DIVISION AUG 04)

Raby, Nigel John Francis, OBE, MSc, jsdc...02 Sep 04
(STLB TEAM LEADER/TEAM LEADER NAVAL ESTATE REVIEW)

Borley, Kim John, MA, CEng, MIEE, rcds, jsdc..07 Sep 04
(FLAG OFFICER TRAINING)

Mark, Robert Alan, MSc, FRIN, MNI, MInsD...06 Jan 05
(SENIOR NAVAL MEMBER RCDS DIRECTING STAFF)

Parry, Christopher John, CBE, MA, rcds, pce, pcea, psc..25 Jan 05
(DIRECTOR GENERAL DEVELOPMENT, CONCEPTS & DOCTRINE)

Latham, Neil Degge, MSc, CEng, Hf, MIMechE, jsdc..28 Feb 05
(COMMANDANT OF THE COLLEGE OF MANAGEMENT AND TECHNOLOGY)

Kimmons, Michael, BA, rcds...15 Mar 05
(CHIEF OF STAFF (PERSONNEL & SUPPORT) TO COMMANDER-IN-CHIEF FLEET/CHIEF NAVAL
LOGISTICS OFFICER (AS HEAD OF SPECIALISATION) APR 06)

Mathews, Andrew David Hugh, MSc, CEng, MIMechE, rcds, psc......................................24 Mar 05
(DIRECTOR GENERAL NUCLEAR MAR 05/CONTROLLER OF THE NAVY APR 06)

Ibbotson, Richard Jeffery, DSC, MSc, CGIA, pce ....23 Jun 05
(NAVAL SECRETARY JUN 05)

Massey, Alan Michael, CBE, BA, PGCE, rcds, pce, psc..05 Jul 05
(ACNS JUL 05)

Leaman, Richard Derek, OBE, pce, psc(j), hcsc...06 Sep 05
(COS TO CDR ALLIED NAVAL FORCES S.EUROPE SEP 05)

Morisetti, Neil, BSc, jsdc, pce, hcsc...18 Nov 05
(COMMANDER UNITED KINGDOM MARITIME FORCES NOV 05)

Henley, Simon Michael, MBE, BSc, CEng, MRAeS, jsdc ....30 Jan 06
(TECHNICAL DIRECTOR JUN 06)

COMMODORES

X	Johnstone-Burt, C.A.	10 Jan
E	Tibbitt, I.P.G.	15 Apr
E	Alabaster, M.B.	30 Apr
X	Snow, C.A.	14 May
MS	Reed, F.	12 Jun
X	Avery, M.B.	24 Jun
X	Richards, A.D.	24 Jun
E	Hussain, A.M.	09 Jul
X	Cooling, R.G.	28 Aug
X	Jermy, S.C.	10 Sep
X	Zambellas, G.M.	29 Nov
X	Kirby, S.R.	06 Dec

2003

E	Thwaites, G.J.	01 Apr
X	Walpole, P.K.	07 Jul
X	Bennett, A.R.C.	15 Jul
E	Jackman, R.W.	26 Aug
X	Robinson, P.H.	30 Sep
E	Van Beek, L.	07 Oct
X	Adair, A.A.S.	04 Nov
X	Moncrieff, I.	10 Nov
E	Graves, M.E.L.	11 Nov

X	Montgomery, C.P.R.	25 Nov
E	Rymer, A.R.	11 Dec

2004

E	McFarlane, A.L.	05 Jan
E	Miklinski, A.S.	02 Mar
X	Anderson, M.	30 Mar
E	Kidd, J.C.	19 Apr
E	Love, R.T.	04 May
W	Stait, C.J.	22 Jun
X	Harris, T.R.	24 Jun
E	Baldwin, S.F.	01 Jul
E	Lister, S.R.	06 Jul
X	Docherty, P.T.	16 Jul
X	Harland, N.J.G.	13 Sep
X	Corder, I.F.	09 Nov
X	Charlier, S.B.	16 Nov
X	Jones, P.A.	13 Dec
X	Hudson, P.D.	31 Dec

2005

S	Fraser, R.W.	11 Jan
E	Patrick, J.	08 Feb

X	Cunningham, T.A.	22 Feb
E	Whyntie, A.	01 Apr
E	Keegan, W.J.	26 Apr
X	Williams, S.T.	03 May
E	Hockley, C.J.	01 Jun
X	Cleary, S.P.	09 Jul
S	Whalley, S.D.	01 Nov
E	Christie, C.S.	08 Nov
S	Steel, D.G.	21 Nov
X	Palmer, C.L.	24 Nov
X	Mathias, P.B.	13 Dec
E	Jess, I.M.	15 Dec

2006

X	Scorer, S.J.	09 Mar
E	Lloyd, S.J.	27 Mar
E	Brunton, S.B.	03 Apr
E	Johns, T.	06 Apr
X	Williams, B.N.B.	27 Apr
X	Cameron, A.J.B.	20 Jun

CAPTAINS

1996

X	Covington, W.M.	31 Dec

1997

E	Potter, M.J.	30 Jun
X	Gass, C.J.	30 Jun
X	Rix, A.J.	30 Jun
E	Wills, J.R.	31 Dec
E	Green, J.A.	31 Dec
X	Butler, N.A.M.	31 Dec

1998

X	Martin, S.C.	30 Jun
E	Little, R.M.	31 Dec
X	Ramm, S.C.	31 Dec
X	Davies, P.N.M.	31 Dec
S	Martin, T.F.W.	31 Dec

1999

X	Knowles, J.M.	30 Jun
S	Rayner, B.N.	30 Jun
E	Hyldon, C.J.	30 Jun
X	Croke, A.	30 Jun
E	Rees, J.B.M.	31 Dec
E	Jarvis, D.J.	31 Dec
X	Mervik, C.F.	31 Dec
X	Hart, J.	31 Dec
X	Sloan, M.U.	31 Dec
X	Gower, J.H.J.	31 Dec
X	Winstanley, K.	31 Dec

2000

E	Williams, N.L.	30 Jun
S	Quinn, P.A.	30 Jun
E	Leeming, R.J.	30 Jun
X	Mansergh, R.J.	30 Jun
E	Wilkinson, R.M.	30 Jun
S	MacDonald, G.E.	30 Jun
X	Peach, G.L.	30 Jun
X	Lambert, N.R.	30 Jun
X	Halliday, D.A.	30 Jun
X	Potts, D.L.	30 Jun
E	Watts, R.F.	31 Dec
X	Mansergh, M.P.	31 Dec
X	Karsten, T.M.	31 Dec
E	Penny, A.D.	31 Dec
X	Windsor, M.	31 Dec
X	Fraser, T.P.	31 Dec

2001

X	Dedman, N.J.K.	30 Jun
X	Steel, P.ST.C.	30 Jun
X	Hawkins, R.C.	30 Jun
E	Mason, R.W.	30 Jun
E	Langbridge, D.C.	30 Jun
E	Neave, C.B.	30 Jun
X	Stanford, J.H.	30 Jun
X	Best, R.R.	30 Jun
X	Chick, S.J.	30 Jun

2002

S	Ross, A.A.	30 Jun
X	Turner, I.	30 Jun

E	Tate, A.J.	30 Jun
X	Dickens, D.J.R.	30 Jun
X	Collins, P.N.	30 Jun
E	Hughes, R.I.	30 Jun
E	Stratton, J.D.	30 Jun
X	Tarr, M.D.	30 Jun
S	Albon, R.	30 Jun
E	Sealey, N.P.	30 Jun
E	Gosden, S.R.	30 Jun
X	Brown, R.A.M.	30 Jun
X	Fraser, E.	30 Jun
X	Westwood, M.W.	30 Jun
E	Burrell, P.M.	30 Jun
X	Stanley, N.P.	30 Jun
X	Westbrook, J.S.	30 Jun
E	Holloway, J.T.	30 Jun
X	Wolfe, D.E.	30 Jun
X	Cochrane, M.C.N.	30 Jun
E	Dearden, S.R.	30 Jun
X	Parr, M.J.	30 Jun
X	Bell, A.S.	30 Jun
E	Parker, H.H.	30 Jun
MS	Bootland, E.G.	24 Jul

2003

X	Wilson, S.G.	30 Jun
X	Bramley, S.	30 Jun
X	Durston, D.H.	30 Jun
X	Welborn, C.G.	30 Jun
X	Upright, S.W.	30 Jun
E	Bishop, P.R.	30 Jun
X	Hennessey, T.P.D.	30 Jun
E	Dannatt, T.M.	30 Jun

CAPTAINS

X	Bevan, S.	30 Jun
X	Edgell, J.N.	30 Jun
S	Marsh, D.J.	30 Jun
E	Costello, G.T.	30 Jun
S	Chelton, S.R.L.	30 Jun
X	Finney, M.E.	30 Jun
E	McElwaine, R.I.	30 Jun
X	Wellesley, R.C.R.	30 Jun
E	Evans, D.J.	30 Jun
E	Rusbridger, R.C.	30 Jun
X	Wallace, M.R.B.	30 Jun
E	Thompson, R.J.	30 Jun
E	Burton, D.S.	30 Jun
X	Harding, R.G.	30 Jun
X	Lowe, T.M.	30 Jun
E	Beverstock, M.A.	30 Jun
E	King, E.M.	30 Jun
X	Moores, J.K.	30 Jun
X	Morse, J.A.	30 Jun
X	Williams, S.P.	30 Jun
S	Atherton, M.J.	30 Jun
X	Johnstone, C.C.C.	30 Jun
X	Ancona, S.J.	30 Jun

2004

S	Davis, B.J.	01 Apr
X	Chambers, N.M.C.	30 Jun
E	King, A.M.	30 Jun
S	Hosker, T.J.	30 Jun
E	Steel, C.M.H.	30 Jun
E	Allwood, C.	30 Jun
X	Humphrys, J.A.	30 Jun
E	Usborne, C.M.	30 Jun
X	Wallace, G.W.A.	30 Jun
E	Molyneaux, D.G.	30 Jun
E	Rowell, G.E.	30 Jun
X	Archibald, B.R.	30 Jun
X	James, D.R.	30 Jun
X	Davies, A.R.	30 Jun
X	Evans, M.C.	30 Jun
E	Holberry, A.P.	30 Jun
X	Richards, C.M.	30 Jun
X	Beaumont, I.H.	30 Jun

X	Harrap, N.R.E.	30 Jun
X	Davis-Marks, M.L.	30 Jun
X	Murphie, J.D.D.	30 Jun
E	Fulford, J.P.H.	30 Jun
S	King, C.E.W.	30 Jun
X	Hamp, C.J.	30 Jun
X	Thicknesse, P.J.	30 Jun
X	Stewart, R.G.	30 Jun
E	Holdsworth, H.W.	30 Jun
X	Tarrant, R.K.	30 Jun
E	Slawson, J.M.	30 Jun
E	Beckett, K.A.	30 Jun
E	Bennett, P.M.	30 Jun
X	Darlington, M.R.	30 Jun
MS	Holyer, R.J.	06 Jul
MS	Jackson, S.K.	31 Aug

2005

X	Greenlees, I.W.	30 Jun
E	Coulthard, J.K.	30 Jun
S	Nelson, D.T.	30 Jun
X	Fletcher, N.E.	30 Jun
E	Kenward, P.D.	30 Jun
E	Jagger, P.R.A.	30 Jun
E	Forsey, C.R.	30 Jun
X	Pegg, R.M.	30 Jun
X	Keble, K.W.L.	30 Jun
S	Bullock, M.P.	30 Jun
E	Watts, G.M.	30 Jun
S	Smith, M.	30 Jun
X	Warren, B.H.	30 Jun
E	Taylor, J.J.	30 Jun
X	Blunden, J.J.F.	30 Jun
E	Lofthouse, I.	30 Jun
X	Handley, J.M.	30 Jun
E	Wilson, K.P.	30 Jun
E	Thistlethwaite, M.H.	30 Jun
X	Buckley, P.J.A.	30 Jun
E	Farrage, M.E.	30 Jun
E	Hay, J.D.	30 Jun
E	Newell, J.M.	30 Jun
S	Cunningham, P.	30 Jun
X	Garrett, S.W.	30 Jun

X	Hawthorne, M.J.	30 Jun
X	Lemkes, P.D.	30 Jun
X	Kenny, S.J.	30 Jun
X	Kings, S.J.N.	30 Jun
X	Sutton, G.B.	30 Jun
E	Toy, M.J.	30 Jun
X	Sanguinetti, H.R.	30 Jun
X	Clink, J.R.H.	30 Jun
X	Kingwell, J.M.L.	30 Jun
E	Woodcock, S.J.	30 Jun

2006

E	Ratcliffe, J.P.	30 Jun
X	Brocklebank, G.P.	30 Jun
X	Arthur, I.D.	30 Jun
E	Pendle, M.E.J.	30 Jun
S	Storrs-Fox, R.N.	30 Jun
E	Powell, D.C.	30 Jun
X	Corrigan, N.R.	30 Jun
S	Finlayson, A.G.	30 Jun
X	Richmond, I.J.M.	30 Jun
E	Spalding, R.E.H.	30 Jun
E	Derrick, G.G.J.	30 Jun
X	Morgan, P.T.	30 Jun
X	Baum, S.R.	30 Jun
E	O'Neill, P.J.	30 Jun
E	Braham, S.W.	30 Jun
X	Nail, V.A.	30 Jun
X	MacKay, G.A.	30 Jun
X	McBarnet, T.F.	30 Jun
X	Lloyd, P.R.	30 Jun
X	Cree, M.C.	30 Jun
E	Stokes, R.	30 Jun
X	Adams, A.J.	30 Jun
X	McAlpine, P.A.	30 Jun
S	Brown, N.L.	30 Jun
S	Gardner, C.R.S.	30 Jun
E	French, S.A.	30 Jun
E	Wareham, M.P.	30 Jun
E	Hammond, P.A.	30 Jun
X	Key, B.J.	30 Jun

COMMANDERS

1989

X	Scoles, J.C.	31 Dec
X	Williams, T.N.E.	31 Dec
E	Harrison, R.A.	31 Dec

1990

X	Turner, S.M.	30 Jun
X	Simmonds, R.M.	31 Dec
X	Crabtree, I.M.	31 Dec
E	Firth, S.K.	31 Dec
X	Vaughan, D.M.	31 Dec

1991

X	Ferguson, J.N.	30 Jun

X	MacDonald, D.H.L.	30 Jun
E	Hume, C.B.	31 Dec
X	Williams, N.D.B.	31 Dec
X	Stoneman, T.J.	31 Dec
X	Johnson, G.P.	31 Dec

1992

E	Stanley, P.	30 Jun
X	Gregan, D.C.	30 Jun
X	Lankester, P.	30 Jun
X	Herman, T.R.	30 Jun
X	Thoburn, R.	30 Jun
X	Pepper, M.R.	31 Dec
E	Usborne, A.C.	31 Dec
E	Ayers, R.P.B.	31 Dec

X	Marshall, R.A.	31 Dec
S	Peilow, B.F.	31 Dec
X	Spalton, G.M.S.	31 Dec
E	Arnold, B.W.H.	31 Dec
X	Bartholomew, I.M.	31 Dec
X	Gibson, I.A.	31 Dec
E	Wormald, R.E.	31 Dec

1993

S	Williams, R.E.	30 Jun
X	Grant, A.K.	30 Jun
X	Bell-Davies, R.W.	30 Jun
X	Chambers, W.J.	30 Jun
X	Snow, M.C.P.	30 Jun
X	Holihead, P.W.	30 Jun

COMMANDERS

E	Wright, G.N.	30 Jun
S	Cowdrey, M.C.	30 Jun
X	Harvey, K.	30 Jun
E	Cox, P.W.S.	30 Jun
X	Bateman, S.J.F.	30 Jun
X	Goodwin, D.R.	31 Dec
X	Thomas, S.A.	31 Dec
E	Stenhouse, N.J.	31 Dec
E	Lunn, J.F.C.	31 Dec
X	Trevithick, A.R.	31 Dec
X	Bosshardt, R.G.	31 Dec
X	Churchill, T.C.	31 Dec
E	Parker, I.R.	31 Dec
X	Riley, M.J.	31 Dec

1994

E	Fisher, M.A.L.	30 Jun
E	Fox, K.A.	30 Jun
E	Whitehorn, I.J.	30 Jun
X	Cutt, J.J.D.	30 Jun
X	Reid, M.	30 Jun
X	Humphreys, J.I.	30 Jun
X	Brown, M.K.	20 Sep
E	Wakeling, J.L.	31 Dec
X	Hosking, D.B.	31 Dec
X	Murgatroyd, A.C.	31 Dec
E	Faulconbridge, D.	31 Dec
E	Horne, T.K.	31 Dec
X	Stallion, I.M.	31 Dec
X	Clark, K.I.M.	31 Dec
E	Brough, G.A.	31 Dec
E	White, A.R.	31 Dec
S	Airey, S.E.	31 Dec

1995

X	Carter, K.	30 Jun
E	Podger, K.G.R.	30 Jun
X	Phillips, D.G.	30 Jun
X	McNair, E.A.	30 Jun
X	Wilson, C.D.	30 Jun
X	Shrives, M.P.	30 Jun
X	Thomas, R.P.	30 Jun
X	Gasson, N.S.C.	30 Jun
E	Price, F.E.F.	30 Jun
E	Young, S.S.	30 Jun
X	Lander, M.C.	30 Jun
X	Clarke, C.M.L.	30 Jun
X	Bull, A.J.	01 Oct
X	Holmes, R.	31 Dec
E	Smith, M.A.	31 Dec
E	Spicer, C.G.	31 Dec
S	Ireland, R.C.	31 Dec
E	Sewry, M.R.	31 Dec
X	Stonor, P.F.A.	31 Dec
X	Seatherton, E.F.K.	31 Dec
S	Keefe, P.C.	31 Dec
E	Anderson, R.G.	31 Dec
E	Wyatt, S.P.	31 Dec

1996

X	Nicholson, S.C.L.	30 Jun
E	Nixon, P.W.	30 Jun
X	Betteridge, J.T.	30 Jun
X	Langhorn, N.	30 Jun
X	Ayres, C.P.	30 Jun
E	Lovett, M.J.	30 Jun
X	Funnell, N.C.	30 Jun
E	Price, J.P.	30 Jun
E	Bridger, D.W.	30 Jun
X	Sibbit, N.T.	30 Jun
X	Furness, S.B.	30 Jun
E	Haley, T.J.	30 Jun
X	Rycroft, A.E.	30 Jun
E	Gourlay, J.S.	30 Jun
X	Perkins, M.J.	30 Jun
X	Farrington, R.	30 Jun
E	Erskine, P.A.	30 Jun
E	Yuill, I.A.	01 Oct
X	Lee, D.J.	31 Dec
E	Palmer, J.E.	31 Dec
X	Sullivan, C.	31 Dec
X	Terry, J.M.	31 Dec
X	Lambourn, P.N.	31 Dec
S	Church, A.D.	31 Dec
X	Edney, A.R.	31 Dec
X	Pearey, M.S.	31 Dec
X	Hughes, N.J.	31 Dec
S	Tinsley, G.N.	31 Dec
X	Lilley, D.J.	31 Dec
X	Hugo, I.D.	31 Dec
E	Jenkin, A.M.H.	31 Dec
X	Abraham, P.	31 Dec
E	Wise, S.D.	31 Dec

1997

X	Horne, T.G.	30 Jun
X	Robinson, A.	30 Jun
X	Balston, D.C.W.	30 Jun
E	Whitaker, M.J.	30 Jun
E	Graham, G.R.	30 Jun
E	Page, D.M.	30 Jun
X	Spence, N.A.	30 Jun
X	Scarth, W.	30 Jun
X	Pickles, I.S.	30 Jun
X	Barker, R.D.J.	30 Jun
X	Brand, S.M.	30 Jun
S	Crook, A.S.	30 Jun
X	Garratt, M.D.	30 Jun
X	Smithson, P.E.	30 Jun
E	Waterman, J.H.	31 Dec
S	Charlton, C.R.A.M.	31 Dec
E	Greenwood, S.	31 Dec
E	Wrightson, H.M.	31 Dec
E	Straughan, H.	31 Dec
E	Peck, I.J.	31 Dec
X	Brooksbank, R.J.	31 Dec
X	Taylor, K.A.	31 Dec
S	White, S.N.	31 Dec
E	Sunderland, J.D.	31 Dec
E	Pickthall, D.N.	31 Dec

X	Ameye, C.R.	31 Dec
X	Pettitt, G.W.	31 Dec

1998

X	Pope, C.M.	24 Jun
X	Snook, R.E.	30 Jun
E	Enticknap, K.	30 Jun
E	Clark, D.K.	30 Jun
X	Jardine, G.A.	30 Jun
X	Lade, C.J.	30 Jun
E	McLennan, R.G.	30 Jun
X	Steeds, S.M.	30 Jun
X	Jackman, A.W.	30 Jun
X	Gaunt, N.R.	30 Jun
E	Russell, S.J.	30 Jun
E	Main, E.S.	30 Jun
X	Ewence, M.W.	30 Jun
E	MacDonald, A.I.	30 Jun
E	Taylor, S.A.	30 Jun
X	Cassar, A.P.F.	30 Jun
S	Pattinson, I.H.	30 Jun
E	Quaye, D.T.G.	30 Jun
X	Robertson, K.F.	30 Jun
X	McDonnell, P.W.	30 Jun
E	Wiles, S.J.	30 Jun
X	Reynolds, T.E.	30 Jun
E	Shipperley, I.	30 Jun
X	Ingram, R.G.	30 Jun
X	Alcock, C.	30 Jun
E	Elford, D.G.	30 Jun
S	Litchfield, J.F.	30 Jun
E	Gulley, T.J.	30 Jun
E	Danbury, I.G.	30 Jun
E	Hobbs, R.	01 Oct
X	Trundle, N.R.E.	31 Dec
E	Davies, T.G.	31 Dec
S	Spiller, M.F.	31 Dec
X	Newton, D.J.	31 Dec
X	White, M.W.	31 Dec
X	Percharde, M.R.	31 Dec
E	Mason, N.H.	31 Dec
E	Curnow, M.D.	31 Dec
E	Gray, A.J.	31 Dec
X	Woods, R.P.	31 Dec
X	Clark, A.W.C.	31 Dec
E	Stanley-Whyte, B.J.	31 Dec
S	Beard, G.T.C.	31 Dec
E	Fry, J.M.S.	31 Dec
X	Williams, M.H.	31 Dec
S	Redstone, C.	31 Dec
X	Hatch, G.W.H.	31 Dec
X	Evans, K.N.M.	31 Dec
E	Green, A.R.	31 Dec
X	McKendrick, A.M.	31 Dec
E	Chidley, T.J.	31 Dec
X	Muir, K.	31 Dec
E	Green, S.N.	31 Dec
X	McCartain, M.B.W.	31 Dec
X	Shield, S.J.	31 Dec
X	Cook, P.R.	31 Dec
S	Skidmore, C.M.	31 Dec
X	Green, T.J.	31 Dec

COMMANDERS

E	O'Reilly, T.M.	31 Dec	X	Reid, C.I.	31 Dec	X	Malcolm, S.R.	31 Dec
X	McQuaker, S.R.	31 Dec	S	Murdoch, S.J.	31 Dec	E	Stidston, I.J.	31 Dec
E	Morritt, D.C.	31 Dec	X	Race, N.J.	31 Dec	X	Connolly, C.J.	31 Dec
S	Jameson, A.C.	31 Dec	E	Hodgson, T.C.	31 Dec	E	Parsons, C.G.	31 Dec
E	Hayes, J.V.B.	31 Dec	X	Brown, H.S.	31 Dec	E	Deaney, M.N.	31 Dec
			X	Hopper, S.O.	31 Dec	S	Hughes, G.L.	31 Dec

1999

			E	Morris, A.J.	31 Dec	E	Marmont, K.L.	31 Dec
E	Merriman, P.O.	30 Jun	X	McMichael-Phillips, S.J.	31 Dec	E	Abbey, M.K.	31 Dec
E	Hadfield, D.	30 Jun	E	Stubbings, P.R.	31 Dec	X	Thomas, W.G.	31 Dec
X	Drewett, R.E.	30 Jun	E	Harrison, M.S.	31 Dec	X	Blowers, M.D.	31 Dec
X	Haley, C.W.	30 Jun	E	Johnson, J.C.	31 Dec	E	Risley, J.	31 Dec
E	Ellis, R.W.	30 Jun	X	Sullivan, A.G.	31 Dec	X	Powell, R.L.	31 Dec
E	Fear, R.K.	30 Jun	X	Porter, S.P.	31 Dec	E	Cargen, M.R.	31 Dec
X	Alexander, R.S.	30 Jun	X	Healy, A.J.	31 Dec	E	Parsons, B.R.	31 Dec
E	Ranson, C.D.	30 Jun	X	Walliker, M.J.D.	31 Dec	S	Bond, N.D.	31 Dec
E	Darwent, A.	30 Jun	S	Rance, M.G.W.	31 Dec	X	Durkin, M.T.G.	31 Dec
E	Pett, J.G.	30 Jun	X	Bone, D.N.	31 Dec	E	Martyn, A.W.	31 Dec
X	Clarke, N.J.	30 Jun	E	Tate, S.J.	31 Dec	X	Davies, J.H.	31 Dec
E	Haworth, J.	30 Jun	X	McGhie, I.A.	31 Dec	S	Walker, C.L.	31 Dec
E	Bisson, I.J.P.	30 Jun				X	Williams, A.P.	31 Dec
E	Vandome, A.M.	30 Jun		**2000**		E	Glennie, A.M.G.	31 Dec
X	Spencer, E.A.	30 Jun				S	Buchan-Steele, M.A.	31 Dec
X	Knibbs, M.	30 Jun	X	Daniels, S.A.	30 Jun	S	Merchant, I.C.	31 Dec
X	Jervis, N.D.	30 Jun	E	Blake, G.E.	30 Jun	S	Rigby, J.C.	31 Dec
S	Thomas, F.S.	30 Jun	E	McKenzie, D.	30 Jun	E	Corry, S.M.	31 Dec
X	Carden, P.D.	30 Jun	E	Moreland, M.J.	30 Jun	E	Jones, H.A.	31 Dec
X	Northwood, G.R.	30 Jun	X	Snowball, S.J.	30 Jun	X	Reed, A.W.	31 Dec
E	Ramshaw, G.W.L	30 Jun	X	Stewart, A.C.	30 Jun	X	Williamson, T.J.L.	31 Dec
E	Simmons, N.D.	30 Jun	X	Tilley, D.S.J.	30 Jun	X	Denham, N.J.	31 Dec
X	Ireland, A.R.	30 Jun	X	Newton, G.A.	30 Jun	E	Heley, J.M.	31 Dec
X	Horn, P.B.	30 Jun	X	Sephton, J.R.	30 Jun	X	Ashcroft, A.C.	31 Dec
S	Morton, N.P.B.	30 Jun	X	Cunningham, R.A.	30 Jun	X	Milburn, P.K.	31 Dec
X	Robinson, C.E.T.	30 Jun	E	Basson, A.P.	30 Jun	X	Fulton, C.P.	31 Dec
X	Moore, C.I.	30 Jun	X	Broadley, K.J.	30 Jun	E	Jessop, P.E.	31 Dec
E	Lewis, J.K.	30 Jun	E	Atkinson, S.R.	30 Jun	E	Moore, M.N.	31 Dec
E	Barton, P.G.	30 Jun	E	Argent-Hall, D.	30 Jun	E	Frankham, P.J.	31 Dec
X	Titterton, P.J.	30 Jun	E	Short, G.C.	30 Jun	X	Cooper, M.A.	31 Dec
E	Daws, R.P.A.	30 Jun	S	Tothill, N.M.	30 Jun	E	Clough, C.R.	31 Dec
X	Allen, R.M.	30 Jun	S	Fergusson, H.J.	30 Jun	X	Fancy, R.	31 Dec
X	Pollock, D.J.	30 Jun	E	Harvey, C.A.	30 Jun	X	Blount, K.E.	31 Dec
X	Weale, J.S.	30 Jun	X	Hayes, S.J.	30 Jun	X	Dutton, D.	31 Dec
E	Roberts, N.S.	30 Jun	E	Vanderpump, D.J.	30 Jun			
S	Lavery, J.P.	30 Jun	S	Wunderle, C.A.	30 Jun		**2001**	
X	Millward, J.P.	31 Dec	X	Entwistle, S.C.	30 Jun			
E	Tindall-Jones, L.D.	31 Dec	X	Spence, A.B.	30 Jun	E	Parker, M.N.	30 Jun
X	Buckland, R.J.F.	31 Dec	X	Carter, I.P.	30 Jun	X	Faulkner, J.J.	30 Jun
X	Ovens, J.J.	31 Dec	X	Stockings, T.M.	30 Jun	X	Corbett, W.R.	30 Jun
E	Treanor, M.A.	31 Dec	X	Chivers, P.A.	30 Jun	E	Gordon, D.	30 Jun
E	Maltby, M.R.J.	31 Dec	E	Walker, N.J.	30 Jun	X	Knight, D.A.	30 Jun
S	Isaac, P.	31 Dec	E	Walker, M.	30 Jun	E	Martin, M.T.	30 Jun
E	Crossley, C.C.	31 Dec	X	Heley, D.N.	30 Jun	X	Sheehan, M.A.	30 Jun
S	Tulley, J.R.	31 Dec	X	Pearson, S.J.	30 Jun	E	Grieve, S.H.	30 Jun
E	Greene, M.J.	31 Dec	X	Allibon, M.C.	30 Jun	S	O'Grady, M.J.	30 Jun
X	Chalmers, D.P.	31 Dec	S	Bath, M.A.W.	30 Jun	E	Raybould, A.G.	30 Jun
E	Mason, A.H.	31 Dec	E	Williams, M.J.	30 Jun	X	Payne, R.C.	30 Jun
X	Tuppen, R.M.	31 Dec	E	Little, G.T.	30 Jun	X	Greenwood, P.	30 Jun
X	Johnson, A.S.	31 Dec	E	Talbot, R.P.	30 Jun	E	Grantham, S.M.	30 Jun
E	Plant, J.N.M.	31 Dec	E	Dyer, M.D.J.	30 Jun	X	Jones, M.C.	30 Jun
X	Doyle, G.L.	31 Dec	E	Hine, N.W.	30 Jun	E	Martin, M.P.	30 Jun
E	Thompson, S.J.	31 Dec	S	Rees, J.H.	01 Jul	X	Mitchell, H.G.M.	30 Jun
X	Harris, A.I.	31 Dec	X	McKie, A.	31 Dec	E	Charlesworth, G.K.	30 Jun
S	Gray, R.S.	31 Dec	E	Kerchey, S.J.V.	31 Dec	X	Doolan, M.	30 Jun
			E	Welburn, R.S.	31 Dec	E	Wood, J.L.	30 Jun

COMMANDERS

S	Crozier, S.R.M.	30 Jun	E	Float, R.A.	30 Jun	E	Dustan, A.J.	30 Jun
E	Borland, S.A.	30 Jun	E	Waddington, J.	30 Jun	X	Hall, R.L.	30 Jun
E	Podmore, A.	30 Jun	E	Dabell, G.L.	30 Jun	X	Aiken, S.R.	30 Jun
E	Haines, P.R.	30 Jun	E	Grindel, D.J.S.	30 Jun	E	Knight, P.R.	30 Jun
X	Pritchard, G.S.	30 Jun	X	Thompson, B.D.	30 Jun	X	Smith, M.R.K.	30 Jun
S	Shaw, S.M.	30 Jun	E	Haywood, S.A.	30 Jun	E	Stewart, J.N.	30 Jun
X	Foreman, J.L.R.	30 Jun	X	Evans, W.Q.F.	30 Jun	X	Hinch, N.E.	30 Jun
X	Burton, A.J.	30 Jun	E	Magan, M.J.C.	30 Jun	S	Flynn, M.T.	30 Jun
X	Nolan, A.L.	30 Jun	X	Turner, D.B.	30 Jun	X	Cunningham, J.G.	30 Jun
E	St Aubyn, J.D.E.	30 Jun	E	French, J.T.	30 Jun	E	Adams, P.	30 Jun
X	Wallace, A.	30 Jun	E	Streeten, C.M.	30 Jun	E	Blackman, N.T.	30 Jun
E	Casson, P.R.	30 Jun	E	Rhodes, A.G.	30 Jun	X	Brown, W.C.	30 Jun
X	Barker, D.C.K.	30 Jun	E	Thompson, A.	30 Jun	E	Salter, J.A.	30 Jun
E	Phenna, A.	30 Jun	S	Renwick, J.	30 Jun	E	Kirkup, J.P.	30 Jun
X	Warwick, P.D.	30 Jun	E	Clifford, T.J.	30 Jun	X	Robertson, M.G.	30 Jun
MS	Coulton, I.C.	30 Jun	X	Haywood, G.	30 Jun	X	Fields, D.G.	30 Jun
X	Hardern, S.P.	30 Jun	E	Dorricott, A.J.	30 Jun	E	Cropley, A.	30 Jun
E	Prescott, S.	30 Jun	S	Lines, J.M.	30 Jun	E	Sumner, M.D.	30 Jun
E	Kershaw, S.	30 Jun	X	Entwisle, W.N.	30 Jun	S	David, S.E.J.	30 Jun
S	Noyes, D.J.	30 Jun	X	Tindal, N.H.C.	30 Jun	E	Clark, I.D.	30 Jun
E	Corderoy, J.R.	30 Jun	X	Burke, P.D.	30 Jun	E	Saxby, C.J.	30 Jun
X	Schwarz, P.M.G.	30 Jun	E	Scott, N.L.J.	30 Jun	X	Hutchison, G.B.	30 Jun
E	Dawson, S.L.	30 Jun	E	Wise, G.J.	30 Jun	X	Stangroom, A.	30 Jun
S	Faulks, D.J.	30 Jun	X	Wallis, A.J.	30 Jun	E	Smith, K.A.	30 Jun
E	MacKay, C.R.	30 Jun	E	Jarvis, L.R.	30 Jun	X	Amphlett, N.G.	30 Jun
E	Dumbell, P.	30 Jun	E	Childs, D.G.	30 Jun	E	Harding, D.M.	30 Jun
E	Birchall, S.J.	30 Jun	S	Hall, E.C.	30 Jun	X	Hawkins, M.A.J.	30 Jun
X	Layland, S.	30 Jun	X	Thomas, R.K.	30 Jun	X	Webb, A.J.	30 Jun
X	Cheesman, C.J.	30 Jun	X	Reindorp, D.P.	30 Jun	E	Green, D.P.S.	30 Jun
X	Petheram, M.J.	30 Jun	E	Adams, A.M.	30 Jun	X	Gurmin, S.J.A.	30 Jun
E	Tarr, B.S.	30 Jun	X	Swannick, D.J.	30 Jun	X	Johnston, T.A.	30 Jun
E	Naden, A.C.K.	30 Jun	MS	Murphy, A.	30 Jun	X	Nisbet, J.H.T.	30 Jun
E	Warden, J.M.	30 Jun	X	Hodkinson, C.B.	30 Jun	E	Roberts, T.J.	30 Jun
E	King, R.W.	30 Jun	E	Robinson, M.P.	30 Jun	E	Kennedy, I.J.A.	30 Jun
E	Sykes, M.	30 Jun	X	Radakin, A.D.	30 Jun	E	Beardall, M.J.D.	30 Jun
X	Hardy, L.C.	30 Jun	E	Thompson, R.C.	30 Jun	E	Jenkins, G.W.	30 Jun
X	Hodgkins, J.M.	30 Jun	E	Course, A.J.	30 Jun	E	Burlingham, B.L.	30 Jun
X	Roberts, I.T.	30 Jun	E	Annett, I.G.	30 Jun	X	Aspden, A.M.	30 Jun
S	Laws, P.E.A.	30 Jun	X	Robinson, G.A.	30 Jun	X	Waddington, A.K.	30 Jun
E	Jones, R.W.	30 Jun	X	Wainhouse, M.J.	30 Jun	X	Pentreath, J.P.	30 Jun
E	Ryan, D.G.	30 Jun	X	Bewick, D.J.	30 Jun	X	Sherriff, D.A.	30 Jun
X	Mair, B.	30 Jun	S	Lustman, A.M.	30 Jun	E	Munns, A.R.	30 Jun
E	Crago, P.T.	30 Jun	X	Blackmore, M.S.	30 Jun	X	Dyke, C.L.	30 Jun
X	Fitter, I.S.T.	30 Jun	X	Gilmour, C.J.M.	30 Jun	X	Salisbury, D.P.	30 Jun
X	Lacey, S.P.	30 Jun	S	Anderson, H.A.	30 Jun	E	Fieldsend, M.A.	30 Jun
X	Gray, A.J.	30 Jun	X	Thomas, R.A.A.	30 Jun	E	Gilbert, P.D.	30 Jun
X	Davies, C.J.	30 Jun	S	Aplin, A.T.	30 Jun	X	Straw, A.N.	30 Jun
X	Kelbie, E.	30 Jun				X	Chrishop, T.I.	30 Jun
E	Moffatt, N.R.	30 Jun		**2003**		X	Mahony, D.G.	30 Jun
X	Turnbull, S.J.L.	30 Jun	X	Murray, S.J.	30 Jun	X	Corbett, A.S.	30 Jun
S	Watts, A.D.	30 Jun	X	Lightfoot, C.D.	30 Jun	X	Coles, A.L.	30 Jun
X	Hare, N.J.	30 Jun	E	Wyatt, J.M.	30 Jun	X	Meakin, B.R.	30 Jun
S	Randall, D.F.	30 Jun	X	Corner, G.C.	30 Jun	MS	Lloyd, C.J.	30 Jun
X	Barrand, S.M.	30 Jun	E	Cochrane, M.D.	30 Jun	X	Newland, M.I.	30 Jun
X	Cluett-Green, S.M.	30 Jun	X	Leaning, M.V.	30 Jun	S	Aitken, K.M.	30 Jun
X	Gordon, S.R.	30 Jun	X	Stanton, D.V.	30 Jun	X	Briers, M.P.	30 Jun
E	Shaw, K.N.G.	30 Jun	X	Shawcross, P.K.	30 Jun	E	Cran, B.C.	30 Jun
X	Gething, J.B.	30 Jun	E	Peacock, S.	30 Jun	S	Hollins, R.P.	30 Jun
E	Archer, G.W.	30 Jun	X	Randall, R.D.	30 Jun	S	Kyte, A.J.	30 Jun
X	Falk, B.H.G.	30 Jun	X	Suddes, L.A.	30 Jun	S	Wintle, G.L.	30 Jun
X	Turnbull, G.D.	30 Jun	E	Upton, I.D.	30 Jun	S	Hill, R.K.J.	30 Jun
X	Skeer, M.R.	30 Jun	E	Claxton, M.G.	30 Jun	X	Harvey, R.M.M.J.	30 Jun

COMMANDERS

E Dailey, P.G.J. 30 Jun	X Dible, J.H. 30 Jun	X Haycock, T.P. 30 Jun
X Holt, S. 30 Jun	X Lister, M. 30 Jun	X Abernethy, L.J.F. 30 Jun
E Kissane, R.E.T. 30 Jun	E Bartlett, D.S.G. 30 Jun	E Dowell, P.H.N. 30 Jun
X Scott, J.A. 30 Jun	X Ireland, P.C. 30 Jun	X Swift, R.D. 30 Jun
E Knight, P.J. 30 Jun	S Murrison, R.A. 30 Jun	X Dane, R.M.H. 30 Jun
E Rowse, M.L. 30 Jun	E Bull, C.M.S. 30 Jun	X George, A.P. 30 Jun
E Graham, D.W.S. 30 Jun	S Edge, J.H. 30 Jun	E Boyd, N. 30 Jun
X White, J.A.P. 30 Jun	E Titcomb, A.C. 30 Jun	X Thomson, D. 30 Jun
S Burningham, M.R. 30 Jun	X Breckenridge, I.G. 30 Jun	E Grenfell-Shaw, M.C. 30 Jun
S Hood, K.C. 30 Jun	X Woods, J.B. 30 Jun	E McInnes, J.G.K. 30 Jun
S Trump, N.W. 30 Jun	E MacDonald, J.R. 30 Jun	E Pollock, M.P. 30 Jun
E Petitt, S.R. 30 Jun	E Mather, G.P. 30 Jun	X Jones, G.R. 30 Jun
X Titcomb, M.R. 30 Jun	X Kyd, J.P. 30 Jun	X Williams, D.S. 30 Jun
E Roberts, S.D. 30 Jun	E Reynolds, A.G. 30 Jun	X Lawler, J.A. 30 Jun
X Axon, D.B. 30 Jun	X Vitali, R.C. 30 Jun	E Rippingale, S.N. 30 Jun
E Pomeroy, M.A. 30 Jun	X Bourne, C.M. 30 Jun	X Cunningham, D.A. 30 Jun
X Betton, A. 30 Jun	E Cree, A.M. 30 Jun	S Walmsley, E.A. 30 Jun
	X Hibberd, N.J. 30 Jun	S Hayle, J.K. 30 Jun
2004	X Rolph, A.P.M. 30 Jun	E Winkle, S.J. 30 Jun
	X Allen, S.M. 30 Jun	E Harrop, I. 30 Jun
X Rich, J.G. 30 Jun	X Halton, P.V. 30 Jun	E Merritt, J.J. 30 Jun
X Dawson, P.J. 30 Jun	E Coulson, P. 30 Jun	X Maher, M.P. 30 Jun
X Riches, I.C. 30 Jun	X Young, G.L. 30 Jun	E Short, J.J. 30 Jun
E Gibson, A. 30 Jun	E Hill, G.F. 30 Jun	E Prior, G.M. 30 Jun
E Ball, M.P. 30 Jun	X Dunn, R.P. 30 Jun	E Buckle, I.L. 30 Jun
X Moss, P. 30 Jun	X Hatcher, R.S. 30 Jun	X Green, P.J. 30 Jun
E Townshend, J.J. 30 Jun	S Wood, R. 30 Jun	E Geary, T.W. 30 Jun
X Bridger, R.J. 30 Jun	X Dainton, S. 30 Jun	E Foster, G.J. 30 Jun
X Jones, P. 30 Jun	X Biggs, W.P.L. 30 Jun	E Cooper, K.P. 30 Jun
S Giles, A.R. 30 Jun	E Ferris, D.P.S. 30 Jun	X Bowen, N.T. 30 Jun
S Mellor, B.J. 30 Jun	X Burns, D.I. 30 Jun	E Stirzaker, M. 30 Jun
E Giles, D.W. 30 Jun	X Merewether, H.A.H. 30 Jun	E Jackson, A.S. 30 Jun
E Tarr, R.N.V. 30 Jun	X Long, A.D. 30 Jun	X Honnoraty, M.R. 30 Jun
E Shirley, W.P. 30 Jun	X Graham, I.E. 30 Jun	S Chapell, A. 30 Jun
X Howell, S.B. 30 Jun	E Band, J.W. 30 Jun	E Mallinson, R. 30 Jun
E Denovan, P.A. 30 Jun	X Haslam, P.J. 30 Jun	X Swain, A.V. 30 Jun
X Hunter, N.M. 30 Jun	E Tritschler, E.L. 30 Jun	X Barker, P.T. 30 Jun
X Poole, J.L. 30 Jun	MS McAuslin, T.M. 30 Jun	X Bowbrick, R.C. 30 Jun
E Saunders, T.M. 30 Jun	X Thomas, J.E. 30 Jun	X Bower, N.S. 30 Jun
X Davison, A.P. 30 Jun	S Fisher, C.R.A. 30 Jun	E Martin, B.A. 30 Jun
X Swarbrick, R.J. 30 Jun	X Groves, C.K. 30 Jun	S Mearns, C.M. 30 Jun
X Hart, M.A. 30 Jun	E Lison, A.C. 30 Jun	X Robertson, D.C. 30 Jun
X Sutcliffe, J. 30 Jun	X Sparkes, P.J. 30 Jun	S Wright, S.H. 30 Jun
S Shaw, P.J. 30 Jun	X Morley, J.D. 30 Jun	X Spiller, V.J. 30 Jun
X Lochrane, A.E.R. 30 Jun	MS Durning, W.M. 30 Jun	E McHale, K. 30 Jun
S Willis, A.J. 30 Jun	E Methven, P. 30 Jun	E White, R.F. 30 Jun
S Carter, S.N. 30 Jun	X Warrender, W.J. 30 Jun	E Matthews, D.W. 30 Jun
E Mace, S.B. 30 Jun	X Connell, M.J. 30 Jun	S Parry, A.K.I. 30 Jun
S Notley, L.P. 30 Jun	E Halliwell, D.C. 30 Jun	E Russell, P.R. 30 Jun
E Toft, M.D. 30 Jun	X Macleod, J.N. 30 Jun	E Helliwell, M.A. 30 Jun
X Kilby, S.E. 30 Jun	X Chatwin, N.J. 30 Jun	X Anstey, R.J. 30 Jun
E Hill, P.J. 30 Jun	X Finnemore, R.A. 30 Jun	E Shutts, D. 30 Jun
X Bellfield, R.J.A. 30 Jun	X Price, T.W. 30 Jun	S Walsh, M.A. 30 Jun
E Stace, I.S. 30 Jun	X Smith, S.L. 30 Jun	X Hurrell, P.R. 30 Jun
X Abernethy, J.R.G. 30 Jun	X Fox, R.G. 30 Jun	X Cryar, T.M.C. 30 Jun
E Harrison, P.G. 30 Jun	X Langley, E.S. 30 Jun	X Cartwright, D. 30 Jun
E O'Brien, P.M.C. 30 Jun	E McTear, K. 30 Jun	E Manson, T.E. 30 Jun
X Salmon, M.A. 30 Jun	E Murdoch, A.W. 30 Jun	E Forer, D.A. 30 Jun
E Lovegrove, R.A. 30 Jun	E Smith, G.K. 30 Jun	S Oliphant, W. 30 Jun
E Rodgers, S. 30 Jun	E Janaway, P. 30 Jun	X Ward, S.I. 30 Jun
X Thorburn, A. 30 Jun	X Deller, M.G. 30 Jun	X Price, D.W. 30 Jun
S Philpott, N.E. 30 Jun	E Duncan, I.S. 30 Jun	X Huntington, S.P. 30 Jun
E Higgins, G.N. 30 Jun		

COMMANDERS

S	Clark, M.T.	30 Jun	X	Carretta, M.V.	30 Jun	X	Hancock, A.P.	30 Jun
X	Olive, P.N.	30 Jun	X	Collins, D.A.	30 Jun	X	Goodsell, C.D.	30 Jun
E	Davey, G.S.	30 Jun	S	Smith, C.J.	30 Jun	X	Moss, R.A.	30 Jun
S	Clark, S.M.	30 Jun	X	Lindsay, I.G.	30 Jun	S	Turner, J.S.H.	30 Jun
X	Orchard, A.P.	30 Jun	E	Worthington, J.M.F.	30 Jun	E	Scott, M.	30 Jun
E	Osmond, J.B.	30 Jun	X	Masters, J.C.	30 Jun	S	Rees, J.P.	30 Jun
X	Harris, K.J.	30 Jun	E	Scott, J.B.	30 Jun	X	Allen, R.	30 Jun
X	Duffy, H.	30 Jun	E	Woodford, G.I.	30 Jun	X	Brown, P.A.E.	30 Jun
S	Goldthorpe, M.	30 Jun	E	Young, M.S.	30 Jun	X	Churcher, J.E.	30 Jun
X	Verney, P.S.	30 Jun	E	Coles, C.J.	30 Jun	E	Punton, I.M.	30 Jun
X	Beard, H.D.	30 Jun	X	Munro-Lott, P.R.J.	30 Jun	X	Hayde, P.J.	30 Jun
X	Millen, I.S.	30 Jun	X	Slocombe, C.A.	30 Jun	X	Howard, D.G.	30 Jun
X	Watt, A.J.L.	30 Jun	E	Lias, C.D.	30 Jun	X	Horne, A.	30 Jun
S	Cole, A.C.	30 Jun	X	Seymour, K.W.	30 Jun	S	Ackland, H.K.	30 Jun
E	Cameron, M.J.	30 Jun	S	McGarel, D.F.	30 Jun	E	Towell, P.J.	30 Jun
X	Burns, A.P.	30 Jun	X	Davies, M.B.	30 Jun	S	Talbott, A.H.	30 Jun
X	Guy, T.J.	30 Jun	X	Drysdale, S.R.	30 Jun	X	Washer, N.B.J.	30 Jun
X	Perks, J.LE.S.	30 Jun	X	Chandler, N.J.	30 Jun	E	Higham, J.G.	30 Jun
X	Henry, T.M.	30 Jun	X	Morris, R.J.	30 Jun	E	Kelly, J.A.	30 Jun
X	Jordan, A.A.	30 Jun	E	Carrick, R.J.	30 Jun	E	O'Brien, K.J.	30 Jun
X	Paterson, M.P.	30 Jun	E	King, N.W.	30 Jun	S	Pomeroy, P.M.	30 Jun
			S	Evans, E.M.	30 Jun	X	Dominy, D.J.D.	30 Jun
	2006		X	Hutchinson, O.J.P.	30 Jun	E	Long, A.M.	30 Jun
			E	Morris, S.T.	30 Jun	X	Gray, J.A.	30 Jun
E	Eastaugh, A.C.	30 Jun	X	Fleming, K.P.	30 Jun	E	Gregory, A.S.	30 Jun
E	Perry, R.	30 Jun	E	Hellyn, D.R.	30 Jun	E	Ewen, A.P.	30 Jun
X	Roper, M.	30 Jun	S	Gibson, A.D.	30 Jun	E	Marshall, P.	30 Jun
X	Harvey, P.A.	30 Jun	S	Towler, A.	30 Jun	S	Waterhouse, P.	30 Jun
X	Dunn, N.G.	30 Jun	X	Peacock, T.J.	30 Jun	X	Utley, M.K.	30 Jun
X	Woolley, M.J.	30 Jun	X	Romney, P.D.	30 Jun	X	Dunn, P.E.	30 Jun
E	Sneyd, E.P.B.	30 Jun	E	Hemsworth, K.J.	30 Jun	MS	Phillips, I.M.	30 Jun
X	Acland, D.D.	30 Jun	E	MacGillivray, I.	30 Jun	X	Roberts, P.S.	30 Jun
X	Elvin, A.J.	30 Jun	X	Albon, M.	30 Jun	MS	Dell, I.M.	30 Jun
E	Blount, D.R.	30 Jun	X	Hawkins, J.S.	30 Jun			
X	Stuttard, M.C.	30 Jun	X	May, N.P.	30 Jun			
X	Thompson, N.J.	30 Jun	E	McCue, D.	30 Jun			
E	Gibbs, N.D.	30 Jun	X	Hughes, G.G.H.	30 Jun			
E	Juckes, M.A.	30 Jun	E	Hall, B.J.	30 Jun			
X	Evans, M.J.	30 Jun	E	Vickers, J.	30 Jun			
X	Mathieson, K.R.	30 Jun	E	Guy, M.A.	30 Jun			

LIEUTENANT COMMANDERS

1982

E	Helby, P.F.H.	16 Jul

1984

X	Sinclair, A.B.	01 Feb
X	Thornton, M.C.	08 Feb
E	Smith, A.C.	16 Mar
X	Fraser, D.K.	01 Jul
E	Lemon, R.G.A.	01 Sep

1985

X	Archdale, P.M.	16 Mar
X	Stone, C.R.M.	01 May
E	Pilsworth, D.S.	01 Jun
X	Wilson, C.G.T.	01 Aug
S	Craven, J.A.G.	01 Sep

1987

X	Chandler, S.A.	01 Jan
E	Fiander, P.J.	01 Feb
X	Taylor, N.F.	16 Feb
X	Jenks, A.W.J.	16 Apr
X	MacNaughton, F.G.	01 May
X	Martin, N.D.	01 Jun
E	Lord, A.S.	01 Sep
X	Crudgington, P.	01 Sep
E	Newton, M.R.	22 Sep
X	Goddard, D.J.S.	01 Oct
X	Gaskin, S.E.	01 Nov
X	Holmes, G.	01 Dec
E	Trotter, S.	01 Dec

1988

S	Billington, N.S.	01 Feb

E	Edwards, A.D.P.	01 Feb
X	Sharpe, G.J.	01 Feb
X	Pamphilon, M.J.	01 Mar
E	Honey, J.P.	01 Mar
E	O'Brien, P.C.	23 Apr
X	Johnson, B.	01 May
X	Speller, N.S.F.	01 May
E	Nurse, M.T.	01 Jun
X	Woznicki, S.J.	16 Jun
X	Davis, M.P.	01 Jul
X	Abbey, M.P.	01 Oct
E	Dinham, A.C.	01 Oct
X	Chambers, T.G.	01 Oct
X	Smith, K.M.	16 Nov
E	Quine, N.J.	01 Dec
E	Tweed, C.J.	01 Feb
X	Gibbs, P.N.C.	01 Feb
E	Denison, A.R.V.T.	01 Feb

LIEUTENANT COMMANDERS

X	O'Riordan, M.P.	01 Apr
X	Pollitt, D.N.A.	01 Apr
X	Baudains, T.J.	01 Apr
S	Ramsey, J.S.	16 Apr
E	Cooper, P.F.	21 Apr
X	Newman, P.H.	01 May
E	Carver, A.G.	01 May
X	Kent, M.D.	01 May
E	Davey, P.J.	01 Jun
X	Yates, N.P.	01 Jun
S	Almond, D.E.M.	01 Jul
E	Jackson, S.H.	01 Jul
X	Palmer, P.A.	01 Jul
E	Faulkner, R.I.	01 Aug
X	Watson, R.J.	01 Aug
S	Lewis, G.D.	01 Sep
X	Carr, D.L.	01 Oct
E	Williams, R.C.	01 Oct
E	Mant, J.N.	01 Oct
X	Grimley, D.M.J.	01 Nov

1990

X	Wade, N.C.	01 Jan
X	Knight, A.W.	01 Feb
X	Little, C.S.A.	01 Feb
X	Beats, K.A.	16 Feb
X	Leaney, M.J.	01 Mar
X	Kerr, W.M.M.	09 Mar
X	Currie, D.W.	01 Apr
X	Britton, N.J.	01 Apr
E	Fowler, P.J.S.	01 Apr
X	Griffiths, D.T.	01 Apr
E	Boraston, P.J.	01 Apr
X	Chapple, C.P.	01 May
X	Barker, N.J.	01 May
X	Chapman, N.J.	01 May
S	Cropper, M.A.K.	16 May
X	Howarth, D.W.	01 Jun
X	Clegg, M.L.	01 Jun
E	Howard, K.A.	01 Jul
E	Plant, I.R.	01 Jul
E	Pringle, A.	01 Jul
X	Davies, C.S.	01 Sep
X	Murphy, N.	01 Sep
X	Burgess, S.	01 Oct
X	Saunders, J.N.	01 Oct
X	Slade, C.	01 Oct
E	Squire, P.A.	01 Oct
X	Bell, R.P.W.	01 Oct
X	Chichester, M.A.R.	01 Oct
X	Straughan, C.J.	01 Dec
X	Evans, G.R.	01 Dec
E	Maw, M.J.	01 Dec
E	Walton, J.C.	01 Dec

1991

S	Pike, M.S.	01 Mar
X	Eedle, R.J.	01 Mar
X	Crowther, K.W.	29 Mar
X	Henderson, T.M.P.	01 Apr
X	Dobson, R.A.	01 Apr

X	Dunlop, P.F.	01 Apr
X	Roberts, D.H.W.	01 Apr
X	Kelly, R.	03 Apr
X	Naismith, D.H.	01 May
E	Trewhella, G.G.	01 May
X	MacDonald, G.D.	01 May
E	Quick, N.H.	01 May
E	Stott, J.A.	26 May
E	Gibson, D.T.	01 Jun
E	Gomm, K.	01 Jun
E	James, C.	01 Jun
E	Stewart, R.W.	01 Jul
X	Smith, N.P.	01 Jul
E	Canty, N.R.	01 Sep
X	Lawson, S.J.	01 Sep
S	Lloyd, D.P.J.	01 Sep
X	Donaldson, S.B.	01 Sep
X	Clark, A.N.	01 Sep
E	Shaw, I.B.	15 Sep
X	Hawkins, R.H.	01 Oct
X	Carrington-Wood, C.G.	01 Oct
X	Graham, D.E.	01 Oct
X	Bernau, J.C.	01 Nov
X	Metcalfe, A.P.W.	01 Dec
X	McHale, G.J.	01 Dec

1992

E	Masters, R.H.	01 Jan
X	Morse, A.C.	01 Jan
X	Drylie, A.J.	01 Feb
X	Potts, K.M.	01 Feb
X	Trathen, N.C.	01 Feb
E	White, P.A.	16 Feb
E	Mundin, A.J.	01 Apr
X	Jenkin, J.R.S.L.	01 May
X	Deighton, D.S.	01 May
E	Kennedy, N.H.	01 May
X	Roberts, D.A.	01 May
X	Giles, K.D.L.	01 May
E	Bone, C.J.	01 May
X	Bromige, T.R.J.	19 May
X	Williams, D.I.	29 May
E	Burdett, R.W.	01 Jun
S	Murphy, J.	01 Jun
X	Morris, P.J.	10 Jun
S	Barnes-Yallowley, J.J.H.	16 Jul
E	Sennitt, J.W.	01 Aug
E	West, M.W.	05 Aug
E	John, G.D.	01 Sep
E	King, P.C.	01 Sep
X	Mardon, K.F.	02 Sep
X	Thomas, K.I.	01 Oct
X	Shepherd, P.R.	01 Oct
W	Price, T.L.	01 Oct
X	Nelson, D.L.	01 Oct
E	Toon, J.R.	01 Oct
X	Maude, C.P.	01 Oct
E	Shepherd, A.	01 Oct
X	Howorth, K.	01 Dec

1993

X	Bilson, J.M.F.	01 Jan
S	Teasdale, R.M.	16 Jan
X	Walker, N.L.	01 Feb
X	Chesterman, G.J.	01 Feb
X	Fortescue, R.C.	01 Mar
S	Chilman, P.W.H.	01 Mar
X	Hall, A.P.	01 Mar
E	Loring, A.	01 Mar
S	Lister, S.R.	01 Apr
X	Price, D.J.	01 Apr
E	Tulloch, F.M.	01 Apr
E	Fogg, D.S.	01 Apr
X	Dodds, R.S.	01 May
X	Smith, R.W.R.	01 May
E	Sutton, G.D.	01 Jun
X	Collier, A.S.	01 Jun
X	Witton, J.W.	01 Jun
E	Mullin, P.N.	01 Jul
X	Bennett, G.L.N.	01 Jul
X	Russell, T.	01 Jul
X	French, K.L.	09 Jul
S	Tyler, P.L.	10 Jul
E	Burnip, J.M.	01 Aug
S	Wiltcher, R.A.	01 Aug
X	Green, D.P.	13 Aug
X	Godfrey, K.R.	01 Sep
X	Landrock, G.J.	01 Sep
E	Udensi, E.A.A.A.	01 Sep
E	Anderson, F.B.	01 Oct
X	Chartres, D.I.	01 Oct
X	Thornton, P.J.	01 Oct
X	Doherty, K.	01 Oct
X	Mills, T.C.	01 Oct
X	Lawrence, S.P.	01 Oct
E	Franks, P.D.	01 Oct
X	Stacey, H.A.	01 Oct
E	Hamilton, R.A.	01 Oct
X	Robertson, D.M.	01 Oct
X	Bowker, G.N.	01 Oct
X	Bird, D.E.	01 Oct
W	Silver, C.K.	01 Oct
S	McKnight, N.W.	01 Oct
X	Watts, A.P.	01 Oct
S	Burt, P.R.	01 Oct
X	James, C.W.	27 Oct
X	Taylor, S.M.	01 Nov
X	Wyatt, D.J.	01 Nov
X	Gladwell, T.J.	01 Dec

1994

X	McGrenary, A.	01 Jan
X	Neve, P.C.	11 Feb
X	Saxby, K.A.	24 Feb
X	Newall, J.A.	01 Mar
X	Moorey, C.G.	01 Mar
E	Cattroll, I.M.	01 Mar
X	Meredith, N.	01 Apr
X	Crispin, T.A.B.	01 Apr
X	Eaton, P.G.	01 Jun
E	Bolam, A.G.	01 Jun

LIEUTENANT COMMANDERS

X	Andrews, P.N.	01 Jun	E	Reynolds, T.P.	30 Apr	X	Hill, M.R.	22 Jun
X	Lunn, A.C.	01 Jun	X	Birley, J.H.	01 May	E	Kempsell, I.D.	26 Jun
X	Hardacre, P.V.	01 Jun	E	Mills, A.	01 May	X	Taylor, B.D.	01 Jul
X	Towler, P.J.B.	01 Jun	X	Marshall, R.G.C.	01 May	X	McDonough, A.G.	01 Jul
X	Horsley, A.M.R.	01 Jul	X	Goldsmith, S.V.W.	01 May	X	Simpson, M.J.	01 Jul
X	Houghton, P.J.	01 Jul	X	Schnadhorst, J.C.	01 May	X	Tetlow, H.S.G.	01 Jul
S	Smerdon, C.D.E.	01 Jul	S	Willis, M.S.	02 May	X	McCall, I.R.	01 Jul
E	Westwood, M.R.T.	01 Jul	E	Hewitt, A.	01 Jun	X	Pooley, S.W.	01 Jul
E	Griffiths, A.J.	26 Jul	E	Brown, P.S.J.	01 Jun	E	Rimmer, H.E.	22 Jul
X	Horner, P.A.	01 Aug	X	Mannion, R.V.	01 Jun	E	Hope, K.	01 Sep
X	Denholm, I.G.	13 Aug	X	Woodward, D.J.	01 Jul	X	Benton, A.M.	01 Sep
X	Glass, J.E.	01 Sep	X	Cornish, M.C.	01 Jul	E	Geddis, R.D.	01 Sep
X	Robin, C.C.E.	01 Sep	X	Foster, D.G.S.	01 Jul	X	Brady, S.E.	01 Sep
X	Fleming, S.A.	30 Sep	E	Smith, M.R.	14 Jul	X	Bark, J.S.	01 Sep
X	Hands, A.P.	01 Oct	E	Rawlings, D.P.	01 Aug	X	Corbett, G.J.	01 Oct
E	Alison, L.A.	01 Oct	X	Greenaway, N.M.	01 Aug	X	Hibbert, M.C.	01 Oct
X	Monger, P.D.	01 Oct	E	Collins, P.R.	01 Sep	X	Creech, R.D.	01 Oct
X	Scott-Dickins, C.A.	01 Oct	X	Burke, M.C.	01 Sep	X	Jefferson, P.M.	01 Oct
X	Taylor, L.	01 Oct	X	Hill, R.A.	01 Sep	E	Johns, S.A.B.	01 Oct
X	Sewed, M.A.	01 Oct	X	Fitzsimmons, M.B.	01 Sep	X	Sykes, R.A.	01 Oct
X	Walker, M.C.	01 Oct	X	Martin, R.G.	01 Sep	X	Hoper, P.R.	01 Oct
X	Dowdell, R.E.J.	01 Oct	E	Murphy, P.W.	01 Sep	X	Biggs, D.M.	01 Oct
E	Franks, D.I.	01 Oct	X	Evans, A.W.	01 Oct	X	Webb, C.M.	01 Oct
E	Naden, J.R.	01 Oct	X	Moffatt, R.	01 Oct	X	Wilkinson, P.M.	01 Oct
X	Burrows, M.J.	01 Oct	X	Dean, W.M.H.	01 Oct	E	Ashton Jones, G.	01 Oct
E	Sugden, M.R.	01 Oct	X	Daniels, I.J.R.	01 Oct	X	Armstrong, N.P.B.	01 Oct
X	Savage, S.	01 Oct	X	Carter, R.I.	01 Oct	W	Whetton, J.B.D.	01 Oct
X	Lee, J.C.	01 Oct	X	Smith, K.J.	01 Oct	E	Clarke, R.	01 Oct
X	Elliman, S.M.	01 Oct	X	Callister, D.R.	01 Oct	E	Bracher, H.	01 Oct
E	Snow, P.F.	01 Oct	X	Pipkin, S.C.	01 Oct	X	Hudson, P.T.	01 Oct
X	Hamilton, G.R.	01 Oct	X	Brundle, P.R.	01 Oct	S	Olliver, A.J.	01 Oct
X	Disney, P.W.	01 Oct	E	Nelson, A.	01 Oct	X	Leitch, I.R.	01 Oct
E	De Jonghe, P.T.	01 Oct	X	Daniell, C.J.	01 Oct	X	Saynor, R.M.	01 Oct
X	Francis, J.	01 Oct	X	Fincher, K.J.	01 Oct	E	Galvin, D.	01 Oct
E	Howard, N.	31 Oct	X	Bate, D.I.G.	01 Oct	E	Mockford, J.A.	01 Oct
X	Gunn, W.J.S.	01 Nov	E	Roberts, E.W.	01 Oct	E	Fraser, W.C.	01 Oct
X	Clark, K.C.	01 Nov	X	Welch, A.	13 Oct	E	Marson, G.M.	14 Oct
X	Hurry, A.P.	01 Nov	E	Lipscomb, P.	01 Nov	E	Watson, P.G.C.	25 Oct
E	Bull, G.C.	01 Nov	X	Vickery, T.K.	01 Nov	E	Burwin, H.L.	01 Nov
E	Harding, G.A.	01 Dec	S	Porrett, J.A.	14 Nov	S	Toomey, N.J.	01 Nov
X	Hills, A.A.	01 Dec	E	Stephenson, D.	22 Nov	X	Gale, S.P.	01 Nov
			X	Boddington, J.D.L.	16 Dec	E	Wilson, C.J.	01 Dec
			X	Meeds, K.	16 Dec	S	Blackwell, R.E.	01 Dec
			X	Bath, E.G.	27 Dec	X	Barnbrook, J.C.	16 Dec

1995

E	Campbell, R.D.H.	01 Feb
X	Ovenden, N.S.P.	01 Feb
X	Hunt, J.S.P.	05 Feb
X	Lewis, T.J.	05 Feb
X	Baldwin, C.M.	01 Mar
E	Dathan, T.J.	01 Mar
X	Pillar, C.D.	01 Mar
X	Firth, N.R.	01 Mar
X	Jones, M.	01 Mar
E	Gillham, P.R.	02 Mar
X	Law, J.	27 Mar
E	Gray, D.K.	01 Apr
E	Munro, K.	01 Apr
X	Egeland-Jensen, F.A.	01 Apr
E	Gill, M.R.	01 Apr
E	Holmes, R.W.	01 Apr
X	Reed, J.H.	01 Apr
X	Greenland, M.R.	16 Apr
X	Smith, C.P.	26 Apr

1996

X	Atkinson, M.	01 Feb
X	Bankier, S.	19 Feb
X	Draper, S.P.	26 Feb
X	Furlong, K.	01 Mar
E	Jackson, I.A.	01 Apr
E	Withers, J.W.	01 Apr
X	Collins, G.J.S.	07 Apr
S	Waters, N.R.	16 Apr
S	McConochie, A.D.	16 Apr
E	Walker, P.R.	01 May
E	Shepherd, R.G.	01 May
E	Carter, J.M.	01 Jun
X	Moore, P.H.G.	01 Jun
X	Gazzard, J.H.	01 Jun
X	Freeman, D.R.	01 Jun
X	Hayward, C.E.W.	01 Jun

1997

X	Shepherd, C.S.	01 Jan
X	Adam, I.K.	01 Jan
E	Harrison, D.	05 Jan
X	Irwin, M.A.	09 Jan
X	Noyce, N.R.	15 Jan
E	Parvin, P.S.	01 Feb
S	Stanton, P.C.M.	16 Feb
X	Hulme, T.M.	01 Mar
X	Bell, R.D.	01 Mar
X	Cummings, A.T.	01 Mar
X	Hogg, C.W.	01 Mar
X	Williams, M.S.	29 Mar
X	Cowley, R.M.	01 Apr
E	New, C.M.	01 Apr
E	Patterson-Hollis, C.	01 Apr
X	Toothill, J.S.	01 Apr

LIEUTENANT COMMANDERS

X	Lowson, R.M.	01 Apr	E	Faulkner, D.W.	29 Nov	X	Bird, R.A.J.	01 Jul
X	Ryan, R.M.	01 Apr	X	Dale-Smith, G.	01 Dec	E	O'Shea, E.P.	01 Jul
X	Wilson-Chalon, L.M.	01 Apr	X	Ince, D.P.	01 Dec	X	Badrock, B.	05 Jul
E	Harris, A.G.	12 Apr	X	Montgomery, M.H.	01 Dec	E	Hall, A.J.	01 Aug
E	Finch, R.L.	01 May	X	Venables, A.N.	01 Dec	X	Ford, M.J.	05 Aug
E	Feeney, M.L.	01 May	X	Prentice, D.C.	22 Dec	X	McGuire, M.J.	31 Aug
E	Clark, S.R.	01 May				E	Stewart, K.C.	01 Sep
X	Pethybridge, R.A.	01 May		**1998**		X	Toor, J.J.S.	01 Sep
X	Rich, D.C.	20 May				X	Murphy, S.R.A.	01 Sep
E	Thomson, I.R.	22 May	X	Carroll, P.J.	01 Jan	X	Savage, M.R.	01 Sep
X	Woollcombe-Gosson, D.J.	01 Jun	E	Bartlett, I.D.	01 Jan	E	Humphrey, I.J.	17 Sep
X	South, D.J.	15 Jun	X	Kitchen, S.A.	01 Jan	E	Wallace, D.J.	01 Oct
X	Irons, P.A.	01 Jul	X	Lea, J.	01 Jan	E	Hart, P.A.	01 Oct
E	Peace, R.W.	02 Jul	X	Smith, G.C.S.	01 Jan	W	Hayle, E.A.	01 Oct
X	Ellis, N.M.	18 Jul	E	Ward, S.D.	01 Jan	X	Manson, C.R.	01 Oct
X	Forester-Bennett, R.M.W.	24 Jul	X	Haseldine, S.G.	01 Feb	X	Reed, M.	01 Oct
X	Wells, J.M.C.	01 Aug	X	Allen, A.D.	01 Feb	X	Haynes, J.W.	01 Oct
E	Pearson, N.	01 Aug	X	Bence, D.E.	01 Feb	E	Krosnar-Clarke, S.M.	01 Oct
X	Woollven, A.H.	01 Aug	X	Carroll, B.J.	01 Feb	X	Tyack, T.J.	01 Oct
X	Stannard, M.P.	01 Aug	E	Hughesdon, M.D.	01 Feb	E	Mills, G.W.	01 Oct
X	Webber, C.J.	26 Aug	X	Mugridge, D.R.	01 Feb	W	Whittingham, D.J.	01 Oct
X	Hare, J.H.	01 Sep	E	Rogers, A.G.	01 Feb	X	Neave, A.M.	01 Oct
E	Richardson, M.A.	01 Sep	E	Thomas, J.H.	01 Feb	X	Thompson, R.A.	01 Oct
X	Wynn, S.R.	01 Sep	E	Wellington, S.	01 Feb	E	Bourne, D.S.	01 Oct
X	Petheram, A.J.	01 Sep	E	Franks, C.S.	01 Feb	X	Wilkinson, R.N.	01 Oct
X	Tebbet, P.N.	01 Sep	E	Blackburn, S.A.	01 Mar	X	Shallcroft, J.E.	01 Oct
X	Llewelyn, K.	01 Oct	X	Goodman, A.T.	01 Mar	X	Spayne, N.J.	01 Oct
X	Stringer, R.A.	01 Oct	X	Mules, A.J.	01 Mar	E	Dawson, S.N.	01 Oct
X	Daw, S.J.	01 Oct	X	Scott, R.J.	02 Mar	S	Cunane, J.R.	01 Oct
X	Lambourne, D.J.	01 Oct	X	McKenzie, M.	03 Mar	X	Chapman, D.A.	01 Oct
X	Clucas, M.R.	01 Oct	X	Stowell, P.I.M.	01 Apr	X	Franklin, B.J.	01 Oct
X	James, A.J.	01 Oct	E	Lynn, S.R.	01 Apr	X	Wheaton, B.J.S.	01 Oct
E	Morgan, S.A.	01 Oct	X	MacDonald-Robinson, N.U.S.	01 Apr	E	Hill, G.A.	01 Oct
X	Moys, A.J.	01 Oct	X	Petherick, J.S.	01 Apr	X	Lewis, D.J.	01 Oct
X	Cook, D.J.	01 Oct	E	Rook, G.I.	01 Apr	X	Barrick, P.V.	01 Oct
E	Price, T.P.	01 Oct	X	Smith, A.P.	01 Apr	S	MacDougall, G.R.	01 Oct
X	Cornick, R.M.	01 Oct	X	Chapman, S.J.	01 Apr	X	Strathern, R.J.	01 Oct
X	Hargreaves, N.	01 Oct	E	Hood, K.M.	01 Apr	X	Simmonds, G.F.	01 Oct
E	Leonard, M.	01 Oct	E	Bone, R.C.	01 May	E	Clarke, J.	01 Oct
E	Rowe, P.E.	01 Oct	E	Green, A.J.	01 May	E	Grace, T.P.	01 Oct
E	Davies, T.M.	01 Oct	E	Fawcett, F.P.	01 May	E	Jordan, N.S.	01 Oct
E	Cole, S.P.	01 Oct	E	Hepworth, A.W.D.	01 May	E	Birbeck, K.	01 Oct
E	Downie, A.J.	01 Oct	X	Goodacre, I.R.	01 May	E	Rimmer, R.	01 Oct
X	Harper, J.A.	01 Oct	E	Hutchison, P.G.	01 May	E	Stokes, A.W.	01 Oct
X	Yarker, D.L.	01 Oct	E	Winter, T.M.	01 May	E	Ferguson, G.H.	01 Oct
X	Stuttard, S.E.	01 Oct	E	Dunn, G.R.	01 May	S	Case, P.	01 Oct
S	Bennett, A.J.	01 Oct	X	Royston, S.J.	01 May	X	Dawson, W.	01 Nov
S	Finch, T.S.A.	01 Oct	X	Morshead, C.H.	14 May	S	McNally, N.J.	01 Nov
X	Morris, P.J.	01 Oct	E	Millar, G.C.	15 May	X	Reidy, P.A.	01 Nov
E	Moss, T.E.	01 Oct	S	Evans, M.D.	16 May	X	Smith, M.M.	01 Nov
X	Ward, D.S.	01 Oct	E	Philo, J.Q.	01 Jun	X	Taylor, A.R.	01 Nov
E	Morrison, R.W.	01 Oct	E	Murray, G.M.	01 Jun	E	Corps, S.D.	11 Nov
X	Griffiths, A.	01 Oct	E	Baker, M.J.	01 Jun	E	Boulton, N.A.	20 Nov
S	Knill, R.L.	01 Oct	E	Bosustow, A.M.	01 Jun	E	Donnelly, J.S.	22 Nov
E	O'Flaherty, J.S.	03 Oct	E	Evans, G.	01 Jun	X	Redman, C.J.R.	23 Nov
X	Surgey, I.C.	26 Oct	X	Payne, J.D.	01 Jun	S	Stoffell, D.P.	27 Nov
X	Tabeart, G.W.	01 Nov	X	Deacon, S.	01 Jun	E	Windsar, P.A.	27 Nov
X	Jones, A.D.	01 Nov	E	Hanson, N.A.	01 Jun	X	Davies, I.E.	01 Dec
E	Morgan, F.S.	01 Nov	X	Kimberley, R.	01 Jul	X	MacKay, P.	01 Dec
X	Houlberg, K.M.T.	01 Nov	X	Lowther, J.M.	01 Jul	X	Rogers, T.H.G.	04 Dec
S	Asbridge, J.I.	16 Nov	X	Powell, S.R.	01 Jul	E	Foster, B.M.T.	07 Dec
S	Hewitt, L.R.	16 Nov	X	Beech, C.M.	01 Jul	X	Warn, C.J.	09 Dec
			X	Price, T.A.	01 Jul			

LIEUTENANT COMMANDERS

X	Powell, W.G.	16 Dec	E	Roberts, D.	04 Apr	X	Murray, A.S.	01 Oct
			X	Foster, D.H.	01 May	X	Miller, C.R.	01 Oct
	1999		E	Bowhay, S.	01 May	E	Gunther, P.T.	01 Oct
			X	Burstow, R.S.	01 May	E	Nicholls, G.A.	01 Oct
S	Dudley, S.M.T.	01 Jan	X	Bravery, M.A.E.	01 May	X	Ash, T.C.V.	01 Oct
X	Millard, A.R.	01 Jan	X	Garratt, J.K.	01 May	E	Milsom, J.	01 Oct
E	Twine, J.H.	01 Jan	E	Sansford, A.J.	27 May	E	Appelquist, P.	01 Oct
E	Greatwood, I.M.	01 Jan	X	Golden, D.S.C.	01 Jun	X	Blythe, P.C.	01 Oct
X	Ponsford, P.K.	01 Jan	X	Bush, A.J.T.	01 Jun	X	Bougourd, M.A.	01 Oct
E	Roberts, K.E.	01 Jan	X	Allen, P.L.	01 Jun	X	Lower, I.S.	01 Oct
X	Lees, E.C.	01 Feb	S	Ferns, T.D.	01 Jun	E	McDermott, O.D.	01 Oct
X	Osborn, R.M.	01 Feb	X	Mackey, M.C.	01 Jun	E	Gazard, P.N.	01 Oct
X	Staley, S.P.L.	01 Feb	X	Whitley, I.D.B.	01 Jun	X	Talbot, C.M.	01 Oct
E	Copeland, S.N.	01 Feb	X	Young, A.	01 Jun	X	Dutton, P.J.	01 Oct
X	Godwin, C.A.	01 Feb	E	West, G.G.	06 Jun	E	Glennie, B.W.	01 Oct
E	Hancox, M.J.	01 Feb	E	Proud, A.D.	11 Jun	S	Freegard, I.P.	01 Oct
E	Jackson, P.N.	01 Feb	X	Hewitt, D.L.	01 Jul	E	Maude, D.H.	01 Oct
X	Jones, N.P.	01 Feb	E	Jones, D.B.	01 Jul	S	Twist, D.C.	01 Oct
X	Kerslake, R.W.	01 Feb	E	Parkin, M.I.	01 Jul	X	Woodruff, A.D.	01 Oct
S	Nairn, A.B.	01 Feb	S	Percival, M.C.	01 Jul	X	Bassett, N.E.	01 Oct
E	Smith, A.G.	01 Feb	X	Bushell, G.R.	09 Jul	X	Thomas, L.	01 Oct
X	Taylor, M.A.	01 Feb	X	Southorn, M.D.	21 Jul	E	Jones, D.A.	01 Oct
X	Welford, R.C.	01 Feb	E	Richardson, P.S.M.	01 Aug	X	Stephens, R.P.	01 Oct
E	Wright, N.S.	01 Feb	E	Lee, P.A.	01 Aug	E	Norman, P.D.	01 Oct
E	Fergusson, N.A.	01 Feb	E	Collis, M.J.	01 Aug	E	Sugden, S.R.	01 Oct
E	Crofts, D.J.	01 Feb	E	Currie, S.M.	01 Aug	E	Taylor, K.J.	01 Oct
X	Holmes, J.D.	04 Feb	X	Dreelan, M.J.	01 Aug	S	Harris, M.T.	01 Oct
X	Pitt, J.M.	17 Feb	E	Owens, D.T.	01 Aug	S	Holland, N.R.	01 Oct
W	Kent, I.M.	20 Feb	E	Quekett, I.P.S.	01 Aug	W	Graham, P.J.	22 Oct
E	Southern, P.J.	27 Feb	E	Lowe, J.C.	01 Aug	X	Jones, C.A.	01 Nov
X	Lee, N.F.	01 Mar	X	Barnes, J.R.	01 Aug	X	Necker, C.D.	01 Nov
E	Lauste, W.E.	01 Mar	E	Dyer, J.D.T.	01 Sep	X	Baker, A.P.	01 Nov
E	Casson, N.P.	01 Mar	E	Grears, J.	01 Sep	X	Joyce, T.J.	01 Nov
X	Hussain, S.	01 Mar	E	McLarnon, C.P.C.	01 Sep	E	Lancaster, R.M.	01 Nov
X	Burns, R.D.J.	01 Mar	E	Tatham, S.A.	01 Sep	E	White, I.F.	18 Nov
X	McDonnell, D.S.	01 Mar	E	Bolton, J.P.	01 Sep	E	Chapman, C.L.	29 Nov
X	Bingham, D.S.	01 Mar	X	Goode, A.N.	01 Sep	X	Smith, B.J.	01 Dec
E	Hill, D.	01 Mar	E	Greener, C.	01 Sep	E	Easterbrook, K.I.E.	01 Dec
X	Waller, S.A.	01 Mar	E	Taylor, R.	01 Sep	E	McRae, P.C.	01 Dec
X	Currass, T.D.	01 Mar	X	Whitworth, R.M.	01 Oct	X	Tennuci, R.G.	01 Dec
E	Douglass, M.C.M.	01 Mar	X	Luscombe, M.D.	01 Oct	E	Woodruff, D.A.	01 Dec
E	Groom, I.S.	01 Mar	X	Johns, M.G.	01 Oct	X	Hunkin, D.J.	01 Dec
E	Henderson, S.P.	01 Mar	X	Marsh, B.H.	01 Oct	X	Gayfer, M.E.	01 Dec
E	Mackie, D.F.S.	01 Mar	X	Hartley, J.L.	01 Oct	X	Moore, C.R.	05 Dec
E	Rawlinson, S.J.	01 Mar	X	Callaghan, P.F.	01 Oct	E	Rose, M.F.	28 Dec
X	O'Flaherty, C.P.J.	01 Mar	E	Morris, N.	01 Oct			
E	Bywater, R.L.	01 Mar	E	Sergeant, N.R.	01 Oct		**2000**	
X	Hogben, A.L.	01 Mar	E	Barrett, S.J.	01 Oct			
X	Briggs-Mould, T.P.	16 Mar	X	Rae, A.J.W.	01 Oct	X	Harcourt, R.J.	01 Jan
X	Brooks, G.L.	01 Apr	X	Goldsmith, D.	01 Oct	E	Stamper, J.C.H.	01 Jan
X	Beck, S.K.	01 Apr	X	Cooke, G.J.	01 Oct	E	Nickolls, K.P.	01 Jan
X	Collighan, G.T.	01 Apr	E	Preston, M.R.	01 Oct	E	Baxter, I.M.	01 Jan
X	Dodd, K.M.	01 Apr	X	Holden, R.J.	01 Oct	X	Bryan, R.J.L.	01 Jan
E	Goldman, P.H.L.	01 Apr	E	Weir, S.D.	01 Oct	X	Parsons, A.D.	01 Jan
S	Mardlin, S.A.	01 Apr	E	Barker, J.W.	01 Oct	E	Rowland, P.N.	01 Jan
X	Mimpriss, G.D.	01 Apr	E	Mason, M.	01 Oct	X	Walker, N.M.	01 Jan
X	Roscoe, R.D.	01 Apr	X	Pegrum, T.A.	01 Oct	X	Kerr, J.	04 Jan
S	Dodd, N.C.	01 Apr	X	Cowie, K.M.	01 Oct	X	Griffiths, M.O.J.	16 Jan
E	Foster, S.J.H.	01 Apr	E	Linderman, I.R.	01 Oct	X	Aylott, P.R.F.D.	29 Jan
X	Wood, U.G.S.	01 Apr	E	Matthews, P.B.	01 Oct	X	Crosbie, D.E.F.	01 Feb
E	Waring, J.R.	01 Apr	X	Avison, M.J.	01 Oct	X	Pierce, A.K.M.	01 Feb
X	Mahony, C.D.C.	03 Apr	E	Roberts, S.C.	01 Oct	E	Burgess, G.T.M.	01 Feb
S	Athayde Banazol, C.V.N.	04 Apr				E	Gale, M.A.	01 Feb

LIEUTENANT COMMANDERS

E	Greenway, S.A.	01 Feb	X	Duff, A.P.	01 Sep	X	Beaumont, S.J.	01 Oct
E	Martin, S.J.	01 Feb	X	Oulds, K.A.	01 Sep	X	Whitlam, J.	01 Oct
S	Rae, S.G.	01 Feb	E	Walton, C.P.	01 Sep	S	Young, S.W.	01 Oct
E	Lewis, G.D.	03 Feb	E	Wheal, A.J.	01 Sep	S	Bunt, K.J.	01 Oct
E	Bolton, M.T.W.	06 Feb	X	Wyper, J.R.	01 Sep	S	Pocock, D.	16 Oct
E	Shaw, M.L.	11 Feb	X	Wilson, R.	01 Sep	E	Norris, J.G.	01 Nov
S	Brenchley, N.G.	17 Feb	E	Taylor, A.	01 Oct	X	Ramsey, R.T.	01 Nov
S	Ashman, R.G.	28 Feb	X	Watkins, T.C.	01 Oct	X	O'Byrne, P.B.M.	01 Nov
S	Sparke, P.R.W.	01 Mar	X	Cook, G.E.	01 Oct	E	Wylie, I.C.H.	01 Nov
E	Cotterill, B.M.	01 Mar	X	Clarke, A.P.	01 Oct	S	Hally, P.J.	01 Nov
E	Balhetchet, A.S.	01 Mar	X	Williams, M.A.	01 Oct	X	Stockton, K.G.	19 Nov
S	Murphy, P.A.	01 Mar	X	Higgs, R.J.	01 Oct	E	Ballard, M.L.	01 Dec
E	Reece, N.D.	01 Mar	S	Walker, N.A.	01 Oct	E	Lowe, S.M.	01 Dec
E	Teideman, I.C.	01 Mar	X	Oddy, D.M.	01 Oct	E	Rayner, A.	01 Dec
E	Whitehead, S.J.	01 Mar	X	Gardiner, P.F.D.	01 Oct	X	Broadhurst, M.R.	01 Dec
E	Jackson, D.J.	01 Mar	X	Robertson, P.N.	01 Oct	X	Douglas, P.J.	01 Dec
E	Whitfield, K.D.	01 Mar	X	O'Sullivan, B.O.	01 Oct	X	Knight, D.W.	01 Dec
E	Hartley, A.P.	02 Mar	E	Pears, I.J.	01 Oct	X	Douglas, P.G.	03 Dec
E	Pugh, J.	08 Mar	X	Grindon, M.G.	01 Oct	S	Beresford-Green, P.M.	16 Dec
E	Bedding, S.W.E.	01 Apr	X	Phillips, J.P.	01 Oct	S	Gale, C.V.	24 Dec
E	Bignell, S.	01 Apr	X	Smith, R.C.V.	01 Oct	E	Rutherford, T.J.	30 Dec
X	Bruford, R.M.C.	01 Apr	E	Cook, C.B.	01 Oct			
X	Buck, J.E.	01 Apr	E	Orton, D.M.	01 Oct		**2001**	
E	Curlewis, A.J.	01 Apr	E	Lacey, C.M.	01 Oct	E	McMullan, N.L.	01 Jan
X	Firth, R.J.G.	08 Apr	E	Moss, P.J.	01 Oct	E	Kerr, A.N.	01 Jan
X	Lindsey, R.J.	30 Apr	X	Hart, T.G.DE.B.	01 Oct	E	Malley, M.P.	01 Jan
X	Gurr, A.W.G.	01 May	X	Bennett, W.D.	01 Oct	X	Smith, G.D.J.	01 Jan
X	Parry, J.D.F.	01 May	X	Lynch, S.	01 Oct	E	Thomas, S.M.	01 Jan
E	Russell, B.	01 May	X	Howell, H.R.G.	01 Oct	S	Donovan, R.J.	01 Jan
E	Strutt, J.F.	01 May	E	Bissett, I.M.	01 Oct	X	MacKinnon, D.J.	01 Jan
X	Wilson, D.R.	01 May	E	Bissett, P.K.	01 Oct	X	Varley, I.G.	01 Jan
E	Bye, M.D.	01 May	MS	Trasler, M.F.	01 Oct	X	Wills, P.J.	01 Jan
E	Reah, S.	02 May	X	Finn, G.J.	01 Oct	S	Lawrence, S.P.	14 Jan
E	Prinsep, T.J.	01 Jun	S	Bell, M.	01 Oct	X	Brown, S.H.	15 Jan
E	Bradley, P.M.	01 Jun	E	Dyke, K.A.	01 Oct	E	Sellers, G.D.	01 Feb
E	Howard, N.H.	01 Jun	S	Axon, G.M.	01 Oct	X	Stanton-Brown, P.J.	01 Feb
E	Rogers, C.M.	01 Jun	E	Hutchings, J.S.	01 Oct	X	Hopper, S.M.	01 Feb
E	Fleisher, S.M.	01 Jun	E	Joyce, D.A.	01 Oct	X	Knott, M.B.	01 Feb
X	Moore, M.	01 Jun	S	Turner, R.F.	01 Oct	X	Miller, P.D.	01 Feb
E	Mulvaney, P.A.	01 Jun	E	Burge, R.G.	01 Oct	X	Thomson, C.D.	01 Feb
E	Nicklas, C.J.	01 Jun	E	Hatcher, T.R.	01 Oct	X	Tredray, T.P.	01 Feb
X	Wilkinson, D.H.	01 Jun	E	Rundle, A.L.	01 Oct	E	Woods, T.C.	01 Feb
X	Williams, J.P.	01 Jun	X	Barron, P.J.	01 Oct	X	Chaston, S.P.	01 Mar
X	Campbell, L.M.	01 Jul	X	Billington, T.J.	01 Oct	X	Cox, R.J.	01 Mar
X	Gardner, J.E.	01 Jul	S	Hall, D.A.	01 Oct	S	Hallett, S.J.	01 Mar
E	Barton, M.A.	01 Jul	E	Aniyi, C.B.J.	01 Oct	E	Head, S.A.	01 Mar
E	Crundell, R.J.	01 Jul	E	Love, T.S.N.	01 Oct	X	Nelson, C.S.	01 Mar
E	Lunn, M.H.B.	01 Jul	X	Lett, J.D.	01 Oct	X	Pearson, M.F.	01 Mar
E	Moody, D.C.	01 Jul	E	Prince, M.E.	01 Oct	X	Bristowe, P.A.	01 Mar
E	Panther, A.M.	01 Jul	E	Pearson, C.P.B.	01 Oct	E	Giles, R.K.	01 Mar
E	Atkins, I.	01 Jul	S	Pheasant, J.C.S.	01 Oct	X	George, D.M.	13 Mar
E	Etchells, S.B.	03 Jul	E	Phesse, J.P.L.	01 Oct	X	Williams, S.W.L.	01 Apr
E	Philpot, D.J.	18 Jul	S	Stillwell-Cox, A.D.R.	01 Oct	X	Holden, N.	01 Apr
E	Lauchlan, R.A.	01 Aug	E	Game, P.G.	01 Oct	E	Whyte, I.P.	01 Apr
X	Dando, J.N.	01 Aug	E	Hobson, I.S.	01 Oct	E	Adams, G.H.	01 Apr
X	Ley, J.A.	01 Aug	E	Finn, I.R.	01 Oct	E	Parnell, A.D.	01 Apr
E	Ross, I.	01 Aug	MS	Gerrell, F.J.	01 Oct	X	Ryan, S.J.	01 Apr
E	Miles, G.J.	07 Aug	S	Grocott, P.C.	01 Oct	E	Drywood, T.	01 Apr
E	Thrippleton, M.G.	15 Aug	E	Cowper, I.R.	01 Oct	E	Reid, J.C.J.	01 Apr
S	Tothill, R.C.	17 Aug	X	Taylor, M.R.	01 Oct	S	Whalley, R.J.	01 Apr
X	Hutchinson, C.J.	01 Sep	X	Dufosee, S.W.	01 Oct	E	Holland, S.M.W.	01 May
E	Richter, A.S.B.	01 Sep	X	Ahlgren, E.G.	01 Oct	E	Rand, M.J.	01 May

LIEUTENANT COMMANDERS

X	Russell, P.	01 May	E	Stobie, P.L.	01 Oct	E	Hutton, K.D.	21 Jan
X	Bessell, D.A.	01 Jun	S	West, A.W.	01 Oct	E	Lang, A.J.N.	01 Feb
X	Williams, C.N.O.	01 Jun	E	Bannister, A.N.	01 Oct	E	Barnett, A.C.	01 Feb
E	Bonnar, J.A.	01 Jun	X	Griffin, N.R.	01 Oct	X	Fryer, A.C.	01 Feb
E	Hutchins, R.F.	01 Jun	E	Langrill, M.P.	01 Oct	S	Higgs, T.A.	01 Feb
E	Keen, N.	01 Jun	X	Beattie, P.S.	01 Oct	E	Macleod, M.S.	01 Feb
X	Newell, P.R.	01 Jun	X	Dennis, M.J.	01 Oct	X	Hesling, G.	28 Feb
E	Cropper, F.B.N.	24 Jun	S	Knock, G.P.	01 Oct	X	Wuidart-Gray, S.R.	01 Mar
X	Norgan, D.J.	01 Jul	X	Houston, D.J.M.	01 Oct	E	Carroll, P.C.	01 Mar
X	Watts, R.	01 Jul	S	Joll, S.M.	01 Oct	E	Clarke, R.W.	01 Mar
S	Richardson, G.N.	01 Jul	X	Cooke, G.S.	01 Oct	E	Jose, S.	01 Mar
E	Green, A.M.	01 Jul	E	Barrett, D.L.	01 Oct	E	Meek, C.S.	01 Mar
E	Napier, G.A.	01 Jul	E	Leaning, D.J.	01 Oct	E	Proctor, W.J.G.	01 Mar
E	Sullivan, M.	01 Jul	E	Rowan, N.A.	01 Oct	X	Stephen, B.M.	01 Mar
E	Shirley, A.J.	01 Aug	E	Hancock, R.T.A.	01 Oct	X	Wallace, S.J.	01 Mar
X	Bower, A.J.	01 Aug	E	Baggaley, J.A.L.	01 Oct	S	Brock, R.F.	01 Mar
S	Finch, B.A.	01 Aug	E	Farrington, J.L.	01 Oct	S	Bugg, K.J.	01 Mar
X	O'Sullivan, M.L.J.	01 Aug	S	Wilman, D.M.	01 Oct	E	Broadbent, P.S.	01 Mar
X	Coyle, G.J.	01 Aug	X	Weightman, N.E.	01 Oct	S	Burns, A.C.	04 Mar
E	Graham, A.N.S.	01 Aug	E	Dewsnap, M.D.	01 Oct	X	Walker, S.P.	09 Mar
S	Preece, D.G.	01 Aug	E	Cunnane, K.J.	01 Oct	X	Ritchie, J.N.	01 Apr
E	Winter, R.J.	01 Aug	X	Green, T.C.	01 Oct	X	Derby, B.D.	01 Apr
X	Wood, C.	01 Aug	S	Melville-Brown, M.G.	01 Oct	X	Kohler, A.P.	01 Apr
X	Markey, A.P.	01 Aug	X	Howe, J.P.	01 Oct	E	Cubbage, J.	01 Apr
X	Campbell, J.C.	01 Sep	S	Walker, D.W.A.	01 Oct	S	Goudge, S.D.P.	01 Apr
E	Lewis, D.J.	01 Sep	E	Cox, D.J.	01 Oct	S	Johnson, C.C.B.	01 Apr
E	Laing, I.	01 Sep	X	Clink, A.D.	01 Oct	E	Kelly, H.C.	01 Apr
X	Dowsett, P.G.	01 Sep	X	West, A.B.	01 Oct	X	Offord, M.R.	01 Apr
E	Chapman, P.	01 Sep	X	Lintern, R.D.	01 Oct	X	Childs, J.R.	01 Apr
X	Downes, C.H.	01 Sep	E	Walton, S.P.	01 Oct	X	Dineen, J.M.G.	01 Apr
X	Yelland, C.B.	01 Oct	X	Jaggers, G.G.	01 Oct	X	Hopper, I.M.	09 Apr
X	Nicholas, B.J.	01 Oct	S	Taylor, I.K.	01 Oct	X	Lynch, R.D.F.	16 Apr
X	Turner, K.A.	01 Oct	E	Evans, S.	01 Oct	X	Brotherton, J.D.	16 Apr
X	Deverson, R.T.M.	01 Oct	X	Kerr, A.T.F.	01 Oct	E	Flint, H.A.	01 May
X	Graham, M.A.	01 Oct	MS	Stead, R.A.	01 Oct	E	Mandley, P.J.	01 May
X	Knight, A.R.	01 Oct	E	Dunsby, N.B.	01 Oct	X	Cull, I.	01 May
E	Taylor, S.J.	01 Oct	E	Mitchell, S.D.	01 Oct	X	Blackburn, S.J.	01 May
S	Cottis, M.C.	01 Oct	X	Clarke, I.B.	01 Oct	X	Hygate, A.M.	01 May
X	Hannigan, P.F.	01 Oct	X	Wilson, G.J.	01 Oct	X	Maxwell, R.	01 May
X	Scivier, J.S.	01 Oct	E	Phillips, A.R.	01 Oct	X	Bradley, M.T.	01 May
X	Bowers, J.P.	01 Oct	E	Walsh, D.G.	01 Oct	X	Craig, J.A.	01 May
X	Duncan, J.	01 Oct	S	Jackson, P.A.	01 Oct	X	Noakes, K.M.	01 May
X	Forster, R.A.	01 Oct	X	Smith, N.J.	01 Oct	S	Porter, T.B.	01 May
E	Horwell, B.B.	01 Oct	E	Stanham, C.M.	01 Oct	X	West, R.J.	01 Jun
X	Tattersall, R.B.	01 Oct	X	Smallwood, R.I.	12 Oct	X	Osborn, C.G.	01 Jun
X	Westley, D.R.	01 Oct	E	Wroblewski, J.A.	31 Oct	X	Hempsall, A.M.	01 Jun
X	Noblett, P.G.A.	01 Oct	X	Moore, S.K.	01 Nov	X	Hurley, C.	01 Jun
E	Baines, D.M.L.	01 Oct	X	Noyce, V.R.A.	01 Nov	X	McGlory, S.J.	01 Jun
E	Morgan-Hosey, J.N.	01 Oct	E	Palmer, M.E.	01 Nov	X	Stacey, A.M.	01 Jun
E	Rowlands, K.	01 Oct	X	Curry, R.E.	01 Nov	X	Waterfield, S.J.	01 Jun
X	Richardson, G.A.	01 Oct	E	Chamberlain, N.R.L.	01 Nov	E	Prendergast, S.A.	25 Jun
X	Gough, S.R.	01 Oct	X	Castle, A.S.	01 Dec	S	Moorhouse, S.M.	29 Jun
X	Rogers, A.	01 Oct	E	Buckingham, G.	01 Dec	X	Cook, M.C.	01 Jul
X	Brunsden-Brown, S.E.	01 Oct	E	Ford, J.D.	01 Dec	E	Fraser, I.D.	01 Jul
E	Davies, S.P.	01 Oct	X	Edey, M.J.	01 Dec	E	Doran, S.E.	01 Jul
E	Mountjoy, B.J.	01 Oct	X	Currie, D.G.	16 Dec	X	O'Nyons, Y.I.	01 Jul
E	Wray, A.D.	01 Oct	X	Gritt, L.A.	17 Dec	X	Raeburn, M.	01 Jul
X	Sneddon, R.N.	01 Oct	E	Browning, R.S.	01 Jan	X	Jacques, M.J.	01 Jul
E	Mills, I.	01 Oct	E	Davies, L.	01 Jan	X	Block, A.W.G.	01 Jul
E	Procter, J.E.	01 Oct	E	Onyike, C.E.	01 Jan	X	Gill, M.H.	01 Jul
E	Wharrie, E.K.B.	01 Oct	X	Pink, S.E.	01 Jan	E	Mincher, D.J.F.	01 Jul
S	Wooller, M.A.H.	01 Oct	E	Goldsmith, D.T.	01 Jan	X	Payne, P.J.	01 Jul

LIEUTENANT COMMANDERS

X	Doyle, N.P.	01 Aug
X	Goldstone, R.S.	01 Aug
S	Nicholson, K.J.	01 Aug
S	Dickson, J.I.	01 Aug
S	Taylor, C.R.	01 Aug
X	Carter, K.S.	27 Aug
E	Rose, C.M.	30 Aug
E	Marratt, R.J.	01 Sep
X	Stephens, R.J.	01 Sep
E	Choules, B.	01 Sep
S	Moore, S.	01 Sep
X	Aitken, A.J.	01 Sep
E	MacDonald, A.J.	01 Sep
E	Voyce, J.E.	01 Sep
X	Reese, D.M.	01 Sep
X	Roberts, M.	01 Oct
E	Mason, L.C.	01 Oct
X	Suckling, R.L.	01 Oct
X	D'Arcy, P.A.	01 Oct
E	Thomas, A.L.	01 Oct
E	Walker, M.J.	01 Oct
X	Crimmen, D.J.	01 Oct
X	Davison, G.J.	01 Oct
E	Taylor, N.R.	01 Oct
X	Gray, P.R.	01 Oct
X	Richardson, G.L.	01 Oct
X	Windebank, S.J.	01 Oct
X	Slocombe, N.R.	01 Oct
X	Richardson, P.	01 Oct
E	Ball, S.J.	01 Oct
X	Canning, C.P.	01 Oct
X	Sparkes, S.N.	01 Oct
X	Birse, G.J.	01 Oct
E	Solly, M.M.	01 Oct
E	Craib, A.G.	01 Oct
E	Radbourne, N.I.	01 Oct
W	Mayell, J.A.	01 Oct
X	Wallis, J.S.	01 Oct
X	Brian, N.	01 Oct
X	Langrish, G.J.	01 Oct
X	Gibbons, N.P.	01 Oct
E	Cooke, M.J.	01 Oct
E	Daly, J.M.	01 Oct
E	Warr, R.F.	01 Oct
X	Soar, G.	01 Oct
X	Mould, P.	01 Oct
X	Jacques, N.A.	01 Oct
X	Sutton, R.M.J.	01 Oct
E	McLachlan, M.P.	01 Oct
X	Harper, I.L.	01 Oct
E	Lees, S.N.	01 Oct
E	Ireland, J.M.	01 Oct
E	Price, T.E.	01 Oct
S	Arnold, A.S.	01 Oct
X	Miller, G.	01 Oct
E	Cheshire, T.E.	01 Oct
E	Bradshaw, K.T.	01 Oct
E	Wells, B.C.	01 Oct
E	Wrenn, M.R.W.	01 Oct
S	Hart, N.L.W.	01 Oct
E	Stephenson, K.J.M.	01 Oct
X	Drodge, A.P.F.	01 Oct
E	Snelling, P.D.	01 Oct
E	Boyle, J.B.	01 Oct
S	Bryant, D.J.G.	01 Oct
X	Morgan, D.H.	01 Oct
X	Sharpe, T.G.	01 Oct
X	Barry, J.P.	01 Oct
X	Pitcher, P.P.	01 Oct
E	Doull, D.J.M.	01 Oct
X	Lamb, A.G.	01 Oct
E	Patterson, D.	01 Oct
X	Pledger, D.	01 Oct
E	McCarthy, S.J.	01 Oct
E	Benn, S.W.	01 Oct
E	Harwood, C.G.	01 Oct
E	Jones, D.L.	01 Oct
X	Seward, S.A.	01 Oct
MS	Wagstaff, N.	01 Oct
S	Ablett, E.L.	01 Oct
E	Malkin, S.L.	01 Oct
E	Shaughnessy, S.L.	01 Oct
E	Keeley, S.P.	01 Oct
X	Nash, P.D.	01 Oct
E	Holden, P.A.	01 Oct
E	Reed, J.C.	01 Oct
X	Horne, J.R.	01 Oct
S	Dean, J.R.	01 Oct
X	Bassett, D.A.	01 Oct
X	Rackham, A.D.H.	01 Oct
X	Byrne, T.M.	01 Oct
X	Marsh, M.P.A.	01 Oct
X	Morrison, P.	01 Oct
E	Bailey, J.J.	01 Oct
X	Smith, M.D.	01 Oct
S	Hanson, M.N.	01 Oct
X	Capes, S.G.	01 Oct
MS	Bradford, T.H.C.	01 Oct
X	Easton, D.W.	01 Oct
MS	Walton, A.P.	01 Oct
X	Smith, A.B.D.	01 Oct
S	Scandling, R.J.	01 Oct
S	Harris, R.P.	01 Oct
S	Barratt, S.M.	01 Oct
S	Darlow, P.R.	01 Oct
S	Dunne, M.G.	01 Oct
X	Weaver, N.	01 Oct
S	Bower, J.W.	01 Oct
X	Jones, A.E.	01 Nov
X	Brown, S.D.	01 Nov
E	Cummings, D.J.	01 Nov
E	Bird, M.G.J.	01 Nov
X	Ripley, B.E.	01 Nov
S	White, J.E.	01 Nov
X	Kirkwood, T.A.H.	01 Nov
S	Murdoch, A.P.	01 Nov
X	Sillers, B.	01 Dec
X	Brodie, R.W.J.	01 Dec
E	Scopes, D.	01 Dec
S	Titmuss, J.F.	01 Dec
E	Trott, E.A.	01 Dec

2003

E	Frost, M.A.	01 Jan
X	Braithwaite, J.S.	01 Jan
X	Lunn, T.R.	01 Jan
X	Allfree, J.	01 Jan
X	Jones, M.D.	01 Jan
E	Nelson, L.M.	01 Jan
X	Laverty, R.E.	01 Feb
X	Gray, Y.M.	01 Feb
X	Bowden, M.T.E.	01 Feb
E	Boyes, M.R.	01 Feb
S	Dutton, A.C.	01 Feb
E	Gair, S.D.H.	01 Feb
X	Maynard, C.I.	01 Feb
X	Wiseman, I.C.	01 Feb
X	Borbone, N.	01 Feb
X	Cooke, J.E.	01 Feb
X	Rogers, J.C.E.	01 Mar
E	Adams, R.J.	01 Mar
X	Foulis, N.D.A.	01 Mar
S	Gennard, A.	01 Mar
X	Tanner, R.C.	01 Mar
E	Burvill, J.P.	01 Mar
E	Coope, P.J.	01 Mar
X	Goulding, J.P.	01 Mar
E	Jennings, W.	01 Mar
E	Large, S.A.	01 Mar
E	Phillips, J.N.	01 Mar
E	Stagg, A.R.	01 Mar
X	Thompson, M.G.	01 Mar
S	Wales, B.D.	01 Mar
X	Watson, I.	01 Mar
X	Skelley, A.N.M.	01 Mar
E	Rawson, S.M.	01 Apr
X	Foster, T.G.	01 Apr
X	Lovatt, G.J.	01 Apr
X	Stride, J.C.	01 Apr
E	Bowman, R.J.	01 Apr
G	Oliver, G.	01 May
E	Taylor, A.L.	01 May
E	Hardiman, N.A.	01 May
X	Whitfield, R.M.P.	01 May
X	Byron, J.D.	01 May
E	Coulthard, A.J.	11 May
E	Durham, P.C.L.	18 May
X	Peppe, A.G.	01 Jun
X	Asquith, S.P.	01 Jun
X	Euden, C.P.	01 Jun
E	Sharkey, E.R.	01 Jun
X	Ward, A.J.	01 Jun
X	Lee, N.D.	16 Jun
X	Lynn, I.H.	30 Jun
X	Leaver, C.E.L.	01 Jul
X	McKnight, D.J.S.	01 Jul
E	May, S.C.	01 Jul
X	Beacham, P.R.	01 Jul
E	Edward, G.J.	01 Jul
E	Lincoln, K.J.	01 Jul
X	Ruddock, G.W.D.	01 Jul
E	Ryan, N.J.	01 Jul
X	Chatfield-Smith, R.D.	01 Jul
E	Paulson, R.B.	01 Aug
E	Sandle, N.D.	01 Aug
X	Syrett, M.E.	01 Aug

LIEUTENANT COMMANDERS

X	Cahill, K.A.	01 Aug	E	Bryce, N.A.	01 Oct	X	Taylor, J.P.	01 Oct
E	Hickson, M.S.H.	01 Aug	E	Midmore, M.J.	01 Oct	X	Wilson, A.J.	01 Oct
E	Letts, A.J.	01 Aug	E	Craggs, S.	01 Oct	E	Fitzgerald, C.	01 Oct
S	Russell, G.S.	01 Aug	X	Elston, A.J.	01 Oct	X	Holloway, S.A.	01 Oct
E	Storey, C.L.	01 Aug	E	Deakin, J.	01 Oct	S	Noon, D.	01 Oct
E	Sweeney, K.P.M.	01 Aug	E	Kellett, A.	01 Oct	S	Stephenson, P.G.	01 Oct
E	Veal, A.E.	01 Aug	E	Dawson, A.J.	01 Oct	X	Lea, S.A.P.	01 Nov
X	Tregunna, G.A.	08 Aug	E	Eddie, A.G.W.	01 Oct	X	Ley, A.B.	01 Nov
E	Jones, G.D.	01 Sep	E	Knight, K.J.	01 Oct	X	Ingram, G.J.	01 Dec
E	Edwards, A.G.	01 Sep	X	Gold, J.W.	01 Oct	X	Rees, R.T.	01 Dec
X	McWilliams, J.E.	01 Sep	E	Barrows, D.M.	01 Oct	X	Foreman, S.L.	24 Dec
E	Stowell, R.B.M.	01 Sep	E	Knight, R.H.	01 Oct			
E	Collins, S.J.	01 Oct	E	Dalton, F.J.	01 Oct		**2004**	
X	Cobbett, J.F.	01 Oct	X	Cunningham, N.J.W.	01 Oct			
X	Bhattacharya, D.	01 Oct	E	Palmer, J.	01 Oct	E	Beadnell, R.M.	01 Jan
X	Crockatt, S.R.J.	01 Oct	E	Harrington, J.B.H.	01 Oct	E	Rostron, D.W.	01 Jan
E	Vincent, A.	01 Oct	E	O'Neill, P.J.	01 Oct	E	Pakes, D.T.	01 Jan
X	Harrison, P.D.	01 Oct	X	Bosley, B.D.	01 Oct	E	Hendrickx, C.J.	01 Jan
E	Williams, P.M.	01 Oct	X	Irons, R.C.S.	01 Oct	E	Field, C.R.H.	01 Jan
X	Davidson, N.R.	01 Oct	S	Matthews, P.K.	01 Oct	X	Brown, A.P.	01 Feb
X	Whitfield, J.A.	01 Oct	X	Wheeler, N.J.	01 Oct	X	Atkinson, G.C.	01 Feb
X	Tetley, M.	01 Oct	X	Jardine, D.S.	01 Oct	X	Dale, A.	01 Feb
X	Hayward, G.	01 Oct	X	Neild, T.	01 Oct	E	Powles, D.A.	01 Feb
X	Ellwood, P.G.	01 Oct	E	Mallen, D.J.	01 Oct	S	MacKay, A.C.	01 Feb
X	Lindsay, D.J.	01 Oct	X	Lawson, G.J.	01 Oct	X	Moorhouse, S.M.R.	01 Feb
X	Logan, J.M.	01 Oct	X	Woodrow, K.J.	01 Oct	X	Peters, W.R.	01 Mar
E	Roberts, I.G.	01 Oct	S	Bollen, J.M.	01 Oct	X	Clark, M.H.	01 Mar
X	Neal, S.M.	01 Oct	E	Thompson, M.J.	01 Oct	E	Ling, C.	01 Mar
X	Shrimpton, M.W.	01 Oct	X	Rimington, A.K.	01 Oct	X	Rae, D.G.	01 Mar
E	Plackett, A.J.	01 Oct	X	Stride, J.A.	01 Oct	E	Screaton, R.M.	01 Mar
X	Bird, J.M.	01 Oct	E	Stubbs, M.A.	01 Oct	E	Lewis, A.J.	01 Mar
E	Wilkins, R.R.	01 Oct	X	Hunt, F.B.G.	01 Oct	X	Lockett, D.J.	01 Apr
E	Hunt, P.E.R.D.	01 Oct	X	Clay, J.C.	01 Oct	X	Readwin, R.R.	01 Apr
X	Lambert, A.	01 Oct	S	Nelson, V.	01 Oct	E	Shepherd, M.P.	01 Apr
S	Fogell, A.D.	01 Oct	X	Backus, R.I.K.	01 Oct	X	Battrick, R.R.	01 Apr
X	Woodard, J.R.A.	01 Oct	E	Barrows, S.M.	01 Oct	X	Hains, J.	01 Apr
X	Haigh, A.J.	01 Oct	X	Walker, M.J.	01 Oct	X	Laughton, P.	01 Apr
W	Green, J.L.	01 Oct	E	Fraser, P.	01 Oct	E	Robertshaw, I.W.	01 Apr
E	Higson, B.L.	01 Oct	X	Riggall, A.D.	01 Oct	E	Spooner, R.S.	01 Apr
E	Bedelle, S.J.	01 Oct	S	Evans, C.A.	01 Oct	X	Hammond, P.J.	01 May
E	MacDougall, S.J.	01 Oct	E	Grant, D.J.	01 Oct	E	Bell, J.M.	01 May
X	Payne, M.J.	01 Oct	E	King, G.C.	01 Oct	E	Blair, G.J.L.	01 May
E	Byrne, A.C.	01 Oct	X	Hourigan, M.P.	01 Oct	E	Parry, M.R.R.	01 May
E	McQueen, J.B.	01 Oct	E	Leach, S.J.	01 Oct	E	Smith, M.J.	01 May
X	Crascall, S.J.	01 Oct	MS	Miller, D.E.	01 Oct	E	York, G.R.J.	01 May
E	Butler, L.P.	01 Oct	X	Richards, F.C.	01 Oct	E	Flynn, A.	01 May
S	Johnson, M.D.	01 Oct	S	Percival, F.	01 Oct	X	Mowatt, P.	01 May
E	Kies, L.N.	01 Oct	E	Day, S.N.	01 Oct	X	Steadman, R.P.	01 May
X	Haywood, P.J.	01 Oct	E	Gullett, H.R.	01 Oct	X	Griffiths, R.H.	01 Jun
X	Allen, D.J.K.	01 Oct	E	Fulford, R.N.	01 Oct	E	Ubhi, W.G.	01 Jun
X	Clarke, D.	01 Oct	X	Clark, A.S.	01 Oct	E	Hedgecox, D.C.	01 Jun
X	Mailes, I.R.A.	01 Oct	MS	Finn, D.W.	01 Oct	E	Lyons, M.J.	01 Jun
X	Stembridge, D.P.T.	01 Oct	X	Lewis, K.A.	01 Oct	E	Rowlands, A.R.	01 Jun
E	Wicking, G.S.	01 Oct	X	McGrane, R.J.	01 Oct	X	Sturdy, C.C.M.	01 Jun
S	Park, B.C.	01 Oct	S	Moores, J.	01 Oct	X	May, C.	01 Jul
X	Hunt, S.C.	01 Oct	E	Murchie, A.D.	01 Oct	X	Atkinson, R.J.	01 Jul
E	Hamilton, S.M.	01 Oct	X	Ellison, T.G.	01 Oct	E	Fraser, H.L.	01 Jul
X	Hopkins, S.D.	01 Oct	E	Turle, P.J.	01 Oct	E	Hope, M.R.	01 Jul
E	Dawson, N.J.F.	01 Oct	X	Collins, M.C.	01 Oct	E	Jones, D.M.	01 Jul
E	Beautyman, A.J.	01 Oct	X	McEvoy, L.P.	01 Oct	S	Parrott, J.P.	01 Jul
X	Vartan, M.R.	01 Oct	X	Morris, K.I.	01 Oct	E	Thorp, B.T.	01 Jul
X	Woolhead, A.L.	01 Oct	S	Strudwick, R.	01 Oct	X	Tyler, J.C.	01 Jul
						X	Dennis, P.E.	01 Jul

LIEUTENANT COMMANDERS

E	Woodbridge, R.G. ...... 01 Aug	MS	Follington, D.C. ...... 01 Oct	MS	Smith, M.P. ...... 01 Oct
E	McNamara, I.M. ...... 01 Aug	S	Goldsworthy, E.T. ...... 01 Oct	E	Brunell, P.J. ...... 01 Oct
X	Stroude, P.A. ...... 01 Aug	X	Lucocq, N.J. ...... 01 Oct	E	Sibley, A.K. ...... 01 Oct
E	Murphy, S.M. ...... 01 Aug	X	Armstrong, S.T. ...... 01 Oct	E	Slimmon, K.W. ...... 01 Oct
X	Patterson, J.D. ...... 01 Aug	E	Le Gassick, P.J. ...... 01 Oct	X	Trubshaw, C. ...... 01 Oct
X	Moules, M.A.J. ...... 01 Aug	E	Vincent, D. ...... 01 Oct	E	Purvis, D.M. ...... 16 Oct
X	McGuire, J. ...... 24 Aug	X	Rhodes, M.J. ...... 01 Oct	E	Gordon, N.L. ...... 01 Nov
E	Harding, C.S. ...... 01 Sep	X	Harrison, R.S. ...... 01 Oct	X	Balletta, R.J. ...... 01 Nov
E	McCombe, J. ...... 01 Sep	X	Newton, J.L. ...... 01 Oct	X	McBratney, J.A.G. ...... 01 Nov
E	Wright, D.I. ...... 01 Sep	X	Jones, P.D. ...... 01 Oct	X	Walsh, K.M. ...... 01 Nov
E	Puxley, M.E. ...... 01 Sep	X	Knight, J.D. ...... 01 Oct	W	Elborn, T.K. ...... 01 Dec
X	Read, A.J. ...... 01 Oct	E	Pinder, C.D. ...... 01 Oct	W	McBain, M.S. ...... 01 Dec
X	Bance, N.D. ...... 01 Oct	E	Watson, C.R. ...... 01 Oct	E	Mullins, A.D. ...... 01 Dec
E	Forward, D.J. ...... 01 Oct	X	Smith, D.L. ...... 01 Oct	X	Wood, M.L. ...... 01 Dec
X	Imrie, P.B. ...... 01 Oct	S	Woodard, N.A. ...... 01 Oct	X	Mitchell, C.D. ...... 01 Dec
E	Diver, P.H. ...... 01 Oct	X	Crabb, A.J. ...... 01 Oct	E	Ankah, G.K.E. ...... 01 Dec
X	Allen, P.M. ...... 01 Oct	MS	Blocke, A.D. ...... 01 Oct	E	Brown, A.M. ...... 01 Dec
X	McIntyre, A.W. ...... 01 Oct	S	Carter, S.P. ...... 01 Oct	S	Reed, D.K. ...... 01 Dec
X	Morrell, A.J. ...... 01 Oct	E	McCloskey, I.M. ...... 01 Oct	E	Whitehouse, N.R. ...... 01 Dec
X	Hilson, S.M. ...... 01 Oct	X	Monk, S.R. ...... 01 Oct	E	Boston, J. ...... 01 Jan
X	Hutton, G. ...... 01 Oct	E	Sanderson, L.D. ...... 01 Oct	E	Lewis, S.J. ...... 01 Jan
X	Tidball, I.C. ...... 01 Oct	E	Haworth, J.H.T. ...... 01 Oct	X	Ottewell, P.S. ...... 01 Jan
X	Quinn, S.A. ...... 01 Oct	X	Stuart, E.E.A. ...... 01 Oct	X	Wood, C.R. ...... 01 Jan
E	Dyer, G.R. ...... 01 Oct	X	Dickins, B.R. ...... 01 Oct	E	Cleminson, M.D. ...... 01 Feb
E	Mitchell, P. ...... 01 Oct	X	Essenhigh, A.N.P. ...... 01 Oct	E	Kendrick, A.M. ...... 01 Feb
X	King, S.J. ...... 01 Oct	E	Ashworth, H.J. ...... 01 Oct	X	Robertson Gopffarth, A.A.J. ...... 01 Feb
X	Rasor, A.M. ...... 01 Oct	X	Grieve, L.H. ...... 01 Oct	X	Parr, M.J.E. ...... 02 Feb
X	Allen, L.B. ...... 01 Oct	E	Smith, C.J.H. ...... 01 Oct	E	Haddow, T.R. ...... 01 Mar
E	Dickens, D.S. ...... 01 Oct	E	Dow, C.S. ...... 01 Oct	E	McHugh, R.H. ...... 01 Mar
S	Cogan, R.E.C. ...... 01 Oct	X	Harper, P.R. ...... 01 Oct	E	Thorne, D.J. ...... 01 Mar
X	Julian, T.M. ...... 01 Oct	E	Jefferson, T.S. ...... 01 Oct	X	Tilden, P.J.E. ...... 01 Mar
E	Sargent, P.M. ...... 01 Oct	E	Miller, M.C. ...... 01 Oct	S	Wells, M.P. ...... 01 Mar
E	Rowe, A.J. ...... 01 Oct	E	Cain, C.W. ...... 01 Oct	X	Rackham, K.L.M. ...... 01 Mar
X	MacNeil, S.W. ...... 01 Oct	E	Ridge, M.H. ...... 01 Oct	X	Small, R.J. ...... 01 Mar
X	Simpson, C.C. ...... 01 Oct	E	Wildin, A. ...... 01 Oct	X	Dale-Smith, V.G. ...... 15 Mar
X	Stock, C.M. ...... 01 Oct	E	Mealing, D.W. ...... 01 Oct	E	Rae, A.L. ...... 01 Apr
X	Massey, P. ...... 01 Oct	X	Conway, M.J. ...... 01 Oct	E	Foreman, S.M. ...... 01 Apr
E	Ellis, J.P. ...... 01 Oct	MS	McGunigall, R.J. ...... 01 Oct	E	Boxall, P. ...... 01 Apr
X	Bolton, S.J. ...... 01 Oct	S	Exworthy, D.A.G. ...... 01 Oct	X	Brooks, G.C.G. ...... 01 Apr
X	Scott, M.R. ...... 01 Oct	S	Vogel, L.D. ...... 01 Oct	X	Hounsom, T.R. ...... 01 Apr
X	Tite, A.D. ...... 01 Oct	E	Cattroll, D. ...... 01 Oct	X	Lumsden, P.I. ...... 01 Apr
X	Chadfield, L.J. ...... 01 Oct	E	Shuttleworth, S. ...... 01 Oct	E	Nicoll, A.J. ...... 01 Apr
S	Lewins, G. ...... 01 Oct	E	Sargent, L.M. ...... 01 Oct	X	Jacques, K.M. ...... 01 May
X	Hoare, P.J.E. ...... 01 Oct	S	Welch, K.A. ...... 01 Oct	X	Oakley, S.E. ...... 01 May
S	Sellars, S.J. ...... 01 Oct	E	Richards, J.I.H. ...... 01 Oct	E	Kirk, A.C. ...... 01 May
E	Skelton, J.S. ...... 01 Oct	S	Cox, M.B. ...... 01 Oct	X	Loane, M.M. ...... 01 Jun
X	Kirkham, S.P. ...... 01 Oct	X	Corkett, K.S. ...... 01 Oct	E	Lee, W. ...... 01 Jun
E	Hodge, C.M. ...... 01 Oct	E	Butler, I.A. ...... 01 Oct	E	McCallum, N.R. ...... 01 Jun
E	Ajala, A.R.A. ...... 01 Oct	E	Hendy, R. ...... 01 Oct	E	Burley, M.R. ...... 01 Jun
X	Mullen, J.J. ...... 01 Oct	X	Pedre, R.G. ...... 01 Oct	E	Harvey, B. ...... 01 Jun
E	Ford, G.R. ...... 01 Oct	S	Bull, C.V.R. ...... 01 Oct	E	O'Shaughnessy, D.J. ...... 01 Jun
E	White, R.L. ...... 01 Oct	S	Carrigan, J.A. ...... 01 Oct	X	Saunders, C.E.M. ...... 01 Jun
X	Russell, N.A.D. ...... 01 Oct	E	Benstead, N.W.J. ...... 01 Oct	X	Fitzpatrick, J.A.J. ...... 01 Jul
X	Soul, N.J. ...... 01 Oct	X	Higham, S.W.J.A. ...... 01 Oct	S	Patterson, S.D. ...... 01 Jul
E	Carpenter, B.H. ...... 01 Oct	S	Watson, S.B.C. ...... 01 Oct	E	Selway, M.A. ...... 01 Jul
E	Lovering, T.T.A. ...... 01 Oct	E	Curtis, D. ...... 01 Oct	X	Birrell, G.C. ...... 01 Jul
E	Cragg, R.D. ...... 01 Oct	E	Henderson, R.J. ...... 01 Oct	X	Spinks, D.W. ...... 01 Aug
E	Abbott, D.A. ...... 01 Oct	E	Vollentine, L. ...... 01 Oct	X	Northover, A.F. ...... 01 Aug
X	Atkinson, C.P. ...... 01 Oct	S	Thomas, D.J. ...... 01 Oct	E	Spiller, S.N. ...... 01 Aug
E	Youp, A.T. ...... 01 Oct	S	Prest, N.A. ...... 01 Oct	X	Ward, S. ...... 01 Sep
X	Noyce, R.G. ...... 01 Oct	MS	Manwaring, R.G. ...... 01 Oct	S	Hayes, C.L. ...... 01 Sep
X	Doran, I.A.G. ...... 01 Oct	S	Reed, N. ...... 01 Oct	E	Skittrall, S.D. ...... 15 Oct

LIEUTENANT COMMANDERS

E	Stevenson, J.P.	01 Nov	X	Hutchings, R.P.H.	01 Dec	E	Hay, M.	01 Mar
X	Howe, T.	01 Nov	S	Webster, R.J.	01 Dec	X	Richardson, P.C.	01 Mar
E	Morley, J.I.	01 Nov				E	Thorp, D.B.	01 Mar
S	Sheikh, N.	01 Nov		**2006**		E	Harrington, L.B.	01 Mar
E	Dunn, A.J.P.	07 Nov				E	Nicholas, S.P.	01 Apr
X	Witte, R.H.	01 Dec	E	Ablett, S.D.	01 Jan	X	Brotton, P.J.	01 Apr
X	Allan, C.R.	01 Dec	S	Butterworth, C.L.	01 Feb	E	Mountford, P.C.	01 Apr
E	Bamforth, C.J.M.	01 Dec	X	Dempsey, S.P.	01 Feb	E	Goodall, M.A.	01 May

LIEUTENANTS

1984

E	Maskell-Bott, J.M.	16 Feb

1985

E	Schillemore, P.C.	18 Oct

1987

X	Carne, R.J.P.	16 May
X	Tribe, J.D.	16 Oct

1988

E	Fisher, R.	10 Jun
E	White, S.P.	10 Jun

1989

X	Boyes, R.A.	01 Mar
E	Griffiths, A.R.	09 Jun
X	Swann, J.I.	28 Jul

1990

E	Smart, S.J.	23 Feb
E	Young, K.H.	23 Feb
E	Allen, D.P.	15 Jun
E	Davies, G.P.	15 Jun
X	Davies, A.J.A.	01 Aug

1991

X	Clucas, P.R.	04 Apr
X	May-Clingo, M.S.	04 Apr
E	Gilliland, S.S.	13 Jun
X	Christmas, S.P.	16 Aug
X	Carnell, G.J.	01 Sep
X	Haworth, C.L.N.	01 Sep
X	Milne, P.B.	16 Sep
S	Gill, S.C.	12 Dec

1992

E	Ritsperis, A.	01 Jan
X	Moulton, S.J.	01 Jan
X	Poole, T.J.	16 Jan
X	Thompson, A.R.	01 Feb
X	Hatchard, J.P.	04 Mar
X	Murphy, D.A.	01 Apr
X	Milligan, R.J.C.	16 Apr
X	Radford, A.J.	01 Jun

X	Jameson, R.M.	16 Jul	X	Naylor, A.J.	16 Jun
X	Jaques, D.A.	16 Aug	X	Sheils, D.E.T.	16 Jul
E	Parry, R.J.	16 Oct	X	Lee, P.M.	16 Jul
X	Steele, T.G.	11 Dec	X	Wingfield, M.J.	16 Jul
			X	Laycock, A.	16 Jul

1993

E	Wooding, G.A.	19 Feb	X	Wright, D.A.	29 Jul
E	Edson, M.A.	22 Feb	X	Garner, S.M.	01 Aug
X	Darwent, S.A.	01 Mar	E	Scott, R.A.	01 Aug
X	Gates, N.S.	16 Mar	E	Saunders, J.M.	01 Sep
X	Bramwell, J.G.	01 Apr	X	Cottee, B.R.J.	01 Sep
X	Moreby, M.F.	02 Apr	X	Mutch, J.R.	01 Sep
X	Gamble, P.	15 May	X	Webber, J.P.	01 Sep
X	White, S.H.W.	16 Jun	X	Lord, R.J.	01 Oct
X	Morris, A.M.	01 Jul	X	Ellerton, P.	16 Oct
X	Rodgers, D.	01 Jul	X	Roberts, M.A.	01 Nov
X	Brosnan, M.A.	16 Jul	X	Webster, A.P.	01 Nov
X	Norris, G.P.	16 Jul	X	Peachey, R.M.	01 Nov
E	Evison, T.	27 Jul	X	Allison, G.	16 Nov
X	Willing, N.P.	16 Aug	X	Roster, S.P.	16 Nov
X	Duncan, C.J.	01 Sep	X	Young, R.	01 Dec
X	Elwell-Deighton, D.C.	16 Sep	X	Hardy, L.B.	16 Dec
X	Rutherford, K.J.	01 Oct			
E	Burrows, J.C.	15 Oct		**1995**	
X	May, P.J.	29 Oct			
X	Gamble, N.	01 Nov	E	Rogers, P.S.	01 Jan
X	MacFarlane, I.S.D.	01 Nov	X	Mills, S.D.G.	01 Jan
X	Polding, M.	01 Nov	X	Jones, M.D.	16 Jan
X	Marquis, A.C.	01 Dec	X	Satterthwaite, B.J.	01 Feb
X	Spence, R.G.	16 Dec	E	Langrill, T.J.	01 Feb
X	Wardle, M.	17 Dec	X	McCutcheon, G.	01 Feb
S	Wyatt, C.	17 Dec	X	Barber, C.J.H.	01 Feb
			E	Fallowfield, J.P.	24 Feb

1994

X	Sims, D.L.	01 Jan	X	Bainbridge, S.D.	01 Mar
X	Gotke, C.T.	16 Jan	X	Gray, J.N.S.	01 Apr
X	Buckley, D.D.G.	01 Feb	X	Stratford, P.J.	01 Apr
X	Bunney, G.J.	01 Feb	X	Reid, M.R.	01 Apr
E	Brothers, A.H.G.	18 Feb	X	McLennan, A.	01 Apr
X	Hinchcliffe, A.	01 Mar	X	Inge, D.J.	01 May
X	Knight, A.C.F.	01 Mar	X	Stubbs, I.	16 May
X	Barnes, P.A.L.	01 Apr	X	Woolsey, K.E.K.	16 May
S	Austen, R.M.	08 Apr	X	Turner, D.N.	01 Jun
X	Lister, S.	08 Apr	X	Watson, A.H.	01 Jun
X	Evans, G.B.	01 May	E	Wilson, J.A.	15 Jun
X	Townsend, G.P.	01 May	X	Day, M.K.	15 Jun
X	Kennington, L.A.	01 May	X	May, J.W.	01 Jul
X	Matthews, J.	16 May	X	Parrock, N.G.	01 Jul
X	Hedworth, A.J.	01 Jun	X	Deavin, M.J.	01 Jul
			X	Bishop, G.C.	27 Jul
			X	Higgins, A.J.	01 Aug
			E	Mehta, K.L.	01 Sep

LIEUTENANTS

E	Hambly, B.J.	01 Sep
E	Cullen, N.L.	01 Sep
X	Baxter, J.C.	27 Sep
E	Welsh, J.	15 Oct
E	Parker, T.S.	01 Nov
X	Chick, N.S.	16 Nov
E	Lee, S.Y.L.	01 Dec
X	Tacey, R.H.	01 Dec
X	Evans, D.A.	20 Dec

1996

E	Collins, T.L.	01 Jan
E	Harrison, T.I.	01 Jan
E	Heighway, M.R.	01 Jan
X	Okukenu, D.	01 Jan
S	Trinder, S.J.	30 Jan
X	Officer, R.L.	01 Feb
X	Wookey, M.	01 Feb
X	Wilkinson, M.F.	01 Feb
X	Watts, J.N.	01 Feb
X	Thomas, S.M.	16 Feb
X	Packham, C.N.R.	01 Mar
X	Simms, D.M.	16 Mar
X	Flintham, J.E.	16 Mar
X	Long, M.S.	01 Apr
X	Ford, A.J.	04 Apr
X	Campbell, I.A.	16 Apr
X	Fraser, I.E.	16 Apr
E	Evans, P.C.	01 May
X	MacColl, A.A.J.	01 May
E	Taylor, I.J.	05 May
X	Robley, W.F.	01 Jun
X	Strathie, G.S.	01 Jun
X	Criddle, G.D.J.	01 Jun
X	Fisher, R.J.	01 Jun
X	Gilmore, M.P.	01 Jun
E	Hutchinson, P.	14 Jun
X	Vorley, S.W.	15 Jun
X	Wiseman, N.C.	16 Jun
X	Platt, J.H.	16 Jun
E	Deeks, P.J.	01 Jul
X	Fox, T.M.	01 Jul
X	Spillane, P.W.	01 Jul
X	Davies, H.G.A.	01 Jul
X	Church, S.C.	16 Jul
X	Forbes, P.T.	16 Jul
X	Brember, P.B.	25 Jul
X	Smith, S.R.F.	28 Jul
X	Abel, N.P.	16 Aug
X	Clarke, R.J.	16 Aug
X	Hall, D.	16 Aug
X	Whitlum, A.C.	16 Aug
E	Edwards, J.	01 Sep
E	Kelly, G.J.	01 Sep
X	Terry, N.P.	01 Sep
X	Enever, S.A.	01 Sep
X	Williams, R.J.S.	01 Sep
X	Campbell, M.A.M.	01 Sep
X	Hindmarch, S.A.	01 Sep
X	Raeburn, C.	01 Sep
E	Bottomley, S.	06 Sep
E	Dunbar, S.	17 Sep

X	Hill, A.J.	01 Oct
X	Bonnar, S.M.	01 Nov
E	Gothard, A.M.	01 Nov
X	Webber, K.J.	01 Nov
X	Bradley, R.L.	01 Nov
X	Ollerton, J.C.	16 Nov
X	Hayden, T.W.	01 Dec

1997

E	Collins, D.R.	01 Jan
E	Dick, C.M.	01 Jan
E	Taylor, C.S.	01 Jan
X	Long, S.G.	01 Jan
X	Clague, J.J.	15 Jan
X	Johnson, S.R.D.	16 Jan
E	Smith, K.D.	01 Feb
X	Thomsen-Rayner, L.L.	01 Feb
E	McTaggart, D.A.	07 Feb
X	Owen, G.	16 Feb
E	Thomson, P.D.	24 Feb
E	Read, P.S.	01 Mar
X	Jackson, I.	01 Mar
X	Philip, A.D.	01 Mar
X	Compain, C.H.	21 Mar
E	Cumming, R.A.	01 Apr
X	Bernard, R.A.	01 Apr
X	Green, I.A.	01 Apr
X	Alcindor, D.J.	01 Apr
X	Norford, M.A.	03 Apr
X	Stretton, D.G.	03 Apr
X	Tomlinson, D.C.	03 Apr
E	Brooks, K.M.L.	06 Apr
X	Heaney, M.J.	16 Apr
X	Bennett, D.P.	01 May
E	Adams, G.	01 May
E	Straughan, S.R.	01 May
X	Lewis, B.C.	16 May
E	Briggs, M.D.	01 Jun
X	Gamble, S.B.	01 Jun
X	Leighton, M.R.	01 Jun
S	Porter, D.L.	01 Jun
X	Jones, M.A.	13 Jun
E	White, K.F.	01 Jul
X	Baines, A.R.	01 Jul
X	McKee, H.M.	01 Jul
X	Pedler, M.D.	01 Jul
E	Saward, J.R.E.	01 Jul
X	Wilson, J.	01 Jul
E	Wood, A.G.	01 Jul
X	Boughton, T.F.	01 Jul
X	Hughes, S.M.	16 Jul
X	Potter, D.J.	24 Jul
X	Vowles, M.J.	24 Jul
X	Young, J.N.	24 Jul
E	Mallabone, J.J.K.	01 Aug
X	Chawira, D.N.	01 Aug
E	Evans, M.E.	01 Aug
X	Mennecke-Jappy, G.W.G.	01 Aug
E	Brutton, J.H.	01 Aug
X	Holder, J.M.	01 Aug
S	Robb, M.E.	01 Aug
X	Fuller, C.E.	16 Aug

X	Scott, M.	16 Aug
E	Clark, S.R.	01 Sep
E	Pettigrew, T.R.	01 Sep
E	Ashby, K.J.	01 Sep
X	Clay, T.C.D.C.	01 Sep
X	Palethorpe, N.	01 Sep
X	Prole, N.M.	16 Sep
E	Jenner, A.C.	16 Sep
X	Walton, S.P.	01 Oct
X	Mansfield, J.A.	01 Oct
X	Davey, T.J.	01 Oct
X	Hudson, M.	10 Oct
X	Alexander, O.D.D.	01 Nov
X	Hancock, Z.M.A.	01 Nov
X	Goulder, J.D.	01 Nov
X	Leadbetter, A.J.	01 Nov
S	Rickard, J.	12 Nov
E	Hawkins, S.R.	01 Dec
X	Davies, G.W.T.	01 Dec
E	Collen, S.J.	01 Dec
X	Wallace, S.A.	01 Dec
X	Doig, B.J.	01 Dec
E	Chambers, P.D.	01 Dec
E	Stevens, A.J.	04 Dec
X	Davies, J.J.	12 Dec
X	Rose, A.D.	16 Dec

1998

E	Auld, D.M.	01 Jan
E	Watkins, K.J.	01 Jan
X	Stilwell, J.M.	01 Jan
X	Spoors, B.M.	01 Jan
X	Steen, K.M.	01 Jan
X	Willis, A.S.	01 Jan
E	Goodship, M.T.	01 Jan
X	Blackmore, J.	16 Jan
E	D'Silva, D.M.	01 Feb
X	Gibbs, D.J.E.	01 Feb
E	Millard, J.R.	01 Feb
X	Roberts, N.D.	10 Feb
X	Eastwood, R.N.	15 Feb
X	Priest, J.E.	15 Feb
X	Holroyd, J.E.J.	16 Feb
E	Lyons, A.G.	01 Mar
X	Guy, C.R.	01 Mar
S	Haggard, A.	01 Mar
X	White, D.J.	01 Mar
X	Gray, J.A.	01 Mar
X	Calhaem, R.T.	15 Mar
X	McCormick, P.E.	15 Mar
X	Beech, D.J.	16 Mar
X	Samuels, N.J.	01 Apr
X	Lippitt, S.T.	01 Apr
X	Birchall, J.C.	01 Apr
X	Peak, M.	03 Apr
S	Platt, N.	03 Apr
X	Wood, J.A.	03 Apr
X	Bates, A.J.	16 Apr
X	Haggo, J.R.	16 Apr
X	Tremelling, P.N.	16 Apr
E	Cameron, F.	24 Apr
E	Buck, S.R.	01 May

LIEUTENANTS

E	Eveling, R.J.	01 May
E	Hartley, J.H.D.	01 May
X	Rushworth, B.J.	01 May
X	McWilliams, A.R.	01 May
E	Clarke, M.D.	01 May
X	Riggall, L.J.	01 May
E	Beaver, R.M.S.	01 May
E	Grennan, E.F.	01 May
X	Vallance, M.S.	01 May
S	Sutcliffe, E.D.	01 May
X	Yates, S.E.	01 May
X	Full, R.J.	01 Jun
E	Humphery, D.	01 Jun
X	Denham, D.J.	01 Jun
S	Gilbert, R.G.	01 Jun
X	Hicks, N.J.I.	01 Jun
X	Coulton, J.R.S.	16 Jun
X	Jenkins, A.R.	16 Jun
E	Jones, R.K.	19 Jun
E	Paton, A.J.M.	19 Jun
E	Stone, R.J.	19 Jun
X	Bainbridge, J.R.	30 Jun
E	Simm, C.W.	01 Jul
X	Johnson, M.R.E.	01 Jul
X	Howe, C.M.	01 Jul
X	Mason, A.C.	01 Jul
X	Pressdee, S.J.	01 Jul
E	Chilton, J.	01 Jul
X	Rogers, S.J.P.	01 Jul
X	Beale, M.D.	23 Jul
X	Johns, L.E.	23 Jul
X	Louden, C.A.	23 Jul
X	Parkinson, A.P.	23 Jul
X	Kewley, I.D.	01 Aug
E	Taylor, K.M.	01 Aug
E	Burns, E.P.	01 Aug
X	Mansergh, F.A.	01 Aug
X	Craven, M.W.	01 Aug
X	Heirs, G.G.	01 Aug
X	MacLaughlin, R.A.	01 Aug
X	Muirhead, B.G.	01 Aug
S	Miles, P.J.	01 Aug
S	Park, I.D.	01 Aug
X	Pollard, A.E.	01 Aug
X	Hammock, S.G.	16 Aug
E	Bird, T.S.V.	01 Sep
E	Bristow, P.C.	01 Sep
E	Coles, S.P.	01 Sep
E	Jameson, A.J.	01 Sep
E	MacCorquodale, M.A.	01 Sep
E	Rees, A.M.	01 Sep
E	Salim, M.	01 Sep
X	Bagshaw, J.R.W.	01 Sep
X	Davies, N.M.S.	01 Sep
X	Berry, T.J.	01 Sep
X	Griffiths, N.	01 Sep
X	Howard, N.A.	01 Sep
X	Hutchins, I.D.M.	01 Sep
E	McDonald, D.J.	01 Sep
X	Thomas, M.	01 Sep
X	Williams, A.S.	01 Sep
X	Arkle, N.J.	01 Sep

X	Burbidge, K.	01 Sep
X	Ingham, A.R.	01 Sep
E	Brodier, M.I.	04 Sep
E	Metcalfe, R.J.	04 Sep
X	Raynes, C.	16 Sep
X	Ashlin, J.M.	16 Sep
X	Walton, S.D.	01 Oct
X	Osbaldestin, R.A.	01 Oct
X	Anderson, G.S.	01 Oct
X	Crane, O.R.	01 Oct
X	Fletcher, I.J.	01 Oct
X	Gould, J.D.	01 Oct
X	Thomas, D.W.	01 Oct
X	Varty, J.A.	01 Oct
X	Benzie, N.J.E.	01 Oct
X	Densham, M.P.J.	01 Oct
X	Drodge, K.N.	01 Oct
X	Wyness, C.J.	01 Oct
X	Wappner, G.D.	10 Oct
X	Gaskell, H.D.	16 Oct
X	Tazewell, M.R.	16 Oct
X	Doubleday, S.	16 Oct
X	Gillett, D.A.	01 Nov
X	Instone, M.J.	01 Nov
X	Chacksfield, E.N.	01 Nov
X	Cowin, T.J.	01 Nov
S	Curwood, J.E.	01 Nov
X	McCall, G.	01 Nov
E	McCoy, M.	01 Nov
X	Norgate, A.T.	01 Nov
X	Stein, G.K.	01 Nov
S	Ward, D.J.	01 Nov
X	Baldie, S.A.H.	15 Nov
X	Iliffe, D.I.	16 Nov
X	Nelson, M.R.	16 Nov
E	Greig, J.A.	27 Nov
E	McLaughlin, S.	01 Dec
X	Whitehead, P.J.	01 Dec
E	Sangha, R.S.	01 Dec
E	Walsh, A.H.	01 Dec
X	Hartley, B.P.I.	01 Dec
X	Johnston, G.S.	01 Dec
X	Alsop, S.H.	01 Dec
X	Astle, D.S.	01 Dec
E	Blackburn, A.R.J.	01 Dec
X	Crabbe, R.J.	01 Dec
X	Lilly, D.M.	01 Dec
E	McCann, T.	01 Dec
X	Meyer, A.J.	01 Dec
S	Terry, J.H.	01 Dec
X	Webster, R.J.	01 Dec
X	Wright, D.J.	01 Dec
E	Pine, P.M.	06 Dec
X	Beard, R.G.	10 Dec
X	Egerton, S.B.	10 Dec
X	Martin, A.J.	10 Dec
X	Routledge, W.D.	10 Dec
X	Singleton, M.D.	10 Dec
X	Smith, R.E.	10 Dec

1999

E	Gibson, S.J.	01 Jan

X	Ball, A.D.	01 Jan
E	Carroll, S.L.	01 Jan
X	Clarke, D.	01 Jan
X	Conlin, J.A.	01 Jan
X	Wood, I.L.	01 Jan
X	Brazier, L.F.	01 Jan
E	Newman, D.J.	01 Jan
E	Ruston, M.R.	01 Jan
X	Ansell, C.N.	01 Jan
S	Arend, F.M.	01 Jan
X	Croft, D.F.	01 Jan
E	Hunt, P.S.	01 Jan
X	Johnson, A.D.	01 Jan
E	McClement, D.L.	01 Jan
E	O'Shaughnessy, P.C.	01 Jan
E	Ruddock, J.	01 Jan
X	Thomson, J.C.	01 Jan
X	Watts, Z.A.	01 Jan
E	Smith, A.	09 Jan
E	Dry, I.	31 Jan
E	Hiscock, S.R.B.	01 Feb
E	Burns, J.E.	01 Feb
X	Greenwood, A.W.	01 Feb
S	Haines, R.J.	01 Feb
E	Turner, P.L.	01 Feb
X	Wade, J.M.R.	01 Feb
X	Bell, C.M.	01 Feb
X	Denney, J.R.	01 Feb
X	Hirons, F.D.	01 Feb
X	Johnson, P.R.	01 Feb
X	Mullowney, P.	01 Feb
E	Moody, A.C.	01 Feb
X	Wall, S.N.	01 Feb
X	Morgan, E.J.A.	12 Feb
X	Sweeney, C.	16 Feb
E	Todd, D.B.	01 Mar
X	Gibbs, A.M.	01 Mar
X	Brewin, D.J.	01 Mar
S	Conway, S.H.	01 Mar
X	Fisher, S.J.	01 Mar
X	Hume, K.J.	01 Mar
X	Middleton, D.M.	01 Mar
S	Robertson, S.T.	01 Mar
X	Wadsworth, R.Y.	01 Mar
E	Barton, K.J.A.	01 Mar
X	Mains, G.	18 Mar
X	Dodds, M.L.	01 Apr
X	Rawles, J.R.	01 Apr
X	Twigg, K.L.	01 Apr
X	Ward, M.T.	01 Apr
X	Smith, A.J.E.	01 Apr
X	Stait, B.G.	01 Apr
E	Thomson, M.L.	01 Apr
X	Beavis, J.A.	01 Apr
X	Hilton, S.T.	01 Apr
S	Stait, E.J.	01 Apr
X	Hutchings, J.R.	01 Apr
X	Percy, N.A.	01 Apr
E	Grey, E.J.W.	03 Apr
X	Sparrow, M.J.	16 Apr
X	Thompson, D.A.	16 Apr
S	Case, A.	26 Apr

LIEUTENANTS

	Name	Date		Name	Date		Name	Date
X	Dunkley, S.C.	26 Apr	E	Booth, W.N.	02 Sep	S	Carcone, P.N.	01 Dec
X	Harriman, P.	26 Apr	E	Brennan, P.A.	02 Sep	X	Griffiths, C.S.H.	01 Dec
X	Lovett, S.A.	26 Apr	E	Flatt, L.D.	02 Sep	X	Holden, J.L.	01 Dec
X	Pearch, S.M.	26 Apr	E	Forshaw, D.R.	02 Sep	X	Morse, J.	01 Dec
X	Toon, P.G.	26 Apr	E	MacLean, M.T.	02 Sep	E	Pollard, J.R.	01 Dec
E	Johnston, K.I.	01 May	E	Millar, K.I.	02 Sep	E	Hamilton, M.I.	01 Dec
X	Ellis, A.C.	01 May	E	Nicholson, J.C.	02 Sep	X	Taylor, A.I.	01 Dec
S	Clements, E.J.	01 May	E	Nursey, A.P.	02 Sep	X	Breen, D.A.	11 Dec
S	Titcombe, A.J.	01 May	E	Penketh, M.G.	02 Sep	X	Bevan, J.R.	16 Dec
X	Daly, P.	01 May	E	Quirk, A.T.	02 Sep			
X	Dransfield, J.A.J.	01 May	E	Rom, S.P.	02 Sep		**2000**	
E	Stratton, M.P.	01 May	E	Saywell-Hall, S.E.	02 Sep			
X	Flatman, T.D.	16 May	E	Scholes, N.A.	02 Sep	E	Blethyn, H.P.	01 Jan
X	Mann, D.M.	01 Jun	E	Spencer, J.C.	02 Sep	E	Gill, P.S.	01 Jan
E	Deal, C.	01 Jun	E	Stead, J.A.	02 Sep	E	Hemingway, D.G.	01 Jan
X	Hughes, C.B.	01 Jun	E	Torney, C.J.	02 Sep	E	Muyambo, N.N.	01 Jan
X	Moran, R.J.	01 Jun	E	Ward, N.A.	02 Sep	E	Perryman, I.T.C.	01 Jan
X	Redmayne, M.E.	01 Jun	E	Watson, A.P.	02 Sep	E	Priestley, C.	01 Jan
E	Stead, A.M.	01 Jul	X	Bull, M.A.J.	11 Sep	E	White, S.P.	01 Jan
X	Kennedy, R.J.	01 Jul	X	Netherwood, L.D.	15 Sep	E	Wood, C.T.	01 Jan
E	Blackburn, E.C.	01 Jul	X	Lawrence, L.J.	16 Sep	X	Kitteridge, D.J.	01 Jan
S	Christian, J.	01 Jul	X	Adams, E.S.	16 Sep	X	Mason, M.J.	01 Jan
X	Fennell, C.B.	01 Jul	X	Llewellyn, J.G.	20 Sep	X	Brewer, C.E.	01 Jan
X	Gillard, V.A.	01 Jul	MS	Welch, A.	20 Sep	X	Crew, J.M.	01 Jan
E	Goodship, J.S.	01 Jul	X	Martin, N.	20 Sep	S	Lanning, K.A.	01 Jan
S	Murphy, V.J.	01 Jul	E	Osborne, J.M.	01 Oct	X	Williams, D.L.	01 Jan
S	Relf, K.M.	01 Jul	X	Cutler, A.R.	01 Oct	X	Mortlock, P.A.	01 Jan
X	Saltonstall, P.J.R.	01 Jul	E	Buckenham, P.J.	01 Oct	E	Russell, C.M.L.	01 Jan
X	Thomas, D.H.	01 Jul	X	Cornford, M.	01 Oct	X	Slattery, D.J.	01 Jan
X	Kelly, S.P.	01 Jul	S	Cutler, T.P.	01 Oct	E	Bennett, W.E.	01 Jan
X	Whitwell, N.S.	01 Jul	X	Hammon, M.A.	01 Oct	X	Gill, C.D.	01 Jan
X	Swindells, M.	16 Jul	S	Rees, K.M.M.	01 Oct	E	Hatchard, P.	01 Jan
E	Epps, M.P.	17 Jul	X	Rex, C.A.	01 Oct	E	Law, R.	01 Jan
E	Bailey, S.	01 Aug	X	Sanderson, C.P.	01 Oct	X	Mabbott, K.I.	01 Jan
X	Hughes, J.J.	01 Aug	X	Hardman, M.J.	01 Oct	X	McIntyre, L.	01 Jan
X	Sambrooks, R.J.	01 Aug	S	Knox, G.P.	01 Oct	E	Miller, I.	01 Jan
X	Clark, R.A.	01 Aug	X	Thomas, O.H.	16 Oct	E	Nicklin, G.J.E.	01 Jan
X	Crowe, D.M.	01 Aug	X	Greenwood, P.A.	16 Oct	X	Phillips, R.M.	01 Jan
X	Hannam, D.B.	01 Aug	X	Barker, T.J.	16 Oct	X	Boeckx, T.J.F.	01 Jan
E	Holmwood, M.A.G.	01 Aug	E	Clear, N.J.	01 Nov	X	Green, R.R.	08 Jan
E	Martin, S.W.	01 Aug	X	Finch, I.R.	01 Nov	X	Francis, D.E.	10 Jan
X	Rogers, J.A.	01 Aug	E	Andrew, P.	01 Nov	X	Lester, R.L.	10 Jan
X	Weston, K.N.N.	01 Aug	X	Cannell, G.M.	01 Nov	X	Moran, C.A.	10 Jan
X	Woollven, C.D.	01 Aug	X	Hayashi, L.R.	01 Nov	E	Stafford, B.R.	01 Feb
X	Frazer, H.F.	01 Aug	E	Hubschmid, S.R.	01 Nov	S	Brimacombe, L.M.	01 Feb
E	Molyneux, I.T.	01 Aug	E	Orr, K.J.	01 Nov	S	Wall, I.J.	01 Feb
X	Currie, M.J.	16 Aug	X	Aldous, B.W.	01 Nov	X	Considine, K.J.	01 Feb
E	Scotter, C.M.	01 Sep	S	Clarke, A.G.	01 Nov	X	Harford-Cross, P.J.	01 Feb
X	Jordan, A.F.	01 Sep	E	Jones, I.M.	01 Nov	X	Jackson, P.	01 Feb
E	Alexander, A.L.	01 Sep	E	Lee, S.E.	01 Nov	E	Martin, R.J.	01 Feb
X	Barr, S.P.	01 Sep	S	Black, S.B.	05 Nov	E	Risley, J.G.	01 Feb
X	Birleson, P.D.	01 Sep	X	Rowson, M.J.	16 Nov	X	Thompson, W.A.	01 Feb
X	Carnie, M.J.	01 Sep	X	O'Neill, J.	22 Nov	E	Timbrell, I.P.J.	01 Feb
X	Livsey, A.E.J.	01 Sep	E	Cessford, R.I.	01 Dec	X	Whitehall, S.	01 Feb
X	Green, J.H.	01 Sep	E	Derrick, M.J.G.	01 Dec	X	Wooller, L.F.V.	01 Feb
E	Healey, M.J.	01 Sep	X	Marshall, A.J.	01 Dec	E	Jones, L.H.	13 Feb
E	Hepplewhite, M.B.	01 Sep	X	Chambers, C.P.	01 Dec	E	Quinn, M.E.	01 Mar
X	Johnson, S.	01 Sep	X	Gray, N.J.	01 Dec	X	Coverdale, P.	01 Mar
E	Leivers, A.J.	01 Sep	E	Jenkins, R.C.	01 Dec	X	Winsor, J.	01 Mar
S	Matthew, M.J.	01 Sep	S	Oliver, G.J.	01 Dec	X	Bennett, C.D.	01 Mar
S	Weare, J.B.	01 Sep	X	Sloan, I.A.	01 Dec	E	Ellis, C.R.	01 Mar
S	Curtis, S.E.H.	01 Sep	E	Ball, M.P.	01 Dec	X	Lanning, R.M.	01 Mar
						E	Mathieson, N.B.	01 Mar

LIEUTENANTS

E	McDonald, A.W.	01 Mar	E	Hodgson, J.R.	02 May	X	Armstrong, S.M.	01 Sep
E	Milne, W.J.C.	01 Mar	E	Liddell, M.L.	02 May	E	Blackburn, L.R.	01 Sep
X	Richardson, I.H.	01 Mar	E	Moy, D.K.	02 May	E	Dawson, G.A.E.	01 Sep
X	Madigan, L.	01 Mar	X	Paget, S.J.	02 May	E	Dixon, A.K.	01 Sep
X	Brown, A.R.A.	01 Mar	E	Ryan, J.P.	02 May	E	Dominy, V.L.	01 Sep
X	Holmes, A.M.	15 Mar	E	Smart, M.J.	02 May	S	Lear, S.F.	01 Sep
X	McGannity, C.S.	16 Mar	E	Pearmain, S.R.	14 May	X	Bailes, K.P.	01 Sep
X	Barritt, O.D.	01 Apr	E	Whetter, R.S.	14 May	X	Bullock, R.A.	01 Sep
E	Pipkin, P.J.	01 Apr	X	O'Kane, R.J.	16 May	X	Hearn, S.P.	01 Sep
E	Winbolt, N.I.	01 Apr	E	Mantri, A.H.	22 May	X	Lynas, J.F.A.	01 Sep
X	Lloyd, B.J.	01 Apr	X	George, S.D.	01 Jun	X	Armstrong, C.D.	01 Sep
X	MacLean, J.A.	01 Apr	X	Beanland, P.L.	01 Jun	S	Johnson, A.C.	01 Sep
X	Moore, N.J.	01 Apr	X	Bedding, D.	01 Jun	S	Peyman, T.A.	01 Sep
X	Murgatroyd, K.J.	01 Apr	X	Campbell, T.R.	01 Jun	X	Ransom, B.R.J.	01 Sep
E	Barker, P.D.	01 Apr	E	Grant, W.G.	01 Jun	E	Rooney, M.	01 Sep
X	Bates, N.S.	01 Apr	X	Higginson, N.J.	01 Jun	X	Wick, H.M.S.	01 Sep
X	Chambers, R.	01 Apr	X	Ives, D.J.	01 Jun	E	Pickard, S.R.	01 Sep
X	Feeney, M.B.	01 Apr	X	Money, C.J.	01 Jun	X	Finn, S.A.	01 Sep
E	Gilmore, S.J.	01 Apr	X	Mount, J.B.	01 Jun	S	Flegg, K.G.	01 Sep
X	Hammond, M.M.V.	01 Apr	X	Randles, S.	01 Jun	X	Stanway, C.A.	01 Sep
X	Liddle, R.D.	01 Apr	X	Urwin, S.J.	01 Jun	E	Geneux, N.S.	01 Sep
X	Whitehouse, D.S.	01 Apr	X	Varley, P.G.S.	01 Jun	X	Boon, G.J.	19 Sep
X	Bodman, S.A.	01 Apr	X	Irwin, S.G.	01 Jun	X	Castle, C.D.	19 Sep
E	England, P.M.	01 Apr	E	Lovett, A.R.	01 Jun	X	Cowan, A.R.	19 Sep
X	Griffen, D.J.	01 Apr	E	Jones, M.R.	01 Jun	X	Howells, S.M.	19 Sep
X	Headley, M.J.	01 Apr	E	Prest, S.F.	01 Jun	S	Love, J.D.	19 Sep
S	McLocklan, L.M.	01 Apr	X	Williams, D.E.	08 Jun	X	Lynn, H.W.	19 Sep
X	Shearn, M.A.	01 Apr	X	Sims, A.R.	15 Jun	X	Mills, G.A.	19 Sep
S	Turner, D.J.	01 Apr	X	Milles, O.K.	16 Jun	X	Parton, A.	19 Sep
S	West, N.K.	01 Apr	E	Quinn, A.D.	01 Jul	X	Pirrie, J.A.	19 Sep
E	Bartholomew, D.J.	01 May	E	Wallace, I.S.	01 Jul	X	Stringer, G.E.	19 Sep
E	Free, A.S.	01 May	X	Lewis, K.E.	01 Jul	X	Walker, R.S.	19 Sep
E	Goodall, J.C.	01 May	E	Dickinson, P.H.	01 Jul	X	Wilson, G.J.	19 Sep
E	Hollyfield, P.R.	01 May	X	Gare, C.J.	01 Jul	X	Stobo, A.	01 Oct
E	Holt, J.D.	01 May	X	Humphries, M.	01 Jul	E	Gould, A.A.	01 Oct
E	Padget, J.L.	01 May	E	Kitchen, B.	01 Jul	X	Hancock, J.H.	01 Oct
E	Ussher, J.H.D.	01 May	X	Retter, R.L.	01 Jul	S	Henderson, S.C.	01 Oct
S	Halsey, K.E.	01 May	X	Bane, N.S.J.	01 Jul	X	Fyfe, K.S.	01 Oct
E	Andrews, C.	01 May	X	Bull, L.P.	01 Jul	X	Hadland, G.V.	01 Oct
E	Baillie, R.W.	01 May	X	Jacob, A.W.	01 Jul	X	Hampshire, T.	01 Oct
X	Firth, J.S.	01 May	S	Stone, N.J.J.	01 Jul	S	Richards, A.J.	01 Oct
S	Forge, S.M.	01 May	E	Elliott, J.A.	01 Jul	X	Robey, J.C.	01 Oct
X	Gardner, M.P.	01 May	X	Kohn, P.A.	01 Jul	X	Winn, J.P.	01 Oct
E	Newth, C.S.	01 May	X	Rea, S.D.	01 Jul	X	Dodd, S.E.	01 Oct
X	Page, M.R.	01 May	E	Casson, R.F.	01 Jul	X	Gallimore, R.M.	01 Oct
E	Austin, S.T.	01 May	E	Foote, A.S.	01 Jul	X	Kroon, Z.	01 Oct
E	Coles, C.P.	01 May	X	Harcombe, A.	16 Jul	X	Filtness, D.M.	01 Oct
X	Keith, B.C.	01 May	E	Treharne, M.A.	01 Aug	X	King, W.R.C.	01 Oct
S	Lane, N.	01 May	X	Coulton, S.L.	01 Aug	E	Grantham, G.J.	01 Nov
S	Wood, S.A.H.	01 May	X	Hewitson, J.G.A.	01 Aug	X	Parsons, R.J.	01 Nov
X	Woolhead, C.M.	01 May	S	Potts, R.E.	01 Aug	X	Bartram, R.J.	01 Nov
X	Stratton, N.C.	01 May	X	Sturman, R.W.	01 Aug	X	Bouyac, D.R.L.	01 Nov
X	Brown, J.A.	01 May	X	Ainsley, A.M.J.	01 Aug	X	Collins, A.C.	01 Nov
X	Cromie, J.M.	01 May	X	Anderson, S.R.	01 Aug	X	Crompton, P.J.	01 Nov
X	Hember, M.J.C.	01 May	S	Clark, C.L.	01 Aug	X	Owen, S.T.L.	01 Nov
X	Reid, J.L.	01 May	S	Middleton, W.T.	01 Aug	S	Rollason, C.A.	01 Nov
X	Winand, F.M.J.	01 May	X	Mc Currach, R.H.	01 Aug	X	Burton, A.	01 Nov
S	Ashley, P.D.	01 May	E	Reeves, P.K.	01 Aug	X	Doran, K.E.	01 Nov
E	Trueman, B.D.	01 May	X	Brown, S.G.	04 Aug	X	Horton, J.R.	01 Nov
E	Burton, P.R.	02 May	X	Farr, I.R.	16 Aug	S	MacDonald, S.B.	01 Nov
E	Collins, D.A.	02 May	E	Collins, L.J.	01 Sep	E	Seagrave, S.J.	01 Nov
E	Edwins, M.R.	02 May	E	Holmes, R.M.	01 Sep	X	Spears, A.G.	01 Nov

LIEUTENANTS

X	Simmonite, G.I.	16 Nov	X	Whitson-Fay, C.D.	15 Feb	E	Toone, S.A.	01 Apr
X	Hall, C.J.	01 Dec	X	Lightfoot, R.A.	16 Feb	E	Turner, A.J.	01 Apr
X	Partridge, S.C.	01 Dec	S	Broadbent, S.E.	01 Mar	X	Tutchings, A.	01 Apr
E	Wharrie, C.G.	01 Dec	X	Dowling, A.J.	01 Mar	E	Whitehouse, S.R.	01 Apr
X	Dermody, R.T.	01 Dec	X	Knowles, C.J.	01 Mar	X	Wood, N.R.	01 Apr
X	Pearson, J.C.	01 Dec	E	Wallace, R.P.	01 Mar	E	Cheyne, R.D.	01 Apr
X	Summers, A.J.	01 Dec	X	Price, J.C.	05 Mar	E	Clapham, G.T.	01 Apr
X	Fillmore, R.J.	01 Dec	X	Twigg, N.R.	16 Mar	E	Dodd, L.	01 Apr
X	Northcote, M.R.	01 Dec	E	Alberts, P.W.	01 Apr	E	Flegg, M.J.	01 Apr
X	Milne, A.P.	16 Dec	E	Barron-Robinson, D.P.	01 Apr	E	Heal, T.S.	01 Apr
			S	Baxter, F.J.	01 Apr	X	Godfrey, S.D.W.	01 Apr
	2001		S	Bell, S.W.	01 Apr	E	Bleasdale, D.R.	01 Apr
			E	Blois, S.D.	01 Apr	X	Gibbs, A.E.	08 Apr
E	Blackler, S.	01 Jan	S	Brady, T.W.	01 Apr	E	Anderson, C.J.	13 Apr
E	Oakley, A.J.	01 Jan	E	Carter, P.	01 Apr	S	Brint, I.	29 Apr
E	Kierstan, S.J.J.	01 Jan	S	Chilton, D.J.	01 Apr	X	Carter, N.R.	29 Apr
X	Aitken, S.R.	01 Jan	X	Clarke, M.	01 Apr	S	Christie, A.B.	29 Apr
E	Alexander, P.M.D.	01 Jan	S	Cotton, E.L.	01 Apr	E	Cooke, R.N.	29 Apr
X	Butler, P.M.	01 Jan	E	Crawley, D.A.	01 Apr	X	Dainty, R.C.	29 Apr
X	Finn, J.S.	01 Jan	X	Daniels, S.P.	01 Apr	E	Finch, S.	29 Apr
X	Gladwin, M.D.	01 Jan	E	Dawson, P.	01 Apr	E	Griffiths, C.J.J.	29 Apr
E	Morphet, K.	01 Jan	E	Dumbleton, D.W.	01 Apr	X	Gwatkin, N.J.	29 Apr
X	Turner, J.S.	01 Jan	X	Dunn, A.	01 Apr	E	Hamilton, G.D.	29 Apr
X	Dingley, P.A.	01 Jan	X	Edmondson, J.A.	01 Apr	E	Hardy, R.J.	29 Apr
X	Dixon, R.A.	01 Jan	E	Freeman, M.J.	01 Apr	E	Harrison, A.D.	29 Apr
X	Howie, E.J.	01 Jan	X	Gallimore, J.M.	01 Apr	X	Hattle, P.M.	29 Apr
S	Ledward, K.L.	01 Jan	E	Gibson, M.J.S.	01 Apr	E	Hewitt, M.J.	29 Apr
X	Pickles, D.R.	01 Jan	S	Gosling, D.J.	01 Apr	E	Loughrey, N.C.	29 Apr
X	Wragg, G.T.	01 Jan	MS	Haughey, J.P.	01 Apr	E	Newell, G.D.	29 Apr
E	Richardson, A.P.	01 Jan	E	Havron, P.R.	01 Apr	E	Nicholson, B.H.	29 Apr
X	Punch, J.M.	01 Jan	E	Hocking, M.J.E.	01 Apr	E	Richards, P.	29 Apr
E	Robinson, S.L.	01 Jan	E	Holvey, P.J.	01 Apr	E	Robert, I.A.	29 Apr
E	Satterly, R.J.	01 Jan	E	James, M.	01 Apr	S	Viney, P.M.	29 Apr
X	Davis, G.R.	01 Jan	X	Jayes, N.J.	01 Apr	E	Wrennall, E.P.	29 Apr
X	Nicholson, D.A.G.	01 Jan	X	Jones, S.S.	01 Apr	E	Drew, C.	01 May
E	Thomson, J.M.	01 Jan	MS	Jones, T.M.	01 Apr	E	Farr-Voller, E.M.	01 May
X	Way, R.A.	01 Jan	X	Jones-Thompson, M.J.	01 Apr	E	Fortt, P.D.J.	01 May
S	Grigg, S.K.	08 Jan	X	Kay, P.S.	01 Apr	E	Tilsley, D.J.	01 May
S	Harvey, P.J.	08 Jan	E	Matthews, P.R.	01 Apr	X	Leason, N.C.	01 May
X	Lewis, P.L.	08 Jan	X	Meikle, R.B.	01 Apr	X	Reynolds, M.J.	01 May
S	McGrath, W.J.	08 Jan	X	Meikle, S.A.	01 Apr	X	Wilkins, D.P.	01 May
E	Austin, P.N.	09 Jan	E	Metcalf, S.W.	01 Apr	E	Barron, J.M.	01 May
E	Collins, D.	09 Jan	MS	Milburn, V.	01 Apr	X	Binns, J.F.	01 May
E	Collins, M.A.	09 Jan	X	Molnar, R.M.	01 Apr	E	Buchanan, R.M.	01 May
E	Conneely, S.A.	09 Jan	X	Moore, M.J.	01 Apr	S	Carthew, R.J.	01 May
E	Donaldson, A.M.	09 Jan	S	Northeast, P.	01 Apr	X	Crouch, M.	01 May
X	Flynn, S.J.	09 Jan	E	Nottley, S.M.	01 Apr	X	Duce, M.	01 May
X	Gray, M.J.H.	09 Jan	E	Parmenter, A.J.	01 Apr	X	Evans, L.S.	01 May
S	Johnson, K.	09 Jan	E	Pollard, A.J.	01 Apr	X	Fabik, A.N.	01 May
E	Murphy, A.	09 Jan	E	Prior, I.A.	01 Apr	X	Garreta, C.E.	01 May
E	Stafford, W.	09 Jan	E	Prowse, D.G.	01 Apr	X	Gordon, D.I.	01 May
X	White, S.J.	09 Jan	E	Rawlings, G.A.	01 Apr	X	Hall, K.J.D.	01 May
X	Collins, S.J.P.	16 Jan	E	Rhodes, A.W.	01 Apr	E	Holford, S.J.	01 May
X	Laurence, S.T.	16 Jan	MS	Robinson, A.	01 Apr	X	Hopkins, C.	01 May
E	Topham, N.E.	01 Feb	X	Robinson, R.J.	01 Apr	X	Humphries, G.D.	01 May
S	New, R.A.	01 Feb	X	Santry, P.M.	01 Apr	X	Jackson, H.C.	01 May
X	Paulet, M.R.	01 Feb	E	Shaw, N.A.	01 Apr	E	Jordan, M.D.	01 May
X	Simpson, S.F.	01 Feb	X	Smith, P.A.	01 Apr	E	Kent, M.J.	01 May
E	Welsh, R.M.K.	01 Feb	S	Somerville, S.J.	01 Apr	X	Klidjian, M.J.	01 May
X	White, J.P.	01 Feb	E	Temple, D.C.	01 Apr	E	Layton, C.	01 May
X	Hurst, C.N.S.	01 Feb	E	Thomson, D.F.	01 Apr	X	Little, M.I.G.	01 May
E	Eaglestone, S.	01 Feb	E	Thomson, I.W.	01 Apr	S	Lucocq, C.M.	01 May
S	Walsh, D.	01 Feb						

LIEUTENANTS

X	Martyn, D.	01 May	X	Lewis, A.B.	01 Sep	X	Brock, M.J.	01 Jan
S	McCowen, P.A.C.	01 May	S	Manning, G.P.	01 Sep	E	Brodie, D.J.	01 Jan
E	Miller, K.R.	01 May	X	Martin, D.C.S.	01 Sep	E	Bukhory, H.	01 Jan
E	Moon, I.L.	01 May	X	Mitchell, J.D.	01 Sep	E	Carbery, S.J.	01 Jan
X	Noonan, C.D.	01 May	X	Monnox, J.	01 Sep	S	Chadwick, K.	01 Jan
X	Nunnen, C.R.	01 May	X	Morris, P.J.	01 Sep	X	Chandler, P.J.	01 Jan
X	Oakley, C.M.	01 May	MS	Murray, A.	01 Sep	X	Chapman, J.L.J.	01 Jan
S	Ollis, V.	01 May	E	Palmer, C.R.	01 Sep	X	Clarke, M.	01 Jan
S	Pearson, S.	01 May	X	Rankin, G.J.	01 Sep	X	Cooke, S.N.	01 Jan
X	Pickles, M.R.	01 May	E	Ritchie, D.B.	01 Sep	E	Cowie, A.D.	01 Jan
X	Sherwood, G.A.F.	01 May	X	Scott, N.	01 Sep	E	Creek, S.B.	01 Jan
X	Spencer, A.C.	01 May	E	Slowther, S.J.	01 Sep	X	Dawson, P.M.D.	01 Jan
X	Spinks, R.J.	01 May	X	Sterry, J.E.B.	01 Sep	X	Eaton, D.C.	01 Jan
E	Stratton, S.J.	01 May	X	Stewart, C.H.	01 Sep	MS	Edwards, D.	01 Jan
X	Vickery, B.R.	01 May	MS	Wade, A.	01 Sep	X	Filshie, S.J.	01 Jan
X	Waite, T.G.	01 May	X	Wells, J.D.	01 Sep	X	French, J.H.	01 Jan
X	Watson, B.L.	01 May	X	Wilson-Smith, R.A.	01 Sep	E	Fry, T.G.	01 Jan
X	Wickham, R.J.	01 May	MS	Witt, A.K.	01 Sep	S	Garbutt, H.J.	01 Jan
X	Wielopolski, M.L.C.C.	01 May	X	Colley, R.	01 Sep	E	Gibson, T.A.	01 Jan
X	Williams, P.G.	01 May	X	Ingham, L.	01 Sep	E	Godley, D.J.	01 Jan
X	Winterbon, A.R.	01 May	S	Mawdsley, G.R.	01 Sep	X	Grey, C.S.	01 Jan
X	Youldon, L.J.	01 May	X	Stack, E.F.	01 Sep	E	Hawkins, S.	01 Jan
E	Bland, C.D.	01 May	E	Cunningham, D.B.	01 Sep	X	Holliehead, C.L.	01 Jan
E	Woods, M.J.P.	01 May	X	Griffin, S.	01 Sep	S	Horwood, N.A.	01 Jan
E	Hayden, J.M.L.	01 May	E	Grinnell, J.	01 Oct	E	Hughes, G.D.	01 Jan
E	Wadge, G.D.E.	08 May	S	Whale, V.A.	01 Oct	E	Hutchinson, N.J.	01 Jan
X	Goodman, D.F.	09 May	X	Renaud, G.A.R.	16 Oct	X	Inglis, D.J.	01 Jan
S	Guilfoyle, V.M.	15 May	E	Bennett, B.C.H.	01 Nov	X	Issitt, B.D.	01 Jan
E	Crossey, M.D.	01 Jun	E	Grierson, A.D.	01 Nov	E	Jarman, P.R.	01 Jan
E	Cantellow, S.J.	01 Jun	X	Hesketh, J.J.	01 Nov	E	Jones, C.D.	01 Jan
X	Menzies, B.	01 Jul	X	James, R.M.	01 Nov	S	Kingdon, S.C.	01 Jan
E	Perkins, B.	01 Jul	X	Woad, J.P.R.	01 Nov	X	Ladislaus, C.J.	01 Jan
X	Henaghen, S.J.	13 Jul	X	Goddard, I.A.	16 Nov	X	Latus, S.H.	01 Jan
X	Malone, J.M.	29 Jul	E	Lewis, D.	01 Dec	X	Leeper, J.S.	01 Jan
X	Wightwick, K.H.T.	01 Aug	X	Blythe, J.	01 Dec	E	Louw, L.	01 Jan
X	Prosser, M.J.	01 Aug	X	Briggs, C.E.	01 Dec	E	MacIntyre, I.D.	01 Jan
X	Burghall, R.C.	01 Aug	S	Harman, S.J.	01 Dec	E	Mann, A.W.	01 Jan
E	Barnard, T.J.	01 Aug	E	Laidler, P.J.	01 Dec	S	Marland, E.E.	01 Jan
X	Perryment, C.P.	01 Aug	X	Higgins, P.M.	16 Dec	E	Marshall, G.P.	01 Jan
X	Robey, S.J.	01 Aug	S	Jackson, A.	21 Dec	X	Mc Allister, S.E.	01 Jan
S	Underwood, R.A.H.	01 Aug				E	McCamphill, P.J.	01 Jan
X	Antrobus, S.R.	05 Aug		**2002**		X	McKay, T.W.	01 Jan
E	Simpson, M.G.	05 Aug	E	Atwal, K.S.	01 Jan	X	Moran, B.M.	01 Jan
E	Booth, D.P.P.	01 Sep	E	Butler, R.A.	01 Jan	X	Morgan, B.P.	01 Jan
E	Maxwell, M.S.	01 Sep	E	Moss, R.M.	01 Jan	E	Morris, D.W.	01 Jan
E	Miah, J.H.	01 Sep	E	Priddle, A.C.	01 Jan	X	Nash, R.D.C.	01 Jan
X	Sienkiewicz, M.K.	01 Sep	E	Ralston, W.A.	01 Jan	X	Nash, R.P.	01 Jan
X	Andrews, I.S.	01 Sep	E	Ross, P.W.	01 Jan	X	O'Neill, T.J.	01 Jan
E	Bass, E.M.	01 Sep	E	Saleh, J.	01 Jan	X	Parsons, R.M.J.	01 Jan
E	Beadling, D.J.	01 Sep	E	Stevens, D.G.	01 Jan	X	Pearce, R.J.	01 Jan
E	Breen, J.E.	01 Sep	S	Truelove, S.	01 Jan	MS	Pinhey, A.D.	01 Jan
E	Brooks, N.R.	01 Sep	E	Walker, M.J.E.	01 Jan	X	Quinn, M.G.	01 Jan
X	Brown, A.S.	01 Sep	E	Whitehead, R.J.	01 Jan	E	Rand, M.A.	01 Jan
S	Chapman, M.S.	01 Sep	S	Chesters, D.M.B.	01 Jan	E	Richards, S.C.A.	01 Jan
MS	Davies, J.L.	01 Sep	X	Barrow, C.M.	01 Jan	E	Rider, J.C.R.	01 Jan
S	De La Rue, A.N.	01 Sep	X	Beegan, C.F.	01 Jan	X	Rimmer, O.F.	01 Jan
X	Fraser, M.J.S.	01 Sep	E	Berry, S.M.	01 Jan	X	Rowberry, A.G.	01 Jan
S	Gray, E.J.	01 Sep	X	Binns, J.R.	01 Jan	X	Russell, M.S.	01 Jan
X	Hirstwood, J.L.	01 Sep	X	Black, E.J.	01 Jan	S	Sargent, D.R.	01 Jan
X	Hulston, L.M.	01 Sep	X	Blick, S.L.	01 Jan	E	Sawford, G.N.	01 Jan
X	Jenkins, D.G.	01 Sep	S	Boardman, S.J.	01 Jan	E	Simpson, W.J.S.	01 Jan
E	King, W.T.P.	01 Sep	X	Boulind, M.A.	01 Jan	S	Smith, L.	01 Jan

LIEUTENANTS

	Name	Date
E	Smye, M.A.	01 Jan
E	Snell, D.M.	01 Jan
X	Stevenson, S.R.	01 Jan
X	Suter, F.T.	01 Jan
E	Tait, S.J.	01 Jan
X	Tappin, S.J.	01 Jan
X	Van Duin, M.I.A.	01 Jan
X	Wallace, A.R.	01 Jan
S	Wild, R.J.	01 Jan
E	Williams, P.A.	01 Jan
X	Wood, J.T.	01 Jan
S	Cleary, C.M.	01 Jan
X	Ludlow, J.A.	01 Jan
E	Rooke, Z.S.	01 Jan
E	Canty, T.A.	01 Feb
E	Marden, T.	01 Feb
S	Huynh, C.C.	01 Mar
X	Fuller, J.E.	01 Mar
E	McClurg, R.J.	01 Mar
E	Peck, S.R.	01 Mar
E	Reynolds, H.F.	01 Mar
E	Wickett, R.J.	01 Mar
S	Parry, S.D.	05 Mar
E	Peasley, H.S.	01 Apr
E	Smallwood, R.J.	01 Apr
E	Barr, D.D.	01 Apr
E	Smith, O.J.	01 Apr
X	Crawford, V.E.	01 Apr
X	Day, B.T.	01 Apr
E	Gaytano, R.T.M.	01 Apr
X	Hopkins, A.E.T.	01 Apr
X	Mountney, G.A.	01 Apr
X	Rawlins, S.T.	01 Apr
E	Abbotts, M.C.	01 Apr
E	Gibbs, M.P.	01 Apr
X	Steadman, R.A.J.	01 Apr
E	Trewinnard, R.M.	01 Apr
E	Walker, S.J.	01 Apr
E	Williams, C.L.	01 Apr
E	Cheal, A.J.	01 Apr
E	Edwards, R.P.	01 Apr
S	Kirwan, J.A.	07 Apr
X	Pearce, E.A.	09 Apr
E	Sharp, C.	12 Apr
E	Jones, G.A.	01 May
E	Jones, N.H.	01 May
E	Sennett, M.C.	01 May
X	Adams, W.J.	01 May
X	Adamson, S.E.	01 May
E	Ainscow, A.J.	01 May
E	Anderson-Cooke, D.C.J.	01 May
E	Andrews, J.P.	01 May
X	Atkinson, L.V.	01 May
X	Ballantyne, C.	01 May
E	Bartram, G.J.	01 May
E	Bastiaens, P.A.	01 May
E	Baxter, A.C.	01 May
X	Biggs, P.	01 May
E	Boakes, P.J.	01 May
X	Bond, J.E.	01 May
E	Bowie, R.	01 May
E	Bradley, T.A.	01 May
E	Brooking, R.R.	01 May
X	Buggins, B.	01 May
E	Carey, T.J.	01 May
E	Collins, D.A.	01 May
S	Cook, N.J.H.	01 May
E	Coyle, R.D.	01 May
S	Elkins, S.S.	01 May
X	Ellis-Morgan, R.T.	01 May
X	Fergusson, I.B.	01 May
X	Flaherty, C.L.	01 May
E	Fuller, S.P.	01 May
E	Fulton, D.M.	01 May
E	Goddard, P.	01 May
X	Hall, S.L.	01 May
X	Hamiduddin, I.	01 May
X	Heaton, H.G.	01 May
S	Holland, C.C.	01 May
X	Holmes, P.J.M.	01 May
X	Hughes, G.E.	01 May
S	Johnston, D.R.	01 May
E	Kestle, M.E.	01 May
X	Kiernan, C.G.	01 May
E	Leeder, T.R.	01 May
E	Leese, J.F.	01 May
X	Lindeyer, M.J.	01 May
E	Livingston, M.P.J.	01 May
E	Lock, W.J.	01 May
E	Lucas, D.P.	01 May
X	Luxford, C.A.	01 May
E	MacCormick, J.	01 May
E	MacQuarrie, G.A.	01 May
X	Marsh, S.D.	01 May
X	Masson, N.G.	01 May
X	Minall, M.L.	01 May
X	Morgan, C.W.	01 May
X	Morgan, D.	01 May
MS	Mundy, A.R.	01 May
X	Newman, C.R.S.	01 May
X	O'Callaghan, P.F.	01 May
S	O'Rourke, R.M.	01 May
X	Oakes, M.C.	01 May
X	Olivey, T.D.	01 May
X	Orme, W.B.	01 May
X	Owen, V.F.	01 May
X	Paston, W.A.	01 May
MS	Patton, R.R.	01 May
S	Peattie, I.W.	01 May
E	Porritt, C.J.	01 May
E	Powne, S.P.W.	01 May
E	Roberts, A.P.	01 May
X	Round, M.J.	01 May
X	Saltonstall, H.F.R.	01 May
E	Sharp, A.P.	01 May
MS	Smyth, C.R.	01 May
E	Snell, A.J.	01 May
X	Spike, A.J.	01 May
E	Standen, G.D.	01 May
X	Steele, M.S.	01 May
X	Stone, J.W.G.	01 May
X	Storey, A.E.	01 May
S	Sturgeon, D.M.	01 May
X	Talbot, K.E.F.	01 May
X	Talbot, R.J.	01 May
E	Tate, N.M.	01 May
X	Taylor, R.P.	01 May
X	Veal, D.J.	01 May
X	Voke, H.L.	01 May
S	Wagstaff, A.	01 May
X	Ware, A.T.	01 May
X	Welsh, G.L.	01 May
E	Woolfe, K.D.	01 May
X	Wynn Jones, I.	01 May
E	Gubby, A.W.	01 May
E	Hale, B.W.	01 May
E	Saywell, J.N.	01 Jun
S	Kennan, N.P.	01 Jun
X	Bradford, G.J.	01 Jun
E	Cooch, T.J.	01 Jul
E	Cross, N.	01 Jul
E	Ramsay, A.J.D.	01 Jul
E	Edge, H.R.	01 Jul
E	Gwilliam, E.K.	01 Jul
X	Tok, C.F.L.	03 Jul
S	Bell, L.J.	01 Aug
X	Donovan, S.J.	01 Aug
X	Ritchie, I.D.	01 Aug
X	Smith, E.G.G.	01 Aug
X	Unwin, N.R.F.	01 Aug
X	Voke, C.A.	01 Aug
X	Bullock, J.R.	01 Aug
E	Chang, H.W.	01 Aug
X	Hart, S.D.	01 Aug
E	Holgate, J.A.	01 Aug
X	Leeson, A.R.	01 Aug
X	Walker, N.M.C.	01 Aug
E	French, P.	02 Aug
X	Lippe, P.W.	02 Aug
E	Marrison, G.R.	02 Aug
E	Patch, S.J.	02 Aug
X	Wylie, D.	02 Aug
E	Tait, M.D.	27 Aug
E	Davis, P.H.	01 Sep
E	Munro, H.L.	01 Sep
E	Nix, C.J.	01 Sep
E	Rogers, P.R.	01 Sep
X	Morey, K.N.	01 Sep
X	Parkinson, J.H.G.	01 Sep
E	Ashton, J.	01 Sep
E	Best, R.M.	01 Sep
X	Botting, N.A.	01 Sep
E	Brierley, S.P.J.	01 Sep
E	Bromwell, M.S.	01 Sep
X	Burrell, D.J.	01 Sep
E	Callis, G.J.	01 Sep
E	Carvosso-White, A.L.	01 Sep
E	Causton, J.F.	01 Sep
E	Chatterjee, S.	01 Sep
E	Cripps, M.J.	01 Sep
X	Crompton, A.P.J.	01 Sep
X	Elliot-Smith, T.J.	01 Sep
E	Ellis, D.R.	01 Sep
X	Evans, L.J.	01 Sep
X	Feasey, I.D.	01 Sep
X	Fullman, G.	01 Sep

LIEUTENANTS

X	Garner, M.E.	01 Sep
E	Gooch, M.D.	01 Sep
E	Goodenough, R.H.	01 Sep
X	Gorman, D.A.	01 Sep
X	Gulliver, J.W.	01 Sep
E	Hall, C.L.	01 Sep
E	Handoll, G.N.G.	01 Sep
E	Harding, D.V.	01 Sep
E	Heath, S.P.R.	01 Sep
E	Horsted, J.A.	01 Sep
S	Hunt, R.J.C.	01 Sep
E	Hyde, J.W.	01 Sep
E	James, A.G.	01 Sep
X	Johnson, M.W.	01 Sep
E	Keenan, B.F.	01 Sep
X	King, I.A.	01 Sep
X	Kingston, E.A.	01 Sep
E	Lewis, M.D.	01 Sep
S	Lloyd, M.R.	01 Sep
X	Malcolm, P.S.	01 Sep
X	Marriott, M.J.	01 Sep
X	Masterman, A.P.	01 Sep
E	McCarthy, D.J.	01 Sep
E	McEwan, R.D.	01 Sep
X	Molloy, L.	01 Sep
S	Morris, H.S.	01 Sep
X	Moseley, S.H.	01 Sep
X	Murray, G.M.	01 Sep
E	Newall, P.J.	01 Sep
E	Nguyo, D.N.	01 Sep
E	Northcott, P.J.	01 Sep
E	Norton, A.L.E.	01 Sep
X	Owen, D.P.C.	01 Sep
E	Reynolds, A.C.J.	01 Sep
X	Riddett, A.O.	01 Sep
E	Rose, A.	01 Sep
X	Ryan, P.D.B.	01 Sep
X	Ryan, P.J.	01 Sep
E	Sturgeon, M.	01 Sep
X	Taylor, J.E.H.	01 Sep
X	Wallace, R.S.	01 Sep
S	Ward, A.J.	01 Sep
S	Webb, E.L.	01 Sep
X	Westwood, A.J.	01 Sep
E	Woodley, S.L.	01 Sep
X	Zipfell, A.J.	01 Sep
X	Abel, L.	01 Sep
X	Baker, J.E.G.	01 Sep
S	Mettam, S.R.	01 Sep
X	Southworth, M.	01 Sep
X	Sykes, M.J.	01 Sep
X	Ward, M.B.	01 Oct
X	Hudson, A.I.	01 Oct
X	Clee, J.S.	01 Oct
E	Mann, C.A.	01 Oct
X	Baverstock, A.P.	01 Oct
E	Burt, D.J.	01 Oct
E	Ford, B.E.	01 Oct
MS	Green, P.G.	01 Oct
X	Harrison, I.	01 Oct
X	Little, C.M.	01 Oct
X	May, D.M.	01 Oct
X	Monk, K.N.	01 Oct
S	Robinson, D.	01 Oct
E	Stanley, A.B.	01 Oct
X	Vout, D.K.	01 Oct
X	Watson, R.D.	01 Oct
X	Webb, J.P.	01 Oct
E	Inness, M.J.	01 Oct
X	Morris, D.R.	01 Oct
X	Sloan, G.D.	01 Oct
X	Williamson, P.J.	01 Oct
X	Carpenter, G.E.	01 Oct
X	Doe, J.R.	01 Oct
X	Lupini, J.M.	01 Oct
MS	Channon, K.D.	01 Nov
E	Hallett, D.J.	01 Nov
X	Skipper, J.A.	01 Nov
S	Harding, E.L.	12 Nov
X	Green, J.	16 Nov
S	Anderson, L.A.	01 Dec
X	Ayrton, R.E.	01 Dec
X	Shepherd, A.C.	01 Dec
MS	Vines, N.O.	01 Dec
S	Lanigan, B.R.	01 Dec

2003

X	Compain, B.F.	01 Jan
E	Evans, C.P.	01 Jan
X	Holland, R.J.	01 Jan
E	Alderton, P.A.	01 Jan
X	Armstrong, R.J.	01 Jan
E	Bailey, T.D.	01 Jan
E	Bass, P.W.	01 Jan
S	Beales, N.S.	01 Jan
X	Bickley, G.N.	01 Jan
X	Birch, P.L.	01 Jan
E	Brindley, M.W.	01 Jan
E	Brooks, P.N.	01 Jan
E	Brown, J.A.	01 Jan
S	Bulmer, W.E.	01 Jan
X	Burns, A.J.	01 Jan
X	Cantellow, R.B.	01 Jan
E	Clarkson, A.M.	01 Jan
S	Conran, N.W.D.	01 Jan
S	Coppin, N.J.	01 Jan
E	Craven, D.	01 Jan
S	Cunnell, R.L.	01 Jan
X	Day, A.	01 Jan
S	Di Maio, M.D.	01 Jan
X	Gater, J.C.	01 Jan
E	Goodsell, D.L.	01 Jan
E	Griffiths, N.C.	01 Jan
X	Hall, G.W.R.	01 Jan
E	Harvey, G.A.	01 Jan
X	Hayes, M.A.	01 Jan
S	Hughes, B.F.M.	01 Jan
E	Hughes, F.C.	01 Jan
X	Hunt, R.E.	01 Jan
X	Jones, E.N.L.	01 Jan
X	Kelly, S.	01 Jan
E	Kiff, I.W.	01 Jan
X	L'Amie, C.A.	01 Jan
X	Lancaster, J.H.D.	01 Jan
S	Lawson, A.F.	01 Jan
X	Ligale, E.	01 Jan
X	Lovell, J.E.C.	01 Jan
X	MacPherson, C.A.C.	01 Jan
X	Malone, R.W.	01 Jan
X	McGreal, B.	01 Jan
E	McQuire, D.E.A.	01 Jan
S	Mowat, A.D.J.	01 Jan
X	Notley, E.J.	01 Jan
E	O'Connor, D.P.	01 Jan
X	O'Neill, H.L.	01 Jan
S	Pallett, A.J.	01 Jan
X	Palmer, M.D.	01 Jan
S	Pitman, L.J.	01 Jan
X	Pitt, W.T.	01 Jan
E	Prodger, A.P.	01 Jan
X	Quaite, D.G.	01 Jan
S	Reaves, C.E.	01 Jan
X	Redmayne, M.J.	01 Jan
X	Reynolds, J.	01 Jan
E	Rostron, J.H.	01 Jan
S	Roue, J.L.	01 Jan
E	Savage, D.L.	01 Jan
X	Semple, B.	01 Jan
X	Shanks, D.Z.	01 Jan
E	Sidebotham, S.C.	01 Jan
E	Trotman, S.P.	01 Jan
E	Walker, I.M.	01 Jan
E	Walker, J.	01 Jan
X	Weaver, T.H.	01 Jan
X	Wheatley, N.S.	01 Jan
X	Wilson, G.P.	01 Jan
E	Wilson, M.G.	01 Jan
X	Worley, T.F.	01 Jan
E	Griffiths, G.	01 Jan
E	Coates, A.J.	01 Jan
E	Maddison, H.R.	01 Jan
E	Reeves, A.P.	01 Jan
E	Holdsworth, R.A.	01 Jan
E	Floyd, R.E.	01 Jan
E	Beverley, A.P.	01 Feb
E	Eldridge, S.J.	01 Feb
E	Ffoulkes, W.M.	01 Feb
E	Moore, S.	01 Feb
E	Stubbs, I.	01 Feb
E	Dyter, R.C.	01 Feb
X	Bannister, J.	01 Feb
X	Benarr, C.M.	01 Feb
E	Boughton, J.A.L.	01 Feb
S	Farrant, J.D.	01 Feb
X	Lynn, S.L.	01 Feb
E	Tomlin, I.S.	01 Feb
E	Cooper, A.	01 Mar
E	Maude, C.D.	01 Mar
E	Peskett, D.M.	01 Mar
E	Thomas, A.J.	01 Mar
S	Roberts, S.	23 Mar
X	Hackland, A.S.	01 Apr
X	Stephenson, C.J.	01 Apr
X	Duffy, M.L.	01 Apr
X	Kilbane, D.K.J.	01 Apr
X	Dobson, A.C.	01 Apr

LIEUTENANTS

X	Harrison, L.E.	01 Apr	E	Nicholls, L.R.	01 May	S	Isaac, S.M.	01 Sep
X	Meacher, P.G.	01 Apr	X	Ottaway, T.A.	01 May	X	Shropshall, I.J.	01 Sep
X	Norman, T.B.	01 Apr	X	Payne, M.	01 May	X	Abbot, R.L.	01 Sep
E	Dillon, B.	01 Apr	X	Payne, W.D.	01 May	E	Anderson, L.C.	01 Sep
E	Grice, M.G.	01 Apr	E	Pond, R.J.	01 May	E	Bailey, I.J.	01 Sep
E	Parker, J.D.	01 Apr	S	Proctor, N.S.	01 May	X	Baird, G.M.	01 Sep
E	Hearty, S.P.	11 Apr	X	Riches, A.I.	01 May	X	Barber, M.	01 Sep
E	Morey, R.G.	11 Apr	X	Ronald, E.T.	01 May	X	Barfoot, P.M.	01 Sep
X	Anderson, A.E.	01 May	S	Rose, S.	01 May	X	Berry, J.T.	01 Sep
E	Andrews, D.M.	01 May	X	Ross, G.D.A.	01 May	S	Boon, S.E.	01 Sep
E	Atkins, P.R.	01 May	E	Royle, N.A.	01 May	E	Butler, J.E.	01 Sep
E	Ball, W.J.E.	01 May	E	Russell, M.J.	01 May	S	Byron, D.C.	01 Sep
S	Barnes, N.J.	01 May	MS	Scarborough, D.C.	01 May	E	Caddick, A.	01 Sep
X	Becker, R.K.	01 May	X	Scott, N.	01 May	X	Carnew, S.F.	01 Sep
E	Bingham, A.A.J.	01 May	X	Shanahan, L.A.	01 May	X	Cassidy, S.M.	01 Sep
X	Botterill, H.W.S.	01 May	X	Simmonds, D.D.H.	01 May	X	Cloney, J.W.J.	01 Sep
X	Bowker, J.M.	01 May	X	Skinsley, T.J.	01 May	X	Coughlan, S.	01 Sep
E	Briscoe, J.W.A.	01 May	X	Smith, C.J.	01 May	X	Cumming, F.S.	01 Sep
E	Buchanan, D.C.	01 May	X	Smith, D.J.	01 May	E	Dymond, J.R.M.	01 Sep
MS	Burnett, P.H.	01 May	E	Southwood, S.C.	01 May	E	Earle-Payne, G.E.	01 Sep
X	Campbell-Baldwin, J.W.	01 May	X	Spark, S.M.	01 May	E	Faulkner, S.G.	01 Sep
S	Chang, C.J.	01 May	X	Stewart, B.C.	01 May	X	Fearon, D.J.	01 Sep
X	Chudley, I.V.	01 May	X	Thompson, S.L.	01 May	X	Gaskin, D.E.	01 Sep
E	Courtney, T.P.	01 May	X	Thornley, J.G.C.	01 May	X	Gilmore, J.E.	01 Sep
X	Craig, M.J.	01 May	MS	Todd, G.A.	01 May	E	Gray, J.M.	01 Sep
X	Dray, J.M.	01 May	E	Tonge, M.S.	01 May	X	Gray, R.L.	01 Sep
X	Edwards, T.H.H.	01 May	E	Turner, N.B.	01 May	X	Hodder, P.J.	01 Sep
E	Emery, C.S.	01 May	E	Twiselton, M.J.	01 May	S	Hughes, G.A.	01 Sep
X	Evans, C.A.	01 May	X	Walton, G.J.	01 May	X	Hulse, R.M.	01 Sep
X	Fairclough-Kay, M.	01 May	X	White, P.D.	01 May	X	Hunt, B.P.	01 Sep
E	Fanshawe, E.L.	01 May	E	White, S.	01 May	S	Imrie, S.J.	01 Sep
X	Fitzpatrick, N.J.	01 May	E	Wilkins, R.L.	01 May	E	Jerrold, W.H.	01 Sep
E	Foster, A.J.	01 May	E	Wilshaw, G.I.	01 May	X	Jones, G.J.L.	01 Sep
X	Glendinning, C.J.A.	01 May	X	Wilson, N.A.	01 May	E	Kadinopoulos, B.A.	01 Sep
X	Gordon, J.	01 May	E	Wright, D.W.	01 May	X	Kirkby, S.J.	01 Sep
S	Gott, S.B.	01 May	E	O'Sullivan, P.B.	01 May	S	Law, S.J.	01 Sep
E	Gould, I.	01 May	E	Wills, R.H.	01 May	X	Lewis, W.D.	01 Sep
E	Green, L.D.	01 May	E	Black, J.M.	15 May	X	MacDonald, K.L.	01 Sep
X	Hall, J.E.	01 May	E	Anderson, K.B.	01 Jun	X	MacLean, G.F.	01 Sep
S	Hannam, S.J.	01 May	E	Atkinson, A.	01 Jun	X	Marjoribanks, C.	01 Sep
X	Hill, T.E.	01 May	E	Hignett, G.	01 Jun	X	McCallum, G.P.	01 Sep
X	Hogg, A.J.	01 May	E	Sampson, J.P.	01 Jun	E	McCormack, G.	01 Sep
E	Holland, C.J.R.	01 May	S	Wragg, H.C.	01 Jun	X	McGannity, S.E.K.	01 Sep
S	Irving, T.C.	01 May	E	Vaughan, J.R.	01 Jun	E	Mole, A.J.	01 Sep
S	James, G.C.M.	01 May	E	Williams, B.	01 Jun	X	Petch, A.N.	01 Sep
E	Jemmeson, S.H.	01 May	E	Smart, C.R.	01 Jul	E	Peterson, K.A.	01 Sep
S	Jones, D.K.	01 May	E	Chappell, M.W.	01 Jul	X	Phillips, R.E.	01 Sep
E	Jones, S.	01 May	S	Lai-Hung, J.J.P.	01 Jul	X	Plenty, A.J.	01 Sep
E	Keane, B.M.	01 May	E	Fiddock, M.L.	01 Jul	E	Reynolds, M.E.	01 Sep
X	Keane, G.A.	01 May	X	Fraser, J.M.	01 Jul	S	Richardson, S.C.	01 Sep
X	Kerley, B.J.	01 May	X	Samways, M.J.	01 Jul	X	Roberts, B.	01 Sep
E	Law, J.S.	01 May	X	McKenna, D.R.	01 Jul	S	Royston, J.L.	01 Sep
X	Leslie, B.D.	01 May	X	Sharp, J.V.	01 Jul	E	Sharkey, P.J.	01 Sep
E	Love, J.J.	01 May	E	Forbes, R.G.	01 Jul	X	Sharrott, C.	01 Sep
MS	MacPhail, N.M.	01 May	S	Fuller, R.	01 Jul	X	Shears, G.R.	01 Sep
S	Mallinson, L.J.	01 May	X	Brown, S.	01 Jul	E	Sobers, S.	01 Sep
S	Malone, M.T.	01 May	X	Wrigglesworth, S.M.	01 Jul	E	Stevens, J.I.	01 Sep
E	Markwick, K.W.	01 May	S	Boot, S.	01 Jul	X	Stubbs, B.D.	01 Sep
E	McCallum, M.D.	01 May	E	Bullock, J.B.	01 Jul	E	Tantam, R.J.G.	01 Sep
X	Miall, M.C.	01 May	E	Bowers, M.R.	01 Aug	E	Tough, I.S.	01 Sep
X	Mitchell, P.J.	01 May	E	Burlingham, A.C.R.	01 Aug	X	Trent, T.	01 Sep
X	Mittins, S.	01 May	E	Robertson, I.W.	01 Aug	X	Warren, R.A.	01 Sep

LIEUTENANTS

X	Weston, H.L.	01 Sep
S	Woosey, D.A.	01 Sep
X	Workman, R.J.	01 Sep
S	Yates, L.O.	01 Sep
E	Woodman, D.P.	01 Sep
E	Lee, D.A.	01 Sep
X	Pugh, G.N.J.	01 Oct
X	Parry, G.R.	01 Oct
E	Baddeley, R.	01 Nov
E	Selden, J.D.A.	01 Nov
E	Steiger, R.C.	01 Nov
MS	Storey, A.	01 Nov
X	George, C.A.	01 Nov
X	McLeod, K.Y.L.	01 Dec
X	Reynolds, Z.A.	01 Dec
X	Voigt, M.A.	01 Dec
X	Bettles, J.	01 Dec
E	Hetherington, T.A.	01 Dec

2004

E	Cripps, N.J.	01 Jan
E	Devlin, C.J.	01 Jan
E	Sweeney, R.J.	01 Jan
E	Webster, A.J.	01 Jan
X	Vincent, P.H.	01 Jan
X	Walker, J.J.	01 Jan
X	Armstrong, D.M.	01 Jan
X	Banks, M.J.	01 Jan
X	Barrett, S.	01 Jan
X	Barron, P.R.	01 Jan
X	Beard, S.A.	01 Jan
E	Bennett, M.A.	01 Jan
MS	Birkin, K.	01 Jan
E	Boud, C.S.	01 Jan
X	Brace, A.F.	01 Jan
X	Brazenall, B.C.	01 Jan
E	Ciaravella, T.J.	01 Jan
E	Clark, P.A.	01 Jan
S	Clark, S.M.	01 Jan
E	Crosland, S.A.	01 Jan
E	Daly, M.P.	01 Jan
E	Daniel, B.J.E.	01 Jan
X	Davey, C.S.	01 Jan
X	Dewar, M.J.	01 Jan
E	Dixon, M.E.	01 Jan
E	Dodd, P.M.	01 Jan
E	Dooley, M.E.	01 Jan
E	Elliott, S.P.	01 Jan
X	Evans, B.G.	01 Jan
X	Evans, R.P.	01 Jan
X	Fisher, R.V.	01 Jan
S	Flannagan, D.L.	01 Jan
X	Fox, D.J.	01 Jan
S	Gershater, S.C.	01 Jan
E	Gibson, A.	01 Jan
X	Gillett, N.D.	01 Jan
X	Goscomb, P.A.	01 Jan
X	Griffiths, N.M.	01 Jan
E	Harvey, P.G.	01 Jan
MS	Hazard, L.	01 Jan
X	Heward, M.G.	01 Jan
X	Hewitt, R.P.	01 Jan

E	Hogben, M.J.	01 Jan
E	Hopper, G.	01 Jan
X	Hounsome, J.R.	01 Jan
E	Hughes, T.W.	01 Jan
X	Ingamells, S.D.	01 Jan
E	Lee, R.A.	01 Jan
E	Lettington, P.D.W.	01 Jan
X	Marsh, D.R.	01 Jan
S	Marsh, S.W.	01 Jan
X	Marshall, J.M.	01 Jan
X	McMahon, D.S.	01 Jan
E	Mortimer, P.R.	01 Jan
E	Munday, S.W.	01 Jan
E	Nash, R.F.R.	01 Jan
X	Nekrews, A.N.L.M.	01 Jan
X	Norwood, J.K.	01 Jan
E	O'Brien, T.P.	01 Jan
X	Parker, M.J.	01 Jan
X	Pate, C.M.	01 Jan
X	Pearce, J.	01 Jan
X	Penalver, W.C.	01 Jan
E	Pike, R.T.	01 Jan
S	Richards, G.B.	01 Jan
S	Riggs, M.G.W.	01 Jan
X	Roy, C.A.	01 Jan
E	Rucinski, P.G.	01 Jan
E	Say, R.G.	01 Jan
E	Scarlett, C.J.	01 Jan
X	Sedgwick, H.G.	01 Jan
X	Seton, J.	01 Jan
E	Sheehan, T.J.	01 Jan
S	Shortland, K.	01 Jan
E	Shrestha, S.	01 Jan
X	Simpson, C.J.	01 Jan
X	Stead, A.	01 Jan
X	Syson, C.F.	01 Jan
E	Thomas, M.A.	01 Jan
X	Thompson, A.J.	01 Jan
X	Thorley, G.	01 Jan
S	Tibballs, L.R.	01 Jan
E	Torbet, L.	01 Jan
X	Tretton, J.E.	01 Jan
E	Tumilty, K.	01 Jan
S	Turberville, C.T.L.	01 Jan
E	Turner, M.	01 Jan
E	Vardy, K.J.	01 Jan
X	Visram, A.H.	01 Jan
X	Walker, D.H.	01 Jan
S	Walker, M.D.J.	01 Jan
X	Waugh, R.P.	01 Jan
X	Westwood, T.P.	01 Jan
X	Wheen, C.J.D.	01 Jan
E	White, D.	01 Jan
X	White, K.J.	01 Jan
X	Wilkinson, J.R.	01 Jan
X	Wilson, S.A.	01 Jan
X	Yarham, N.P.	01 Jan
S	Jennings, C.R.	01 Jan
X	Gorman, G.K.	15 Jan
E	McLachlan, A.C.	19 Jan
E	Youngman, P.G.	01 Feb
X	Laing, N.A.	01 Feb

X	Thompson, D.J.	20 Feb
E	Curtiss, C.J.	01 Mar
E	Loadman, D.R.	01 Mar
X	Snee, P.	01 Mar
E	Braithwaite, G.C.	01 Apr
X	Claxton, A.G.D.	01 Apr
X	Cox-Tregale, J.	01 Apr
X	Hill, C.J.	01 Apr
X	Leightley, S.M.	01 Apr
X	Scanlon, M.P.	01 Apr
MS	Wernham, W.F.	01 Apr
E	Ashcroft, K.T.	01 Apr
E	Anderson, N.	09 Apr
E	Collins, M.R.	01 May
E	Erhahiemen, P.E.	01 May
E	Fulthorpe, S.D.	01 May
E	Hudson, T.A.J.	01 May
E	Wilson, D.J.	01 May
X	Hart, S.J.	01 May
E	Alder, M.C.	01 May
S	Baker, H.M.H.	01 May
X	Bell, D.J.	01 May
X	Bell, N.A.G.	01 May
X	Benbow, J.A.K.	01 May
X	Bladen, C.S.	01 May
S	Blair, L.D.	01 May
X	Bligh, S.L.	01 May
X	Brann, R.W.	01 May
E	Bush, D.J.	01 May
X	Byne, N.	01 May
X	Campbell, A.	01 May
X	Coleman, T.J.A.	01 May
X	Coles, A.J.	01 May
X	Colvin, M.A.T.	01 May
X	Cooper, E.S.	01 May
S	Cooper, L.J.	01 May
X	Cory, N.J.	01 May
X	Cox, M.S.	01 May
E	Crockett, S.K.	01 May
X	Crosby, D.W.M.	01 May
X	Cuthbert, G.	01 May
E	Cutler, D.T.	01 May
X	Dalgleish, G.A.	01 May
X	Dixon, S.P.	01 May
X	Frisby, P.	01 May
X	Gardner, L.P.	01 May
X	Gillard, K.E.	01 May
S	Goddard, D.S.	01 May
X	Goosen, R.D.	01 May
E	Gordon, D.E.	01 May
X	Greenhill, M.C.	01 May
S	Hackman, J.D.	01 May
X	Hanson, S.J.	01 May
S	Harriott, C.L.	01 May
X	Heap, G.G.	01 May
E	Howell, P.C.H.	01 May
X	Hudson, R.E.	01 May
X	Hunnibell, J.R.	01 May
X	Hunt, A.J.	01 May
X	Inglis, G.D.	01 May
X	Isaacs, N.J.	01 May
X	Isherwood, C.R.	01 May

LIEUTENANTS

X	Jardine, I.	01 May	E	Frost, L.J.	01 Jul	E	Ripley, S.L.	01 Jul
X	Jewson, B.D.	01 May	E	Grant, R.	01 Jul	E	Roe, R.J.	01 Jul
E	Johansen, S.P.	01 May	S	Grayson, S.	01 Jul	E	Screen, J.W.	01 Jul
X	Johnston, A.I.	01 May	X	Grove, J.J.	01 Jul	E	Stancliffe, A.E.	01 Jul
X	Koheeallee, M.C.R.C.	01 May	X	Hawkins, S.	01 Jul	E	Street, P.M.	01 Jul
X	Leaker, D.T.	01 May	S	Hine, M.J.	01 Jul	X	Walker, R.P.	01 Jul
X	Lindley, J.	01 May	X	James, R.	01 Jul	E	Whittington, R.	01 Jul
X	Lowe, G.J.	01 May	E	Jones, M.R.	01 Jul	E	Whyte, G.	01 Jul
X	Lucas, N.H.	01 May	E	King, J.M.	01 Jul	E	Young, D.A.	01 Jul
E	Maskell, B.M.	01 May	E	Lockhart, J.B.	01 Jul	MS	Klar, P.A.	01 Jul
X	Mason, R.J.	01 May	MS	Macey, K.	01 Jul	MS	Thornhill, S.M.	01 Jul
E	Maunder, J.G.	01 May	E	MacMillan, S.J.	01 Jul	X	Williams, A.C.	01 Jul
X	McKee, R.W.	01 May	E	McDougall, W.	01 Jul	X	Ryder, T.	13 Jul
X	McPhail, T.C.	01 May	E	Munro, M.	01 Jul	X	Barrett, B.T.	01 Aug
S	McPherson, A.	01 May	X	Pirie, I.T.	01 Jul	X	Cochrane, D.S.	01 Aug
X	Morris, P.W.	01 May	X	Reid, D.R.	01 Jul	X	Gray, S.D.	01 Aug
S	Morrison, J.	01 May	E	Robinson, L.D.	01 Jul	X	Morton, B.A.	01 Aug
E	Mountjoy-Row, R.E.	01 May	S	Searle, C.R.	01 Jul	X	Ray, L.B.	01 Aug
X	Murray, W.J.	01 May	E	Sneesby, N.J.	01 Jul	X	Thomson, S.M.	01 Aug
S	O'Reilly, C.A.	01 May	E	Tall, I.T.G.	01 Jul	X	Westoby, G.T.R.	01 Aug
X	Oliver, C.J.	01 May	E	Thwaites, L.W.	01 Jul	X	Dicker, N.M.	01 Aug
S	Overington, M.T.	01 May	E	Utting, R.C.	01 Jul	X	Greaves, M.R.	01 Aug
E	Paton, M.S.	01 May	S	Vivian, P.	01 Jul	S	Wright, H.J.	13 Aug
E	Phillippo, D.G.	01 May	E	Williams, L.J.	01 Jul	MS	Burcham, V.L.	13 Aug
MS	Pickering, D.A.	01 May	X	Ennis, J.L.	01 Jul	MS	Fowler, J.E.	13 Aug
X	Robinson, M.S.	01 May	X	Evans, A.	01 Jul	X	Haley, C.J.	13 Aug
X	Scott, A.J.	01 May	X	Ivill, S.	01 Jul	E	Keam, I.	13 Aug
X	Shaw, M.A.	01 May	MS	Parker, D.S.	01 Jul	E	Wright, N.D.	13 Aug
X	Smith, K.M.	01 May	MS	Redding, A.M.	01 Jul	X	Berry, M.G.	25 Aug
X	Smith, S.C.	01 May	X	Walker, J.J.	01 Jul	E	Parkinson, H.M.L.	01 Sep
E	Stanistreet, G.C.	01 May	X	Wall, K.	01 Jul	E	Weedon, G.A.	01 Sep
X	Stewart, N.J.	01 May	X	Wotton, A.C.	01 Jul	X	Martin, R.L.	01 Sep
S	Street, S.C.	01 May	MS	Abey, J.A.	01 Jul	E	Almond, N.A.B.	01 Sep
X	Thomas, J.M.	01 May	X	Allen, R.W.	01 Jul	X	Attwood, K.A.	01 Sep
X	Thompson, J.	01 May	X	Packer, R.G.	01 Jul	X	Ballard, A.P.V.	01 Sep
S	Tomlinson, A.R.	01 May	MS	Peake, S.P.	01 Jul	X	Banfield, S.D.	01 Sep
X	Warren, M.J.	01 May	S	Ward, J.M.	01 Jul	E	Barrie, S.	01 Sep
X	White, A.J.M.	01 May	S	Wright, J.R.	01 Jul	X	Bird, A.W.	01 Sep
X	White, R.E.	01 May	X	Bayliss, R.E.	01 Jul	X	Blackburn, C.J.	01 Sep
S	Williams, G.	01 May	S	Brown, S.M.J.	01 Jul	E	Blake, S.	01 Sep
X	Winterton, P.	01 May	X	Gunter, J.J.	01 Jul	E	Bond, R.D.A.	01 Sep
X	Wood, M.W.	01 May	X	Hind, K.N.	01 Jul	E	Bowers, K.J.	01 Sep
E	Wooding, S.J.	01 May	X	Scott, J.V.	01 Jul	X	Brannighan, I.D.	01 Sep
E	Thompson, E.E.	01 May	S	Whittles, G.W.	01 Jul	X	Browett, J.J.	01 Sep
E	Harrison, S.	10 May	X	Wren, S.J.	01 Jul	E	Brown, A.D.	01 Sep
E	Williams, T.G.E.	01 Jun	E	Belcher, D.R.	01 Jul	E	Burgess, P.G.	01 Sep
E	Reilly, P.	08 Jun	E	Broster, L.J.	01 Jul	E	Colley, I.P.	01 Sep
X	Elliott, M.E.	25 Jun	E	Caddick, S.A.	01 Jul	X	Dacombe, C.A.	01 Sep
X	Louis, D.R.A.	01 Jul	E	Davidson, J.D.	01 Jul	X	Dale, N.A.	01 Sep
X	McKeever, S.A.	01 Jul	E	Evans, C.C.	01 Jul	E	Dalglish, K.M.	01 Sep
E	Ainsworth, A.J.	01 Jul	E	Flitcroft, M.	01 Jul	X	Darlington, A.	01 Sep
X	Bailey, M.	01 Jul	E	Green, W.J.	01 Jul	X	Dart, D.J.	01 Sep
X	Balfour, R.D.	01 Jul	E	Hardy-Hodgson, D.N.	01 Jul	X	Davies, S.J.	01 Sep
E	Cheema, S.S.	01 Jul	E	Heap, S.A.	01 Jul	X	Davis, P.H.	01 Sep
E	Collier, M.J.	01 Jul	E	Henson, A.J.	01 Jul	E	Dennard, K.J.	01 Sep
S	Collins, D.I.	01 Jul	E	Leaver, A.D.	01 Jul	E	Downie, D.R.M.	01 Sep
E	Collins, G.V.	01 Jul	E	Maddison, P.	01 Jul	X	Duke, A.J.	01 Sep
X	Cowlishaw, N.D.	01 Jul	E	Martin, G.	01 Jul	X	Easterbrook, C.	01 Sep
X	Edmondson, M.	01 Jul	E	McNally, N.A.	01 Jul	X	Elliott, T.D.	01 Sep
E	Evans, P.J.	01 Jul	E	Morrison, S.	01 Jul	E	Fickling, J.W.A.	01 Sep
E	Fidler, M.M.G.	01 Jul	E	Norton, I.A.	01 Jul	E	Fisher, N.D.	01 Sep
MS	Flynn, M.C.	01 Jul	E	Prideaux, R.J.	01 Jul	X	Fleming, D.P.	01 Sep

LIEUTENANTS

E	Foers, P.S.	01 Sep	E	Wain, A.W.	01 Sep	X	Garey, E.J.	01 Jan
X	Fooks-Bale, M.E.	01 Sep	E	Warrick, M.	01 Sep	X	Hampson, A.G.	01 Jan
E	Gahan, R.J.	01 Sep	S	Westwood, M.J.	01 Sep	X	Haskins, B.S.	01 Jan
X	Gaunt, A.V.	01 Sep	X	Williams, A.M.	01 Sep	S	Hooper, T.	01 Jan
E	Groves, R.	01 Sep	E	Wood, J.R.	01 Sep	X	Hopkins, N.S.	01 Jan
E	Harris, R.A.	01 Sep	X	Wood, R.R.T.	01 Sep	X	Houlston, I.J.E.	01 Jan
E	Hatton-Brown, O.R.	01 Sep	S	Wright, J.S.	01 Sep	E	Husband, J.	01 Jan
E	Hobbs, T.P.	01 Sep	X	Mason-Matthews, A.	01 Sep	X	Hutchinson, M.R.	01 Jan
X	Hodgkinson, S.P.	01 Sep	X	Schofield, J.C.	01 Sep	X	Laidlaw, J.M.	01 Jan
X	Ingham, N.H.	01 Sep	X	Aldous, R.J.	01 Oct	X	Lang, A.J.M.	01 Jan
E	Joyce, D.J.	01 Sep	X	Orton, T.	01 Oct	X	Mattock, N.J.	01 Jan
X	Keillor, S.J.	01 Sep	X	Anderson-Hanney, P.	01 Oct	X	McDermott-Evans, R.	01 Jan
X	Kemp, R.L.	01 Sep	X	Crichton, G.S.	29 Oct	X	McDonald, M.J.	01 Jan
X	King, D.A.	01 Sep	X	Eacock, J.P.	29 Oct	X	Mifflin, M.J.	01 Jan
X	Knowles, D.	01 Sep	S	Brown, L.E.M.	29 Oct	X	Minnikin, S.B.	01 Jan
X	Lipson, C.N.	01 Sep	S	Parker, A.R.	29 Oct	S	Mitchell, S.E.	01 Jan
E	Locke, N.M.	01 Sep	X	Elesmore, J.D.	29 Oct	X	Newby, C.	01 Jan
E	Longman, M.S.	01 Sep	X	Evans, K.	29 Oct	X	Nightingale, S.D.	01 Jan
S	MacKenow, H.R.	01 Sep	X	Thurston, M.S.	29 Oct	X	Norriss, M.W.	01 Jan
X	MacLean, S.M.	01 Sep	E	Hale, A.D.	01 Nov	X	Owens, J.W.	01 Jan
X	Mallinson, I.P.	01 Sep	S	Jones, A.L.	01 Nov	X	Pearson, A.J.	01 Jan
X	Martin, R.J.W.	01 Sep	S	Frost, U.E.	01 Nov	X	Pope, K.D.	01 Jan
E	Mawer, K.J.	01 Sep	E	Montgomery, H.E.	01 Nov	S	Savage, A.F.	01 Jan
S	Mawer, S.L.	01 Sep	X	Birkby, C.	01 Dec	S	Searle, E.L.	01 Jan
X	Mayberry, P.J.	01 Sep	X	Briant-Evans, T.A.H.	01 Dec	X	Sherwin, A.J.	01 Jan
X	McGivern, R.P.	01 Sep	X	Carman, F.S.D.	01 Dec	X	Smith, L.A.	01 Jan
E	McLaughlin, V.	01 Sep	X	Duffy, J.C.	01 Dec	X	Sutcliffe, P.M.	01 Jan
X	McMillan, N.	01 Sep	X	Dunne, J.	01 Dec	X	Tawse, L.O.J.	01 Jan
X	McQueen, P.G.	01 Sep	X	Ealey, N.J.	01 Dec	X	Tuffin, M.G.	01 Jan
X	Meigh, P.D.	01 Sep	X	Furmston, G.H.	01 Dec	X	Ware, P.J.	01 Jan
X	Morgan, G.L.	01 Sep	X	Green, A.J.	01 Dec	X	Warr, C.H.	01 Jan
E	Mullins, N.E.	01 Sep	X	Hastings, S.B.	01 Dec	X	Waters, M.R.	01 Jan
E	Murphy, C.J.	01 Sep	X	Toland, M.J.	01 Dec	E	Wykes, T.E.V.	01 Jan
X	Neyland, D.A.	01 Sep	X	Wilton, M.	01 Dec	E	Ziolo, J.M.C.	01 Jan
E	Pearson, I.T.	01 Sep	X	Marshall, C.G.	01 Dec	X	Sheals, E.J.	18 Jan
X	Phillips, L.C.	01 Sep	E	Argent, D.J.T.C.	01 Dec	X	Carter, C.A.	18 Feb
S	Phillips, M.R.	01 Sep	X	Hopwood, A.P.	17 Dec	X	Richardson, G.	18 Feb
E	Piaggesi, G.F.	01 Sep	X	Sandy, D.J.	17 Dec	X	Scales, D.R.	18 Feb
X	Pimm, A.R.	01 Sep	E	Gregory, J.E.	01 Jan	X	Taylor, A.	18 Feb
X	Preece, S.E.	01 Sep	E	McDiarmid, D.A.	01 Jan	E	Mulroy, P.J.	18 Feb
E	Pryce, H.C.	01 Sep	E	Mounsey, C.A.	01 Jan	E	Wilshire, N.L.	18 Feb
E	Purdy, R.J.	01 Sep	E	Pawsey, S.P.J.	01 Jan	X	Lewis, J.M.	25 Feb
E	Ralls, D.W.	01 Sep	E	Telford, J.	01 Jan	E	Perry, C.S.L.	01 Mar
X	Richardson, J.F.	01 Sep	X	Wells, M.N.	01 Jan	E	Wood, M.D.J.	01 Mar
S	Roberts, M.J.	01 Sep	X	Coughlin, P.J.L.	01 Jan	S	Byrd, L.B.	17 Mar
E	Roffey, K.D.	01 Sep	X	Aitken, L.	01 Jan	S	Moore, N.G.A.	17 Mar
X	Rugg, C.P.	01 Sep	E	Allan, O.J.	01 Jan	X	Bessant, M.	01 Apr
E	Samwell, M.G.	01 Sep	X	Armand-Smith, P.H.	01 Jan	X	Cunningham, S.I.	01 Apr
X	Seal, M.O.	01 Sep	X	Attwater, R.P.	01 Jan	X	Davies, D.T.	01 Apr
E	Searle, A.J.A.	01 Sep	X	Bailey, S.G.	01 Jan	E	Shakespeare, B.	01 Apr
E	Shakespeare, C.A.	01 Sep	X	Barber, A.S.L.	01 Jan	X	Williams, L.A.J.	01 Apr
S	Smith, M.D.	01 Sep	X	Boulton, G.R.	01 Jan	S	Austen, T.V.	01 Apr
X	Stevenson, A.P.	01 Sep	S	Brown, E.L.	01 Jan	X	Dawe, C.J.	01 Apr
E	Stevenson, P.M.	01 Sep	X	Bulgin, M.R.	01 Jan	S	Stephenson, R.J.E.	08 Apr
X	Strawbridge, C.M.	01 Sep	X	Capps, J.A.	01 Jan	X	Angliss, R.J.	08 Apr
X	Stuart, S.A.	01 Sep	E	Coffey, R.B.D.	01 Jan	E	Blatchford, T.P.	08 Apr
S	Swift, R.D.	01 Sep	X	Corbally, M.L.	01 Jan	E	Cloherty, A.	08 Apr
X	Taylor, J.E.	01 Sep	X	Curd, M.C.	01 Jan	E	Deakin, S.M.	08 Apr
X	Taylor, J.T.	01 Sep	S	Davies, D.J.	01 Jan	E	Duthie, A.G.	08 Apr
X	Trosh, N.	01 Sep	X	Dixon, S.J.	01 Jan	MS	Eden, J.R.H.	08 Apr
X	Tucker, P.J.	01 Sep	X	Emerson, M.J.	01 Jan	E	Evans, R.G.	08 Apr
X	Vaughan, E.A.	01 Sep	X	Franklin, R.W.	01 Jan	E	Hadley, C.M.	08 Apr

LIEUTENANTS

E	Herzberg, M.J.	08 Apr	X	Chisholm, P.J.H.	01 Jul	X	Keegan, A.C.	01 Sep
E	Hewitt, N.W.	08 Apr	X	Driscoll, M.S.	01 Jul	E	King, I.J.	01 Sep
E	Holland, S.W.	08 Apr	X	Hairsine, W.	01 Jul	E	McBeth, G.	01 Sep
MS	Horlock, A.	08 Apr	X	Hay, R.H.I.	01 Jul	X	McCavour, B.D.	01 Sep
E	Maden, S.G.	08 Apr	X	Higgins, D.J.	01 Jul	E	Mellor, D.P.	01 Sep
E	Parkin, B.A.	08 Apr	X	Hopton, M.J.	01 Jul	E	Minty, D.	01 Sep
E	Parnell, D.C.	08 Apr	X	Jane, S.C.	01 Jul	X	Neale, D.F.	01 Sep
E	Porteous, R.A.	08 Apr	X	Johnson, T.P.	01 Jul	E	Nicol, A.M.	01 Sep
E	Reynolds, D.P.	08 Apr	E	Lawrenson, T.A.H.	01 Jul	E	Oldfield, C.A.W.	01 Sep
E	Rooney, T.M.	08 Apr	X	Mahoney, A.J.	01 Jul	S	Page, C.A.	01 Sep
E	Stephens, C.P.	08 Apr	X	McKeen, S.A.	01 Jul	X	Pierce, S.L.	01 Sep
E	Trigwell, S.P.	08 Apr	X	Morgan, F.C.F.	01 Jul	X	Poole, D.C.	01 Sep
E	Walter, S.R.	08 Apr	X	Peschardt, C.W.H.	01 Jul	E	Ridgwell, D.R.	01 Sep
E	Wyper, J.	08 Apr	X	Shaw, S.A.	01 Jul	E	Robertson, A.J.	01 Sep
S	Hynde, C.L.	22 Apr	X	Stacey, E.J.	01 Jul	S	Robinson, P.J.	01 Sep
X	Betchley, J.W.	01 May	X	Stephens, P.G.	01 Jul	E	Rudkin, A.L.	01 Sep
E	Winborn, D.J.	01 May	X	Wilcocks, D.N.	01 Jul	E	Rushworth, A.W.E.	01 Sep
X	Blake, M.G.	01 May	X	Willsmore, S.A.	01 Jul	E	Shepherd, C.E.	01 Sep
S	Boyd, E.M.	01 May	X	Wordsworth, J.D.	01 Jul	X	Shrubsole, G.M.	01 Sep
X	Brettell, J.D.	01 May	X	Cox, A.D.	01 Aug	X	Taborda, M.A.	01 Sep
S	Brooksbank, R.	01 May	X	Herridge, D.J.	01 Aug	E	Thomson, P.A.	01 Sep
S	Coles-Hendry, F.A.	01 May	X	Shropshall, K.A.	01 Aug	E	Tuhey, J.J.G.	01 Sep
X	Cooke, D.P.	01 May	S	Clewes, S.	12 Aug	E	Watson, J.R.	01 Sep
X	Cox, S.J.	01 May	S	Bainbridge, P.A.	12 Aug	E	Watson, S.C.	01 Sep
X	Frost, T.S.	01 May	S	Crawford, R.I.	12 Aug	S	West, T.L.	01 Sep
X	Greenwood, S.J.	01 May	E	Brennan, J.P.	12 Aug	E	Whitaker, R.E.	01 Sep
S	Hanks, O.T.	01 May	E	Dodds, S.	12 Aug	X	Whitehouse, A.P.	01 Sep
X	Harris, H.J.L.	01 May	E	McQuaid, I.T.	12 Aug	X	Slight, O.W.L.	11 Sep
X	Hazlehurst, J.A.	01 May	MS	Simpson, J.N.	12 Aug	X	Johnson, A.M.	01 Oct
S	Hulse, R.J.	01 May	E	Amorosi, R.G.F.L.	01 Sep	X	Montague, A.D.	01 Oct
E	Leckey, E.H.	01 May	E	Bell, F.J.	01 Sep	X	Smith, M.R.T.	01 Oct
S	Leech, S.L.	01 May	E	Bowen, R.J.	01 Sep	X	Rowley, T.P.	28 Oct
X	Macaulay, S.C.	01 May	E	Golden, C.A.	01 Sep	X	Trevethan, C.J.	28 Oct
X	Malster, D.A.	01 May	E	Gordon, D.J.	01 Sep	S	Caswell, N.C.	28 Oct
X	McCallum, N.	01 May	E	Jubb, C.L.	01 Sep	X	Cowpe, P.	28 Oct
E	McCrea, M.J.	01 May	X	O'Neill, C.M.	01 Sep	X	Dougan, D.S.	28 Oct
X	McLone, S.P.	01 May	E	Tatton-Brown, H.T.	01 Sep	X	Medlicott, N.	28 Oct
S	Parker, D.J.	01 May	E	Weil, D.G.	01 Sep	MS	Middleton, M.A.	28 Oct
X	Purvis, S.G.	01 May	X	Barr, D.J.	01 Sep	X	Walker, J.	28 Oct
X	Relf, E.M.	01 May	X	Brown, M.A.	01 Sep	S	Burt, M.T.	28 Oct
X	Scorer, A.J.	01 May	E	Carpenter, G.J.	01 Sep	E	Abel, J.A.	01 Nov
X	Shortall, J.J.	01 May	X	Clark, P.J.	01 Sep	X	Coleman, J.M.P.	01 Nov
S	Smedley, R.L.	01 May	E	Cochrane, C.D.	01 Sep	E	Farrant, S.	01 Nov
X	Smith, B.	01 May	E	Cole, S.P.	01 Sep	E	Hankin, R.S.	01 Nov
X	Talbot, S.E.	01 May	X	Cornelio, S.M.	01 Sep	X	Haywood, A.J.	01 Nov
X	Talbot, S.J.	01 May	S	Costain, K.A.	01 Sep	E	Hewlett, P.J.E.	01 Nov
X	Tasker, A.M.	01 May	X	Coxon, H.E.M.	01 Sep	E	Ivory, T.J.	01 Nov
X	Thomas, D.J.	01 May	X	Craven, O.E.	01 Sep	E	Lipczynski, B.J.	01 Nov
X	Vierow, M.K.	01 May	X	Crombie, S.	01 Sep	X	Low, S.A.S.	01 Nov
X	Riley, R.A.	01 Jun	X	Dallas, L.I.	01 Sep	X	Perks, A.B.	01 Nov
X	Bowman, S.K.J.	01 Jun	X	Davidson, S.R.	01 Sep	X	Pollock, B.J.	01 Nov
X	Cursiter, J.D.	12 Jun	E	Dickson, K.G.	01 Sep	X	Sharples, J.H.	01 Nov
X	Billings, A.J.	25 Jun	X	Dixon, R.J.	01 Sep	X	Shaw, S.J.	01 Nov
X	Harrison, A.K.	25 Jun	E	Gearing, R.M.	01 Sep	X	Stant, M.S.	01 Nov
X	Higson, G.R.	25 Jun	E	Goodenough, R.E.	01 Sep	E	Sutcliff, J.D.	01 Nov
E	Holt, R.J.	25 Jun	X	Hagger, M.J.	01 Sep	E	Sweetman, D.J.	01 Nov
E	Kantharia, P.	25 Jun	E	Hammock, E.R.F.	01 Sep	X	Taylor, N.S.C.	01 Nov
E	Smith, N.D.	25 Jun	E	Hougham, T.N.	01 Sep	E	Teasdale, J.P.	01 Nov
E	Winstone, N.P.	25 Jun	X	Hurman, R.N.	01 Sep	E	Telfer, D.D.	01 Nov
X	Batho, W.G.P.	01 Jul	X	Insley, A.D.	01 Sep	E	Tetchner, D.J.	01 Nov
X	Borrett, J.E.	01 Jul	X	Irving, P.J.	01 Sep	X	Whitehouse, M.L.	01 Nov
X	Cantrell, S.R.D.	01 Jul	X	Jenkins, T.R.	01 Sep			

LIEUTENANTS

E	Wright, G.J.T.	01 Nov	X	Martin, J.N.	01 Jan	X	Roberts, S.M.	01 Feb
X	McSavage, R.I.	01 Dec	X	Paterson, J.M.A.	01 Jan	X	Royce, R.H.	01 Feb
X	Reid, J.A.W.	01 Dec	X	Patrick, J.A.	01 Jan	E	Ryder, M.R.	01 Feb
X	Hough, P.J.	01 Dec	E	Philips, T.J.	01 Jan	X	Sidoli, L.T.A.	01 Feb
X	Warren, A.J.L.	01 Dec	X	Rogers, M.S.	01 Jan	X	Skinner, J.J.	01 Feb
X	Rees, S.G.	01 Dec	E	Shaw, C.R.	01 Jan	E	Smith, C.A.	01 Feb
E	Botham, A.M.	16 Dec	X	Shields, K.N.	01 Jan	X	Starkey, D.S.	01 Feb
E	Davis, R.	16 Dec	X	Snel, K.E.	01 Jan	X	Veti, M.A.	01 Feb
E	Fowler, C.D.	16 Dec	X	Southworth, C.	01 Jan	X	Walker, M.J.	01 Feb
X	Hadden, D.W.	16 Dec	X	Stephens, S.J.R.	01 Jan	X	Yemm, M.A.	01 Feb
X	Liddle, M.R.	16 Dec	X	Story, R.S.	01 Jan	X	Bebbington, D.M.	17 Feb
			E	Turner, D.L.	01 Jan	X	Hannigan, J.D.	17 Feb

2006

			X	Vereker, R.J.P.	01 Jan	S	Howarth, M.C.	17 Feb
			X	Vessey, L.M.	01 Jan	E	Harris, R.	20 Feb
E	Chaudhary, R.	01 Jan	X	Sauer, A.C.	01 Feb	S	Stamper, V.L.	01 Mar
X	Carr, D.J.	01 Jan	X	Arbuthnott, E.A.H.	01 Feb	X	Milner, L.D.	01 Mar
X	Ormshaw, M.A.	01 Jan	E	Baugh, A.J.E.	01 Feb	X	Swann, A.P.D.	01 Mar
X	Akers, S.J.	01 Jan	X	Bell, L.G.	01 Feb	X	Bond, R.J.	01 Apr
X	Alexander, W.A.D.	01 Jan	E	Bent, P.M.	01 Feb	X	Parrott, S.S.	01 Apr
X	Beedle, J.D.S.	01 Jan	X	Brady, M.V.	01 Feb	X	Seal, M.R.	01 Apr
X	Bird, M.P.	01 Jan	S	Croxton, D.P.	01 Feb	X	Seddon, J.D.	01 Apr
X	Burton, J.H.	01 Jan	X	Dean, J.P.	01 Feb	X	Sheppard, H.C.	01 Apr
X	Ellison, P.J.P.	01 Jan	X	Fox, J.P.	01 Feb	E	Carlton, P.D.	01 May
X	Gill, A.B.	01 Jan	X	Freeman, E.M.R.	01 Feb	E	Chisholm, D.T.	01 May
X	Haynes, J.G.	01 Jan	S	Frith, A.M.	01 Feb	E	Offord, S.J.J.	01-May
X	Hooper, W.R.	01 Jan	X	Hamblin, P.A.	01 Feb			
X	Jamieson, P.A.	01 Jan	X	Harris, A.M.	01 Feb			
X	Knight, J.M.	01 Jan	X	Hucker, O.C.	01 Feb			
X	Lamb, R.J.F.	01 Jan	E	Muir, A.	01 Feb			

SUB LIEUTENANTS

2002

			X	Cackett, T.E.R.	01 May	S	Bird, T.M.	01 Jun
			S	Carver, C.A.	01 May	S	Buchan, L.H.	01 Jun
E	Simpson, E.L.	01 Jan	X	Collie, J.A.	01 May	S	Carr, J.	01 Jun
X	Wood, C.	01 Jan	X	Corcoran, R.M.	01 May	S	Charnock, S.J.	01 Jun
X	Neil, D.A.	01 May	X	Cumberland, N.S.	01 May	X	Crowe, P.D.	01 Jun
E	Peters, M.K.	01 Jul	X	Dobson, S.C.S.	01 May	X	Drewett, B.J.H.	01 Jun
X	Brown, A.P.	01 Sep	X	Ellicott, M.J.	01 May	X	Duncan, J.E.	01 Jun
X	Byers, H.R.	01 Sep	X	Evered, J.F.	01 May	X	Leaphard, D.P.	01 Jun
E	Cheater, C.J.	01 Sep	X	Farrow, R.D.	01 May	X	Lorenz, R.	01 Jun
X	Coatalen-Hodgson, R.	01 Sep	X	Harper, K.J.	01 May	S	McIntyre, C.	01 Jun
E	Errington, R.J.B.	01 Sep	X	Keane, J.P.	01 May	X	Moore, J.P.	01 Jun
E	Fletcher, A.S.	01 Sep	X	Langmead, B.	01 May	X	Paul, G.M.	01 Jun
E	King, M.A.	01 Sep	X	Marshall, A.	01 May	X	Quick, B.P.	01 Jun
E	Magzoub, M.M.M.	01 Sep	S	Miller, A.D.	01 May	X	Taylor, S.A.	01 Jun
E	Thomas, A.G.	01 Sep	X	Pariser, A.M.	01 May	X	Bretten, N.J.	01 Jul
E	Turner, V.M.	01 Sep	X	Parkin, M.J.	01 May	X	Camplisson, O.G.	01 Jul
X	Verrecchia, J.R.	01 Sep	X	Peacock, L.G.J.	01 May	X	Parry, S.J.	01 Jul
E	Vowles, I.R.	01 Sep	X	Piper, B.J.	01 May	X	Rolls, E.C.	01 Jul
X	Elliott, O.L.	01 Nov	X	Pollitt, A.W.	01 May	X	Storton, G.H.	01 Jul
E	Kay, V.J.	01 Nov	X	Rawlinson, K.E.	01 May	S	Harwood, A.J.	01 Aug
			S	Rogerson, A.E.	01 May	X	Leigh, C.J.	01 Aug

2003

			X	Sharples, M.J.	01 May	X	Proudman, M.P.	01 Aug
S	Knight, S.	01 Jan	X	Thomas, M.P.	01 May	X	Allan, V.E.	01 Sep
S	Grimley, T.P.	01 Apr	X	Tickle, M.J.	01 May	X	Austin, S.A.	01 Sep
X	Westlake, K.J.	01 Apr	X	Tyacke, R.S.	01 May	X	Barham, E.J.	01 Sep
X	Baker, J.K.	01 May	S	Wright, J.N.	01 May	E	Betts, A.T.J.	01 Sep
X	Bell, R.J.	01 May	X	Askham, M.T.	01 Jun	E	Betts, P.R.	01 Sep
X	Bentley, G.S.	01 May	X	Bate, R.C.	01 Jun	E	Binns, J.B.	01 Sep
X	Burgoyne, W.L.	01 May	X	Batley, J.T.	01 Jun	X	Blackett, W.P.H.	01 Sep

SUB LIEUTENANTS

E	Blackmore, A.M.	01 Sep	X	Collins, C.A.	01 Nov	X	Gardner, E.S.E.	01 Feb
X	Booth, T.O.	01 Sep	X	Edwards, M.I.	01 Nov	X	Giles, P.A.I.	01 Feb
X	Cave, J.	01 Sep	X	Flegg, W.J.	01 Nov	X	Hardy, J.	01 Feb
E	Church, S.J.	01 Sep	X	Fletcher, J.H.G.	01 Nov	X	Hollingworth, C.R.	01 Feb
E	Cox, M.J.	01 Sep	S	Holburt, R.M.	01 Nov	X	Jones, T.	01 Feb
E	Cutlan, S.L.	01 Sep	X	Mason, D.	01 Nov	X	Jones, W.C.	01 Feb
X	Dale, J.R.	01 Sep	X	Muir, K.M.	01 Nov	X	Knott, T.M.	01 Feb
E	Davies, J.S.A.	01 Sep	X	Roberts, D.S.	01 Nov	X	McArdle, M.J.	01 Feb
S	Davison, L.M.	01 Sep				S	McKenzie, H.K.	01 Feb
E	Dix, C.P.	01 Sep		**2004**		X	Mileusnic, C.J.	01 Feb
X	Dyer, S.D.	01 Sep				X	Phillips, E.H.L.	01 Feb
X	Ebbern, G.J.	01 Sep	E	Allen, A.P.	01 Jan	X	Pilkington, B.M.	01 Feb
S	Evans, T.W.	01 Sep	X	Bakewell, R.A.	01 Jan	X	Pyette, M.D.V.C.	01 Feb
X	Ferguson, I.	01 Sep	S	Barker, P.R.	01 Jan	X	Scott, P.D.	01 Feb
E	Flannigan, A.	01 Sep	E	Barter, E.C.	01 Jan	X	Skinner, A.L.	01 Feb
X	Flatt, L.B.	01 Sep	X	Black, K.J.	01 Jan	X	Taylor, N.R.	01 Feb
E	Forward, K.L.	01 Sep	X	Bradley, M.J.	01 Jan	X	Tiebosch, N.K.	01 Feb
E	Fowler, R.	01 Sep	S	Chatterley, D.A.	01 Jan	X	Vincent, C.	01 Feb
X	Fredrickson, C.A.	01 Sep	X	Cheshire, T.S.	01 Jan	X	Welsh, M.P.	01 Feb
X	Gilbertson, C.J.	01 Sep	X	Cocks, A.E.J.	01 Jan	X	West, D.M.	01 Feb
X	Greaves, T.M.	01 Sep	E	Cullum, W.E.	01 Jan	X	Williams, J.L.	01 Feb
E	Guild, I.W.	01 Sep	X	Curnock, T.C.R.	01 Jan	E	Adamson, H.J.	01 Mar
X	Hancox, J.	01 Sep	X	Fellows, C.R.	01 Jan	X	Allinson, M.D.	01 Mar
E	Heywood, R.H.	01 Sep	X	Fitzgibbon, J.P.	01 Jan	E	Jones, H.	01 Mar
E	Hitchings, M.J.	01 Sep	S	Forbes, M.P.	01 Jan	X	Langford, T.D.	01 Mar
E	Howe, J.K.A.	01 Sep	X	Gillingham, G.	01 Jan	E	Smith, P.M.	01 Mar
E	Jones, D.P.	01 Sep	X	Gooding, D.C.	01 Jan	X	Horn, N.R.	01 Apr
E	Kendall-Torry, G.C.	01 Sep	X	Guy, F.L.	01 Jan	X	Strickland, T.J.	01 Apr
E	Lister, M.J.L.	01 Sep	S	Hammond, C.R.	01 Jan	X	Webster, M.	01 Apr
E	London, N.J.	01 Sep	E	Hannaby, P.B.	01 Jan	E	Wood, J.T.S.	01 Apr
E	Marlor, A.	01 Sep	X	Henderson, A.G.	01 Jan	X	Aitken, N.D.	01 May
X	Martin, D.L.	01 Sep	X	Inglis, W.S.	01 Jan	X	Anderson, M.I.C.	01 May
X	McEwen, C.J.	01 Sep	S	Jones, M.R.	01 Jan	S	Bassett, N.	01 May
E	Moran, J.	01 Sep	X	Kelley, A.L.	01 Jan	X	Beck, A.J.	01 May
X	Moss-Ward, E.G.	01 Sep	X	Lake, A.	01 Jan	X	Blenkinsop, G.J.	01 May
X	Munns, E.N.	01 Sep	X	Latchem, A.J.	01 Jan	X	Burch, M.H.	01 May
X	Nokes, O.	01 Sep	X	MacRae, K.	01 Jan	X	Carter, A.J.M.	01 May
E	North, A.C.	01 Sep	X	Mason, A.E.	01 Jan	X	Clark, P.	01 May
E	Patten, M.L.	01 Sep	E	McAllister, A.W.	01 Jan	X	Durston, A.P.	01 May
E	Payne, J.O.	01 Sep	X	McCormack, S.	01 Jan	X	Evans, P.A.	01 May
E	Pearsall, M.J.S.	01 Sep	X	Mehlsen, N.M.N.	01 Jan	X	Gatenby, D.	01 May
E	Philipson, M.J.	01 Sep	X	Montagu, T.B.E.P.	01 Jan	X	Haynes, Z.E.	01 May
X	Plunkett, G.N.	01 Sep	X	Morrow, O.J.	01 Jan	S	Holloway, B.S.V.	01 May
X	Power, B.	01 Sep	E	Mullis, G.	01 Jan	X	Keenan, D.J.	01 May
E	Riordan, S.P.	01 Sep	X	Patterson, P.X.	01 Jan	X	Leaman, T.P.	01 May
E	Rooke, A.E.	01 Sep	X	Pearson, R.J.	01 Jan	S	MacDonald, F.J.	01 May
E	Rooke, K.E.	01 Sep	S	Pearson, S.I.	01 Jan	X	Martin, B.R.	01 May
E	Rose, M.E.	01 Sep	E	Percival, V.H.	01 Jan	X	McLaughlan, C.T.	01 May
E	Ryan, S.J.	01 Sep	X	Pinnington, A.J.	01 Jan	X	Moloney, B.G.	01 May
S	Slayman, E.	01 Sep	X	Powell, G.M.J.	01 Jan	X	Murray, J.C.	01 May
E	Spacey, C.D.	01 Sep	X	Preston, J.N.	01 Jan	S	Poynton, C.M.F.	01 May
E	Stafford-Shaw, D.V.	01 Sep	X	Ray, B.T.	01 Jan	S	Prissick, M.A.	01 May
E	Taberham, H.	01 Sep	E	Rose, S.P.	01 Jan	X	Rodgers, B.M.	01 May
E	Taylor, S.R.	01 Sep	X	Smith, J.C.	01 Jan	X	Skinner, N.D.	01 May
X	Thompson, G.C.	01 Sep	X	Stackhouse, M.C.	01 Jan	X	Spalding, T.S.	01 May
E	Westbrook, K.	01 Sep	X	Sykes, H.E.	01 Jan	S	Tudor, O.J.	01 May
X	Weston, G.K.	01 Sep	X	Waskett, D.	01 Jan	E	Wason, J.M.	01 May
X	Wilcox, C.R.	01 Sep	X	Whitaker, M.J.	01 Jan	X	Webber, A.A.	01 May
X	Williams, O.C.L.	01 Sep	E	Wilkinson, S.L.	01 Jan	E	Zitkus, J.J.	01 May
S	Wilson, C.K.	01 Sep	E	Wright, M.G.	01 Jan	X	Berry, D.H.	01 Jun
X	Adam, M.W.	01 Nov	X	Broadwith, J.L.	01 Feb	X	Breckenridge, R.J.M.	01 Jun
X	Ayers, O.R.B.	01 Nov	X	Crocker, D.T.A.	01 Feb	X	Johnson, M.D.	01 Jun
			S	Flinton, A.R.	01 Feb			

SUB LIEUTENANTS

X	Kelly, P.J.	01 Jun	E	Little, J.I.	01 Sep	X	Williams, J.E.	01 Nov
X	Laird, I.A.	01 Jun	S	Locke, K.C.	01 Sep	X	Neave, J.R.	01 Dec
X	Lawrence-Archer, S.E.S.	01 Jun	X	Mawdsley, O.R.T.C.	01 Sep			
X	Loewendahl, S.	01 Jun	E	McBride, A.R.	01 Sep		**2005**	
X	Macleod, A.M.	01 Jun	S	McLean, D.J.	01 Sep			
X	Manning, D.S.	01 Jun	X	Moon, B.J.	01 Sep	S	Adams, S.J.	01 Jan
X	Moss, J.E.	01 Jun	E	Mouatt, D.M.	01 Sep	X	Bayliss, J.E.L.	01 Jan
X	Murray, G.P.	01 Jun	X	Nugent, H.A.	01 Sep	S	Bennett, E.C.	01 Jan
X	Rock, J.A.	01 Jun	X	Pellecchia, D.N.	01 Sep	S	Brocklebank, B.M.C.	01 Jan
X	Rowntree, P.J.	01 Jun	S	Pepper, N.R.	01 Sep	X	Casey, A.M.	01 Jan
X	Shouler, M.F.	01 Jun	X	Perera-Stack, E.	01 Sep	E	Chisholm, D.C.	01 Jan
X	Taylor, C.P.	01 Jun	E	Pethrick, J.F.	01 Sep	S	Clark, O.R.	01 Jan
X	Weller, J.K.	01 Jun	X	Richards, R.D.	01 Sep	E	Davidson, G.J.	01 Jan
X	Coleman, A.P.G.	01 Jul	X	Roberts, G.E.	01 Sep	E	Davies, A.	01 Jan
X	Hall, R.S.	01 Jul	X	Rutter, J.C.	01 Sep	E	Dewhirst, M.A.	01 Jan
X	Leonard, T.A.	01 Jul	S	Shaves, T.D.L.	01 Sep	E	Dimmock, G.N.	01 Jan
X	Magill, A.F.	01 Jul	E	Shirvill, M.J.	01 Sep	E	Eldridge, J.W.C.	01 Jan
X	Kidd, A.N.	01 Aug	E	Stephen, C.E.	01 Sep	E	Epsom, O.	01 Jan
X	Sinha, R.	01 Aug	X	Thomas, S.	01 Sep	X	Forrest, D.J.	01 Jan
E	Andrews, R.	01 Sep	E	Twiss, P.J.	01 Sep	E	Fox-Roberts, P.K.	01 Jan
E	Archibald, K.E.	01 Sep	X	Vowles, A.L.D.	01 Sep	X	Gibbs, A.P.	01 Jan
S	Barker, H.A.	01 Sep	E	Walker, G.H.	01 Sep	S	Goy, S.E.	01 Jan
E	Bartlett, D.L.	01 Sep	X	Ward, A.J.	01 Sep	X	Graddon, G.J.	01 Jan
E	Beck, E.A.	01 Sep	X	White, C.G.	01 Sep	X	Grossett, K.M.	01 Jan
X	Bennett, I.J.	01 Sep	X	Williams, N.M.	01 Sep	X	Guest, C.A.	01 Jan
X	Booth, A.K.	01 Sep	E	Williams-Allden, L.A.	01 Sep	E	Harland, S.J.	01 Jan
E	Bowman, D.E.	01 Sep	E	Wylie, J.J.	01 Sep	E	Hayes, J.D.	01 Jan
S	Bray, A.J.	01 Sep	S	Kearsley, I.P.	01 Oct	E	Hitchcock, B.	01 Jan
X	Brian, S.A.	01 Sep	X	Abbott, D.A.J.	01 Nov	E	Holmes, C.	01 Jan
X	Bryden, D.G.	01 Sep	X	Arnall-Culliford, E.C.	01 Nov	X	Jackson, A.R.	01 Jan
X	Campbell, J.G.	01 Sep	X	Bannon, W.J.J.	01 Nov	E	Jones, C.D.	01 Jan
E	Chapman, N.J.	01 Sep	X	Brewer, C.W.G.	01 Nov	E	Kelway, J.R.	01 Jan
E	Clarke, J.P.	01 Sep	X	Campbell-Wilson, C.J.	01 Nov	E	Kent, R.A.J.	01 Jan
S	Coleman, G.W.	01 Sep	X	Cooper, D.T.	01 Nov	E	Lees, A.C.S.	01 Jan
E	Collier, D.E.	01 Sep	X	Coupar, D.R.	01 Nov	X	Luke, C.J.	01 Jan
X	Critchley, I.J.	01 Sep	X	Court, M.R.	01 Nov	X	McClelland, P.W.	01 Jan
E	Crook, R.F.	01 Sep	X	Crawford, A.A.	01 Nov	X	McNair, K.	01 Jan
X	De'Maine, R.J.	01 Sep	X	Darcy, J.D.	01 Nov	X	Morton, N.	01 Jan
S	De'Silva, O.A.	01 Sep	X	Flood, L.J.	01 Nov	X	Mowthorpe, S.L.	01 Jan
X	Dore, C.L.	01 Sep	X	Floyer, H.G.	01 Nov	X	Newman, A.M.	01 Jan
X	Drennan, D.G.	01 Sep	X	Freeth, D.J.	01 Nov	X	Parker, J.R.	01 Jan
X	Duncan, E.M.	01 Sep	X	Gleave, R.D.	01 Nov	X	Parkinson, N.	01 Jan
E	Edwards, G.R.	01 Sep	X	Goose, S.J.	01 Nov	E	Peachey, N.D.	01 Jan
E	Fenwick, S.G.	01 Sep	X	Kennedy, M.P.	01 Nov	X	Powell, A.D.	01 Jan
X	Flint, G.F.	01 Sep	X	Knapp, V.E.	01 Nov	S	Price, M.W.	01 Jan
X	Gilbert, M.A.	01 Sep	X	Marston, R.M.	01 Nov	X	Rofe, S.A.	01 Jan
S	Graham, B.R.	01 Sep	X	Mathieson, C.M.	01 Nov	E	Scott, R.B.	01 Jan
E	Guy, R.J.	01 Sep	X	Napier, A.A.	01 Nov	X	Smalley, P.J.	01 Jan
E	Hamlet, M.C.	01 Sep	X	Norman, S.J.	01 Nov	X	Smith, J.A.	01 Jan
X	Hardwick, A.J.	01 Sep	X	Reid, J.R.	01 Nov	X	Spackman, L.C.	01 Jan
E	Harvey, A.	01 Sep	X	Rich, D.	01 Nov	X	Spearpoint, D.M.	01 Jan
X	Henderson, H.A.	01 Sep	X	Roberts, M.T.	01 Nov	X	Stevens, M.J.	01 Jan
E	Hodges, P.R.	01 Sep	X	Sawicki, A.J.	01 Nov	X	Stocker, J.T.	01 Jan
X	Howard, M.J.	01 Sep	X	Shattock, J.D.	01 Nov	X	Stopps, G.A.M.	01 Jan
E	Hunter, D.J.	01 Sep	X	Short, K.J.	01 Nov	X	Swales, R.	01 Jan
S	Isted, L.R.	01 Sep	X	Skelley, R.	01 Nov	X	Symcox, C.M.	01 Jan
X	Jackson, J.C.A.	01 Sep	X	Skelton, R.S.	01 Nov	X	Thomas, C.M.	01 Jan
X	Johnson, C.J.	01 Sep	X	Southall, N.C.J.	01 Nov	S	Thompson, D.J.	01 Jan
E	Kelley, V.L.	01 Sep	X	Taylor, M.G.	01 Nov	E	Tilson, D.R.	01 Jan
E	Lane, R.J.	01 Sep	X	Taylor, M.R.	01 Nov	S	Tuckett, C.S.E.	01 Jan
X	Latham, D.G.	01 Sep	X	Thompson, C.F.	01 Nov	X	Unsworth, B.M.	01 Jan
E	Lister, S.	01 Sep	X	White, K.T.	01 Nov	X	Venner, S.J.	01 Jan
						X	Ward, J.A.	01 Jan

SUB LIEUTENANTS

E	Wilson, G.H.C.	01 Jan	X	McManus, A.J.	01 Feb	X	Smith, A.M.	01 Sep
X	Woods, J.D.	01 Jan	X	Mitchell, A.J.	01 Feb	S	Thomas, R.D.	01 Sep
X	Wotton, R.J.	01 Jan	X	Newton, O.R.A.	01 Feb	X	Revell, A.D.	10 Sep
X	Wright, J.A.H.	01 Jan	X	Nottingham, J.M.	01 Feb	X	Bratt, J.R.	01 Nov
S	Wynn, I.A.	01 Jan	X	Oxley, J.D.	01 Feb	X	Brown, S.S.	01 Nov
X	Allison, G.	01 Feb	MS	Pitchford, S.	01 Feb	X	Collins, S.J.	01 Nov
X	Beeching, L.G.	01 Feb	X	Raval, V.	01 Feb	X	Knight, A.J.	01 Nov
X	Benn, G.I.	01 Feb	X	Stewart, S.T.	01 Feb	X	Whittington, C.C.	01 Nov
X	Blunt, C.L.	01 Feb	X	Townsend, A.M.	01 Feb	X	Peacock, J.D.	01 Dec
X	Braycotton, E.J.	01 Feb	X	Walford, L.S.	01 Feb			
X	Brolls, G.G.	01 Feb	X	Wall, T.C.	01 Feb			
X	Carrott, D.L.	01 Feb	X	Wardley, H.D.M.P.	01 Feb		**2006**	
X	Cattanach, J.I.	01 Feb	X	Watson, R.W.	01 Feb			
E	Coogan, T.	01 Feb	X	Woodward, A.J.	01 Feb	X	Clayton, A.L.	01 Jan
X	Drummond, A.S.	01 Feb	X	Sawyer, J.L.	20 Feb	X	Marshall, N.K.	01 Jan
X	Gardiner, L.M.	01 Feb	X	Godwin, L.D.	01 Mar	X	Phelan, S.C.	01 Jan
X	Harkin, J.P.	01 Feb	X	Ferris, N.	01 May	X	Holt, T.D.	03 Jan
X	Hazell, E.V.	01 Feb	X	Glover, T.F.	01 May	X	Crewdson, R.P.	01 Feb
X	Hazelwood, S.	01 Feb	X	Kopsahilis, A.	01 May	X	Howard, J.W.	01 Feb
X	Herron, R.P.	01 Feb	X	Davison, W.M.	01 Jun	X	Kerr, M.	01 Feb
X	Holbrook, S.J.	01 Feb	S	Hastings, C.S.	01 Jun	X	Moore, A.L.	01 Feb
X	Holland, R.	01 Feb	S	Whatley, M.	01 Jul	X	Smith, E.J.	01 Feb
X	Hunter, D.J.C.	01 Feb	X	Lane, E.H.	01 Aug	E	Stevenson, L.L.	01 Feb
X	Ingram, D.D.	01 Feb	X	Amos, J.L.	01 Sep	X	George, J.A.	13 Feb
X	Instrell, C.B.	01 Feb	X	Burrows, T.G.	01 Sep	X	Duff, A.J.	01 Mar
X	Kendall, N.R.	01 Feb	X	Butcher, M.W.	01 Sep	X	Martindale, H.	01 Apr
X	Loughran, O.A.G.	01 Feb	X	Dart, M.P.	01 Sep	X	Ridley, G.E.	01 Apr
X	McInerney, D.F.	01 Feb	X	Edwards, L.	01 Sep			

SUB LIEUTENANTS (UCE)

2001			**2004**			**2005**		
E	Reed, P.K.	01 Sep	E	Blatcher, D.J.	01 Sep	X	Brown, R.J.	01 Sep
			E	Main, M.G.	01 Sep	X	Gibson, M.J.	01 Sep
2003			E	Myatt, M.	01 Sep	E	Johnson, T.	01 Sep
			X	Webb, A.F.	01 Sep	E	Middleditch, T.C.	01 Sep
E	Willmore, S.	01 Jan	S	Wright, J.S.	01 Sep	X	Stone, N.S.	01 Sep
E	Griffiths, F.M.	01 Sep	X	Yates, S.P.	01 Sep	X	Tottenham, G.J.	01 Sep
E	Westley, A.J.R.	01 Sep				X	Witton, O.E.N.J.C.	01 Sep

MIDSHIPMEN

2004								
X	Evans, M.R.	01 Jan	X	Gilbert, J.S.D.	01 Nov	X	Denyer, A.C.	01 Sep
X	Bracken, C.D.	01 May	X	Jeffs, S.G.	01 Nov	X	Fraser, M.J.	01 Sep
X	Craig, A.P.	01 May	X	Kenchington, R.A.W.	01 Nov	X	Jones, C.	01 Sep
X	Edge, T.W.	01 May	X	McGlone, F.R.	01 Nov	X	Targett, E.G.	01 Sep
X	King, M.	01 Jun	X	Southern, V.	01 Nov	X	Taylor, A.I.	01 Sep
X	McMorrow, K.M.	01 Jun	X	White, D.J.	01 Nov	X	Prollins, M.R.	01 Nov
X	Dando, B.J.	01 Sep	X	Winskell, T.R.	01 Nov			
X	Edwards, J.D.	01 Sep					**2006**	
X	Garner, R.J.	01 Sep		**2005**				
X	Richardson, D.M.	01 Sep				X	Askew, D.T.	01 Jan
X	Shepherd, O.J.	01 Sep	X	Flynn, C.	01 Jan	S	Cooper, N.J.W.	01 Jan
X	Smith, L.M.	01 Sep	X	Lane, M.J.	01 Jan	X	Mould, C.W.	01 Jan
X	Stevens, C.K.	01 Sep	X	Maumy, J.M.	01 Jan	X	Oram, C.	01 Jan
X	Wallington-Smith, J.	01 Sep	X	Fearn, D.C.T.	01 Feb	X	Pullin, K.M.	01 Jan
X	White, P.K.L.	01 Sep	X	Knight, A.J.L.	01 Feb	X	Sewell, L.E.	01 Jan
X	Young, M.N.W.	01 Sep	X	Pettit, S.A.	01 Feb	X	Withers, D.M.	01 Jan
			X	Morgan, A.K.	01 May	X	Yarker, S.	01 Jan
			X	Cooper, J.W.	01 Sep			

MEDICAL OFFICERS

SURGEON VICE ADMIRAL

Jenkins, Ian Lawrence, CB, CVO, MB, BCH, FRCS .... 21 Oct 02
(SURGEON GENERAL (SL 01) OCT 02)

SURGEON REAR ADMIRALS

Farquharson-Roberts, Michael Atholl, CBE, QHS, MB, BS, MA(Lond), LRCP, FRCS, rcds .... 9 Dec 03
(MEDICAL DIRECTOR GENERAL(NAVAL) DEC 03)

Raffaelli, Philip Iain, MSc, MB, BCH, MRCGP, FFOM, rcds, jsdc .... 4 May 04
(CHIEF EXECUTIVE DEFENCE MEDICAL TRAINING AGENCY)

SURGEON CAPTAINS

1994	2000	2004
- Howard, O.M. ....31 Dec	- Morgan, N.V. .... 30 Jun	
	- Gabb, J.H. ....31 Dec	- Hughes, A.S. .... 30 Jun
1995	- Johnston, C.G. ....31 Dec	- Pipkin, C. .... 30 Jun
- Tolley, P.F.R. ....31 Dec		- Walker, A.J. .... 30 Jun
	2002	
1996	- Brown, D.C. .... 30 Jun	**2005**
- Douglas-Riley, T.R. ....31 Dec	- Campbell, J.K. .... 30 Jun	
	- McArthur, C.J.G. .... 30 Jun	- Hett, D.A. .... 01 Jun
1998		- Waugh, P.J. .... 30 Jun
	2003	- Johnston, R.P. .... 19 Aug
- Mugridge, A.R. .... 30 Jun	- Ashton, R.E. .... 01 Apr	- Buxton, P.J. .... 01 Oct
- Sykes, J.J.W. ....31 Dec	- Kershaw, C.R. ....01 Apr	
	- Runchman, P.C. .... 01 Apr	
1999	- Allison, A.S.C. .... 30 Jun	**2006**
- Bevan, N.S. ....31 Dec	- Butterfield, N.P. .... 30 Jun	
- Jarvis, L.J. ....31 Dec	- Dean, M.R. .... 30 Jun	- Lunn, D.V. .... 30 Jun

SURGEON COMMANDERS

1993	1998	2001
- Benton, P.J. ....31 Dec	- Hughes, P.A. .... 30 Jun	- Townsend, J.S. ....31 Jan
	- Midwinter, M.J. ....31 Dec	- Nichols, E.A. ....27 May
1994	- Risdall, J.E. ....31 Dec	- Turnbull, P.S. .... 30 Jun
- Nicol, P.J.S. .... 30 Jun		- Birt, D.J. .... 30 Jun
- Baker, A.B. .... 30 Jun	**1999**	
	- Lambert, A.W. .... 30 Jun	**2002**
1996	- Howell, M.A. .... 30 Jun	- Pearson, C.R. .... 30 Jun
- Aitchison, K.J. .... 04 Feb	- Ross, R.A. ....31 Dec	- Campbell, D.J. .... 30 Jun
- Burgess, A.J. .... 30 Jun		- Clarke, J.M. .... 30 Jun
- McNeill Love, R.M.C. .... 30 Jun	**2000**	- Stapley, S.A. .... 30 Jun
- Perry, J.N. ....31 Dec	- Groom, M.R. .... 30 Jun	- Evershed, M.C. .... 30 Jun
	- Bree, S.E.P. .... 30 Jun	- Sharpley, J.G. .... 30 Jun
1997	- Burkett, J.A. ....01 Jul	- Millar, S.W.S. .... 30 Jun
- Norwood, J.M. .... 01 Mar	- Hill, G.A. ....31 Dec	**2003**
- Edwards, C.J.A. ....31 Dec	- Nicholson, G. ....31 Dec	- Haddon, R.W.J. ....01 Apr
	- Foster, C.R.M. ....31 Dec	- Wylie, R.D.S. ....01 Apr

SURGEON COMMANDERS

- Whitehouse, D.P. ....01 Apr
- Terry, M.C.G. .... 30 Jun
- Hand, C.J. .... 30 Jun
- Smith, S.R.C. .... 30 Jun
- Miles, R. .... 30 Jun
- Tanser, S.J. .... 30 Jun
- Mellor, A.J. .... 30 Jun
- Blair, D.G.S. .... 30 Jun
- Fisher, N.G. .... 30 Jun
- Campbell, A.D.K. .... 03 Aug
- Thomson, R.G. ....05 Nov

2004

- Wood, G. .... 30 Jun

- Leigh-Smith, S.J. .... 30 Jun
- Cannon, L.B. .... 30 Jun
- Connor, D.J. .... 30 Jun
- Pimpalnerkar, A.L. .... 30 Jun
- Craner, M.J. .... 30 Jun
- Matthews, G.A. .... 30 Jun
- Thomas, L.M. .... 30 Jun
- Rickard, R.F. .... 30 Jun
- Batham, D.R. ....01 Sep

2005

- Rawal, K.M. .... 30 Jun
- Whittaker, M.A. .... 30 Jun
- Taylor, P.J. .... 30 Jun

- Smith, J.E. .... 30 Jun
- Haworth, K.J. .... 30 Jun
- Shrimpton, H.D. .... 30 Jun
- Randle, M.P. ....01 Sep
- Evans, G.W.L. .... 17 Oct
- Bowie, A.N. .... 28 Oct

2006

- Daramola, O. .... 30 Jun
- Dekker, B.J. .... 30 Jun
- Heames, R.M. .... 30 Jun
- Greenberg, N. .... 30 Jun

SURGEON LIEUTENANT COMMANDERS

1996

- Ramaswami, R.A. ....27 Jul
- Fowler, P.J. .... 03 Aug
- Neary, J.M. .... 01 Oct

1997

- Palmer, A.C. .... 01 Mar
- Yarnall, N.J. .... 01 Aug

1998

- Masilamani, N.S. ....14 Jan
- Streets, C.G. .... 01 Aug
- Freshwater, D.A. .... 09 Aug

1999

- Baden, J.M. .... 17 Mar
- Duby, A. .... 23 Apr
- Counter, P.R. .... 01 Aug
- Snowden, M.B.S. .... 01 Aug
- Brinsden, M.D. .... 01 Aug
- Tamayo, B.C.C. .... 01 Aug
- Houlberg, K.A.N. .... 01 Aug
- Gibson, A.R. .... 01 Aug
- Hughes, D.J. .... 01 Aug
- Parry, C.A. .... 12 Aug

2000

- Shah, R.R. ....12 Jan
- Coltman, T.P. .... 01 Aug
- McCabe, S.E.T. .... 01 Aug
- Hudson, J.D.P. .... 02 Aug
- Siggers, B.R.C. .... 02 Aug
- Bateman, R.M. .... 02 Aug
- Sowden, L.M. .... 02 Aug
- Dickson, S.J. .... 02 Aug
- Mercer, S.J. .... 03 Aug
- Ayers, D.E.B. .... 03 Aug
- McLachlan, J.K. .... 17 Aug

- Lew-Gor, S.T.W. ....05 Sep
- Tennant, M.I. .... 14 Sep
- Kehoe, A.D. ....01 Dec

2001

- Webber, R.J. .... 01 Feb
- Crowson, E. ....06 May
- Matthews, J.J. .... 01 Aug
- Porter, S. .... 01 Aug
- Mantle, M. .... 07 Aug
- Marshall, F.T. .... 07 Aug
- Denholm, J.L. .... 07 Aug
- Smith, J.J. .... 07 Aug
- Reston, S.C. .... 07 Aug
- Bland, S.A. .... 07 Aug
- Milner, R.A. .... 07 Aug
- McLean, C.R. .... 07 Aug
- Schofield, S.R. .... 08 Aug
- Mackie, S.J. .... 12 Aug
- Imm, N.D.H. ....23 Nov

2002

- Armstrong, E.M. .... 05 Feb
- Pickard, R.J. .... 23 Apr
- Dewar, J.C. .... 30 Apr
- Norris, W.D. .... 20 May
- Prior, K.R.E.J. .... 06 Aug
- Hutchings, S.D. .... 06 Aug
- Henry, M.F. .... 06 Aug
- Mair, E.J. .... 06 Aug
- Dow, W.A.M. .... 06 Aug
- Rees, P.S.C. .... 06 Aug
- McIntosh, J.D. .... 26 Aug
- Phillips, S.M. ....03 Sep
- Whybourn, L.A. ....28 Nov

2003

- Brown, A. .... 05 Aug
- Gay, D.A.T. .... 05 Aug

- Welch, J.F. .... 05 Aug
- Brims, F.J.H. .... 05 Aug
- Allsop, A.R.L. .... 05 Aug
- Evans, G.C. .... 05 Aug
- Cormack, A.J.R. .... 05 Aug
- Collett, S.M. .... 05 Aug
- Doran, C.M.C. .... 07 Aug

2004

- Nelstrop, A.M. .... 11 Feb
- Carey, D.B. .... 01 Jun
- Turner, M.J. .... 01 Aug
- Price, V.J. .... 04 Aug
- Franklyn-Miller, A.D. .... 04 Aug
- Barton, S.J. .... 04 Aug
- Martin, N. .... 04 Aug
- Scott, T.E. .... 04 Aug
- Grainge, C.L. .... 04 Aug
- Leason, J.M.E. .... 04 Aug
- Read, J.A.J.M. .... 04 Aug
- Coates, P.J.B. .... 04 Aug
- Cooke, J.M. .... 02 Aug
- Hayton, J.C. .... 02 Aug
- Harrison, J.C. .... 02 Aug
- Stannard, A. .... 02 Aug
- Dew, A.M. .... 02 Aug
- Lamont, S.N.J. .... 02 Aug
- Mercer, S.J. .... 02 Aug
- Robin, J.I. .... 02 Aug
- Guyver, P.M. .... 04 Aug
- Martin, N.P. .... 26 Aug
- Gardner, C.B. .... 29 Sep

2005

- MacKay-Brown, A.L. .... 01 Aug
- Pardoe, E.R. .... 06 Aug

SURGEON LIEUTENANTS

2001

- Bennett, S.A.F.J. .... 01 Aug
- Wild, G. .... 01 Aug
- Proctor, A.R. .... 01 Aug
- Khan, M.A. .... 01 Aug
- Hamilton, S.C. .... 01 Aug
- Mercer, A.J. .... 01 Aug
- Maples, A.T. .... 01 Aug
- Patel, D.R. .... 01 Aug
- Yates, E.H. .... 01 Aug
- Bray, K.E. .... 01 Aug
- Beard, D.J. .... 01 Aug
- Bains, B.S. .... 01 Aug
- Arthur, C.H.C. .... 01 Aug
- Bonner, T.J. .... 09 Aug

2002

- Pointon, B.M. .... 04 May
- Miles, S.A. .... 17 May
- Cordner, M.A. .... 01 Aug
- Phillips, J.C. .... 01 Aug
- Wood, A.M. .... 01 Aug
- Taylor, R.S. .... 07 Aug
- Kershaw, R.J. .... 07 Aug
- Barker, V.S. .... 07 Aug
- Picken, C.R. .... 07 Aug
- Ambrose, R.E.F. .... 07 Aug
- Allcock, E.C. .... 07 Aug
- Evans, T.E. .... 07 Aug
- Edward, A.M. .... 07 Aug
- Hemingway, R. .... 07 Aug
- Vale, A.J. .... 07 Aug

- Hunter, C.R. .... 07 Aug
- Westerman, R.W. .... 13 Aug
- Gregory, A.E. .... 01 Sep

2003

- Calvin, A.J. .... 04 Feb
- Leather, N.W.F. .... 07 Apr
- Pengelly, S.P. .... 06 Aug
- Gardiner, D.R.C. .... 06 Aug
- Sargent, D.S. .... 06 Aug
- Isbister, E.J. .... 06 Aug
- McMenamin, D.M. .... 06 Aug
- Gilmartin, K.P. .... 06 Aug
- Newton, N.J.P. .... 06 Aug
- Lindsay, M.H. .... 06 Aug
- Shearman, A.J. .... 06 Aug
- Boddy, K.L. .... 06 Aug
- Morris, L.E. .... 06 Aug
- Jaques, S.C.D. .... 06 Aug
- Strachan, R.P. .... 06 Aug
- Jones, A.L. .... 06 Aug
- Dewynter, A.M. .... 06 Aug
- Gordon, D.A. .... 06 Aug
- Middleton, S.W.F. .... 11 Sep
- Henning, D.C.W. .... 19 Sep
- Penn-Barwell, J.G. .... 07 Oct
- MacFarlane, G.T. .... 08 Oct

2004

- Scutt, M.J. .... 04 Feb
- Cockram, A.L. .... 04 Feb
- Ralph, J.M. .... 16 Mar

- Tayal, M. .... 01 Aug
- Morris, A.J. .... 03 Aug
- Wrigley, A.J. .... 03 Aug
- Hillman, C.M. .... 03 Aug
- Roue, K.S. .... 03 Aug
- Gokhale, S.G. .... 04 Aug
- Potter, D.L. .... 04 Aug
- Roscoe, D. .... 04 Aug
- Longmore, D. .... 04 Aug
- Barnard, E.B.G. .... 04 Aug
- O'Shea, M.K. .... 06 Sep
- Mellor, R.G. .... 01 Dec

2005

- Philpott, M.C. .... 04 Jan
- McKinlay, J.A.C. .... 01 Feb
- Fries, C.A. .... 02 Feb
- Barker, R.J. .... 01 Aug
- Evans, H.J. .... 01 Aug
- Durkin, J.L. .... 02 Aug
- Halpin, A.C. .... 02 Aug
- Martin, L.C. .... 02 Aug
- Robinson, T.G. .... 02 Aug
- Minshall, D.M. .... 02 Aug
- Davey, K.L. .... 02 Aug
- Rainey, O.H. .... 02 Aug
- Gibbens, C.J. .... 02 Aug
- Hughes, C.L. .... 02 Aug
- Herbert, L.J. .... 03 Aug
- Lim, F.C. .... 01 Sep
- Proffitt, A. .... 16 Sep

ACTING SURGEON LIEUTENANTS

2005

- Droog, S.J. .... 19 Jun
- Bell, C.S. .... 12 Jul
- Dowlen, H.T.B. .... 18 Jul
- Hornby, S.A. .... 27 Jul

- Dickie, A.K. .... 01 Aug
- Howes, R.J. .... 01 Aug
- Tomkins, B.M. .... 01 Aug
- Williams, R.J. .... 01 Aug
- Wood, I.M. .... 01 Aug
- Andersson, J.L. .... 02 Aug

- Booth, R.M. .... 02 Aug
- Brogden, T.G. .... 02 Aug
- Wells, L.C. .... 02 Aug
- Weale, J.H. .... 03 Aug

MEDICAL CADETS SURGEON SUB LIEUTENANTS RN

2002

- Warren, J.M. ....01 Jul

2003

- Bourn, S.J.N. ....01 Jul
- Evans, C.V. ....01 Jul
- Evans, J.T. ....01 Jul
- Hughes, R.W. ....01 Jul
- Oxlade, A.T. ....01 Jul
- Rennie, R.A. ....01 Jul
- Scorer, T.G. ....01 Jul
- Skyrme, L.L. ....01 Jul
- Smith, A.H. ....01 Jul
- Steer, R.R. ....01 Jul
- Bleakley, C.I. ....02 Jul
- Holland, T.J. ....23 Sep
- Ritson, J.E. ....19 Oct

2004

- Smith, F.E. ....11 Mar
- Watchorn, J.C. ....15 May

- Leong, M.J.L.J. ....23 Jun
- Jeffery, S.M.T. ....30 Jun
- Edgar, I.A.M.M. ....31 Aug
- Shaw, A.F.H. ....06 Sep
- Jamieson, S. ....13 Sep
- Towner, S.D.P. ....13 Sep
- Lee, R.K. ....15 Sep
- Robinson, M.W. ....16 Sep
- Fry, R.L. ....20 Sep
- Henderson, A.H. ....20 Sep
- Kemp, P.G. ....20 Sep
- Pillai, S.N. ....20 Sep
- Reilly, J.J. ....20 Sep
- Denby, W.J. ....25 Sep
- Angus, D.J.C. ....28 Sep
- Jowett, A.G. ....05 Nov
- Hale, A.L. ....20 Nov
- Castledine, B.C. ....28 Dec

2005

- Wake, C.E.V. ....19 Jan
- Ahuja, V.Y. ....22 Jan

- Herod, T.P. ....22 Jan
- Thomas, R.C. ....26 Mar
- Millar, J.A. ....22 Apr
- Sharp, W.M.J. ....01 Jun
- Shaw, E.J. ....05 Sep
- Simpson, M.A. ....05 Sep
- Nobbs, C.G. ....07 Sep
- Thompson, M.H.W. ....08 Sep
- Freer, J.M. ....10 Sep
- O'Brien, D.J. ....10 Sep
- McIntosh, S.J. ....12 Sep
- Glennie, J.S. ....14 Sep
- Tanzer, W.J.C.E. ....08 Oct
- Lundie, A.J. ....14 Oct
- Neil-Gallacher, E.H.M.D. ....25 Nov
- Nixon, S.W. ....15 Dec
- Saffin, J.R. ....16 Dec

2006

- Morgan, R.E. ....12 Jan
- Stanning, A.J. ....02 Feb

DENTAL OFFICERS

SURGEON CAPTAINS (D)

1996
- Morrison, G.L. ....31 Dec

2000
- Sanderson, R.C. .... 30 Jun

2002
- Weston, M.W. .... 30 Jun

2003
- Thomas, D.L. ....01 Apr

2004
- Norris, R.E. .... 26 Oct

2005
- Sidoli, G.E. ....01 Jan
- Stevenson, R.M. 06-Aug

SURGEON COMMANDERS (D)

1995
- Gall, M.R.C. .... 30 Jun

1996
- Culwick, P.F. ....31 Dec

1997
- Aston, M.W. .... 30 Jun

1998
- Howe, S.E. ....31 Dec

- Jordan, A.M. ....31 Dec

1999
- Hall, D.J. ....31 Dec

2000
- McJarrow, D.J. .... 30 Jun
- Redman, C.D.J. ....31 Dec

2001
- Smith, B.S. .... 30 Jun

2002
- Elmer, T.B. .... 30 Jun

2003
- Turnbull, N.R. .... 30 Jun

2005
- Fenwick, J.C. .... 30 Jun
- James, I. .... 30 Jun
- McMeekin, N.S. 15-Jul

SURGEON LIEUTENANT COMMANDERS (D)

1996
- Minall, P.A. ....24 Jul

1997
- Davenport, N.J. ....16 Jan
- Everitt, C.J. .... 11 Mar

1998
- Moore, P.G. ....31 Dec

1999
- Leyshon, R.J. ....09 Jan
- Stevenson, G.S. ....14 Jan
- Winch, E.J. ....24 Jan

2001
- Wingfield, M.H. ....01 Jul
- Madgwick, E.C.C. ....23 Jul

2002
- Doherty, M. ....05 Jan
- Scott, W.A. ....13 Jan
- Jessiman, S.I. .... 20 Jun
- Hands, A.J. .... 26 Jun
- Verney, K.H. ....09 Jul
- Chittick, W.B.O. ....10 Jul
- Dean, T.C. ....22 Jul

2003
- Drummond, K.B. ....13 Jul
- Murdoch, G.A. ....20 Jul
- Holmes, P.S. ....20 Jul

2004
- Foulger, T.E. .... 11 Jun

2005
- Williams, B.R. .... 27 Jun
- Cole, C.V. .... 29 Jun
- Bryce, G.E. .... 29 Jun
- Hamilton, M.S. 30-Aug
- Jenks, J.C.B. .... 24 Sep

SURGEON LIEUTENANTS (D)

2001
- Kershaw, S.H.C. ....18 Jul

2002
- McNab, G.J. .... 19 Jun

- Cordner, K.J. ....04 Jul
- Wells, J.P. ....04 Jul

2003
- Lovell, A.D. .... 25 Jun
- Williams, D.S. .... 25 Jun

- Stevenson, L.J. ....27 Jun
- Park, L.K. ....27 Jun

2004
- Pepper, T.D. 13-Jul

ACTING SURGEON LIEUTENANTS (D)

2004	2005
- Chan, A. .... 25 Jun	- Hickey, R.M. .... 24 Jun
- Hesketh, M.J. .... 25 Jun	- Macleod, A.M. 24-Jun

SURGEON SUB LIEUTENANTS (D)

2005	2006
- Westwood, A.J. ....26 Jul	- Hall, J.M. ....01 Jan
- Valender, C.J.A. .... 18 Aug	

CHAPLAINS

DIRECTOR GENERAL NAVAL CHAPLAINCY SERVICE
AND THE CHAPLAIN OF THE FLEET

Green, John, QHC..04 Jun 91

PRINCIPAL ANGLICAN CHAPLAIN

Green, John, QHC..04 Jun 91
(DGNCS-PERSONAL APR 06)

CHAPLAINS

1978

CE   Barlow, D. ....04 Apr

1980

CE   Hilliard, R.G.............................01 Aug

1981

CE   Clarke, B.R. ....30 Jun

1982

CE   Howard, C.W.W. ....28 Sep

1983

CE   Jackson, M.H.............................19 Apr

1984

CE   Brotherton, M. ....04 Sep

1986

CE   Elmore, G.M.............................30 Sep

1987

CE   Luckraft, C.J. ....05 Aug

1988

CE   Thomas, D.W.W. ....18 Oct

1990

CE   Pyne, R.L. ....23 Jan
CE   Callon, A.M...............................05 Jun
CE   Poll, M.G. ....14 Jun

1991

CE   Scott, P.J.D.S............................03 Sep
CE   Springett, S.P. ....10 Sep

1992

CE   Kelly, N.J...................................26 May
CE   Bromage, K.C...........................02 Aug
CE   Morris, J.O. ....06 Oct

1993

CE   Beveridge, S.A.R.......................28 Apr

1994

CE   Hill, J. ....17 Jan

1997

CE   Wheatley, I.J. ....08 Apr

1998

CE   Hills, M.J. ....21 Apr
CE   Evans, M.L................................01 Sep
CE   Gough, M.J................................01 Sep

CE   Wylie, D.V. ....01 Dec

2000

CE   Phillips, A.G...............................14 Feb

2002

CE   Hallam, S.P. ....05 May

2003

CE   Hitchins, E.G.D. ....06 Jan
CE   Lamb, S.I...................................06 Jan

2004

CE   Stewart, M.P.M.........................29 Mar
CE   Petzer, G.S................................01 Aug
CE   Corness, A.S..............................06 Sep
CE   Duff, A.J....................................04 Oct

2005

CE   Simpson, D.J. ....07 Mar
CE   Beardsley, N.A. ....03 May
CE   Parselle, S.P...............................30 Aug
CE   Hillier, A. ....13 Sep

2006

CE   Keith, G.M.W. ....03 Jan

PRINCIPAL CHURCH OF SCOTLAND AND FREE CHURCHES CHAPLAIN

Rae, Scott MacKenzie, MBE, QHC, BD.. 02 Feb 81
(DGNCS-DNCS PPO PCSFCC N APR 06)

CHAPLAINS

1990

SF   Eglin, C.A.................................. 10 Sep

1992

SF   Britchfield, A.E.P. .... 01 Oct

1993

SF   Brown, S.J. ....20 Apr
SF   Shackleton, S.J.S. ....20 Apr
SF   Wort, R.S. ....27 Jul

1995

SF   Beadle, J.T. .... 30 Mar

1996

SF   Martin, R.C.J.R. ....03 Sep

1997

SF   Wilkinson, T.L. .... 04 Mar
SF   Meachin, M.C. ....07 Jul

2000

SF   Ellingham, R.E. .... 17 Apr
SF   Grimshaw, E............................02 May
SF   Kennon, S. .... 17 Sep
SF   Rowe, R.D. ....24 Sep

2002

SF   Goodwin, T. .... 05 May

SF   Botwood, T.J. ....09 Sep

2003

SF   Devenney, D.J.............................06 Jan
SF   Dalton, M.F. ....12 Jan

2004

SF   McCulloch, A.J.R. .... 12 Jun
SF   Thomson, S. .... 13 Sep

2005

SF   Gates, W.C................................06 Sep

2006

SF   Roissetter, D.A..........................03 Jan

PRINCIPAL ROMAN CATHOLIC CHAPLAIN

Madders, Brian Richard, MBE, QHC.. 09 Sep 85
(DGNCS-DNCS FD E   PRCC N APR 06)

CHAPLAINS

1985

RC   Donovan, P.A.............................22 Apr

1990

RC   Sharkey, M. .... 01 Oct

1996

RC   Bradbury, S............................... 18 Sep

RC   McLean, D.................................18 Sep

1998

RC   McFadden, A..............................01 Sep
RC   Yates, D.M. ....01 Sep

2000

RC   Cassidy, M.J..............................24 Sep

RC   Conroy, D.A. ....24 Sep

2005

RC   Blythen, R.A. ....06 Sep

NAVAL CAREERS SERVICE OFFICERS (RN)

LIEUTENANTS (CS)

1998	1999
- Drewett, C.E. .... 19 Sep	- Jones, C.R. ....08 Jan
	- Concarr, D.T. .... 19 Sep

NAVAL CAREERS SERVICE OFFICERS (RM)

LIEUTENANTS (CS)

1999	
- Wilcockson, R............................07 May	

FAMILY SERVICE

LIEUTENANTS (FS)

1999	
FS Butterworth, L............................16 Jan	

ROYAL MARINES

CREST - The Globe surrounded by a Laurel wreath and surmounted by the Crowned Lion and Crown with 'Gibraltar' on a scroll. The Fouled Anchor imposed on the wreath below the Globe. Motto - 'Per Mare Per Terram'.

THE QUEEN'S COLOUR - The Union. In the centre the Fouled Anchor with the Royal Cypher interlaced ensigned with the St Edward's Crown and 'Gibraltar' above; in base the Globe surrounded by a Laurel wreath. Motto - 'Per Mare Per Terram'. In the case of Royal Marines Commando units the distinguishing colour of the units is interwoven in the gold cords and tassles.

THE REGIMENTAL COLOUR - Blue. In the centre the Fouled Anchor interlaced with the Royal Cypher 'G.R.IV' ensigned with the St Edward's Crown and 'Gibraltar' above, in base the Globe surrounded by a Laurel wreath. Motto - 'Per Mare Per Terram'. In the dexter canton the Union in the remaining three corners the Royal Cypher. In the case of Royal Marines Commando units the numerical designation of the unit is shown immediately below the insignia. The distinguishing colour of the unit is interwoven in the gold cords and tassles.

ROYAL MARINES SECRETARY - Whale Island, Portsmouth Hants PO2 8ER.

CORPS JOURNAL - 'The Globe and Laurel,' Whale Island Portsmouth, Hants PO2 8ER

ROYAL MARINES ASSOCIATION - General Secretary, Southsea, Hants, PO4 9PX.

ROYAL MARINES MUSEUM - Southsea, Hants, PO4 9PX.

ROYAL MARINES

CAPTAIN GENERAL

His Royal Highness The Prince Philip Duke of Edinburgh, KG, KT, OM, GBE, AC, QSO

HONORARY COLONEL

His Majesty King Harald V of Norway, KG, GCVO

COLONELS COMMANDANT

Brigadier S P Hill , OBE .... 14 Sep 02
(COLONEL COMMANDANT ROYAL MARINES)

Lieutenant General Fulton, Sir Robert Henry Gervase, KBE, BA, rcds, psc(m), hcsc ....3 Jun 03
(REPRESENTATIVE COLONEL COMMANDANT ROYAL MARINES)

LIEUTENANT GENERALS

Fulton, Sir Robert Henry Gervase, KBE, BA, rcds, psc(m), hcsc..3 Jun 03
(DEP CHIEF OF DEFENCE STAFF (EQUIP CAPABILITY) JUN 03)

Fry, Sir Robert Allan, KCB, CBE, BSc, MA, psc(m) ....7 Jul 03
NP IRAQ (MAR 06)

MAJOR GENERALS

Dutton, James Benjamin, CBE, BSc, rcds, psc(m)... 4 May 04
(COMMANDANT GENERAL ROYAL MARINES/COMMANDER UK AMPHIBIOUS FORCES MAY 04)

Rose, John Gordon, MBE, psc(m), hcsc... 06 Feb 06
(DGIC FEB 06)

BRIGADIERS

2001	2004	2005
- Thomas, J.H. .... 17 Sep	- Salmon, A. .... 13 Apr	- Mason, J.S.....................................01 Jul
	- Shadbolt, S.E............................. 01 Oct	
2003	- Capewell, D.A. .... 18 Oct	
- Robison, G.S. .... 15 Sep		

COLONELS

1996
- Heaver, D.G.V. .... 30 Jun

1998
- Hartnell, S.T. .... 30 Jun

1999
- Robbins, J.M.F. .... 30 Jun
- Heal, J.P.C. .... 31 Dec
- Noble, M.J.D. .... 31 Dec

2000
- Haddow, F. .... 30 Jun
- Bibbey, M.W. .... 31 Dec
- Chicken, S.T. .... 31 Dec

2001
- Thomson, A.B. .... 30 Jun

2002
- Howes, F.H.R. .... 30 Jun
- Dunham, M.W. .... 30 Jun
- Huntley, I.P. .... 30 Jun
- Messenger, G.K. .... 30 Jun

2003
- Stearns, R.P. .... 30 Jun
- Denning, P.R. .... 30 Jun
- Pickup, R.A. .... 30 Jun
- Hook, D.A. .... 30 Jun

2004
- Taylor, W.J. .... 30 Jun
- Davis, E.G.M. .... 30 Jun
- Bevis, T.J. .... 30 Jun

2005
- Stewart, D.J. .... 30 Jun
- Scott, C.R. .... 30 Jun
- Watts, R.D. .... 30 Jun

2006
- Brown, N.P. .... 30 Jun
- Ellis, M.P. .... 30 Jun
- Dechow, W.E. .... 30 Jun
- Salzano, G.M. .... 30 Jun

LIEUTENANT COLONELS

1988
- Nunn, C.J. .... 30 Jun

1990
- Roy, A.C. .... 31 Dec

1991
- Grant, I.W. .... 30 Jun

1992
- Balm, S.V. .... 30 Jun
- McCabe, J. .... 31 Dec
- Armstrong, R.I. .... 31 Dec

1993
- Crosby, J.P. .... 30 Jun
- Canning, W.A. .... 30 Jun
- Gelder, G.A. .... 31 Dec
- Martin, P.J. .... 31 Dec

1994
- Beadon, C.J.A. .... 30 Jun
- Hughes, S.J. .... 30 Jun
- Lovelock, R.B. .... 30 Jun
- Wilson, S.R. .... 30 Jun
- Wotherspoon, S.R. .... 30 Jun
- Taylor, M.K. .... 30 Jun

1995
- Guyer, S.T.G. .... 30 Jun
- Wilson, A.C. .... 31 Dec
- Tasker, G. .... 31 Dec
- Heatly, R.J. .... 31 Dec

1996
- Leigh, J. .... 31 Dec
- Musto, E.C. .... 31 Dec

1997
- Sampson, P.H. .... 30 Jun
- Hutton, J.K. .... 30 Jun
- Foster, G.R. .... 31 Dec
- Walker, R.E. .... 31 Dec

1998
- Herring, J.J.A. .... 30 Jun
- Newing, S.G. .... 30 Jun
- Davies, J.R. .... 31 Dec
- Price, M.J. .... 31 Dec

1999
- Cusack, N.J. .... 30 Jun
- Mudford, H.C. .... 30 Jun
- Page, M.C. .... 30 Jun
- Smith, M.L. .... 31 Dec
- Hall, S.J. .... 31 Dec
- Lindley, N.P. .... 31 Dec
- Spencer, R.A.W. .... 31 Dec

2000
- Summerfield, D.E. .... 30 Jun
- Webster, T.J.C. .... 30 Jun
- Cawthorne, M.W.S. .... 30 Jun
- Burnell, J.R.J. .... 31 Dec
- Barnes, R.W. .... 31 Dec
- Bruce-Jones, N.W. .... 31 Dec
- Middleton, T.P.W. .... 31 Dec
- Matthews, G. .... 31 Dec

2001
- Paul, R.W.F. .... 30 Jun
- Syvret, M.E.V. .... 30 Jun
- Evans, D.M.M. .... 30 Jun
- King, D.C.M. .... 30 Jun

2002
- McCardle, J.A. .... 30 Jun
- Hudson, J.D. .... 30 Jun
- Copinger-Symes, R.S. .... 30 Jun
- Harradine, P.A. .... 30 Jun
- Marok, J. .... 30 Jun
- Maddick, M.J. .... 30 Jun
- Cameron, P.S. .... 30 Jun
- Ross, J.H. .... 30 Jun
- Manger, G.S.C. .... 30 Jun
- Curry, B.R. .... 30 Jun
- Gray, M.N. .... 30 Jun
- Maynard, A.T.W. .... 30 Jun
- BS Davis, C.J. .... 30 Jun

2003
- Daniels, T.N. .... 30 Jun
- Taylor, P.G.D. .... 30 Jun
- Wilson, D.W.H. .... 30 Jun
- Francis, S.J. .... 30 Jun
- Birrell, S.M. .... 30 Jun
- Holmes, M.J. .... 30 Jun
- Pulvertaft, R.J. .... 30 Jun
- Stephens, R.J. .... 30 Jun
- Magowan, R.A. .... 30 Jun
- O'Donnell, I.M. .... 30 Jun
- Dewar, D.A. .... 30 Jun

2004
- Phillips, S.J. .... 30 Jun
- Green, M.G.H. .... 30 Jun
- Bennett, N.M. .... 30 Jun
- Cundy, R.G. .... 30 Jun
- Livingstone, A.J. .... 30 Jun
- Kassapian, D.L. .... 30 Jun
- Oliver, K.B. .... 30 Jun
- Joyce, P. .... 30 Jun
- Stickland, C.R. .... 30 Jun
- Porter, M.E. .... 30 Jun
- Everritt, R. .... 30 Jun

LIEUTENANT COLONELS

- Pierson, M.F. .... 30 Jun

2005

- Forster, R.M. .... 30 Jun
- Ross, A.C.P. .... 30 Jun
- Scott, S.J. .... 30 Jun
- Saddleton, A.D. .... 30 Jun
- Greedus, D.A. .... 30 Jun
- Maybery, J.E. .... 30 Jun
- White, H.J. .... 30 Jun

- Pressly, J.W. .... 30 Jun
- Morris, J.A.J. .... 30 Jun
- Holt, J.S. .... 30 Jun
- Evans, P.J. .... 30 Jun
- May, D.P. .... 30 Jun

2006

- Pritchard, S.A. .... 30 Jun
- Price, A.M. .... 30 Jun
- Hughes, J-P.H. .... 30 Jun

- Ritchie, W.J. .... 30 Jun
- Holmes, C.J. .... 30 Jun
- Litster, A. .... 30 Jun
- Crouden, S.F. .... 30 Jun
- Case, A.C. .... 30 Jun
- Armour, G.A. .... 30 Jun
- Cunningham, J.T. .... 30 Jun
- McInerney, A.J. .... 30 Jun
- Bestwick, M.C. .... 30 Jun
- James, P.M. .... 30 Jun
- Green, G.E. .... 30 Jun

MAJORS

1984

- Rye, J.W. .... 01 Sep

1986

- Tyrrell, R.K. .... 01 Sep

1987

- Ebbens, A.J. .... 01 Sep

1988

- Underwood, N.J. .... 01 Sep
- Milne, A.R. .... 01 Sep

1989

- Milner, H.C. .... 01 Sep

1990

- Gittoes, M.A.W. .... 01 Sep
- Hall, R.M. .... 01 Sep
- Parks, E.P. .... 01 Sep
- Grixoni, M.R.R. .... 01 Sep
- Sharland, S.P. .... 01 Sep

1992

- Corrin, C.ST.J. .... 01 Sep
- Bentham-Green, N.R.H. .... 01 Sep

1993

- MacDonald, I.R. .... 08 Feb
- Gwillim, V.G. .... 01 Sep

1995

- Smallwood, J.P. .... 05 Sep

1996

- Hood, M.J. .... 25 Apr
- Pelly, G.R. .... 25 Apr
- Cullis, C.J. .... 25 Apr
- Freeman, M.E. .... 01 Sep
- Willson, N.J. .... 01 Sep
- Thomas, P.W. .... 01 Oct

1997

- Gadie, P.A. .... 01 May
- Thurstan, R.W.F. .... 01 May
- Morris, P.E.M. .... 01 May
- Searight, M.F.C. .... 01 May
- Slack, J.M. .... 01 May
- Cook, T.A. .... 01 Sep
- Hembrow, T. .... 01 Oct
- Maese, P.A. .... 01 Oct
- Corbidge, S.J. .... 01 Oct

1998

- Kenworthy, R.A. .... 30 Apr
- Mc Laren, J.P. .... 30 Apr
- Kemp, P.J. .... 01 Sep
- Sear, J.J. .... 01 Sep
- Amos, J.H.J. .... 01 Sep
- Gilding, D.R. .... 01 Sep
- Green, G.M. .... 01 Sep
- Chapman, S. .... 01 Sep
- Jones, M.R. .... 01 Sep
- Cunningham, J.S. .... 01 Oct

1999

- Kettle, R.A. .... 24 Apr
- Fergusson, A.C. .... 01 May
- Hills, R.B. .... 01 May
- Manson, P.D. .... 01 Sep
- Baxendale, R.F. .... 01 Sep
- Hussey, S.J. .... 01 Sep
- Skuse, M. .... 01 Sep
- Stovin-Bradford, M. .... 01 Sep
- Richards, S.W. .... 01 Oct
- Beazley, P. .... 01 Oct

2000

- Murray, A.B. .... 26 Apr
- Robertson, N.B. .... 01 May
- Mattin, P.R. .... 01 May
- Bucknall, R.J.W. .... 01 May
- Cooper-Simpson, R.J. .... 01 May
- Hammond, M.C. .... 01 May
- Walls, K.F. .... 01 May
- Chattin, A.P. .... 01 May
- Congreve, S.C. .... 01 May
- Cook, M.F. .... 01 May

- Murchison, E.A. .... 01 Sep
- Blythe, T.S. .... 01 Sep
- Wraith, N. .... 01 Sep
- Kern, A.S. .... 01 Sep
- Bakewell, T.D. .... 01 Sep
- Jermyn, N.C. .... 01 Sep
- Davies, H.C.A. .... 01 Sep
- Bulmer, R.J. .... 01 Oct
- Perry, R.W. .... 01 Oct
- BS Watson, P.F. .... 01 Oct

2001

- Reed, J.J. .... 01 Jan
- Geldard, M.A. .... 01 May
- Walker, A.J. .... 01 May
- Craig, K.M. .... 01 May
- King, R.J. .... 01 May
- Spanner, P. .... 01 May
- Page, D.C.M. .... 01 Sep
- Daukes, N.M. .... 01 Sep
- Dowd, J.W. .... 01 Sep
- Hedges, J.W. .... 01 Sep
- Liddle, S.J. .... 01 Sep
- Hermer, J.P. .... 01 Sep
- Hughes, M.J. .... 01 Sep
- Jenkins, G. .... 01 Sep
- Taylor, M.A.B. .... 01 Sep
- Coomber, J.M. .... 01 Sep
- De Reya, A.L. .... 01 Sep
- Harris, C.C. .... 01 Sep
- Roylance, J.F. .... 01 Sep
- Thomsett, H.F.J. .... 01 Sep
- Twist, M.T. .... 01 Sep
- Fuller, S.R. .... 01 Sep
- Venn, N.S.C. .... 30 Sep
- Fraser, G.W. .... 01 Oct
- Hannah, W.F. .... 01 Oct
- Kelly, A.P. .... 01 Oct

2002

- Brighouse, N.G. .... 24 Apr
- Dresner, R.J. .... 24 Apr
- Moorhouse, E.J. .... 24 Apr
- Balmer, G.A. .... 24 Apr
- Sutherland, N. .... 24 Apr
- Hardy, D.M. .... 24 Apr
- Kearney, P.L. .... 27 Apr

MAJORS

- Hale, J.N. ...27 Apr
- Plewes, A.B. ...27 Apr
- Lee, S.P. ...27 Apr
- Roddy, M.P. ...27 Apr
- Summers, J.A.E. ...24 May
- Tanner, M.J. ...01 Sep
- Blanchford, D. ...01 Sep
- Read, R.J. ...01 Sep
- Turner, S.A. ...01 Sep
- Bailey, D.S. ...01 Sep
- Harris, T. ...01 Sep
- Hammond, D.E. ...01 Sep
- Jackson, M.J.A. ...01 Sep
- Kelly, P.M. ...01 Sep
- McGhee, C. ...01 Sep
- Paton, C.M. ...01 Sep
- Preston, R.W. ...01 Sep
- O'Herlihy, S.I. ...01 Sep
- Manning, D. ...01 Sep
- Goodridge, T.J. ...01 Oct
- Smith, S.F. ...01 Oct

2003

- Gray, J.A. ...01 May
- Maltby, R.J. ...01 May
- Morley, A. ...01 May
- Parvin, R.A. ...01 May
- Watkins, A.P.L. ...01 May
- Brown, L.A. ...01 Sep
- O'Hara, G.C. ...01 Sep
- Jepson, N.H.M. ...01 Sep
- Muddiman, A.R. ...01 Sep
- Whitfield, P.M. ...01 Sep
- Devereux, M.E. ...01 Sep
- Ethell, D.R. ...01 Oct
- Rearden, R.J. ...01 Oct
- Stafford, D.B. ...01 Oct
- Wilson, A.C. ...01 Oct
- Todd, M.A. ...01 Oct
- Bowra, M.A. ...01 Oct

- Scott, S.C. ...01 Oct
- Ward, C.D. ...01 Oct

2004

- Burrell, A.M.G. ...01 Apr
- Collin, M. ...01 Apr
- Lock, A.G.D. ...01 Apr
- Lee, O.A. ...01 May
- Crawford, A.T.S. ...01 May
- Duncan, G.S. ...01 May
- Somerville, N.J.P. ...01 May
- Williamson, A.K. ...01 May
- Cheesman, D.J.E. ...01 Sep
- Wilson, J.G. ...01 Sep
- Cantrill, R.J. ...01 Sep
- Penkman, W.A.V. ...01 Sep
- Stemp, J.E. ...01 Sep
- Nicholls, B.A. ...01 Oct
- Parry, J.A. ...01 Oct
- Pilkington, A.G.H. ...01 Oct
- Thompson, G.M. ...01 Oct
- Tulloch, S.W. ...01 Oct
- Clark, P.A. ...01 Oct
- Fenwick, R.J. ...01 Oct
- Rochester, R.W. ...01 Oct
- Atherton, B.W. ...01 Oct
- Brady, S.P. ...01 Oct
- Taylor, S.D. ...01 Oct
- Lugg, J.C. ...01 Oct
- Merchant, J.M. ...01 Oct
- Watson, R.I. ...01 Oct
- Alderson, R.J. ...01 Oct
- Churchward, M.J. ...01 Oct
- Davies, C.R. ...01 Oct
- Haw, C.E. ...01 Oct
- Lynch, P.P. ...01 Oct
- Pruden, I. ...01 Oct
- Janzen, A.N. ...01 Oct
- Houvenaghel, I.M. ...01 Oct
- Jess, A.E.K. ...01 Oct

- Middleton, C.S. ...01 Oct
- Urry, S.R. ...01 Oct
- Clare, J.F. ...01 Oct
- Smith, D.M. ...01 Oct
- Phillips, M.C. ...01 Oct
- BS Thornhill, A.P. ...01 Oct
- Tarnowski, T.A. ...12 Nov

2005

- Bubb, J.D. ...01 May
- Gibson, A.J. ...01 May
- Hill, J.P. ...01 May
- Nicholson, D.P. ...01 Sep
- Hart, S.J.E. ...01 Sep
- Leyden, T.N. ...01 Sep
- Ordway, C.N.M.P. ...01 Sep
- Thompson, D.H. ...01 Sep
- Howarth, S.J. ...01 Sep
- Richardson, M.C. ...01 Oct
- Tyce, D.J. ...01 Oct
- Kilmartin, S. ...01 Oct
- Lancashire, A.C. ...01 Oct
- Maddison, J.D. ...01 Oct
- Westlake, S.R. ...01 Oct
- Murphy, K.S. ...01 Oct
- Baker, M.B. ...01 Oct
- Fisher, A.G. ...01 Oct
- Ross, G. ...01 Oct
- Gosney, C.J. ...01 Oct
- Cowan, K.G. ...01 Oct
- Edmondson, S.P. ...01 Oct
- Boschi, P.H. ...01 Oct
- Dennis, J.A. ...01 Oct
- Fuller, J.B. ...01 Oct
- Johnson, M. ...01 Oct
- Wiseman, G.R. ...01 Oct
- Garland, A.N. ...01 Oct
- Howarth, J. ...01 Oct
- Cooper, N. ...01 Oct
- BS Grace, N.J. ...01 Oct

CAPTAINS

1993

- Sharpe, G.A. ...01 Jan

1995

- Ginn, R.N. ...01 Jan

1996

- Nicoll, S.K. ...01 Jan

1997

- Shergold, P.J. ...01 Jan
- Sellar, T.J. ...01 Jan

1998

- Holloway, N. ...01 Jan

- Coats, D.S. ...01 Sep

1999

- Lawton, P. ...01 Jan
- Moffat, J.W. ...23 Apr
- Moran, J.T. ...28 Apr
- Hasted, D. ...01 May
- Bird, G.M. ...01 Sep

2000

- Hazelwood, C.D. ...01 Jan
- Kenneally, S.J. ...01 Jan
- Read, C.D. ...01 May
- Atkinson, N.C. ...01 May
- Edye, R.F. ...01 May
- Foster, N.P. ...01 May
- Gray, K.D. ...01 May

- Howard, R.D. ...01 May
- Mears, R.J. ...01 May
- Todd, J.W. ...01 May
- Bowyer, R.J. ...01 May
- Griffiths, N.A. ...01 May
- Oura, A.N. ...01 Sep
- Turner, A.R. ...01 Sep
- Hardie, M.J. ...01 Sep
- Totten, P.M. ...01 Sep
- Foster, B. ...01 Sep
- Brain, W.J.W. ...01 Sep
- Durup, J.M.S. ...01 Sep
- Huntingford, D.J. ...01 Sep
- Kelly, T.J. ...01 Sep
- Muncer, R.A. ...01 Sep
- Todd, O.J. ...01 Sep
- Davies, R.T. ...01 Sep
- Hopkins, R.M.E. ...01 Sep

CAPTAINS

- Smith, G.K. .... 01 Oct	- Nolan, P.E. .... 01 Apr	- Pascoe, J.R.M. .... 01 Sep
	- Cross, A.G. .... 01 Apr	- Allan, F.S. .... 01 Sep
2001	- MacPherson, W.G.C. .... 01 Apr	- Archer, T.W.K. .... 01 Sep
	- Mewes, D.B. .... 01 Apr	- Bennet, G.C. .... 01 Sep
- Stonier, P.L. ....01 Jan	- Morton, J.C. .... 01 Apr	- Buczkiewicz, M.J. .... 01 Sep
- Baines, G.A. ....01 Jan	- Paterson, T.J. .... 01 Apr	- Caldwell, D.J. .... 01 Sep
- Adcock, G.E. ....01 Jan	- Price, R.T. .... 01 Apr	- Copsey, N.R.B. .... 01 Sep
- Collins, J. ....01 Jan	- Usher, A.T. .... 01 Apr	- Coryton, O.C.W.S. .... 01 Sep
- Fitzpatrick, P.S. ....01 Jan	- Usher, B. .... 01 Apr	- Elliott, M.F. .... 01 Sep
- Standen, C.A. ....01 Jan	- Weir, J.R. .... 01 Apr	- Eve, L. .... 01 Sep
- Lucas, S.U. ....01 Jan	- Orr, S.D. .... 03 Apr	- Ferrey, R.M. .... 01 Sep
- Giles, G.J. ....01 Jan	- Melbourne, S. .... 15 Apr	- Galbraith, L.A. .... 01 Sep
- Price, D.G. ....01 Jan	- Fitzpatrick, P.J. .... 19 Jul	- Southern, M.J. .... 01 Sep
- Tapp, S.J. ....01 Jan	BS Smallwood, A.J. .... 19 Jul	- Whitmarsh, A.T. .... 01 Sep
- Frost, M.J. ....01 Jan	- West, D.J. .... 19 Jul	- Johnston, K.G. .... 01 Sep
- Hunt, D. ....01 Jan	- Abbott, G.P. .... 01 Sep	- MacRae, J.R. .... 01 Sep
BS Kelly, J.A. ....01 Jan	- Alston, R. .... 01 Sep	- Metcalfe, L.M. .... 01 Sep
- Sutton, D. .... 01 Apr	- Brocklehurst, K.P. .... 01 Sep	- Moffatt, D. .... 01 Sep
- Hulse, A.W. .... 01 Apr	- Butler, S. .... 01 Sep	- Morris, R.C. .... 01 Sep
- Hall, C.M.I. .... 01 Apr	- Dean, S.I.R. .... 01 Sep	- Newton, R.W. .... 01 Sep
- McCulley, S.C. .... 01 Apr	- Delahay, J.E. .... 01 Sep	- Payne, M.T. .... 01 Sep
- Howe, S. .... 01 Apr	- Fidler, J.Q. .... 01 Sep	- Shaw, A.T. .... 01 Sep
- Wallace, R.S. .... 01 Apr	- Gray, S.A.N. .... 01 Sep	- Simmons, R.L. .... 01 Sep
- Wilcox, T.C. .... 01 Apr	- Hecks, I.J. .... 01 Sep	- Stitson, P. .... 01 Sep
- Fomes, C.J.H. .... 01 Apr	- Menzies, G.M. .... 01 Sep	- Thomas, J.G. .... 01 Sep
- Cavill, N.R.D. .... 01 May	- Norman, J.M. .... 01 Sep	- Thorpe, R.M. .... 01 Sep
- Hanson, S.C. .... 01 May	- Parker, M.C. .... 01 Sep	- Tottenham, T.W. .... 01 Sep
- Lindsay, J.M. .... 01 May	- Preston, T.E. .... 01 Sep	- Waldmeyer, E. .... 01 Sep
- Roskilly, M. .... 01 May	- Price, J.E.O. .... 01 Sep	- Williams, M.C. .... 01 Sep
- Samuel, C.D.R. .... 01 May	- Rochester, A.D. .... 01 Sep	- Williams, P.M. .... 01 Sep
- Scanlon, M.J. .... 01 May	- Rogers, S.M. .... 01 Sep	- Witts, C.I. .... 01 Sep
- Tamlyn, S.J. .... 01 May	- Schleyer, J. .... 01 Sep	- Hilton, J.N. .... 01 Sep
- Baker, A.J. ....01 Jul	- Spink, D.A. .... 01 Sep	
- Hoare, P.F. ....21 Jul	- Taylor, N.J. .... 01 Sep	**2004**
- Rhodes, P.E. ....21 Jul	- Tucker, S.J.W. .... 01 Sep	
- Tinsley, P. ....21 Jul	- Waite, M.T. .... 01 Sep	- Brading, R.D. .... 01 Mar
- Barnwell, A.F. ....21 Jul	- Venables, D.M. .... 01 Sep	- Bourne, S.W. .... 01 Apr
- Tidman, M.D. ....21 Jul		- Breach, C.E.M. .... 01 Apr
- Perrin, M.S. .... 01 Sep	**2003**	- Buston, D.C. .... 01 Apr
- Bonney, J.E. .... 01 Sep		- Campbell, K.R. .... 01 Apr
- Darley, M.E. .... 01 Sep	- Bryars, P.M. .... 01 Apr	- Chapple, S. .... 01 Apr
- Forbes, D.G. .... 01 Sep	- Butcher, D. .... 01 Apr	- Gibbins, P. .... 01 Apr
- Francis, T.D.H. .... 01 Sep	- Dawson, A. .... 01 Apr	- Knowles, G.R. .... 01 Apr
- Halsted, B.E. .... 01 Sep	- Gibb, A.K.B. .... 01 Apr	- Latham, M.A. .... 01 Apr
- Hester, J.F.W. .... 01 Sep	- Hembury, L. .... 01 Apr	BS Long, R.P. .... 01 Apr
- Hopkins, R. .... 01 Sep	- Nicholas, J.R. .... 01 Apr	- Priddle, S.M.R. .... 01 Apr
- Thompson, P.L. .... 01 Sep	- Peters, A.D. .... 01 Apr	- Roberts, P.A. .... 01 Apr
- Mansergh, A.C. .... 01 Sep	- Phillips, D.G. .... 01 Apr	- Rudd, P. .... 01 Apr
- Maynard, P.A. .... 01 Sep	- Sharpe, M.R. .... 01 Apr	- Watkins, D.T. .... 01 Apr
- Morgan, H.L. .... 01 Sep	- Stanton, K.V. .... 01 Apr	- Curry, P.T. .... 01 Apr
- Pennington, C.E. .... 01 Sep	- Flinn, J.A. .... 01 Apr	- Barden, P.E. ....01 Jul
- Robinson, P.J.O. .... 01 Sep	- Abbott, D. .... 01 Apr	- Collinson, N.P. ....01 Jul
- Wallace, S.P. .... 01 Sep	- Burgess, M.J. .... 01 Apr	- Fenton, G.M. ....01 Jul
- Liva, A.J. .... 01 Sep	- Flower, N.P. .... 01 Apr	- Gray, T. ....01 Jul
	BS Burcham, J.R. .... 01 Apr	- Mawer, P.R. ....01 Jul
2002	BS Dowrick, M.P. .... 01 Apr	- Nielsen, E.M. ....01 Jul
	- Gordon, R.S. .... 01 Apr	- O'Connor, D.M. ....01 Jul
- Clarke, P.M. ....01 Jan	- Noble, K.L. .... 01 Apr	- Titerickx, A.T. ....01 Jul
- Cross, E.J. ....01 Jan	- Carr, P. ....01 Jul	- Williams, D.A. ....01 Jul
- Robbins, H.V. ....01 Jan	- Gellender, P.S. .... 24 Jul	- Brown, R. .... 24 Jul
- Watson, B.R. ....01 Jan	- Norton, T.C.H. .... 01 Sep	BS Curtis, P.J. .... 24 Jul
- Kemp, A.C. .... 01 Apr	- Jones, R.P.M. .... 01 Sep	- Gannon, D.R. .... 24 Jul
- May, D.J. .... 01 Apr	- Axcell, M.F. .... 01 Sep	- Giles, S. .... 24 Jul

CAPTAINS

- Milne, J.R. ....24 Jul
- Rand, M.C. ....24 Jul
- Ridley, J. ....24 Jul
- Rutherford, A.T. ....24 Jul
- Ubaka, P.B.N. ....24 Jul
- Watson, G.B. ....24 Jul
- O'Sullivan, M.R.J. ....01 Sep
- Pinckney, M.R.N. ....01 Sep
- Apps, J.C. ....01 Sep
- Bradford, M.H. ....01 Sep
- Carns, A.S. ....01 Sep
- Catton, I.C. ....01 Sep
- Finn, T.A. ....01 Sep
- George, N.D. ....01 Sep
- Higham, D.J. ....01 Sep
- Jamison, J.S. ....01 Sep
- Kenny, L.E. ....01 Sep
- Lerwill, S.S.G. ....01 Sep
- Lewis, B.M. ....01 Sep
- Lewis, J.A.E. ....01 Sep
- MacDonald, M.J. ....01 Sep
- McLaren, S.C. ....01 Sep
- Moore, W.I. ....01 Sep
- Norcott, W.R. ....01 Sep
- Pengelley, T.A.H. ....01 Sep
- Pennefather, D.C.J. ....01 Sep
- Precious, A.P. ....01 Sep
- Renshaw, P.A. ....01 Sep
- Reynolds, B.K.M. ....01 Sep

- Ryall, T.A.S. ....01 Sep
- Simpson, T.W. ....01 Sep
- Sparks, S. ....01 Sep
- Suchet, R.J. ....01 Sep
- Thomson, L.G. ....01 Sep
- Uprichard, A.J. ....01 Sep
- Vickers, C.H. ....01 Sep
- Winch, J.A. ....01 Sep
- Murray, S.D. ....01 Sep
- Pilkington, W.J. ....01 Sep

2005

- Heenan, M. ....01 Apr
- Beaumont, D.M. ....19 Jul
- Donaghey, M. ....19 Jul
- Ferguson, C. ....19 Jul
- Foreman, N.A. ....19 Jul
- Hibbert, O.A. ....19 Jul
- Hill, C.J. ....19 Jul
- Richardson, S.J. ....19 Jul
- Starling, C.M. ....19 Jul
- Kirk, K.R. ....19 Jul
- Purser, L.J. ....19 Jul
- King, R.E. ....19 Jul
- O'Callaghan, P.P. ....19 Jul
- Nixon, N.P. ....19 Jul
- Horton, M.P. ....19 Jul
- Keay, G.M. ....19 Jul
- Carty, M.G. ....01 Sep

- Dow, A.J.R. ....01 Sep
- Postgate, M.O. ....01 Sep
- MacLean, R.G. ....01 Sep
- Thornton, D.M. ....01 Sep
- Hamilton, S.J.D. ....01 Sep
- Hogg, G.D. ....01 Sep
- Anderson, B.W.D. ....01 Sep
- Armstrong, R.F. ....01 Sep
- Crisp, D.J.D. ....01 Sep
- Davies, L.M.A. ....01 Sep
- Drinkwater, R. ....01 Sep
- Duckitt, J.N. ....01 Sep
- Evans-Jones, T.M. ....01 Sep
- Goss, J.R.C. ....01 Sep
- Lee-Gallon, T.J. ....01 Sep
- Hall, E.C.M. ....01 Sep
- Kyle, R. ....01 Sep
- Lewis, M.J. ....01 Sep
- Long, H.A. ....01 Sep
- MacCrimmon, S.S. ....01 Sep
- Gaffney, B. ....01 Sep
- Morris, J.E.D. ....01 Sep
- Morton, J.H. ....01 Sep
- Noble, T.M.D. ....01 Sep
- Reed, E.C.D. ....01 Sep
- Reid, B.W. ....01 Sep
- Simpson, R.F. ....01 Sep
- Pinney, R.F. ....01 Sep
- Speedie, A.C. ....01 Sep

LIEUTENANTS

2003

- Ginn, R.D. ....01 Sep
- O'Keefe, T.D. ....01 Sep
- Sharman, M.C. ....01 Sep
- Sutherland, I.D. ....01 Sep

- Trafford, M. ....01 Sep
- White, J.W. ....01 Sep

2004

- Fearn, S.R. ....01 Sep

2005

- Rogers, O. ....01 Sep

SECOND LIEUTENANTS

2000

- Pritchard, L.B. ....01 Aug

2001

- Air, C.T.L. ....01 Aug
- Anderson, J.H. ....01 Aug
- Barrow, J.M. ....01 Aug
- Bowes, N.E. ....01 Aug
- Burr, C.J. ....01 Aug
- Clews, A. ....01 Aug
- Clarke, D.W.D. ....01 Aug
- Cottrell, R.F.G. ....01 Aug
- Cox, S.T. ....01 Aug
- Christie, N.E. ....01 Aug
- Denise, A.M. ....01 Aug
- Dingwall, N.T. ....01 Aug
- Dinsmore, S.J. ....01 Aug
- Eden, C.J. ....01 Aug

- Forrest, P.M. ....01 Aug
- Sayer, R.J. ....01 Aug
- Gray, O.W.J. ....01 Aug
- Hands, E.W.H. ....01 Aug
- Kestle, R.J. ....01 Aug
- Little, G.J.R. ....01 Aug
- MacKenzie-Green, W.H.M.G. ......01 Aug
- Marshall, L. ....01 Aug
- Okell, P.M.C. ....01 Aug
- Scott, T. ....01 Aug
- Seaman, A.L. ....01 Aug
- Sweny, G.L.H. ....01 Aug
- Waller, R.M. ....01 Aug
- Glancy, J.A. ....01 Sep

2002_

- Badenoch, W.J.C. ....01 Aug
- Ballinger, A.R. ....01 Aug
- Barlow, M.J. ....01 Aug

- Barrow, M.C. ....01 Aug
- Beete, J.E. ....01 Aug
- Bird, P.R.K. ....01 Aug
- Blackford, O.D. ....01 Aug
- Clark, D.R. ....01 Aug
- Eaton, D.T. ....01 Aug
- Fleet, R.P. ....01 Aug
- Forrest, E.R. ....01 Aug
- Gloak, J.M. ....01 Aug
- Hammond, M.J. ....01 Aug
- Hardman, D.I. ....01 Aug
- Harrison, M.A.C. ....01 Aug
- Hills, M. ....01 Aug
- Holder, S.A. ....01 Aug
- Hughes, S.E. ....01 Aug
- Jemmett, S.B. ....01 Aug
- Kerr, R.M. ....01 Aug
- Law, D.J.F. ....01 Aug
- Lee, A.J. ....01 Aug

SECOND LIEUTENANTS

- Moore, C.J.P. .... 01 Aug
- Moses, C. .... 01 Aug
- Musgrove, J.D. .... 01 Aug
- O'Sullivan, N.J. .... 01 Aug
- Pastouna, J.D.A. .... 01 Aug
- Payne, C.M. .... 01 Aug
- Pounds, A.N. .... 01 Aug
- Pyke, D.G. .... 01 Aug
- Quinn, T.J. .... 01 Aug
- Schwarz, W.H. .... 01 Aug
- Sharp, R.S. .... 01 Aug
- Shaw, A.P. .... 01 Aug
- Sisson, C.J.M. .... 01 Aug
- Steel, G.D. .... 01 Aug

- Sylvan, C. .... 01 Aug
- Thomson, L.I. .... 01 Aug
- Whiteman, J.W.T. .... 01 Aug
- Yapp, R.W. .... 01 Aug
- Ouseley, D.M.G. .... 01 Sep

2003

- Goodman, W. .... 01 Aug
- Nixon, A.J. .... 01 Aug
- Thornton, J.D. .... 01 Aug

2004

- Argles, E.V. .... 01 Aug

- Disney, L.I.W.P. .... 01 Aug
- Kidd, R.S. .... 01 Aug
- Knight, J. .... 01 Aug
- Mallows, J.A. .... 01 Aug
- Moore, R.G. .... 01 Aug
- Richardson, B.F. .... 01 Aug
- Cooling, B.R. .... 01 Aug
- Heaver, J.D. .... 01 Aug
- Denning, O.W. .... 31 Aug

2005

- Taylor, R.A.P. .... 01 Aug

QUEEN ALEXANDRA'S ROYAL NAVAL NURSING SERVICE

DIRECTOR NAVAL NURSING SERVICE AND MATRON-IN-CHIEF

Gibbon, Lynne, ARRC, QHNS ....28 Jul 03

CAPTAINS

Bowen, Michael, ARRC, BA, MSc ....27 Mar 01

COMMANDERS

2002
Onions, J.M. .... 30 Jun

2003
Allkins, H.L... 30 Jun

2004
Duke, R.M. .... 30 Jun
Howes, N.J.. 30 Jun

2005
Smith, B.C. .... 30 Jun
Williams, C.M.A................................ 30 Jun
Kennedy, I.J....................................... 30 Jun

LIEUTENANT COMMANDERS

1999
Thain-Smith, J.C............................... 31 Mar
Stinton, C.A.. 01 Oct

2000
Robson, C.J.. 01 Oct
Spencer, S.J....................................... 01 Oct

2001
Baird, E.H... 11 Mar
Aldwinckle, T.W. .... 01 Oct
Knight, D.J.. 01 Oct

2002
Ferguson, V.S. .... 01 Oct
Charlton, K.W..................................... 25 Oct

2003
Piper, N.D. .... 01 Oct
Rankin, S.J. .... 01 Oct

2004
England, L... 01 Oct
Hofman, A.J.. 01 Oct
Briggs, C.S.. 01 Oct

Bagnall, S.E.. 01 Oct
Holland, A.L.. 01 Oct
Chilvers, L.D....................................... 01 Oct

2005
Thompson, F. .... 01 Oct
Newby Stubbs, R.L............................ 01 Oct

LIEUTENANTS

1996
Johnson, V. ....25 Jan
O'Maoil-Mheana, P.J. .... 30 Mar
Logan, J.G. ....
27 Jul
James, K.J. ....26 Nov
Dilloway, P.J. ....07 Dec

1997
Ouvry, J.E.D....................................... 25 Mar
Kiernan, M.D. .... 30 May
Wilkinson, G....................................... 06 Oct

1998
Kennedy, C.H..................................... 07 May
Lang, J.S. .... 30 Sep
Gardner-Clark, S.L.............................05 Nov
Carnell, R.P. ....06 Nov
Blakeley, A.L.......................................17 Nov.

1999
McFarland, N. ....14 Jan
Kenworthy, L.K. ....01 Apr
Hurley, K.A..26 May
Taylor, L.M. ....05 Jul
Thorpe, E. .... 03 Aug
France, S.C. .... 25 Aug
Morgan, R.S.. 06 Sep
Scott, C.R. .... 12 Sep
Stevens, A.J. .... 24 Sep

2000
McConville, C.W. .... 28 Mar
Brown, B.C.. 11 Jun
Emmerson, D.M.................................. 22 Jun
Geraghty, F... 01 Sep
Sutherland, G. .... 25 Oct
Simpson, P.E....................................... 27 Oct

2001
Glendinning, A.S.................................12 Jan

Selwood, P.J. .... 26 Feb
Brodie, S.D.. 08 Mar
Brocklehurst, J.E................................. 26 Apr
Clarkson, A.M...................................... 04 May
Bryce-Johnston, F.L.S.........................16 Jul
Falconer, L.M. .... 16 Sep
Cooper, J.L...01 Nov

2002
Despres, J.P. ....19 Nov
Kelly, F.A. .... 01 Feb
Gray, S.E. .... 20 Feb
Kennedy, I.C....................................... 26 May
D'Arcy, T. ....14 Jul
Swire, B.J. ....26 Jul
Hodds, S.L. ....01 Nov
Huggins, K.E....................................... 01 Nov
Fraser-Smith, S.A................................23 Nov
Wright-Jones, A.E.M...........................29 Nov

LIEUTENANTS

2003

Wagstaff, S.E.	01 Jan
Warburton, A.M.	26 Feb
Martyn, J.M.	01 Mar
Claridge, A.M.	12 Apr
Adams, S.A.	01 Jun
Wesson, M.I.	01 Jul
Johnson, S.V.	01 Sep
Edwards, S.P.	01 Nov
Thompson, S.K.	01 Nov

2004

Ward, C.J.	01 May
Jefferis, B.A.	01 Sep
McCullough, K.M.	01 Nov

2005

Wardley, T.E.	01 Mar
Hale, S.D.	01 Apr

SUB LIEUTENANTS

2002

James, V.H.	01 Aug
Lees, S.E.	01 Sep
Clark, G.R.	01 Nov

2005

Humphrey, D.P.	01 Nov

KEY ROYAL NAVAL PERSONNEL, ATTACHES AND ADVISERS

(See Sec. 1 for Admiralty Board Members and Defence Council Members)

MOD/CENTRAL STAFF

1SL/CNS	Admiral Sir Jonathon Band KCB ADC
CE DEA	Vice Admiral P A Dunt CB
DCDS(C)	Vice Admiral C R Style CBE
DCDS(EC)	Lieutenant General Sir Robert Fulton KBE
DCDS(H)	Vice Admiral R A I McLean CB OBE
DG CAP (CS)	Rear Admiral N C F Guild CB
ACNS	Rear Admiral A M Massey CBE
CM (PA)	Rear Admiral T A Soar OBE
ACDS(RP)	Rear Admiral T J H Laurence MVO
SNM RCDS	Rear Admiral R A Mark
DS SEC	Rear Admiral P J Wilkinson
DG JDC	Rear Admiral C J Parry CBE
Cmdt DCMT	Rear Admiral N D Latham

CINCFLEET

CINCFLEET	Admiral Sir James Burnell-Nugent KCB CB
DCINC	Vice Admiral Sir Timothy P McClement KCB OBE
COS(Cap)	Rear Admiral D G Snelson CB
COM(OPS)	Rear Admiral P Lambert
COS(P&S)	Rear Admiral M Kimmons
FOSNNI/FOR	Rear Admiral P L Wilcocks DSC
COMUKMARFOR	Rear Admiral N Morisetti
FOST	Rear Admiral R S Ainsley
CGRM/COMUKAMPHIBFOR	Major General J B Dutton CBE
STLB TL	Rear Admiral N J F RabyOBE

SECOND SEA LORD

2SL/CNH	Vice Admiral A J Johns CBE
NAVSEC	Rear Admiral R J Ibbotson DSC
FOTR	Rear Admiral K J Borley
DGNCS	The Venerable J Green QHC

DLO

DG Def Logistics Fleet	Rear Admiral R P Boissier
CE DCSA	Rear Admiral R G J Ward CB
DG Nuclear	Rear Admiral A D H Mathews

PROCUREMENT EXECUTIVE

Technical Director	Rear Admiral S M Henley MBE

NATO

UKMILREP	Vice Admiral A K Dymock CB
COS MARCOMAFSOUTH	Rear Admiral R D Leaman OBE
DEP COMSTRIKFORSTH	Rear Admiral D J Cooke MBE
DCOM HRF(I)	Major General R G T Lane CBE

AFPAA

CE AFPAA	Rear Admiral T A Spires

MEDICAL

Surgeon General	Surgeon Vice Admiral I L Jenkins CB CVO QHS
MDG(Navy)	Surgeon Rear Admiral M A Farquharson-Roberts
CE DMETA	Surgeon Rear Admiral P I Raffaelli

ATTACHES AND ADVISERS

OFFICERS PROVIDING A NAVAL SERVICE IN FOREIGN COUNTRIES

A full and comprehensive listing of Attaches and Advisers can be accessed through the MoD intranet (Directorate of Defence Diplomacy - Overseas Directory (Yellow Book)), the URL is:

http://defenceintranet.diiweb.r.mil.uk/DefenceIntranet/Library/BrowseDocumentCategories/
OrgsRollHist/OverseasCommandsAndOverseasDefenceStaff/DefenceAndServiceAttaches/
DirectorateOfDefenceDiplomacy-OverseasDirectoryyellowBook.htm

Service Mail

All official service mail is to be forwarded in accordance with current instructions.

Albania	China	Georgia
Defence Attaché	Naval Attaché	Defence Attaché
Tirana	Peking	Tbilisi
Angola	Colombia	Germany
Defence Attaché	Defence Attaché	Naval Attaché
Luanda	Bogota	Bonn
Argentina	Congo (Democratic Republic)	Greece
Defence Attaché	Defence Attaché	Defence Attaché
Buenos Aires	Kinshasa	Athens
Austria	Croatia	Guatemala
Defence Attaché	Defence Attaché	Defence Attaché
Vienna	Zagreb	Guatemala City
Bahrain	Czech Republic	Hungary
Defence Attaché	Defence Attaché	Defence Attaché
Manama	Prague	Budapest
Belgium	Denmark	Indonesia
Defence Attaché	Defence Attaché	Defence Attaché
Brussels	Copenhagen	Jakarta
Brazil	Egypt	Ireland
Naval Attaché	Naval & Air Attaché	Defence Attaché
Brasilia	Cairo	Dublin
Bulgaria	Finland	Israel
Defence Attaché	Defence Attaché	Naval & Air Attaché
Sofia	Helsinki	Tel Aviv
Chile	France	Italy
Defence Attaché	Naval Attaché	Naval Attaché
Santiago	Paris	Rome

Japan
Defence Attaché
Tokyo

Jordan
Defence Attaché
Amman

Kazakhstan
Defence Attaché
Almaty

Korea
Naval & Air Attaché
Seoul

Kuwait
Defence Attaché
Kuwait City

Latvia
Defence Attaché
Riga

Lebanon
Defence Attaché
Beirut

Lithuania
Defence Attaché
Vilnius

Macedonia
Defence Attaché
Skopje

Morocco
Defence Attaché
Rabat

Nepal
Defence Attaché
Kathmandu

Netherlands
Defence Attaché
The Hague

Norway
Defence Attaché
Oslo

Oman
Naval & Air Attaché
Muscat

Philippines
Defence Attaché
Manila

Poland
Naval & Military Attaché
Warsaw

Portugal
Defence Attaché
Lisbon

Qatar
Defence Attaché
Doha

Romania
Defence Attaché
Bucharest

Russia
Naval Attaché
Assistant Naval Attaché
Moscow

Saudi Arabia
Naval Attaché
Riyadh

Slovakia
Defence Attaché
BratislSlovakia

Slovakia
Defence Attaché
Ljubljana

Spain
Defence Attaché
Madrid

Sweden
Defence Attaché
Stockholm

Switzerland
Defence Attaché
Berne

Syria
Defence Attaché
Damascus

Thailand
Defence Attaché
Bangkok

Turkey
Naval & Air Attaché
Ankara

Ukraine
Defence Attaché
Kiev

United Arab Emirates
Defence Attaché
Abu Dhabi

United States of America
Naval Attaché
Assistant Naval Attaché
Washington DC

Uzbekistan
Defence Attaché
Tashkent

Venezuela
Defence Attaché
Caracas

Yugoslavia (Federal Republic)
Defence Attaché
Belgrade

OFFICERS PROVIDING A NAVAL SERVICE IN COMMONWEALTH COUNTRIES

Australia
Defence & Naval Adviser
Canberra

Barbados
Defence Adviser
Bridgetown

Brunei
Defence Adviser
Bandar Seri Begawan

Canada
Naval & Air Adviser
Ottawa

Cyprus
Defence Adviser
Nicosia

Ghana
Defence Adviser
Accra

India
Naval and Air Adviser
New Delhi

Jamaica
Defence Adviser
Kingston

Kenya
Defence Adviser
Nairobi

Malaysia
Defence Adviser
Kuala Lumpur

New Zealand
Defence Adviser
Wellington

Nigeria
Defence Adviser
Abuja

Pakistan
Naval & Air Adviser
Islamabad

Singapore
Assistant Defence Adviser &
Royal Navy
Liaison Officer
Singapore

South Africa
Naval & Air Adviser
Pretoria

Sri Lanka
Defence Adviser
Colombo

Uganda
Defence Adviser
Kampala

Zimbabwe
Defence Adviser
Harare

NON-RESIDENTIAL ACCREDITATIONS

Attaches accredited to the following countries are non-residential

Algeria
(Is resident London (DOMA))

Anguilla
(Is resident Barbados)

Antigua & Barbuda
(Is resident Barbados)

Armenia
(Is resident Georgia)

Azerbaijan
(Is resident Georgia)

Bahamas
(Is resident Jamaica)

Bangladesh
(Is resident India)

Belarus

(Is resident Russia)

Belize
(Is resident Jamaica)

Bermuda
(Is resident USA)

Bolivia
(Is resident Chile)

Botswana
(Is resident Zimbabwe)

British Virgin Islands
(Is resident Barbados)

Burundi
(Is resident Uganda)

Cayman Islands
(Is resident Jamaica)

Cuba
(Is resident Venezuela)

Curacao
(Is resident Barbados)

Dominica
(Is resident Barbados)

Algeria
(Is resident London (DOMA))

Anguilla
(Is resident Barbados)

Antigua & Barbuda
(Is resident Barbados)

Armenia
(Is resident Georgia)

Azerbaijan

(Is resident Georgia)

Bahamas
(Is resident Jamaica)

Bangladesh
(Is resident India)

Belarus
(Is resident Russia)

Belize
(Is resident Jamaica)

Ecuador
(Is resident Venezuela)

El Salvador
(Is resident Guatemala)

Eritrea
(Is resident Kenya)

Estonia
(Is resident Finland)

Ethiopia
(Is resident Kenya)

Fiji
(Is resident New Zealand)

Gabon
(Is resident Congo DR)

Granada
(Is resident Barbados)

Guadeloupe
(Is resident Barbados)

Guinea
(Is resident Sierra Leone)

Guyana
(Is resident Barbados)

Honduras
(Is resident Guatemala)

Ivory Coast
(Is resident Ghana)

Kyrgyzstan
(Is resident Russia)

Lesotho
(Is resident South Africa)

Luxembourg
(Is resident Belgium)

Madagascar
(Is resident London (DOMA))

Malawi
(Is resident Zimbabwe)

Maldives
(Is resident Sri Lanka)

Mauritania
(Is resident Morocco)

Mauritius
(Is resident Kenya)

Mexico
(Is resident Guatemala

Moldova
(Is resident Romania)

Mongolia
(Is resident China)

Montserrat
(Is resident Barbados)

Mozambique
(Is resident Zimbabwe)

Namibia
(Is resident South Africa)

Nicaragua
(Is resident Guatemala)

Panama
(Is resident Venezuela)

Papua New Guinea
(Is resident Australia)

Paraguay
(Is resident Argentina)

Peru
(Is resident Colombia)

Rwanda
(Is resident Uganda)

St Kitts & Nevis
(Is resident Barbados)

St Lucia

(Is resident Barbabos)

St Vincent
(Is resident Barbados)

Senegal
(Is resident Morocco)

Seychelles
(Is resident Kenya)

Suriname
(Is resident Barbados)

Swaziland
(Is resident South Africa)

Tajikistan
(Is resident Kazakhstan)

Tanzania
(Is resident Kenya)

The Gambia
(Is resident Morocco)

Togo
(Is resident Ghana)

Tonga
(Is resident New Zealand)

Trinidad & Tobago
(Is resident Barbados)

Tunisia
(Is resident London (DOMA))

Turkmenistan
(Is resident Russia)

Turks & Caicos Islands
(Is resident Jamaica)

Uruguay
(Is resident Argentina)

Vietnam
(Is resident Malaysia)

Yemen
(Is resident Saudi Arabia)

Zambia
(Is resident London (DOMA))

INTERPRETERS

Name	Date of Rank Re-qualifying	Qualifying or	Name	Date of Rank Re-qualifying	Qualifying or
ARABIC			Rooke, Z.S., ...LT	May-05	
Rand, M.C., ...CAPT RM	Mar-00		Stewart, A.C., ... CDR	Mar-04	
			Stonor, P.F.A., ... CDR	Mar-88	
CHINESE			Stride, J.A., ... LT CDR	Apr-99	
Rayner, B.N., ...CAPT	Dec-83		Turner, J.S.H., ... CDR	Mar-94	
White, S.N., ... CDR	Sep-90		Underwood, R.A.H., ...LT	Mar-04	
			Wallace, M.R.B., ...CAPT	Jun-03	
DANISH			**GERMAN**		
Watson, P.H., ...CAPT	Oct-76		Airey, S.E., ... A/CAPT	Apr-81	
DUTCH			Durston, D.H., ...CAPT	Mar-83	
Cox, P.W.S., ... CDR	Dec-04		Finch, B.A., ... LT CDR	Mar-96	
Davies, A.R., ...CAPT	Mar-84		Gibbs, N.D., ... CDR	Mar-04	
Ewence, M.W., OBE............... CDR	Mar-88		Hill, D., ... LT CDR	Mar-98	
Shipperley, I., ... CDR	Oct-93		Hollins, R.P., ... CDR	Mar-98	
			Howard, D.G., ... CDR	Apr-00	
FRENCH			Knight, P.J., ... CDR	Apr-97	
Adair, A.A.S., ...CDRE	Dec-99		Massey, A.M., CBE.............. RADM	Mar-80	
Airey, S.E., ... A/CAPT	Mar-80		McGuire, M.J., ... LT CDR	Sep-02	
Bernard, R.A., ...A/LT CDR	Jun-97		Mennecke-Jappy, G.W.G., ...LT	Dec-04	
Braithwaite, G.C., ...LT	Jul-00		Nurse, M.T., ...A/CDR	Mar-86	
Butcher, M.W., ... SLT	Jul-04		Pillar, C.D., ... LT CDR	Jul-05	
Butler, N.A.M., ...CAPT	Mar-04		Pitcher, P.P., ... LT CDR	Nov-97	
Cook, T.A., ... MAJ	Jun-01		Robertson Gopffarth, A.A.J., LT CDR	Mar-95	
Craven, J.A.G., ... LT CDR	Mar-90		Robin, C.C.E., ... LT CDR	Mar-98	
Cree, M.C., ...CAPT	Feb-95		Shropshall, I.J., ...LT	May-03	
Davies, H.C.A., ... MAJ	Jun-04		Sparke, P.R.W., ... LT CDR	Mar-92	
Dermody, R.T., ...LT	Mar-98		Williams, N.L., ...CAPT	Mar-85	
Elliman, S.M., ... LT CDR	Oct-92				
Ewence, M.W., OBE............... CDR	Mar-98		**GREEK**		
Fieldsend, M.A., ... CDR	May-95		Ritsperis, A., ...LT	Jul-96	
Gray, E.J., ...LT	Sep-02				
Gubbins, V.R., MBE............... CDR	Jul-96		**ITALIAN**		
Harlow, S.R., ... LT CDR	Jun-01		Amorosi, R.G.F.L., ...LT	Sep-00	
Hollins, R.P., ... CDR	Apr-99				
Irwin, S.G., ...LT	Mar-02		**JAPANESE**		
Kettle, R.A., ... MAJ	Jun-98		Chelton, S.R.L., ...CAPT	Oct-88	
Lawrence, L.J., ...LT	Mar-04		Norgate, A.T., ...LT	Oct-03	
Mansergh, M.P., ...CAPT	Mar-91				
Newell, J.M., MBE.................CAPT	Mar-89		**NORWEGIAN**		
Paton, C.M., ... MAJ	May-05		Stallion, I.M., ... CDR	Mar-79	
Roddy, M.P., MBE.................. MAJ	Jun-03		Taylor, W.J., OBE ....COL	Mar-91	

Name	Date of Rank Re-qualifying	Qualifying or	Name	Date of Rank Re-qualifying	Qualifying or

POLISH

Tarnowski, T.A., ... MAJ	Mar-99

PORTUGUESE

Harrison, R.A., ... CDR	Dec-03
McGlory, S.J., ... LT CDR	Jul-96

RUSSIAN

Airey, S.E., ... A/CAPT	Mar-94
Connolly, C.J., ... CDR	Mar-89
Davies, A.R., ...CAPT	Mar-89
Drewett, R.E., MBE .... CDR	Mar-91
Fields, D.G., ... CDR	Mar-90
Foreman, J.L.R., ... CDR	Mar-92
Green, T.J., ... CDR	Mar-89
Gwillim, V.G., ... MAJ	Mar-94
Hodgson, T.C., MBE .... CDR	Mar-94
Lister, S.R., OBE....................CDRE	Mar-90
McTear, K., MBE................... CDR	Mar-91
Newton, G.A., ... CDR	Mar-94
Peters, W.R., ... LT CDR	Mar-00
Priddle, A.C., ...LT	Jul-04
Tarnowski, T.A., ... MAJ	Mar-00

SPANISH

Adam, I.K., ... LT CDR	Mar-91
Baker, M.J., ... LT CDR	Dec-03
Croke, A., ...CAPT	Jul-00
Curry, B.R., MBE .... LT COL	Mar-98
Dedman, N.J.K., ...CAPT	Dec-02
Eedle, R.J., ... LT CDR	Sep-98
Gannon, D.R., ...CAPT RM	Jan-00
Humphrys, J.A., ...CAPT	Mar-98
Lawrence, L.J., ...LT	Mar-04
Lynch, R.D.F., ... LT CDR	Mar-91
Marsh, B.H., MBE.............. LT CDR	Jun-03
McGlory, S.J., ... LT CDR	Mar-94
McLennan, R.G., ... CDR	Mar-94
Reed, J.H., ... LT CDR	Jun-02
Sanguinetti, H.R., ...CAPT	Mar-90
Turner, J.S.H., ... CDR	Nov-94
Wolfe, D.E., ...CAPT	Mar-95

SWEDISH

Rigby, J.C., ... CDR	Mar-86

OFFICERS OF THE LOGISTICS SPECIALISATION PRACTISING AS NAVAL BARRISTERS

COMMODORES

Fraser R.W. MVO
(Director Naval Legal Services)

CAPTAINS

Crabtree, P D, OBE
Steel, D G
Davis, B J, OBE

COMMANDERS

Williams, R E, OBE
Jameson, A C
Brown, N L
Gray, R S
Spence, A B
Crozier, S R M
Anderson, H A
Hollins, R P
Wright, S H
Cole, A C

Wood, R
Taylor, S J

LIEUTENANT COMMANDERS

Kingsbury, J A T
Towler, A
Turner, J S H
Murdoch, A P
Dow, C S
Pheasant, J C S
Axon, G M
Wilman, D M
Reed, D K

LIEUTENANTS

Atwill, J W O
Gilbert, R G
Sheikh, N
Butterworth, C L
Park, I D
Knox, G P

HM SHORE ESTABLISHMENTS

AFPAA(CENTURION)
Centurion Building
Grange Road
GOSPORT
Hants
PO13 9XA

DARTMOUTH BRNC
Britannia Royal Naval College
DARTMOUTH
Devon
TQ6 0HJ

DRAKE SFM
Tyne Building
HM Naval Base Devonport
Plymouth
Devon
PL2 2BG

JSU NORTHWOOD
Joint Support Unit
Northwood Headquarters
Sandy Lane
Northwood
Middlesex
HA6 3HP

MWS COLLINGWOOD
Maritime Warfare School
HMS COLLINGWOOD
Newgate Lane
FAREHAM
Hants
PO14 1AS

MWS EXCELLENT
HMS EXCELLENT
PORTSMOUTH
Hants
PO2 8ER

MWS SOUTHWICK PK
MWS (Southwick Park)
Southwick
FAREHAM
Hampshire
PO17 6EJ

NELSON
UPO (PA)
HMS NELSON
Portsmouth
Hants
PO1 3HH

NEPTUNE DLO
HMNB Clyde
Faslane
Argyll and Bute
G84 8HL

RALEIGH
HMS RALEIGH
TORPOINT
Cornwall
PL11 2PD

RNAS CULDROSE
RNAS Culdrose
HELSTON
Cornwall
TR12 7RH

RNAS YEOVILTON
RNAS Yeovilton
ILCHESTER
Somerset
BA22 8HT

SULTAN
HMS Sultan
Gosport
Hants
PO12 3BY

SULTAN AIB
Admiralty Interview Board
HMS SULTAN
GOSPORT
Hants
PO12 3BY

TEMERAIRE
HMS TEMERAIRE
Burnaby Road
PORTSMOUTH
Hants
PO1 2HB

VICTORY
HMS VICTORY
HM Naval Base
PORTSMOUTH
Hants
PO1 3PZ

HM SHIPS

For those with access to the internal MoD intranet and seeking more indepth information on HM Ships, the URL is:
http://royalnavy.defence.mod.uk/fleet_reference/Fleet_Publications/BCard/index.htm

ALBION (Fearless)
BFPO 204

ARCHER (Attacker)
BFPO 208

ARGYLL (Type 23)
BFPO 210

ARK ROYAL (Invincible)
BFPO 212

ATHERSTONE (Hunt)
BFPO 215

BANGOR (Sandown)
BFPO 222

BITER (Attacker)
BFPO 229

BLAZER (Attacker)
BFPO 231

BLYTH (Sandown)
BFPO 221

BROCKLESBY (Hunt)
BFPO 241

BULWARK (Fearless)
BFPO 243

CAMPBELTOWN (Type 22)
BFPO 248

CATTISTOCK (Hunt)
BFPO 251

CHARGER (Attacker)
BFPO 252

CHATHAM (Type 22)
BFPO 253

CHIDDINGFOLD (Hunt)
BFPO 254

CORNWALL (Type 22)
BFPO 256

CUMBERLAND (Type 22)
BFPO 261

DASHER (Attacker)
BFPO 271

DUMBARTON CASTLE
BFPO 274

ECHO (Misc)
BFPO 275

EDINBURGH (Type 42)
BFPO 277

ENDURANCE (Ice Patrol)
BFPO 279

ENTERPRISE (Misc)
BFPO 276

EXAMPLE (Attacker)
BFPO 281

EXETER (Type 42)
BFPO 278

EXPLOIT (Attacker)
BFPO 285

EXPLORER (Attacker)
BFPO 280

EXPRESS (Attacker)
BFPO 282

GLEANER (Gleaner)
BFPO 288

GLOUCESTER (Type 42)
BFPO 289

GRIMSBY (Sandown)
BFPO 292

HURWORTH (Hunt)
BFPO 300

ILLUSTRIOUS (Invincible)
BFPO 305

IRON DUKE (Type 23)
BFPO 309

KENT (Type 23)
BFPO 318

LANCASTER (Type 23)
BFPO 323

LEDBURY (Hunt)
BFPO 324

LIVERPOOL (Type 42)
BFPO 327

MANCHESTER (Type 42)
BFPO 331

MERSEY (River)
BFPO 334

MIDDLETON (Hunt)
BFPO 335

MONMOUTH (Type 23)
BFPO 338

MONTROSE (Type 23)
BFPO 339

NORTHUMBERLAND (Type 23)
BFPO 345

NOTTINGHAM (Type 42)
BFPO 346

OCEAN (LPH)
BFPO 350

PEMBROKE (Sandown)
BFPO 357

PENZANCE (Sandown)
BFPO 358

PORTLAND (Type 23)
BFPO 361

PUNCHER (Attacker)
BFPO 362

PURSUER (Attacker)
BFPO 363

QUORN (Hunt)
BFPO 366

RAIDER (Attacker)
BFPO 377

RAMSEY (Sandown)
BFPO 368

RANGER (Attacker)
BFPO 369

RICHMOND (Type 23)
BFPO 375

ROEBUCK (Bulldog)
BFPO 376

SABRE (Archer P2000)
BFPO 378

SCEPTRE (Swiftsure)
BFPO 380

SCIMITAR (Archer P2000)
BFPO 384

SCOTT (Hecla)
BFPO 381

SEVERN (River)
BFPO 382

SHOREHAM (Sandown)
BFPO 386

SMITER (Attacker)
BFPO 387

SOMERSET (Type 23)
BFPO 395

SOUTHAMPTON (Type 42)
BFPO 389

SOVEREIGN (Swiftsure)
BFPO 390

SPARTAN (Swiftsure)
BFPO 391

SPLENDID (Swiftsure)
BFPO 393

ST ALBANS (Type 23)
BFPO 399

SUPERB (Swiftsure)
BFPO 396

SUTHERLAND (Type 23)
BFPO 398

TALENT (Trafalgar)
BFPO 401

TIRELESS (Trafalgar)
BFPO 402

TORBAY (Trafalgar)
BFPO 403

TRACKER (Attacker)
BFPO 409

TRAFALGAR (Trafalgar)
BFPO 404

TRENCHANT (Trafalgar)
BFPO 405

TRIUMPH (Trafalgar)
BFPO 406

TRUMPETER (Attacker)
BFPO 407

TURBULENT (Trafalgar)
BFPO 408

TYNE (River)
BFPO 412

VANGUARD (PORT) (Trident)
BFPO 418

VANGUARD (STBD) (Trident)
BFPO 418

VENGEANCE (STBD) (Trident)
BFPO 421

VICTORIOUS (PORT) (Trident)
BFPO 419

VIGILANT (PORT) (Trident)
BFPO 420

VIGILANT(STBD) (Trident)
BFPO 420

WALNEY (Sandown)
BFPO 423

WESTMINSTER (Type 23)
BFPO 426

YORK (Type 42)
BFPO 430

RN FISHERY PROTECTION &
MINE COUNTERMEASURES SQUADRONS

FISHERY PROTECTION SQN

LT X   G Cuthbert

FIRST MCM SQN

CDR..............X   M S   Blackmore

SECOND MCM SQN

CDR..............X   A P Williams

THIRD MCM SQN

CDR..............X   C J Davies

ROYAL NAVAL AIR SQUADRONS

CO CHF
A/LtCol X   J McCardle

700(M) SEAHAWK
LT CDR..........X   J D L Boddington

727 SQN
LT CDR..........X   K M Potts

750 SQN SEAHAWK (FAA)
LT CDR..........X   C J Daniell

771 SQN (FAA)
LT CDR..........X   J C Barnbrook

792 SQN HERON
LT CDR..........X   A Rogers

800 SQN (GR7 Harrier)
CDR.............. E   K W Seymour

801 SQN (GR7 Harrier)
CDR..............X   E A F Orchard

814 SQN SEAHAWK
CDR..............X   P R J MUNRO-LOTT

815 SQN Heron
CDR..............X   W N Entwisle OBE MVO

820 SQN SEAHAWK
CDR.............. E   K W Seymour

824 SQN (Merlin)
LT CDR..........X   K M Dodd

829 SQN SEAHAWK
LT CDR..........X   S Deacon

845 SQN (Sea King Mk4)
CDR..............X   C A Slocombe

846 SQN (Sea King Mk4)
CDR..............X   M V Carretta

847 SQN (CDO Support)
LT CDR..........X   D A Chapman

848 SQN HERON (FAA)
A/CDR X   M C Walker

849 SQN A FLT (Sea King AEW)
LT CDR..........X   D M Biggs

849 SQN B FLT (Sea King AEW)
LT CDR..........X   P M Jefferson

849 SQN HQ
CDR..............X   M A J H

GANNET SAR Detachment
LT CDR..........X   R A Stringer

ROYAL NAVAL RESERVE UNITS

HMS CALLIOPE
South Shore Road
GATESHEAD
Tyne & Wear
NE8 2BE

HMS CAMBRIA
Hayes PointSully
PENARTH
CF6 2XU

HMS CAROLINE
BFPO 806

HMS DALRIADA (MOB
Navy Buildings
Eldon Street
GREENOCK
PA16 7SL

HMS EAGLET
RNHQ Merseyside
Brunswick Dock
LIVERPOOL
Merseyside
L3 4DZ

HMS FERRET
Chicksands
SHEFFORD
Bedfordshire
SG17 5PR

HMS FLYING FOX
Winterstoke Road
BRISTOL
BS3 2NS

HMS FORWARD
Trafalgar House
10/20 Sampson Road North
BIRMINGHAM
B11 1BL

HMS KING ALFRED
Whale Island
PORTSMOUTH
Hants
PO2 8ER

HMS NORTHWOOD
Brackenhill House
The Woods
NORTHWOOD
HA6 3EX

HMS PRESIDENT
72 St Katherine's Way
LONDON
E1 9UQ

HMS SCOTIA
Pitreavie
DUNFERMLINE
KY11 5QE

HMS SHERWOOD
Chalfont Drive
NOTTINGHAM
NG8 3LT

HMS VIVID
Mount Wise
DEVONPORT
PL1 4JH

HMS WILDFIRE
Brackenhill House
The Woods
NORTHWOOD
Middlesex
HA6 3EX

HMS WILDFIRE
Collingwood Block
Khyber Road
CHATHAM
Kent
ME4 4TT

ROYAL MARINES ESTABLISHMENTS AND UNITS

CDO LOG REGT RM
Commando Logistics Regiment
Royal Marines
RMB Chivenor
BARNSTAPLE
Devon
EX31 1AZ

CTCRM
Commando Training Centre
Royal Marines
Lympstone
Nr EXMOUTH
Devon
EX8 5AR

CTCRM (SEA)
Commando Training Centre
Royal Marines
Lympstone
Nr Exmouth
Devon
EX8 5AR

FLEET HQ PORTS 2
The Admiral Sir Henry Leach Bldg
Guardroom Road
Whale Island
PORTSMOUTH
PO2 8BY

HQ 3 CDO BDE RM
Headquarters 3 Commando Brigade
Royal Marines
RM Barracks
Stonehouse
PLYMOUTH
Devon
PL1 3QS

RM CONDOR
Royal Marines Condor
ARBROATH
Angus
Scotland
DD11 3SJ

RMB STONEHOUSE
Royal Marines Stonehouse
RM Barracks
Stonehouse
PLYMOUTH
Devon
PL1 3QS

UKLFCSG RM
UKLF CSG
RM Barracks
Stonehouse
Plymouth
Devon
PL1 3QS

1 ASSLT GP RM
1 Assault Group Royal Marines
Hamworthy
POOLE
Dorset
BH15 4NQ

11 (ATT) SQN
11 (ATT) Sqn
Royal Marines
Instow
BIDEFORD
Devon
EX39 4JH

148 FOU BTY RA
RM Poole
Hamworthy
Poole
Dorset
BH15 4NQ

29 CDO REGT RA
29 Commando Regiment Royal
Artillery
The Royal Citadel
Plymouth
Devon
PL1 2PD

40 CDO RM
40 Commando Royal Marines
Norton Manor Camp
TAUNTON
Somerset
TA2 6PF

42 CDO RM
42 Commando Royal Marines
Bickleigh Barracks
PLYMOUTH
Devon
PL6 7AJ

45 CDO RM
45 Commando Royal Marines
RM CONDOR
ARBROATH
Angus
Scotland
DD11 3SJ

ROYAL MARINES BAND SERVICE
BRNC BAND
Britannia Royal Naval College
DARTMOUTH
Devon
TQ6 0MJ

ROYAL MARINES BAND SERVICE
CTCRM BAND
EXMOUTH
Devon
EX8 5AR

ROYAL MARINES BAND SERVICE
HQ BAND SERVICE
HQ Band Service RM
Eastney Block
HMS Nelson
PORTSMOUTH
Hants
PO1 3HH

ROYAL MARINES BAND SERVICE
MWS RM SCH MUSIC
Maritime Warfare School
Royal Marines School of Music
Eastney Block
HMS NELSON
HM Naval Base
PORTSMOUTH
PO1 3HH

ROYAL MARINES BAND SERVICE
RM BAND PLYMOUTH
RM BAND Plymouth
HMS RALEIGH
TORPOINT
Cornwall
PL11 2PD

ROYAL MARINES BAND SERVICE
RM BAND PTSMTH
RM BAND Portsmouth
HMS NELSON
PORTSMOUTH
Hants
PO1 3HH

ROYAL MARINES BAND SERVICE
RM BAND SCOTLAND
RM BAND Scotland
RNSE
HMS CALEDONIA
ROSYTH
Fife
Scotland
KY11 2XH

ROYAL MARINES RESERVE UNITS

RMR BRISTOL
Royal Marines Reserve Bristol
Dorset House
Litfield Place
BRISTOL
BS8 3NA

RMR LONDON
Royal Marines Reserve
City of London
2 Old Jamaica Road
Bermondsey
LONDON
SE16 4AN

RMR MERSEYSIDE
Royal Marines Reserve Merseyside
RNHQ Merseyside
East Brunswick Dock
LIVERPOOL
Merseyside
L3 4DZ

RMR SCOTLAND
Royal Marines Reserve Scotland
37-51 Birkmyre Road
Govan
GLASGOW
G51 3JH

RMR TYNE
Royal Marines Reserve Tyne
Anzio HouseQuayside
NEWCASTLE-UPON-TYNE
NE6 1BU

ROYAL FLEET AUXILIARY SERVICE

ARGUS, Aviation Training & Primary Casualty Reception Ship

BAYLEAF, Support Tanker, (AO)

BLACK ROVER, Small Fleet Tanker, (AORL)

BRAMBLELEAF, Support Tanker, (AO)

DILIGENCE, Forward Repair Ship, (AR)

FORT AUSTIN, Support Stores Ship (AFS)

FORT VICTORIA, Combined Fleet Support Tanker & Store Ship(AOR)

FORT GEORGE, Combined Fleet Support Tanker & Store Ship,(AOR)

FORT ROSALIE, Support Stores Ship (AFS)

GOLD ROVER, Small Fleet Tanker, (AORL)

GREY ROVER, Small Fleet Tanker, (AORL)

OAKLEAF, Support Tanker, (AO)

ORANGELEAF, Support Tanker, (AO)

SIR BEDIVERE, Landing Ship Logistics, (LSL)

SIR GALAHAD, Landing Ship Logistics, (LSL)

SIR PERCIVALE, Landing Ship Logistics, (LSL)

SIR TRISTRAM, Landing Ship Logistics, (LSL)

WAVE KNIGHT, Support Tanker,(AO)

WAVE RULER, Support Tanker,(AO)

LARGS BAY, Landing Ship Dock, (Auxiliary)

LYME BAY, Landing Ship Dock, (Auxiliary)

CARDIGAN BAY, Landing Ship Dock, (Auxiliary)

MOUNTS BAY, Landing Ship Dock, (Auxiliary)

KEY ADDRESSES

ARMED FORCES PERSONNEL ADMINISTRATION AGENCY HEADQUARTERS (AFPAA HQ)

AFPAA (Central Office)
Building 182
RAF Innsworth
GLOUCESTER
Gloucestershire
GL3 1HW

AFPAA (Centurion)
Centurion Building
Grange Road
GOSPORT
Hants
PO13 9XA

COMBINED CADET FORCE

Director of Naval Reserves
South Terrace
HM Naval Base
PORTSMOUTH
Hants
PO1 3LS

COMMITTEES

UNITED KINGDOM COMMANDERS IN CHIEF COMMITTEE (HOME)(UKCICC)(H)
Erskine Barracks
Wilton
SALISBURY
Wiltshire
SP2 0AG
(01722 433208)

COMMONWEALTH LIAISON OFFICES
AUSTRALIA
Australia House
Strand
London
WC2B 4LA
BANGLADESH
28 Queens Gate
LONDON
SW7 5JA

CANADA
Macdonald House
Grosvenor Square
LONDON
W1K 4AB

GHANA
13 Belgrave Square
LONDON
SW1X 8PN
INDIA
India House
Aldwych
LONDON
WC2B 4NA

MALAYSIA
45 Belgrave Square
LONDON
SW1X 8QT
NEW ZEALAND
New Zealand House
Haymarket
LONDON
SW1Y 4TQ

NIGERIA
Nigeria House
9 Northumberland Avenue
LONDON
WC2N 5BX

EDUCATIONAL ESTABLISHMENTS

THE ROYAL COLLEGE OF DEFENCE STUDIES
Seaford House
37 Belgrave Square
LONDON
SW1 X8NS
(020 7915 4804)

THE JOINT SERVICES COMMAND AND STAFF TRAINING COLLEGE
BRACKNELL
Berkshire
RG12 9DD
(01344 457271)

JSCSC SHRIVENHAM
Faringdon Road
Watchfield
Swindon
Wiltshire
SN6 8LA
(01793 788001)

MEDICAL SERVICES

The Medical Director General (Naval)
Victory Building
HM Naval Base
PORTSMOUTH
PO1 3LS

**Ministry of Defence Hospital Unit
Portsmouth**
Royal Hospital Haslar
Haslar Road
GOSPORT
Hants
PO12 2AA

**Ministry of Defence Hospital Unit
Derriford**
Derriford Hospital
PLYMOUTH
Devon
PL6 8DH
Institute of Naval Medicine
ALVERSTOKE
Hants
PO12 2DL

MINISTRY OF DEFENCE POLICE
HEADQUARTERS

Ministry of Defence Police Headquarters
MDP Wethersfield
BRAINTREE
Essex
CM7 4AZ
(01371 854000)

NAVAL BASES AND SUPPLY AGENCY

CDIRECTOR GENERAL LOG. FLEET
Birch
1-N54c
#3131
FOXHILL
Bath
BA1 5AB

NAVAL BASE COMMANDER CLYDE
HM Naval Base
Clyde
Dunbartonshire
G84 8HL
Defence Munitions
BEITH
Ayrshire
KA15 1JT

CAMPBELTOWN (NATO POL Depot)
Glen Ramskill, Campbeltown
PA28 6RD

COULPORT (RN Armament Depot)
PO Box 1
Cove
Helensburgh
Dunbartonshire
G84 0PD

CROMBIE (RN Armament Depot)
Main Depot
Ordnance Road
Crombie
KY12 8LA

FASLANE (RN Store Depot)
HM Naval Base
Faslane
G84 8HL

**GLEN DOUGLAS (NATO Ammunition
Depot)**
PO Box 1
Arrochar
Dunbartonshire
G83 7BA

LOCH EWE (NATO POL Depot)
Aultbea
Achnasheen
Ross Shire
IV22 2HU

LOCH STRIVEN (NATO POL Depot)
Loch Striven
Scotland
PA23 7UL
ROSYTH (RN Store Depot)
Fife
KY11 2XP

NAVAL BASE COMMANDER DEVONPORT
HM Naval Base
DEVONPORT
Plymouth
PL1 4SL

Devonport (RN Store Depot)
HM Naval Base
DEVONPORT
Plymouth
PL1 4SL

Ernesettle (RN Armament Depot)
Ernesettle Lane
PLYMOUTH
PL5 2TX

Exeter (Support Engineering Facility)
Topsham
EXETER
Devon
EX2 7AH

**NAVAL BASE COMMANDER
PORTSMOUTH**
HM Naval Base
PORTSMOUTH
Hants
PO1 3LT

DIRECTOR SUPPLY (SOUTH)
South Office Block
HM Naval Base
PORTSMOUTH
PO1 3LU

Colerne (RN Store Depot)
Doncombe Lane
Colerne
Wiltshire
SN14 8QY

GOSPORT (RN Armament Depot)
Fareham Road
Gosport
Hants
PO13 0AH

PORTSMOUTH (RN Armament Depot)
Hants
PO1 3LU

MARINE SERVICES SUPPORT

Deputy Director Marine Services Support
Room 92A
Block E
ENSLEIGH
Bath
BA1 5AB

General Manager
HM Mooring Depot
Pembroke Dock
Pembrokeshire
SA72 6TB

NAVY, ARMY AND AIR FORCE INSTITUTES

NAAFI HQ
LONDON Road
Amesbury
SALISBURY
Wiltshire
SP4 7EN

NATO HEADQUARTERS-MILITARY COMMITTEE (UKMILREP)

UKMILREP
NATO Headquarters
BFPO 49

ALLIED COMMAND TRANSFORMATION (ACT)

HEADQUARTERS, SUPREME ALLIED COMMANDER TRANSFORMATION (SACT)
Naval Party 1964
(SACT)
BFPO 493

CC MAR HQ NORTHWOOD
Eastbury Park
Northwood
Middlesex
HA6 3HP

REGIONAL HEADQUARTERS SOUTH ATLANTIC (RHQ SOUTHLANT)
BFPO 6

COMSUBNORTH
Eastbury Park
NORTHWOOD
Middlesex
HA6 3HP

ANTI-SUBMARINE WARFARE STRIKING FORCE
Office of COMUKMARFOR
Fieldhouse Building
Whale Island
PORTSMOUTH
Hants

SACT UNDERSEA RESEARCH CENTRE
Viale San Bartolomeo 400
I-19026 San Bartolomeo
Italy

ALLIED COMMAND OPERATIONS (ACO)

SUPREME HEADQUARTERS ALLIED POWERS EUROPE (SHAPE)
BFPO 26

NATO SCHOOL (SHAPE)
Oberammergau
Box 2003
BFPO 105

JFC HQ NAPLES
BFPO 8

STRIKEFORNATO JFC NAPLES
BFPO 8

JFC HQ NAPLES
BFPO 8

FRENCH COMMANDER-IN-CHIEF MEDITERRANEAN
(CECMED)
Prefecture Maritime
83800 Toulon Naval
France

JFC HQ BRUNSSUM
BPFO 28

NAVAL PERSONAL AND FAMILY SERVICE (NPFS)

Area Office (NPFS) Eastern
Swiftsure Block
HMS Nelson
Queen Street
PORTSMOUTH
Hants
PO1 3HH
(02392 722712)

Area Office (NPFS) Western
Fenner Block
H M Naval Base Devonport
HMS DRAKE
PLYMOUTH
Devon
PL2 2BG
(01752 555041)

Area Office (NPFS) Northern
Triton House
1-5 Churchill Square
HELENSBURGH
Argyll and Bute
G84 9HL
(01436 672798)

NAVAL REGIONAL OFFICES

SCOTLAND & NORTHERN IRELAND REGIONS
HMS CALEDONIA
ROSYTH
Fife
KY11 2XH
(01383 425532)

NORTHERN ENGLAND REGION
Royal Naval Headquarters Merseyside
Brunswick Dock
LIVERPOOL
L3 4DZ
(0151 707 3400/3401/3402)

Naval Regional Sub-Office
HMS CALLIOPE
South Shore Road
GATESHEAD
Tyne & Wear
NE8 2BE
(0191 477 8607 and 0191 478 7067)

WALES & WESTERN REGIONS
Naval Regional Management Centre
HMS FLYING FOX
Winterstoke Road
BRISTOL
BS3 2NS
(0117 953 0996)

EASTERN ENGLAND REGION
HMS PRESIDENT
72 St Katharine's Way
LONDON
E1W 1UQ
(020 7481 7324)

REGULAR FORCES EMPLOYMENT ASSOCIATION

(NATIONAL ASSOCIATION FOR EMPLOYMENT OF REGULAR SAILORS SOLDIERS AND AIRMEN)
49 Pall Mall
LONDON
SW1Y 5JG
(020 7321 2011)

ABERDEEN
46A Union Street
ABERDEEN
AB10 1BD

BEDFORD
TA Centre
28 Bedford Road
KEMPSTON
Beds
MK42 8AJ

BELFAST
Northern Ireland War Memorial Building
Waring Street
BELFAST
BT1 2EU

BIRMINGHAM
2nd Floor
Cornwall Buildings
45 Newhall Street
BIRMINGHAM
B3 3QR

BRISTOL
Borough Park Business Centre
Borough Park
Romney Avenue
BRISTOL
BS7 9ST

BURY ST. EDMUNDS
Room 4
90 Guildhall Street
BURY ST EDMUNDS
IP33 1PR

CARDIFF
Maindy Barracks
CARDIFF
CF4 3YE

CHELMSFORD
Springfield Tyrells House
250 Springfield Road
CHELMSFORD
Essex
CM2 6BY

CHELTENHAM
Potter House
St Annes Road
CHELTENHAM
Glos
GL52 2SS

DARLINGTON
67 Duke Street
Darlington
Co. Durham
DL3 7SD

DERBY
Room 18
The College Business Centre
Uttoxeter New Road
DERBY
DE22 3WZ

EDINBURGH
New Haig House
Logie Green Road
EDINBURGH
EH7 4HQ

EXETER
Wyvern Barracks
EXETER
Devon
EX2 6AR

GLASGOW
2nd Floor, The Pentagon Centre
36 Washington Street
GLASGOW
G3 8AZ

LEEDS
Carlton Barracks
Carlton Gate
LEEDS
LS7 1HE

LINCOLN
Unit 4, Oak House
Witharn Park
Waterside South
LINCOLN
LN5 7FB

LIVERPOOL
Suite 43 Oriel Chambers
14 Water Street
LIVERPOOL
L2 8TD

LONDON
49 Pall Mall
LONDON
SW1Y 5JG

MAIDSTONE
Royal British Legion Industries
Royal British Legion Village
Aylesford
Nr MAIDSTONE
Kent
ME20 7NL

MANCHESTER
TA Centre
Belle Vue Street
MANCHESTER
M12 5PW

NEWCASTLE-ON-TYNE
c/o The Queen's Own Yeomanry
Fenham Barracks
Barrack Road
NEWCASTLE-UPON-TYNE
NE2 4NP

NORTHAMPTON
TA Centre
28 Bedford Road
KEMPSTON
Beds
MK42 8AJ

NORWICH
TA Centre
Britannia House
325 Aylsham Road
NORWICH
NR3 2AB

PLYMOUTH
Flat 10
MOD Mt Wise Business Park
Devonport
PLYMOUTH
PL1 4JH

PORTSMOUTH
2B Tipner Road
Stamshaw
PORTSMOUTH
PO2 8QP

PRESTON
Fulwood Barracks
Fulwood
PRESTON
Lancs
PR2 8AA

READING
Watlington House
Watlington Street
READING
RG1 4RJ

SALISBURY
27 Castle Street
SALISBURY
Wilts
SP1 1TT

SHEFFIELD
2nd Floor
9 Paradise Square
SHEFFIELD
S1 2DE

SWANSEA
See Cardiff Branch

QINETIQ

HEAD OFFICE
QINETIQ
Cody Technology Park
Ively Road
FARNBOROUGH
Hampshire
GU14 0LX

DSTL Portsdown West
Portsdown Hill Road
FAREHAM
Hampshire
PO17 6AD

QINETIQ
Winfrith Technology Centre
Newburgh
DORCHESTER
Dorset
DT2 8XJ

DSTL Porton Down
SALISBURY
Wiltshire
SP4 0JQ

QINETIQ
Malvern Technology Park
St Andrews Road
MALVERN
Worcs
WR14 3PS

DSTL Fort Halstead
SEVENOAKS
Kent
TN14 7BP

DEFENCE AVIATION REPAIR AGENCY

HEAD OFFICE
DARA St Athan
St Athan
BARRY
Vale of Glamorgan
CF62 4WA

DARA Almondbank
Almondbank
PERTH
PH1 3NQ

DARA Fleetlands
Fareham Road
GOSPORT
Hampshire
PO13 0AA

DARA Sealand
Welsh Road
DEESIDE
Flintshire
CH5 2LS

DIRECTORATE OF NAVAL RECRUITING REGIONAL CAREERS HEADQUARTERS (RCHQS) AND ARMED FORCE CAREERS OFFICES (AFCOs)

RCHQ NORTH
RN Support Establishment
HMS Caledonia
ROSYTH
KY11 2XH
(01383 425516)

AFCOs NORTH REGION
63 Belmont Street
ABERDEEN
AB10 1JS
(01224 639666)

Palace Barracks
Holywood
BELFAST
Co. Down
BT18 9RA
(02890 423840)

94-96 English Street
CARLISLE
CA3 8ND
(01228 523958)

148 Northgate
DARLINGTON
DL1 1QT
(01325 461850)

29/31 Bank Street
DUNDEE
DD1 1RW
(01382 227198)

TA Centre
Elgin Street
DUNFERMLINE
KY12 7SB
01383 625283

67-83 Shandwick Place
EDINBURGH
EH2 4SN
(0131 221 1111)

Charlotte House
78 Queen Street
GLASGOW
G1 3DN
(0141 221 4852

Britannia Suite
Norwich House
Savile Street
KINGSTON-UPON-HULL
HU1 3ES
(01482 325901)

3 Bridge Street
INVERNESS
IV1 1HG
(01463 233668)

10 - 14 Bond Street
Park Row
LEEDS
LS1 2JY
(0113 2458195)

15 James Street
LIVERPOOL
L2 7NX
(0151 236 1566)
Petersfield House

29 Peters Street
MANCHESTER
M2 5QJ
(0161 835 2923)

67 Borough Road
MIDDLESBROUGH
Cleveland
TS1 3AE
(01642 211749)

New England House
20 Ridley Place
NEWCASTLE UPON TYNE
NE1 8JW
(0191 2327048)

63 College Street
St Helens
MERSEYSIDE
WA10 1TN
(01744 753560)

46 Edward VII Quay
Navigation Way
Ashton on Wibble
PR2 2YF
(01772 555675)

Central Buildings
1A Church Street
SHEFFIELD
S1 1FZ
(0114 272 1476)
RCHQ SOUTH

Ladywood House
45/46 Stephenson Street
BIRMINGHAM
B2 4DY
(0121 634 8508)

AFCOs SOUTH REGION
Unit 46
The Pallasades
BIRMINGHAM
B2 4XN
(0121 633 4995)

244 Holdenhurst Road
BOURNEMOUTH
BH8 8AZ
(01202 311224)

120 Queen's Road
BRIGHTON
BN1 3XQ
(01273 325386)

4 Colston Avenue
BRISTOL
BS1 4TY
(0117 9260233)

2 Glisson Road
CAMBRIDGE
CB1 2HD
(01223 315118)

South Gate House
84 Wood Street
CARDIFF
CF10 1GR
(02920 727626)

3 Dock Road
CHATHAM
ME4 4SJ
(01634 826206)

Sir Henry Parks Road
Canley
COVENTRY
CV5 6TA
(02476 226513)

Fountain House
Western Way
EXETER
EX1 2DQ
(01392 274040)

4th Floor
Britannia Warehouse
The Docks
GLOUCESTER
GL1 2EH
(01452 521676)

Stanford House
91 Woodbridge Road
GUILDFORD
GU1 4LN
(01483 302304)

180A Cranbrook Road
ILFORD
Essex
IG1 4LR
(020 851 858855)

37 Silent Street
IPSWICH
IP1 1TF
(01473 254450)

St George's House
6 St George's Way
LEICESTER
LE1 1SH
(01162 543233)

Sibthorpe House
350/352 High Street
LINCOLN
LN5 7BN
(01522 525661)

Ground Floor
Zone D
St Georges Court

2-12 Bloomsbury Way
LONDON
WC1A 2SH
(020 7305 3329)

Dunstable House
Dunstable Road
LUTON
LU1 1EA
(01582 721501)

22 Unthank Road
NORWICH
NR2 2RA
(01603 620033)

70 Milton Road
Victoria Centre
NOTTINGHAM
NG1 3QX
(0115 9419503)

35 St Giles Street
OXFORD
OX1 3LJ
(01865 553431)

21 - 23 Hereward Cross
PETERBOROUGH
PE1 1TB
(01733 568833)

Mount Wise
Devonport
PLYMOUTH
PL1 4JH
(01752 501790)

Cambridge Road
PORTSMOUTH
PO1 2EN
(023 9282 6536)

Oak House
Chapel Street
REDRUTH
TR15 2BY
(01209 314143)

2nd Floor
Princess House
The Square
SHREWSBURY
Shropshire
SY1 1JZ
(01743 232541)

152 High Street
Lower Bar
SOUTHAMPTON
Hants
SO14 2BT
(023 8063 0486)

36 - 38 Old Hall Street
Hanley
STOKE-ON-TRENT
ST1 3AP
(01782 214688)

Llanfair Buildings
17-19 Castle Street
SWANSEA
SA1 1JF
(01792 654208/642516)

35 East Street
TAUNTON
Somerset
TA1 3LS
(01823 354430)

43A Queens Street
WOLVERHAMPTON
WV1 3BL
(01902 715395)
Halkyn House

21 Rhosddu Road
WREXHAM
LL11 1NE
(01978 263334)

OFFICER CAREERS LIAISON CENTRES (OCLCs)

OCLCs NORTH REGION

RN Support Establishment
HMS CALEDONIA
ROSYTH
KY11 2XH
(01383 425515)

Petersfield House
29-31 St Peter's Street
MANCHESTER
M2 5QJ
(0161 8352916

Palace Barracks
Holywood
County Down
BELFAST or BFPO 806
BT18 9RA
(028 9042 3832)

OCLCs SOUTH REGION

Ladywood House
45/46 Stephenson Street
BIRMINGHAM
B2 4DY
(0121 66348508)

JHQ Building
Northwood HQ
Northwood
MIDDLESEX
HA6 3HP
(01923 833140)

HMS FLYING FOX
Winterstoke Road
BRISTOL
BS3 2NS
(0117 9655251)

ROYAL NAVAL FILM CHARITY

Registered Office
HM Naval Base (PP23)
PORTSMOUTH
PO1 3NH
(023 927 23108)

SEA CADET CORPS

HEADQUARTERS
202 Lambeth Road
LONDON
SE1 7JF
(020 7928 8978)

NORTHERN AREA
HMS CALEDONIA
ROSYTH
Fife
KY11 2XH
(01383 416300)

NORTH WEST AREA
Royal Naval Headquarters Merseyside
East Brunswick Dock
LIVERPOOL
L3 4DZ
(0151 707 3440)

SOUTH WEST AREA
HMS FLYING FOX
Winterstoke Road
BRISTOL
Avon
BS3 2NS
(0117 953 1991)

EASTERN AREA
The Drill Hall
Ropery Road
GAINSBOROUGH
Lincolnshire
DN21 2NS
(01427 614441)

LONDON AREA
HMS PRESIDENT
72 St. Katharine's Way
LONDON
E1W 1UQ
(020 7481 7372)

SOUTHERN AREA
HMS NELSON
PORTSMOUTH
Hants
PO1 3HH
(023 927 24263)

SHIPPING POLICY DIVISION

(DEFENCE PLANNING AND EMERGENCIES BRANCH)
Department for Transport, Local Government and the Regions
Zone 4/21
Great Minster House
76 Marsham Street
LONDON
SW1P 4DR
(020 7944 5148)

YACHT CLUBS USING A SPECIAL ENSIGN

Yachts belonging to members of the following Yacht Clubs may, subject to certain conditions, obtain a Warrant to wear a Special Ensign.

Club	Address

WHITE ENSIGN

Royal Yacht Squadron	Royal Yacht Squadron, Castle Cowes PO31 7QT

BLUE ENSIGN

Royal Albert Yacht Club	17 Pembroke Road, Portsmouth, PO1 2NT
Royal Brighton Yacht Club	253 St Kilda Street,Middle Brighton, 3186, Victoria,Australia
Royal Cinque Ports Yacht Club	4-5 Waterloo Crescent, Dover, CT6 1LA
Royal Cruising Club	Bywaters, Taylors Lane, Bosham, West Susex, PO18 8QQ
Royal Dorset Yacht Club	11 Custom House Quay, Weymouth, Dorset, DT4 8BG
Royal Engineer Yacht Club	86 Training Squadron, Army Apprentice College, Chepstow, Gwent, NP6 7YG
Royal Geelong Yacht Club	PO Box 156, Geelong, 3220 Victoria, Australia
Royal Gourock Yacht Club	Ashton Gourock PA19 1DA
Royal Highland Yacht Club	Westmanse House, Lichrenan Tanyuilt, Argyl, PH35 1HG
Royal Marines Sailing Club	Poole, Dorset, BH15 4NQ
Royal Melbourne Yacht Club	Lower Esplanade, St Kilda, 3182
Royal Motor Yacht Club	Panorama Road, Sandbanks, Poole, Dorset, BH13 7RN
Royal Naval Sailing Association	Royal Naval Club, 10 Haslar Marina, Haslar Road, Gosport, PO12 1NU
Royal Naval Volunteer Reserve Yacht Club	The Naval Club, 38 Hill Street, London, W1X 8DB
Royal New Zealand Yacht Squadron	Squadron Rooms, Westhaven, PO Box 46128 Herne Bay, Auckland, New Zealand

Royal Northern and Clyde Yacht Club .... The Club House, Rhu, Dumbartonshire, G84 8NG

Royal Perth Yacht Club of Western Australia .... PO Box 5, Nedlands, West Australia 6009

Royal Port Nicholas Yacht Club .... Clyde Quay Boat Harbour, PO Box 9674, Wellington, New Zealand

Royal Queensland Yacht Club .... PO Box 21, Manly, Queensland 4179, Australia

Royal Scottish Motor Yacht Club .... 5 St Vincent Place, Glasgow, G1 2DJ

Royal Solent Yacht Club .... Yarmouth, Isle of Wight, PO41 0NS

Royal South Australia Yacht Club .... North Haven 5018, South Australia

Royal Southern Yacht Club .... Hamble, Southampton, SO3 5HB

Sussex Motor Yacht Club .... 7 Ship Street, Brighton, East Sussex, BN1 1AD

Royal Sydney Yacht Squadron .... PO Box 484, Milsons' Point, NSW 2061, Australia

Royal Temple Yacht Club .... 6 West Cliff Mansions, Ramsgate, Kent, CT11 9WY

Royal Thames Yacht Club .... 60 Knightsbridge, London, SW1X 7LF

Royal Western Yacht Club of England .... West Hoe, Plymouth, PL1 3DG

Royal Western Yacht Club of Scotland .... Lochabar, 20 Barclay Drive, Helensburgh, Dunbartonshire, G84 9RB

Royal Yacht Club of Tasmania .... Marieville Esplanade, Sandy Bay, Tasmania 7005

Royal Yacht Club of Victoria .... 120 Nelson Place, Williamstown, 3016, Australia

BLUE ENSIGN DEFACED BY BADGE OF CLUB

Aldburgh Yacht Club .... Aldebrugh, Suffolk

Army Sailing Association .... c/o MOD (ASCB), M Block, Clayton Barracks, Aldershot, Hants

Bar Yacht Club .... 1 Mitre Court Buildings, Temple, London, EC4Y 7BS

City Livery Yacht Club .... Shortlands, Bromley, Kent BR2 0LG

Cruising Yacht Club of Australia .... New Beach Road, Darling Point, New South Wales 2027

Royal Air Force .... Yacht Club Riverside House, Hamble, Southampton,SO3 5HD

Royal Akrana Yacht Club .... PO Box 42004, Orakei, Auckland 5, New Zealand

Royal Anglesey Yacht Club .... 3 Cadnant Court, Rating Row, Beaumaris, Anglesey, Gwynnedd, LL58 8AL

Royal Armoured Corps Yacht Club .... Bovington Camp, Wareham, Dorset, BH20 6ND

Royal Artillery Yacht Club .... Tamberton, Upton Lovell, Warminster, Wilts, BA12 0JP

Royal Australian Navy Sailing Association .... New Beach Road, Edgecliffe, New South Wales 2027, Australia

Royal Bermuda Yacht Club .... PO Box 894, Hamilton HM DX, Bermuda

Royal Bombay Yacht Club .... PO Box 206, Apollo Bunder, Fort Bombay 400039

Royal Burnham Yacht Club .... The Quay, Burnham-on-Crouch, Essex, CM0 8AO

Royal Channel Islands Yacht Club .... Le Boulevard, Bulwark, St Aubin, Jersey, Channel Islands, JE5 8AD

Conway Club Cruising Association .... 5 Furlong Lane, Totternhoe, Nr Dunstable, BEds

Royal Corinthian Yacht Club .... Burnham-on-Crouch, Essex

Royal Cornwall Yacht Club .... Greenbank, Falmouth, Cornwall

Royal Dee Yacht Club .... 16 Holford Crescent, Knutsford, Cheshire, WA16 8DZ

Royal Forth Yacht Club .... Middle Pier, Granton Harbour, Edinburgh

Royal Freshwater Bay Yacht Club of Western Australia . Keane's Point, Peppermint Grove, Western Australia 6011

Royal Gibraltar Yacht Club .... Queensway, Gibraltar

Royal Harwich Yacht Club .... Woolverstone, Ipswich, IP9 1AT

Royal Hong Kong Yacht Club .... Kellet Island, Hong Kong

Household Division Yacht Club .... HQ Welsh Guards, Wellington Barracks, Birdcage Walk, London SW1E 6HQ

Royal Irish Yacht Club .... Dun Loaghaire, Co Dublin

Royal Jamaica Yacht Club..Kingston, Jamaica

Little Ship Club ....Bell Wharfe Lane, Upper Thames Street, London EC4R 3TB

Little Ship Club (Queensland Squadron) ....119 Bank Street, Newmarket, Queensland 4051, Australia

Royal London Yacht Club ....The Parade, Cowes, Isle of Wight, PO31 7QS

Medway Cruising Club...Boyses Hill Farm, Newington, Sittingbourne, Kent, ME9 7JF

Royal Malta Yacht Club...Couvre Port, Fort Manoel, Manoel Island, Gzira, Malta

Royal Mersey Yacht Club..Bedford Road East, Rockferry, Birkenhead, Merseyside, L42 1LS

Royal Motor Yacht Club of New South Wales..........Wunulla Road, Point Piper, New South Wales 2027

Royal Nassau Sailing Club ....PO Box SS 6891, Nassau, Bahamas

Royal North of Ireland Yacht Club ....Cultra, 7 Seaford Road, Co Down, Ireland

Royal Northumberland Yacht Club ....36 Longridge Drive, Whitley Bay, Tyne & Wear

Royal Ocean Racing Club ....20 St James's Place SW1A 1NN

Parkstone Yacht Club..Pearce Avenue, Parkstone, Poole, Dorset, BH14 8EN

Royal Plymouth Corinthian Yacht Club ....Madeira Road, Plymouth, PL1 2NY

Poole Yacht Club ....New Harbour Road West, Hamworthy, Poole, Dorset

Royal Prince Alfred Yacht Club ....PO Box 99,   Newport Beach, New South Wales 2106, Australia

Royal Prince Edward Yacht Club.............................160 Wolseley Road, Point Piper, 2027 New South Wales, Australia

Severn Motor Yacht Club ....Bath Road, Broomhall, Worcester, WR5 3HR

Royal Southampton Yacht Club...............................1 Channel Way, Ocean Village, Southampton, SO1 1XE

Sussex Motor Yacht Club ....Medina House, Brighton Marine, Brighton, BN2 5UF

Royal Suva Yacht Club ....PO Box 335, Suva, Fiji

The Cruising Association ....Ivory House, St Katherine's Dock, London
E1 9AT

The House of Lords Yacht Club ....House of Lords, London, SW1A 0PW

The Medway Yacht Club ....Upnor, Rochester, Kent

The Poole Harbour Yacht Club ....38 Salterns Way, Lilliput, Poole, Dorset,
BH14 8JR

Thames Motor Yacht Club ....The Green, Hampton Court, East Molesey,
Surrey

Royal Torbay Yacht Club..Beacon Hill, Torquay, Devon

Royal Ulster Yacht Club..101 Clifton Road, BANGOR, Co Down

Royal Welsh Yacht Club ....Porth yr Aur, Caernarvon, Gwynedd

Royal Yorkshire Yacht Club......................................1 Windsor Crescent, Bridlingtonn, YO15
3HY

Old Worcesters Yacht Club......................................Les Heches, St Peter in the Wood,
Guernsey, Channel Islands

RED ENSIGN DEFACED BY BADGE OF CLUB

Brixham Yacht Club ....Overgang, Brixham, Devon, TQ5 8AR

Royal Dart Yacht Club ....Kingswear, South Devon, TQ6 0AB

Royal Fowey Yacht Club...Fowey, Cornwall, PL23 8IH

House of Commons Yacht Club ....RYA House, Romsey Road, Eastleigh,
Hants, SO5 4YA

Lloyd's Yacht Club...London, SW6 5DP

Royal Hamilton Amateur Dinghy Club.....................PO Box 298, Paget PG BX, Bermuda

Royal Lymington Yacht Club....................................Bath Road, Lymington, Hants, S41 9SE

Royal Norfolk and Suffolk Yacht Club......................Royal Plain, Lowestoft, Suffolk, NR33 0AQ

Royal St George Yacht Club ....Dun Laoghaire, Co Dublin

St Helier Yacht Club ....South Pier, St Helier, Jersey

Royal Victoria Yacht Club ....Fishbourne, Isle of Wight, PO33 4EU

Royal Windermere Yacht Club.................................Fallbarrow Road, Bowness in Windermere,
Cumbria, LA33 3DJ

Royal Yachting Association.......................................RYA House, Romsey Road, Eastleigh,
Hants, SO5 4YA

West Mersea Yacht Club..116 Coast Road, West Mersea, Colchester,
Essex

HONORARY OFFICERS OF THE ROYAL NAVAL RESERVE

Honorary Rear Admiral HRH Prince Michael of Kent, GCVO

Honorary Commodore The Right Honourable The Lord Sterling of Plaistow, GCVO CBE

Honorary Commodore Sir Donald Gosling KCVO

Honorary Captain Mrs Mary Fagan JP

Honorary Captain Mr Eric Dancer CBE JP

Honorary Captain The Lord Browne of Madingley

Honorary Captain Robert B Woods CBE

Honorary Captain Lady Carswell OBE

Honorary Captain R Warwick

Honorary Captain (Supernumerary) The Duke of Buccleugh and Queensberry KT VRD JP

Honorary Commander E J Billington

Honorary Commander P R Moore RD*

Honorary Commander Angus Buchanan

Honorary Commander Stephen Howarth

Honorary Lieutenant-Commander Bear Grylls

Honorary Lieutenant-Commander Dame Ellen MacArthur DBE

Honorary Lieutenant- Commander James Stevens BSc FRIN

Honorary Lieutenant-Commander Ian Robinson

Honorary Commander (Supernumerary) Sir Robin Gillett Bt GBE RD

Honorary Commander (Supernumerary) F A Mason MBE

Honorary Chaplain The Right Reverend Bill Ind

Honorary Chaplain The Reverend John Williams MBE

Honorary Chaplain (Supernumerary) The Right Reverend M A P Woods, DSC, MA, (CofE)

HONORARY OFFICERS OF THE ROYAL MARINES RESERVE

Honorary Colonel E P R Cautley .... 1 Jul 99

Honorary Colonel G M Simmers, CBE, CA.. 01 Apr 00

Honorary Colonel J N Tidmarsh, MBE, JP... 01 Jan 98

Honorary Colonel Sir David Trippier RD JP DL... 01 Jan 96

Honorary Colonel Sir Neville Trotter, FCA, JP, DL .... 1 Sep 98

OFFICERS OF THE ACTIVE LIST
OF THE ROYAL NAVAL RESERVE,
ROYAL MARINES RESERVE, THE QUEEN ALEXANDRA'S
ROYAL NAVAL NURSING RESERVE,
SEA CADET CORPS AND
COMBINED CADET FORCE

ROYAL NAVAL RESERVE

Name	Rank	Branch	Unit	Seniority
Abdel - Khalek, Adham Ahmad,	ASG SLT		PRESIDENT	29.11.01
Ace-Hopkins, Serena,	MID	URNU	U/A	12.10.04
Ackerman, Richard,	LT	SM	CAMBRIA	09.05.99
Ackroyd, James,	MID	URNU	U/A	13.10.05
Adair, Jonathan,	ASL	NE	WILDFIRE RNR	05.10.05
Adair, Richard,	ASL	NE	WILDFIRE RNR	05.05.05
Adams, Danielle,	MID	URNU	U/A	17.10.05
Adams, Shawn,	MID	URNU	U/A	10.10.05
Adlam, Charlotte,	MID	URNU	U/A	25.08.03
Adusei, Atta Anane,	MID	URNU	U/A	29.09.05
Aggett, Emily,	CADET	URNU	U/A	17.10.02
Ah-Yave, Sophie,	MID	URNU	U/A	12.10.04
Aitchison, Ian James,	LT CDR	SM	PRESIDENT	31.03.03
Alberts, Ian,	LT CDR	URNU	U/A	01.10.03
Alcock, Charles Edward Hayes, RD	LT CDR	AW	PRESIDENT	31.03.00
Alcock, David John, RD	LT CDR	MW	KING ALFRED	18.02.87
Alexander, Anne,	MID	URNU	U/A	16.10.03
Alexander, Louise Marie,	MID	URNU	U/A	20.10.05
Alexandrou, Natasha,	MID	URNU	U/A	11.10.05
Ali, Filson,	MID	URNU	U/A	06.10.05
Allan, Richard Michael,	LT CDR	SEA	FERRET (RNR)	31.03.02
Allan, William, RD	LT CDR	HQ	SCOTIA	02.09.88
Allen, Elinor Jane,	LT CDR	HQ	VIVID	30.09.91
Allen, Ian James, RD	ACDR	MWHQ	CAROLINE	31.03.97
Allinson, Michael David,	ASL	NE	CAMBRIA	27.11.03
Alvis, Jonathan Geoffrey,	ASL	NE	PRESIDENT	15.10.03
Anderson, Isobel,	CADET	URNU	U/A	01.10.02
Anderson, John Christopher,	LT	MW	DALRIADA	06.03.99
Anderson, Kerry McGowan, BSC	LT CDR	HQ	CAROLINE	31.03.99
Andersson, James,	MID	URNU	U/A	14.10.99
Andrews, Mark David,	LT	LOGS	FLYING FOX	03.11.00
Andrews, Rick,	MID	URNU	U/A	05.09.02
Angliss, Timothy,	MID	URNU	U/A	11.10.04
Antrobus, Richard,	MID	URNU	U/A	20.10.04
Ap Robert, Tomos,	MID	URNU	U/A	11.10.04

Name	Rank	Branch	Unit	Seniority
Arbeid, Mark Leon,	ALT	COMM	PRESIDENT	26.09.03
Armour, Fraser,	MID	URNU	U/A	07.10.04
Armstrong, John,	ASL	NE	U/A	05.12.02
Armstrong, Michael,	LT	AIR	RNR AIR BR VL	14.03.96
Armstrong, Sally,	LT	CS(O)	VIVID RNR	09.04.04
Arrell, Christopher,	MID	URNU	U/A	15.10.02
Asaolu, Ebunoluwa,	MID	URNU	U/A	01.10.03
Ashby, Maxine,	LT	MEDIA	RNR MEDIA RELTNS	03.12.97
Ashley, Stephen,	MID	URNU	U/A	17.10.02
Ashley-Smith, Richard,	MID	URNU	U/A	25.08.03
Ashpole, Richard David,	SG LTCDR		SHERWOOD	01.08.90
Ashton, Jonathan Richard,	SG CDR		CALLIOPE	11.11.00
Ashton, Paul,	MID	URNU	U/A	01.10.03
Ashwood, Lindsey,	ASL	NE	VIVID RNR	13.11.04
Ashworth, Ryan,	MID	URNU	U/A	20.10.04
Askey, Rebekah,	MID	URNU	U/A	07.10.05
Aslam, Zabeada,	CADET	URNU	U/A	22.10.98
Aspden, Mark Charles,	ALT	AWNIS	WILDFIRE	
Aspinell, Charles Jonathan, RD*,	CDR	NCAGS	KING ALFRED	30.09.97
Aspinell, (Pamela Ann), RD,	LT CDR	Q	KING ALFRED	31.03.96
Athol, Stuart Charles,	SLT	MS(M)	PRESIDENT	20.11.01
Atkinson, James Donald,	ASL	NE	SHERWOOD	23.01.03
Attrill, Alexander,	LT CDR	AIR	RNR AIR BR VL	11.05.97
Austin, Caroline,	MID	URNU	U/A	16.10.03
Austin, Elizabeth,	MID	URNU	U/A	12.10.04
Austin, Kevin, RD	LT CDR	AW	PRESIDENT	31.03.98
Avery, Philip,	LT CDR	AIR	RNR AIR BR VL	31.03.97
Avis, Robert Graeme, RD*,	CAPT	AW	PRESIDENT	30.09.02
Aygun, Karyn Stewart, RD,	LT CDR	NCAGS	FLYING FOX	31.03.01

B

Name	Rank	Branch	Unit	Seniority
Babu, Suresh,	ASL	NE	EAGLET	18.09.03
Bacon, David,	MID	URNU	U/A	03.10.02
Baden, Richard,	MID	URNU	U/A	04.10.04
Bagguley, Timothey,	MID	URNU	U/A	11.10.04
Bailey, David,	MID	URNU	U/A	16.10.03
Bailey, Onathan,	MID	URNU	U/A	18.10.02
Bailey, Jonathan,	MID	URNU	U/A	14.10.04
Baines, Mark,	LT CDR	AIR	RNR AIR BR VL	01.02.93
Baird, Andrew,	LT	HQ	CAROLINE	07.08.90
Baker, Luke,	MID	URNU	U/A	12.10.04
Baker, Peter Alan,	CDR	NCAGS	PRESIDENT	30.09.03
Baker, Sarah,	MID	URNU	U/A	14.10.04
Baker, Thomas,	MID	URNU	U/A	08.10.03
Bakewell, Hannah,	MID	URNU	U/A	16.10.03
Baldock, Duncan,	MID	URNU	U/A	11.10.05
Ballance, Theo,	ACDR	AIR	RNR AIR BR VL	04.10.02
Balmain, Stephen Service,	LT	SEA	DALRIADA	01.07.94
Bancroft, David Gideon,	LT	AW	CALLIOPE	20.12.94
Banks, Iain,	LT CDR	AIR	RNR AIR BR VL	31.03.01
Bannister, Mark,	ASL	NE	WILDFIRE RNR	27.01.05
Barfield, Kevin Lloyd, RD	LT CDR	COMM	FORWARD	31.03.96
Barker, Elizabeth Charlotte,	LT	NCAGS	PRESIDENT	28.04.02
Barkhuysen, Edward David,	ASL	NE	FLYING FOX	06.09.02
Barlow, Edward,	MID	NE	U/A	05.09.02
Barlow, Pauline Elizabeth,	ASL	NE	VIVID	09.03.02
Barnes, David,	MID	URNU	U/A	18.07.04
Barnes, David,	MID	URNU	U/A	07.10.99
Barnes, Judith Margaret,	LT	COMM	EAGLET	15.03.03
Barnett, Alison Elaine,	ASL	NE	CAROLINE	15.10.03
Barnett, Caila,	MID	URNU	U/A	20.10.04
Barnett, Neil,	MID	URNU	U/A	06.10.05

Name	Rank	Branch	Unit	Seniority
Barraclough, Ross,	MID	URNU	U/A	24.10.01
Barrand, William,	MID	URNU	U/A	07.10.98
Barratt, Stephen James,	ASL	NE	FORWARD	23.01.02
Barrell, Katie,	CADET	URNU	U/A	03.10.02
Barrett, Mark,	LT CDR	AIR	RNR AIR BR VL	31.03.01
Barrie, James,	MID	URNU	U/A	17.11.04
Barron, Carine,	MID	URNU	U/A	06.10.05
Barth, Alan,	LT	URNU	U/A	03.10.03
Bartlett, David Christopher,	ASG SLT		VIVID	24.01.01
Bartlett, David,	MID	URNU	U/A	10.09.01
Bashir, Fahim,	MID	URNU	U/A	06.10.05
Bassett, Nigel Peter, RD	LT CDR	AW	KING ALFRED	31.03.97
Bateson, Paul,	MID	URNU	U/A	18.10.04
Battle, Richard,	ASL	NE	EAGLET	27.11.03
Baughan, Philip John, RD	LT CDR	HQ	SHERWOOD	01.11.89
Baxter, Ross John, RD	LT	NCAGS	FORWARD	01.09.91
Beales, Jeremy,	MID	URNU	U/A	11.10.05
Beaton, Iain William,	ASL	NE	DALRIADA	24.03.99
Beattie, Jane Elizabeth,	LT CDR	Q	WILDFIRE	31.03.93
Beattie, Teri,	MID	URNU	U/A	10.10.05
Beaumont, Andrew John, RD	LT CDR	MWHQ	EAGLET	31.03.04
Beaumont, Richard,	MID	URNU	U/A	10.09.01
Beckwith, Gordon,	MID	URNU	U/A	07.10.05
Bedford, Jonathan,	SG CDR		SCOTIA	30.09.00
Beech, Eric Edward, RD	LT CDR	DIS	FERRET (RNR)	03.06.87
Beel, Megan,	MID	URNU	U/A	12.10.04
Beer, Christine,	MID	URNU	U/A	25.08.03
Bellamy, Simon,	LT	URNU	U/A	01.10.97
Benmayor, Dinah Elizabeth,	ASL	NE	PRESIDENT	04.03.04
Benn, Peter Quentin,	LT	MW	PRESIDENT	28.02.98
Bennet, Niall,	ALT	MW	SCOTIA RNR	22.11.04
Bennison, Maria,	MID	URNU	U/A	06.10.05
Bentley, David Scott Arthur,	ASL	NE	FLYING FOX	09.05.00
Bereznyckyj, (Susan Dorothy), Sd	LT CDR	Q	SHERWOOD	31.03.94
Berkowicz, Susie,	CADET	URNU	U/A	24.10.02
Berry, Eleanor,	CADET	URNU	U/A	17.10.02
Berry, Ian, RD	LT CDR	MW	CALLIOPE	31.03.96
Berry, James,	MID	URNU	U/A	05.11.03
Best, Angela Dawn,	ASL	NE	EAGLET	19.11.03
Bewley, Geoffrey, RD	LT CDR	MW	KING ALFRED	31.03.99
Bhanumurthy, Sanapla,	PSURGLCDR		CAMBRIA	03.06.03
Bicknell, Richard Anthony,	LT CDR	MW	KING ALFRED	31.03.01
Biggerstaff, Adam Graham,	LT CDR	HQ	DALRIADA	03.04.85
Biggs, Nigel,	LT	SEA	PRESIDENT	31.07.95
Binstead, Kenneth,	LT	AIR	RNR AIR BR VL	01.02.93
Birch, Megan,	MID	URNU	U/A	16.10.03
Birse, Bronwen Louise,	LT	LOGS	SCOTIA	
Bishop, Jonathon,	MID	URNU	U/A	16.10.03
Bishop, Jonathon,	LT CDR	AIR	RNR AIR BR VL	31.03.96
Bissett, Leigh Robert,	ASL	NE	SCOTIA	25.10.01
Bithell, Ian,	LT CDR	AIR	RNR AIR BR VL	01.10.00
Black, Karen,	MID	URNU	U/A	24.10.01
Black, Simon Mitchell, RD	LT CDR	HQ	SCOTIA	30.06.83
Blackall, Peter,	MID	URNU	U/A	14.10.04
Blackburn, John Adam Francis,	ASL	NE	KING ALFRED	12.06.01
Blackwell, Jason,	LT CDR	AIR	RNR AIR BR VL	16.01.98
Blagden, David,	MID	URNU	U/A	14.10.04
Blatherwick, Gemma,	MID	URNU	U/A	09.10.03
Blee, Kirtsty,	MID	URNU	U/A	01.10.05
Bloom, Michael,	ALT	URNU	U/A	06.12.02
Blyth, Anne Scotland,	SG LTCDR	MEDF	PRESIDENT	14.08.83
Blythe, Wendy Elizabeth,	LT	LOGS	DALRIADA	29.01.96

Name	Rank	Branch	Unit	Seniority
Boak, Philip,	MID	URNU	U/A	07.10.05
Boal, Michael,	LT	MW	CAROLINE	23.02.98
Boarder, Richard,	MID	URNU	U/A	11.07.05
Boardman, Andrew,	MID	URNU	U/A	10.09.01
Boardman, Sarah,	CADET	URNU	U/A	16.10.97
Boey, Xianiie,	MID	URNU	U/A	06.10.05
Bolton, Adam,	ASL	NE	VIVID RNR	24.11.04
Bond, Frances,	MID	URNU	U/A	13.10.05
Bond, Thomas,	ASL	NE	SHERWOOD RNR	28.09.05
Bone, Matthew,	MID	URNU	U/A	11.07.05
Bonham-Smith, Rupert,	MID	URNU	U/A	05.11.98
Booth, Victoria,	MID	URNU	U/A	22.10.03
Boswell, Emily Charlotte,	ASL	NE	WILDFIRE	03.06.03
Boulton, Jeremy Charles,	LT CDR	SM	PRESIDENT	31.03.01
Bovington, Thomas,	MID	URNU	U/A	29.09.05
Bowden, Anthony,	MID	URNU	U/A	07.10.03
Bowen, Michael Leslie,	SG LTCDR		PRESIDENT	30.09.98
Bower, Laura,	MID	URNU	U/A	01.10.03
Bowker, Rebecca,	MID	URNU	U/A	11.10.04
Bowkett, James,	MID	URNU	U/A	20.10.05
Bowler, Thomas,	MID	URNU	U/A	14.10.04
Bowmer, Christopher,	MID	URNU	U/A	05.09.02
Bown, Anthony Mark,	LT CDR	HQ	CAMBRIA	08.03.91
Bown, Carol Diane, BA, RD	LT CDR	HQ	CAMBRIA	31.03.03
Boyd, Edward Russell,	LT CDR	AWNIS	KING ALFRED	31.03.03
Boyd, Keeley,	MID	URNU	U/A	16.10.03
Boyd, Lindsay,	MID	URNU	U/A	07.10.04
Boyle, Abigail Elder,	ASL	NE	FERRET (RNR)	12.12.00
Boyle, Kirk,	LT	DIS	FERRET (RNR)	11.05.96
Brabner, Susan,	LT CDR	DIS	FERRET (RNR)	31.03.94
Bracewell, Anna,	MID	URNU	U/A	09.10.00
Bradburn, James,	MID	URNU	U/A	24.10.00
Bradbury, Louise,	MID	URNU	U/A	29.10.03
Bradbury, Miles,	LT	URNU	U/A	01.06.04
Bradford, Christine Mary Patricia,	ACDR	NCAGS	EAGLET	04.10.02
Bradford, Nigel Stuart,	LT	SM	EAGLET	18.12.87
Bradley, Alan,	ASL	NE	U/A	15.02.06
Bradshaw, James,	MID	URNU	U/A	06.10.05
Braine, David,	LT CDR	AIR	RNR AIR BR VL	31.03.98
Braithwaite, Joanna,	MID	URNU	U/A	16.10.03
Brampton, Susan,	LT	Q	PRESIDENT	08.01.97
Brannighan, David Matthew Thomas,	MID	NE	CALLIOPE	16.02.04
Branyan, Lawrence Ode, RD	LT	HQ	EAGLET	06.09.89
Breyley, Nigel,	LT CDR	AIR	RNR AIR BR VL	31.03.98
Bridges, Lauren,	CADET	URNU	U/A	14.11.02
Bridgman, Megan,	MID	URNU	U/A	01.10.03
Brigden, Kevin,	LT CDR	AIR	RNR AIR BR VL	16.04.92
Briggs, Andrew,	SLT	SM	PRESIDENT RNR	01.03.05
Bright, Jack,	MID	NE	PRESIDENT	27.11.03
Bright, William,	MID	URNU	U/A	07.10.05
Brimacombe, Shaun,	MID	URNU	U/A	29.10.03
Brockie, Alan,	LT	Q	SCOTIA RNR	02.03.01
Broderick, Matthew,	MID	URNU	U/A	30.09.05
Broderick, Samuel,	MID	URNU	U/A	18.10.04
Brogan, Gary Edward,	LT	NCAGS	EAGLET	12.10.02
Brokenshire, Sarah Isobel,	ASL	NE	VIVID	06.02.02
Brooking, Stephen,	LT CDR	AIR	RNR AIR BR VL	11.05.87
Brooks, Alexandra,	ASL	NE	FLYING FOX	03.02.99
Brooks, Richard John,	ASL	NE	PRESIDENT	01.04.04
Brooksbank, Oliver,	MID	URNU	U/A	11.10.05
Brooman, Martin,	LT	AIR	RNR AIR BR VL	16.08.95
Broster, Mark,	LT	AW	U/A	03.05.02

Name	Rank	Branch	Unit	Seniority
Brothwood, Michael,	LT CDR	AIR	RNR AIR BR VL	03.04.99
Brousil, James Joseph,	ASL	NE	SHERWOOD	18.09.03
Brown, Andrew David,	PSURGLCDR		SCOTIA	30.05.02
Brown, Andrew,	LT CDR	AIR	RNR AIR BR VL	01.10.90
Brown, Colin,	LT CDR	AIR	RNR AIR BR VL	30.04.97
Brown, Charles David,	LT	X	U/A	01.10.81
Brown, John Erskine, RD	LT CDR	AWNIS	WILDFIRE	31.03.96
Brown, Oliver,	MID	URNU	U/A	12.10.04
Brown, Rebecca,	MID	URNU	U/A	13.10.04
Brown, Steven,	MID	URNU	U/A	24.09.05
Brown, Timothy,	LT CDR	AIR	RNR AIR BR VL	19.03.93
Brown, Thomas,	LT CDR	AW	VIVID RNR	01.07.00
Browne, Alastair Grant,	ASL	NE	SCOTIA	13.02.03
Browne, Thomas,	MID	URNU	U/A	14.10.99
Browne, Tom,	SLT	URNU	U/A	13.10.04
Browning, James Chapman Corbet,	ASL	NE	PRESIDENT	16.01.02
Brunskill, John,	LT	AIR	RNR AIR BR VL	01.06.91
Bryning, Christopher,	LT CDR	AIR	RNR AIR BR VL	01.03.85
Bubbins, Eleanor,	MID	URNU	U/A	06.10.05
Buchan, John,	LT	OPINT	EAGLET RNR	28.03.00
Buchanan, Craig,	MID	URNU	U/A	06.12.01
Buchanan, Stuart Bruce,	PSG LT		VIVID	16.07.99
Buckley, Jonathan Mark,	LT	MW	CAMBRIA	08.11.97
Bucknell, David Ian,	LT CDR	SEA	FLYING FOX	
Buglass, Rachel,	MID	URNU	U/A	16.10.03
Bulusu, Rita,	MID	URNU	U/A	29.09.05
Bunyan, Hlaire,	MID	URNU	U/A	09.10.03
Burden, Fraser,	LT	AIR	RNR AIR BR VL	01.04.88
Burke, Michelle,	MID	URNU	U/A	04.10.04
Burke, Samuel,	MID	URNU	U/A	08.11.05
Burne, Penelope Jane, RD	CDR	DIS	VIVID	27.06.01
Burstall, James,	ASL	NE	WILDFIRE RNR	24.11.05
Burt, James,	MID	URNU	U/A	14.10.04
Bush, Sarah,	MID	URNU	U/A	12.10.04
Bustin, Nicholas,	MID	URNU	U/A	14.10.04
Butcher, Alexander,	MID	URNU	U/A	29.10.03
Butler, Adam,	MID	URNU	U/A	12.10.04
Butterworth, Sophie,	MID	URNU	U/A	06.10.05

C

Name	Rank	Branch	Unit	Seniority
Cable, Phillip,	LT	MW	PRESIDENT RNR	23.08.05
Cadden, Edward,	ALT	URNU	U/A	01.03.00
Caddock, Matthew,	MID	URNU	U/A	09.10.97
Caddy, Paul,	MID	URNU	U/A	01.10.03
Calhaem, Sarah,	ASL	NE	FORWARD RNR	22.11.05
Cambell-Balcombe, Andre,	LT	URNU	U/A	18.09.03
Cambrook, Laura,	MID	URNU	U/A	14.10.04
Cameron, Anne Louise, RD	LT CDR	NCAGS	KING ALFRED	31.03.01
Cameron, Christopher,	LT	URNU	U/A	01.07.04
Cameron, Iain,	LT CDR	AIR	RNR AIR BR VL	01.09.99
Cameron, James,	LT	H INT	FERRET (RNR)	01.12.99
Cameron, Sam,	MID	URNU	U/A	14.10.03
Cameron, Shaun,	ASL	NE	EAGLET RNR	02.11.05
Campbell, Graham John,	LT	COMM	FORWARD	24.01.97
Campbell, Scott,	MID	URNU	U/A	09.10.03
Canham, Wendy Jacqueline, RD	LT CDR	COMM	SHERWOOD	31.03.98
Cardy, Thomas,	MID	URNU	U/A	17.10.05
Carew, Louise,	MID	URNU	U/A	06.10.05
Carey, Andrew William,	ASL	NE	WILDFIRE	13.06.01
Carlin, Christina,	MID	URNU	U/A	14.10.04
Carnie, Christopher,	MID	URNU	U/A	07.10.05
Carnie, Edward,	MID	URNU	U/A	07.10.05

Name	Rank	Branch	Unit	Seniority
Carpenter, David, RD	LT CDR	MEDIA	U/A	
Carpenter, Philip,	LT	AIR	RNR AIR BR VL	01.02.94
Carr, Amy,	MID	URNU	U/A	08.10.05
Carr, Robert,	LT	AIR	RNR AIR BR VL	13.04.91
Carre, Jane,	LT	URNU	U/A	11.02.05
Carss, George Alexander,	SG CDR		KING ALFRED	30.09.01
Carter, David,	ALT	AW	EAGLET	22.03.99
Carter, Richard,	LT CDR	AIR	RNR AIR BR VL	31.03.03
Cartland, James,	MID	URNU	U/A	14.10.04
Carvalho, Elaine,	ASL	NE	DALRIADA	01.11.02
Carver, Andrew,	LT CDR	AIR	RNR AIR BR VL	31.03.98
Casey, Graham Peter,	LT CDR	DIS	FERRET (RNR)	31.03.00
Casey, Neil,	LT CDR	AIR	RNR AIR BR VL	31.03.00
Caskie, Iain Neil,	LT CDR	SM	SCOTIA	16.05.92
Cass, Geoffrey Philip,	LT CDR	NA	FORWARD	03.06.95
Cassells, Jason Bern Costello,	ASL	NE	CAROLINE	12.04.00
Casson, Hilary Patricia, RD	LT CDR	NCAGS	VIVID	31.03.96
Castle, Stephen,	MID	URNU	U/A	16.10.03
Castleford, Lauren,	MID	URNU	U/A	07.10.04
Caulfield, Lee,	CADET	URNU	U/A	01.10.99
Cavanagh, Sophie,	MID	URNU	U/A	29.09.05
Chakrawertti, Sandeepan,	MID	URNU	U/A	17.10.05
Chalmers, Amalia Lourdes, RD	LT CDR	MWHQ	FERRET (RNR)	31.03.95
Chalmers, Paul,	LT CDR	AIR	RNR AIR BR VL	01.10.99
Chamberlain, Moira,	LT	Q	KING ALFRED	02.06.97
Chambers, Catherine Louise,	SG LT	MEDF	KING ALFRED	16.03.04
Chambers, Joanne,	MID	URNU	U/A	25.08.03
Chan-A-Sue, Stephen,	LT CDR	AIR	RNR AIR BR VL	15.04.02
Chapman, Anthony,	LT CDR	MW	PRESIDENT	31.03.03
Charles, Emma,	MID	URNU	U/A	14.10.04
Charlton, Noel,	LT	NCAGS	KING ALFRED	
Chauvelin, David Coulson Wyllie,	LT	MW	SCOTIA	26.11.98
Cheetham, Ian,	ASL	NE	WILDFIRE RNR	10.11.03
Chetwynd, Alan,	MID	URNU	U/A	14.10.04
Cheyne, Steven,	CDR	AIR	RNR AIR BR VL	15.05.04
Christian-Edward, Julia,	MID	URNU	U/A	14.10.03
Church, Elizabeth Ann, RD	LT	SM	PRESIDENT	16.11.88
Churchley, Richard,	LT CDR	AIR	RNR AIR BR VL	31.03.97
Clareboets, Steven,	MID	URNU	U/A	22.10.03
Claricoats, James,	MID	URNU	U/A	14.10.04
Claridge, Sarah,	MID	URNU	U/A	04.10.04
Clark, Alison,	ASL	NE	PRESIDENT RNR	24.11.05
Clark, Eleanor,	MID	URNU	U/A	13.10.05
Clark, Suzanne,	LT CDR	AIR	RNR AIR BR VL	31.03.97
Clark, Thomas,	MID	URNU	U/A	11.10.04
Clarke, Danielle,	MID	URNU	U/A	16.10.03
Clarke, Henry Edmund Alexander,	ASL	NE	FLYING FOX	11.10.02
Clarke, Kathryn Jane,	ASL	NE	EAGLET	18.09.03
Clarke, Peter,	LT CDR	AIR	RNR AIR BR VL	01.10.90
Clarke, Rory,	MID	URNU	U/A	11.07.05
Clarke, Roger Derek, RD	LT CDR	NCAGS	VIVID	31.03.96
Clarke, William Stephen, RD	LT CDR	MWHQ	CAROLINE	31.03.00
Clarkson, David,	MID	URNU	U/A	13.10.04
Clayton, Steven,	LT CDR	AIR	RNR AIR BR VL	01.07.96
Cleary, Deidre, RD	LT CDR	MEDIA	PRESIDENT	31.03.99
Cleaver, Ian,	MID	URNU	U/A	20.10.04
Cleeve, Felicity Sarah,	ASL	NE	FORWARD	30.01.02
Clews, Harriet Christine,	ASL	NE	WILDFIRE	03.10.02
Cliffe, Daniela Maria,	LT	Q	VIVID	18.05.01
Clifford, Martin,	LT CDR	AIR	RNR AIR BR VL	09.05.98
Clissold, Patrick,	MID	URNU	U/A	25.08.03
Coatsworth, Robert,	MID	URNU	U/A	03.10.02

Name	Rank	Branch	Unit	Seniority
Cobbold, Andrew Reginald,	LT CDR	DIS	FERRET (RNR)	31.03.03
Cockburn, Frank,	LT CDR	MS(M)	CALLIOPE	
Cockeram, Chris,	MID	NCAGS	U/A	16.10.03
Cocks, Steven,	ASL	NE	U/A	07.06.05
Cocksworth, Ben,	MID	URNU	U/A	20.10.04
Cody, William Jonathan Kinsborough,	LT CDR	DIS	FERRET (RNR)	01.07.97
Coe, Morgan,	ASL	NE	PRESIDENT	02.06.99
Cohen, James Seymour Lionel, BSC, RD	LT CDR	NCAGS	PRESIDENT	31.03.97
Coldham, David,	MID	URNU	U/A	21.10.99
Coley, Simon John,	LT CDR	MEDIA	KING ALFRED	
Collier, David John,	ASL	NE	FLYING FOX	20.10.03
Collins, David,	SLT	URNU	U/A	08.12.05
Collins, Steven, RD	CDR	AW	FORWARD	30.09.01
Collis, Andrew,	MID	URNU	U/A	13.10.05
Colton, Ian, RD	LT CDR	AIR	RNR AIR BR VL	22.11.92
Colyer, Michael,	LT	SEA	FORWARD	22.06.94
Condy, Sallie Louise,	LT CDR	DIS	FERRET (RNR)	31.03.02
Connell, John,	LT CDR	AIR	RNR AIR BR VL	01.10.91
Considine, Pierre,	MID	URNU	U/A	18.10.04
Constable, Thomas,	MID	URNU	U/A	13.10.05
Constant, David,	LT CDR	AIR	RNR AIR BR VL	31.03.02
Conway, James,	MID	URNU	U/A	11.10.05
Conway, Keith Alexander,	LT CDR	MWHQ	SCOTIA	31.03.99
Cook, Helen Jane,	ASL	NE	CALLIOPE	02.09.02
Cook, Simon Hugh Home,	LT	MW	PRESIDENT	31.03.98
Cook, William John,	LT CDR	AW	SCOTIA	01.03.85
Cooke, Holly,	MID	URNU	U/A	10.10.05
Coombes, Kirsty,	CADET	URNU	U/A	28.06.99
Cooney, Graham,	MID	URNU	U/A	10.10.02
Cooper, David John,	LT CDR	HQ	PRESIDENT	31.03.99
Cooper, Eiran,	MID	URNU	U/A	07.10.04
Cooper, Juan,	MID	URNU	U/A	29.10.03
Cooper, Katheryn,	MID	URNU	U/A	14.10.04
Cooper, Susan, BSC	LT CDR	HQ	PRESIDENT	31.03.01
Copeland-Davis, Terence,	LT CDR	AIR	RNR AIR BR VL	31.03.03
Copleston, Charlotte,	MID	URNU	U/A	08.11.01
Corbett, Jennifer,	MID	URNU	U/A	10.10.05
Corbett, Paul,	LT	AIR	RNR AIR BR VL	01.10.02
Corden, Adam,	MID	URNU	U/A	26.10.05
Cornes, John,	LT	URNU	U/A	01.01.92
Corrigan, Nicholas Timothy,	ASL	NE	SHERWOOD	17.01.04
Corson, Robert John,	SG LTCDR		CALLIOPE	13.10.98
Cory-Wright, Christopher,	MID	URNU	U/A	26.10.05
Cottam, Simon Roscoe,	LT CDR	AWNIS	FLYING FOX	31.03.97
Cottey, Laura,	MID	URNU	U/A	13.10.05
Cottingham, Neil,	LT CDR	AIR	RNR AIR BR VL	01.10.98
Cotton, Matthew,	MID	URNU	U/A	29.10.03
Coupland, Mark,	LT	AIR	RNR AIR BR VL	01.03.89
Courtney, Kurt David,	SLT	NA	CAROLINE	14.04.99
Cowan, (Andrew Stuart), As	LT CDR	MWHQ	DALRIADA	31.03.97
Coward, Suzanne,	MID	URNU	U/A	14.10.04
Cox, Craig,	MID	URNU	U/A	01.10.03
Cox, Hugh Jeremy,	SG CDR		KING ALFRED	30.05.94
Cox, Matthew,	ASL	NE	VIVID	20.05.02
Cox, Rhoderick,	LT CDR	AIR	RNR AIR BR VL	01.12.88
Cox, Timothy,	ASL	NE	CNH(R)	20.01.05
Coyle, Mark Francis,	LT	SEA	CALLIOPE	14.09.01
Coyne, John,	LT	AIR	RNR AIR BR VL	17.12.93
Craig, Caroline Alexandra,	ASL	NE	PRESIDENT	08.02.00
Cramp, Louise,	MID	URNU	U/A	04.10.04
Crane, Matthew,	MID	URNU	U/A	17.10.05
Crawford, Andrew John, RD	CDR	AW	VIVID	30.09.01

Name	Rank	Branch	Unit	Seniority
Crees, David,	LT CDR	NA	U/A	01.01.05
Creighton, Robert,	MID	URNU	U/A	29.09.05
Crewick, Joseph,	MID	URNU	U/A	13.10.04
Cribley, Michael,	LT CDR	AIR	RNR AIR BR VL	01.10.91
Crickmar, Kieran,	MID	URNU	U/A	18.10.04
Critchlow, Angela,	MID	URNU	U/A	13.10.05
Crockett, Victor Andrew, RD	LT CDR	DIS	FERRET (RNR)	31.03.95
Crombie, Nicholas,	LT	AIR	RNR AIR BR VL	01.02.93
Crone, David James Edward, RD	ACDR	MWHQ	CAROLINE	02.07.99
Cronk, Joanna,	MID	URNU	U/A	25.08.03
Crook, Richard,	MID	URNU	U/A	05.09.02
Crookston, Neil,	MID	URNU	U/A	05.11.03
Crossley, Megan,	MID	URNU	U/A	07.10.04
Crossley, Samuel Neil Thomas,	ASL	NE	PRESIDENT	07.01.99
Cruickshanks, Charlie,	MID	URNU	U/A	26.10.05
Crump, Peter Charles, RD*	CDR	AW	KING ALFRED	30.09.97
Cuff, Samuel,	MID	URNU	U/A	25.08.03
Cundy, Abigail,	MID	URNU	U/A	11.10.05
Currie, Katherine,	CADET	URNU	U/A	15.10.97
Curris, Stephen,	MID	URNU	U/A	14.10.04
Curtis, Roger Stafford,	LT	SEA	SCOTIA	

D

Name	Rank	Branch	Unit	Seniority
Dace, Katherine Elizabeth, RD	LT CDR	DIS	FERRET (RNR)	31.03.95
Dady, Simon James,	ASL	NE	PRESIDENT	29.09.98
Dalby, Russell,	ASL	NE	SHERWOOD	06.11.02
Dalgliesh, Chrstopher,	MID	URNU	U/A	24.10.01
Dalrymple, James,	MID	URNU	U/A	13.10.04
Dalton, Ebony,	ASL	NE	FORWARD RNR	06.09.05
Dalton, (Neil Jarvis), N	ASL	NE	PRESIDENT	02.10.89
Daly, Karen Lesley,	ALT CDR	NCAGS	KING ALFRED	
Daly, Paul, RD,	LT CDR	AIR	RNR AIR BR VL	31.03.95
Daly, Shane,	MID	URNU	U/A	13.10.05
Dalziel, Simon,	LT CDR	MEDIA	KING ALFRED	
Dann, Adrian Stuart,	LT CDR	MCDO	U/A	
Dark, Helen Wright, H, W, WELDON	LT	HQ	DALRIADA	16.03.89
Darville, Makeba,	MID	URNU	U/A	06.10.05
Dashfield, Adrian Kenneth,	SG CDR		VIVID	30.06.00
Davies, George,	LT CDR	AIR	RNR AIR BR VL	31.03.03
Davies, Jennifer,	CADET	URNU	U/A	24.10.01
Davies, Julia,	MID	URNU	U/A	11.10.05
Davies, Nicola,	ASL	NE	KING ALFRED	07.01.00
Davies, Richard Myall,	LT	MW	PRESIDENT	17.09.03
Davies, Sarah Elizabeth,	LT	AWNIS	PRESIDENT	19.02.99
Davies, Sarah,	MID	URNU	U/A	06.10.05
Davies, Simon Lovat,	LT	MW	KING ALFRED	15.09.95
Davies, Timoths,	MID	URNU	U/A	22.10.03
Davies, William,	SLT	URNU	U/A	31.07.95
Davis, Andrew,	LT CDR	AIR	RNR AIR BR VL	02.10.94
Davis, Bryan,			EAGLET	
Davis, Mark,	MID	URNU	U/A	05.09.02
Dawson, Chloe,	MID	URNU	U/A	14.10.04
Day, Henry Ralph Benet,	ASL	NE	PRESIDENT	22.01.02
De Burgh, Hugo,	MID	URNU	U/A	11.10.05
De Castro, Tracy,	MID	URNU	U/A	07.10.04
De La Rue, Michael,	MID	URNU	U/A	17.10.05
Deacon, James,	MID	URNU	U/A	24.10.02
Dean, Georgina,	ASL	URNU	U/A	30.10.01
Dean, Nicola,	ALT	MEDF	EAGLET	22.06.01
Deboys, Leighanne,	MID	URNU	U/A	08.10.05
Deeney, Stephen,	LT CDR	AIR	RNR AIR BR VL	01.10.99
Deighton, Alistair,	LT	URNU	PPPA(C)-RESERVES	01.06.00

Name	Rank	Branch	Unit	Seniority
Deighton, Graeme,	SLT	LOGS	CALLIOPE RNR	29.09.04
Dembrey, Mark,	LT	AIR	RNR AIR BR VL	16.12.94
Denison-Davies, Edward,	MID	URNU	U/A	12.10.99
Dent, John George,	ASL	NE	SCOTIA	15.07.03
Denton, Stacey,	MID	URNU	U/A	16.10.03
Dibb-Dimkin, James,	MID	URNU	U/A	06.10.05
Dickens, Charles,	SLT	CIS	FORWARD RNR	02.11.04
Dickin, Arnie,	MID	URNU	U/A	11.10.01
Dickinson, Dorothy Emily,	ALT	Q	CALLIOPE	06.06.00
Dickson, Hannah,	MID	URNU	U/A	17.10.05
Dietz, Laura,	MID	URNU	U/A	25.08.03
Diment, Stephanie,	MID	URNU	U/A	06.10.05
Dinsmore, Simon,	MID	URNU	U/A	01.02.01
Dismore, Oliver,	ACAPT	AIR	RNR AIR BR VL	15.01.05
Ditton, Nathan John,	ASL	NE	KING ALFRED	29.01.02
Dixon, Kate,	MID	URNU	U/A	06.10.05
Dixon, Michael,	MID	URNU	U/A	16.10.03
Doar, Christopher,	MID	URNU	U/A	06.10.05
Dobson, Christopher,	MID	URNU	U/A	01.10.03
Docherty, Zoe,	MID	URNU	U/A	26.10.05
Donaldson, John Richard,	LT CDR	DIS	FERRET (RNR)	12.08.94
Donnelly, Adam,	ASL	H INT	FERRET (RNR)	14.02.05
Donnelly, Matthew,	MID	URNU	U/A	06.10.05
Donohue, Paul John,	ASL	NE	KING ALFRED	10.12.03
Dorman, Nicholas Roger Vause,	LT CDR	MWHQ	SCOTIA	31.03.97
Douglas, Benedict,	MID	URNU	U/A	17.10.02
Douthwaite, Lisa,	SLT	Q	SHERWOOD	13.11.97
Downie, Anne Louise, RD	LT	SEA	SCOTIA	01.12.95
Downie, James,	MID	URNU	U/A	08.10.05
Downing, Carl,	LT CDR	AIR	RNR AIR BR VL	16.11.92
Downing, James,	MID	URNU	U/A	16.10.03
Downing, Neil Edmond,	LT CDR	MW	CAROLINE	31.03.00
Downing, Rebecca,	MID	URNU	U/A	28.10.00
Doyle, Allan,	MID	URNU	U/A	08.10.05
Drake, Peter,	MID	URNU	U/A	20.10.05
Drake, Roderick Allan, RD	LT CDR	NCAGS	FLYING FOX	31.03.98
Drewett, Brian,	SLT	URNU	U/A	17.06.02
Driscoll, Claire,	ASL	NE	CAMBRIA	19.07.02
Drummond, Andrew,	SG LT		EAGLET	07.06.03
Dudill, Louise,	ASL	NE	SHERWOOD	27.09.00
Dudley, Edward,	MID	URNU	U/A	29.09.05
Duerden, Thomas,	MID	URNU	U/A	18.10.02
Duff, Heather Janine Rosemarie,	SLT	MW	SCOTIA	03.08.96
Duff, Joseph,	MID	URNU	U/A	17.10.05
Duff, Jennifer,	MID	URNU	U/A	07.10.04
Duffus, Philippa,	MID	URNU	U/A	14.10.04
Duffy, Patrick,	MID	URNU	U/A	07.10.04
Duggua, Rodney, RD	LT CDR	COMM	KING ALFRED	31.03.93
Dunbar, Ross,	MID	URNU	U/A	23.09.02
Duncan, Barbara Mary,	LT	AWNIS	EAGLET	31.03.92
Duncan, Keith Julian, RD	LT CDR	AW	EAGLET	31.03.94
Dunn, Edward,	MID	URNU	U/A	09.10.02
Dunn, Josephine,	LT	NCAGS	U/A	10.11.03
Dunn, Karl,	MID	URNU	U/A	14.10.04
Dunne, Lawrence John,	LT CDR	SEA	FORWARD	31.03.04
Durbin, Stephen,	MID	URNU	U/A	04.10.04
Duthie, Charles Euan,	ASL	NE	SCOTIA	25.06.03
Duthie, David James Ralph,	SG CDR		SHERWOOD	30.09.00
Duthie, Ruth Mary Mitchell,	LT	AWNIS	KING ALFRED	16.04.94

E

| Eagles, Susan, | CDR | MEDIA | FLYING FOX | 30.09.95 |

Name	Rank	Branch	Unit	Seniority
Eaglesham, Phillip,	ASL	NE	CAROLINE	16.01.02
Earl, Nicholas,	LT CDR	AIR	RNR AIR BR VL	31.03.04
East, John Howard,	ASL	NE	DALRIADA	10.10.02
Eastaugh, Timothy,	LT CDR	AIR	RNR AIR BR VL	30.06.02
Eastham, Allan Michael, BSC, RD	LT CDR	NCAGS	SHERWOOD	31.03.94
Edwards, Craig,	MID	URNU	U/A	21.10.03
Edwards, Elizabeth,	MID	URNU	U/A	06.10.05
Edwards, Michael Steven De La Warr,	PSURGLCDR		SHERWOOD	07.09.99
Edwards, Nathan,	MID	URNU	U/A	22.09.04
Edwards, Pamela,	MID	URNU	U/A	14.10.04
Eggett, Louise,	CADET	URNU	U/A	18.10.02
El Basha, John,	MID	URNU	U/A	10.07.04
Elby, Tristan,	MID	URNU	U/A	06.10.05
Eldridge, James,	MID	URNU	U/A	10.09.01
Elliott, Robin,	LT CDR	AIR	RNR AIR BR VL	01.04.97
Ellis, Christopher,	MID	URNU	U/A	05.10.04
Ellis, Richard Alwyn, Lt	LT	HQ	PRESIDENT	18.08.90
Ellis, Simon Christopher,	PSG SLT		SCOTIA	19.03.02
Ellison-Lomax, Jodie,	MID	URNU	U/A	08.10.03
Ellison-Smith, Stephen,	MID	URNU	U/A	20.10.05
Emanuel, Josse,	MID	URNU	U/A	16.10.03
England, Robert,	LT	Q	KING ALFRED	30.08.96
Errington, Laura,	MID	URNU	U/A	22.10.03
Esfahani, Shahrokh, RD	LT CDR	HQ	WILDFIRE	31.03.02
Esmonde, Sean,	MID	URNU	U/A	10.10.05
Evans, Ann, RD	LT CDR	DIS	FORWARD	31.03.94
Evans, Alex,	LT CDR	AIR	RNR AIR BR VL	31.03.99
Evans, Carol,	LT	MEDIA	FLYING FOX	12.01.92
Evans, Catherine,	MID	URNU	U/A	13.10.03
Evans, Louisa,	MID	URNU	U/A	09.10.00
Evans, Michael,	LT CDR	AIR	RNR AIR BR VL	17.05.88
Everatt, Ruth,	MID	URNU	U/A	14.10.04
Everest, Becky,	MID	URNU	U/A	07.10.03
Eves, Daniel,	MID	URNU	U/A	15.10.03
Ewen, Joseph,	MID	URNU	U/A	06.10.05

F

Name	Rank	Branch	Unit	Seniority
Fagan, Louise,	MID	URNU	U/A	22.10.03
Fairbairn, Oliver,	MID	URNU	U/A	11.10.05
Fairclough, Simon,	ASL	NE	CAMBRIA RNR	03.08.05
Falconer, Alistair James,	LT	MEDIA	KING ALFRED	
Farmer, Gary, RD	LT	HQ	SCOTIA	28.06.92
Farrall, Keith,	MID	URNU	U/A	26.11.03
Faull, Caroline,	MID	URNU	U/A	07.10.03
Fearnley, David George, B.ED, RD*	LT CDR	MW	EAGLET	31.03.89
Fearon, John,	ASL	NE	EAGLET	12.07.99
Fedorowicz, Richard,	LT CDR	AIR	RNR AIR BR VL	16.10.00
Fell, James,	MID	URNU	U/A	17.10.05
Ferens, Samantha,	CADET	URNU	U/A	18.10.00
Ferguson, Alistair,	ASL	URNU	U/A	17.10.05
Ferguson, Adam,	MID	URNU	U/A	11.10.04
Ferguson, Jonathan,	MID	URNU	U/A	14.10.04
Ferguson, Nicholas Alistair Malcolm,	LT CDR	HQ	VIVID	31.03.99
Fidler, Steven,	MID	URNU	U/A	16.10.03
Filochowski, Kate,	CADET	URNU	U/A	18.10.02
Filtness, Rosemary Jane, RD	LT CDR	DIS	FERRET (RNR)	31.03.93
Finch, Christopher,	MID	URNU	U/A	20.10.04
Findlay, Ronald,	ASL	NE	WILDFIRE RNR	19.12.05
Finn, Katherine,	MID	URNU	U/A	06.10.05
Finn, Mark,	LT CDR	NA	U/A	01.01.05
Fisher, Florence,	MID	URNU	U/A	06.10.05
Fisher, Simon,	MID	URNU	U/A	25.10.01

Name	Rank	Branch	Unit	Seniority
Fitchsampson, Steven R,	LT	SEA	FLYING FOX	18.10.02
Fittes, Mark,	MID	URNU	U/A	10.09.01
Fitton, Daniel,	MID	URNU	U/A	07.10.05
Fitzgerald, Elizabeth Jane,	ASL	NE	WILDFIRE	03.06.03
Fitzgerald, Nicholas,	LT	AIR	RNR AIR BR VL	01.12.92
Flack, Melissa,	MID	URNU	U/A	13.10.05
Flanagan, Martin,	LT CDR	AIR	RNR AIR BR VL	01.02.92
Fleming, Samuel Andrew,	LT CDR	HQ	KING ALFRED	31.03.02
Fletcher, Catriona Rose,	ASL	NE	CALLIOPE	29.04.04
Fletcher, Richard Paul,	LT	COMM	EAGLET	31.03.04
Flint, Chris,	MID	URNU	U/A	17.11.05
Flint, Grahame,	MID	URNU	U/A	18.10.01
Flintoff, Susan Ellen,	ASL	NE	DALRIADA	24.11.99
Flynn, Ingrid,	MID	URNU	U/A	06.10.05
Flynn, Nicola Jane,	LT	MEDIA	VIVID	06.12.01
Flynn, Stephen Andrew,	ASL	NE	CALLIOPE	21.05.02
Fontaine, Barney,	MID	URNU	U/A	07.10.03
Ford, Katy,	MID	URNU	U/A	07.10.04
Ford, Suzanne,	CADET	URNU	U/A	10.09.01
Foreman, Kerry,	MID	URNU	U/A	29.09.05
Foreman, Louisa,	MID	URNU	U/A	23.02.05
Foreman, Timothy,	LT CDR	AIR	RNR AIR BR VL	31.03.03
Forrester, Michael,	MID	URNU	U/A	18.10.04
Forsey, Daniel,	MID	URNU	U/A	06.10.05
Forsyth, Adam,	MID	URNU	U/A	05.09.02
Fortey, Melissa,	ASL	URNU	U/A	19.10.05
Foster, James,	ASL	URNU	U/A	12.10.04
Foster, Nicholas,	ASL	NE	CALLIOPE RNR	27.05.05
Foster, Stephen Edward, RD	CDR	NCAGS	FORWARD	03.06.97
Fouracre, Andrew Mark George,	ASL	NE	CAMBRIA	22.09.99
Fox, Samantha,	MID	URNU	U/A	14.10.04
Frampton, Charles,	MID	URNU	U/A	13.10.05
Francis, Garry,	ASL	NE	WILDFIRE RNR	15.02.06
Frim, Chaslav,	MID	URNU	U/A	14.10.03
Frodin, David,	ASL	AW	WILDFIRE RNR	18.03.05
Frost, Robert,	MID	URNU	U/A	11.10.05
Fry, Christopher Wesley,	LT	HQ	FORWARD	28.07.95
Fry, Stephen Michael,	LT	NCAGS	CAMBRIA	15.06.95
Fulford, Mark,	LT CDR	AIR	RNR AIR BR VL	01.01.96
Funnell, Lee,	MID	URNU	U/A	14.10.04
Furse, Michael,	SLT	AW	U/A	15.02.05

G

Name	Rank	Branch	Unit	Seniority
Gaffney, Francis Eugene David,	ASL	NE	VIVID	16.06.04
Galley, Anna,	MID	URNU	U/A	07.10.03
Gammon, Bernard,	MID	URNU	U/A	20.10.05
Gammon, Jenny,	MID	URNU	U/A	29.09.05
Gandhi, Sophia,	MID	URNU	U/A	16.10.03
Gardiner, George, RD	SG LTCDR		CAROLINE	31.03.97
Gardner, Helen,	MID	URNU	U/A	16.10.03
Garrett-Jones, John,	MID	URNU	U/A	12.10.04
Garton, Hazelle,	MID	URNU	U/A	03.10.05
Gaskin, Matthew,	MID	URNU	U/A	13.10.03
Gatenby, Christopher David,	LT	AW	EAGLET	
Gatland, David,	MID	URNU	U/A	07.10.04
Gaunt, Emma,	MID	URNU	U/A	06.10.05
Gausden, Christine, RD	LT CDR	SM	PRESIDENT	31.03.00
Gavey, Stephen John, RD	LT CDR	HQ	VIVID	01.08.88
Gayle, Matthew,	MID	URNU	U/A	13.10.05
Geary, Michael,	LT CDR	AIR	RNR AIR BR VL	31.03.05
Gee, Michael,	ASL	NE	EAGLET	18.07.00
Gemmell, Philip,	MID	URNU	U/A	14.10.04

Name	Rank	Branch	Unit	Seniority
Georgeson, Ian, RD	LT CDR	AIR	RNR AIR BR VL	01.06.91
Gerrard, Richard,	MID	URNU	U/A	06.10.05
Ghost, Richard Lyell,	ASL	NE	EAGLET	23.07.03
Gibb, Peter,	LT CDR	AIR	RNR AIR BR VL	31.03.93
Giblett, James Anthony,	ASL	NE	VIVID	10.10.02
Gibson, Alice,	SLT	URNU	U/A	10.11.05
Gibson, Stephen,	LT CDR	AIR	RNR AIR BR VL	31.03.94
Gilbert, Antony,	ASL	NE	FLYING FOX RNR	07.10.04
Gilbertson, Cheryl Jane,	ASL	NE	SCOTIA	16.07.02
Gillet, Edward,	MID	URNU	U/A	11.10.04
Gillman, Jennifer,	MID	URNU	U/A	14.10.03
Gladston, Stephen,	LT	AIR	RNR AIR BR VL	01.04.99
Glanville, David,	MID	URNU	U/A	10.10.05
Gleave, Anthony,	SLT	URNU	U/A	09.11.05
Gleave, James, RD	LT CDR	COMM	DALRIADA	31.03.04
Glover, David,	MID	URNU	U/A	06.11.97
Glover, Martyn Richard Timothy, MARD	LT CDR	NCAGS	PRESIDENT	31.03.01
Gobey, Christopher,	LT CDR	SM	SCOTIA RNR	01.10.95
Gobey, Richard John Allen,	ASL	NE	FLYING FOX	03.06.04
Goldthorpe, Sally Louise,	LT CDR	MEDIA	PRESIDENT	31.03.95
Goode, Wendy,	LT	URNU	U/A	01.02.00
Goodes, Simon Newbury, RD	LT CDR	NCAGS	WILDFIRE	31.03.97
Goodwin, Jade,	CADET	URNU	U/A	17.10.02
Goodwin, Timothy,	MID	URNU	U/A	08.10.05
Goram, Malcolm,	LT	AIR	RNR AIR BR VL	05.05.87
Gorrod, Richard George,	PSURGLCDR		PRESIDENT	28.09.00
Gosnell, Thomas,	MID	URNU	U/A	11.10.05
Gould, Andrew Edward,	CDR	LOGS	SCOTIA	30.09.97
Gouldson, Elizabeth J,	ASL	NE	FLYING FOX	15.03.00
Grace, Jonathan,	LT CDR	AIR	RNR AIR BR VL	31.03.00
Graham, (Adrian William), A	LT CDR	DIS	FERRET (RNR)	19.02.89
Graham, Richard,	SLT	URNU	U/A	01.10.95
Grainger, Darren,	MID	URNU	U/A	18.10.04
Grainger, Julia Catherine Ishbel,	SLT	NCAGS	EAGLET	05.04.99
Grainger, Serena Jane,	ASL	NE	VIVID	01.05.01
Grant, Andrew,	MID	URNU	U/A	06.10.05
Grantham, Jonathan,	MID	URNU	U/A	07.10.05
Gray, Andrew Crispian,	LT CDR	AW	PRESIDENT	31.03.99
Gray, John,	MID	URNU	U/A	16.10.03
Gray, James,	MID	URNU	U/A	13.10.05
Greaves, Christopher,	LT CDR	AIR	RNR AIR BR VL	01.10.95
Greaves, Jeremy Justin,	LT	MEDIA	FLYING FOX	
Greaves, Michael,	MID	URNU	U/A	25.08.03
Greaves, Michael,	LT CDR	AIR	RNR AIR BR VL	01.04.94
Greenacre, Richard Paul, RD	LT CDR	AWNIS	VIVID	31.03.97
Greenaway, Ben,	MID	URNU	U/A	20.10.05
Greene, Alistair Michael Iyan,	SLT	NCAGS	PRESIDENT	13.04.99
Greenwood, Elizabeth Jane,	LT CDR	MEDIA	PRESIDENT	31.03.99
Greenwood, Jeanette,	LT	LOGS	EAGLET	30.03.01
Greenwood, Justine,	MID	URNU	U/A	26.10.05
Greenwood, Lauren,	MID	URNU	U/A	07.10.04
Greenwood, Oliver,	MID	URNU	U/A	03.11.03
Greenwood, Robert,	MID	URNU	U/A	29.09.05
Gregg, Martin,	MID	URNU	U/A	18.07.04
Grierson, Andrew,	ASL	URNU	U/A	29.10.99
Griffin, Danielle Louise,	ASL	NE	KING ALFRED	14.01.03
Griffith, Peter,	MID	URNU	U/A	14.10.04
Griffiths, Emily,	CADET	URNU	U/A	24.10.02
Griffiths, Gareth,	LT	URNU	U/A	01.10.98
Griffiths, Lindsay,	CADET	URNU	U/A	24.10.02
Griffiths, Linnett,	MID	URNU	U/A	10.10.05
Griffiths, Michael Edward, BSC, RD	LT CDR	SM	CAMBRIA	31.03.02

Name	Rank	Branch	Unit	Seniority
Grimes, Keith, ...MID	URNU	U/A	23.10.03
Grimes, Mathew, ...SLT	URNU	U/A	27.06.03
Grist, David Francis Neil, ...LT	MS(M)	KING ALFRED	05.07.00
Guckian, Paul, ...MID	URNU	U/A	14.10.04
Guest, Ryan, ...MID	URNU	U/A	06.10.05
Guild, Ian, ...MID	URNU	U/A	16.01.01
Guild, Malcolm, ...SG LTCDR		SCOTIA	12.07.87
Gunn, Debra Ann, RD ....LT CDR	HQ	SCOTIA	31.03.94
Gunson, Edward, ...MID	URNU	U/A	07.10.04
Gwilliam, Simon, ...MID	URNU	U/A	14.10.04

H

Name	Rank	Branch	Unit	Seniority
Habergham, Stacey, ...ASL	NE	EAGLET RNR	22.11.05
Hadnett, Edmund Robert, ...LT CDR	AW	PRESIDENT	29.01.93
Haffenden, Simon, BSC, MIEE, C.ENG..LT	SM	FLYING FOX	26.04.96
Haikin, Peter Harry, BSC ....LT	DIS	FERRET (RNR)	02.02.96
Halblander-Smyth, Craig James Michael, HALBLANDER, BA, LLB, ...LT	MW	KING ALFRED	06.05.94
Hale, Amanda Diane, ...ASL	NE	KING ALFRED	06.03.03
Hall, Howard, ...MID	URNU	U/A	13.10.05
Hall, Jessica, ...MID	URNU	U/A	14.10.04
Hall, Neil, ...LT CDR	INFOP	U/A	01.03.93
Hall, Stephen Scott, ...ASL	NE	FERRET (RNR)	16.04.02
Hamblin, James, ...ASL	NE	PRESIDENT RNR	23.12.05
Hamilton, Andrew Robert, ...SG LTCDR		SCOTIA	01.08.86
Hamilton, Ivan, ...LT	AIR	RNR AIR BR VL	16.11.91
Hamilton, Neil David, ...ASL	NE	PRESIDENT	21.01.03
Hamilton, Ronald, RD..LT	LOGS	DALRIADA	14.10.95
Hamilton, Richard, ...ASL	NE	PRESIDENT RNR	02.11.05
Hamilton, Seonaid, ...MID	URNU	U/A	06.10.05
Hamlet, Max, ...MID	URNU	U/A	05.09.02
Hammett, Simon, ...MID	URNU	U/A	08.10.03
Hancock, Angela Margaret, ...LT CDR	MEDIA	VIVID	31.03.00
Hancock, Kim, ...MID	URNU	U/A	08.10.03
Handley, Dane, ...LT CDR	AIR	RNR AIR BR VL	31.03.96
Hankey, Mark, RD ....LT	SEA	PRESIDENT	31.07.95
Hannah, Andrew, ...MID	URNU	U/A	16.10.03
Hanrahan, Martin, ...LT CDR	AIR	RNR AIR BR VL	01.06.01
Hanratty, Shaun, ...MID	URNU	U/A	14.10.04
Harding, David, ...MID	URNU	U/A	12.10.00
Harding, James Alexander, ...ASL	NE	PRESIDENT	16.03.04
Hardinge, Christopher Harry, MBE..LT CDR	SM	KING ALFRED	31.03.98
Hardman, Andrew, ...MID	URNU	U/A	14.10.03
Hardman, Micheal, ...MID	URNU	U/A	29.09.05
Hare, Timothy, ...MID	URNU	U/A	04.10.04
Hargreaves, Simon, ...CDR	AIR	RNR AIR BR VL	01.07.02
Harkin, James Paul, ...ASL	NE	SCOTIA	05.02.02
Harmon, Anna, ...MID	URNU	U/A	13.10.05
Harper, Alexander, ...ASL	NE	PRESIDENT RNR	06.12.05
Harper, Robert Simon, RD ....LT	HQ	CAROLINE	27.01.95
Harper, Stephen, ...MID	URNU	U/A	11.10.01
Harris, Adrian, ...LT	SM	WILDFIRE	30.07.95
Harris, Adam, ...MID	URNU	U/A	11.10.05
Harris, Joanna, ...MID	URNU	U/A	07.10.03
Harris, Martyn, ...MID	URNU	U/A	13.10.05
Harris, Raymond Leo, RD..LT CDR	ME	U/A	23.10.80
Harrison, Laura, ...ASL	NE	WILDFIRE RNR	07.07.05
Harrison, Mark Alasdair Timothy, ...ASL	NE	WILDFIRE	12.04.00
Harrison, Peter, ...LT CDR	SEA	KING ALFRED	30.05.90
Harrison, Richard William, ...SG LTCDR		SHERWOOD	30.09.96
Hart, Daniel, ...MID	URNU	U/A	25.08.03
Hart, Keith, RD..CDR	AWNIS	WILDFIRE	30.09.01
Hart, Sarah, ...MID	URNU	U/A	07.10.04

Name	Rank	Branch	Unit	Seniority
Hartley, Ann, RD	LT CDR	DIS	FERRET (RNR)	30.09.87
Hartley, David,	CDR	SM	WILDFIRE	30.09.02
Hartley, Philip Terence,	LT CDR	DIS	FERRET (RNR)	16.12.88
Hartley, Sheila Ann, RD	LT	HQ	VIVID	20.01.89
Haslett, Matthew,	MID	URNU	U/A	12.10.04
Hassan, Ramin,	MID	URNU	U/A	22.01.04
Hathorn, Andrew,	MID	URNU	U/A	20.10.04
Hawes, Alison Linda,	LT CDR	MEDIA	VIVID	31.03.98
Hawker, Charles,	MID	URNU	U/A	12.10.04
Hawkins, Duncan,	LT	URNU	U/A	01.03.03
Hawkins, John David,	LT	AW	KING ALFRED	
Hawksley, Alex,	MID	URNU	U/A	20.10.00
Hawksworth, Jamie,	MID	URNU	U/A	07.10.04
Hawley, James,	MID	URNU	U/A	26.10.05
Hawley, Victoria,	MID	URNU	U/A	14.10.04
Hawthorne, Gillian Louise,	LT	Q	CAROLINE	26.07.03
Hay, Sharlene,	MID	URNU	U/A	14.10.04
Hayes, Anthony,	MID	URNU	U/A	13.10.05
Hayes, Jennifer,	MID	URNU	U/A	16.10.03
Hayes, James,	MID	URNU	U/A	20.10.04
Haynes, Jennifer,	MID	URNU	U/A	14.10.04
Hayton, Carrie Jane, RD	LT CDR	MEDIA	WILDFIRE	30.09.91
Hayward, James Douglas, RD, MA, B.ENG	ACDR	LOGS	FORWARD	31.03.00
Haywood, Andrew,	MID	URNU	U/A	28.10.00
Haywood, Paul,	LT CDR	AIR	RNR AIR BR VL	28.08.93
Healey, Jonathon,	MID	URNU	U/A	26.10.05
Healy, Pamela, OBE, RD	LT CDR	MEDIA	KING ALFRED	30.09.90
Heap, Matthew James,	ASL	NE	PRESIDENT	03.05.00
Heap, Stephen,	MID	URNU	U/A	06.10.05
Heath-Thompson, Edward,	MID	URNU	U/A	06.10.05
Heavyside, Andrew,	MID	NE	WILDFIRE RNR	01.10.03
Hedges, Matthew,	MID	URNU	U/A	29.10.03
Heffron, Kirsty,	CADET	URNU	U/A	14.11.95
Heley, Rachel,	MID	URNU	U/A	14.10.04
Hellawell, Sara,	MID	URNU	U/A	06.10.03
Helsby, Edward,	LT CDR	AIR	RNR AIR BR VL	31.03.96
Hendicott, Bridget,	MID	URNU	U/A	14.10.04
Henwood, A, RD	CDR	AW	PRESIDENT	30.09.98
Hepenstal, Samuel,	MID	URNU	U/A	06.10.05
Heritage, Francis,	MID	URNU	U/A	05.12.03
Hermanson, Stephen,	ASL	NE	WILDFIRE RNR	28.10.04
Hetherington, Simon David Francis,	ASL	NE	PRESIDENT	30.01.01
Hewins, Clive William,	LT CDR	AW	SHERWOOD	20.05.91
Hewitt, Andrew,	MID	URNU	U/A	14.10.04
Hibling, Russell,	LT CDR	URNU	U/A	19.09.95
Hick, David,	LT CDR	AIR	RNR AIR BR VL	31.03.02
Hicks, John David, RD	ALT CDR	HQ	EAGLET	31.03.00
Hicks, Thomas,	MID	URNU	U/A	06.10.05
Hickson, Craig,	LT CDR	AIR	RNR AIR BR VL	31.03.03
Higgins, Edward,	MID	URNU	U/A	25.08.03
Higgs, Jane Ann,	LT	Q	EAGLET	25.01.98
Higgs, Nick,	MID	URNU	U/A	14.10.04
Higson, Rennie Malcolm,	ASL	NE	SHERWOOD	10.01.02
Hill, Douglas,	ASL	NE	PRESIDENT	22.11.01
Hill, Jamie,	MID	URNU	U/A	11.07.05
Hill, Michael,	MID	URNU	U/A	03.10.02
Hill, Paul Terence,	LT CDR	SM	PRESIDENT	31.03.00
Hill, Robin,	MID	URNU	U/A	05.09.02
Hill, Sarah,	ASL	NE	SHERWOOD	13.04.00
Hillard, Christopher,	MID	URNU	U/A	07.10.03
Hilliard, John Stephen,	ASGLTCDR		CAMBRIA	15.03.00
Hindle, Sean,	LT	SM	EAGLET	18.09.91

Name	Rank	Branch	Unit	Seniority
Hines, Stephen Frederic, RD	LT CDR	AW	KING ALFRED	01.08.86
Hirst, Matthew,	MID	URNU	U/A	17.10.02
Hiscox, Lee,	ASL	NE	FLYING FOX	04.03.04
Hitchcock, Beth,	MID	URNU	U/A	05.09.02
Hitchlock, Kevin,	ASL	URNU	U/A	15.12.02
Ho, Layla,	MID	URNU	U/A	11.10.04
Hodges, Delwen,	MID	URNU	U/A	20.10.04
Hodges, Matthew,	MID	URNU	U/A	17.10.02
Hodges, Philip,	MID	URNU	U/A	10.09.01
Hodgkinson, Gail,	MID	URNU	U/A	26.10.05
Hodkinson, Alice Clare,	PSG LT		PRESIDENT	26.09.01
Hodkinson, Krista,	ASL	NE	CAMBRIA RNR	17.11.04
Hogan, Ambrose Dominic,	ASL	NE	PRESIDENT	15.05.01
Hogan, Francis John, RD	LT CDR	MWHQ	EAGLET	31.03.01
Holborn, Carl,	LT CDR	AIR	RNR AIR BR VL	31.03.03
Holbrook, Bryony St Clair,	ASL	NE	PRESIDENT	27.11.02
Holland, Dominique,	MID	URNU	U/A	26.10.05
Holley, Steven,	ASL	NE	U/A	15.11.01
Hollis, Robert Leslie Graham,	LT CDR	AWNIS	EAGLET	31.03.02
Holloway, Steven,	MID	URNU	U/A	13.10.04
Holmes, Robert,	LT CDR	AIR	RNR AIR BR VL	01.03.03
Holmes, Rosamund,	MID	URNU	U/A	26.11.03
Holt, Timothy,	ASL	NE	CAMBRIA	01.12.03
Homer, Lisa,	MID	URNU	U/A	29.10.03
Hook, Samantha Elisabeth,	SG LT		FLYING FOX	29.06.99
Horgan, Andrew,	ASL	NE	U/A	13.11.03
Horne, Martin,	LT	SEA	PRESIDENT	23.05.97
Horner, Benjamin Brian Harold,	LT	SM	PRESIDENT	13.05.02
Horner, Ian David,	LT CDR	DIS	FERRET (RNR)	01.11.83
Horswill, Laura,	MID	URNU	U/A	07.10.03
House, Andrew,	MID	URNU	U/A	07.10.04
Howard, Benjamin,	LT	AWNIS	U/A	01.04.98
Howard, Peter,	LT CDR	AIR	RNR AIR BR VL	16.08.96
Howard-Pearce, Tamar,	MID	URNU	U/A	29.10.03
Howarth, Georgina,	LT	URNU	U/A	14.10.04
Howden, Malcolm,	MID	URNU	U/A	14.11.02
Howe, Michael,	MID	URNU	U/A	16.10.03
Howell, Colin, RD	LT CDR	HQ	KING ALFRED	31.03.99
Howels, Matthew,	MID	NE	U/A	05.09.02
Howes, Simon Tee, RD	LT CDR	DIS	FERRET (RNR)	28.03.84
Hoyle, Stephen,	LT CDR	SM	EAGLET	31.03.03
Hubbard, Paul Andrew,	LT CDR	LOGS	SCOTIA	22.05.98
Hubble, Robert,	LT CDR	AIR	RNR AIR BR VL	01.10.97
Huey, Joanne,	CADET	URNU	U/A	01.12.00
Hughes, Adam,	MID	URNU	U/A	11.07.05
Hughes, Clare Yvonne, RD*	ACDR	COMM	PRESIDENT	30.09.90
Hughes, Jill Elizabeth,	LT CDR	NCAGS	CAROLINE	31.03.95
Hughes, John Fraser,	LT CDR	MEDIA	KING ALFRED	
Hughes, Kai,	LT CDR	DIS	FERRET (RNR)	01.05.92
Hughes, Paul James, RD	SG CDR		KING ALFRED	30.09.95
Hughes, Ralph,	MID	URNU	U/A	07.10.04
Hull, Andrew,	MID	URNU	U/A	20.10.05
Humphreys, Christopher,	MID	URNU	U/A	09.10.03
Humphreys, John Martyn, PHD	LT CDR	MW	KING ALFRED	31.03.01
Humphreys, Rosemary,	SLT	Q	CAMBRIA	13.05.97
Hunt, Paul Roland,	ASL	NE	VIVID	27.01.04
Hunt, Stephen Neil,	LT	MEDIA	KING ALFRED	
Hunt, Tom,	MID	URNU	U/A	07.10.04
Hunter, Rosemary,	MID	URNU	U/A	04.10.04
Hurst, Thomas,	MID	URNU	U/A	17.10.05
Hussain, Imran,	MID	URNU	U/A	04.10.04
Hutchings, Thomas,	MID	URNU	U/A	10.02.05

Name	Rank	Branch	Unit	Seniority
Hutchinson, (Janice Elizabeth), J	LT CDR	NCAGS	EAGLET	31.03.93
Hutchison, Peter Patrick,	LT	AW	SCOTIA	
Hynes, Anthony,	MID	URNU	U/A	04.10.04

I

Iliffe, Mark,	MID	URNU	U/A	26.10.05
Inman, Kieron,	MID	URNU	U/A	06.10.05
Inwood, John Maxwell,	SG CDR		SCOTIA	30.09.98
Ismael, Salam,	MID	URNU	U/A	07.10.03
Ivory, Daniel,	ASL	NE	U/A	30.10.03

J

Jabbar, Zarif,	MID	URNU	U/A	17.10.02
Jacklin, John,	LT CDR	NA	U/A	01.01.05
Jackson, Alasdair,	MID	URNU	U/A	10.01.06
Jackson, Graham,	LT CDR	AIR	RNR AIR BR VL	01.10.88
Jackson, Philip,	MID	URNU	U/A	07.10.04
Jackson, Trevor,	LT CDR	AIR	RNR AIR BR VL	01.10.91
Jacques, Kathryn,	ASL	NE	SHERWOOD RNR	24.05.05
Jaffier, Robert Gary,	ASL	NE	FORWARD	13.10.01
Jagger, Joanna,	MID	URNU	U/A	06.10.05
James, John,	MID	URNU	U/A	12.10.04
James, Roy Arthur, BSC	CDR	SM	FORWARD	30.09.00
Jameson, Susan Catherine,	LT CDR	HQ	FLYING FOX	31.03.00
Jarvis, Benjamin,	MID	URNU	U/A	13.10.05
Jarvis, Victoria,	MID	URNU	U/A	07.10.04
Jefferies, Sam,	MID	URNU	U/A	17.10.05
Jefferys, Louise,	MID	URNU	U/A	11.10.05
Jeffries, Felicity,	ASL	NE	PRESIDENT RNR	12.04.05
Jemmett, Nicola,	MID	URNU	U/A	03.10.02
Jensen, Iain,	MID	URNU	U/A	06.10.05
Jermy, Richard,	LT	H INT	FERRET (RNR)	
Jesuthasan, Jananee,	MID	URNU	U/A	11.10.05
Joakim, Ben,	MID	URNU	U/A	10.10.05
Johnson, David G,	ASL	NE	EAGLET	05.06.99
Johnson, Edward,	MID	URNU	U/A	20.10.99
Johnson, Graham,	MID	URNU	U/A	11.10.04
Johnson, James,	MID	URNU	U/A	16.10.03
Johnson, (Jill Ena), J	LT CDR	Q	CAMBRIA	31.03.01
Johnston, Bryan,	MID	URNU	U/A	25.10.02
Johnstone, Peter Hughes, RD	LT CDR	LOGS	PRESIDENT	31.03.97
Jones, Anthony,	LT CDR	NA	U/A	01.11.04
Jones, Andrew David,	ASL	NE	KING ALFRED	30.04.02
Jones, Alexander,	MID	URNU	U/A	20.10.05
Jones, Christopher, RD	LT CDR	AW	PRESIDENT	01.05.88
Jones, Charles David, RD	LT CDR	SM	DALRIADA	31.03.00
Jones, Carolyn,	LT	MEDIA	FLYING FOX RNR	04.07.95
Jones, Dilwyn,	MID	URNU	U/A	03.10.03
Jones, Danielle,	MID	URNU	U/A	07.10.04
Jones, Geoffrey Mark,	LT CDR	AW	EAGLET	31.03.02
Jones, Helen,	PASG LT	MEDF	EAGLET	17.05.00
Jones, Iain Stuart,	ASL	NE	KING ALFRED	15.01.04
Jones, Kerrie,	MID	URNU	U/A	26.10.05
Jones, Keith Williams,	LT	LOGS	FORWARD	11.06.03
Jones, Leslie,	LT CDR	H INT	FERRET (RNR)	
Jones, Nicholas Thomas Edward,	ASL	NE	FORWARD	15.02.02
Jones, Phillip,	MID	URNU	U/A	14.10.04
Jones, Pauline Lesley, R, D	LT CDR	LOGS	CALLIOPE	31.03.98
Jones, Rebecca,	MID	URNU	U/A	07.10.05
Jordan-Rowell, Isaac,	MID	URNU	U/A	09.10.03
Jose, Sian,	MID	URNU	U/A	22.10.03

Name	Rank	Branch	Unit	Seniority
Journeaux, Simon Francis,	ASGLTCDR		EAGLET	28.09.99
Joy, Cherrie,	MID	URNU	U/A	24.10.02
Judd, Simon,	LT CDR	AIR	RNR AIR BR VL	01.10.96

K

Name	Rank	Branch	Unit	Seniority
Kadera, Stephen John,	LT CDR	MEDIA	PRESIDENT	
Karlsen, Fiona,	MID	URNU	U/A	10.07.04
Kashita, Stephen,	MID	URNU	U/A	04.10.04
Kay, David,	ACDR	LOGS	FLYING FOX	01.01.02
Kay, Nichola,	MID	URNU	U/A	20.10.05
Kearney, Melian Jane, RD	LT CDR	HQ	VIVID	31.03.97
Keating, Fergus Stephen Jonathon,	PSURGLCDR		PRESIDENT	10.01.02
Kedge, Jennifer Claire,	ASL	NE	WILDFIRE	24.03.03
Keenan, Gregory,	MID	URNU	U/A	06.10.05
Kehoe, Rowan,	MID	URNU	U/A	07.10.04
Kelly, Nanette,	ASL	NE	SHERWOOD RNR	22.09.04
Kelly, Sarah Louise,	ASL	NE	SCOTIA	01.05.01
Kelly, Timothy,	LT CDR	X	RNR AIR BR VL	04.07.92
Kelway, Jenna,	MID	URNU	U/A	05.09.02
Kembery, Simon John,	LT	AW	CAMBRIA	11.06.93
Kemp, Stuart,	MID	URNU	U/A	08.10.03
Kemp, Simon Michael,	LT CDR	DIS	FERRET (RNR)	31.03.99
Kendrick, Katherine Sonia,	ASL	NE	PRESIDENT	18.02.03
Kenney, Dawn Elizabeth, OBE, RRC	CDR	Q	WILDFIRE	30.09.99
Kent, Thomas William Henry, RD	CDR	AW	SHERWOOD	30.09.99
Kenyon, Christopher,	LT CDR	HQ	PRESIDENT	03.04.82
Keough, James,	MID	URNU	U/A	04.10.04
Ker, Stuart,	MID	URNU	U/A	17.10.02
Kerrigan, Gareth,	MID	URNU	U/A	01.03.04
Kersting, Alexandra,	MID	URNU	U/A	14.10.04
Kesteven, Ralph,	ASL	NE	EAGLET	24.01.02
Kilbride, Paul,	MID	URNU	U/A	27.09.01
Kim, Michael,	LT	DIS	FORWARD	08.10.02
King, Andrew,	MID	URNU	U/A	14.10.03
King, Andrew Stephen, RD	LT CDR	MW	KING ALFRED	31.03.99
King, Charles Guy Hall,	LT CDR	SEA	KING ALFRED	31.03.02
King, Ian, RD	LT	HQ	EAGLET	05.12.97
King, Lindsay,	SLT	URNU	U/A	22.10.01
King, Samuel,	MID	URNU	U/A	18.10.04
Kinsella, Kevin, QVRM, RD*	CDR	MW	KING ALFRED	30.09.96
Kirk, William Walter,	LT	NCAGS	SHERWOOD	31.03.96
Kistruck, David,	LT CDR	AIR	RNR AIR BR VL	31.03.00
Kite, Edwin,	MID	URNU	U/A	06.10.05
Knapper, James,	MID	URNU	U/A	20.10.05
Knight, Jane,	MID	URNU	U/A	06.10.05
Knight, Richard,	MID	URNU	U/A	25.02.03
Knott, Clive,	LT CDR	AIR	RNR AIR BR VL	31.03.98
Knotts, George William,	LT CDR	COMM	CALLIOPE	31.03.02
Knowles, Donna Maureen,	LT CDR	MW	CAROLINE	31.03.01
Knowles, Thomas,	ASL	NE	PRESIDENT	21.05.02
Koonsombat, Manwaad,	MID	URNU	U/A	16.10.03
Kordowski, Nicholas,	ASL	NE	PRESIDENT	01.11.00
Krasun, Charles Robert,	ASL	NE	KING ALFRED	30.10.01
Kwek, Kon,	MID	URNU	U/A	16.10.03
Kyme, Michael John,	LT	DIS	FERRET (RNR)	30.11.93
Kyte, Andrew,	MID	URNU	U/A	07.10.05

L

Name	Rank	Branch	Unit	Seniority
Ladbrooke-Chartres, Wrettham,	MID	URNU	U/A	12.10.04
Ladislaus, Paul James,	ASL	NE	CALLIOPE	30.05.02
Laird, Suzanna,	MID	URNU	U/A	13.10.05

Name	Rank	Branch	Unit	Seniority
Laity, Emma,	MID	URNU	U/A	13.10.04
Lalley, Andrea,	MID	URNU	U/A	20.10.05
Lalli, Tegjit,	MID	URNU	U/A	14.10.04
Lancaster, Gavin,	SLT	CS(O)	FLYING FOX RNR	24.08.02
Land, Benjamin,	MID	URNU	U/A	06.10.05
Langmead, Clive Francis, RD	LT CDR	AW	FORWARD	01.07.90
Lapage-Norris, Thomas,	ALT CDR	LOGS	FLYING FOX	31.10.97
Larsen, Thomas,	MID	URNU	U/A	11.10.01
Last, Nicholas, AFC	LT CDR	AIR	RNR AIR BR VL	01.10.91
Lathrope, Jennifer,	CADET	URNU	U/A	30.09.99
Lau, Eddie,	MID	URNU	U/A	29.09.05
Laundy, Nicholas,	PSG LT		EAGLET	23.05.00
Lauretani, Andrew Stephen David,	LT	MEDIA	VIVID	
Laverick, Helen Tanya,	LT	LOGS	PRESIDENT	14.10.02
Lavis-Jones, Mark,	ASL	NE	WILDFIRE RNR	24.11.05
Lawrence, Ian Martin,	ASL	AW	KING ALFRED	03.06.01
Lawrence, Jenna,	MID	URNU	U/A	30.05.01
Lawrenson, Alexandre,	MID	URNU	U/A	06.10.05
Lawson, Rosemary,	ASL	NE	EAGLET	14.11.02
Lawson, Zoe,	MID	URNU	U/A	17.10.02
Le Poidevin, Ian,	MID	URNU	U/A	25.08.03
Leach, Helen,	MID	URNU	U/A	11.07.05
Leach, Simon,	LT	AIR	RNR AIR BR VL	22.09.93
Leask, Clare,	MID	URNU	U/A	16.10.03
Leather, Roger,	LT CDR	AW	EAGLET	01.06.87
Lecumberri Adamson, Nora,	MID	URNU	U/A	29.10.03
Ledochowski, Konrad,	MID	URNU	U/A	29.10.03
Ledwidge, Francis Andrew,	LT CDR	SEA	FERRET (RNR)	31.03.02
Lee, David Antony,	ACDR	SM	DALRIADA	02.04.03
Lee, John,	CDR	NCAGS	CALLIOPE	30.09.03
Lee, Kirsty,	MID	URNU	U/A	16.10.03
Lee, Robert,	LT CDR	AIR	RNR AIR BR VL	31.03.02
Lee, Thomas William Robert,	LT	H INT	FERRET (RNR)	
Lee Sin Tsong, Jesse,	MID	URNU	U/A	16.10.03
Lehmann, Tobias,	MID	URNU	U/A	07.10.04
Leigh, Daniel,	MID	URNU	U/A	12.10.00
Leiserach, Joseph,	MID	URNU	U/A	25.08.03
Lemkes, James,	MID	URNU	U/A	10.10.05
Lentell, Heather,	LT	Q	EAGLET	03.05.01
Leonard, John,	SG CDR		KING ALFRED	30.09.01
Leonard, Jeanette,	LT	MEDIA	RNR MEDIA RELTNS	07.05.99
Lester, Richard,	MID	URNU	U/A	16.10.03
Lever, Thomas,	MID	URNU	U/A	25.08.03
Levine, Andrew,	LT	AIR	RNR AIR BR VL	07.02.98
Lewellen, Susan,	MID	URNU	U/A	26.10.05
Lewis, Catrin,	MID	URNU	U/A	12.10.05
Lewis, John Charles, RD	LT CDR	SEA	PRESIDENT	31.03.02
Lewis, Kathryn Elizabeth,	LT	MW	PRESIDENT	31.07.95
Lewis, Richard,	LT CDR	AIR	RNR AIR BR VL	31.03.01
Lewis, Richard,	ASL	NE	CAMBRIA	27.11.03
Lewis, Simon, RD	LT CDR	LOGS	EAGLET	31.03.04
Leyland, Paula,	MID	URNU	U/A	14.10.04
Leyshon, Sally Louise,	LT CDR	AWNIS	FLYING FOX	31.03.93
Liddel, Ross,	MID	URNU	U/A	06.10.05
Liggins, Michael,	LT CDR	AIR	RNR AIR BR VL	01.10.01
Liles, Julie,	MID	URNU	U/A	16.10.03
Linden, Roy Stephen,	ASL	NE	VIVID	01.11.00
Line, Matthew,	ASL	NE	PRESIDENT RNR	23.11.05
Ling, Peter,	MID	URNU	U/A	18.07.04
Linton, Andrew,	ASL	NE	EAGLET RNR	08.03.05
Lintott, Mark,	MID	URNU	U/A	14.10.04
Lippell, Sabrina Rose, BSCRD	LT CDR	MEDIA	WILDFIRE	30.09.89

Name	Rank	Branch	Unit	Seniority
Lister, Andrew,	LT	AIR	RNR AIR BR VL	16.06.93
Lister, Robert,	MID	URNU	U/A	06.10.05
Little, John,	MID	URNU	U/A	14.10.04
Lloyd, David Vernon,	LT CDR	AW	KING ALFRED	31.03.99
Lloyd, Gareth, RD	LT CDR	HQ	EAGLET	31.03.98
Lloyd, Peter John, RD	LT CDR	AW	KING ALFRED	31.03.00
Lloyd, Susan,	LT	MEDIA	PRESIDENT	01.09.90
Loates, Mark,	ALT	URNU	U/A	17.06.04
Lock, Richard,	MID	URNU	U/A	06.10.05
Lockwood, Neville,	ASL	NE	VIVID	06.05.02
Lodge, Claire,	MID	URNU	U/A	30.09.05
Lomas, David,	MID	URNU	U/A	29.09.05
Lort, Timothy,	LT CDR	AIR	RNR AIR BR VL	01.10.95
Lorton, Jonathan, RD	LT CDR	HQ	FLYING FOX	31.03.94
Loudoun, Fiona,	MID	URNU	U/A	09.10.03
Loughran, Cedric Grenville, RD	CDR	AW	EAGLET	30.09.98
Lovegrove, Richard Edward,	PSG LT		WILDFIRE	05.06.01
Loyo Mayo, Rebecca,	MID	URNU	U/A	20.10.04
Luke, Warren Munro, RD	SG CDR		SCOTIA	30.09.99
Lumley, Richard,	ASL	NE	U/A	22.11.05
Lundie, Andrew,	MID	URNU	U/A	14.10.03
Lunn, Thomas,	MID	URNU	U/A	16.10.03
Lutman, Charles,	ALT CDR	NA	CALLIOPE	07.08.01
Lyall, Kenneth Alexander,	LT CDR	HQ	SCOTIA	31.03.97
Lydon, Michael, RD	LT	LOGS	CALLIOPE	30.09.96
Lynch, Richard,	MID	URNU	U/A	10.10.05
Lynch, Suzanne, RD	LT	LOGS	CAMBRIA	28.05.02

M

Name	Rank	Branch	Unit	Seniority
MacDonald, Alasdair,	MID	URNU	U/A	10.10.02
MacDonald, Fiona,	CADET	URNU	U/A	14.10.99
MacDonald, Julie Anne,	LT	Q	KING ALFRED	18.05.01
Mace, Stephen,	MID	URNU	U/A	20.10.04
Machin, Peter Charles Clive, RD*	CDR	HQ	CAMBRIA	30.09.00
MacIntyre, Kirsty,	MID	URNU	U/A	10.10.05
MacIver, Iain,	ASL	NE	U/A	27.03.03
MacKay, David,	LT CDR	AIR	RNR AIR BR VL	01.10.93
MacKay, Evan George,	PALT	AW	DALRIADA	06.12.96
MacKay, Richard,	MID	URNU	U/A	13.10.05
MacKenzie, David,	MID	URNU	U/A	17.11.05
MacKenzie, Hannah Louise,	ASL	NE	WILDFIRE	17.06.02
MacKenzie, Kate,	MID	URNU	U/A	18.10.04
MacKenzie-Philps, Linda,	LT CDR	MEDIA	KING ALFRED	31.03.99
Mackie, Robert Charles Gordon,	ASL	NE	FORWARD	19.05.99
MacKintosh, Zemma,	PSG LT		EAGLET	25.06.03
MacLean, Duncan,	MID	URNU	U/A	09.10.03
MacLean, Graeme Paul,	ASL	NE	DALRIADA	15.10.03
MacLean, Marjory,	CHAPLAIN (R)	CE	SCOTIA RNR	25.11.04
MacLean, Nicholas Peter, RD	LT CDR	SM	PRESIDENT	31.03.97
Macleod, Alistair David,	SG LTCDR		SCOTIA	17.10.78
MacMillan, Alasdair Iain Macaulay,	SG LTCDR		SCOTIA	04.03.97
MacNae, Bridget,	MID	URNU	U/A	16.10.03
MacRae, Eilidh,	CADET	URNU	U/A	14.11.02
MacRae, Kirk,	MID	URNU	U/A	14.10.99
MacSephney, Tracey Lee Helen,	LT	AWNIS	KING ALFRED	
MacTaggart, Alasdair Donald, RD	CDR	COMM	DALRIADA	01.09.02
MacWilliam, Ronald,	MID	URNU	U/A	10.10.02
Mair, Barbara,	MID	URNU	U/A	26.10.05
Malkin, Roy Vyvian,	LT	AW	PRESIDENT	03.07.01
Mallinson, Stuart Jeffry, MSC	LT	MW	PRESIDENT	31.03.96
Malone, Keith,	ASGLTCDR		EAGLET	07.01.00
Malpas, Peter,	LT CDR	NCAGS	KING ALFRED	31.03.02

Name	Rank	Branch	Unit	Seniority
Mann, Barbara Louise,	LT CDR	MEDIA	VIVID	31.03.01
Manning, Jacqueline Vera,	LT CDR	SM	PRESIDENT	31.03.02
Mannion, Christopher,	MID	URNU	U/A	04.10.04
Manser, Darren,	LT	AIR	RNR AIR BR VL	01.04.94
Manson, Sinclair,	MID	URNU	U/A	18.11.04
Manuel, Laura,	MID	URNU	U/A	14.10.04
March, Marissa,	ASL	NE	PRESIDENT RNR	23.11.05
Markham, Christopher,	MID	URNU	U/A	06.10.05
Markwell, Jonathan,	MID	URNU	U/A	22.10.01
Marlow, Stephen, QGM, RD	CDR	AIR	RNR AIR BR VL	15.01.05
Marlowe, Joe,	MID	URNU	U/A	29.09.05
Marple, Natalie,	CADET	URNU	U/A	19.10.00
Marr, David,	LT CDR	AIR	RNR AIR BR VL	01.10.94
Marriott, Anna,	MID	URNU	U/A	18.10.04
Marsh, Richard,	MID	URNU	U/A	14.10.04
Marshall, Deirdre,	MID	URNU	U/A	14.10.04
Marshall, Stephen Michael,	LT	MCDO	U/A	17.04.88
Marsland, Andrew,	MID	URNU	U/A	14.10.04
Martin, Andrew,	MID	URNU	U/A	14.10.04
Martin, Darren Hinna,	LT CDR	AW	PRESIDENT	31.03.01
Martin, Emma,	MID	URNU	U/A	14.10.04
Martin, Kelly,	MID	URNU	U/A	07.10.04
Martin, Nicholas John, RD	LT CDR	MWHQ	CALLIOPE	31.03.95
Martin, Sara-Jane,	MID	URNU	U/A	14.10.04
Martin, Samuel,	MID	URNU	U/A	14.10.04
Maryon, Karen Anne, RD	LT	Q	SHERWOOD	24.12.87
Mason, Ann Margaret, RD	LT CDR	LOGS	EAGLET	01.04.99
Mason, Andrew Robert,	ASL	NE	PRESIDENT	11.06.99
Mason, Christopher,	MID	URNU	U/A	14.10.03
Mason, Grace Victoria,	ASL	NE	PRESIDENT	25.09.01
Mason, John,	MID	URNU	U/A	06.10.05
Mason, Thomas,	LT CDR	AIR	RNR AIR BR VL	01.10.88
Massey, Steven,	LT CDR	AIR	RNR AIR BR VL	31.03.02
Mathers, Fiona Catherine,	ASL	NE	VIVID	27.11.03
Maturi, Careen,	MID	URNU	U/A	06.10.05
Maxwell, Malcolm Scott,	ASL	NE	SCOTIA	15.01.04
May, Simon,	MID	URNU	U/A	30.09.05
May Brown, Gemma,	MID	URNU	U/A	07.01.03
Mc Alear, Stuart Douglas,	LT CDR	MW	KING ALFRED	25.10.95
Mc Kenzie, Gary,	ASL	NE	CAMBRIA	10.10.02
McAlpine, Jeffrey,	ASL	NE	EAGLET	28.07.03
McArdell, Steven,	LT	AIR	RNR AIR BR VL	01.04.90
McAuley, Nicholas,	MID	URNU	U/A	18.10.05
McCabe, Matthew James,	ASL	NE	PRESIDENT	03.10.03
McCabe, Rebecca,	MID	URNU	U/A	01.10.03
McCartney, William Robert,	LT	LOGS	PRESIDENT	26.03.03
McCormack, Patrick, RD	LT CDR	NCAGS	DALRIADA	15.07.92
McCormick, Damion Kevin,	ASL	NE	SHERWOOD	20.04.99
McCrea, Mark,	ASL	NE	CNH(R)	14.11.02
McCready, Heather,	ASL	NE	DALRIADA RNR	22.09.04
McCreery, Robert George,	LT	SEA	CAROLINE	20.06.89
McCullough, Karen Margaret,	ALT	Q	CAROLINE	12.05.03
McDermott, Mark,	LT CDR	AIR	RNR AIR BR VL	18.10.01
McDonald, Ian,	LT	AIR	RNR AIR BR VL	01.05.91
McDonald, John,	MID	URNU	U/A	16.10.03
McDonald, Stewart Neil,	ASL	NE	DALRIADA	19.02.04
McDowell, Kirsten,	MID	URNU	U/A	14.10.04
McFadden, Jaime,	MID	URNU	U/A	06.10.05
McFarland, Kezia,	MID	URNU	U/A	07.10.04
McGeever, Mark,	MID	URNU	U/A	08.10.05
McGhee, Stephen James,	LT	HQ	DALRIADA	18.12.01
McGinley, Mark Patrick,	LT	LOGS	KING ALFRED	

Name	Rank	Branch	Unit	Seniority
McGwinn, Daniel Michael,	ASL	NE	CALLIOPE	27.11.03
McHardy-Roberts, Jaqueline Carole,	ASL	NE	EAGLET	10.10.01
McInnes, Vivian,	LT	Q	KING ALFRED	14.12.92
McIntyre, James,	MID	URNU	U/A	16.10.03
McKay, Christopher,	MID	URNU	U/A	16.10.03
McKeating, John Brendan,	SG CDR		SHERWOOD	31.12.99
McKinley, Mairi,	LT	Q	DALRIADA RNR	02.01.04
McKinley, Mairi Catriona,	ASL	NE	DALRIADA	19.10.00
McKinty, Gareth,	ASL	NE	CNH(R)	05.05.05
McKnight, Edward,	ASL	X	U/A	17.10.90
McLaverty, Karen Anne,	LT	NCAGS	CAROLINE	17.03.99
McLellan, Moira,	MID	URNU	U/A	06.10.05
McLeman, Leo,	MID	URNU	U/A	16.10.03
McMenemy, Scott,	MID	URNU	U/A	06.10.05
McMinn, Sandra,	ASL	URNU	U/A	01.10.98
McMullan, Frances,	MID	URNU	U/A	10.10.05
McMurran, Robert Campbell, RD	LT CDR	HQ	CAROLINE	31.03.97
McNally, Barry,	MID	URNU	U/A	18.10.02
McNaught, Edward William Gordon,	LT CDR	MWHQ	CALLIOPE	31.03.97
McPherson, Emma,	LT	Q	CAROLINE	15.06.00
McWilliams, Esther Carole,	ASL	NE	SCOTIA	03.09.02
Meadows, Brian,	LT CDR	MEDIA	CAMBRIA RNR	01.10.98
Meakin, Matthew,	MID	URNU	U/A	18.10.00
Medland, Elizabeth Ellen,	ASL	NE	VIVID	20.02.01
Meharg, Neil, RD	LT	MW	CAROLINE	11.08.96
Meldram, Sheryl Christine Anne,	LT	Q	PRESIDENT	30.10.93
Melson, Janet,	LT	LOGS	KING ALFRED	25.02.96
Menadue, Henrietta,	MID	URNU	U/A	29.09.05
Meropoulos, John,	ALT	MW	FERRET (RNR)	16.09.04
Merryweather, Lee,	MID	URNU	U/A	07.10.04
Mhar, Sabrina,	MID	URNU	U/A	11.10.05
Miller, Benjamin,	ASL	NE	SHERWOOD	02.06.01
Miller, David,	MID	URNU	U/A	08.10.05
Miller, David,	LT CDR	AIR	RNR AIR BR VL	01.04.95
Miller, Iain,	MID	URNU	U/A	06.10.05
Millington, Hayley,	MID	URNU	U/A	17.10.04
Millward, Jonathan,	LT CDR	SM	KING ALFRED	01.09.91
Millyard, Matthew,	MID	URNU	U/A	16.10.03
Milne, David,	MID	URNU	U/A	14.10.04
Milne, Iain,	ASL	URNU	U/A	16.05.02
Milner, Thomas,	MID	URNU	U/A	14.10.04
Minto, Paul,	MID	URNU	U/A	21.10.00
Mitchell, John,	MID	URNU	U/A	14.10.04
Mitchell, Natalie,	ASL	NE	WILDFIRE	19.09.01
Mitchell, Ross,	MID	URNU	U/A	16.10.03
Mitchell, Robert,	LT CDR	AIR	RNR AIR BR VL	31.03.93
Mitchell, Samantha,	MID	URNU	U/A	09.11.00
Moir, Euan,	MID	URNU	U/A	12.10.04
Mollard, Michael,	LT	AIR	RNR AIR BR VL	01.07.94
Molyneux, Giles Bassingthwaighte,	PSG SLT		SCOTIA	24.01.01
Monroe, James,	MID	URNU	U/A	13.10.03
Montgomery, William George,	LT CDR	SEA	FLYING FOX	31.03.00
Moore, Chris,	ASL	NE	FORWARD	16.07.03
Moore, Joseph,	MID	URNU	U/A	20.10.04
Moore, Tristan,	MID	URNU	U/A	13.10.05
Moorthy, Roham Michael,	LT	SM	PRESIDENT	02.03.02
Moran, Simon,	LT	AIR	RNR AIR BR VL	18.02.94
Morgan, (Eugene Peter), E	LT	DIS	FERRET (RNR)	31.07.95
Morgan, Gareth, RD	LT CDR	LOGS	CAMBRIA	31.03.01
Morgan, John,	MID	URNU	U/A	06.10.05
Morgan, Kelly,	MID	URNU	U/A	07.10.03
Morgan, Linda Frances,	LT	Q	WILDFIRE	26.09.96

Name	Rank	Branch	Unit	Seniority
Morgan, Lyndsey,	MID	URNU	U/A	12.10.04
Morgan, Phillip,	MID	URNU	U/A	17.10.05
Morgans, Daniel James,	LT	MW	PRESIDENT	09.05.99
Moriarty, Helen Jean,	LT	Q	PRESIDENT	03.07.97
Morientes, Yusuf,	MID	URNU	U/A	13.10.05
Morley, Dietmar Allen,	LT	NCAGS	SHERWOOD	20.10.98
Morris, Alan Philip,	LT CDR	MEDIA	DALRIADA	
Morris, David John, RD	CDR	SM	WILDFIRE	30.09.01
Morrisey, Huw,	MID	URNU	U/A	07.10.04
Morton, William,	MID	URNU	U/A	26.10.05
Moseley, Allison,	ASL	NE	CALLIOPE	10.03.98
Mowbray, Roger, QCVSA	LT CDR	AIR	RNR AIR BR VL	01.10.88
Muir, Jonathan,	MID	URNU	U/A	09.10.03
Munro, Greg,	MID	URNU	U/A	14.10.03
Munson, Eileen Patricia,	LT	Q	CAMBRIA	23.09.95
Munt, Marcus,	MID	URNU	U/A	08.10.98
Murphy, Samantha,	ASL	URNU	U/A	16.06.99
Murray, Abigail,	ASL	URNU	U/A	16.10.03
Murray, Anita May,	ASL	NE	VIVID	09.05.00
Murray, Catherine,	MID	URNU	U/A	02.11.05
Murray, Edward Charles, RD	LT CDR	H INT	FERRET (RNR)	
Murray, Emma,	MID	URNU	U/A	11.10.05
Murrison, Andrew William,	SG CDR		PRESIDENT	31.12.97
Murrison, Mark P, RD	LT CDR	AW	PRESIDENT	31.03.99
Musgrove, Christopher,	MID	URNU	U/A	11.10.05
Myerscough, Andrew,	LT CDR	AIR	RNR AIR BR VL	01.10.96

N

Name	Rank	Branch	Unit	Seniority
Nadin, Robert,	LT CDR	AIR	RNR AIR BR VL	01.09.95
Napier, Gary,	MID	URNU	U/A	10.10.02
Nash, Adrian,	MID	URNU	U/A	06.10.05
Nath, Vishaal,	MID	URNU	U/A	16.10.03
Naylor, Cathy,	MID	URNU	U/A	06.10.05
Naylor, Raymond Dean,	ASL	NE	SHERWOOD	31.10.02
Neale, Kirsty A,	LT	NCAGS	EAGLET	30.11.94
Neale, Richard,	MID	URNU	U/A	30.09.05
Neave, Rosemary,	MID	URNU	U/A	07.10.04
Neave, Thomas,	MID	URNU	U/A	02.02.05
Nelson, Jennifer,	MID	URNU	U/A	06.10.05
Newby-Grant, William, MBE, RD	LT CDR	H INT	FERRET (RNR)	26.03.80
Newman, Andrew,	MID	URNU	U/A	17.10.02
Newson, Laura,	MID	URNU	U/A	18.10.02
Newton, David Jason,	LT	SEA	PRESIDENT	28.03.96
Newton, Ingrid Catherine,	LT CDR	LOGS	EAGLET	31.03.99
Newton, Mark,	LT CDR	AIR	RNR AIR BR VL	31.03.01
Newton, Russell Scott Henry,	ASL	NE	PRESIDENT	22.05.01
Nicholls, Graham,	MID	URNU	U/A	07.10.04
Nicholls, Rachel,	MID	URNU	U/A	22.10.03
Nicholson, Ashley,	MID	URNU	U/A	08.10.05
Nicholson, David,	LT CDR	AIR	RNR AIR BR VL	31.03.05
Nicholson, Emma Sarah,	ASL	NE	DALRIADA	22.01.98
Nicholson, Jeremy David,	LT CDR	AW	FLYING FOX	01.10.84
Nicholson, John,	SLT	H INT	FERRET (RNR)	26.03.03
Nicolson, Vernon,	AB(HQ)2		DALRIADA	04.09.96
Nimmo Scott, Sarah,	LT	URNU	U/A	01.11.99
Nisbet, James Thornton,	ASL	NE	PRESIDENT	24.01.02
Noakes, David Anthony,	LT	LOGS	PRESIDENT	06.10.00
Noble, Alexander Peter,	ASL	NE	KING ALFRED	09.01.02
Noble, Freddie,	MID	URNU	U/A	17.10.05
Noble, Robert Howard, BSC, RD	LT CDR	NCAGS	FORWARD	31.03.97
Norris, Andrew Michael,	ALT	NCAGS	KING ALFRED	01.10.90
Norris, Ciaran,	MID	URNU	U/A	18.10.04

Name	Rank	Branch	Unit	Seniority
Northcott, John, RD	LT CDR	LOGS	CALLIOPE	31.03.98
Norton, Omar,	MID	URNU	U/A	13.10.04
Norwich, Roger Peter,	SG LTCDR		FLYING FOX	12.09.02
Nunn, James,	LT CDR	AIR	RNR AIR BR VL	31.03.99
Nwokora, Dal,	MID	URNU	U/A	07.10.03

O

Name	Rank	Branch	Unit	Seniority
O'Brien, Helen,	MID	URNU	U/A	29.10.03
O'Callaghan, Penelope Jane,	LT CDR	Q	KING ALFRED	31.03.96
O'Connell, Daniel,	MID	URNU	U/A	12.10.04
O'Dell, Phillip,	LT CDR	AIR	RNR AIR BR VL	23.09.98
O'Dooley, Paul Patrick,	ASL	NE	SHERWOOD	01.11.02
O'Driscoll, Edward Hugh,	LT	SEA	PRESIDENT	25.01.03
O'Hara, Katherine,	CADET	URNU	U/A	11.10.01
O'Neill, Steven,	MID	URNU	U/A	14.10.04
O'Rorke, Alice,	MID	URNU	U/A	14.10.04
O'Sullivan, James,	MID	URNU	U/A	18.10.02
O'Sullivan, Kathryn Winifred, RD	LT	SEA	VIVID	26.07.96
Oakeshott, Luke,	MID	URNU	U/A	12.10.04
Oakley, Richard,	LT	AW	PRESIDENT	22.05.02
Oaten, Timothy,	LT	COMM	SHERWOOD	03.06.87
Oates, Edward,	LT CDR	AIR	RNR AIR BR VL	16.02.93
Oatway, Paul,	SLT	LOGS	U/A	01.01.05
Obasi, Ambrose,	MID	URNU	U/A	07.10.04
Ogden, Braddan,	LT	AIR	RNR AIR BR VL	01.04.95
Ogilvie, Mark,	LT	AIR	RNR AIR BR VL	18.03.97
Oldfield, Paul,	LT CDR	CIS	WILDFIRE RNR	22.07.04
Oliphant, Helen,	CADET	URNU	U/A	18.10.02
Olivant, David Francis, RD	LT CDR	COMM	SHERWOOD	31.03.99
Olsen, Alexander,	MID	URNU	U/A	06.10.05
Ord, Elizabeth,	LT	DIS	FERRET (RNR)	23.05.97
Ormshaw, Andrew,	CDR	AIR	RNR AIR BR VL	15.07.04
Osborne, Matthew,	MID	URNU	U/A	07.10.03
Osbourne, Ruth,	MID	URNU	U/A	14.10.04
Overton, Thomas,	MID	URNU	U/A	07.10.04
Owen, David,	MID	URNU	U/A	06.10.05

P

Name	Rank	Branch	Unit	Seniority
Packer, James,	MID	URNU	U/A	14.10.04
Packer, Stephen,	MID	URNU	U/A	06.10.05
Paddock, Lee David,	LT	SM	FORWARD	01.03.94
Padgham, Philip,	LT	URNU	U/A	30.06.97
Paget, Sarah,	MID	URNU	U/A	07.10.04
Paget-Tomlinson, John Edward,	ASL	NE	KING ALFRED	28.08.02
Pain, Sarah Louise,	ASL	NE	KING ALFRED	30.01.02
Palmer, Alon, RD	LT CDR	AW	SCOTIA	09.05.91
Palmer, Helen,	ASL	URNU	U/A	01.10.90
Palmer, Helen,	LT	URNU	U/A	26.07.03
Palmer, James,	SLT	URNU	U/A	13.10.04
Palmer, Matthew,	MID	URNU	U/A	20.10.05
Pardoe, Christopher Richard,	LT CDR	MEDIA	VIVID	
Park, Lindsay,	CADET	URNU	U/A	08.02.01
Parker, Gavin,	MID	URNU	U/A	16.10.03
Parkinson, Gareth,	MID	NE	U/A	13.02.03
Parmar, Kishan,	MID	URNU	U/A	29.09.05
Parnell, Rebecca Ann,	LT	AWNIS	KING ALFRED	
Parris, John, RD	CDR	NCAGS	FLYING FOX	30.09.01
Parry, Angela Lynn,	ASL	NE	KING ALFRED	11.12.01
Parry, Christopher,	ASL	NE	WILDFIRE	10.10.01
Parry, Louise,	MID	URNU	U/A	14.10.03
Parsonage, Neil David, LLM	ALT CDR	NCAGS	EAGLET	31.03.00

Name	Rank	Branch	Unit	Seniority
Patel, Umar,	MID	URNU	U/A	29.09.05
Patel, Kavita,	MID	URNU	U/A	01.10.03
Paterson, Gordon Laird,	LT CDR	AWNIS	KING ALFRED	02.11.84
Paterson, Mathew Robert,	ASL	NE	FORWARD	27.10.02
Paterson, Stuart,	MID	URNU	U/A	08.10.01
Patten, Michelle Louise,	ASL	NE	FORWARD	03.09.02
Patten, Mark Thomas,	SG LTCDR		WILDFIRE	29.03.96
Patten, Nicholas William,	LT CDR	NCAGS	FORWARD	31.03.00
Patterson, Jarrod Lee,	LT CDR	S	PRESIDENT	31.03.01
Patterson, Paul,	MID	URNU	U/A	13.10.05
Paxton, Alan,	MID	URNU	U/A	14.10.99
Payne, Christopher,	ASL	NE	WILDFIRE RNR	05.05.05
Payton, Philip John,	CDR	MEDIA	VIVID	
Peace, Catherine,	MID	URNU	U/A	06.10.05
Peachey, Jason,	MID	URNU	U/A	12.10.04
Pearce, Alexandra,	CADET	URNU	U/A	12.11.01
Pearson, Craig Antony,	ASL	AW	CAMBRIA	25.10.01
Pearson, Paul Austin Kevin,	LT CDR	SM	VIVID	31.03.00
Pearson, Robert James,	ASL	NE	VIVID	25.09.03
Peasley, Helen Susan,	ASL	NE	U/A	13.11.01
Pedder, Gregg,	MID	URNU	U/A	14.10.04
Pedley, Michael,	ASL	NE	FORWARD	16.01.02
Pegram, Katie,	MID	URNU	U/A	16.10.03
Pellegrini, Lucy,	MID	URNU	U/A	11.10.05
Penn, James,	MID	URNU	U/A	13.10.05
Pepper, Philip,	LT	H INT	FERRET (RNR)	03.10.02
Percharde, Michelle,	MID	URNU	U/A	12.10.04
Pereora-Rego, Angharad,	MID	URNU	U/A	26.10.05
Perrin, Myles,	MID	URNU	U/A	20.10.05
Perrin, Roanne,	MID	URNU	U/A	26.10.05
Perry, Jessica,	MID	URNU	U/A	30.09.05
Peter, Kathleen Elizabeth,	ASL	NE	WILDFIRE	04.04.01
Pethick, Ian,	LT CDR	LOGS	VIVID	31.03.04
Petrie, Lindsay,	MID	URNU	U/A	08.10.05
Petrie, Melville,	LT CDR	LOGS	FLYING FOX	09.01.87
Petzold, Andrea,	MID	URNU	U/A	06.10.05
Phillips, Alexander,	MID	URNU	U/A	08.10.03
Phillips, Nicholas James,	ASL	NE	PRESIDENT	23.04.02
Phillips, Sophia,	ASL	NE	WILDFIRE	13.11.01
Picton, Georgina,	MID	URNU	U/A	14.10.04
Piggot, Carline,	MID	URNU	U/A	16.10.03
Pike, Christine Margaret, RD	LT CDR	DIS	FERRET (RNR)	31.03.95
Pike, Stuart,	LT CDR	AIR	RNR AIR BR VL	31.03.05
Pillow, Daniel,	MID	URNU	U/A	16.10.03
Pink, Karen,	ASL	NE	CALLIOPE RNR	02.12.03
Piper, Sarah,	MID	URNU	U/A	07.10.03
Pitchford, Ian,	LT CDR	AIR	RNR AIR BR VL	31.03.04
Pittaway, Ernest,	MID	URNU	U/A	21.10.97
Platts, Emily,	MID	URNU	U/A	14.10.03
Platts, Oliver,	MID	URNU	U/A	06.10.05
Plumley, Laura,	MID	URNU	U/A	16.10.03
Pogson, Andrew David,	ASL	NE	U/A	25.05.04
Poionter, Louise,	MID	URNU	U/A	07.10.04
Polley, Christopher,	MID	URNU	U/A	14.10.04
Poole, Crystal,	MID	URNU	U/A	13.10.05
Porteous, Cameron,	MID	URNU	U/A	11.07.05
Porter, Jonathan Mitchell Alexander,	ASL	NE	EAGLET	22.02.00
Posnett, Dickon,	LT CDR	AIR	RNR AIR BR VL	31.03.99
Poulson, Christopher,	MID	URNU	U/A	13.10.05
Poulton-Watt, Andrew Ritchie,	LT	COMM	SCOTIA	03.03.00
Powell, Robert,	MID	URNU	U/A	20.10.04
Powell, Rebecca,	MID	URNU	U/A	14.10.03

Name	Rank	Branch	Unit	Seniority
Powell, Stephen,	LT CDR	AIR	RNR AIR BR VL	01.10.93
Powell, William,	LT CDR	AIR	RNR AIR BR VL	31.03.99
Powley, Simon Owen Maxwell, RD	LT CDR	DIS	FERRET (RNR)	31.03.98
Pragnell, Katie,	MID	URNU	U/A	13.10.05
Pratt, Ian Heggie,	LT CDR	MEDIA	KING ALFRED	
Preston, Andrew,	MID	URNU	U/A	09.10.03
Prew, Jennifer,	MID	URNU	U/A	20.10.05
Price, Alistair,	MID	URNU	U/A	01.12.05
Price, Susan Elizabeth, MBE	LT CDR	NCAGS	VIVID	31.03.97
Proom, Edward,	MID	URNU	U/A	13.10.03
Pryce, Mark,	MID	URNU	U/A	13.10.05
Pryce, Simon,	LT CDR	AIR	RNR AIR BR VL	31.03.02
Pugh, James,	MID	URNU	U/A	11.07.05
Pugh, Neil,	LT	LOGS	CAMBRIA	15.05.91
Pullin, Stuart,	MID	URNU	U/A	14.10.04
Puritz, Sophie,	MID	URNU	U/A	22.10.03
Purser, Jacqueline,	MID	URNU	U/A	07.10.03
Pye, Steven,	ALT	URNU		21.10.97

Q

Name	Rank	Branch	Unit	Seniority
Quilter, George,	MID	URNU	U/A	26.10.05
Quinn, Luke,	MID	URNU	U/A	26.10.05
Quinn, Martin,	LT CDR	MEDIA	CAROLINE	
Quinn, Michael,	MID	URNU	U/A	13.10.04

R

Name	Rank	Branch	Unit	Seniority
Radjenovic, Zeljko,	ASL	NE	EAGLET RNR	28.10.04
Raffle, Edward,	MID	URNU	U/A	21.10.04
Rainford, Kate,	MID	URNU	U/A	07.10.05
Rajah, Pamela,	MID	URNU	U/A	16.10.03
Ramsay, Brian P., RD, MA	LT CDR	SM	PRESIDENT	31.03.01
Ramsdale, Timothy,	LT CDR	AIR	RNR AIR BR VL	31.03.02
Randall, Jeremy,	MID	URNU	U/A	13.10.05
Randall Orr, Jacqueline,	MID	URNU	U/A	06.10.05
Randles, Philip Neil,	LT	NCAGS	CALLIOPE	22.03.04
Rawlins, Michael,	MID	URNU	U/A	06.10.05
Rayer, Steven,	MID	URNU	U/A	22.10.03
Read, David Arthur, BSC	LT CDR	HQ	PRESIDENT	31.03.97
Redbourn, James,	MID	URNU	U/A	17.10.05
Reddin, Laura,	MID	URNU	U/A	13.10.05
Redmond, Robert,	LT CDR	COMM	PRESIDENT	31.03.00
Redpath, Scott,	MID	URNU	U/A	17.10.05
Redwood, Benjamin,	MID	URNU	U/A	14.10.04
Reen, Stephen,	LT	AIR	RNR AIR BR VL	01.10.92
Rees, Christopher,	MID	NE	U/A	22.11.05
Rees, Edward,	MID	URNU	U/A	17.10.05
Rees, Joseph,	MID	URNU	U/A	12.10.05
Rees, Joanne,	MID	URNU	U/A	07.10.04
Reid, Crawford,	ASGLTCDR		SCOTIA RNR	19.04.05
Reid, Iain,	LT CDR	AIR	RNR AIR BR VL	31.03.03
Rennell, Ian Joseph,	LT	SEA	EAGLET	19.11.96
Rennie, Ewan,	MID	URNU	U/A	08.10.05
Renouf, Robert Jeffery John,	ASL	NE	SCOTIA	29.01.03
Reynolds, Louisa,	CADET	URNU	U/A	09.10.97
Reynolds, Nelson James Elliott, RD	CDRE	MWHQ	CAROLINE	05.11.03
Reynolds, Paul,	SLT	URNU	U/A	13.10.05
Reynoldson, Howard, QVRM	LT CDR	AIR	RNR AIR BR VL	03.11.85
Richard-Dit-Leschery, Stanley Ernest, RD	LT CDR	AW	VIVID	22.11.92
Richards, Guy,	LT CDR	SEA	CAMBRIA	31.03.02
Richards, Helen Samantha,	ASL	NE	CAMBRIA	11.11.03
Richards, Jamie,	MID	URNU	U/A	17.10.05

Name	Rank	Branch	Unit	Seniority
Richards, Matthew,	ASL	URNU	U/A	03.10.02
Richards, Steven,	MID	URNU	U/A	25.08.03
Richardson, Ian,	LT CDR	DIS	FERRET (RNR)	15.01.91
Richardson, James,	MID	URNU	U/A	14.10.03
Richardson, Margaret Lynda Maither, RD	CDR	Q	DALRIADA	31.03.04
Richardson, Stuart,	MID	URNU	U/A	18.07.04
Richmond, Rebecca,	MID	URNU	U/A	07.10.03
Rickard, James,	MID	URNU	U/A	20.10.04
Rickard, Matthew,	MID	URNU	U/A	16.10.03
Rickard, Margaret Mary,	LT CDR	MS(F)	KING ALFRED	31.03.03
Ridler, Daniel,	MID	URNU	U/A	14.10.04
Ridley, Glenn,	MID	URNU	U/A	30.09.05
Rigden, James,	ASL	NE	FLYING FOX RNR	29.07.04
Riley, Benjamin,	MID	URNU	U/A	06.10.05
Riley, Heather,	MID	URNU	U/A	13.10.05
Riley, Peter John,	LT CDR	AW	CALLIOPE	31.03.98
Rimay-Muranyi, Gary,	LT	AWNIS	FERRET (RNR)	18.02.00
Ritchie, David,	LT CDR	AIR	RNR AIR BR VL	01.10.00
Roberton, Dominic,	MID	URNU	U/A	25.08.03
Roberts, David,	ASL	URNU	U/A	05.04.96
Roberts, Helena,	ASL	NE	EAGLET	23.01.03
Roberts, James Antony Frederick,	ASL	NE	FERRET (RNR)	20.05.04
Roberts, Robert Ellis,	ASL	NE	SCOTIA	23.09.03
Roberts, William,	MID	URNU	U/A	20.10.05
Robertshaw, Pamela,	LT CDR	AIR	RNR AIR BR VL	10.09.02
Robertson, Jennifer Louise,	ASL	NE	WILDFIRE	10.05.01
Robertson, Lorne, RD	LT CDR	MW	DALRIADA	31.03.96
Robertson, Stuart,	LT CDR	MCDO	U/A	08.11.99
Robinson, Anthony Michael, RD	LT CDR	AW	CAMBRIA	16.06.92
Robinson, Andrew Ronald,	ASL	NE	KING ALFRED	29.01.02
Robinson, Ian Michael, RD	CAPT	NA	SHERWOOD	30.09.01
Robinson, James Brian,	LT	DIS	FERRET (RNR)	24.02.90
Robinson, Martyn Shaun,	LT	SM	WILDFIRE	30.10.97
Robottom, Philip,	MID	URNU	U/A	05.10.04
Rogers, James,	MID	URNU	U/A	18.07.04
Rollings, David Jonathan, RD	LT CDR	HQ	CAMBRIA	30.10.87
Rollins, Anne,	LT	DIS	FERRET (RNR)	20.09.99
Romito, Charles,	ASL	URNU	U/A	28.04.05
Roscoe, Thomas,	MID	URNU	U/A	17.10.05
Rosindale, Philip, RD	LT	SEA	VIVID	19.05.97
Ross, Bruce James,	LT CDR	AW	KING ALFRED	
Ross, Jonathan, RD	LT CDR	MW	DALRIADA	31.03.98
Rowe, Susan Margaret, RD	LT CDR	NCAGS	VIVID	31.03.01
Rowland-Warmann, Mary-Jane,	MID	URNU	U/A	07.10.04
Rowles, Joanne,	LT	COMM	CAMBRIA	21.07.96
Rowley, Andrew,	ASL	URNU	U/A	10.08.00
Ruglys, Matthew,	LT CDR	AIR	RNR AIR BR VL	31.03.02
Rush, Jason,	MID	URNU	U/A	20.10.05
Russ, Philip John,	LT CDR	MWHQ	EAGLET	31.03.96
Ryan, Amy Jemima,	ASL	NE	FLYING FOX	04.08.00
Ryan, Peter,	PALT	AW	EAGLET	18.01.01
Ryan, Simon John D Arcy, QVRM, RD	LT CDR	HQ	EAGLET	31.03.99
Ryde, John,	MID	URNU	U/A	21.10.04
Rydiard, Micheal,	MID	URNU	U/A	10.10.05

S

Salmon, Natalie,	MID	URNU	U/A	12.10.04
Salt, Hedley,	LT	AIR	RNR AIR BR VL	01.09.93
Sambrook, Kate,	MID	URNU	U/A	06.10.05
San, Howald Kin Loong,	LT	SM	PRESIDENT	15.12.90
Sanders, Stephen,	LT	URNU	U/A	24.02.05
Sanderson, Jennifer Patricia,	LT	HQ	KING ALFRED	08.07.96

Name	Rank	Branch	Unit	Seniority
Sard, Alexandra, MBE, RD	LT CDR	LOGS	KING ALFRED	13.12.97
Satchell, Peter James,	LT CDR	MW	PRESIDENT	31.03.00
Sauboorah, Jennifer,	CADET	URNU	U/A	18.10.02
Saunders, Alice,	LT	AIR	RNR AIR BR VL	25.06.91
Saunders, Christopher,	MID	URNU	U/A	22.10.03
Saunders, David James, RD	LT CDR	MW	PRESIDENT	31.03.95
Saunders, Duncan,	ALT	URNU	U/A	03.10.02
Savage, David,	LT	H INT	FERRET (RNR)	16.06.98
Sayers, Emily,	MID	URNU	U/A	13.10.05
Scanlon, Michael Stephen,	ASL	NE	FERRET (RNR)	13.01.99
Scarth, Jessica,	MID	URNU	U/A	13.10.05
Scarth, Richard,	LT	SM	PRESIDENT	18.05.01
Schunke, Michael,	MID	URNU	U/A	06.10.03
Schwab, Robert,	LT CDR	AIR	RNR AIR BR VL	01.10.97
Scorfield, Steven,	MID	URNU	U/A	11.10.05
Scott, Anthony John,	ASL	NE	PRESIDENT	06.10.03
Scott, Alexandra,	MID	URNU	U/A	06.10.05
Scott, Adam,	MID	URNU	U/A	07.10.04
Scott, J G,	LT CDR	AW	PRESIDENT	31.03.99
Scott-Foxwell, Julian, RD	LT CDR	NA	U/A	15.03.98
Scribbins, Christopher John, RD	ACDR	HQ	CALLIOPE	11.10.91
Scrimgeour, John Martin,	ASL	NE	SHERWOOD	31.03.04
Scurlock-Jones, Rhydian,	MID	URNU	U/A	22.10.03
Seaborn, Adam,	LT	AIR	RNR AIR BR VL	01.05.02
Seabrook, Katie,	MID	URNU	U/A	04.10.04
Seager, Benjamin,	MID	URNU	U/A	12.10.04
Seager, Daniel,	MID	URNU	U/A	25.08.03
Seagrave, Martin,	MID	URNU	U/A	13.10.03
Seakins, Patrick Edward,	LT CDR	H INT	PRESIDENT	
Sealy, Douglas,	LT CDR	DIS	FERRET (RNR)	01.10.94
Searle, Geoffrey Derek, RD	LT CDR	MW	KING ALFRED	31.03.00
Seaton, Judith Ann,	SG LT	MEDF	VIVID	15.10.98
Segnatelli, Catherine,	MID	URNU	U/A	29.09.05
Selby, Camilla,	MID	URNU	U/A	30.09.05
Sen, Sohan,	MID	URNU	U/A	11.10.05
Sewell, Mark,	LT	AIR	RNR AIR BR VL	16.10.96
Shakespeare, Edward,	MID	URNU	U/A	20.10.04
Shakespeare, Martin, RD	LT CDR	DIS	FERRET (RNR)	31.03.97
Shannon, Tom, RD	LT CDR	URNU	U/A	01.11.95
Sharland, Craig,	MID	URNU	U/A	05.09.02
Sharp, Christopher,	MID	URNU	U/A	22.10.03
Sharpe, Christian,	ASL	NE	VIVID RNR	28.10.04
Sharples, Derek, RD	CDR	AIR	RNR AIR BR VL	05.03.02
Shaw, James Elliot, RD*	CDR	AW	PRESIDENT	30.09.97
Shawcross, Jayne,	LT CDR	AIR	RNR AIR BR VL	03.01.95
Shears, Stephen,	LT CDR	AIR	RNR AIR BR VL	31.03.00
Shelley, James Charles,	PSG LT		KING ALFRED	12.06.99
Shepherd, Sarah Louise,	ASL	NE	VIVID	10.05.01
Shepherd, Stephen Michael,	ALT	LOGS	KING ALFRED	
Shepherd, William James, RD	LT	DIS	FERRET (RNR)	25.04.95
Sheppard, Adam James,	ASL	NE	CAMBRIA	01.03.00
Sheppard, Edward,	MID	URNU	U/A	07.10.04
Sherman, Christopher James,	LT CDR	HQ	U/A	24.11.91
Sherriff, Jacqueline,	LT	MEDIA	VIVID	
Shilson, Stuart James,	ASL	NE	PRESIDENT	17.01.02
Shiner, David Michael,	LT	DIS	FERRET (RNR)	02.11.99
Shinner, Patrick,	LT CDR	SM	PRESIDENT	31.03.99
Shinner, Stephanie Katherine Fleur,	LT CDR	NCAGS	WILDFIRE	31.03.00
Shinner, Thomas,	MID	URNU	U/A	14.10.04
Shirley, Benjamin,	MID	URNU	U/A	25.08.03
Short, Matthew,	ASL	NE	PRESIDENT RNR	13.12.05
Shouler, Martin Clifford,	ASL	NE	PRESIDENT	27.09.98

Name	Rank	Branch	Unit	Seniority
Sides, James William,	ASL	NE	EAGLET	17.12.03
Sides, Susan, QVRM	LT CDR	HQ	FORWARD	30.09.91
Sigley, Arthur David Martin,	LT	AW	SCOTIA	05.07.04
Silcock, Craig,	ASL	NE	CAMBRIA RNR	13.04.05
Silcox, Anna,	MID	URNU	U/A	20.10.04
Silverton, Charles,	MID	URNU	U/A	18.10.04
Simmonds, Timothy Paul,	LT	MW	PRESIDENT	23.05.97
Simons, David,	MID	URNU	U/A	09.10.00
Simper, Katie,	MID	URNU	U/A	10.10.05
Simpson, Neil,	ASL	NE	SHERWOOD RNR	31.07.03
Simpson-Hayes, Gizella,	ASL	Q	PRESIDENT RNR	02.10.02
Sims, Richmal Jane,	LT	SM	KING ALFRED	16.08.98
Sinclair, Helga,	MID	URNU	U/A	06.10.05
Skeels-Piggins, Talan Stephen,	ALT	SM	FLYING FOX	
Skelly, Andrew James,	ASL	NE	CAROLINE	13.11.03
Skinner, Nigel Guy, BSC, M.ENG	LT	NCAGS	SHERWOOD	15.11.99
Skuriat, Olenka,	CADET	URNU	U/A	23.10.97
Slavin, David Eric,	SG CDR		KING ALFRED	08.05.03
Slocombe, Jane,	LT	AIR	RNR AIR BR VL	01.07.96
Slonecki, Adam,	ASL	NE	PRESIDENT RNR	18.01.05
Small, Pauline,	LT	Q	SCOTIA	15.03.98
Small, Peter Kenneth,	SG CDR		CALLIOPE	30.09.97
Smallpage, Mark,	MID	URNU	U/A	06.10.05
Smith, Benjamin,	MID	URNU	U/A	07.10.03
Smith, Christine,	MID	URNU	U/A	17.10.05
Smith, Christopher,	MID	URNU	U/A	16.10.03
Smith, David,	ALT	LOGS	EAGLET	03.07.01
Smith, Dale,	MID	URNU	U/A	25.08.03
Smith, Darren,	MID	URNU	U/A	26.10.05
Smith, Edward,	MID	URNU	U/A	21.10.04
Smith, Gordon,	LT CDR	AIR	RNR AIR BR VL	31.03.01
Smith, Jennifer,	MID	URNU	U/A	06.10.05
Smith, Jane Marion,	ASL	Q	VIVID	16.04.02
Smith, James,	ASL	NE	U/A	30.10.03
Smith, Karina,	MID	URNU	U/A	16.10.03
Smith, Mark,	MID	URNU	U/A	13.10.05
Smith, Michael,	LT	URNU	U/A	22.01.95
Smith, Martin Richard,	ASL	NE	VIVID	13.11.02
Smith, Peter,	LT CDR	AIR	RNR AIR BR VL	01.10.98
Smith, Rebecca,	ASL	NE	PRESIDENT RNR	03.01.06
Smith, Richard,	MID	URNU	U/A	14.10.04
Smith, Stephen,	LT	COMM	WILDFIRE	03.05.97
Smith, Tegan,	MID	URNU	U/A	30.09.05
Smith, William Charles,	ASL	NE	SCOTIA	02.12.99
Smith, Wilfred Donald Fitzroy, RD	SG CDR		EAGLET	30.09.99
Smithson, Ian,	MID	URNU	U/A	14.10.04
Smyth, Kiaran,	LT	URNU	U/A	11.02.05
Smyth, Michael Paul,	LT	MW	PRESIDENT	
Snalam, Felicity,	MID	URNU	U/A	14.10.03
Snoddon, Robert,	LT CDR	OPINT	CALLIOPE RNR	31.03.01
Solanki, Neha,	MID	URNU	U/A	12.10.04
Soltysiak, Paul,	MID	URNU	U/A	07.10.04
Soltysiak, Rebecca,	MID	URNU	U/A	26.10.05
Souter, Michael David, RD	LT CDR	MEDIA	WILDFIRE	
Southall, Karl,	MID	URNU	U/A	16.10.03
Southern, John,	ASL	NE	EAGLET	28.05.02
Speake, Jonathan,	LT	AIR	RNR AIR BR VL	01.12.90
Speirs, Laura,	MID	URNU	U/A	18.10.04
Spencer, Andrew,	SLT	URNU	U/A	14.10.04
Spencer, Gary,	LT CDR	AIR	RNR AIR BR VL	01.10.94
Spencer, Michael David,	ASL	NE	PRESIDENT	18.04.99

Name	Rank	Branch	Unit	Seniority
Spencer, Philip,	ASL	NE	WILDFIRE RNR	30.11.05
Spray, Alison, RD	LT CDR	NCAGS	VIVID	31.03.93
Spring, Jeremy,	LT CDR	AIR	RNR AIR BR VL	03.08.97
Sprowles, K J, RD	LT CDR	NCAGS	PRESIDENT	04.11.90
Cross, Elizabeth,	LT	H INT	FERRET (RNR)	
Squire, Robert James, RD	LT CDR	COMM	FORWARD	12.05.95
Stafford-Smith, Karen Julie, RD	LT CDR	SM	CAMBRIA	31.03.98
Stainer, Hannah,	MID	URNU	U/A	26.10.05
Stanley, Dermot Alan, RD	LT	SEA	CALLIOPE	12.01.96
Stanley, Nicholas,	LT	AIR	RNR AIR BR VL	16.09.93
Steele, Hannah,	MID	URNU	U/A	04.10.04
Steele, Katie,	MID	URNU	U/A	13.10.03
Stephen, Cameron,	MID	URNU	U/A	11.09.00
Stephen, Lesley,	LT	LOGS	DALRIADA	15.12.01
Stephenson, Michael Edward,	ASL	NE	EAGLET	19.11.98
Stevens, Rupert,	MID	URNU	U/A	22.09.04
Stevenson, Amadeus,	MID	URNU	U/A	11.10.05
Stewart, Allan,	LT CDR	SM	EAGLET	31.03.02
Stewart, Iain Alexander, RD	LT CDR	LOGS	SCOTIA	21.03.87
Stewart, Mathew,	MID	URNU	U/A	16.10.03
Stewart, William,	MID	URNU	U/A	20.10.05
Stickland, Anthony Charles Robert, RD	LT CDR	AW	KING ALFRED	31.03.98
Stidston, David,	LT CDR	AIR	RNR AIR BR VL	01.10.94
Stiles, Maxine,	MID	URNU	U/A	13.10.03
Stock, Rebecca,	MID	URNU	U/A	16.10.03
Stocker, Jeremy,	LT CDR	HQ	CALLIOPE	01.06.89
Stoddart, Craig,	MID	URNU	U/A	10.10.05
Stoffel, Thomas,	MID	URNU	U/A	05.11.03
Stokes, Carrie,	MID	URNU	U/A	20.10.05
Stone, Peter,	MID	URNU	U/A	14.10.04
Stones, Nicholas,	LT	URNU	U/A	09.10.95
Stopps, Jennifer,	MID	URNU	U/A	29.09.05
Storey, Christopher,	MID	URNU	U/A	14.10.03
Strachan, Robin Kinnear,	SG CDR		PRESIDENT	30.09.95
Strachan, Stuart,	MID	URNU	U/A	16.10.03
Strain, Justin Damian Russell,	LT	SEA	KING ALFRED	
Strain, Simon,	MID	URNU	U/A	26.10.05
Stringer, Karl,	LT	AIR	RNR AIR BR VL	16.03.97
Strivens-Joyce, Alexander,	MID	URNU	U/A	06.10.05
Strudwick, Peggy Barbara,	LT	LOGS	VIVID	17.12.96
Stubbs, Gary,	LT	AIR	RNR AIR BR VL	16.09.94
Styles, Sarah Jane,	ASL	NE	PRESIDENT	09.05.00
Suleman, Mohammed,	MID	URNU	U/A	13.10.05
Summerscales, Alison,	MID	URNU	U/A	20.10.05
Surrey, Elizabeth,	MID	URNU	U/A	11.10.05
Sutherland, Frances,	MID	URNU	U/A	16.10.03
Sutton, Anna,	MID	URNU	U/A	01.02.06
Swabey, Matthew,	MID	URNU	U/A	06.09.98
Swann, Judith Helen, QVRM, RD*, JP	CDR	NA	SHERWOOD	03.09.90
Sweenie, John Fraser,	ASG CDR		DALRIADA	21.01.03
Sykes, Danielle,	MID	URNU	U/A	16.10.03
Sykes, Samantha,	MID	URNU	U/A	22.10.03
Syme, Allan, RD*	LT CDR	HQ	DALRIADA	11.02.83
Symington, Anna Dimity Rose,	ASL	NE	FLYING FOX	11.06.02

T

Name	Rank	Branch	Unit	Seniority
Tait, David,	MID	URNU	U/A	14.10.04
Tall, Richard Edward,	LT	SM	FLYING FOX	14.12.97
Tam, Ho Man,	MID	URNU	U/A	01.12.05
Tarrant, David Charles,	LT CDR	AW	KING ALFRED	30.11.93
Tate, Philip,	MID	URNU	U/A	04.10.04
Taylor, Adam,	MID	URNU	U/A	30.09.05

Name	Rank	Branch	Unit	Seniority
Taylor, Alexander,	MID	URNU	U/A	07.10.04
Taylor, Louise Elizabeth, RD	LT CDR	NCAGS	EAGLET	31.03.00
Taylor, Matthew,	MID	URNU	U/A	13.10.05
Taylor, Neville Graham,	LT CDR	INFOP	CALLIOPE	
Taylor, Penelope Jane,	ASL	Q	PRESIDENT	18.05.04
Taylor, Rupert James, RD	LT CDR	AW	KING ALFRED	31.03.99
Taylor, Stewart,	ASL	NE	FORWARD RNR	22.11.05
Taylor, Timothy,	LT CDR	AIR	RNR AIR BR VL	01.10.00
Teasdale, David,	LT CDR	SM	FLYING FOX	31.03.04
Teesdale, William,	MID	URNU	U/A	20.10.04
Telfer, Alison, RD	LT CDR	NCAGS	EAGLET	30.09.91
Temple, Miles,	LT	SEA	WILDFIRE	01.11.94
Theakston, Sally,	CHAPLAIN (R)	CE	WILDFIRE RNR	24.04.99
Thomas, Andrew,	ASL	NE	PRESIDENT	15.10.03
Thomas, Anerin,	MID	URNU	U/A	06.10.05
Thomas, Charlotte Mary,	LT	LOGS	PRESIDENT	29.09.03
Thomas, David Graham,	LT	COMM	KING ALFRED	12.07.02
Thomas, David James,	ASL	NE	CAMBRIA	27.02.02
Thomas, Emma Margaret,	LT CDR	MEDIA	WILDFIRE	31.03.01
Thomas, Kathleen,	MID	URNU	U/A	14.10.04
Thomas, Owen,	MID	URNU	U/A	22.10.03
Thomas, Paul,	SLT	URNU	U/A	11.11.04
Thomas, Richard,	MID	URNU	U/A	21.10.04
Thomas, Stephen Paul,	LT	MW	CAMBRIA	26.01.97
Thomas, Tenny,	MID	URNU	U/A	20.10.99
Thomason, Michael,	LT	LOGS	EAGLET	09.11.97
Thompson, Andrew John, RD	CDR	NCAGS	VIVID	30.09.01
Thompson, Daniel,	MID	URNU	U/A	17.10.05
Thompson, Glenn,	LT CDR	AIR	RNR AIR BR VL	31.03.99
Thompson, Jennifer,	MID	URNU	U/A	11.10.04
Thompson, Mareike,	MID	URNU	U/A	06.10.05
Thomson, Cameron,	MID	URNU	U/A	10.10.02
Thomson, Frederick Davie,	ASL	NE	DALRIADA	23.01.03
Thomson, Paul,	MID	URNU	U/A	07.10.99
Thomson, Susie Jane,	LT CDR	MEDIA	FLYING FOX	31.03.99
Thomson, Sheena Rosemary, BA	LT CDR	MEDIA	SCOTIA	31.03.00
Thorne, Brian John, RD	CDR	COMM	CAMBRIA	30.09.97
Thorne, Lee,	LT CDR	MW	SHERWOOD	31.03.02
Thorne, Stephen Paul, RD	CAPT	COMM	KING ALFRED	30.09.03
Thorpe, Alexander,	ASL	NE	SHERWOOD RNR	24.11.04
Thurston Smith, Carolyn,	MID	URNU	U/A	07.10.04
Tibbitts, James,	MID	URNU	U/A	18.10.04
Tidder, James,	MID	URNU	U/A	06.10.05
Tighe, Gary,	LT CDR	AIR	RNR AIR BR VL	01.02.91
Tilney, Duncan Edward,	LT	MW	WILDFIRE	
Tindall-Jones, Julia Mary, BA	CDR	LOGS	VIVID	30.09.01
Titmus, Aaron,	MID	URNU	U/A	14.10.04
Todd, Andrew Harry Campbell,	LT CDR	NCAGS	SCOTIA	31.03.98
Todd, Christopher,	MID	URNU	U/A	14.10.03
Todd, Susan,	ALT	URNU	U/A	21.10.02
Tonkin, Neil,	LT CDR	AIR	RNR AIR BR VL	01.10.90
Toon, Nicola,	MID	URNU	U/A	20.10.05
Topping, Mark,	LT CDR	HQ	CAMBRIA	31.03.97
Torrens, Victoria,	MID	URNU	U/A	07.10.04
Trangmar, Paul Anthony,	LT	NCAGS	WILDFIRE	22.11.93
Treasure, Samuel,	MID	URNU	U/A	24.10.02
Trehearn, Gareth,	MID	URNU	U/A	01.10.03
Trelawny, Christopher Charles, RD	LT	SEA	PRESIDENT	14.12.89
Trelinska, Victoria Jane, V, J, LOCOCK, RD	ACDR	NA	SHERWOOD	18.12.01
Treloar, Philip Michael,	LT CDR	MEDIA	WILDFIRE	
Tribe, David,	LT CDR	AIR	RNR AIR BR VL	31.03.99
Trimmer, Patrick David Mark,	LT CDR	HQ	CALLIOPE	31.03.96

Name	Rank	Branch	Unit	Seniority
Trott, Craig,	LT CDR	AIR	RNR AIR BR VL	31.03.05
Tubb, Anna,	MID	URNU	U/A	12.10.00
Tucker-Peake, Andrew,	MID	URNU	U/A	07.10.04
Tuckwood, Alex,	MID	URNU	U/A	13.10.05
Tudor, William,	MID	URNU	U/A	13.10.04
Tulloch, Alan,	SLT	X	U/A	08.04.87
Tuppen, Heather,	LT	MEDIA	WILDFIRE	24.10.94
Turnbull, Rhona,	MID	URNU	U/A	09.10.03
Turner, Jonathan Andrew McMahon, RD	SG CAPT		KING ALFRED	30.09.03
Turner, Simon John,	LT CDR	AWNIS	VIVID	31.03.99
Tweed, Jonathan,	MID	URNU	U/A	08.10.02
Tweed, Susan Linda, JP, RD*	CDR	NCAGS	VIVID	30.09.99
Tweedie, Nicola,	ASL	NE	VIVID RNR	01.03.05
Twinn, Richard,	MID	URNU	U/A	11.07.05
Tyrrell, (Carol Marguerite), Cm	LT CDR	DIS	FERRET (RNR)	11.04.90

U

Name	Rank	Branch	Unit	Seniority
Ulriksen, Helena,	MID	URNU	U/A	14.10.04
Upson, James,	MID	URNU	U/A	18.10.04
Ure, Fiona,	ASL	NE	CAROLINE	01.11.02
Urquhart, Nicola,	ASL	NE	DALRIADA RNR	20.01.04
Urquhart, Nicola Jane,	ASL	NE	DALRIADA	20.01.04
Urquhart, Roderick William,	ASL	NE	PRESIDENT	27.11.03
Utting, Penelope Anne,	LT CDR	MEDIA	KING ALFRED	31.03.01

V

Name	Rank	Branch	Unit	Seniority
Valentine, Robert Innes,	LT CDR	SEA	SCOTIA	31.03.99
Vallins, Mark,	MID	URNU	U/A	29.10.03
Van Asch, Edward,	MID	URNU	U/A	24.10.02
Van-Den-Bergh, Mark, M, VAN, DEN, BERGH,	LT	HQ	WILDFIRE	16.12.92
Varley, Peter,	CDR	AIR	RNR AIR BR VL	05.03.02
Vatcher, James,	MID	URNU	U/A	24.10.02
Vellosa, Linda,	CADET	URNU	U/A	08.10.02
Vernon, Michael A, RD	LT CDR	COMM	VIVID	27.08.90
Versallion, Mark,	ASL	NE	WILDFIRE	20.06.02
Vicker-Craddock, Jonathan,	MID	URNU	U/A	29.10.03
Vickers, Mark,	ASL	NE	PRESIDENT RNR	26.10.05
Vickerstaff, Rachel,	MID	URNU	U/A	16.10.03
Vila, Nina,	ASL	NE	WILDFIRE RNR	20.01.05
Vincent, Claire Elaine,	LT CDR	AWNIS	KING ALFRED	31.03.04
Vitali, Julie Elizabeth,	LT	DIS	FERRET (RNR)	08.06.96
Vora, Raju,	MID	URNU	U/A	24.10.02

W

Name	Rank	Branch	Unit	Seniority
Wainwright, Barnaby,	LT CDR	AIR	RNR AIR BR VL	01.09.89
Wake, Christopher,	MID	URNU	U/A	05.10.04
Wake, Thomas Baldwin, RD	LT CDR	COMM	SHERWOOD	31.03.00
Wakefield, David,	ASL	NE	EAGLET RNR	17.11.04
Wakefield, Gary,	CDR	AIR	RNR AIR BR VL	01.07.05
Wakeford, Mark Warren,	LT CDR	MEDIA	KING ALFRED	
Walden, (Geoffery Gerald), G	LT	SM	SHERWOOD	10.12.90
Wale, (Martin Charles Johnson), M C	LT CDR	DIS	FERRET (RNR)	01.08.86
Wales, Frederick Anthony, RD	LT CDR	AW	KING ALFRED	31.03.98
Walker, David,	LT CDR	LOGS	PRESIDENT	31.03.97
Walker, Graeme,	MID	URNU	U/A	10.09.01
Walker, Gregory,	MID	URNU	U/A	16.10.03
Walker, Paul MacKenzie,	LT	DIS	CALLIOPE	14.02.03
Wallace, Stuart Iain,	LT	AW	EAGLET	23.07.99
Wallace, Simon John,	ASL	AW	SHERWOOD	08.06.00
Waller, James,	ASL	NE	PRESIDENT	14.11.00

Name	Rank	Branch	Unit	Seniority
Waller, Vincent Francis, RD	LT CDR	AW	CALLIOPE	01.09.88
Wallom, Anne,	LT	MEDIA	SCOTIA	13.09.92
Walters, Philippa,	MID	URNU	U/A	06.10.05
Walters, Richard,	LT CDR	AW	PRESIDENT	31.03.04
Walthall, Fiona Elizabeth,	LT CDR	NCAGS	SCOTIA	31.03.02
Walworth, William Michael,	CDR	AW	PRESIDENT	30.09.95
Ward, Eleanore Joan,	ASL	NE	KING ALFRED	04.03.03
Ward, Gareth,	MID	URNU	U/A	25.08.03
Ward, Rebecca,	MID	URNU	U/A	14.10.04
Ward, Suzanne,	CADET	URNU	U/A	30.09.97
Warner, M J,	PSG LT		PRESIDENT	07.08.02
Warnock, Gavin,	LT CDR	AIR	RNR AIR BR VL	01.10.95
Warren, David,	MID	URNU	U/A	14.10.04
Warwick, Andrew,	MID	URNU	U/A	26.10.05
Washington, Josephine Jane MacKenzie,	MID	NE	VIVID	09.12.03
Waskett, Daniel,	ASL	NE	VIVID	25.09.02
Waskett, Ellena,	MID	URNU	U/A	06.10.05
Wastnage, Elizabeth,	MID	URNU	U/A	20.10.05
Waters, Anna,	CADET	URNU	U/A	11.10.01
Waters, Christopher Martin,	LT CDR	NCAGS	KING ALFRED	01.05.86
Waterworth, Angela,	ASL	NE	FORWARD RNR	07.12.05
Waterworth, Stephen Norman,	LT	COMM	CAROLINE	01.04.93
Dawson, Melissa,	ASL	NE	SCOTIA	26.06.00
Watkins, Nicola,	MID	URNU	U/A	06.10.05
Watkis, Andrew,	MID	URNU	U/A	18.07.04
Watson, Catherine, RD	LT CDR	HQ	EAGLET	31.03.98
Watson, David,	MID	URNU	U/A	06.11.00
Watson, Andrew,	MID	URNU	U/A	14.10.03
Watson, Lloyd,	LT CDR	AIR	RNR AIR BR VL	01.10.94
Watt, Stuart,	LT CDR	NA	U/A	01.12.03
Watts, Nicholas,	MID	URNU	U/A	11.10.01
Weaver, Peter Malcolm Gerard,	ALT	HQ	VIVID	
Webb, Christopher,	LT CDR	LOGS	KING ALFRED	
Webber, Steven John Anthony Maltravers,	LT CDR	LOGS	FLYING FOX	
Weber, Matthew,	MID	URNU	U/A	24.10.02
Webster, Andrew,	LT CDR	AIR	RNR AIR BR VL	05.05.99
Webster, Elizabeth Lucy,	ASL	NE	CALLIOPE	06.05.04
Wedgwood, Jonathon James,	PSURGLCDR		SCOTIA	26.11.98
Weerapperuma, Sudath,	MID	URNU	U/A	26.10.05
Wells, Christopher Michael,	LT CDR	AW	KING ALFRED	31.03.94
Wells, Rebecca Jane,	ASL	NE	VIVID	08.04.02
Welsh, Audrey,	LT	COMM	WILDFIRE	17.02.97
Welsh, James,	MID	URNU	U/A	14.10.03
Welsh, Nicholas Paul,	ASL	NE	PRESIDENT	17.10.01
Welton, Thomas,	MID	URNU	U/A	20.10.05
Wesley, John R,	LT CDR	HQ	PRESIDENT	12.11.89
West, Alastair,	MID	URNU	U/A	07.10.04
West, Nicholas,	LT CDR	AIR	RNR AIR BR VL	31.03.99
West, Susan Elizabeth,	SG CDR	MEDF	PRESIDENT	30.09.01
Westlake, Simon,	MID	URNU	U/A	29.10.03
Weston, Rowan,	MID	URNU	U/A	01.10.03
Westwood, Amelia,	MID	URNU	U/A	22.10.03
Westwood, Steve,	CDR	AIR	RNR AIR BR VL	30.09.03
Whalley, Simon,	ASL	NE	FLYING FOX RNR	14.04.05
Wheatley, Wendy,	LT CDR	AIR	RNR AIR BR VL	04.10.97
Wheeler, Joanne Natalie,	ASL	NE	KING ALFRED	01.05.01
Wheeler, Robert Alec,	SG CDR		KING ALFRED	30.09.98
Wheeler, Robert Frederick William Georg,	ASL	NE	PRESIDENT	13.02.03
Wheeler, Sophia Rebecca Frances,	LT	SM	PRESIDENT	07.03.03
Whitbread, Jonathon,	ASL	NE	SHERWOOD RNR	07.06.05
Whitby, Philip, VRSM	LT CDR	SM	VIVID	26.12.90
Whitby, Stephen,	LT CDR	HQ	SCOTIA	01.01.92

Name	Rank	Branch	Unit	Seniority
White, Duncan,	MID	URNU	U/A	17.10.05
White, Ian Roy, RD	LT CDR	HQ	CALLIOPE	31.03.96
White, Michael Eaton Lane,	LT	AWNIS	VIVID	
Whitehead, Keith Stuart, BSC, RD	LT CDR	HQ	KING ALFRED	31.03.00
Whitelaw, Darren,	MID	URNU	U/A	14.10.04
Whiting, Mark,	ASL	NE	FLYING FOX RNR	30.11.05
Whitlock, Michael,	LT	NCAGS	U/A	01.11.04
Whitwell, Jonathan,	MID	URNU	U/A	14.10.03
Wickens, Ian,	LT CDR	AIR	RNR AIR BR VL	31.03.00
Widdowson, Matthew,	MID	URNU	U/A	05.09.02
Wilcockson, Alastair Quentin,	SG LTCDR		KING ALFRED	24.07.93
Wilkie, Suzanne Ellen,	LT CDR	HQ	SCOTIA	
Wilkinson, Douglas Allan,	ASGLTCDR		PRESIDENT RNR	28.10.04
Wilkinson, John,	MID	URNU	U/A	04.10.04
Wilkinson, Sarah,	CADET	URNU	U/A	01.12.00
Wilks, Dominic,	MID	URNU	U/A	05.10.04
Williams, Andrew Bruce,	LT CDR	DIS	FERRET (RNR)	01.07.95
Williams, Camellia,	MID	URNU	U/A	14.10.04
Williams, Catherine,	MID	URNU	U/A	13.10.05
Williams, Gareth,	MID	URNU	U/A	20.10.05
Williams, Julia Elisa Maria,	ASL	NE	FORWARD	11.12.03
Williams, Kevin,	SLT	OPINT	FLYING FOX RNR	15.10.03
Williams, Laurent,	MID	URNU	U/A	17.10.05
Williams, Michelle,	MID	URNU	U/A	04.10.04
Williams, Mark Jeremy,	LT	NCAGS	EAGLET	27.10.92
Williams, Matthew,	MID	URNU	U/A	11.10.05
Williams, Matthew,	MID	URNU	U/A	14.10.04
Williams, Rudolf Steven,	ASL	NE	VIVID	01.05.02
Williams, Simon Jeremy,	ASL	NE	FLYING FOX	18.10.02
Williams, Thomas Gerard Jeavon Lytton,	ASL	NE	PRESIDENT	02.12.03
Williams, Timothy Paul,	LT	MW	WILDFIRE	22.09.95
Williams-Allden, Lucy,	MID	URNU	U/A	05.09.02
Williamson, Stephen,	LT	AIR	RNR AIR BR VL	01.03.89
Williamson, Simon,	ASL	NE	SHERWOOD RNR	09.04.02
Willis, Georgina,	MID	URNU	U/A	26.10.05
Wills, Bradley,	MID	URNU	U/A	14.10.04
Wilson, Christopher,	MID	URNU	U/A	11.10.04
Wilson, Gary,	LT CDR	URNU	U/A	10.10.95
Wilson, Iain,	MID	URNU	U/A	08.10.05
Wilson, Jonathan,	ASL	NE	SCOTIA	30.05.99
Wilson, Jennifer,	LT CDR	Q	FLYING FOX	31.03.95
Wilson, Matthew,	MID	URNU	U/A	14.10.04
Wilson, Peter,	LT CDR	AIR	RNR AIR BR VL	07.09.99
Wilson, Stephen John,	SG CDR		PRESIDENT	30.09.02
Winder, Nicholas,	SLT	URNU	U/A	06.12.02
Window, Stephen Harvey,	LT CDR	MCDO	KING ALFRED	
Winfield, Adrian,	LT CDR	AIR	RNR AIR BR VL	31.03.99
Winstanley, Nichola Ann, VRSM	LT CDR	MEDIA	VIVID	31.03.95
Wiseman, Hugo,	MID	URNU	U/A	13.10.05
Wiseman, Kathryn,	CADET	URNU	U/A	11.10.01
Wolfe, Jennifer,	SLT	Q	DALRIADA RNR	24.12.02
Wolstenholme, David,	LT CDR	AIR	RNR AIR BR VL	01.10.93
Wood, John,	LT CDR	COMM	CALLIOPE	31.03.01
Wood, Justin,	LT CDR	AIR	RNR AIR BR VL	01.03.90
Wood, Suzanne,	LT	HQ	PRESIDENT	05.04.93
Woodham, Jeremy,	LT CDR	AIR	RNR AIR BR VL	02.07.92
Woodman, Clive Andrew,	LT CDR	MEDIA	VIVID	
Woodman, Clare Francesca Jane,	LT	LOGS	VIVID	01.09.88
Woods, Fergus,	LT CDR	AIR	RNR AIR BR VL	01.10.88
Woodward, Ian,	MID	URNU	U/A	06.10.05
Wooley, Stephen,	MID	URNU	U/A	20.10.05
Wordie, Andrew George Lyon, RD	LT CDR	COMM	WILDFIRE	31.03.95

Name	Rank	Branch	Unit	Seniority
Wordsworth, Helen,	ALT	MEDF	EAGLET	24.07.01
Worman, Robin,	LT CDR	AIR	RNR AIR BR VL	01.10.98
Worsley, Alistair, RD	LT CDR	MEDIA	WILDFIRE	
Wray, Ronald Maurice,	LT CDR	NCAGS	KING ALFRED	31.03.99
Wreford, Katrine,	LT CDR	MEDIA	SCOTIA	31.03.93
Wrigglesworth, Peter John,	SG LTCDR		SHERWOOD	02.08.88
Wright, Alan Howard,	LT CDR	AW	EAGLET	01.11.91
Wright, Antony,	LT CDR	AIR	RNR AIR BR VL	01.10.97
Wright, Douglas John,	LT	DIS	FERRET (RNR)	26.01.96
Wright, Iain Alistair MacKay,	LT CDR	DIS	FERRET (RNR)	18.08.97
Wright, Matthew,	MID	URNU	U/A	18.10.02
Wright, Stephen,	LT CDR	COMM	KING ALFRED	31.03.00
Wright, Stephen, GM	LT CDR	AIR	RNR AIR BR VL	31.03.01
Wright, Samual,	ASL	NE	PRESIDENT RNR	28.10.05
Wrightson, Ian,	LT CDR	AIR	RNR AIR BR VL	31.03.03
Wring, Matthew Anthony,	LT CDR	MW	FLYING FOX	31.03.03
Wyatt, Mark Edward, RD	CDR	MW	KING ALFRED	30.09.99
Wyglendacz, Jan Andrew, RD	LT CDR	LOGS	CAMBRIA	31.03.03
Hall, Sharon,	LT CDR	AIR	RNR AIR BR VL	31.03.04

X

Xu, Hui,	CADET	URNU	U/A	24.10.01

Y

Yates, Steven,	LT CDR	MW	FLYING FOX	31.03.00
Yibowei, Christophe Amaebi,	ASL	NE	PRESIDENT	06.12.00
Yong, Andrew,	ASL	NE	PRESIDENT RNR	02.12.04
Young, Carl,	LT CDR	AIR	RNR AIR BR VL	31.03.98
Young, Duncan Alexander, RD	LT CDR	MWHQ	CALLIOPE	31.03.98
Young, Gregory Christian,	LT	MW	PRESIDENT	30.11.02
Young, William David,	LT	LOGS	KING ALFRED	11.05.93
Yoxall, William,	MID	URNU	U/A	20.10.05
Yu, Mary Man Wah,	MID	URNU	U/A	12.10.04
Yule, Steven,	MID	URNU	U/A	06.10.05

ROYAL NAVAL RESERVE INTERPRETERS

Name	Date of Rank Re-qualifying	Qualifying or
FRENCH		
Nicholson, P.A.	LT CDR	1980
Pressagh, J.P.	LT CDR	1994
GERMAN		
Cobbold, A.R.	LT	2001
Pressagh, J.P.	LT CDR	1983
ITALIAN		
Pressagh, J.P.	LT CDR	1999
Alcock, M.L.	LT	2001
JAPANESE		
Nicholson, P.A.	LT CDR	1995
PERSIAN		
Cobbold, A.R.	LT	1982

Name	Date of Rank Re-qualifying	Qualifying or
POLISH		
Pressagh, J.P.	LT CDR	1989
RUSSIAN		
Cobbold, A.R.	LT	1989
Pressagh, J.P.	LT CDR	1995
Seakins, P.E.	LT	1995
Jones, L.	LT CDR	1989
SPANISH		
Alcock, M.L.	LT	1995
Nicholson, P.A.	LT CDR	1997
Pressagh, J.P.	LT CDR	1993

ROYAL MARINES RESERVE

Name	Rank	Branch	Unit	Seniority
A				
Ardron, , ...Lt	RM	LONDON	01.07.99
B				
Baker, Al, ...Act Capt	RM	LONDON	26.10.02
Barnwell, Barry, T F .... Lt Col	RM	SCOTLAND	01.08.00
Bates, , ... 2lt	RM	LONDON	20.01.00
Billington, Edward, ...Capt	RM	MERSEYSIDE	07.06.92
Birt, James, ...Capt	RM	LONDON	14.11.02
Blyth, Sandy, ... Lt Col	RM	SCOTLAND	30.06.98
Board, , ...Capt	RM	LONDON	15.05.00
Brooker-Gillespie, Robin, ...Capt	RM	LONDON	01.07.99
Brown, Roger, ...Maj	RM	MERSEYSIDE	15.07.90
Bruce, Rory, ... Lt Col	RM	BRISTOL	30.06.98
Brunskill, , ...Lt	RM	MERSEYSIDE	01.07.99
Burnham, Paul, ...Lt	RM	MERSEYSIDE	
C				
Campbell, Michael, ...Maj	RM	TYNE	01.04.95
Cazeaux, , ... 2lt	RM	BRISTOL	14.10.03
Chamberlain, , ...Capt	RM	BRISTOL	28.04.94
Coard, Thomas, RD................................Maj	RM	SCOTLAND	30.06.98
Cole, Simon, ...Capt	RM	BRISTOL	10.12.02
Crichton, Dayle, ...Capt	RM	SCOTLAND	26.02.03
D				
Darling, Robert, ...Capt	RM	LONDON	02.10.02
Diamond, Nicholas, ...Act Capt	RM	BRISTOL	
Doubleday, , ...Capt	RM	LONDON	15.05.00
Dyer, Andrew, ... 2lt	RM	TYNE	
E				
Edgar, Alastair, ...Act Capt	RM	MERSEYSIDE	
F				
Fielder, , ...Maj	RM	BRISTOL	10.04.02
Figgins, Philip John, ...Maj	RM	FERRET (RNR)	
Finn, , ... 2lt	RM	BRISTOL	11.01.02
Fox Robinson, , ... 2lt	RM	LONDON	06.01.03
Fox-Robinson, John, ...Capt	RM	LONDON	
G				
Gardiner, Andy, ...Capt	RM	SBSR POOLE	
Garnham, Simon, ...Maj	RM	MERSEYSIDE	
Gibson, Mark, ...Maj	RM	MERSEYSIDE	01.02.02
Goldsmith, Andy, ...Capt	RM	SCOTLAND	
H				
Hale, William, ... 2lt	RM	LONDON	
Hall, David, ... Act Maj	RM	TYNE	22.07.96

Name	Rank	Branch	Unit	Seniority
Halls, Montagu,	Maj	RM	BRISTOL	09.11.99
Harker, ,	Capt	RM	TYNE	15.11.01
Hayes, ,	2lt	RM	MERSEYSIDE	23.01.02
Henderson, Andrew,	Maj	RM	LONDON	
Hillman, David,	Capt	RM	SCOTLAND	07.01.00
Holt, Andy,	Lt Col	RM	MERSEYSIDE	31.12.93
Hough, Brian, RD	Col	RM	MERSEYSIDE	01.06.97
Hunter, Karri,	2lt	RM	SCOTLAND	

I

Illingworth, Richard,	Act Capt	RM	TYNE	
Ing, John,	Maj	RM	LONDON	01.09.94

J

Jackson, Fraser,	Capt	RM	SCOTLAND	01.10.92
Jobbins, Paul, OBE, GM, RD*	Lt Col	RM	U/A	01.04.01

K

Kedward, Christopher,	2lt	RM	BRISTOL	
Kilmartin, Steven,	Capt	RM	MERSEYSIDE	06.09.00
Kinninmonth, ,	Lt	RM	SCOTLAND	14.09.01
Knox, David,	Maj	RM	TYNE	01.07.99

L

Lacy, Andrew,	2lt	RM	MERSEYSIDE	
Lacy,	Act Maj	RM	MERSEYSIDE	01.04.91
Lang, Tom,	Brig	RM	BRISTOL	28.02.95
Lewis, ,	2lt	RM	BRISTOL	08.01.02
Lewis, Robbie,	Capt	RM	BRISTOL	01.07.98
Loynes, Philip,	Lt Col	RM	MERSEYSIDE	31.12.94

M

Mannion, Stephen,	Maj	RM	SBSR POOLE	26.03.96
Mantella, Dante,	Act Maj	RM	LONDON	
March, Jefreey,	Lt Col	RM	MERSEYSIDE	01.07.99
Mason, Andrew,	Capt	RM	BRISTOL	17.12.95
Mather, ,	Maj	RM	LONDON	01.07.99
Mawhood, Christopher,	Maj	RM	MERSEYSIDE	01.09.87
May, ,	Maj	RM	MERSEYSIDE	01.05.02
McBride, Robert,	Act Capt	RM	MERSEYSIDE	
McCabe, Garry,	Maj	RM	SCOTLAND	22.09.03
McGovern, James,	Act Capt	RM	LONDON	14.05.01
McKinney, Mark,	Maj	RM	SCOTLAND	
McLaughlin, Stephen,	Capt	RM	SCOTLAND	18.09.91
McNeil, ,	Capt	RM	LONDON	01.07.99
Mirtle, Frank, RD	Col	RM	LONDON	01.06.99
Monk, Christopher,	Maj	RM	BRISTOL	
Moulton, Fred,	Maj	RM	BRISTOL	27.04.92

P

Parker, William,	Lt	RM	BRISTOL	
Player, ,	Col	RM	LONDON	01.07.99
Pott, ,	2lt	RM	LONDON	05.08.97
Pyke, Daniel,	2lt	RM	BRISTOL	

R

Radford, Barry, MBE	Col	RM	BRISTOL	30.06.94
Raitt, James,	Act Maj	RM	TYNE	01.09.97

Name	Rank	Branch	Unit	Seniority
Richards, Gavin, RD	Actltcol	RM	LONDON	16.09.93
Richards, Stephen,	Maj	RM	RNR AIR BR VL	28.04.94
Roberts, John,	Maj	RM	SCOTLAND	22.08.92
Rowlstone, David,	Maj	RM	MERSEYSIDE	01.04.97

S

Name	Rank	Branch	Unit	Seniority
Schofield, Samuel,	Lt	RM	MERSEYSIDE	05.02.03
Scott, John,	Maj	RM	BRISTOL	06.02.04
Sharp, Gordon,	Maj	RM	LONDON	30.06.98
Simpson, Alister,	Capt	RM	RNR AIR BR VL	
Smith, Anthony,	Lt Col	RM	BRISTOL	31.12.85
Smith, Fraser,	Maj	RM	LONDON	03.08.96
Smith, Gregory,	2lt	RM	LONDON	
Storrie, ,	Capt	RM	BRISTOL	24.04.91
Street, Charles,	Maj	RM	TYNE	01.08.94

T

Name	Rank	Branch	Unit	Seniority
Tarnowski, Tom,	Act Maj	RM	LONDON	20.08.01
Tayler, Harry,	Maj	RM	LONDON	04.02.03
Terry, Stuart,	Maj	RM	FERRET (RNR)	
Thompson, Joe,	Capt	RM	TYNE	01.12.00
Tompkins, Richard Michael,	Maj	RM	FERRET (RNR)	
Tonner, Raymond,	Maj	RM	BRISTOL	03.05.95
Travis, Adrian, RD	Maj	RM	LONDON	01.05.96

W

Name	Rank	Branch	Unit	Seniority
Waddell, Ian, RD	Capt	RM	SCOTLAND	01.07.99
Wall, John,	2lt	RM	TYNE	
Watkinson, Neil,	Maj	RM	LONDON	02.09.92
Watkinson, ,	Capt	RM	LONDON	01.07.99
Watt, ,	Maj	RM	BRISTOL	22.01.95
Wilkinson, Andrew,	Lt	RM	SBSR POOLE	02.11.02
Woodbridge, Giles,	Capt	RM	LONDON	
Woodward, Aston,	Act Capt	RM	LONDON	11.02.03
Woosey, ,	Capt	RM	BRISTOL	01.06.02

X

Name	Rank	Branch	Unit	Seniority
Xiberras, Maurice,	Act Capt	RM	MERSEYSIDE	01.02.03

READY AYE READY

SEA CADET CORPS

Name	Rank	Seniority	Name	Rank	Seniority
A			Barras, Hugh	Lt Cdr	01/08/04
			Barron, Edward Richard	Capt	15/10/91
Adams, Thomas Arthur	Lt	07/09/83	Bartleman, Alexander	Lt	26/11/73
Adey, Kay Lorraine	Sub Lt	28/03/04	Bartlett, Jonathan	Lt Cdr	21/09/96
Agnew, Anthony Peter	Capt	01/11/01	Bassett, Gary Terence	Lt	28/11/96
Allam, John Geoffrey	Lt	31/08/87	Bayley, George William	Lt	24/03/99
Allam, Vicki Margaret	Lt	14/05/00	Bayliss, John Albert	Lt Cdr	14/02/87
Allen, Karen Louise	Lt	08/10/88	Bayton, Trevor Edwin	Lt	25/02/00
Allen, Leslie John	Lt Cdr	01/01/99	Beal, Peter David	Lt	26/03/87
Andersen, Kim Aage Victor	Capt	01/07/99	Bedford, Michael Anthony	Lt	01/04/86
Anderson, Alex Jon	Lt	30/03/00	Bell, Brian	Lt	25/02/00
Anderson, Alison Sian	Lt	27/01/06	Bell, Joseph Albert	Lt	13/09/01
Anderson, Robert William Edward	Lt	01/04/99	Bell, Veronica Ann	Lt	29/01/98
Appleby, Keith	Lt	21/02/98	Bennett, Angela Delia	Lt	08/11/98
Archbold, Dennis	Lt Cdr	11/08/99	Bennett, John	Sub Lt	12/06/05
Archbold, Theresa	Lt	20/11/97	Bennett, Stephen	Sub Lt	01/12/00
Archer, Barry Philip	Lt	08/03/94	Bentley, Chris	Sub Lt	22/02/04
Archer, Lynn	Lt	14/11/96	Benton, Anthony Robert Smith	Capt	01/08/99
Argo, James Thomson	Lt	30/11/02	Benton, Ruth Jeannette	Lt Cdr	01/07/04
Aston, Lisa Anne	Sub Lt	12/03/05	Beresford-Hartwell, Christopher William	Sub Lt	09/02/04
Atkins, Doreen E	Lt	08/04/92	Bereznyckyj, Nicholas	Maj	01/12/04
Attwood, Anthony Victor	Lt	22/02/89	Bereznyckyj, Susan Dorothy	Lt Cdr	01/01/05
Avill, Fraser William	Sub Lt	25/09/05	Bickle, Margaret	Sub Lt	05/05/96
Avill, Susan Elizabeth	Lt	01/11/89	Bilby, Glyn Thomas Charles	Lt	20/11/91
Ayers, William Anthony	Lt	04/01/02	Billinghay, Sandra	Lt	03/01/87
			Bilverstone, Brian Keith	Lt Cdr	01/01/01
			Bingham, Keith William	Lt Cdr	01/01/01
B			Binks, Steven Robert	Sub Lt	03/03/06
Bagulay, Alison Louise	Sub Lt	19/10/02	Bird, Sarah Caroline	Sub Lt	23/09/01
Bailey, Arthur Ivan	Sub Lt	03/10/05	Bishop, Peter William	Lt	01/11/95
Bailey, Robert	Lt	12/03/91	Blackburn, Alan	Lt	15/06/04
Bainbridge, Patricia Anne	Lt	03/11/98	Blunt, Victoria Louise	Sub Lt	25/09/05
Baker, Michael William	Lt	01/07/99	Boardman, Richard Cyril	Lt Cdr	27/04/86
Banks, Paul Michael	Lt	06/06/96	Bolton, David Richard	Sub Lt	05/02/99
Barber, Anthony Michael	Lt	12/03/91	Bond, Paul	Lt Cdr	01/01/02
Barker, David Arthur	Lt	21/06/99	Bonfield, Christopher Raymond	Lt	06/11/96
Barker, Sandra	Lt	07/10/98	Bonjour, Andre Paolo	Lt	27/05/92
Barnes, Sarah-Jane	Sub Lt	23/11/03	Boorman, Nicholas	Lt	01/12/88
Barr, William Douglas	Lt	15/02/00	Booth, Christina Penda	Lt	03/12/91

Name	Rank	Seniority	Name	Rank	Seniority
Booth, Kenneth Geoffrey	Lt	06/06/88	Carter, David Alan	Lt	04/03/92
Bourne, Jack	Sub Lt	19/01/03	Carter, Robert James	Lt	18/09/85
Bowen, Terrence Charles	Lt Cdr	01/01/05	Cashmore, Mathew J	Sub Lt	09/05/04
Bowen-Davies, Alison	Sub Lt	12/03/05	Caslaw, Paul	Lt	01/08/94
Bowman, Thomas	Lt Cdr	21/11/98	Catterall, Susan	Lt	20/01/87
Bowskill, Michael Arthur	Lt Cdr	10/11/87	Cea, Franklin Reynold	Lt Cdr	01/01/02
Boyes, Stephen	Lt	25/02/99	Challacombe, Jonathan Andrew	Lt Cdr	27/06/82
Boyne, John Peter	Sub Lt	16/03/94	Challis, Stewart Jay	Sub Lt	09/05/04
Bradbury, David	Lt	07/09/85	Chamberlain, Joanne Mary	Lt	02/04/99
Bradbury, Jason Richard	Lt	05/05/98	Chambers, John	Lt Cdr	19/04/84
Bradbury, Scott Michael	Lt Cdr	09/08/04	Chantler, Michael	Lt	01/01/02
Bradford, David John	Lt Cdr	03/09/85	Cheek, Ronald Stephen	Lt	23/03/05
Bradley, John Stephen	Lt	10/09/91	Chesworth, Howard Edward	Lt	03/12/91
Bratley, Charles Edwin	Lt	16/06/92	Childs, Paul	Lt	01/06/02
Bray, John William	Lt	07/12/99	Chinn, John	Lt Cdr	01/01/83
Brayford, John	Lt Cdr	02/02/84	Chittock, Michael John	Lt	25/03/94
Brazier, Colin Ian	Lt Cdr	01/02/03	Christian, David	Lt	23/03/05
Bridle, Stephen Geoffrey	Lt	12/11/93	Clark, Anne Julie	Lt Cdr	05/11/97
Briscoe, Robert William	Lt	14/11/96	Clark, David Edward	Sub Lt	11/05/03
Britto, Elizabeth	Sub Lt	31/10/00	Clark, Ian Frederic David	Lt Cdr	01/03/92
Broadbent, Graham	Lt Cdr	01/08/84	Clark, Louise Jayne	Sub Lt	25/09/05
Brooks, Henry Robert	Lt Cdr	02/05/87	Clarke, Adam Gregory	Lt	17/12/02
Brotherton, Stephen Anthony	Lt	03/07/97	Clarke, Leonard James	Sub Lt	09/06/94
Brown, Alexander Jnr.	Lt	22/09/86	Clarke, Mark Edward	Lt	03/11/98
Brown, David Martin	Lt Cdr	01/06/86	Clay, John Peter	Lt Cdr	01/04/99
Brown, David Llewellyn	Lt Cdr	30/03/88	Clay, Paul Martin	Sub Lt	05/05/02
Brown, Damien John	Lt	26/03/02	Cleworth, Dean Anthony	Lt	26/03/02
Brown, John Barry	Lt Cdr	04/07/78	Clifford, Ian Alexander	Lt	11/02/99
Brown, Keith	Lt Cdr	27/10/84	Clissold, Mark William	Lt	01/04/93
Brown, Norman James	Lt	01/06/91	Clyburn, Stephen Paul	Lt	19/01/03
Brown, Richard Andrew	Lt	01/05/91	Coast, Philip	Lt Cdr	09/07/90
Brown, Sylvia	Lt	01/08/83	Coates, Margaret Elizabeth	Lt	21/01/06
Browning, Eleanore	Sub Lt	01/06/03	Cockell, Richard Grenville	Lt Cdr	04/12/96
Browning, Martin John	Capt	02/08/02	Cole, Ian Mervyn	Sub Lt	08/06/95
Browning, Sharon Diane	Lt	02/08/02	Coleman, Keith David	Lt	26/11/98
Browning, Tony Paul	Lt	19/12/93	Coles, Thomas Richard S.	Lt Cdr	19/12/87
Broxham, Roy	Lt	21/09/90	Collier, David Michael	Lt	01/09/88
Bryant, Charles Robert	Lt	19/02/87	Collins, Ann Patricia	Lt	25/01/91
Bucknall, Michael Colin	Lt	11/03/83	Collins, Raymond	Sub Lt	31/08/94
Budden, Paul Anthony	Lt	25/01/04	Collins, Timothy John	Sub Lt	27/01/02
Bullock, Lynn Dorothy	Lt	01/12/84	Constable, David	Lt	01/13/81
Burdeyron-Dyster, Ian John	Lt Cdr	18/10/86	Coombes, Paul Michael	Lt	25/01/94
Burns, Desmond Charles	Lt	18/02/78	Copeland, Phillip Ian	Lt	05/10/97
Burns, Philip	Lt Cdr	14/02/03	Copelin, Maureen	Lt Cdr	05/10/88
Burrage, Richard George Rob.	Lt	25/06/90	Cormack, Raymond Stuart	Lt	20/11/97
Burt, Christopher John	Lt	20/08/99	Costerd, David Lloyd	Lt	27/08/94
Burton, Andrew Richard	Sub Lt	01/06/04	Cowell, Christopher	Lt	01/07/99
Burton, Craig Bernard	Lt Cdr	01/06/02	Craig, Neil	Lt	01/04/86
Burton, Philip Alban	Sub Lt	12/06/05	Crawley, Stephen John	Capt	04/06/95
Busby, Roger Charles	Lt	19/12/99	Creighton, Edward William	Lt	26/11/92
Butcher, David Kaye	Lt	17/08/94	Critchlow, Jonathan E. Bates	Lt	19/02/89
Butler, John Thomas	Lt	20/11/97	Cruse, Gillian Audrey	Lt	16/10/98
Butterworth, John Walton	Lt	23/03/87	Cruse, Malcolm Paul	Lt Cdr	17/10/89
			Cumper, Alan James	Lt	01/12/98
			Curran, Paul William	Lt	01/02/88

C

Name	Rank	Seniority
Cadman, John Gordon	Lt Cdr	26/11/86
Cadman, Leslie	Lt Cdr	30/06/99
Calvert, Martin Brian	Lt	19/08/92
Carney, Robert Joseph	Lt	82/08/97
Carr, Barry William	Lt	25/03/05
Carr, Leonard Allen	Lt Cdr	19/02/76
Carroll, Paul James	Maj	01/05/02

D

Name	Rank	Seniority
Dale, Philip Arthur	Sub Lt	01/03/99
Daly, Martin Daniel	Lt	19/11/91
Daniels, Roger	Lt Cdr	14/01/91
Dann, John Charles	Lt	09/07/95
Davies, Colin	Lt	18/09/97

Name	Rank	Seniority
Davies, Peter Jonathan	Lt	19/11/87
Davies, William George	Lt Cdr	01/07/04
Davis, James Edward	Sub Lt	01/06/93
Davison, Henry Robert	Lt	30/01/98
De Bruyne, Jacqueline	Lt	12/03/91
Delderfield, Robin Frederick	Lt	01/12/02
Demellweek, Gilbert	Lt	01/01/92
Derbyshire, David	Lt	03/06/92
Desilva, Michael Anthony	Sub Lt	07/07/92
Devenish, Ian David	Capt	12/02/02
Devereux, Edwin Alexander	Lt Cdr	01/05/87
Dibben, Michael John	Lt	03/11/88
Dibnah, Robert Frederick	Lt	29/10/95
Dickinson, Keith Ian	Lt	10/11/87
Dickinson, Simon	Sub Lt	26/09/04
Dixie, Colin	Lt	15/10/00
Doggart, Norman Ian	Lt	01/07/87
Donnelly, James Paul	Sub Lt	30/10/05
Donovan, Terence William	Lt	06/11/96
Dorricott, Peter Alfred	Lt Cdr	01/10/02
Draper, Philip Terrence	Lt	19/07/99
Dryden, Graeme Anderson	Lt	26/03/02
Dryden, Stephen Foster	Lt	01/03/81
Dublin, Curtis	Sub Lt	01/10/91
Dunkeld, Brian Keith	Lt	04/06/97
Dunnings, Mark	Sub Lt	01/09/04
Dyer, Geoffrey Alan	Maj	01/05/99
Dyer, Paul Edward	Sub Lt	18/03/05
Dyer, Roger Sinclair	Lt	07/06/97

E

Name	Rank	Seniority
Eaton, Trevor Keith	Lt	01/09/96
Edmonds, Annette	Sub Lt	12/03/05
Edmondson, Denis	Lt	28/03/99
Edwards, Stuart Peter	Sub Lt	04/06/95
Elliot, Henry James	Lt	18/05/94
English, Michael Leslie	Lt Cdr	30/03/88
Erskine, Richard Brittain	Lt	23/11/03
Evans, Ivor Kennerley	Sub Lt	17/07/97
Evans, Janet	Lt Cdr	01/07/94
Evans, John Terance	Lt	28/09/98
Evison, Christine Anne	Sub Lt	26/09/04

F

Name	Rank	Seniority
Fairbairn, Rachel Marie Louise	Sub Lt	22/11/00
Farrell, Michael Edward	Sub Lt	05/05/02
Faulkner, Shelley Ann	Sub Lt	26/09/04
Fazey, Kate Elizabeth	Sub Lt	06/05/01
Feist, Ivor Frederick	Lt Cdr	16/02/91
Fenn, Paul Roger	Sub Lt	29/11/99
Fesey, Nicolas	Sub Lt	26/09/04
Fifield, Mark William	Lt	14/06/97
Finlay, David	Lt	21/02/98
Fisher, Barry Raymond	Lt Cdr	26/07/87
Fisher, Hazel Elizabeth	Lt Cdr	26/01/92
Fitch, Michael	Lt	28/02/03
Flaherty, Jeremy	Lt	22/06/03
Fleet, Gordon Edward	Maj	24/06/03
Fleming, Alan Andrew	Lt	10/07/93
Fleming, Andrea Jane	Lt	22/11/02
Fleming, Margaret Sinnickson	Lt	01/01/82

Name	Rank	Seniority
Fletcher, John Malcolm Stuart	Lt Cdr	06/03/87
Fletcher, Malcolm John	Lt	20/02/84
Flett, William Robert	Capt	17/11/96
Ford, Stuart Bruce	Lt	02/08/96
Foreman, Waleria Teresa	Lt	22/09/95
Forrester, Michael	Lt	01/08/81
Fortune, Colin James	Lt	01/10/99
Foster, Andrew Martin	Lt	19/11/91
Foster, Ian James	Lt	05/08/85
Foster, James Michael	Lt	09/05/04
Fowler, Alison Mary	Lt Cdr	01/03/06
Fox, Jane Frances	Sub Lt	27/03/92
Francis, Rebecca Louise	Sub Lt	01/07/02
Franco, Velda Gerthennie Charlatt	Sub Lt	01/06/93
Franklin, Patrick Kenneth	Lt	07/12/02
Freeman, Brian Reginald	Lt	16/06/95
Freestone, Andrew Ray	Lt	07/11/95
Fry, Brian Edward	Lt	26/09/80
Fulcher, Diane	Lt	09/06/94
Fulcher, Graham	Sub Lt	24/04/94
Fuller, Andrew	Lt	26/06/00
Fuller, Keith Duncan	Lt Cdr	04/05/92
Fulton, Karen	Lt Cdr	20/03/02

G

Name	Rank	Seniority
Gale, Ronnie Edwin Gordon	Lt	01/11/90
Gallagher, Eammon	Lt	23/06/92
Gardner, Eric John	Lt	29/01/88
Gardner, Keith John	Lt	22/04/96
Garner, James Herbert	Lt Cdr	02/06/83
Garrett, John David	Lt Cdr	07/05/89
Garrett, Robert Martin	Sub Lt	06/11/94
Gathergood, John Anthony	Lt	17/04/98
Gearing, Robert Russell	Lt Cdr	01/09/77
George, Brian Russell	Lt	01/09/85
Gerald, Anthony David(Tony)	Lt	01/09/98
Gerrard, David William	Lt Cdr	01/12/88
Gerrard, Mary T	Lt Cdr	01/09/98
Gilbert, Robin William James	Maj	01/06/99
Gilbert-Jones, Hilary Dawn	Sub Lt	23/11/03
Gill, Jacqueline Alice	Lt	28/02/95
Gillard, Terence	Lt Cdr	01/12/86
Gillert, Val	Lt	14/11/91
Gilliam, Kevin Mcbrearty	Lt	01/07/93
Gillott, Peter	Sub Lt	23/05/99
Gittins, Susan	Lt	07/12/02
Glanfield, Mark Christopher	Lt	06/02/82
Glanville, Barry Lee	Lt Cdr	14/7/00
Glanville, Debra Louise	Lt	23/05/99
Glendinning, Michael John	Lt	07/07/97
Glover, Stuart	Sub Lt	12/06/05
Goode, Eric Reginald	Lt	13/12/97
Goode, Victoria Gladys Maud	Lt	04/11/00
Goodleff, Deborah Sian	Sub Lt	09/05/04
Goodwin, Michael	Lt	08/12/01
Gordon, Andrew David	Lt	19/02/89
Gorman, Jaqueline Mary	Sub Lt	12/06/05
Gould, Rachael Katharine	Sub Lt	11/05/03
Govier, Adrian Terry	Lt Cdr	27/091999
Grace, RW.	Lt Cdr	13/07/84
Grainge, Andrew	Lt	02/09/98
Grant, Malcolm Wickstead	Lt	28/02/95

Name	Rank	Seniority
Gray, Brian George	Lt	12/12/87
Green, Cecilia Carmel	Sub Lt	02/12/87
Green, Malcom	Lt	16/08/97
Greenaway, Lorna Ann	Sub Lt	09/05/04
Greenfield, Stephen Donald	Lt	23/05/01
Greenhalgh, Peter Noel	Lt	12/05/86
Greenland, Robert Basil	Lt Cdr	10/03/82
Greer, John	Lt Cdr	07/07/76
Gresty, Stephen Anthony	Lt	07/10/98
Grice, Robert	Lt Cdr	08/03/89
Grieve, Derek	Sub Lt	19/11/91
Griffin, Paul Philip	Lt	24/10/86
Griffiths, Meirion William	Lt Cdr	04/11/88
Grogan, Kenneth John	Lt	15/09/78
Groves, Richard George	Lt Cdr	29/08/86
Grundy, Terence Michael	Lt	15/12/92
Guiver, Carl	Maj	01/01/96
Guppy, Graham Leslie	Maj	20/06/84

H

Name	Rank	Seniority
Hackett, Clive George	Lt Cdr	12/10/90
Hadfield, Philip Steven	Capt	09/04/91
Hagan, George Young	Sub Lt	29/11/92
Hailwood, Paul Joseph	Lt Cdr	01/12/92
Haines, Linda J	Lt	01/11/87
Hale, Ronald Alfred	Lt Cdr	11/02/85
Hall, Derek Andrew	Lt Cdr	19/02/98
Hall, Frank Charles	Lt Cdr	01/10/83
Halliday, Angela	Lt	20/03/95
Hamilton, Kerry Lyn	Lt	01/05/92
Hankey, Carol	Lt	29/09/99
Hanley, David Thomas	Lt	18/11/93
Harmer, Robert Iain	Lt	28/10/99
Harper, James	Sub Lt	12/06/05
Harris, Brian Stanley	Lt Cdr	01/01/02
Harris, Trevor James	Lt	05/12/01
Hartwell, Neil John	Lt	26/03/02
Harvey, Brian Paul	Sub Lt	01/11/94
Harvey, Toby	Lt	09/07/05
Hatrick, James William	Lt	29/07/93
Hawkins, Leslie John	Sub Lt	08/11/99
Hayton, Alan	Lt	20/07/89
Hazeldon, Donald Joseph	Sub Lt	28/04/93
Hazzard, Keith	Lt	02/06/98
Headen, Geoffrey	Lt	28/09/98
Healey, Stephen	Lt	15/05/84
Hearl, James	Lt Cdr	01/12/04
Hebbes, Peter Graham	Sub Lt	01/09/91
Helkin, Maggie	Lt Cdr	07/12/85
Henwood, Martin Frederick	Lt Cdr	21/10/80
Herbert, Michael	Lt Cdr	01/01/00
Hercock, Norman George	Lt	03/11/93
Hewitt, Graham Paul	Lt Cdr	07/04/92
Hide, Brenda	Lt	17/05/84
Hill, Anthony Peter	Sub Lt	26/06/85
Hill, Ian	Lt	15/03/89
Hill, Monica Helen	Lt	18/11/93
Hill, Reginald Francis	Lt Cdr	01/03/88
Hillier, Barbara Doreen	Lt	04/09/03
Hinchcliffe, Alan	Sub Lt	28/09/03
Hithersay, John Benjamin	Lt	28/10/78
Holland, Donald Walter	Lt	15/09/84

Name	Rank	Seniority
Holliday, Anthony	Lt Cdr	21/04/93
Hollywell, Gary John	Lt Cdr	01/05/99
Holt, Martin William	Lt Cdr	10/09/85
Holt, Wendy	Lt	29/11/97
Horne, Allan James	Lt	16/09/89
Horner, John Anthony	Lt Cdr	19/09/92
Houlden, Wendy Irene	Lt	01/03/98
Howie, Thomas	Lt Cdr	01/11/88
Hoyle, Keith	Sub Lt	01/10/86
Hudson, Christopher Stanley	Sub Lt	29/11/95
Hughes, Thomas William	Lt Cdr	01/08/83
Hulonce, Michael John	Lt Cdr	01/03/82
Hunter, Lesley Mary	Lt	05/05/98
Hunter, Philip John	Lt	01/12/02
Hurst, Paul Andrew	Lt	06/06/03
Hurst, Thomas William	Lt Cdr	01/06/85
Hutchings, Andrew Neil	Lt	16/11/98
Huyton, Gillian	Lt	07/10/98

I

Name	Rank	Seniority
Iggo, David	Lt	26/01/96
Ingham, Anthony John	Sub Lt	24/02/99
Ingham, David Anthony	Lt Cdr	28/04/98
Ingham, Mark Waller	Sub Lt	22/11/00
Ingram, John Alan	Sub Lt	12/06/05
Ingram, Thomas	Lt	27/01/03
Izzard, Michael Leslie	Lt	25/06/98
Izzard, Thomas Charles	Lt	01/12/06

J

Name	Rank	Seniority
Jaconelli, Nicholas Mario	Lt	12/09/00
James, George Alfred	Lt	22/08/78
James, Robert Martin	Lt Cdr	01/01/95
Janner-Burgess, Mark	Lt	21/01/06
Jardine, Roderick John Mitchell	Lt	05/10/94
Jeffrey, Andrew Alexander	Sub Lt	30/08/94
Jeffries, Leila Bernice	Sub Lt	25/06/05
Jehan, Paula Elizabeth	Sub Lt	19/05/91
Jenkins, Ian	Capt	01/09/91
Jennings, William Andrew	Lt	19/10/84
Jepson, Mary Evelyn G.	Lt	21/03/96
Johnson-Paul, David	Lt	18/04/92
Johnston, Peter Warburton	Lt	02/11/84
Jones, Christopher Antony	Lt Cdr	11/08/99
Jones, Dorothy Edwina	Lt	22/11/94
Jones, Lilly Elizabeth M.	Lt	09/04/91
Jones, Margaret	Lt Cdr	01/07/04
Jones, Mark Allan	Lt	06/11/94
Jones, Nicholas Morgan	Sub Lt	26/09/04
Jones, Neil Roy	Lt	24/03/94
Jones, Neil Royston	Lt	03/01/96
Jones, Peter Ronald	Lt Cdr	01/02/05
Jones, Trevor Eric	Lt	07/04/97
Jordan, Roger Allen	Lt	22/06/94
Jordan, Sheila	Lt	26/07/90
Jupe, Paul	Lt	02/03/88
Justice, David Robert	Lt	10/02/84

K

Name	Rank	Seniority
Kay, Anne Elizabeth	Lt	21/01/06

Name	Rank	Seniority
Kaye, Malcolm	Lt	01/11/89
Kearsey, Peter James	Sub Lt	01/12/04
Keery, Neil William	Lt Cdr	18/05/01
Kenrick, Peter	Lt	23/11/94
Kent, Michael Kevin	Sub Lt	25/09/05
Kilbey, Susan	Sub Lt	16/03/03
Killick, Peter Edward	Lt	08/10/87
Knight, Robert Joseph	Lt	15/02/00
Knowles-Forrest, Norman	Sub Lt	01/10/03
Kristiansen, Karen Shirley	Lt	14/02/98
Kyle, Raymond Alexander	Sub Lt	01/11/90

L

Name	Rank	Seniority
Lamkin, John	Lt	15/02/96
Lampert, Brian Raymond Henrick	Lt Cdr	01/12/84
Lampert, Susan Elizabeth	Lt	01/11/89
Lane, John David	Lt	31/05/91
Larsen, Colin John	Lt	09/05/97
Lawes, Sonia Rachel	Lt	08/03/94
Lawrence, Barrie John	Lt	04/10/92
Lawrence, Kevin Peter	Lt	01/05/01
Lea, Garry John	Sub Lt	05/05/99
Lee, David Howard	Lt Cdr	05/05/80
Lees, Martin	Sub Lt	19/09/92
Legget, Colin Stuart	Sub Lt	19/08/04
Lentle, Robert Norman	Lt	01/11/90
Leslie, Harry Norman	Sub Lt	03/03/91
Lewis, Clifford Bruce	Lt	04/11/92
Lewis, David	Lt	14/04/98
Lewis, Eleanor Ann	Lt	23/11/94
Lewis, John	Capt	17/11/98
Lewis, Peter John	Lt Cdr	01/01/04
Lewis, Walter	Lt	06/05/79
Light, Michael	Sub Lt	28/02/02
Lincoln, David Arthur	Lt Cdr	01/01/06
Lloyd, Terence Arthur	Lt	13/04/84
Lock, Keith Andrew	Sub Lt	01/12/92
Locke, David Leslie	Lt Cdr	01/01/05
Login, Brenda Jay	Lt Cdr	10/11/89
Login, Derek John	Lt Cdr	12/12/88
Long, Adam William	Lt	01/04/97
Lorimer, Deirdre Kathleen	Lt	24/06/98
Loudon, Elizabeth Janet	Sub Lt	07/07/90
Loveland, John Charles	Lt	21/04/93
Loveridge, Anthony Francis	Lt Cdr	01/12/89
Low, William Robert	Sub Lt	05/04/94
Lowe, David Henry	Lt	23/07/77
Lowe, Stuart	Maj	21/04/02
Lucas, Peter	Lt	24/03/99
Luckman, Bruce Innes	Lt	01/10/92
Lumley, Margaret Caroline	Lt	14/06/97
Luxton, Peter James	Lt Cdr	15/04/80
Luxton, Phillip John	Lt	05/11/98
Lyster, Cody	Sub Lt	23/06/03

M

Name	Rank	Seniority
Macausland, Ian Murray	Lt Cdr	01/09/98
Macdonald, Peter John	Lt	07/11/91
Macey, Mark Robert	Lt Cdr	01/09/03
Macgreagh, Shaun	Sub Lt	01/11/84
Machin, Ian James	Maj	01/08/96

Name	Rank	Seniority
Mackay, Charles	Sub Lt	01/12/97
Mackay, David John	Lt	01/07/84
Mackinlay, Colin Russell	Lt	18/04/92
Mackinlay, Sherie Jane	Lt	01/09/93
Maclean, Donald John	Lt	28/03/90
Macleod, Kenneth Mackenzie	Lt	01/11/91
Mahoney-Brown, Jane	Lt Cdr	04/11/93
Main, Paul Leslie	Lt	12/03/91
Mair, Brian George	Lt Cdr	01/01/02
Makepeace, Toby David	Lt	11/05/03
Mannouch, John Henry Thomas	Lt	14/05/90
Mapstone, Arthur	Sub Lt	25/02/02
Marson, Victoria Michele	Lt Cdr	01/02/05
Martin, John Kenneth	Lt Cdr	01/01/87
Martin, Kevin David	Lt	14/03/94
Martin, Peter	Lt	07/09/79
Mathers, David	Lt	15/02/96
Matthews, Christopher Denys	Lt Cdr	01/10/03
Matthews, John Edward	Lt	19/06/95
Matthews, Ronald Edward	Lt	08/10/89
Maxwell-Cox, Michael James	Lt	11/04/05
Maynard, Lisa Jane	Lt	20/03/96
Maynard, Robert Charles	Lt Cdr	21/03/84
Mcavady, Andrew James	Lt	12/06/98
Mcavoy, William John	Lt	16/03/84
Mcdonald, Peter John	Lt	29/06/92
Mcintyre, Rosamund Phyllis	Lt Cdr	01/01/90
Mckaig, Alexander David	Lt	08/01/87
Mckee, David Thomas	Lt Cdr	10/01/66
Mckenna, Paul Michael	Lt	14/03/96
Mckeown, Glenda Karen	Lt	24/04/96
Mcmaster, George Alexander	Lt	06/10/88
Mcvinnie, Elizabeth Jean	Lt	06/11/98
Meadows, Paul Joseph	Lt	02/02/02
Meek, Caroline	Sub Lt	06/05/01
Meikle, John Orr	Lt	06/05/01
Meldon, Michael James	Lt Cdr	01/03/88
Menhams, Angela	Lt	01/12/90
Milby, Stuart Lee	Lt Cdr	27/07/93
Miles, Frederick John	Lt Cdr	01/03/82
Milligan, Kevin Stuart	Lt	08/02/98
Milligan, Victoria Louise	Lt	01/05/98
Mills, William Frederick	Lt	23/06/93
Minett, Clive Stephen	Maj	23/01/05
Mitchell, Barry Colin	Sub Lt	19/01/03
Mitchell, David Albert	Lt	15/05/98
Mitchell, Jane Susan	Lt	04/01/89
Mitchell, Robert Graham	Lt	
Mitchell, Ray Leonard	Lt Cdr	01/01/04
Mitchison, Robert	Sub Lt	12/06/05
Mohammed, Barbara Jean	Lt	07/12/85
Mohammed, John Gholam	Lt Cdr	01/09/82
Moir, Brian	Lt	18/09/95
Money, Alan John	Lt	25/03/94
Monkcom, Susan Patricia	Lt	01/04/98
Mons-White, Margaret Patricia	Lt Cdr	01/11/05
Moody, Roger Anthony	Lt Cdr	01/01/85
Moore, Brian Daniel	Sub Lt	23/11/03
Moore, Robert Jack	Lt Cdr	01/01/01
Morgan, John Howard	Lt	10/02/90
Morgan, Norman John	Lt Cdr	23/07/04
Morgan, Stephen	Lt	13/04/96

N
268

SEA CADET CORPS

Sect.7

Name	Rank	Seniority	Name	Rank	Seniority
Morley, Andrew Roy	Lt	07/10/98	Panchaud, Thomas Christopher	Lt	01/08/95
Morley, Carol Louise	Lt	16/11/01	Park, Martyn Edward	Lt	01/05/99
Morley, Michael Charles	Lt	08/10/85	Parker, Simon Neil	Lt Cdr	01/10/02
Morrin, Kevin Joseph Smythe	Lt	05/04/97	Parks, Edwin	Lt Cdr	01/01/04
Morris, Angela Sheila	Sub Lt	01/07/02	Parr, Geoffrey Laurence	Lt	28/11/92
Morton, Rita	Lt	13/05/98	Parris, Stephen George	Capt	30/01/99
Mould, Peter Reginald	Lt Cdr	21/07/79	Pascoe, William Gunn	Lt	26/07/84
Moulton, Nicholas John	Lt Cdr	21/11/98	Pask, Thomas	Sub Lt	25/09/05
Mountier, Peter Cecil George	Lt	19/11/90	Paterson, Gordon Laird	Lt Cdr	01/12/99
Muggeridge, Edwin Robert	Lt	06/05/84	Patterson, Paul James	Lt	26/10/97
Mugridge, Toni Clare	Lt	15/02/02	Patterson, Phillip John	Lt Cdr	01/12/02
Mullin, Anna Jane	Sub Lt	23/11/03	Paul, Patrick Hugh	Sub Lt	12/08/99
Mullin, William	Lt	10/11/86	Payne, David John	Lt	18/03/98
Murphy, William Joseph	Sub Lt	24/05/99	Payne, David Lawrance	Lt	26/11/98
Musselwhite, Ruth	Lt	19/12/02	Payne, Derek Malcolm	Lt Cdr	23/11/83
			Pearce, Peter Michael	Lt	01/06/98
N			Pearson, James Rodney	Lt	09/03/93
			Penny, Carl Antony	Capt	28/04/01
Newman, Raymond Charles	Lt	20/07/82	Perchard, Ronald Edward	Lt	08/09/05
Newton, Percy Robert	Sub Lt	28/09/03	Perkins, Jonathon Robert	Lt	09/03/03
Newton, Simon Christopher	Lt	25/09/05	Perkins, Kevin Patrick	Lt	05/11/97
Nice, David Alan	Lt	18/10/77	Perry, Kelly Anne	Sub Lt	26/09/04
Nicholls, David John	Lt	11/09/98	Perry, Paul Alan	Lt Cdr	04/02/94
Nichols, David	Sub Lt	15/07/99	Peters, Kenneth John	Lt	25/09/98
Nixon, Joseph	Lt	30/06/84	Pether, Phillip Graham	Lt	04/11/72
Norman, David Richard	Lt	01/04/86	Phillips, Paul Christopher	Lt	06/08/98
Norman, John	Lt Cdr	01/08/87	Pickering, Jean	Lt	03/07/90
Norris, Anthony Alan	Lt Cdr	20/12/92	Picton, Janet	Lt Cdr	18/09/87
Norris, Norman	Lt	01/04/92	Piercy, Peter Robert	Lt Cdr	05/10/86
			Pike, John Rowland	Lt	31/05/96
O			Plummer, Thomas William	Lt	10/11/99
			Pogson, Godfrey Laurence	Lt Cdr	29/05/87
O'Brien, Gary	Lt	30/01/96	Poke, Claire Louise	Lt	14/06/97
O'Donnell, Adrian David	Lt	01/12/96	Poke, David John	Maj	01/06/02
O'Donnell, Wendy Anne	Sub Lt	01/02/05	Pope, Darren Paul	Lt	22/04/93
O'Donoghue, Amanda	Sub Lt	23/11/03	Porter, John	Sub Lt	02/02/76
Oglesby, Simon	Sub Lt	08/12/00	Porter, John Frank	Lt Cdr	03/02/84
O'Hagan, William John	Lt	01/12/85	Postill, John Paul Stephen	Lt	01/07/99
O'Keeffe, Richard William	Lt Cdr	29/04/87	Poth, Anthony William	Lt Cdr	17/03/86
Oldcorn, Geoffrey William	Lt	03/03/97	Pow, David John	Lt	06/10/92
O'Neill, Dawn May	Lt	02/12/94	Powell, Janice Maria	Sub Lt	13/11/85
Orr, Robert Arthur	Lt	26/03/02	Powell, Robert Wilfred	Capt	24/09/01
Orton, Adrian Mark	Capt	01/07/99	Preston, Frank	Sub Lt	01/06/94
Osborne, Brian Paul	Lt	01/01/87	Priest, Derek Richard	Sub Lt	21/11/04
Osborne, Dawn E	Lt	01/02/86	Priestley, Gary	Lt	30/11/02
Osborne, James Dennis	Lt Cdr	01/12/78	Prince, Ramon Melville	Sub Lt	13/04/97
O'Shaughnessy, Helen Ava	Sub Lt	22/05/95	Pritchard, David Michael	Lt Cdr	01/01/95
Owen, Thomas	Lt	01/12/02	Pugh, Heather A.	Lt Cdr	28/04/98
Owen, William Ronald	Lt	05/06/96	Pugh, Mark David	Sub Lt	12/02/06
Owens, Christopher Owen	Lt	30/05/97			
			R		
P			Radcliffe, Brian Alexander	Lt Cdr	15/01/89
			Rawcliffe, Michael	Lt	17/04/98
Packwood, Raymond	Sub Lt	04/07/89	Rawlinson, Martin James	Lt	01/03/98
Packwood, Shelagh	Lt Cdr	01/12/86	Rayson, Trevor John	Lt Cdr	20/10/81
Padbury, John Eric	Sub Lt	12/03/05	Read, Jodie Tiffany	Sub Lt	28/09/03
Page, Helen	Lt	01/10/90	Redhead, Gavin Christopher	Lt	28/09/98
Painter, Lorretta	Lt	28/01/93	Redhead, Julie Elizabeth	Lt	28/03/99
Painting, Peter Michael	Lt	18/03/79	Rees, Andrew David	Lt	01/07/87
Paling, John Philip	Lt Cdr	01/10/96	Reeve, John	Lt	19/11/91
Palmer, Alan James	Capt	20/11/01	Reeves, Angela	Lt Cdr	12/09/88
Palmer, Richard James	Lt	01/12/89	Reeves, Mark Andrew	Lt	11/05/01
Palmer, Robert Allan	Lt Cdr	01/11/05			

Name	Rank	Seniority	Name	Rank	Seniority
Regan, Paul	Maj	01/10/96	Sickelmore, Barry Stephen	Lt Cdr	05/04/99
Reid, Jeffrey James	Lt	04/11/03	Sidwell, Victoria Louise	Sub Lt	09/06/05
Reid, Morag	Lt	01/09/03	Sigley, June	Lt	19/06/96
Rhind, Robert	Lt	22/03/90	Silverthorne, Robert Kenneth	Lt	31/10/91
Richards, Philip Curtis	Lt	14/04/01	Simister, Alan G.m	Lt	23/12/98
Ridgway, Paul Garvin Douglas	Lt Cdr	02/09/77	Simmons, Melvyn George	Lt	10/04/93
Roaf, Alistair David	Sub Lt	07/06/96	Simpson, Alfred	Lt Cdr	08/04/84
Robbins, Alan John	Lt Cdr	18/06/88	Simpson, Leonard Armstrong	Sub Lt	01/05/93
Roberts, Euphemia	Lt Cdr	27/11/03	Simpson, Timothy	Lt	01/02/95
Robinson, Eric William Charles	Lt	09/03/97	Skingle, Stephen Ralph	Lt	05/05/03
Robinson, Paul Leroy	Lt	20/07/99	Small, Stephen George	Sub Lt	25/06/05
Rock, William	Lt	12/11/00	Smart, Claude Anthony	Lt Cdr	23/04/79
Rockey, David John	Sub Lt	11/03/98	Smedley, Montgomery James	Sub Lt	21/08/04
Rodgers, Brian Lee	Sub Lt	28/09/03	Smith, Adrian	Lt	21/08/92
Rodgers, Kevin Anthony	Sub Lt	11/05/03	Smith, Alan Albert Jack	Capt	02/03/02
Rogers, Neil Terence	Lt	30/09/00	Smith, Frank Allan	Lt	08/10/89
Rogers, Sally-Anne	Lt	22/11/97	Smith, Graham Sydney	Lt	05/04/97
Rollins, Linda Elizabeth	Lt	03/11/98	Smith, John Alexander	Sub Lt	12/11/98
Rooney, Frederick John Francis	Lt	08/02/05	Smith, James Christopher	Lt	09/05/94
Roots, Joseph Anthony	Lt	21/09/01	Smith, Stephen	Lt	16/12/82
Ross, David Anthony	Lt	13/10/90	Snedden, David Paul	Sub Lt	25/09/05
Ross, Malcolm Thomas	Lt	09/05/95	Soilleux, Peter	Lt	01/09/02
Rowe, Raymond Allan	Lt	02/04/99	Spear, Keith	Sub Lt	01/04/02
Rowles, David Ezekiel	Lt Cdr	03/05/74	Speariett, Gail Mary	Lt Cdr	16/11/91
Rundle, Trevor	Lt	26/12/87	Spencer, Allan Hugh	Lt	15/10/93
Rushton, Steven Jeffrey	Lt	15/01/97	Spencer, Edward John	Lt	09/09/76
Russell, John Barry	Lt	01/11/89	Spicer, David John	Lt	23/02/87
Rutter, Thomas Frederick	Lt	30/10/87	Spicer, Janice	Lt	01/07/87
Rycroft, Paul	Lt Cdr	09/08/89	Spinks, James Rollings	Lt	02/03/88
Ryder, Ruth Margaret	Lt	03/11/93	Spong, Victor William	Lt Cdr	20/07/76
Salisbury, Linda	Lt	02/04/99	Squires, John Stuart	Lt	06/12/88
			Squirrell, Daren	Sub Lt	21/01/01
S			Standen, Roy Frank Edwin	Lt Cdr	31/12/67
			Stanley, Trevor	Lt	22/01/01
Sandilands, James Graham	Lt	20/12/05	Steggall, Mark Anthony	Lt	01/11/02
Saunders, Donald	Lt	28/08/94	Stevens, Alan	Lt Cdr	01/07/00
Saupe, Peter John	Lt	01/07/87	Stevenson, Iain Paul	Lt	01/03/87
Scanlan, John Edward	Lt	01/04/89	Stewart, James Shaw	Lt	01/03/81
Scarratt, Leslie Thomas	Lt	01/07/99	Stone, Kathleen Jane	Sub Lt	16/07/89
Schofield, George Ewan	Lt	01/04/91	Stone, Terence	Lt	25/05/86
Scholes, David John	Capt	13/03/92	Stott, Barry	Lt	19/01/96
Scholes, Stephen Alan	Capt	01/07/99	Street, Steven Barrie	Lt	14/04/99
Scott, Francis James Martin	Lt Cdr	01/04/92	Strutt, Dupre Alexander	Lt Cdr	28/01/98
Scott, Gordon Macintyre	Lt Cdr	01/12/98	Stubbs, Edward Brian	Lt	18/11/93
Scourfield, Royston Thomas	Lt	02/12/87	Styles, Marc Robert	Sub Lt	21/11/04
Scrivens, Stuart	Lt	03/12/91	Sumner, Robert William	Lt	06/12/99
Seabury, Paul	Lt	16/08/97	Sutherland, Shane Alexander Mcleod	Lt	01/07/94
Searles, Andrew David	Lt	18/04/99	Svendsen, Peter John	Lt Cdr	01/05/02
Sedgwick, Mark	Lt	03/06/98	Swan, Gordon	Lt Cdr	24/01/02
Seggie, Andrew Cave	Sub Lt	26/06/04	Swarbrick, David Rodney	Lt	16/06/83
Servis, Thomas James	Lt	20/08/83	Sydes, Daniel	Capt	21/09/01
Seychell, Charles	Lt	01/07/90			
Sharp, Terence John	Lt Cdr	08/09/80	**T**		
Shaw, David Alan	Lt	14/05/84			
Shaw, James Edward	Lt	14/12/95	Tait, Kevin	Lt Cdr	01/03/04
Shelton, Clive	Lt Cdr	24/04/98	Tannock, Andrew James	Maj	01/12/04
Shelton, Julie	Lt	07/10/89	Tansley, Lorley Margaret	Sub Lt	01/03/04
Shepherd, Carl Andrew	Lt	05/05/02	Tapp, Maria Edna	Lt	23/10/95
Shiel, Gary	Lt	18/03/90	Taylor, Brian	Capt	01/07/91
Shiels, Robert Albert	Lt Cdr	08/09/86	Taylor, John Charles	Lt	01/08/00
Shone, Michael John Paul	Lt	15/06/98	Tebby, Christine Joyce	Lt	05/09/89
Short, Keith	Lt Cdr	06/04/86	Thackery, Richard James	Lt	02/03/96
Shuttleworth, Tye	Lt	16/06/05	Theakston, Flora Maclachlan	Sub Lt	07/09/83

Name	Rank	Seniority
Theobald, Robert John	Lt	10/11/87
Theobald, Wendy Margaret	Lt Cdr	01/01/96
Thickett, David Alan	Sub Lt	11/05/03
Thomas, Alan Brynley Pugh	Lt	14/04/98
Thomas, Michael John	Lt	19/07/80
Thomas, Valerie Ann	Lt	22/11/97
Thomas, William A.	Lt	01/01/84
Thompson, Ian Graham	Lt	01/07/93
Thompson, Joan	Lt	10/02/82
Thompson, Philip	Lt	24/02/00
Thomson, Andrew Duncan	Lt	07/04/95
Thomson, Robert Leck	Lt	21/10/85
Thorne, Christopher John	Lt	13/07/90
Thornton, Peter Kevin	Lt	
Thurland, Joseph Samuel	Mid	25/09/05
Timothy, Emile Augustus	Maj	20/04/92
Titley, John	Lt	04/05/93
Totty, Paul	Maj	22/03/96
Touhey, Martin Paul	Lt	15/07/89
Townsend, Graham	Lt	01/05/98
Townsend, Stephen	Sub Lt	30/03/03
Trahair, Estelle Lorranine	Lt	24/04/96
Trojan, Margaret Ann	Lt	30/11/99
Truelove, Gary Victor	Lt Cdr	01/07/04
Truscott, Gary Denver	Lt Cdr	01/01/96
Tubman, Vernon John	Sub Lt	18/10/91
Tucker, Neil	Lt	03/11/95
Turner, Ian Mark	Lt	04/11/97
Tuson, Barry	Sub Lt	24/03/97
Tyrrell, Richard William Edward	Lt Cdr	19/06/91
Tyson, Michael Derek	Lt	22/03/83

U

Name	Rank	Seniority
Ulrich, Geoffrey Christopher	Lt Cdr	27/11/82
Unsworth, John Paul	Sub Lt	11/05/03
Unwin, Mark	Lt	24/02/01
Urquhart, John	Lt Cdr	01/11/04
Utting, Joseph	Lt	21/09/01

V

Name	Rank	Seniority
Vanns, Jonathan	Lt	04/05/92
Vaughan, Jeffrey	Lt	10/11/95
Villa, Nina Louisa	Lt	08/11/01

W

Name	Rank	Seniority
Waddleton, Michael	Lt	17/07/84
Walker, Keith John	Lt	05/02/88
Walsh, Brian Graham	Lt	11/05/03
Walsh, Edward	Lt Cdr	01/06/82
Ward, John Phillip	Lt Cdr	01/10/03
Waring, Peter	Lt	14/11/96
Warwick, Lynne Michelle	Sub Lt	23/11/03
Warwick, Stephen Peter	Lt	12/03/98
Waterman, Duncan	Sub Lt	01/02/89
Waters, Scott Charles	Lt	21/04/94
Watkins, Colin	Lt Cdr	17/11/03
Watson, Sheila	Lt	06/11/96
Watts, Keith	Sub Lt	26/08/02
Waugh, John	Lt	06/09/80
Waylett, Graham	Lt Cdr	15/02/98

Name	Rank	Seniority
Waylett, Matthew John	Sub Lt	28/09/03
Webb, Colin Peter	Lt	17.11.1995
Webb, John	Lt Cdr	09/11/85
Webster, John Stephen	Lt Cdr	14/12/90
Weightman, Eric James	Lt Cdr	22/05/85
Weller, Katrina	Sub Lt	29/01/86
Welsh, John Anthony	Lt	07/11/93
Welsh, Michelle	Lt	07/11/95
Weobley, Mal John	Maj	28/08/86
Weston, Mark Terence	Lt	07/11/95
Westover, Robert David	Lt	09/06/78
Wheatley, Noel John	Lt Cdr	01/01/95
Wheeler, Michael John	Lt	22/03/75
White, David Michael	Lt	29/11/02
White, Robert David	Lt	07/05/97
White, William	Sub Lt	08/12/00
Whitear, Colin Micheal	Sub Lt	25/09/05
Whitehead, William	Maj	10/12/02
Whiteman, Mark	Lt	05/08/85
Whitley, Roger J B	Lt	14/04/99
Whorwood, Julia Margaret	Lt	07/05/97
Wilde, James Peter Michael	Lt	01/03/93
Wilkinson-Truswell, Jacqueline Anne	Sub Lt	03/11/02
Wilks, Stephen John	Lt	27/07/01
Willett, Marion Christine	Lt	21/12/86
Williams, Alan John	Lt Cdr	01/05/84
Williams, David	Sub Lt	17/09/84
Williams, Derek C	Lt	13/12/88
Williams, David Frank	Lt	15/03/98
Williams, Deborah K	Lt	04/11/92
Williams, David Neil	Sub Lt	26/03/00
Williams, Susan Dawn	Lt	26/03/02
Williams, Susanne Jane	Lt	18/03/81
Williamson, William John	Lt Cdr	26/05/87
Wilson, Dorothy	Lt Cdr	01/03/87
Wilson, Ethel Margaret	Lt	01/11/98
Wilson, Edward John	Sub Lt	08/05/89
Wilson, George Philip	Lt	05/06/96
Wilson, George Thomson	Lt	01/11/95
Wilson, Ian	Lt Cdr	21/02/82
Winchester, John Benjamin	Lt	25/09/05
Winter, Robert Allen	Lt	08/12/83
Wirth, William Simpson	Sub Lt	22/04/87
Wood, Norman John	Lt Cdr	1/3/90
Woodcock, Anthony	Lt Cdr	28/06/84
Woods, Edward Arthur	Lt	01/11/02
Woodward, Stewart Frank	Lt Cdr	26/10/84
Woolgar, Victor John Fredrk.	Lt Cdr	01/04/88
Worrall, Ian	Capt	01/06/99
Wyatt, Donald Allan	Lt	01/03/80
Wylie, William, MBE	Lt Cdr	05/12/83
Wynne, David Paul	Lt	21/04/93

Y

Name	Rank	Seniority
Yates, Daniel Frederick J	Sub Lt	11/05/03
Yorke, Barrie Owen	Lt	01/07/87

Z

Name	Rank	Seniority
Zaccarini, Jason	Lt	26/03/02

COMBINED CADET FORCE

Name	Rank	Date of Appointment	School/College
A			
Adams, Mark	Lt	08.04.99	Churchers
Adams, Steven	A/SLt	01.09.04	Christs College
Adamson, Siobhan	A/SLt	12.12.04	Dollar
Aldridge, Mark	Lt	01.09.92	Trinity
Allan, Richard	A/SLt	17.03.02	St Johns
Allcock, Simon	SLt	15.03.04	Charterhouse
Allen, Brian	Lt	28.02.84	Elizabeth
Allen, Patrick	A/SLt	08.11.04	Scarborough
Anderson, Laurence	A/SLt	01.04.05	Reigate
Anderson, Robyn	SLt	17.09.03	RGS Lancaster
Andrews, Jacqueline	Lt	24.08.93	Recall
Armitage, David	Lt	01.10.98	City Of London
Armstrong, Ivan	Lt Cdr	01.09.90	Bangor
Ash, David	SLt	10.09.03	King Edward
Ashfield, Noel	SLt	28.11.99	Campbell
Ashton, Stephanie	SLt	13.06.01	Recall
Ayers, Tony	Lt Cdr	06.07.00	HQCCF
B			
Baggaley, James Joseph	Lt	24.03.03	Ruthin
Bailey, Nicholas Peter	Lt	05.09.00	HQCCF
Bain, Paul	A/SLt	10.10.05	Seaford
Baker, Piers	Lt	01.01.86	Recall
Barker, Janet Elizabeth	Lt	05.05.87	Recall
Barlow, Katrina	Lt	10.11.00	Recall
Barrett, Rachel	SLt	19.07.02	Recall
Barton, Joanne	SLt	01.09.02	Trinity
Bassett, Paul	Lt	12.07.02	Recall
Batchelder, Mark	Lt	04.03.99	Berkhamstead
Bate, Christopher	Lt Cdr	08.11.04	Reading Blue Coat
Bateson, Victoria	A/SLt	01.08.04	Oundle
Battison, Clare	SLt	17.09.03	Leys
Beaven, Julie	SLt	01.11.02	Recall
Belfield, Peter James	2Lt RMR	01.10.04	Kings Taunton
Bell, Mark Henri	SLt	01.10.03	RGS Newcastle
Benson, Leisle	SLt	01.01.01	Recall
Benson, Roger	Lt	07.11.85	Glenalmond
Birch, James	A/SLt	15.08.04	Uppingham
Bird, Jason	Lt	31.07.99	Trinity
Bland, Martin	A/SLt	14.12.04	Ruthin
Bolam, Laura	A/SLt	25.03.01	Langley
Bone, Robert	SLt	27.02.00	Mill Hill
Borking, Graham	Lt	09.01.90	Queen Victoria
Botterill, Marc Warwick	Lt	01.04.00	HQCCF
Boughton, Charles	SLt	12.09.94	Royal Hospital
Bowen-Walker, Peter	Lt	18.11.01	Perse
Bowles, Michael	Lt	29.10.82	King William
Bownass, Thomas	Lt	19.09.01	Recall
Brazier, Colin	Lt Cdr	16.06.97	HQCCF
Brazie, Lynda	SLt	01.06.03	Recall
Brett, Alison	SLt	15.08.04	Kings Wimbledon
Bridgeman, Keith	Cdr	19.06.84	MTS Northwood
Brierley, Louise	Lt	12.09.90	Prior Park
Brittain, Norman	Lt	30.11.72	Oundle
Brooke, Frank	Lt	15.08.04	Ellesmere
Brooks, John	Lt Cdr	01.09.90	St Peters
Brown, Tony Graham	Cdr	28.09.83	Recall
Brown, Harriet	A/SLt	10.09.05	Exeter
Brown, Thomas	SLt	02.04.01	Arnold
Browne, Niall	SLt	12.10.98	Recall
Bryant, Charles	SLt	01.04.03	St Lawrence
Bryant, Marion	Lt	01.04.00	Bournemouth
Burden, Richard	Lt RMR	23.11.91	Harrow
Burnell, Gareth	A/SLt	10.07.05	Gresham's
Burns, Derek	Lt Cdr	22.10.70	Recall
Burrowes, Christopher	Lt	09.06.90	Winchester

Name	Rank	Date of Appointment	School/College
Butt, Robert	SLt	08.02.00	Downside
Butt, Katherine	A/SLt	14.03.05	Downside
Butterworth, Tiffany	SLt	01.02.05	Recall
Buttriss, Dave	Lt	12.01.03	Recall
Byrom, Matthew	SLt	01.10.04	Newcastle

C

Name	Rank	Date of Appointment	School/College
Caldecott, Arabella	A/SLt	10.10.04	Haileybury
Callow, Martin	Capt RM	29.07.87	Royal Hospital
Campbell, Alexandra	SLt	04.08.01	Recall
Cardwell, Alexander	Lt Cdr	30.10.94	Bangor
Carpenter, Richard	Lt	01.11.97	Nottingham
Carr, Deborah	SLt	01.01.03	Edinburgh
Carter, Micheal	Lt Cdr	01.09.69	Kelly
Carter, Nicholas	Cdr	01.10.82	Newcastle
Carter, Steven Paul	Lt Cdr	01.04.81	Recall
Carter, Sallyanne	SLt	15.11.04	Berkhamstead
Cartmell, Keith	Lt Cdr	23.10.96	Arnold
Caves, Richard	Lt	07.12.98	Recall
Chandler, Lisa Jane	A/SLt	27.09.04	Dean Close
Chapman, Kenneth	SLt	19.06.84	Stamford
Chapman, Russell	SLt	01.03.04	Plymouth
Chetwood, Jim	Lt	17.06.94	Portsmouth
Clark, Daniel	Alt RM	01.09.01	Bradfield
Clarke, Rueben Francis	Lt	12.03.81	Recall
Clayton, Louise	SLt	11.01.02	Haberdashers
Clifford, Karen	SLt	15.01.01	Pangbourne
Clifford, Neil	SLt	01.09.04	Monkton Combe
Clough, Howard	Lt	01.09.97	Recall
Coles, John	SLt	11.03.03	Haileybury
Collier, Anthony	SLt	01.01.93	Recall
Collins, Micheal	SLt	28.02.83	Magdalen
Collins, Wendy Lawray	Lt	26.02.82	Alleyns
Copleston, Micheal	Lt	28.03.99	Taunton
Copplestone, Neil	Lt Cdr	01.09.96	Brentwood
Corbould, Leigh	Lt	01.04.95	Stowe
Cornes, Mary	A/SLt	01.08.04	St Edwards
Cox, Damian	SLt	25.03.01	Prior Park
Cox, Jim	Lt Cdr	17.09.97	Birkenhead
Coyle, David	SLt	04.08.01	Framlingham
Coyne, Lucie	Lt Cdr	01.09.96	Brentwood
Crabtree, John	Lt Cdr	11.01.72	Kings Taunton
Crabtree, Ruth	SLt	15.04.02	Recall
Creasey, Peter	Lt	16.06.91	Royal Hospital
Crees, David	Cdr	01.11.72	HQCCF
Crisp, Victoria	SLt	15.11.04	Duke of York
Crocker, Alan	SLt	11.03.01	Clifton
Crook, Patricia	Lt	28.03.99	Haileybury
Curtis, Berwick	Lt	01.01.75	Epsom

D

Name	Rank	Date of Appointment	School/College
Dale, Simon	A/SLt	23.09.05	Bedford
Daniels, Paul	Capt RM	01.04.05	Bradfield
De Celis Lucas, Elena	2Lt RMR	01.09.04	Strathallan
Delpech, Daniel	Lt	01.09.77	Haberdashers
Dickson, Nathalie	SLt	23.02.05	RGS High Wycombe
Donaldson, Rhona Jane	A/SLt	27.09.04	Dean Close
Doody, Edwin	SLt	05.02.01	HQCCF
Du Vivier, Charles	A/SLt	10.10.05	Fettes
Dubbins, Keith	Lt Cdr	19.09.89	Ryde
Dunn, Alex	Cdr	16.03.95	HQCCF

Name	Rank	Date of Appointment	School/College
Durrans, Howard	Lt	22.05.97	Bridlington
Durrant, Robert Charles	Cdr	01.03.72	Milton Abbey
Dyer, Paul	SLt	12.03.01	Duke of York

E

Name	Rank	Date of Appointment	School/College
Eager, Christopher	Lt	05.09.03	Woodbridge
Eames, Andrew	Lt Col + 8	01.11.95	Hereford
Eaton, Diana	A/SLt	01.10.03	St Dunstan
Eaton, Trevor	Lt	01.09.01	St Dunstan
Elkington, David Herbert	Cdr	12.01.67	Recall
Elliott, Lynnette	Lt	01.03.00	Clifton
Emms, Peter	Lt	01.10.96	Magdalen
Erskine, Randy	SLt	21.02.05	Recall
Evans, Richard	Lt Cdr	16.09.96	Raleigh
Excell, Steven	SLt	01.09.0	Canford
Eyles, Mark	SLt	18.10.99	Colstons
Eyles, Ruth Helen Miss	SLt	01.09.94	Recall

F

Name	Rank	Date of Appointment	School/College
Fabian, Geoffrey	Cdr	15.12.04	Plymouth
Fallone, Paola	SLt	15.02.06	Glasgow Academy
Finn, Mark	Lt Cdr	09.11.93	HQCCF
Ford, Peter	Lt Cdr	01.07.01	HQCCF
Forey, Sarah	SLt	28.06.01	St Peters
Foster, Stella	Lt	07.03.05	Recall
Foulger, Tim Robert	Lt	15.12.89	Recall
Fountain, Evan	SLt	01.09.00	Whitgift
Fowler, Edith	A/SLt	14.03.05	Alleyns
Francis-Jones, Anthony	Lt	01.04.92	Kings Taunton
Fraser, Charles	Lt Cdr	01.06.03	Leys
Freedman, Stephen	Lt Cdr	20.02.91	MTS Crosby
Friend, David	Lt	05.10.90	Kings Bruton
Frost, Rex	Cdr	12.11.79	Exeter
Fullarton, Ian	Lt	07.03.99	Recall
Fuller, David	Lt	26.09.99	Recall
Furse, Michael	Lt	17.01.05	HQCCF
Fyleman, Keith	Lt	01.11.99	Recall

G

Name	Rank	Date of Appointment	School/College
Geddes, George	Cdr	01.08.03	Kelvinside
Georgiakakis, Nikos	Lt	23.11.89	Charterhouse
Gibson, Claire	A/SLt	15.01.05	St Lawrence
Gilchrist, Simon George	Alt RM	01.11.02	Shrewsbury
Gillespie-Payne, Jonathan	Capt RM	06.05.04	Charterhouse
Glasbey, Martyn	Lt	05.09.90	Ryde
Glasspoole, Paul	Lt Cdr	12.06.80	Heles
Goakes, Benjamin	SLt	08.11.04	Kimbolton
Goodwin, Paul	A/SLt	10.10.05	Brighton
Gordon, Robin	Lt	07.04.02	Campbell
Gray, David	Lt Cdr	01.09.05	Bradfield
Gray, John	SLt	18.05.01	Wellingborough
Greatwood, Lisa	SLt	01.02.00	Stowe
Green, George	Cdr	01.01.74	Brighton
Greenhough, Clive Raymond	Lt	16.10.97	RGS High Wycombe
Grice, Kathryn	SLt	01.04.02	Worksop
Griffith, Jill	SLt	01.02.04	Pangbourne
Griffiths, Steven	Alt RM	01.06.02	Harrow

Name	Rank	Date of Appointment	School/College

H

Name	Rank	Date of Appointment	School/College
Hall, Austin Charles	Lt	25.06.81	Recall
Hall, Kevin	SLt	25.03.01	Recall
Hall, Stephen	Lt	01.08.03	Oundle
Halsall, Christopher	SLt	10.07.04	Kings Rochester
Hamill, Jennifer	A/SLt	10.10.05	Campbell
Hamon, Christopher	Lt Cdr	20.05.94	Sherborne
Hannaford, Rowena	A/SLt	14.07.02	Heles
Hanslip, Michael Richard	Lt Cdr	21.03.03	Recall
Harding, Claire	Lt Cdr	07.07.95	Kelly
Hardman, Tom	Lt Cdr	24.02.93	Haberdashers
Harnish, Robert	Lt	17.09.03	Elizabeth
Harris, David	Maj RMR	01.01.01	Recall
Harris, Steven	Lt Cdr	01.08.92	Exeter
Harrison, Anthony	Lt	01.11.88	Recall
Hartley, George	Lt	01.01.91	Ruthin
Hartley, Robin	SLt	03.03.04	Sedbergh
Harvey, Stephen	Capt RM	17.08.97	Bedford Modern
Harvey, MBE, Peter	Lt Cdr	21.05.93	HQCCF
Hatch, Alistair	Capt RM	01.11.01	Sherborne
Hellier, Jeremy	Cdr	01.08.99	Well Sch
Henderson, Joan	Lt Cdr	24.06.93	Recall
Henry, Tom	Lt Cdr	14.09.84	Recall
Hewitt, Richard	Lt	25.06.81	Durham
Hill, Hugh	Lt	15.04.97	Winchester
Hill, Peter	Lt	12.03.98	Sevenoaks
Hocking, Barry	SLt	20.03.99	Royal Hospital
Holland, Clare	Lt	12.10.98	Calday Grange
Holland, Julian	A/SLt	01.03.03	Framlingham
Holmes, Matthew	Lt Cdr	17.11.97	Langley
Hooper, Robin	Lt	01.07.02	Recall
Horley, Philip	SLt	28.06.99	Sutton Valence
Horst, Ellen	SLt	04.07.05	Recall
Houghton, Robert	SLt	08.11.04	Scarborough
Howard, Susan Jayne	A/SLt	22.03.03	Arnold
Hudson, John	Lt Cdr	17.03.94	Recall
Hunt, John	SLt	01.09.02	Loughborough
Hutchings, Alan	Lt RMR	01.09.03	Rugby
Hutchinson, Jeremy James	Cdr	23.01.77	Recall
Huxtable, Nigel	Lt Cdr	31.07.00	Recall

I

Name	Rank	Date of Appointment	School/College
Ibbetson-Price, William	Lt Cdr	17.10.89	Recall
Ing, John	Maj RMR	01.09.89	Harrow
Iredale, Judy	Lt	28.06.83	Taunton

J

Name	Rank	Date of Appointment	School/College
Jacklin, John	Lt Cdr	08.10.99	NCFBO
Jackson, Howard	Lt	19.04.83	Worksop
Jackson, David	Lt	17.04.96	Bedford
Jago, Peter	Lt	01.09.94	RGS Lancaster
Jeans-Jakobsson, Micheal Roy	Lt	23.06.83	Recall
Jenkins, David	Lt Cdr	01.01.80	Recall
Jones, Chris	Lt	07.04.03	Well Sch
Jones, Lily	SLt	24.07.03	Recall

K

Name	Rank	Date of Appointment	School/College
Kay, Anne	SLt	20.03.96	HQCCF
Kearsey, Peter	Lt Cdr	15.09.99	Christs Hospital
Kearsey, Joanne Mary	SLt	18.12.03	Christs Hospital
Kennedy, Caroline Margaret	Lt	01.09.02	Whitgift
Kermode, Erica Jane	Lt	26.08.93	Recall
Killgren, Carl	Lt Cdr	11.10.85	Stamford
Killgren, Susan	SLt	01.09.00	Stamford
King, Stuart John	SLt	02.04.04	Bearwood
Kirby, Michael	SLt	03.06.04	Portsmouth
Kirton, Stephanie	Lt	03.07.98	Berkhamstead
Knight, David	Cdr	24.06.04	Recall

L

Name	Rank	Date of Appointment	School/College
Lauder, David	SLt	01.01.02	St Edwards
Lawrence, Sarah	Lt RMR	01.06.03	Malvern
Lawson, Derick	Lt	01.12.03	RGS Newcastle
Lawson, Edward	Lt Cdr	28.01.97	Arnold
Lawson, Grant	Lt	06.09.97	Shiplake
Lawson, Matthew	Lt Cdr	01.09.98	St Johns
Leaver, Rebecca	Lt	17.11.01	King Edward
Lee, John	Lt	01.09.88	Hereford
Leyshon, Lara	Lt	04.10.00	Haberdashers
Lilford, Jane	SLt	12.03.01	Bridlington
Lingard, David Malcolm	Cdr	02.03.99	HQCCF
Little, John	Lt Cdr	11.09.86	Recall
Little, Peter	SLt	17.03.02	Recall
Lovell, Keith	Lt	07.08.84	Bearwood
Lovell, Stephen	Lt	08.01.92	Royal Hospital
Lowles, Ian	Lt	09.09.02	Exeter
Lowndes, Charles	A/SLt	14.12.04	Shiplake
Lucas, Ian	Cdr	17.11.81	Tonbridge
Lucas, Stuart	SLt	27.02.00	Loretto
Lynch, Jonathan	A/SLt	23.05.05	Harrow

M

Name	Rank	Date of Appointment	School/College
Macbain, Fiona	SLt	01.09.04	Strathallan
Maccarthy, Thomas	SLt	05.11.00	Cheltenham
Macdonald, Fraser	Lt	29.09.67	Trinity
Macgregor, Karen Fiona	Lt	10.10.94	Recall
Macintosh, Richard	A/SLt	15.12.04	Ellesmere
Mackie, Alan	Cdr	20.10.81	Bangor
Mackrell, Robin	A/SLt	01.09.03	City Of London
Macleod, Monica	SLt	06.09.01	Recall
Maddocks, Jane	SLt	14.02.02	Recall
Magrath, Hazel	A/SLt	10.10.05	Langley
Maiden, Philip James	Lt	01.05.02	Christs Hospital
Marsh, Lesley Diane	Lt Cdr	01.01.87	Recall
Martin, Brian	Lt	15.07.02	Liverpool
Martindale, Leslie	Lt Cdr	06.08.00	Recall
Mason, Julie	SLt	07.04.03	Wellingborough
Matthews, Andrew	SLt	11.10.02	St Margare
Matthews, Victoria	Lt	02.09.02	Kings Wimbledon
Maxwell, Peter	A/SLt	16.02.03	Kings Rochester
May, Edward (Ted)	Lt Cdr	05.06.98	HQCCF
Mccann, John	SLt	17.10.00	Brentwood
Mcconnell, Sue Margaret	Lt	05.12.90	Recall
Mcconnell, William Robert	Lt	18.07.88	Recall
Mcdonald, Gary	Lt	03.07.00	Eastbourne
Mcdonald, Richard	Lt	24.06.99	Recall
Mcginty, Michael	Lt	23.09.05	Bedford Modern
Mcguff, Neil	Lt	04.09.91	Well Sch
Mcguirk, Richard	Lt RMR	01.05.03	Wellingborough
Mckay, Pauline	SLt	01.09.05	Taunton
Mcneile, Rory	Cdr	01.05.05	Recall

Name	Rank	Date of Appointment	School/College
Mead, Elizabeth	Lt	30.06.01	Recall
Melville, Graham	Lt	21.01.92	Birkenhead
Mercer, Jane	Lt	18.07.99	Rossall
Middleton, Philip	A/SLt	15.08.04	Loretto
Miles, David	Alt RM	01.01.02	Royal Hospital
Millard, Michelle	Lt	15.02.94	Recall
Mills, Anita	Lt Cdr	01.02.92	Monkton Combe
Milne, Stuart	SLt	25.06.97	HQCCF
Milton, Pippa	Lt	25.06.01	Bedford
Minto, Neil Vickers	Lt	08.01.90	Recall
Mitchell, Ian	Lt	09.09.93	Wellcol
Mitchell, Robert	Cdr	14.11.83	Kings Wimbledon
Montgomery, Paul	Lt Cdr	25.09.92	Dean Close
Moody, Sue Margaret	Lt Cdr	20.09.91	Recall
Moore, Adrian Scott	Lt	04.10.01	Recall
Moore, David John	Lt Cdr	27.05.80	Recall
Moore, Terry Marjorie	SLt	11.07.83	Recall
Morgan, Anthony	SLt	09.09.04	St Johns
Morgan, Bryn John David	Lt	01.05.88	Recall
Morgan, Giles Christopher	Lt Cdr	20.08.01	Recall
Morris, Alwyn	A/SLt	14.03.05	Loughborough
Morton, Hilary	Lt	21.01.00	King William
Moss-Gibbons, David	Cdr	01.08.71	Recall
Mundill, Robin	Lt	02.01.04	Glenalmond
Murray, Richard Glenn	Alt RM	01.10.02	Harrow

N

Name	Rank	Date of Appointment	School/College
Nevin, Paul	A/SLt	17.09.03	Bournemouth
Newton, Ian	Lt Cdr	13.12.95	Recall
Nicholson, Robin	Cdr	01.03.75	Milton Abbey
Nicoll, Andrew	SLt	05.07.03	Recall
Nunn, William	Lt	23.01.06	HQCCF
Nurser, Graham	Lt	28.11.99	Wellington

O

Name	Rank	Date of Appointment	School/College
Oatway, Paul	Lt	25.03.04	Aato
Ogilvie, Fergus	Capt RM	03.11.95	Giggleswick
Oldbury, David John	Cdr	01.06.73	Recall
Olive, Einar	A/SLt	14.12.04	St Edwards
Osmond, Stephen	Cdr	11.01.78	RGS Worcester
Othick, Anthony	SLt	25.05.99	Scarborough
Owen, Elizabeth Harriet	SLt	19.01.98	HQCCF
Owen, John	Lt Cdr	01.01.98	HQCCF

P

Name	Rank	Date of Appointment	School/College
Packer, Thomas Arnold	Lt Cdr	17.05.82	Recall
Parfitt, Sarah	A/SLt	14.03.05	Guildford
Parkinson, Christopher	Lt	06.11.00	Sutton Valence
Parkinson, Michael	SLt	01.06.98	Kings Rochester
Parkinson, Ken	Lt Cdr	26.01.89	HQCCF
Paterson, Sheelagh	SLt	01.09.02	Kelvinside
Paton, Gordon Alexander	Lt Cdr	21.09.72	Recall
Payne, Anthony	Lt	01.12.68	Loughborough
Peak, Edward Ernest	SLt	22.03.03	Calday Grange
Pearsall, Robert	A/SLt	15.11.04	Heles
Pearson-Miles, Edward	Lt RMR	01.09.03	Wellington
Peto-Clark, Tim Andrew Martin	Lt	16.05.96	Recall
Pidoux, John	SLt	21.09.95	Maidstone
Pike, John	Lt	31.01.00	Sandbach
Pitts, Rebecca Louise	A/SLt	01.09.02	Kelly

Name	Rank	Date of Appointment	School/College
Pont, Diana	A/SLt	05.07.03	Churchers
Porter, Fiona	Lt	18.05.98	Sutton Valence
Pouder, George	2Lt RMR	01.12.04	Rugby
Poulet, Gerard	Lt	01.05.01	Trinity
Poulet-Bowden, Geradine	Lt Cdr	18.07.99	Trinity
Powell, Andrew	Lt Cdr	16.02.90	Reigate
Price, Thelma	Lt	28.06.98	Dulwich
Prior, Anthony	Lt	01.12.77	Milton Abbey
Prosser, Nicholas Michael	Lt Cdr	24.09.65	Recall

R

Name	Rank	Date of Appointment	School/College
Ray, James	Lt	01.06.03	Leys
Rennie, Sophie	SLt	27.01.03	Recall
Rennison, Clive	Capt RM	01.10.94	Royal Hospital
Rhodes, Terry	Lt	01.09.94	Recall
Richard, Peter Dalzell	Lt	01.09.82	Recall
Richards, Philip	Lt	16.02.94	Fettes
Ridley-Thomas, Micheal Stuart	Lt	06.11.90	Recall
Ripley, Myles	Lt	22.02.82	Sedbergh
Robarts, Paul John	Lt	26.06.00	MTS Northwood
Roberts, Derek	Lt Cdr	01.11.86	Brighton
Roberts, Martin	Lt Cdr	01.03.67	Recall
Robinson, Nigel	SLt	17.09.03	Bedford Modern
Roby, Ron	Cdr	01.02.64	Recall
Rooms, Lindsay	Cdr	01.12.77	Recall
Rothwell, George	Lt Cdr	07.11.94	HQCCF
Russell, James	A.Maj RM	16.06.93	Malvern

S

Name	Rank	Date of Appointment	School/College
Salmon, Tony	SLt	01.04.05	Recall
Salt, Graeme	SLt	10.05.02	Kings Wimbledon
Sammons, Keith	A/SLt	15.12.04	Tonbridge
Sanders, Bryant	Cdr	15.11.66	Bournemouth
Savage, Anthony	Cdr	01.01.97	Portsmouth
Savage, Kirsty	SLt	01.09.02	Recall
Schofield, Michelle	Lt	23.11.00	Kings Rochester
Scoins, David	SLt	01.07.02	Recall
Scorer, Nicholas	A/SLt	10.10.05	Sherborne
Scorgie, Stuart	Lt Cdr	01.11.89	Clifton
Sell, Roger	Lt	01.07.98	Recall
Shannon, Tom	Lt Cdr	02.09.86	Queen Victoria
Sharpe, Andrew	SLt	01.09.03	Gordons
Shiels, Mary Elizabeth	Lt	01.06.02	Recall
Shone, Michael	Lt	01.03.99	HQCCF
Shorrocks, Jonathan Marsh	Lt Cdr	09.07.81	RGS Worcester
Shortland, Ghislaine	Lt	14.07.02	Gordons
Sibley, Peter Charles	Lt Cdr	15.02.64	Recall
Simiste, Alan	Lt	01.05.01	Eastbourne
Simms, Julie	A/SLt	01.10.04	Newcastle
Simpson, Philip	Lt	12.07.94	Recall
Simpson-Hayes, Gizella	SLt	01.10.01	Recall
Sissons, Stewart	Lt	07.07.95	HQCCF
Smith, Alison	Lt	01.04.97	Dollar
Smith, John Robert	Lt	01.01.01	HQCCF
Smith, Nicholas Edward	SLt	01.09.04	Woodbridge
Smith, Ron	Lt Cdr	30.04.90	Recall
Spall, Christopher	Lt	07.04.02	Loretto
Spear, Keith	SLt	08.07.05	Recall
Spence, Donna	Lt	01.06.95	Bangor
Spence, Richard	Lt	06.09.93	Bangor
Spike, Nigel	Lt	05.10.87	Recall

Name	Rank	Date of Appointment	School/College
Stanley, John	SLt	08.01.02	Sandbach
Stanyer, Richard	SLt	15.11.04	Kelly
Stare, Steve	SLt	01.03.03	Recall
Stevens, Laurence	Lt	05.07.79	St Bartholomews
Stilwell, Valerie	SLt	24.11.93	Recall
Stocker, Paul	Lt	10.09.90	Recall
Storey, John	Capt RM	08.09.05	Sherborne
Stratton-Brown, Colin	Lt Cdr	01.09.96	Maidstone
Streatfeild-James, Adam	Maj RMR	05.09.00	Strathallan
Stringer, Christopher	Capt RM	16.09.86	Malvern
Sugden, Kara	Lt	08.01.02	Canford
Summers, Peter Robert	Lt	01.09.02	Cheltenham
Sutherland, Peter	Lt	28.06.99	Whitgift
Sweetland, Ashley	A/SLt	14.12.04	Bournemouth

T

Name	Rank	Date of Appointment	School/College
Taylor, Liam	A.Maj	03.03.92 RM	Winchester
Taylor, Martyn	SLt	07.03.02	Victoria
Tear, Richard	Lt	03.04.98	Recall
Temple, Robert Howard	Lt Cdr	08.03.01	HQCCF
Tennant, David	Lt Cdr	13.09.85	Tonbridge
Thorn, Simon	SLt	17.10.97	Radley
Tinker, Chris Geoffrey	Cdr	02.06.76	Recall
Tiplady, Rod	SLt	01.09.96	Edinburgh
ToaseL, Stephanie	SLt	01.11.03	Well Sch
Tomlin, Barbara	SLt	04.07.05	Recall
Tomlinson, Steven	A/SLt	12.07.05	Oratory
Toon, Howard	Lt Cdr	21.07.01	Recall
Toy, Jolyon	A/SLt	01.01.03	Eastbourne
Trebble, Dennis	SLt	01.01.04	MTS Northwood
Treharne, Andrew	Lt	01.04.03	Recall
Triggs, Duncan	Lt	12.07.98	Ruthin
Tucker, Vivien	SLt	12.10.98	Hereford
Turner, Clive	Lt	30.08.95	Recall
Turner, Charlotte	SLt	01.07.04	Recall

U

Name	Rank	Date of Appointment	School/College
Ulrich, Jacquelyn	SLt	01.07.04	Recall

V

Name	Rank	Date of Appointment	School/College
Van Der Werff, Tanya	Lt	01.09.91	Reading Blue Coat
Van Zwanenberg, Louise	Lt	15.04.97	Woodbridge
Vanston, Matthew	A/SLt	14.04.05	Langley
Vaughan, Piers	Lt Cdr	05.01.98	Sevenoaks
Vickers, Michael	Lt	02.04.01	Christs College
Vickery, David	Cdr	28.02.84	Recall
Vigers, Rose	Lt	15.01.93	Kings Bruton
Vine, Roger	Lt Cdr	01.01.92	Recall

W

Name	Rank	Date of Appointment	School/College
Walker, Colin	Cdr	16.06.88	Recall
Walker, David	SLt	15.10.01	Woodbridge
Walmsley, Richard	Lt RMR	10.01.01	Strathallan
Walsh, George	Lt Cdr	30.09.99	Recall
Ward, Sarah	SLt	12.12.00	Mill Hill
Warren, Clive	Lt	18.05.98	Colstons
Waugh, Patrick	Lt	24.04.94	Wellingborough
Webb, Victoria	SLt	01.09.99	Maidstone
Whale, Andrew Charles	Lt	20.12.85	Duke of York
Wharton, Neil	2Lt RMR	01.12.04	Giggleswick
Wilkes, Justin	Lt Cdr	29.06.98	Dollar
Wilkinson, Daren	SLt	08.01.02	Bridlington
Wilkinson, Helen	A/SLt	01.09.05	Monkton Combe
Willetts, Jimnah	A/SLt	31.05.05	Adams Gram
Williams, Martin	SLt	17.06.01	Clifton
Williams, Robert	Lt Cdr	30.09.82	Glasgow Academy
Wilson, Andrew	SLt	18.09.02	Oratory
Wright, Duncan	2Lt RMR	01.01.05	Canford
Wright, Matthew	SLt	07.04.03	Haberdashers
Wylie, John	Lt Cdr	31.07.93	Radley

Y

Name	Rank	Date of Appointment	School/College
Yates, Christopher	Capt RM	01.08.97	Winchester
Yetman, Stephen	Lt Cdr	01.09.04	Guildford

ADMIRALTY TRIALS MASTERS

Vice Admiral Sir Fabian MALBON, KBE (Rtd)..6 Jun 99

Captain E.M. HACKETT, FCI, MNI (Rtd)..30 Jun 85

Qualified in accordance with the International Maritime Organisation (IMO) Convention Regulations in Standards of Training, Certification and Watchkeeping (STCW) 1995, the role of the ATM, is to take command of new-build warships on trials. With their wide experience in working with MoD ship builders and DPA Projects, and because of their individual seamanship skills, ATM are uniquely placed to mediate between all parties during sea trials and to promote the highest standards of safety.

ROYAL NAVAL RESERVE AND OTHER VESSELS AUTHORISED TO FLY THE BLUE ENSIGN IN MERCHANT VESSELS (FOREIGN OR HOME TRADE ARTICLES) AND FISHING VESSELS

1. A list of Royal Naval Reserve and other vessels authorised to fly the Blue Ensign will no longer be published in the Navy List.

2. Its inclusion was intended for the information of Captains of Her Majesty's Ships with reference to the provisions of Article 9153 of the Queen's Regulations for the Royal Navy under which they are authorised to ascertain whether British Merchant Ships (including Fishing Vessels) flying the Blue Ensign of Her Majesty's Fleet are legally entitled to do so.

3. However, the usefulness of this list serves only a limited purpose as the list of vessels that could fly the Blue Ensign can change frequently. British merchant ships and fishing vessels are allowed to wear the plain Blue Ensign under the authority of a special Warrant, subject to certain conditions being fulfilled, and which are outlined below.

4. Vessels registered on the British Registry of Shipping may wear a plain Blue Ensign providing the master or skipper is in possession of a warrant issued by the Director of Naval Reserves under the authority of the Secretary of State for Defence, and the additional conditions outlined below are fulfilled. The Blue Ensign is to be struck if the officer to whom the warrant was issued relinquishes command, or if the ship or vessel passes into foreign ownership and ceases to be a British ship as defined by MSA 95.

   a. Vessels on Parts I, II, and IV of the Register. The master must be an officer of the rank of lieutenant RN/RMR or Captain RM/RMR or above in the Royal Fleet Reserve or the maritime forces of a United Kingdom Overseas Territory or Commonwealth country of which Her Majesty is Head of State, or an officer on the Active or Retired Lists of any branch of the maritime reserve forces of these countries or territories.

   b. Vessels on Part II of the Register. This part of the Register is reserved for fishing vessels. The skipper must comply with the same criteria as for sub-Clause 4.a. above, however the crew must contain at least four members, each of whom fulfils at least one of the following criteria:

      Royal Naval or Royal Marines reservists or pensionersReservists or pensioners from a Commonwealth monarchy or United Kingdom Overseas TerritoryEx-ratings or Royal Marines who have completed twenty years service in the ReservesMembers of the Royal Fleet Reserve

5. Action on sighting a merchant ship wearing a Blue Ensign. The Commanding Officer of one of HM ships on meeting a vessel wearing the Blue Ensign may send on board a commissioned officer to confirm that the criteria outlined above are being met in full. If it is found that the ship is wearing a Blue Ensign, without authority of a proper warrant, the ensign is to be seized, taken away and forfeited to The Sovereign and the circumstances reported to the Director Naval Reserves, acting on behalf of the Commander in Chief Naval Home Command, who maintains the list of persons authorised to hold such warrants.

   However, if it is found that, despite the warrant being sighted, the ship is failing to comply with the criteria in some other particular, the ensign is not to be seized but the circumstances are to be reported to the Director Naval Reserves.

OBITUARY

ROYAL NAVAL SERVICE

Commander

Taylor, S..J.	12.12.05
Hibbert, P.N.	14.02.06
Maughan, J.M.C., LVO, OBE	09.04.02

QUEEN ALEXANDRA'S ROYAL NAVAL SERVICE

Lieutenant

Ademokun, G.O.A.	30.12.05

ABBREVIATIONS OF RANKS AND LISTS

A	Acting
A/	Acting
ACT	Acting
ADM	Admiral
ADM OF FLEET	Admiral of the Fleet
ASL	Acting Sub-Lieutenant
AT	Acting Temporary
BRIG	Brigadier
CAND	Candidate
CAPT	Captain
CDT	Cadet
CHAPLAIN-FLT	Chaplain of the Fleet
CDR	Commander
CDRE	Commodore
CNO	Chief Nursing Officer
COL	Colonel
COMDT	Commandant
(CS)	Careers Service
(D)	Dental
E	Engineering
(FS)	Family Service
GEN	General
(GRAD)	Graduate
HON	Honorary
I	Instructor
LOC	Local
LT	Lieutenant
LCDR	Lieutenant-Commander
LT CDR	Lieutenant-Commander
LT COL	Lieutenant-Colonel
LT GEN	Lieutenant-General
MAJ	Major
MAJ GEN	Major-General
MID	Midshipman
(NE)	New Entry
NO	Nursing Officer
OFF	Officer
OFFR	Officer
P/	Probationary
PNO	Principal Nursing Officer
PR	Principal
RADM	Rear-Admiral
REV	Reverend
RM	Royal Marines
S	Supply & Secretariat

(SD) .... Special Duties List
(SDT).. Special Duties List Temporary
SG ....Surgeon
SURG..Surgeon
(SL) ....Supplementary List
SLT.. Sub-Lieutenant
SNO..Senior Nursing Officer
SUPT NO...Superintendent Nursing Officer
T..Temporary
 T/..Temporary
TLT.. Temporary Lieutenant
TSLT .... Temporary Sub-Lieutenant
(UCE).. University Cadet Entrant
VADM..Vice-Admiral
X .... Seaman
2LT ....Second Lieutenant, Royal Marines

ABBREVIATIONS OF SPECIALISATIONS AND QUALIFICATIONS

(Eur Ing)..European Engineer
AAWO.. Anti Air Warfare Officer
ACC/EM ....Accident and Emergency
ACertCM...Archbishops Certificate Church Music
ACGI ....Associate, City and Guilds London Institute
ACIS ....Associate of The Institute of Chartered Secretaries and Administrators
ACMA .... Associate, Institute of Cost & Management Accountants
ACMI...Associate of The Chartered Management Institute
(AD).. Medical and Dental Administration
ADipC..Advanced Post Graduate Diploma in Management Consultancy
ADIPM...Associate, Institute of Data Processing Management
adp..Passed Advanced Adp Course Dadptc
AE .... Air Engineering
AE U/T ....Air Engineering Under Training
AE(L)...Air Engineering (Electrical)
AE(M) ....Air Engineering (Mechanical)
(AE) .... Assault Engineer
AFIMA ....Associate Fellow, Institute Mathematics & Its Applications
AFOM.. Associate, Faculty of Occupational Medicine
AFRIN .... Associate Fellow Royal Institute of Navigation
AGSM.................................... Associate of The Guildhall School of Music and Drama
AIEMA....................Associate Member Institute of Environmental Management & Assessment
AIL... Associate, Institute of Linguists
AIM .... Associate, Institute of Metallurgists
AIMgt.. Associate of The Institute of Management
AInstP...Associate, Institute of Physics
AKC..Associate, King's College London

ALCD	Associate, London College of Divinity
AMASEE	Associate Member, Association of Electrical Engineers
AMBCS	Associate Member, British Computing Society
AMBIM	Associate Member, British Institute of Management
AMHCIMA	Associate Member, Hotel Catering & Institutional Management Association
AMIAM	Associate Member, Institute of Administrative Management
AMICE	Associate Member, Institute of Civil Engineers
AMIEE	Associate Member, Institute of Electrical Engineers
AMIERE	Associate Member, Institution of Electronic and Radio Engineers
AMIIE	Associate Member, Institution of Incorporated Engineers
AMIMarE	Associate Member, Institute of Marine Engineers
AMIMarEST	Associate Member Institute Marine Engineers Science & Technology
AMIMechE	Associate Member, Institute of Mechanical Engineers
AMIMechIE	Associate Member of Institute of Mechanical Incorporated Engineers
AMInstP	Associate Member, Institute of Physics
AMINucE	Associate Member, Institution of Nuclear Engineers
AMIPIE	Associate Member, Institution of Plant Engineers
AMNI	Associate Member, Nautical Institute
AMRAeS	Associate Member, Royal Aeronautical Society
AMRINA	Associate Member. Royal Institution of Naval Architects
ARAM	Associate, Royal Academy of Music
ARCM	Associate, Royal College of Music
ARCS	Associate, Royal College of Science
ARCST	Associate, Royal College of Science and Technology (Glasgow)
ARIC	Associate, Royal Institute of Chemistry
ARICS	Professional Asssociate, Royal Institution of Chartered Surveyors
ATC	Air Traffic Control Officer
ATCU/T	Air Traffic Control Officer Under Training
AV	Aviation
AWO(A)	Advanced Warfare Officer(Above Water)
AWO(C)	Advanced Warfare Officer(Communications)
AWO(U)	Advanced Warfare Officer(Underwater)
aws	Qualified Air Warfare College
BA	Bachelor of Arts
BA(OU)	Bachelor of Arts, Open University
BAO	Bachelor of Art of Obstetrics
BAR	Barrister
BCH	Bachelor of Surgery (Bch)
BCh	Bachelor of Surgery
BChD	Bachelor of Dentistry
BChir	Bachelor of Surgery
BComm	Bachelor of Commerce
BD	Bachelor of Divinity
BDS	Bachelor of Dental Surgery
BEd	Bachelor of Education
BEng	Bachelor of Engineering
BM	Bachelor of Medicine

BMedSc ....Bachelor of Medical Science
BMS..Bachelor of Medical Science
BMus.. Bachelor of Music
BPh..Bachelor of Philosophy
BPharm... Bachelor of Pharmacy
BS..Bachelor of Surgery
BSc ....Bachelor of Science
BSC(EH) ....Bsc Environmental Health
BSc(Eng) ....Bachelor of Science (Engineering)
BTech.. Bachelor of Technology
C ....Communications
C PHYS...Chartered Physicist
C/T .... Clinical Teacher
CA.. Caterer
(CA).. Anaesthetics - Consultant
CC... Coronary Care
(CC).. Paediatrics - Consultant
CDipAF .... The Certified Diploma in Accounting and Finance
(CDO) .... Commando Trained
(CE) .... Otorhinolaryngology - Consultant
(CEM)..Emergency Medicine - Consultant
CEng ....Chartered Engineer
Cert Ed .... Certificate of Education
CertTh .... Certificate in Theology
CGIA .... Insignia Award of The City & Guilds of London Insitute
(CGS)... General Surgery - Consultant
CHB.. Bachelor of Surgery (Chb)
ChB ....Bachelor of Surgery
ChM.. Chartered Mathematician
CITP.. Chartered It Professional
(CK) ....Dermatology - Consultant
(CL)... Pathology - Consultant
(CM)..General Medicine - Consultant
CMA... Management Accountant
CMarSci..Chartered Marine Scientist
CMath .... Chartered Mathematician
(CN/P)..Neuro-Psychiatry - Consultant
(CO/M) .... Occupational Medicine - Consultant
(CO/S)... Orthopaedic Surgery - Consultant
(COSM)...Oral Surgery/Medicine - Consultant
CPDATE .... This Is A 'pay' Only Sq. It Will Not Be Awarded To Personnel.
CPN.. Community Psychiatric Nurse
CQSW .... Certificate of Qualification in Social Work
(CU)..Urology - Consultant
(CX)..Radiology - Consultant
DA...Diploma in Anaesthesia
DAppDy..Diploma in Applied Dynamics

DCH ....Diploma in Child Health
DCHS... Diploma in Community Health Studies
DCL .... Doctor of Civil Law
DCP ....Diploma in Clinical Pathology
DD..Doctor of Divinity
DDPH.. Diploma in Public Dental Health
DEH .... Diploma in Environmental Health
df .... Qualified Defence Fellowship
DGDP RCS(UK).....................................Diploma in General Dental Practice Rcs (Uk)
DGDP(UK).. Diploma in General Dental Practice (Uk)
DGDPRCS(Eng) .... Diploma General Dental Practice Rcs(Eng)
DHC(PO)..Diploma in Remote Health Care - Polar Option
DHMSA ....Diploma in The History of Medicine (Society of Apothecaries)
DIC .... Diploma of The Imperial College
DIH ....Diploma in Industrial Health
Dip FFP ....Diploma of The Facalty of Family Planning
Dip ICN.. Diploma in Infection Control Nursing
Dip OHN .... Diploma in Occupational Health Nursing
Dip OM...Diploma in Occupational Medicine
Dip SM .... Diploma in Sports Medicine
DipA&PPS ....Diploma in Academic & Practical Physiotherapy in Sport
DipAvMed .... Diploma in Aviation Medicine
DIPCM .... Diploma in Clinical Microbiology
DIPCR ....Teaching Diploma in Clinical Radiology
DipEcon .... Diploma in Economics (Open)
DipEd..Diploma in Education
DipEM .... Diploma in Environmental Management
DipEP.. Rs Health Diploma in Environmental Protection
DipFD ....Diploma in Funeral Directing
DipFM.. Diploma in Financial Management
DIPH&S ....Diploma in Health and Safety
DipHE(Paeds) .... Diploma (He)(Paediatrics)
DipIMC RCSED....Diploma in Immmediate Medical Care of Royal College Surgeons (Edinburgh)
DIPRP.. Post Graduate Diploma in Radiation Protection
DipSM ....British Safety Council Diploma in Safety Management
DipTh.. Diploma in Theology
DLitt ....Doctor of Letters
DLO .... Diploma in Laryngology and Otology
DM ....Doctor of Medicine
DMCMP.. Diploma in Medical Centre Practice Management
DMNS...Diploma in Military Nursing Studies
DMRD..Diploma in Medical Radiological Diagnosis
DNE ....Diploma in Nursing Education
DNM.. Diploma in Nuclear Medicine
DO..Diploma in Ophthalmology
DObstRCOG ....Diploma Royal College of Obstetricians and Gynaecologists
DOrth ....Diploma in Orthodontics

DP ....Diploma in Philosophy
DPH ....Diploma in Public Health
DPHC...Dental Public Health - Consultant
DPhil...Doctor of Philosophy
DPHSR .... Dental Public Health - Specialist U/T
DPhysMed .... Diploma in Physical Medicine
DPM ....Diploma in Psychological Medicine
DRCOG................................Diploma Royal College Obstetricians & Gynaecologists
DRD..Diploma in Restorative Dentistry
DRRT ....Diploma in Remedial & Recreational Therapy
DSc...Doctor of Science
DTM&H .... Diploma in Tropical Medicine and Hygiene
ESLog .... European Senior Logistician
Eur Ing...European Engineer
EW ....Electronic Warfare
FBCS.. Fellow, British Computer Society
FBIM... Fellow, British Institute of Management
FC..Fighter Controller
FCILT........................ Fellow of The Chartered Institute of Logistics and Transport
FCIPD...................................... Fellow of The Chartered Institute of Personnel and Development
FCIS.. Fellow, Institute Chartered Secretaries & Administrators
FCMA.............................. Fellow, Chartered Institute of Management Accountants
FCMI...Fellow of The Chartered Management Institute
FDS.. Fellow in Dental Surgery
FDS RCPSGlas .... Fellow in Dental Surgery Royal College of Physicians & Surgeons (Glasgow)
FDS RCS(Eng)...........................Fellow in Dental Surgery, Royal College of Surgeons of England
FDS RCS(Irl).................................. Fellow in Dental Surgery Royal College of Surgeons in Ireland
FDS RCSEdin......................... Fellow in Dental Surgery Royal College of Surgeons of Edinburgh
FDS(RCS)...................................Fellow in Dental Surgery, Royal College of Surgeons of England
FFA ....Fellow, Institute of Financial Accountants
FFAEM.. Fellow of The Faculty of Accident and Emergency Medicine
FFARCS........................ Fellow, Faculty of Anaesthetists, Royal College of Surgeons of England
FFARCSI .... Fellow, Faculty of Anaesthetists, Royal College of Surgeons in Ireland
FFGDP(UK)............................. Fellow of The Faculty of General Dental Practitioners (Uk)
FFOM...Fellow, Faculty of Occupational Medicine
FHCIMA..............................Fellow of The Hotel and Catering Management Association
FIAA ....Fellow, Institute of Actuaries of Australia
FICS ....Fellow of The International College of Surgeons
FIEE... Fellow, Institute of Electrical Engineers
FIEEIE ....Fellow of The Institute of Electrical and Electronic Incorparated Engineer
FIEIE............................ Fellow, Institute of Electrical and Electronic Incorporated Engineers
FIERE............................. Fellow, Institution of Electronic and Radio Engineers
FIIE ....Fellow of The Institution of Incorporated Engineers
FIL.. Fellow, Institute of Linguists
FIM .... Fellow of The Institute of Metals
FIMA..Fellow, Institute of Mathematics and Its Applications
FIMarE ....Fellow, Institute of Marine Engineers

FIMarEST	Fellow Institute Marine Engineers Science & Technology
FIMechE	Fellow, Institution of Mechanical Engineers
FIMgt	Fellow of The Institute of Management
FIMS	Fellow, Institute of Management Specialists Or Mathematical Statistics
FInstAM	Fellow Institute of Administrative Management
FInstLM	Fellow of The Institute of Leadership and Management
FINucE	Fellow, Institute of Nuclear Engineers
FIOSH	Fellow of The Institute Occupational Safety & Health
FIPM	Fellow of The Institute of Personnel Management
FISM	Fellow of The Institute of Supervision and Management
FITE	Fellow, Institution Electrical & Electronics Technician Engineers
FNI	Fellow, Nautical Institute
FRAeS	Fellow, Royal Aeronautical Society
FRAM	Fellow, Royal Academy of Music
FRC.Psych	Fellow of The Royal College of Psychiatrists
FRCA	Fellow of The Royal College of Anaesthetists
FRCGP	Fellow Royal College General Practioners
FRCOG	Fellow, Royal College of Obstetricians and Gynaecologists
FRCP	Fellow, Royal College of Physicians, London
FRCPath	Fellow, Royal College of Pathologists
FRCPEd	Fellow, Royal College of Physicians, Edinburgh
FRCPGlas	Fellow, Royal College of Physicians and Surgeons of Glasgow
FRCR	Fellow, Royal College of Radioligists
FRCS	Fellow, Royal College of Surgeons of England
FRCS(ED)A&E	Fellow of The Royal College of Surgeons (Edinburgh) Accident & Emergency
FRCS(ORL)	Fellow Royal College of Surgeons - Otorhinology
FRCS(ORTH)	Fellow Royal College Surgeons (Orthopaedics)
FRCS(Urol)	Fellow Royal College of Surgeons (Urology)
FRCSEd	Fellow, Royal College of Surgeons of Edinburgh
FRCSGlas	Fellow, Royal College of Physicians and Surgeons of Glasgow
FRCSTr&Orth	Fellowship of The Royal College of Surgeons (Trauma & Orthopaedics)
FRGS	Fellow, Royal Geographical Society
FRHistS	Fellow Royal Historical Society
FRICS	Fellow Royal Institute Chartered Surveyors
FRIN	Fellow of The Royal Institute of Navigation
FRINA	Fellow, Royal Institute of Naval Architects
FRMS	Fellow, Royal Meteorological Society
FRSA	Fellow, Royal Society of Arts
fsc	Qualified Foreign Staff College
GB	The Gilbert Blane Medal
GCIPD	Graduate Chartered Institute Personnel & Development
GCIS	Graduate of The Institute of Chartered Secretaries and Administrators
gdas	General Duties Areo Systems
GDP	General Dental Practitioner
GDP UT	General Dental Practitioner - Specialist U/T
GISVA	Graduate Institute of Surveyors, Valuers and Auctioneers
GMCIPD	Graduate Member Chartered Institute Personnel & Development

GMPP .... General Medical Practitioner
GradIMA............................. Graduate Member, Institute of Mathematics and Its Applications
GradIMS ....Graduate Institute of Management Specialists
GradInstPS .... Graduate Institute of Purchasing and Supply
(GS) .... General Surgery - Senior House Officer
GSX...General Service Executive
gw.. Guided Weapons Systems Course Rmcs Shrivenham
H CH .... Hydrographer (Charge)
HCH .... Hydrographer (Charge)
hcsc.. Higher Command & Staff College
HDCR ....Higher Diploma of College of Radiographers
HDIPCR...Higher Diploma in Clinical Radiology
Hf...Hudson Fellowship
HM...Hydrographer Metoc
HM(AS)... Hydrog/Metoc Advanced Surveyor
HM1 ....Hydrographer/Metoc (First Class)
HM2 ....Hydrographer/Metoc (Second Class)
HNC ....Higher National Certificate
HND ....Higher National Diploma
HULL.. Hull Engineering
H1 .... Hydrographer (First Class)
H2 .... Hydrographer (Second Class)
I(1)Ab .... Interpreter 1st Class Arabic
I(1)Ch ....Interpreter 1st Class Chinese
I(1)Da..Interpreter 1st Class Danish
I(1)Du ....Interpreter 1st Class Dutch
I(1)Fi .... Interpreter 1st Class Finnish
I(1)Fr..Interpreter 1st Class French
I(1)Ge ....Interpreter 1st Class German
I(1)Id.. Interpreter 1st Class Indonesian
I(1)It...Interpreter 1st Class Italian
I(1)Ja.. Interpreter 1st Class Japanese
I(1)Ma.. Interpreter 1st Class Malayan
I(1)No .... Interpreter 1st Class Norwegian
I(1)Pl .... Interpreter 1st Class Polish
I(1)Po..Interpreter 1st Class Portugese
I(1)Ru..Interpreter 1st Class Russian
I(1)Sh .... Interpreter 1st Class Swahili
I(1)Sp .... Interpreter 1st Class Spanish
I(1)Sw .... Interpreter 1st Class Swedish
I(1)Tu .... Interpreter 1st Class Turkish
I(1)Ur ....Interpreter 1st Class Urdu
I(2)Ab ....Interpreter 2nd Class Arabic
I(2)Ch .... Interpreter 2nd Class Chinese
I(2)Da.. Interpreter 2nd Class Danish
I(2)Du .... Interpreter 2nd Class Dutch
I(2)Fi .... Interpreter 2nd Class Finnish

I(2)Fr	Interpreter 2nd Class French
I(2)Ge	Interpreter 2nd Class German
I(2)Id	Interpreter 2nd Class Indonesian
I(2)It	Interpreter 2nd Class Italian
I(2)Ja	Interpreter 2nd Class Japanese
I(2)Ma	Interpreter 2nd Class Malayan
I(2)No	Interpreter 2nd Class Norwegian
I(2)Pl	Interpreter 2nd Class Polish
I(2)Po	Interpreter 2nd Class Portugese
I(2)Ru	Interpreter 2nd Class Russian
I(2)Sh	Interpreter 2nd Class Swahili
I(2)Sp	Interpreter 2nd Class Spanish
I(2)Sw	Interpreter 2nd Class Swedish
I(2)Tu	Interpreter 2nd Class Turkish
I(2)Ur	Interpreter 2nd Class Urdu
IC	Intensive Care
IC/CC	Intensive Care and Coronary Care
idc	Qualified Imperial Defence College
IEng	Incorporated Engineer
ifp	Qualified, International Fellows Programme
IS	Information Systems
IS U/T	Information Systems Under Training
isc	Initial Staff Course
JCPTGP	Certificate of Prescribed Experience in General Practice
jsdc	Joint Service Defence College
jssc	Joint Services Staff College
LC	Landing Craft
LCGI	Licentiate of City and Guilds Institute
LCIPD	Licentiate of The Chartered Institute of Personnel and Development
LDS	Licentiate in Dental Surgery
LDS RCPSGlas	Licenciate in Dental Surgery Royal College of Physicians & Surgeons (Glasgow)
LDS RCS(Eng)	Licentiate in Dental Surgery, Royal College of Surgeons of England
LDS RCS(Irl)	Licenciate in Dental Surgery Royal College of Surgeons in Ireland
LDS RCSEdin	Licenciate in Dental Surgery Royal College of Surgeons of Edinburgh
LGSM	Licentiate, Guildhall School of Music and Drama
LHCIMA	Licentiate Hotel, Catering and Institutional Management Assn
LIEE	Licentiate, Institute Electrical Engineers
LIMA	Licentiate Institute Mathematics & Its Applications
LLB	Bachelor of Law
LLD	Doctor of Laws
LLM	Master of Law
LMCC	Licentiate, Medical Council of Canada
LMHCIMA	Licentiate Member of Hotel,Catering and Institutional Management Assn
LMIPD	Licentiate Member To The Institute of Personnel and Development
LMSSA	Licentiate in Medicine & Surgery, Society of Apothecaries
LRAM	Licentiate, Royal Academy of Music
LRCP	Licentiate, Royal College of Physicians, London

LRCPSGlas .... Licentiate, Royal College of Physicians and Surgeons of Glasgow
LRCS.. Licentiate, Royal College of Surgeons of England
LRPS ....Licentiate, Royal Photographic Society
(LT) .... Laboratory Technician
LTh .... Licentiate in Theology
M ED ....Masters in Education
M.Univ...Master of The University (Ou)
MA...Master of Arts
MA(CANTAB)..Master of Arts Cambridge
MA(Ed) ....Master of Arts in Education
MA(OXON) .... Master of Arts Oxon
MAPM ....Member of The Association of Project Managers
MB .... Bachelor of Medicine
MBA... Master of Business Administration
MBCS .... Member, British Computer Society
MBIM .... Member, British Institute of Management
MCD...Mine Warfare Clearance Diver
MCD/MW ....Mine Clearance Diving & Mine Warfare
MCFA ....Member of The Catering and Food Association
MCGI..Member of City and Guilds Institiute
MCh..Master in Surgery
MChOrth .... Master of Orthopaedic Surgery
MCIEH .... Member Chartered Institute in Environmental Health
MCIPD...............................Chartered Member of The Institute of Personnel and Development
MCIT .... Member, Institute of Training Officers
MCMI.. Member of The Chartered Management Institute
MD ....Doctor of Medicine
MDA...Master of Defence Administration
MDSc.. Master of Dental Science
mdtc.. Maritime Defence Technology Course
ME...Marine Engineering
ME U/T .... Marine Engineering Under Training
ME(L) .... Marine Engineering (Electrical)
MEng...Master of Engineering
MESM.. Marine Engineering (Submarine)
MESMUT ....Marine Engineering (Submarine) Under Training
METOC .... Meteorology & Oceanography
MFCM .... Member, Faculty of Community Medicine
MFDS,RCS ....Membership of The Faculty of Dental Surgery Royal College of Surgeons England
MFGDP(UK) .... Membership in Gen Dent Practice, Facultyof General Dental Practitioners (Uk)
MFOM ....Member, Faculty of Occupational Medicine
MFPM .... Member of Faculty of Pharmaceutical Medicine
MGDS RCS ....Member in General Dental Surgery, Royal College of Surgeons of England
MGDS RCSEd....... Member in General Dental Surgery, Royal College of Surgeons of Edinburgh
MHCIMA .... Member, Hotel Catering & Institutional Management Association
MHSM...Member of The Institute of Health Services Mamagement
MICE .... Member, Institution Civil Engineers

MIDPM .... Member Institute of Data Processing Management
MIEE .... Member, Insitution of Electrical Engineers
MIEEE .... Member of The Institution of Electrical and Electronic Engineers
MIEEIE .... Member of The Institute of Electrical and Electronic Incorporated Engineers
MIERE .... Member, Institution of Electrical & Radio Engineers
MIExpE .... Member, Institute of Explosives Engineers
MIIE .... Member of Institution of Incorporated Engineers
MIIRSM .... Member of The International Institute of Risk & Safety Management
MIIT .... Member of The Institute of Information Technology Training
MIL .... Member, Institute of Linguists
MILDM .... Member of The Institute of Logistics and Distribution Management
MILog ....Member of The Institue of Logistics
MILT .... Member of The Institute of Logistics and Transport
MIM .... Member, Institute of Metals
MIMA ....Member of The Institute of Mathematics and Applications
MIMarA .... Member, Institute of Marine Architects
MIMarE ....Member, Institute of Marine Engineers
MIMarEST ....Member Institute Marine Engineers Science & Technology
MIMechE .... Member, Institution of Mechanical Engineers
MIMechIE .... Member of The Institute of Mechanical Incorporayed Engineers
MIMgt ....Member of The Institute of Management
MIMS .... Member, Institute of Management Specialists
MInsD ....Member of The Institute of Directors
MinstAM ....Member, Institute of Administrative Management
MInstFM .... Member, Institute of Facilities/Resources Management
MINSTP ....Member, Institute of Physics
MInstPS ....Member, Institute of Purchasing and Supply
MINucE ....Member, Institute of Nuclear Engineers
MIOA ....Member of The Institute of Acoustics
MIOSH ....Member, Institute of Occupational Safety and Health
MIPD .... Member of The Institute of Personnel and Development
MIPlantE ....Member, Plant Engineers
MIPM ....Member, Institute of Personnel Management
MIProdE .... Member, Institute of Production Engineers
MISecM ....Member of The Institute of Security Management
MISM .... Member of The Institute of Supervisory Management
MITD ....Member Institute of Training and Development
MITE ....Member, Institute of Technical Engineers
MLDR .... Mountain Leader
MLITT ....Master of Letters
ML2@ .... Mountain Leader 2 (Rm)
MMedSci .... Master of Medical Science
MMus ....Master of Music
MNI .... Member, Nautical Institute
MNZIS ....Member of The New Zealand Institute of Surveyors
MOR ....Heavy Weapons Mortar Course
MOrth ....Master of Orthodontics

MOrth,RCS .... Membership in Othodontics Royal College of Surgeons England
MPH ....Master of Public Health
MPhil.. Master of Philosophy
MPS...Member, Pharmaceutical Society
MRAeS ....Member, Royal Aeronautical Society
MRCGP... Member, Royal College of General Practitioners
MRCOG.................................Member, Royal College Obstetricians & Gynaecologists
MRCP .... Member, Royal College of Physicians, London
MRCP(UK)..Member, Royal College of Physicians
MRCPath ....Member, Royal College of Pathologists
MRCPE ....Member, Royal College of Physicians, Edinburgh
MRCPGlas.................... Member, Royal College of Physicians and Surgeons of Glasgow
MRCPI .... Member, Royal College of Physicians of Ireland
MRCPsych..Member, Royal College of Phsyciatrists
MRCS .... Member, Royal College of Surgeons of England
MRCVS.. Member of The Royal College of Veterinary Surgeons
MRIC ....Member, Royal Institute of Chemistry
MRIN ....Member, Royal Institute of Navigation
MRINA...Member, Royal Institute of Naval Architects
MS... Master of Surgery
MSc .... Master of Science
MSc gw ....Master of Science Guided Weapons
MSc(Econ)... Master of Economic and Social Studies
MScD.. Master of Dental Science
MSE... Member, Society of Engineers
MSRP.. Member of The Society For Radiological Protection
MTh...Master of Theology
MTO.. Motor Transport Officer
MW ....Mine Warfare
n..Frigate Navigating Officer's Course
N .... Navigation
nadc .... Nato Defence College Course
NCAGSA... Naval Cooperation & Guidance For Shipping(A)
NCAGSB ....Naval Cooperation & Guidance For Shipping (B)
NCAGSC.. Naval Cooperation & Guidance For Shipping (C)
ndc..National Defence College
NDipM...National Diploma in Management
NInstC ....Nuclear Instrument Calibration Course
nrf ....Qualified, Nato Research Fellowship
O ....Observer
O LYNX... Observer (Lynx)
O MER.. Observer (Merlin)
O SKW..Observer (Seaking Aew)
O SK6 ....Observer (Seaking 6)
O U/T...Observer Under Training
ocds(Can) .... Qualified Canadian National Defence College
ocds(Ind)... Qualified Indian National Defence College

OCDS(JAP) .... Overseas National Defence College Japanese
ocds(No) ....Qualified, Norwegian Defence College
ocds(Pak) .... Qualified Pakistan National Defence College
ocds(US) ....Qualified The United States National War College
ocds(USN) .... Qualified, United States Naval War College
odc(Aus) .... Qualified Australia Joint Services Staff College
odc(Fr) .... Qualified French Cours Superieur Interarmees
ODC(SWISS) ....International Training in Security and Arms Control
odc(US) ....Qualified United States Armed Forces Staff College
ONC ....Orthopaedic Nursing
ORTHC ....Orthodontics - Consultant
osc .... Qualified Overseas Staff College
osc(Nig) ....Qualified Nigerian Command & Staff College
osc(us) .... Qualified, Usmc Command & Staff College
OStJ .... Order of St. John
OTSPEC ....Operating Theatre Specialist
P ....Pilot
P GAZ ....Pilot (Gazelle)
P GR7 ....Harrier Gr7 Pilot
P LYNX .... Pilot (Lynx)
P LYN7 .... Pilot (Lynx 7)
P MER .... Pilot (Merlin)
P SHAR .... Sea Harrier Pilot
P SKW ....Pilot (Seaking Aew)
P SK4 ....Pilot (Seaking 4)
P SK6 ....Pilot (Seaking 6)
P U/T ....Pilot Under Training
(P) ....Physiotherapist
pce ....Passed Command Examinations
pce(sm) .... Passed Command Examinations (Sm)
pcea ....Passed Command Examinations (Air)
(PD) .... Pharmacy Dispenser
pdm ....Principal Director of Music
PFOM ....President Faculty of Occupational Medicine
PGCE ....Post Graduate Certificate of Education
PGDip ....Post Graduate
PGDIP ....Post Graduate Diploma
PGDIPAN ....Post Graduate Diploma in Applied Navigation
PGDipL ....Post Graduate Diploma in Law
PGDRP ....Post Graduate Diploma in Radiation Protection
PH .... Helicopter Pilot
PhD ....Doctor of Philosophy
PI .... Photographic Interpreter
PR ....Plotting & Radar
psc .... Passed Staff Course
psc(a) .... Passed Staff Course (Raf)
psc(j) ....Passed Staff Course (Joint)

psc(j)(o)... Overseas Staff Colleges Except Ndc Rome
psc(j)o... Overseas Staff Colleges Except Ndc Rome
psc(m)... Passed Staff Course (Army)
PSC(ONDC)... Staff Course (Overseas National Defence College)
psc(or) ....Passed Staff Course Overseas Reserves
PT...Physical Training
ptsc .... Completed Technical Staff Course at The Rmsc Shrivenham
PWO.. Principal Warfare Officer
PWO(A) .... Principal Warfare Officer Above Water
PWO(C) .... Principal Warfare Officer Communications
PWO(N) ....Principal Warfare Officer Navigation
PWO(U) .... Principal Warfare Officer Underwater
rcds .... Royal College of Defence Studies
rcds(fm) ....Royal College of Defence Studies (Foundation Module)
RCPS(Glas)... Royal College of Phsicians and Surgeons of Glasgow
RCS ....Royal College of Surgeons of England
RCSEd.. Royal College of Surgeons of Edinburgh
REG ....Regulating
REGM ....Registered Midwife
(RGN)...Registered General Nurse
RMLE/P .... Senior Corps Commission Pilots Only
RMN.. Registered Mental Nurse
RMP1...Pilot 1
RMP2...Pilot 2
RNT ....Registered Nurse Tutor
S...S
(S).. Stores
(SA) ....Anaesthetics - Specialist Registrar
SALT.. Salt - Nmmis Only
SBS... Special Boat Squadron
SCM ....State Certified Midwife
(SGS) .... General Surgery - Specialist Registrar
SM..Submariner
SM... Sm Qualified
SM U/T .... Submarine Unqualified Under Training
SM(n)... Submarine Navigating Officer
SM(N) ....Submarine (Navigation)
(SM)... General Medicine - Specialist Registrar
SO(LE)...Staff Officer Personnel and Logistics
(SO/M)..Occupational Medicine - Specialist Registrar
SOLE/P...Senior Corps Commission Pilots/General Duties
sondc.. Senior Overseas National Defence College
sowc..Senior Officer's War Course
sq ....Rm Major Staff Qualified After Holding Two Specified Staff Appointments
tacsc .... Territorial Army Command and Staff Course
TAS.. Torpedo Anti-Submarine
TDCR .... Teachers Diploma College of Radiographers

TEng ....Certificate of Technical Engineering
TM...Training Management
TM U/T .... Training Management Under Training
TMSM... Training Management (Sm)
tp .... Qualified Test Pilots Course
(W) ....Writer
WE ....Weapons Engineering
WE U/T ....Weapons Engineering Under Training
WESM .... Weapon Engineering (Submarine)
WESMUT .... Weapons Engineering (Submarine) Under Training
WTO... Weapon Training Officer
X X

ABBREVIATIONS OF PLACE WHERE OFFICER IS SERVING WHEN NOT SERVING AT SEA

AACC MID WALLOP .... HQ School of Army Aviation Middle Wallop
ACDS(POL) USA .... Assistant Chief of Defence Staff (Policy and Nuclear) USA
ADAS BRISTOL..................................... ASSISTANT DIRECTOR ACQUISITION SUPPORT BRISTOL
AFCC..Armed Forces Chaplaincy Centre
AFPAA HQ .... Armed Forces Personnel Administration Agency Headquarters
AFPAA JPA ....AFPAA (Joint Personnel Administration)
AFPAA WTHY DOWN...AFPAA (Worthy Down)
AFPAA(CENTURION)..Directorate of AFPAA (Centurion)
AH IPT ....Attack Helicopter Integrated Project Team
ASM IPT... Attack Submarine Integrated Project Group
BATCIS IPT .... BOWMAN Integrated Project Team
BDLS AUSTRALIA ....British Defence Liaison Staff Australia
BDLS CANADA .... British Defence Liaison Staff Canada
BDLS INDIA ....British Defence Liaison Staff India
BDMT ....Arms CIS Group/Bowman Military Team
BDS WASHINGTON..................................... British Defence Staff Washington
BF BIOT..British Forces, British Indian Ocean Territory
BFPO AGENCY DLO ....BFPO Defence Agency Defence Logistics Organisation
BRNC BAND....................Band of HM Royal Marines Britannia Royal Naval College
CALEDONIA DLO ....HMS Caledonia
CALLIOPE... Royal Naval Reserve Tyne (RN Staff)
CAMBRIA ....Royal Naval Reserve South Wales (RN Staff)
CAPT MCTA....................................Captain Maritime Commissioning Trials & Assessment
CC AIR RAMSTEIN ....CIS Command Air Ramstein
CC MAR AGRIPPA.................HMS Agrippa Mar CC (Allied Naval Forces S. Europe (Italy))
CDO LOG REGT RM ....Commando Logistics Regiment Royal Marines
CENTCOM USA ....Naval Party 1068
CHFHQ(SHORE)..CDO Helo Force Headquarters (Shore)
CHINOOK IPT.. CHINOOK Integrated Project Team
CINCFLEET FIMU .... Fleet Information Management Unit

CINCFLEET FTSU ....Commander-in-Chief (Fleet Technical Support Unit)
CLYDE MIXMAN1 .... Her Majesty's Ship NEPTUNE Mixed Manning
CMT SHRIVENHAM.. DEFAC HQ and DCMT SHRIVENHAM
CNNRP BRISTOL.. Chairman Naval Nuclear Regulatory Panel
COM MCC NWD ....Commander MCC Northwood
COS 2SL/CNH .... Chief of Staff to Second Sea Lord/Commander in Chief Naval Home Co
CSIS IPT ....CSIS Integrated Project Team
CSSE USA .... Chief Strategic Systems Executive (USA)
CTCRM...Commando Training Centre Royal Marines
CTCRM (SEA)... Commando Training Centre Royal Marines (Sea)
CTCRM BAND...............Band of HM Royal Marines Commando Training Centre Royal Marines
CTS.. Corporate Technical Services
CV(F) IPT .... CVF Integrated Project Team
DA ALGIERS...Defence Attache Algiers
DA BRIDGETOWN ....Defence Advisor Bridgetown
DA BRUNEI .... Defence Attache Brunei
DA KIEV...Defence Attache Kiev
DA MANAMA.. Defence Attache Manama
DA SANAA ....Defence Attache Sanaa
DA SOFIA.. Defence Attache Sofia
DA TBILISI ....Defence Attache Tbilisi
DALRIADA .... Her Majesty's Ship DALRIADA
DARTMOUTH BRNC.....................................Britannia Royal Naval College Dartmouth
DASC... Defence Aviation Safety Cell
DCAE COSFORD ....Defence College Aeronautical Engineering (Cosford)
DCCIS BLANDFORD ....Defence College Communications and Information Systems (Blandf
DCCIS FAREHAM .... Defence College of Communication and Information Systems (Fareha
DCL DEEPCUT...Defence College Logistics (Deepcut)
DCPPA....................................... Defence College of Police and Personnel Administration
DCSA DHFCS FMR ....DCSA Defence High Frequency Communications Services Forest Moor
DCSA GIBRALTAR................................... Defence Communications Services Agency Gibraltar
DCSA NWD REGION ....DCSA Northwood Regional Office
DCTS HALTON ....Defence Centre of Training Support (Halton)
DCTS PORTS .... Defence Centre of Training Support (Portsmouth)
DDS HALTON ....Defence Dental Services Halton
DDS PLYMOUTH ....Defence Dental Services Plymouth
DDS PORTSMOUTH.. Defence Dental Services Portsmouth
DDS SCOTLAND...Defence Dental Services Scotland
DEF EXP ORD SCHL.. Defence Ordnance Disposal School
DEF NBC CENTRE... Defence Nuclear Biological Chemical Centre
DEF SCH OF LANG .... Defence School of Languages
DFTE PORTSMOUTH..................................Director Fleet Time Engineering Portsmouth
DGES LAND .... Director General Equipment Support Land
DGIA .... Defence Geographic and Imagery Intelligence Agency
DHFS .... Defence Helicopter Flying School
DISC ....Defence Intelligence & Security Centre
DLO BRISTOL .... Defence Logistics Organisation Bristol

DLO DEF MUN GP.. DLO Defence Munitions Group
DLO TES..DLO Technical Enabling Services
DLO WYTON.. Defence Logistics Organisation Wyton
DLO YEO ....Defence Logistics Organisation Yeovilton
DLO/DG LOG (SC)...DLO/Director General Logistics (Supply Chain)
DMSTC ....Defence Medical Services Training Centre
DNR DISP TEAM..Director of Naval Recruiting Display Team
DNR EC 2... Directorate of Naval Recruiting East Central 2
DNR N IRELAND .... Directorate of Naval Recruiting Northern Ireland
DNR NEE 1 .... Directorate of Naval Recruiting North East England 1
DNR NWE 2 ....Directorate of Naval Recruiting North West England 2
DNR PRES TEAMS .... Director of Naval Recruiting Presentation Teams
DNR RCHQ NORTH ....Director of Naval Recruiting Regional Careers Headquarters (Nor
DNR RCHQ SOUTH .... Director of Naval Recruiting Regional Careers Headquarters (Sou
DNR SEE 1 .... Directorate of Naval Recruiting South East England 1
DNR SWE 2 ....Directorate of Naval Recruiting South West England 2
DNR W CENTRAL..Directorate of Naval Recruiting West Central
DNR WROUGHTON...Director of Naval Recruiting, Wroughton
DOSG BRISTOL..Defence Ordnance Safety Group Bristol
DPA BRISTOL...Defence Procurement Agency Bristol
DPMD... Defence Postgraduate Medical Deanery
DRAKE CBS.. Her Majesty's Ship DRAKE - Captain Base Safety
DRAKE COB..Her Majesty's Ship DRAKE - Captain of the Base
DRAKE DIS..........................Her Majesty's Ship DRAKE - Directorate Infrastructure and Services
DRAKE NBC/DBUS ....Her Majesty's Ship DRAKE - Naval Base Commander/Directorate Bus
DRAKE SFM .... Her Majesty's Ship DRAKE - Superintendent Fleet Maintenance
DSDA..Defence Storage & Distribution Agency
DSFM PORTSMOUTH ....Deputy Superintendent Fleet Maintenance
EAGLET..Royal Naval Reserve Mersey (RN Staff)
EUMS .... European Union Military Staff
EXCH ARMY SC(G) ....Exchange Service British Army On the Rhine
EXCHANGE ARMY UK ....Exchange Service UK Army Units
EXCHANGE AUSTLIA ....Exchange Service Australian Navy
EXCHANGE BRAZIL... Exchange Service Brazilian Navy
EXCHANGE CANADA ....Exchange Service Canadian Armed Forces
EXCHANGE DENMARK .... Exchange Service Denmark
EXCHANGE FRANCE .... Exchange Service France
EXCHANGE GERMANY ....Exchange Service German Navy
EXCHANGE ITALY .... Exchange Italian Navy
EXCHANGE N ZLAND..Exchange Service New Zealand Navy
EXCHANGE NLANDS.. Exchange Service Netherlands Forces
EXCHANGE NORWAY ....Exchange Service Norway
EXCHANGE RAF UK ....Exchange Service with the Royal Air Force
EXCHANGE SPAIN..Exchange Service Spain
EXCHANGE USA .... Exchange Service United States
FDG .... Fleet Diving Group
FDU1 .... Fleet Diving Unit 1

FDU2 .... Fleet Diving Unit 2
FDU3 .... Fleet Diving Unit 3
FLEET AV CRANWEL... Fleet Aviation Cranwell
FLEET AV CU..Fleet Aviation (HMS Seahawk)
FLEET AV HENLOW ....Fleet Aviation Medical Training Wing Henlow
FLEET AV SULTAN... Fleet Aviation (SULTAN)
FLEET AV VALLEY .... Fleet Aviation (RAF Valley)
FLEET AV VL...Fleet Aviation Yeovilton
FLEET CIS PORTS .... Fleet Communication & Information Systems (Portsmouth)
FLEET CMR .... Commander of Maritime Reserves
FLEET COMOPS NWD .... Commander-in-Chief Fleet - Commander Operations Northwood
FLEET COSCAP...................................... Commander-in-Chief Fleet - Chief of Staff(Capability)
FLEET COSP&S .... FLEET Personnel and Support
FLEET FOSNNI ....Fleet FOSNNI
FLEET FOTR ....Fleet Flag Officer Training and Recruiting
FLEET HQ NWD... Fleet Headquarters Northwood
FLEET HQ PORTS ....Fleet Headquarters Portsmouth
FLEET HQ PORTS 2 ....Fleet Headquarters Portsmouth No. 2
FLEET HQ WI... Fleet Headquarters Whale Island
FLEET ISS...Fleet ISS
FLEET PHOT PORTS ....Fleet Photographic Unit Portsmouth
FLEET ROSYTH .... Fleet (Rosyth)
FLYING FOX .... HMS FLYING FOX
FORT BLOCKHOUSE...The Officer in Charge
FORWARD ....RNR Communications Training Centre (Birmingham) (RN Staff)
FOSNNI.. FOSNNI/Commander Clyde Operations Department
FOST DPORT SHORE...................................... Flag Officer Sea Training (Devonport)
FOST DSTF ....Flag Officer Sea Training DSTF
FOST FAS SHORE.....................................Flag Officer Sea Training Faslane Shore
FOST NWD (JMOTS)..............................Joint Maritime Operational Training Staff (Northwood)
FS MASU .... Forward Support Mobile Aircraft Support Unit
FSAST IPT........................... Flt Sim & Synth Trnrs/UK Mil Flying Trg Sys Integrated Project Team
FWO DEVONPORT ....Fleet Waterfront Organisation (Devonport)
FWO FASLANE ....Fleet Waterfront Organisation Faslane
FWO PORTSMOUTH................................ Fleet Waterfront Organisation Portsmouth
GANNET SAR FLT ....Gannet SAR Flight
HANDLING SQN... Handling Squadron
HQ ARRC... HQ Ace Rapid Reaction Corps
HQ BAND SERVICE..Headquarters Band Service
HQ DCSA.. HQ Defence Communication Services Agency
HQ DMETA ....HQ Defence Medical Education & Training Agency
HQ RHINE/EURO SG .... Headquarters Rhine and European Support Group
HQ SACT.............................Headquarters Supreme Allied Comander Transformation
HQ STC..Headquarters Strike Command Ops Support (ATC)
HQ 3 CDO BDE RM.. 3 Commando Brigade Royal Marines
HQBF CYPRUS .... Headquarters British Forces Cyprus
HQ1GP HQSTC .... Headquarters 1 Group

HUMS IPT .... Health & Usage Monitoring Systems Integrated Project Team
IA BRISTOL...Integration Authority Bristol
IMS BRUSSELS...International Military Staff, Brussels
INM ALVERSTOKE ....Institute of Naval Medicine
JACIG ....Joint Arms Control Implementation Group
JARIC..Joint Air Reconnaissance and Intelligence Centre
JATEBRIZENORTON ....Joint Air Transport Establishment - Brize Norton
JCA IPT UK...Joint Combat Aircraft Integrated Project Team
JCA IPT USA................................ Future Carrier Borne Aircraft Integrated Project Team USA
JCTS IPT .... Joint Casualty Treatment Ship Integrated Project Team
JCTTAT..Joint Counter Terrorist Training and Advisory Team
JDCC ....Joint Doctrine and Concepts Centre
JES IPT ....Joint Electronic Surveillance Integrated Project Team
JF HARROLE OFF ....Joint Force Harrier Role Office
JFC HQ AGRIPPA.........................HMS Agrippa JFC HQ (Allied Forces S. Europe (Italy))
JFCHQ BRUNSSUM ....Joint Force Combined Headquarters Brunssum
JHCHQ..Joint Helicopter Command Headquarters
JHCNI .... Joint Helicopter Force (Northern Ireland)
JHQ/CIS LISBON .... Joint Headquarters/Communication Information Systems Lisbon
JHQSW MADRID .... JHQ Southwest Madrid
JPS UK .... Joint Planning Staff UK
JSCSC ....Joint Services Command and Staff College
JSENS IPT ....Joint Sensor Engagement Networks IPT
JSSU CHELTENHAM .... Joint Service Signal Unit - Cheltenham
JSSU CYPRUS...Joint Service Signal Unit CYPRUS
JSU NORTHWOOD .... Joint Support Unit Northwood
JWC/CIS STAVANGR.............Joint Warfare Centre/Communications Information Systems Stava
JWW...Jungle Warfare Wing
KING ALFRED.. Her Majesty's Ship KING ALFRED
LAIPT .... Logistic Applications Integrated Project Team
LN BMATT (CEE)...Loan BMATT (CEE) (Vyskov)
LN BPST SAFRICA...............................Loan British Peace Support Team (South Africa)
LN MTU UKSAT(C) .... Loan Maritime Training Unit UKSAT(C)
LN SIERRA LEONE.. Loan Sierra Leone
LOAN ABU DHABI.. Loan Service in Abu Dhabi
LOAN BMATT GHANA .... British Military Advisory and Training Team (West Africa)
LOAN BRUNEI ....Loan Service in Brunei
LOAN DARA ....Loan DARA
LOAN DSTL... Loan Defence Science & Tech Labs
LOAN HYDROG ....Loan Hydrographer
LOAN JSOC SLOV ....Joint Services Operations Centre Slovakia
LOAN JTEG BSC DN ....Loan Joint Test Evaluation Group Boscombe Down
LOAN KUWAIT...Loan Service Kuwait
LOAN NEW ZEALAND ....Loan Service New Zealand
LOAN OMAN .... Loan Service Oman
LOAN OTHER SVCE...Loan Other Service
LOAN SAUDI ARAB .... Loan Service Saudi Arabia

MARS IPT.....................................Military Afloat Reach & Sustainability Integrated Project Team
MAS BRUSSELS.. Military Agency For Standardisation (Brussels)
MCTC... Military Corrective Training Centre
MDC GIBRALTAR...Maritime Data Centre Gibraltar
MDHU DERRIFORD...Ministry of Defence Hospital Unit (Derriford)
MDHU FRIMLEY .... Ministry of Defence Hospital Unit (Frimley Park)
MDHU NORTH.. MDHU North Allerton
MDHU PETERBRGH ....Ministry of Defence Hospital Unit (Peterborough)
MDHU PORTSMOUTH.......................................Ministry of Defence Hospital Unit (Portsmouth)
MED S IPT...Medical Supplies Integrated Project Team
MERLIN IPT ....Merlin Integrated Project Team
MHRF(F)... Maritime Higher Readiness Force (France)
MTS IPT .... Maritime Trainers and Simulators Integrated Project Team
MWC PORTSDOWN...Maritime Warfare Centre (Portsdown)
MWC SOUTHWICK.. Maritime Warfare Centre Southwick
MWS COLLINGWOOD ....Her Majesty's Ship COLLINGWOOD Maritime Warfare School
MWS DEF DIV SCHL... Maritime Warfare School Defence Diving School
MWS EXC BRISTOL .... Her Majesty's Ship BRISTOL
MWS EXCELLENT................................. Her Majesty's Ship EXCELLENT Maritime Warfare School
MWS HM TG (D)...MWS Hydrographic & Meterological Training Group
MWS RM SCH MUSIC ....Maritime Warfare School Royal Marines School of Music
MWS SOUTHWICK PK ....Maritime Warfare School (Southwick Park)
NAIC NORTHOLT.. Naval Aeronautical Information Cell
NATO DEF COL ....Nato Defence College
NATO MEWSG VL..................NATO Multi-Service Electronic Warfare Support Group Yeovilton
NAVSEC.. Naval Secretary
NBC PORTSMOUTH .... Naval Base Commander (Portsmouth)
NCSA SECTOR NWD... NCSA Sector Northwood
NC3 AGENCY ....NATO C3 Agency
NELSON.. Her Majesty's Ship NELSON
NEPTUNE BNSL .... NEPTUNE - BABCOCK NAVAL SERVICES LTD
NEPTUNE DLO...................................... Captain Base Port (Personnel & Support), HMS NEPTUNE
NEPTUNE DSA.. HMS Neptune - Director of Safety Assurance
NEPTUNE FD ....Facilities Department
NEPTUNE 2SL/CNH.. HMS Neptune (NSC)
NEW IPT...Naval EW Integrated Project Team
NORTH DIVING GRP... Northern Diving Group
NP AFGHANISTAN..Naval Party Afghanistan
NP BOSNIA .... Naval Party BOSNIA Royal Naval Liaison Officer - Banja Luka
NP BRISTOL...Nuclear Propulsion Bristol
NP DNREAY .... Nuclear Propulsion Dounreay
NP 2021 ....Naval Party 2021
NS OBERAMMERGAU.....................................NATO School (SHAPE) Oberammergau
NSRS IPT...Nato Submarine Rescue System Integrated Project Team
NW IPT ....Nuclear Weapons Integrated Project Team
OCLC BIRM.. Officer Careers Liaison Centre, Birmingham
OCLC BRISTOL ....Officer Careers Liaison Centre,Bristol

OCLC MANCH...Officer Careers Liaison Centre, Manchester
OCLC PETERBRGH ....Officer Careers Liaison Centre, Peterborough
OCLC ROSYTH..Officer Careers Liaison Centre, Rosyth
OPTAG.................................... Operational Training and Advisory Group (Warminster)
PAAMS PARIS.....................................Principal Anti Air Missile System Paris
PJHQ....................................Permanent Joint Headquarters (Northwood)
PRESIDENT .... Royal Naval Reserve London (RN Staff)
PSYOPS TEAM ....Psychological Operations Team
QHM CLYDE .... Queens Harbourmaster (Clyde)
RAF AWC ....Air Warfare Centre RAFC Cranwell
RAF COTTESMORE..Royal Air Force Cottesmore
RAF CRANWELL EFS....................Royal Air Force Cranwell (Defence Elementary Flying Training
RAF LINTN/OUSE..Royal Air Force (Linton On Ouse)
RAF SHAWBURY ....Royal Air Force Shawbury
RAF WEST DRAYTON .... Royal Air Force West Drayton
RAF WITTERING .... Royal Air Force Wittering
RALEIGH.. Her Majesty's Ship RALEIGH
RCDM...Royal Centre for Defence Medicine
RCDS..Royal College of Defence Studies
RH HASLAR...The Royal Hospital Haslar
RM BAND PLYMOUTH.. Band of HM Royal Marines Plymouth
RM BAND PTSMTH ....Band of HM Royal Marines Portsmouth
RM BAND SCOTLAND.. Band of HM Royal Marines Scotland
RM BICKLEIGH...Royal Marines BICKLEIGH
RM CHIVENOR...Royal Marines CHIVENOR
RM CONDOR..Royal Marines CONDOR
RM NORTON MANOR...Royal Marines NORTON MANOR
RM WARMINSTER..Royal Marines WARMINSTER
RMB STONEHOUSE..Royal Marine Barracks Stonehouse
RMC OF SCIENCE ....Royal Military College of Science Shrivenham
RMDIV LECONFIELD ....Royal Marines Division Army School of Mechanical Transport
RMR BRISTOL.. Royal Marines Reserve Bristol
RMR LONDON .... Royal Marines Reserve London
RMR MERSEYSIDE.......................................Royal Marines Reserve Merseyside
RMR SCOTLAND .... Royal Marines Reserve Scotland
RMR TYNE ....Royal Marines Reserve Tyne
RN GIBRALTAR ....Royal Navy Gibraltar
RN LOGS SCHOOL .... Royal Naval Logistics School
RN SINGAPORE ....Royal Navy Singapore
RNAS CULDROSE.. Royal Naval Air Station Culdrose
RNAS YEOVILTON ....Royal Naval Air Station Yeovilton
RNEAWC ....Royal Naval Element Air Warfare Centre
RNICG .... Royal Navy Intelligent Customer Group
RNLO GULF...Royal Naval Liaison Officer (Gulf)
RNLO JTF4 .... Royal Naval Liaison Officer for Commander Joint Task Force 4,USN
RNP TEAM .... Royal Naval Presentation Team
RNSR BOVINGTON ....Royal Naval School of Recruiting, Bovington

RNU RAF DIGBY..Royal Naval Unit RAF DIGBY
RNU ST MAWGAN..Royal Naval Unit St Mawgan
SA ANKARA..Service Attache Ankara
SA ATHENS...Service Attache Athens
SA BERLIN...Service Attache Berlin
SA BUENOS AIRES...Service Attache Buenos Aires
SA CAIRO..Service Attache Cairo
SA COPENHAGEN..Service Attache Copenhagen
SA LISBON...Service Attache Lisbon
SA MADRID..Service Attache Madrid
SA MALAYSIA...Service Advisor Malaysia
SA MOSCOW...Service Attache Moscow
SA MUSCAT..Service Attache Muscat
SA OSLO..Service Attache Oslo
SA PARIS...Service Attache Paris
SA PRETORIA..Service Advisor Pretoria
SA RIYADH...Service Attache Riyadh
SA ROME..Service Attache Rome
SA SEOUL...Service Attache Seoul
SA THE HAGUE...Service Attache the Hague
SA TOKYO...Service Attache Tokyo
SACLANT ITALY...Supreme Allied Commander Atlantic, Italy
SACT BELGIUM...Supreme Allied Commander Transformation, Belgium
SANS IPT.............................Sensors, Avionics and Navigation Systems Integrated Project Team
SAT IPT..Satellite Communications Integrated Project Team
SAUDI AFPS SAUDI......................................Saudi Armed Forces Project Sales Saudi
SBS BASE...Headquarters Squadron Royal Marines Base
SCOTIA...Her Majesty's Ship SCOTIA
SCU SHORE..Special Communications Unit (Shore)
SDG PORTSMOUTH..Southern Diving Unit 2 (Portsmouth)
SETT GOSPORT...Submarine Escape Training Tank Gosport
SFSG...Special Forces Support Group
SHAPE BELGIUM..............................Supreme Headquarters Allied Powers In Europe (Belgium)
SHERWOOD...........................RNR Communications Training Centre (Nottingham) (RN Staff)
SONAR 2087 IPT......................................Defence Procurement Agency Peer Group G
STG BRISTOL...Sea Technology Group Bristol
STRIKFORNATO...Strike Force NATO
SULTAN...Her Majesty's Ship SULTAN
SULTAN AIB..Admiralty Interview Board
SUPT OF DIVING..Commanding Officer Fleet Diving Squadron
TDL IPT...Tactical Data Links Integrated Project Group
TEMERAIRE...Her Majesty's Ship TEMERAIRE
TORPEDO IPT..Torpedo Integrated Project Team
T45 IPT...Type 45 Destroyer Integrated Project Team
UDSC IPT....................Underwater Defence Systems and Countermeasures IPT
UKLFCSG RM............United Kingdom Landing Force Command Support Group Royal Marines
UKMCC BAHRAIN...UK Maritime Battle Staff Bahrain

UKMFTS IPT ....UK MILITARY FLYING TRAINING SYSTEM
UKMILREP BRUSS..United Kingdom Military Representative Brussels
UKNMR SHAPE .... United Kingdom Military Representative SHAPE
UKNSU NAPLES..United Kingdom National Support Unit Naples
UKSU JHQ LISBON .... United Kingdom Support Unit Joint Headquarters Lisbon
UKSU JHQ NORTH ....United Kingdom National Support Element Allied Forces Northern
UKSU SHAPE............. United Kingdom Support Unit Supreme Headquarters Allied Powers in E
UN AFRICA ....Naval Party Sierra Leone
UNOMIG...UN Monitoring in Georgia
VICTORY...Her Majesty's Ship VICTORY
VIVID .... Her Majesty's Ship VIVID
WILDFIRE .... Her Majesty's Ship WILDFIRE
1 ASSLT GP RM.. 1 Assault Group Royal Marines
11 (ATT) SQN.....................11 (Amphibious Trials and Training) Squadron Royal Marines
18 (UKSF) SR...18 (UKSF) SR
2SL/CNH...........................Second Sea Lord/Commander-in-Chief Naval Home Command
2SL/CNH FOTR.............................. Flag Officer Training and Recruiting Headquarters
2SL/CNH RNCMC............................. 2SL/CNH Royal Navy Crisis Management Centre
20(R) SQN (RN) .... 20(R) Squadron (RN)
29 CDO REGT RA.....................................29 Commando Regiment Royal Artillery
40 CDO RM... 40 Commando Royal Marines
42 CDO RM... 42 Commando Royal Marines
45 CDO RM... 45 Commando Royal Marines
702 SQN HERON......................... 702 Naval Air Squadron Her Majesty's Ship HERON
727 NAS ....727 Naval Air Squadron
750 SQN HERON...Heron Flight
750 SQN SEAHAWK .... 750 Squadron Seahawk
771 SQN..771 Squadron
815 SQN HQ........................ 815 Headquarters Naval Air Squadron, Her Majesty's Ship HERON
824 SQN..824 Squadron
829 SQN HQ.. 829 Naval Air Squadron Headquarters
848 SQN HERON...848 Naval Air Squadron
849 SQN HQ.. 849 Naval Air Squadron Headquarters

Amendments to Navy List Entry

Editor of the Navy List
DNCM
Room 208
Jago Road
HMNB Portsmouth
PO1 3LU

Please ensure that you state your Service Number and use the spaces provided next to each incorrect field to insert what you believe to be the correct entry. All potential inaccuracies will be investigated.

The information contained in Sections 2 and 3 of this edition was extracted from the Naval Manpower Management Information System and is corrected to include those promotions, appointments etc. promulgated on or before 9 April 2005 which will be effective on or before 30 June 2005.

Service Number (mandatory) ....

Surname ....

Forenames ....

Titular Address ....

Post-Nominals* ....

Rank ....

Commission ....

Branch ....

Spec ....

Seniority ....

* Please note that documentary evidence (for example, a supporting certificate) will be required if any amendments to your post-nominal details are to be made.

Signed ....   Date ....

Once completed, please return this form to the above address, marked for the attention of your Career Manager.

Every effort will be made to correct errors and omissions notified to the Editor but regrettably receipt of this form cannot be acknowledged.